1807
WILEY
2007

BICENTENNIAL · BICENTENNIAL · BICENTENNIAL · BICENTENNIAL

THE WILEY BICENTENNIAL—KNOWLEDGE FOR GENERATIONS

*E*ach generation has its unique needs and aspirations. When Charles Wiley first opened his small printing shop in lower Manhattan in 1807, it was a generation of boundless potential searching for an identity. And we were there, helping to define a new American literary tradition. Over half a century later, in the midst of the Second Industrial Revolution, it was a generation focused on building the future. Once again, we were there, supplying the critical scientific, technical, and engineering knowledge that helped frame the world. Throughout the 20th Century, and into the new millennium, nations began to reach out beyond their own borders and a new international community was born. Wiley was there, expanding its operations around the world to enable a global exchange of ideas, opinions, and know-how.

For 200 years, Wiley has been an integral part of each generation's journey, enabling the flow of information and understanding necessary to meet their needs and fulfill their aspirations. Today, bold new technologies are changing the way we live and learn. Wiley will be there, providing you the must-have knowledge you need to imagine new worlds, new possibilities, and new opportunities.

Generations come and go, but you can always count on Wiley to provide you the knowledge you need, when and where you need it!

WILLIAM J. PESCE
PRESIDENT AND CHIEF EXECUTIVE OFFICER

PETER BOOTH WILEY
CHAIRMAN OF THE BOARD

Microsoft Certified Application Specialist (MCAS)

Approved Courseware

▪ What does this logo mean?

It means this courseware has been approved by the Microsoft® Certified Application Specialist program to be among the finest available for learning Microsoft® Office Word 2007, Microsoft® Office Excel 2007, Microsoft® Office PowerPoint 2007, Microsoft® Office Access 2007, or Microsoft® Office Outlook 2007. It also means that upon completion of this courseware, you may be prepared to take an exam for Microsoft Certified Application Specialist qualification.

▪ What is a Microsoft Certified Application Specialist?

A Microsoft Certified Application Specialist is an individual who has passed exams for certifying his or her skills in one or more of the Microsoft Office desktop applications such as Microsoft Word, Microsoft Excel, Microsoft PowerPoint, Microsoft Outlook, or Microsoft Access. The Microsoft Certified Application Specialist program is the only program approved by Microsoft for testing proficiency in Microsoft Office desktop applications. This testing program can be a valuable asset in any job search or career development.

▪ More Information

To learn more about becoming a Microsoft Certified Application Specialist and exam availability, visit www.microsoft.com/learning/msbc.

Microsoft® Official Academic Course

Microsoft® Office Access® 2007

Credits

EXECUTIVE EDITOR	John Kane
SENIOR EDITOR	Gary Schwartz
DIRECTOR OF MARKETING AND SALES	Mitchell Beaton
MICROSOFT STRATEGIC RELATIONSHIPS MANAGER	Merrick Van Dongen of Microsoft Learning
GLOBAL MOAC MANAGER	Laura McKenna
DEVELOPMENT AND PRODUCTION	Custom Editorial Productions, Inc
EDITORIAL ASSISTANT	Jennifer Lartz
PRODUCTION MANAGER	Kelly Tavares
CREATIVE DIRECTOR/COVER DESIGNER	Harry Nolan
TECHNOLOGY AND MEDIA	Phyllis Bregman/Elena Santa Maria
COVER PHOTO	Corbis

Wiley 200th Anniversary logo designed by: Richard J. Pacifico

This book was set in Garamond by Aptara, Inc. and printed and bound by Bind Rite Graphics. The covers were printed by Phoenix Color.

ISBN-13 978-0-47006950–9

Printed in the United States of America

10 9 8 7 6

Foreword from the Publisher

Wiley's publishing vision for the Microsoft Official Academic Course series is to provide students and instructors with the skills and knowledge they need to use Microsoft technology effectively in all aspects of their personal and professional lives. Quality instruction is required to help both educators and students get the most from Microsoft's software tools and to become more productive. Thus our mission is to make our instructional programs trusted educational companions for life.

To accomplish this mission, Wiley and Microsoft have partnered to develop the highest quality educational programs for Information Workers, IT Professionals, and Developers. Materials created by this partnership carry the brand name "Microsoft Official Academic Course," assuring instructors and students alike that the content of these textbooks is fully endorsed by Microsoft, and that they provide the highest quality information and instruction on Microsoft products. The Microsoft Official Academic Course textbooks are "Official" in still one more way—they are the officially sanctioned courseware for Microsoft IT Academy members.

The Microsoft Official Academic Course series focuses on *workforce development*. These programs are aimed at those students seeking to enter the workforce, change jobs, or embark on new careers as information workers, IT professionals, and developers. Microsoft Official Academic Course programs address their needs by emphasizing authentic workplace scenarios with an abundance of projects, exercises, cases, and assessments.

The Microsoft Official Academic Courses are mapped to Microsoft's extensive research and job-task analysis, the same research and analysis used to create the Microsoft Certified Application Specialist (MCAS) and Microsoft Certified Application Professional (MCAP) exams. The textbooks focus on real skills for real jobs. As students work through the projects and exercises in the textbooks they enhance their level of knowledge and their ability to apply the latest Microsoft technology to everyday tasks. These students also gain resume-building credentials that can assist them in finding a job, keeping their current job, or in furthering their education.

The concept of life-long learning is today an utmost necessity. Job roles, and even whole job categories, are changing so quickly that none of us can stay competitive and productive without continuously updating our skills and capabilities. The Microsoft Official Academic Course offerings, and their focus on Microsoft certification exam preparation, provide a means for people to acquire and effectively update their skills and knowledge. Wiley supports students in this endeavor through the development and distribution of these courses as Microsoft's official academic publisher.

Today educational publishing requires attention to providing quality print and robust electronic content. By integrating Microsoft Official Academic Course products, *WileyPLUS*, and Microsoft certifications, we are better able to deliver efficient learning solutions for students and teachers alike.

Bonnie Lieberman
General Manager and Senior Vice President

Welcome to the Microsoft Official Academic Course (MOAC) program for the 2007 Microsoft Office system. MOAC represents the collaboration between Microsoft Learning and John Wiley & Sons, Inc. publishing company. Microsoft and Wiley teamed up to produce a series of textbooks that deliver compelling and innovative teaching solutions to instructors and superior learning experiences for students. Infused and informed by in-depth knowledge from the creators of Microsoft Office and Windows Vista™, and crafted by a publisher known worldwide for the pedagogical quality of its products, these textbooks maximize skills transfer in minimum time. With MOAC, students are hands on right away—there are no superfluous text passages to get in the way of learning and using the software. Students are challenged to reach their potential by using their new technical skills as highly productive members of the workforce.

Because this knowledgebase comes directly from Microsoft, architect of the 2007 Office system and creator of the Microsoft Certified Application Specialist (MCAS) exams, you are sure to receive the topical coverage that is most relevant to students' personal and professional success. Microsoft's direct participation not only assures you that MOAC textbook content is accurate and current; it also means that students will receive the best instruction possible to enable their success on certification exams and in the workplace.

▪ The Microsoft Official Academic Course Program

The *Microsoft Official Academic Course* series is a complete program for instructors and institutions to prepare and deliver great courses on Microsoft software technologies. With MOAC, we recognize that, because of the rapid pace of change in the technology and curriculum developed by Microsoft, there is an ongoing set of needs beyond classroom instruction tools for an instructor to be ready to teach the course. The MOAC program endeavors to provide solutions for all these needs in a systematic manner in order to ensure a successful and rewarding course experience for both instructor and student—technical and curriculum training for instructor readiness with new software releases; the software itself for student use at home for building hands-on skills, assessment, and validation of skill development; and a great set of tools for delivering instruction in the classroom and lab. All are important to the smooth delivery of an interesting course on Microsoft software, and all are provided with the MOAC program. We think about the model below as a gauge for ensuring that we completely support you in your goal of teaching a great course. As you evaluate your instructional materials options, you may wish to use the model for comparison purposes with available products.

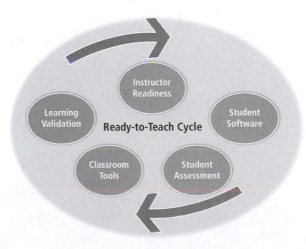

Illustrated Book Tour

■ Pedagogical Features

MOAC for *2007 Microsoft Office system* is designed to cover all the learning objectives in the MCAS exams, referred to as "objective domains." The Microsoft Certified Application Specialist (MCAS) exam objectives are highlighted throughout the textbooks. Many pedagogical features have been developed specifically for *Microsoft Official Academic Course* programs. Unique features of our task-based approach include a Lesson Skills Matrix that correlates skills taught in each lesson to the MCAS objectives; Certification, Workplace, and Internet Ready exercises; and three levels of increasingly rigorous lesson-ending activities: Competency, Proficiency, and Mastery Assessment.

Presenting the extensive procedural information and technical concepts woven throughout the textbook raises challenges for the student and instructor alike. The Illustrated Book Tour that follows provides a guide to the rich features contributing to *Microsoft Official Academic Course* program's pedagogical plan. Following is a list of key features in each lesson designed to prepare students for success on the certification exams and in the workplace:

- Each lesson begins with a **Lesson Skill Matrix.** More than a standard list of learning objectives, the Skill Matrix correlates each software skill covered in the lesson to the specific MCAS "objective domain."

- Every lesson features a real-world **Business Case** scenario that places the software skills and knowledge to be acquired in a real-world setting.

- Every lesson opens with a **Software Orientation.** This feature provides an overview of the software features students will be working with in the lesson. The orientation will detail the general properties of the software or specific features, such as a ribbon or dialog box; and it includes a large, labeled screen image.

- Concise and frequent **Step-by-Step** instructions teach students new features and provide an opportunity for hands-on practice. Numbered steps give detailed, step-by-step instructions to help students learn software skills. The steps also show results and screen images to match what students should see on their computer screens.

- **Illustrations:** Screen images provide visual feedback as students work through the exercises. The images reinforce key concepts, provide visual clues about the steps, and allow students to check their progress.

- **Button images:** When the text instructs a student to click a particular toolbar button, an image of the button is shown in the margin.

- **Key Terms:** Important technical vocabulary is listed at the beginning of the lesson. When these terms are used later in the lesson, they appear in bold italic type and are defined. The Glossary contains all of the key terms and their definitions.

- Engaging point-of-use **Reader aids** located throughout the lessons tell students why this topic is relevant (*The Bottom Line*), provide students with helpful hints (*Take Note*), show alternate ways to accomplish tasks (*Another Way*), or point out things to watch out for or avoid (*Troubleshooting*). Reader aids also provide additional relevant or background information that adds value to the lesson.

- **Certification Ready?** features throughout the text signal students where a specific certification objective is covered. It provides students with a chance to check their understanding of that particular MCAS objective and, if necessary, review the section of the lesson where it is covered. MOAC offers complete preparation for MCAS certification.
- **New Feature:** The New Feature icon appears near any software feature that is new to Office 2007.
- **Competency, Proficiency, and Mastery Assessment** provide three progressively more challenging lesson-ending activities.
- **Internet Ready.** Projects combine the knowledge students acquire in a lesson with a Web-based research task.
- **Circling Back.** These integrated projects provide students with an opportunity to review and practice skills learned in previous lessons.
- **Workplace Ready.** These features preview how the 2007 Microsoft Office system applications are used in real-world situations.
- **Student CD:** The companion CD contains the data files needed for each lesson. These files are indicated by the CD icon in the margin of the textbook.

■ Lesson Features

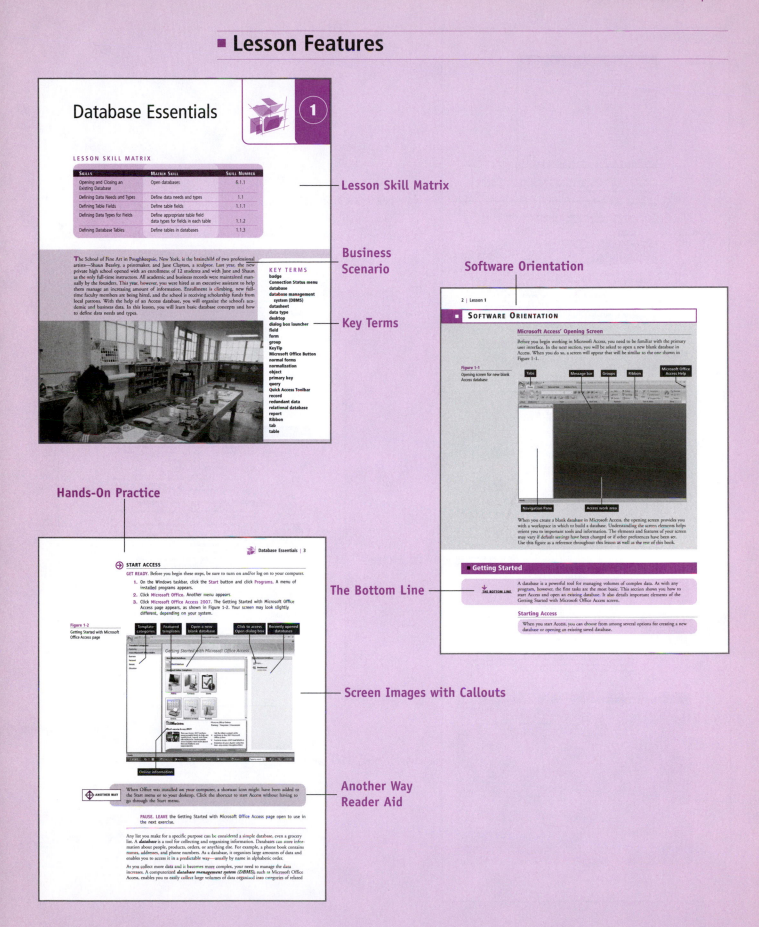

Lesson Skill Matrix

Business Scenario

Software Orientation

Key Terms

Hands-On Practice

The Bottom Line

Screen Images with Callouts

Another Way Reader Aid

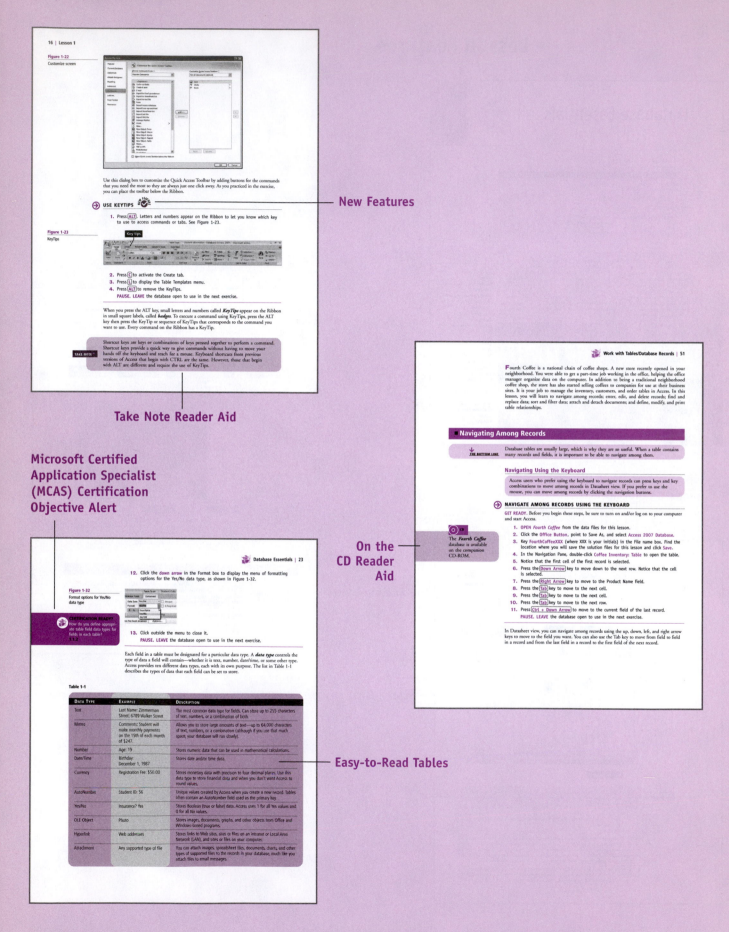

New Features

Take Note Reader Aid

Microsoft Certified
Application Specialist
(MCAS) Certification
Objective Alert

On the
CD Reader
Aid

Easy-to-Read Tables

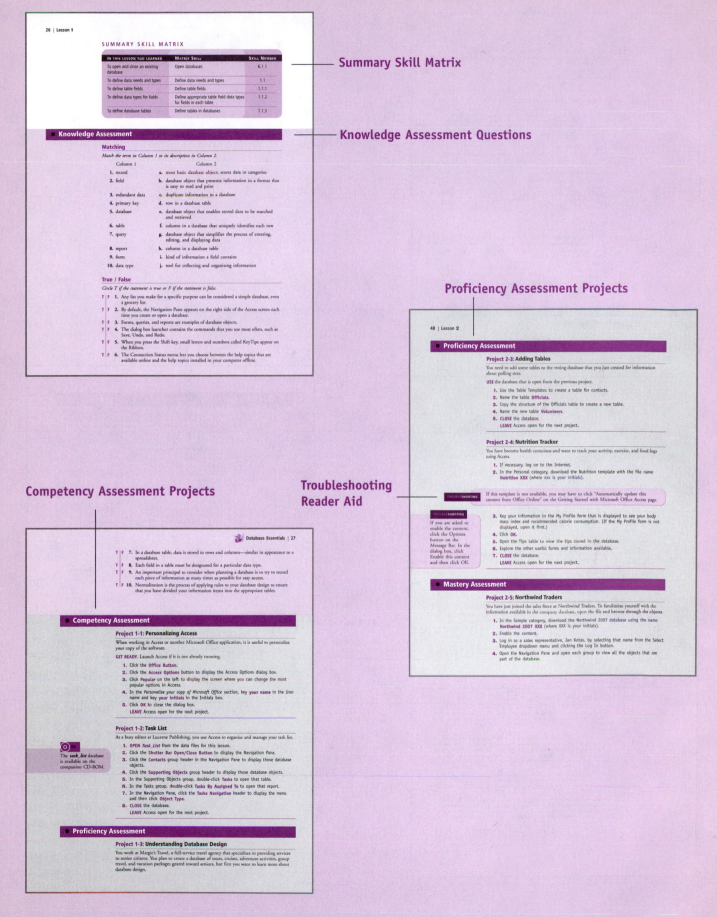

Summary Skill Matrix

Knowledge Assessment Questions

Proficiency Assessment Projects

Competency Assessment Projects

Troubleshooting Reader Aid

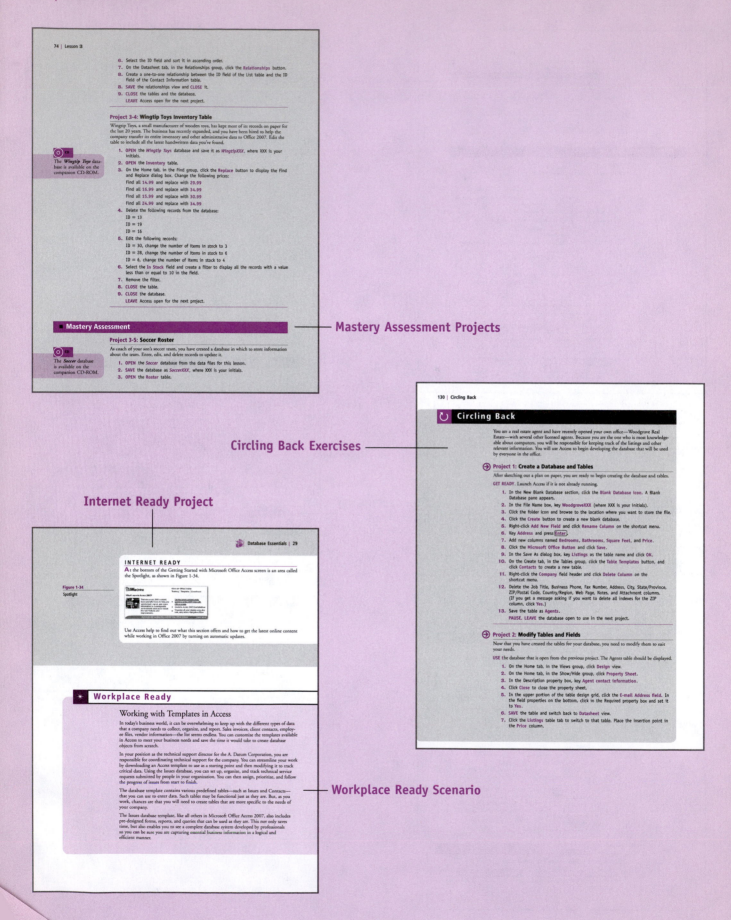

Mastery Assessment Projects

Circling Back Exercises

Internet Ready Project

Workplace Ready Scenario

Conventions and Features Used in This Book

This book uses particular fonts, symbols, and heading conventions to highlight important information or to call your attention to special steps. For more information about the features in each lesson, refer to the Illustrated Book Tour section.

CONVENTION	MEANING
NEW FEATURE ✓	This icon indicates a new or greatly improved Office 2007 feature in this version of the software.
↓ **THE BOTTOM LINE**	This feature provides a brief summary of the material to be covered in the section that follows.
CLOSE	Words in all capital letters and in a different font color than the rest of the text indicate instructions for opening, saving, or closing files or programs. They also point out items you should check or actions you should take.
CERTIFICATION READY?	This feature signals the point in the text where a specific certification objective is covered. It provides you with a chance to check your understanding of that particular MCAS objective and, if necessary, review the section of the lesson where it is covered.
◎ **CD**	This indicates a file that is available on the student CD.
TAKE NOTE	Reader aids appear in shaded boxes found in your text. *Take Note* provides helpful hints related to particular tasks or topics.
◆ **ANOTHER WAY**	*Another Way* provides an alternative procedure for accomplishing a particular task.
TROUBLESHOOTING	*Troubleshooting* covers common problems and pitfalls.
X REF	These notes provide pointers to information discussed elsewhere in the textbook or describe interesting features of Office 2007 that are not directly addressed in the current topic or exercise.
SAVE 🖫	When a toolbar button is referenced in an exercise, the button's picture is shown in the margin.
Alt + **Tab**	A plus sign (+) between two key names means that you must press both keys at the same time. Keys that you are instructed to press in an exercise will appear in the font shown here.
A *cell* is the area where data is entered.	Key terms appear in bold italic.
Key **My Name is.**	Any text you are asked to key appears in color.
Click **OK.**	Any button on the screen you are supposed to click on or select will also appear in color.
OPEN *FitnessClasses.*	The names of data files will appear in bold, italic, and color for easy identification.

Instructor Support Program

The *Microsoft Official Academic Course* programs are accompanied by a rich array of resources that incorporate the extensive textbook visuals to form a pedagogically cohesive package. These resources provide all the materials instructors need to deploy and deliver their courses. Resources available online for download include:

- **6-Month Office 2007 Trial Edition (available in North America only).** Students receive 6-months' access to Microsoft Office Professional 2007 when you adopt a MOAC 2007 Microsoft Office system textbook. The textbook includes the trial CD and a product key that allows students to activate the CD for a 6-month period.

- The **Instructor's Guide** contains Solutions to all the textbook exercises, Syllabi for various term lengths, Data Files for all the documents students need to work the exercises. The Instructor's Guide also includes chapter summaries and lecture notes. The Instructor's Guide is available from the Book Companion site (http://www.wiley.com/college/microsoft) and from WileyPLUS.

- The **Test Bank** contains hundreds of multiple-choice, true-false, and short answer questions and is available to download from the Instructor's Book Companion site (http://www.wiley.com/college/microsoft) and from WileyPLUS. A complete answer key is provided. It is available as a computerized test bank and in Microsoft Word format. The easy-to-use test-generation program fully supports graphics, print tests, student answer sheets, and answer keys. The software's advanced features allow you to create an exam to meet your exact specifications. The computerized test bank provides:

  - Varied question types to test a variety of comprehension levels—multiple-choice, true-false, and short answer.

  - Allows instructors to edit, randomize, and create questions freely.

  - Allows instructors to create and print different versions of a quiz or exam.

- **PowerPoint Presentations and Images.** A complete set of PowerPoint presentations is available on the Instructor's Book Companion site (http://www.wiley.com/college/microsoft) and in WileyPLUS to enhance classroom presentations. Approximately 50 PowerPoint slides are provided for each lesson. Tailored to the text's topical coverage and Skills Matrix, these presentations are designed to convey key Office 2007 concepts addressed in the text.

  All figures from the text are on the Instructor's Book Companion site (http://www.wiley.com/college/microsoft) and in WileyPLUS. You can incorporate them into your PowerPoint presentations, or create your own overhead transparencies and handouts.

  By using these visuals in class discussions, you can help focus students' attention on key elements of Office 2007 and help them understand how to use it effectively in the workplace.

- **Microsoft Business Certification Pre-Test and Exams**. With each MOAC textbook, students receive information allowing them to access a Pre-Test, Score Report, and Learning Plan, either directly from Certiport, one of Microsoft's exam delivery partners, or through links from WileyPLUS Premium. They also receive a code and information for taking the certification exams.

- The **MSDN Academic Alliance** is designed to provide the easiest and most inexpensive way for university departments to make the latest Microsoft software available to faculty and students in labs, classrooms, and on student PCs. A free 1-year membership is available to qualified MOAC adopters.

- **The Wiley Faculty Network** lets you tap into a large community of your peers effortlessly. Wiley Faculty Network mentors are faculty like you, from educational institutions around the country, who are passionate about enhancing instructional efficiency and effectiveness through best practices. Faculty Network activities include technology training and tutorials, virtual seminars, peer-to-peer exchanges of experience and ideas, personal consulting, and sharing of resources. To register for a seminar, go to www.wherefacultyconnect.com or phone 1-866-4FACULTY.

WileyPLUS

Broad developments in education over the past decade have influenced the instructional approach taken in the Microsoft Official Academic Course programs. The way that students learn, especially about new technologies, has changed dramatically in the Internet era. Electronic learning materials and Internet-based instruction is now as much a part of classroom instruction as printed textbooks. *WileyPLUS* provides the technology to create an environment where students reach their full potential and experience academic success that will last them a lifetime!

WileyPLUS is a powerful and highly-integrated suite of teaching and learning resources designed to bridge the gap between what happens in the classroom and what happens at home and on the job. *WileyPLUS* provides Instructors with the resources to teach their students new technologies and guide them to reach their goals of getting ahead in the job market by having the skills to become certified and advance in the workforce. For students, WileyPLUS provides the tools for study and practice that are available to them 24/7, wherever and whenever they want to study. *WileyPLUS* includes a complete online version of the student textbook; PowerPoint presentations; homework and practice assignments and quizzes; links to Microsoft's Pre-Test, Learning Plan, and a code for taking the certification exam (in WileyPLUS Premium); image galleries; test-bank questions; gradebook; and all the instructor resources in one easy-to-use website.

Organized around the everyday activities you and your students perform in the class, *WileyPLUS* helps you:

- **Prepare & Present** outstanding class presentations using relevant PowerPoint slides and other *WileyPLUS* materials—and you can easily upload and add your own.
- **Create Assignments** by choosing from questions organized by lesson, level of difficulty, and source—and add your own questions. Students' homework and quizzes are automatically graded, and the results are recorded in your gradebook.
- **Offer context-sensitive help to students, 24/7.** When you assign homework or quizzes, you decide if and when students get access to hints, solutions, or answers where appropriate—or they can be linked to relevant sections of their complete, online text for additional help whenever—and wherever they need it most.
- **Track Student Progress:** Analyze students' results and assess their level of understanding on an individual and class level using the *WileyPLUS* gradebook, or export data to your own personal gradebook.
- **Administer Your Course:** Wiley PLUS can easily be integrated with another course management system, gradebook, or other resources you are using in your class, providing you with the flexibility to build your course, your way.
- **Seamlessly integrate all of the rich WileyPLUS content and resources with WebCT and Blackboard**—with a single sign-on.

Please view our online demo at **www.wiley.com/college/wileyplus**. Here you will find additional information about the features and benefits of Wiley PLUS, how to request a "test drive" of Wiley PLUS for this title, and how to adopt it for class use.

MICROSOFT BUSINESS CERTIFICATION PRE-TEST AND EXAMS AVAILABLE THROUGH WILEY*PLUS* PREMIUM

Enhance your students' knowledge and skills and increase their performance on Microsoft Business Certification exams with adoption of the Microsoft Official Academic Course program for Office 2007.

With the majority of the workforce classified as *information workers*, certification on the 2007 Microsoft Office system is a critical tool in terms of validating the desktop computing knowledge and skills required to be more productive in the workplace. Certification is the primary tool companies use to validate the proficiency of desktop computing skills among employees. It gives organizations the ability to help assess employees' actual computer skills and select job candidates based on verifiable skills applying the latest productivity tools and technology.

Microsoft Pre-tests, delivered by Certiport, provide a simple, low-cost way for individuals to identify their desktop computing skill level. Pre-Tests are taken online, making the first step towards certification easy and convenient. Through the Pre-Tests, individuals can receive a custom learning path with recommended training.

To help students to study for and pass the Microsoft Certified Application Specialist, or MCAS exam, each MOAC textbook includes information allowing students to access a Pre-Test, Score Report, and Learning Plan, either directly from Certiport or through links from the Wiley*PLUS* Premium course. Students also receive a code and information for taking the certification exams. Students who do not have access to Wiley*PLUS* Premium can find information on how to purchase access to the Pre-Test and a code for taking the certification exams by clicking on their textbook at:

http://www.wiley.com/college/microsoft.

The Pre-Test can only be taken once. It provides a simple, low-cost way for students to evaluate and identify their skill level. Through the Pre-Test, students receive a recommended study plan that they can print out to help them prepare for the live certification exams. The Pre-Test is comprised of a variety of selected response questions, including matching, sequencing exercises, "hot spots" where students must identify an item or function, and traditional multiple-choice questions. After students have mastered all the certification objectives, they can use their code to take the actual Microsoft Certified Application Specialist (MCAS) exams for Office 2007.

Wiley*PLUS* Premium includes a complete online version of the student textbook, PowerPoint® presentations, homework and practice assignments and quizzes, links to Microsoft's Pre-Test, Learning Plan and a certification voucher, image galleries, test bank questions, gradebook, and all the instructor resources in one, easy-to-use website. Together, with Wiley*PLUS* and the MCAS Pre-Test and exams delivered by Certiport, we are creating the best of both worlds in academic learning and performance based validation in preparation for a great career and a globally recognized Microsoft certification—the higher education learning management system that accesses the industry-leading certification pre-test.

Contact your Wiley rep today about this special offer.

MSDN ACADEMIC ALLIANCE—FREE 1-YEAR MEMBERSHIP AVAILABLE TO QUALIFIED ADOPTERS!

MSDN Academic Alliance (MSDN AA) is designed to provide the easiest and most inexpensive way for universities to make the latest Microsoft software available in labs, classrooms, and on student PCs. MSDN AA is an annual membership program for departments teaching Science, Technology, Engineering, and Mathematics (STEM) courses. The membership provides a complete solution to keep academic labs, faculty, and students on the leading edge of technology.

As a bonus to this free offer, faculty will be introduced to Microsoft's Faculty Connection and Academic Resource Center. It takes time and preparation to keep students engaged while giving them a fundamental understanding of theory, and the Microsoft Faculty Connection is designed to help STEM professors with this preparation by providing articles, curriculum, and tools that professors can use to engage and inspire today's technology students.

Software provided in the MSDN AA program carries a high retail value but is being provided here through the Wiley and Microsoft publishing partnership and is made available to your department free of charge with the adoption of any Wiley qualified textbook.*

* Contact your Wiley rep for details.

For more information about the MSDN Academic Alliance program, go to:

http://msdn.microsoft.com/academic/

Adoption Options

To provide you and your students with the right choices for learning, studying, and passing the MCAS certification exams, we have put together various options for your adoption requirements.

All selections include the student CD. Please contact your Wiley rep for more information:
- Textbook with 6-month Microsoft Office Trial
- Textbook, 6-month Microsoft Office Trial, WileyPLUS
- Textbook, 6-month Microsoft Office Trial, WileyPLUS Premium (includes access to Certiport)
- WileyPLUS (includes full e-book)
- WileyPLUS Premium (includes full e-book and access to Certiport)

Important Web Addresses and Phone Numbers

To locate the Wiley Higher Education Rep in your area, go to the following Web address and click on the "*Who's My Rep?*" link at the top of the page.

http://www.wiley.com/college

Or Call the MOAC Toll Free Number: 1 + (888) 764-7001

To learn more about becoming a Microsoft Certified Application Specialist and exam availability, visit www.microsoft.com/learning/msbc.

http://www.wiley.com/college/microsoft *or* call the MOAC Toll-Free Number: 1+(888) 764-7001

Student Support Program

Book Companion Website (www.wiley.com/college/microsoft)

The book companion site for the MOAC series includes the Instructor Resources and Web links to important information for students and instructors.

Wiley*PLUS*

Wiley*PLUS* is a powerful and highly-integrated suite of teaching and learning resources designed to bridge the gap between what happens in the classroom and what happens at home and on the job. For students, Wiley*PLUS* provides the tools for study and practice that are available 24/7, wherever and whenever they want to study. Wiley*PLUS* includes a complete online version of the student textbook; PowerPoint presentations; homework and practice assignments and quizzes; links to Microsoft's Pre-Test, Learning Plan, and a code for taking the certification exam (in Wiley*PLUS* Premium); image galleries; test bank questions; gradebook; and all the instructor resources in one easy-to-use website.

Wiley*PLUS* provides immediate feedback on student assignments and a wealth of support materials. This powerful study tool will help your students develop their conceptual understanding of the class material and increase their ability to answer questions.

- A **Study and Practice** area links directly to text content, allowing students to review the text while they study and answer. Access to Microsoft's Pre-Test, Learning Plan, and a code for taking the MCAS certification exam is available in Study and Practice. Additional Practice Questions tied to the MCAS certification that can be re-taken as many times as necessary, are also available.

- An **Assignment** area keeps all the work you want your students to complete in one location, making it easy for them to stay on task. Students have access to a variety of interactive self-assessment tools, as well as other resources for building their confidence and understanding. In addition, all of the assignments and quizzes contain a link to the relevant section of the multimedia book, providing students with context-sensitive help that allows them to conquer obstacles as they arise.

- A **Personal Gradebook** for each student allows students to view their results from past assignments at any time.

Please view our online demo at www.wiley.com/college/wileyplus. Here you will find additional information about the features and benefits of WileyPLUS, how to request a "test drive" of Wiley*PLUS* for this title, and how to adopt it for class use.

6-MONTH MICROSOFT OFFICE 2007 TRIAL EDITION

MOAC textbooks provide an unparalleled value to students in today's performance-based courses. All MOAC 2007 Microsoft Office system textbooks sold in North America are packaged with a 6-month trial CD of Microsoft Office Professional 2007. The textbook includes the CD and a product key that allows students to activate Microsoft Office Professional 2007 for the 6-month trial period. After purchasing the textbook containing the Microsoft Office Professional 2007 Trial CD, students must install the CD onto their computer and, when prompted, enter the Office Trial product key that allows them to activate the software.

Installing the Microsoft Office Professional 2007 Trial CD provides students with the state-of-the-art 2007 Microsoft Office system software, allowing them to use the practice files on the Student CD and in WileyPLUS to learn and study by doing, which is the best and most effective way to acquire and remember new computing skills.

TAKE NOTE *

For the best performance, the default selection during Setup is to uninstall previous versions of Office. There is also an option to remove previous versions of Office. With all trial software, Microsoft recommends that you have your original CDs available to reinstall if necessary. If you want to return to your previous version of Office, you need to uninstall the trial software. This should be done through the Add or Remove Programs icon in Microsoft Windows Control Panel (or Uninstall a program in the Control Panel of Windows Vista).

Installation of Microsoft Office Professional 2007 6-Month Trial software will remove your existing version of Microsoft Outlook. However, your contacts, calendar, and other personal information will not be deleted. At the end of the trial, if you choose to upgrade or to reinstall your previous version of Outlook, your personal settings and information will be retained.

Installing the 2007 Microsoft Office System 6-Month Trial

1. Insert the trial software CD-ROM into the CD drive on your computer. The CD will be detected, and the Setup.exe file should automatically begin to run on your computer.
2. When prompted for the Office Product Key, enter the Product Key provided with the software, and then click **Next.**
3. Enter your name and organization user name, and then click **Next.**
4. Read the End-User License Agreement, select the *I Accept the Terms in the License Agreement* check box, and then click **Next.**
5. Select the install option, verify the installation location or click **Browse** to change the installation location, and then click **Next.**
6. Verify the program installation preferences, and then click **Next.**
7. Click **Finish** to complete the setup.

Upgrading Microsoft Office Professional 2007 6-Month Trial Software to the Full Product

You can convert the software into full use without removing or reinstalling software on your computer. When you complete your trial, you can purchase a product license from any Microsoft reseller and enter a valid Product Key when prompted during Setup.

Uninstalling the Trial Software and Returning to Your Previous Office Version

If you want to return to your previous version of Office, you need to uninstall the trial software. This should be done through the Add or Remove Programs icon in Control Panel (or Uninstall a program in the Control Panel of Windows Vista).

Uninstall Trial Software

1. Quit any programs that are running.
2. In Control Panel, click **Add or Remove Programs** (or **Uninstall a program** in Windows Vista).
3. Click **Microsoft Office Professional 2007,** and then click **Remove** (or **Uninstall** in Windows Vista).

TAKE NOTE * If you selected the option to remove a previous version of Office during installation of the trial software, you need to reinstall your previous version of Office. If you did not remove your previous version of Office, you can start each of your Office programs either through the Start menu or by opening files for each program. In some cases, you may have to recreate some of your shortcuts and default settings.

Student CD

The CD-ROM included with this book contains the practice files that you will use as you perform the exercises in the book. By using the practice files, you will not waste time creating the samples used in the lessons, and you can concentrate on learning how to use Microsoft Office 2007. With the files and the step-by-step instructions in the lessons, you will learn by doing, which is an easy and effective way to acquire and remember new skills.

IMPORTANT This course assumes that the 2007 Microsoft Office system has already been installed on the PC you are using. Note that Microsoft Product Support does not support this trial version.

Copying the Practice Files

Your instructor might already have copied the practice files before you arrive in class. However, your instructor might ask you to copy the practice files on your own at the start of class. Also, if you want to work through any of the exercises in this book on your own at home or at your place of business after class, you may want to copy the practice files. Note that you can also open the files directly from the CD-ROM, but you should be cautious about carrying the CD-ROM around with you as it could become damaged.

◆ ANOTHER WAY

If you only want to copy the files for one lesson, you can open the Data folder and right-click the desired Lesson folder within the Data folder.

1. Insert the CD-ROM in the CD-ROM drive of your computer.
2. Start Windows Explorer.
3. In the left pane of Explorer, locate the icon for your CD-ROM and click on this icon. The folders and files contained on the CD will appear listed on the right.
4. Locate and select the **Access Data** folder. This is the folder that contains all of the practice files, separated by Lesson folders.
5. Right-click on the **Access Data** folder and choose **Copy** from the menu.
6. In the left pane of Windows Explorer, locate the location to which you would like to copy the practice files. This can be a drive on your local PC or an external drive.
7. Right-click on the drive/location to which you want to copy the practice files and choose **Paste.** This will copy the entire Data folder to your chosen location.
8. Close Windows Explorer.

Deleting the Practice Files

Use the following steps when you want to delete the practice files from your hard disk or other drive. Your instructor might ask you to perform these steps at the end of class. Also, you should perform these steps if you have worked through the exercises at home or at your place of business and want to work through the exercises again. Deleting the practice files and then reinstalling them ensures that all files and folders are in their original condition if you decide to work through the exercises again.

1. Start Windows Explorer.
2. Browse through the drives and folders to locate the practice files.
3. Select the **Access Data** folder.
4. Right-click on the **Access Data** folder and choose **Delete** from the menu.
5. Close Windows Explorer.

Locating and Opening Practice Files

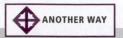

ANOTHER WAY

If you only want to delete only the files for one lesson, you can open the Data folder and right-click the desired Lesson folder within the Data folder.

After you (or your instructor) have copied the practice files, all the files you need for this course will be stored in a folder named Data located on the disk you choose.

1. Click the **Office Button** in the top left corner of your application.
2. Choose **Open** from the menu.
3. In the Open dialog box, browse through the Folders panel to locate the drive and folder where you copied the files.
4. Double-click on the **Access Data** folder.
5. Double-click on the **Lesson** folder for the lesson in which you are working.
6. Select the file that you want and click **Open** or double-click on the file that you want.

Wiley Desktop Editions

ANOTHER WAY

You can use the Search function in the Open dialog box to quickly find the specific file for which you are looking.

Wiley MOAC Desktop Editions are innovative, electronic versions of printed textbooks. Students buy the desktop version for 60% off the price of the printed text, and get the added value of permanence and portability. Wiley Desktop Editions provide students with numerous additional benefits that are not available with other e-text solutions:

Wiley Desktop Editions are NOT subscriptions; students download the Wiley Desktop Edition to their computer desktops. Students own the content they buy to keep for as long as they want. Once a Wiley Desktop Edition is downloaded to the computer desktop, students have instant access to all of the content without being online. Students can also print out the sections they prefer to read in hard copy. Students also have access to fully integrated resources within their Wiley Desktop Edition. From highlighting their e-text to taking and sharing notes, students can easily personalize their Wiley Desktop Edition as they are reading or following along in class.

Microsoft® Office Online

Please visit Microsoft Office Online for help using Office 2007, Clip Art, Templates, and other valuable information:
http://office.microsoft.com/

Preparing to Take the Microsoft Certified Application Specialist (MCAS) Exam

The Microsoft Certified Application Specialist program is part of the new and enhanced Microsoft Business Certifications. It is easily attainable through a series of verifications that provide a simple and convenient framework for skills assessment and validation.

For organizations, the new certification program provides better skills verification tools that help with assessing not only in-demand skills on the 2007 Microsoft Office system, but also the ability to quickly complete on-the-job tasks. Individuals will find it easier to identify and work towards the certification credential that meets their personal and professional goals.

To learn more about becoming a Microsoft Certified Application Specialist and exam availability, visit www.microsoft.com/learning/msbc.

Microsoft Certified Application Specialist (MCAS) Program

The core Microsoft Office Specialist credential has been upgraded to validate skills with the 2007 Microsoft Office system as well as the new Windows Vista operating system. The Application Specialist certifications target information workers and cover the most popular business applications such as Word 2007, PowerPoint 2007, Excel 2007, Access 2007, and Outlook 2007.

By becoming certified, you demonstrate to employers that you have achieved a predictable level of skill in the use of a particular Office application. Employers often require certification either as a condition of employment or as a condition of advancement within the company or other organization. The certification examinations are sponsored by Microsoft but administered through exam delivery partners like Certiport.

Preparing to Take an Exam

Unless you are a very experienced user, you will need to use a test preparation course to prepare to complete the test correctly and within the time allowed. The *Microsoft Official Academic Course* series is designed to prepare you with a strong knowledge of all exam topics, and with some additional review and practice on your own. You should feel confident in your ability to pass the appropriate exam.

After you decide which exam to take, review the list of objectives for the exam. This list can be found in the MCAS Objectives Appendix at the back of this book. You can also easily identify tasks that are included in the objective list by locating the Lesson Skill Matrix at the start of each lesson and the Certification Ready sidebars in the margin of the lessons in this book.

To take the MCAS test, visit *www.microsoft.com/learning/msbc* to locate your nearest testing center. Then call the testing center directly to schedule your test. The amount of advance notice you should provide will vary for different testing centers, and it typically depends on the number of computers available at the testing center, the number of other testers who have already been scheduled for the day on which you want to take the test, and the number of times per week that the testing center offers MCAS testing. In general, you should call to schedule your test at least two weeks prior to the date on which you want to take the test.

When you arrive at the testing center, you might be asked for proof of identity. A driver's license or passport is an acceptable form of identification. If you do not have either of these items of documentation, call your testing center and ask what alternative forms of identification will be accepted. If you are retaking a test, bring your MCAS identification number, which will have been given to you when you previously took the test. If you have not prepaid or if your organization has not already arranged to make payment for you, you will need to pay the test-taking fee when you arrive.

Test Format

All MCAS certification tests are live, performance-based tests. There are no multiple-choice, true/false, or short-answer questions. Instructions are general: you are told the basic tasks to perform on the computer, but you aren't given any help in figuring out how to perform them. You are not permitted to use reference material other than the application's Help system.

As you complete the tasks stated in a particular test question, the testing software monitors your actions. An example question might be:

Open the file named *Wiley Guests* and select the word *Welcome* in the first paragraph. Change the font to 12 point, and apply bold formatting. Select the words *at your convenience* in the second paragraph, move them to the end of the first paragraph using drag and drop, and then center the first paragraph.

When the test administrator seats you at a computer, you will see an online form that you use to enter information about yourself (name, address, and other information required to process your exam results). While you complete the form, the software will generate the test from a master test bank and then prompt you to continue. The first test question will appear in a window. Read the question carefully, and then perform all the tasks stated in the test question. When you have finished completing all tasks for a question, click the Next Question button.

You have 45 to 60 minutes to complete all questions, depending on the test that you are taking. The testing software assesses your results as soon as you complete the test, and the test administrator can print the results of the test so that you will have a record of any tasks that you performed incorrectly. A passing grade is 75 percent or higher. If you pass, you will receive a certificate in the mail within two to four weeks. If you do not pass, you can study and practice the skills that you missed and then schedule to retake the test at a later date.

Tips for Successfully Completing the Test

The following tips and suggestions are the result of feedback received from many individuals who have taken one or more MCAS tests:

- Make sure that you are thoroughly prepared. If you have extensively used the application for which you are being tested, you might feel confident that you are prepared for the test. However, the test might include questions that involve tasks that you rarely or never perform when you use the application at your place of business, at school, or at home. You must be knowledgeable in all the MCAS objectives for the test that you will take.

- Read each exam question carefully. An exam question might include several tasks that you are to perform. A partially correct response to a test question is counted as an incorrect response. In the example question on the previous page, you might apply bold formatting and move the words *at your convenience* to the correct location, but forget to center the first paragraph. This would count as an incorrect response and would result in a lower test score.

- You are allowed to use the application's Help system, but relying on the Help system too much will slow you down and possibly prevent you from completing the test within the allotted time. Use the Help system only when necessary.

- Keep track of your time. The test does not display the amount of time that you have left, so you need to keep track of the time yourself by monitoring your start time and the required end time on your watch or a clock in the testing center (if there is one). The test program displays the number of items that you have completed along with the total number of test items (for example, "35 of 40 items have been completed"). Use this information to gauge your pace.

- If you skip a question, you cannot return to it later. You should skip a question only if you are certain that you cannot complete the tasks correctly.

- As soon as you are finished reading a question and you click in the application window, a condensed version of the instruction is displayed in a corner of the screen. If you are unsure whether you have completed all tasks stated in the test question, click the Instructions button on the test information bar at the bottom of the screen and then reread the question. Close the instruction window when you are finished. Do this as often as necessary to ensure you have read the question correctly and that you have completed all the tasks stated in the question.

If You Do Not Pass the Test

If you do not pass, you can use the assessment printout as a guide to practice the items that you missed. There is no limit to the number of times that you can retake a test; however, you must pay the fee each time that you take the test. When you retake the test, expect to see some of the same test items on the subsequent test; the test software randomly generates the test items from a master test bank before you begin the test. Also expect to see several questions that did not appear on the previous test.

Acknowledgments

MOAC Instructor Advisory Board

We would like thank to our Instructor Advisory Board, an elite group of educators who has assisted us every step of the way in building these products. Advisory Board members have acted as our sounding board on key pedagogical and design decisions leading to the development of these compelling and innovative textbooks for future Information Workers. Their dedication to technology education is truly appreciated.

Catherine Binder, Strayer University & Katharine Gibbs School–Philadelphia

Catherine currently works at both Katharine Gibbs School in Norristown, PA and Strayer University in King of Prussia, PA. Catherine has been at Katharine Gibbs School for 4 years. Catherine is currently the Department Chair/Lead instructor for PC Networking at Gibbs and the founder/advisor of the TEK Masters Society. Since joining Strayer University a year and a half ago she has risen in the ranks from adjunct to DIT/Assistant Campus Dean.

Catherine has brought her 10+ year's industry experience as Network Administrator, Network Supervisor, Professor, Bench Tech, Manager and CTO from such places as Foster Wheeler Corp, KidsPeace Inc., Victoria Vogue, TESST College, AMC Theatres, Blue Mountain Publishing and many more to her teaching venue.

Catherine began as an adjunct in the PC Networking department and quickly became a full-time instructor. At both schools she is in charge of scheduling, curricula and departmental duties. She happily advises about 80+ students and is committed to Gibbs/Strayer life, her students, and continuing technology education every day.

Penny Gudgeon, CDI College

Penny is the Program Manager for IT curriculum at Corinthian Colleges, Inc. Until January 2006, Penny was responsible for all Canadian programming and web curriculum for five years. During that time, Corinthian Colleges, Inc. acquired CDI College of Business and Technology in 2004. Before 2000 she spent four years as IT instructor at one of the campuses. Penny joined CDI College in 1997 after her working for 10 years first in programming and later in software productivity education. Penny previously has worked in the fields of advertising, sales, engineering technology and programming. When not working from her home office or indulging her passion for life long learning, and the possibilities of what might be, Penny likes to read mysteries, garden and relax at home in Hamilton, Ontario, with her Shih-Tzu, Gracie, and husband, Al.

Jana Hambruch, School District of Lee County

Ms. Hambruch currently serves as Director for the Information Technology Magnet Programs at The School District of Lee County in Ft Myers, Florida. She is responsible for the implementation and direction of three schools that fall under this grant program. This program has been recognized as one of the top 15 most innovative technology programs in the nation. She is also co-author of the grant proposal for the IT Magnet Grant prior to taking on the role of Director.

Ms. Hambruch has over ten years experience directing the technical certification training programs at many Colleges and Universities, including Barry University, the University of

South Florida, Broward Community College, and at Florida Gulf Coast University, where she served as the Director for the Center for Technology Education. She excels at developing alternative training models that focus on the tie between the education provider and the community in which it serves.

Ms. Hambruch is a past board member and treasurer of the Human Resources Management Association of SW Florida, graduate of Leadership Lee County Class of 2002, Steering Committee Member for Leadership Lee County Class of 2004 and a former board member of the Career Coalition of Southwest Florida. She has frequently lectured for organizations such as Microsoft, American Society of Training and Development, Florida Gulf Coast University, Florida State University, University of Nevada at Las Vegas, University of Wisconsin at Milwaukee, Canada's McGill University, and Florida's State Workforce Summit.

Dee Hobson, Richland College

Dee Hobson is currently a faculty member of the Business Office Systems and Support Division at Richland College. Richland is one of seven colleges in the Dallas County Community College District and has the distinction of being the first community college to receive the Malcolm Baldrige National Quality Award in 2005. Richland also received the Texas Award for Performance Excellence in 2005.

The Business Office Systems and Support Division at Richland is also a Certiport Authorized Microsoft Office testing center. All students enrolling in one of Microsoft's application software courses (Word, Excel, PowerPoint, and Access) are required to take the respective Microsoft certification exam at the end of the semester.

Dee has taught computer and business courses in K-12 public schools and at a proprietary career college in Dallas. She has also been involved with several corporate training companies and with adult education programs in the Dallas area. She began her computer career as an employee of IBM Corporation in St. Louis, Missouri. During her ten-year IBM employment, she moved to Memphis, Tennessee, to accept a managerial position and to Dallas, Texas, to work in a national sales and marketing technical support center.

Keith Hoell, Katharine Gibbs School–New York

Keith has worked in both non-profit and proprietary education for over 10 years, initially at St. John's University in New York, and then as full-time faculty, Chairperson and currently Dean of Information Systems at the Katharine Gibbs School in New York City. He also worked for General Electric in the late 80's and early 90's as the Sysop of a popular bulletin board dedicated to ASCII-Art on GE's pioneering GEnie on-line service before the advent of the World Wide Web. He has taught courses and workshops dealing with many mainstream IT issues and varied technology, especially those related to computer hardware and operating system software, networking, software applications, IT project management and ethics, and relational database technology. An avid runner and a member of The New York Road Runners, he won the Footlocker Five Borough Challenge representing Queens at the 2005 ING New York City Marathon while competing against the 4 other borough reps. He currently resides in Queens, New York.

Michael Taylor, Seattle Central Community College

Michael worked in education and training for the last 20 years in both the public and private sector. He currently teaches and coordinates the applications support program at Seattle Central Community College and also administers the Microsoft IT Academy. His experience outside the educational world is in Travel and Tourism with wholesale tour operations and cruise lines.

Interests outside of work include greyhound rescue. (He adopted 3 x-racers who bring him great joy.) He also enjoys the arts and is fortunate to live in downtown Seattle where there is much to see and do.

MOAC Office 2007 Reviewers

We also thank the many reviewers who pored over the manuscript, providing invaluable feedback in the service of quality instructional materials.

Access

Susan Fry, Boise State University
Leslie Jernberg, Eastern Idaho Technical College
Dr. Deborah Jones, South Georgia Technical College
Suzanne Marks, Bellevue Community College
Kim Styles, Tri-County Technical College & Anderson School District 5
Fred Usmani, Conestoga College

Excel

Bob Gunderson, TriOS College
Christie Hovey, Lincoln Land Community College
Barbara Lave, Portland Community College
Trevor McIvor, Bow Valley College
Donna Madsen, Kirkwood Community College
James M. Veneziano, Davenport University—Caro
Dorothy Weiner, Manchester Community College

PowerPoint

Barbara Gillespie, Cuyamaca College
Caroline de Gruchy, Conestoga College
Tatyana Pashnyak, Bainbridge College
Michelle Poertner, Northwestern Michigan College
Janet Sebesy, Cuyahoga Community College

Outlook

Julie Boyles, Portland Community College
Joe LaMontagne, Davenport University—Grand Rapids
Randy Nordell, American River College
Echo Rantanen, Spokane Community College
Lyndsey Webster, TriOS College

Project

Janis DeHaven, Central Community College
Dr. Susan Jennings, Stephen F. Austin State University
Jack Maronowski, Curriculum Director, CDI College
Diane D. Mickey, Northern Virginia Community College
Linda Nutter, Peninsula College
Marika Reinke, Bellevue Community College

Word

Diana Anderson, Big Sandy Community & Technical College
Donna Hendricks, South Arkansas Community College
Dr. Donna McGill-Cameron, Yuba Community College—Woodland Campus
Patricia McMahon, South Suburban College
Jack Maronowski, Curriculum Director, CDI College
Nancy Noe, Linn-Benton Community College
Teresa Roberts, Wilson Technical Community College

Focus Group and Survey Participants

Finally, we thank the hundreds of instructors who participated in our focus groups and surveys to ensure that the Microsoft Official Academic Courses best met the needs of our customers.

Jean Aguilar, Mt. Hood Community College

Konrad Akens, Zane State College

Michael Albers, University of Memphis

Diana Anderson, Big Sandy Community & Technical College

Phyllis Anderson, Delaware County Community College

Judith Andrews, Feather River College

Damon Antos, American River College

Bridget Archer, Oakton Community College

Linda Arnold, Harrisburg Area Community College– Lebanon Campus

Neha Arya, Fullerton College

Mohammad Bajwa, Katharine Gibbs School–New York

Virginia Baker, University of Alaska Fairbanks

Carla Bannick, Pima Community College

Rita Barkley, Northeast Alabama Community College

Elsa Barr, Central Community College – Hastings

Ronald W. Barry, Ventura County Community College District

Elizabeth Bastedo, Central Carolina Technical College

Karen Baston, Waubonsee Community College

Karen Bean, Blinn College

Scott Beckstrand, Community College of Southern Nevada

Paulette Bell, Santa Rosa Junior College

Liz Bennett, Southeast Technical Institute

Nancy Bermea, Olympic College

Lucy Betz, Milwaukee Area Technical College

Meral Binbasioglu, Hofstra University

Catherine Binder, Strayer University & Katharine Gibbs School–Philadelphia

Terrel Blair, El Centro College

Ruth Blalock, Alamance Community College

Beverly Bohner, Reading Area Community College

Henry Bojack, Farmingdale State University

Matthew Bowie, Luna Community College

Julie Boyles, Portland Community College

Karen Brandt, College of the Albemarle

Stephen Brown, College of San Mateo

Jared Bruckner, Southern Adventist University

Pam Brune, Chattanooga State Technical Community College

Sue Buchholz, Georgia Perimeter College

Roberta Buczyna, Edison College

Angela Butler, Mississippi Gulf Coast Community College

Rebecca Byrd, Augusta Technical College

Kristen Callahan, Mercer County Community College

Judy Cameron, Spokane Community College

Dianne Campbell, Athens Technical College

Gena Casas, Florida Community College at Jacksonville

Jesus Castrejon, Latin Technologies

Gail Chambers, Southwest Tennessee Community College

Jacques Chansavang, Indiana University–Purdue University Fort Wayne

Nancy Chapko, Milwaukee Area Technical College

Rebecca Chavez, Yavapai College

Sanjiv Chopra, Thomas Nelson Community College

Greg Clements, Midland Lutheran College

Dayna Coker, Southwestern Oklahoma State University– Sayre Campus

Tamra Collins, Otero Junior College

Janet Conrey, Gavilan Community College

Carol Cornforth, West Virginia Northern Community College

Gary Cotton, American River College

Edie Cox, Chattahoochee Technical College

Rollie Cox, Madison Area Technical College

David Crawford, Northwestern Michigan College

J.K. Crowley, Victor Valley College

Rosalyn Culver, Washtenaw Community College

Sharon Custer, Huntington University

Sandra Daniels, New River Community College

Anila Das, Cedar Valley College

Brad Davis, Santa Rosa Junior College

Susan Davis, Green River Community College

Mark Dawdy, Lincoln Land Community College

Jennifer Day, Sinclair Community College

Carol Deane, Eastern Idaho Technical College

Julie DeBuhr, Lewis-Clark State College

Janis DeHaven, Central Community College

Drew Dekreon, University of Alaska–Anchorage

Joy DePover, Central Lakes College

Salli DiBartolo, Brevard Community College

Melissa Diegnau, Riverland Community College

Al Dillard, Lansdale School of Business

Marjorie Duffy, Cosumnes River College

Sarah Dunn, Southwest Tennessee Community College

Shahla Durany, Tarrant County College–South Campus

Kay Durden, University of Tennessee at Martin

Dineen Ebert, St. Louis Community College–Meramec

Donna Ehrhart, State University of New York–Brockport

Larry Elias, Montgomery County Community College

Glenda Elser, New Mexico State University at Alamogordo

Angela Evangelinos, Monroe County Community College

Angie Evans, Ivy Tech Community College of Indiana

Linda Farrington, Indian Hills Community College

Dana Fladhammer, Phoenix College

Richard Flores, Citrus College

Connie Fox, Community and Technical College at Institute of Technology West Virginia University

Wanda Freeman, Okefenokee Technical College

Brenda Freeman, Augusta Technical College

Susan Fry, Boise State University

Roger Fulk, Wright State University–Lake Campus

Sue Furnas, Collin County Community College District

Sandy Gabel, Vernon College

Laura Galvan, Fayetteville Technical Community College

Candace Garrod, Red Rocks Community College

Sherrie Geitgey, Northwest State Community College

Chris Gerig, Chattahoochee Technical College

Barb Gillespie, Cuyamaca College

Jessica Gilmore, Highline Community College

Pamela Gilmore, Reedley College

Debbie Glinert, Queensborough Community College

Steven Goldman, Polk Community College

Bettie Goodman, C.S. Mott Community College

Mike Grabill, Katharine Gibbs School–Philadelphia

Francis Green, Penn State University

Walter Griffin, Blinn College

Fillmore Guinn, Odessa College

Helen Haasch, Milwaukee Area Technical College

John Habal, Ventura College

Joy Haerens, Chaffey College

Norman Hahn, Thomas Nelson Community College

Kathy Hall, Alamance Community College

Teri Harbacheck, Boise State University

Linda Harper, Richland Community College

Maureen Harper, Indian Hills Community College

Steve Harris, Katharine Gibbs School–New York

Robyn Hart, Fresno City College

Darien Hartman, Boise State University

Gina Hatcher, Tacoma Community College

Winona T. Hatcher, Aiken Technical College

BJ Hathaway, Northeast Wisconsin Tech College

Cynthia Hauki, West Hills College – Coalinga

Mary L. Haynes, Wayne County Community College

Marcie Hawkins, Zane State College

Steve Hebrock, Ohio State University Agricultural
   Technical Institute

Sue Heistand, Iowa Central Community College

Heith Hennel, Valencia Community College

Donna Hendricks, South Arkansas Community College

Judy Hendrix, Dyersburg State Community College

Gloria Hensel, Matanuska-Susitna College University
   of Alaska Anchorage

Gwendolyn Hester, Richland College

Tammarra Holmes, Laramie County Community College

Dee Hobson, Richland College

Keith Hoell, Katharine Gibbs School–New York

Pashia Hogan, Northeast State Technical
   Community College

Susan Hoggard, Tulsa Community College

Kathleen Holliman, Wallace Community College Selma

Chastity Honchul, Brown Mackie College/Wright
   State University

Christie Hovey, Lincoln Land Community College

Peggy Hughes, Allegany College of Maryland

Sandra Hume, Chippewa Valley Technical College

John Hutson, Aims Community College

Celia Ing, Sacramento City College

Joan Ivey, Lanier Technical College

Barbara Jaffari, College of the Redwoods

Penny Jakes, University of Montana College of Technology

Eduardo Jaramillo, Peninsula College

Barbara Jauken, Southeast Community College

Susan Jennings, Stephen F. Austin State University

Leslie Jernberg, Eastern Idaho Technical College

Linda Johns, Georgia Perimeter College

Brent Johnson, Okefenokee Technical College

Mary Johnson, Mt. San Antonio College

Shirley Johnson, Trinidad State Junior College–
   Valley Campus

Sandra M. Jolley, Tarrant County College

Teresa Jolly, South Georgia Technical College

Dr. Deborah Jones, South Georgia Technical College

Margie Jones, Central Virginia Community College

Randall Jones, Marshall Community and Technical College

Diane Karlsbraaten, Lake Region State College

Teresa Keller, Ivy Tech Community College of Indiana

Charles Kemnitz, Pennsylvania College of Technology

Sandra Kinghorn, Ventura College

Bill Klein, Katharine Gibbs School–Philadelphia

Bea Knaapen, Fresno City College

Kit Kofoed, Western Wyoming Community College

Maria Kolatis, County College of Morris

Barry Kolb, Ocean County College

Karen Kuralt, University of Arkansas at Little Rock

Belva-Carole Lamb, Rogue Community College

Betty Lambert, Des Moines Area Community College

Anita Lande, Cabrillo College

Junnae Landry, Pratt Community College

Karen Lankisch, UC Clermont

David Lanzilla, Central Florida Community College

Nora Laredo, Cerritos Community College

Jennifer Larrabee, Chippewa Valley Technical College

Debra Larson, Idaho State University

Barb Lave, Portland Community College

Audrey Lawrence, Tidewater Community College

Deborah Layton, Eastern Oklahoma State College

Larry LeBlanc, Owen Graduate School–
   Vanderbilt University

Philip Lee, Nashville State Community College

Michael Lehrfeld, Brevard Community College

Vasant Limaye, Southwest Collegiate Institute for the
   Deaf – Howard College

Anne C. Lewis, Edgecombe Community College

Stephen Linkin, Houston Community College

Peggy Linston, Athens Technical College

Hugh Lofton, Moultrie Technical College

Donna Lohn, Lakeland Community College

Jackie Lou, Lake Tahoe Community College

Donna Love, Gaston College

Curt Lynch, Ozarks Technical Community College
Sheilah Lynn, Florida Community College–Jacksonville
Pat R. Lyon, Tomball College
Bill Madden, Bergen Community College
Heather Madden, Delaware Technical & Community College
Donna Madsen, Kirkwood Community College
Jane Maringer-Cantu, Gavilan College
Suzanne Marks, Bellevue Community College
Carol Martin, Louisiana State University–Alexandria
Cheryl Martucci, Diablo Valley College
Roberta Marvel, Eastern Wyoming College
Tom Mason, Brookdale Community College
Mindy Mass, Santa Barbara City College
Dixie Massaro, Irvine Valley College
Rebekah May, Ashland Community & Technical College
Emma Mays-Reynolds, Dyersburg State Community College
Timothy Mayes, Metropolitan State College of Denver
Reggie McCarthy, Central Lakes College
Matt McCaskill, Brevard Community College
Kevin McFarlane, Front Range Community College
Donna McGill, Yuba Community College
Terri McKeever, Ozarks Technical Community College
Patricia McMahon, South Suburban College
Sally McMillin, Katharine Gibbs School–Philadelphia
Charles McNerney, Bergen Community College
Lisa Mears, Palm Beach Community College
Imran Mehmood, ITT Technical Institute–King of Prussia Campus
Virginia Melvin, Southwest Tennessee Community College
Jeanne Mercer, Texas State Technical College
Denise Merrell, Jefferson Community & Technical College
Catherine Merrikin, Pearl River Community College
Diane D. Mickey, Northern Virginia Community College
Darrelyn Miller, Grays Harbor College
Sue Mitchell, Calhoun Community College
Jacquie Moldenhauer, Front Range Community College
Linda Motonaga, Los Angeles City College
Sam Mryyan, Allen County Community College
Cindy Murphy, Southeastern Community College
Ryan Murphy, Sinclair Community College
Sharon E. Nastav, Johnson County Community College
Christine Naylor, Kent State University Ashtabula
Haji Nazarian, Seattle Central Community College
Nancy Noe, Linn-Benton Community College
Jennie Noriega, San Joaquin Delta College
Linda Nutter, Peninsula College
Thomas Omerza, Middle Bucks Institute of Technology
Edith Orozco, St. Philip's College
Dona Orr, Boise State University
Joanne Osgood, Chaffey College
Janice Owens, Kishwaukee College
Tatyana Pashnyak, Bainbridge College

John Partacz, College of DuPage
Tim Paul, Montana State University–Great Falls
Joseph Perez, South Texas College
Mike Peterson, Chemeketa Community College
Dr. Karen R. Petitto, West Virginia Wesleyan College
Terry Pierce, Onandaga Community College
Ashlee Pieris, Raritan Valley Community College
Jamie Pinchot, Thiel College
Michelle Poertner, Northwestern Michigan College
Betty Posta, University of Toledo
Deborah Powell, West Central Technical College
Mark Pranger, Rogers State University
Carolyn Rainey, Southeast Missouri State University
Linda Raskovich, Hibbing Community College
Leslie Ratliff, Griffin Technical College
Mar-Sue Ratzke, Rio Hondo Community College
Roxy Reissen, Southeastern Community College
Silvio Reyes, Technical Career Institutes
Patricia Rishavy, Anoka Technical College
Jean Robbins, Southeast Technical Institute
Carol Roberts, Eastern Maine Community College and University of Maine
Teresa Roberts, Wilson Technical Community College
Vicki Robertson, Southwest Tennessee Community College
Betty Rogge, Ohio State Agricultural Technical Institute
Lynne Rusley, Missouri Southern State University
Claude Russo, Brevard Community College
Ginger Sabine, Northwestern Technical College
Steven Sachs, Los Angeles Valley College
Joanne Salas, Olympic College
Lloyd Sandmann, Pima Community College–Desert Vista Campus
Beverly Santillo, Georgia Perimeter College
Theresa Savarese, San Diego City College
Sharolyn Sayers, Milwaukee Area Technical College
Judith Scheeren, Westmoreland County Community College
Adolph Scheiwe, Joliet Junior College
Marilyn Schmid, Asheville-Buncombe Technical Community College
Janet Sebesy, Cuyahoga Community College
Phyllis T. Shafer, Brookdale Community College
Ralph Shafer, Truckee Meadows Community College
Anne Marie Shanley, County College of Morris
Shelia Shelton, Surry Community College
Merilyn Shepherd, Danville Area Community College
Susan Sinele, Aims Community College
Beth Sindt, Hawkeye Community College
Andrew Smith, Marian College
Brenda Smith, Southwest Tennessee Community College
Lynne Smith, State University of New York–Delhi
Rob Smith, Katharine Gibbs School–Philadelphia
Tonya Smith, Arkansas State University–Mountain Home
Del Spencer – Trinity Valley Community College

Jeri Spinner, Idaho State University

Eric Stadnik, Santa Rosa Junior College

Karen Stanton, Los Medanos College

Meg Stoner, Santa Rosa Junior College

Beverly Stowers, Ivy Tech Community College of Indiana

Marcia Stranix, Yuba College

Kim Styles, Tri-County Technical College

Sylvia Summers, Tacoma Community College

Beverly Swann, Delaware Technical & Community College

Ann Taff, Tulsa Community College

Mike Theiss, University of Wisconsin–Marathon Campus

Romy Thiele, Cañada College

Sharron Thompson, Portland Community College

Ingrid Thompson-Sellers, Georgia Perimeter College

Barbara Tietsort, University of Cincinnati–Raymond Walters College

Janine Tiffany, Reading Area Community College

Denise Tillery, University of Nevada Las Vegas

Susan Trebelhorn, Normandale Community College

Noel Trout, Santiago Canyon College

Cheryl Turgeon, Asnuntuck Community College

Steve Turner, Ventura College

Sylvia Unwin, Bellevue Community College

Lilly Vigil, Colorado Mountain College

Sabrina Vincent, College of the Mainland

Mary Vitrano, Palm Beach Community College

Brad Vogt, Northeast Community College

Cozell Wagner, Southeastern Community College

Carolyn Walker, Tri-County Technical College

Sherry Walker, Tulsa Community College

Qi Wang, Tacoma Community College

Betty Wanielista, Valencia Community College

Marge Warber, Lanier Technical College–Forsyth Campus

Marjorie Webster, Bergen Community College

Linda Wenn, Central Community College

Mark Westlund, Olympic College

Carolyn Whited, Roane State Community College

Winona Whited, Richland College

Jerry Wilkerson, Scott Community College

Joel Willenbring, Fullerton College

Barbara Williams, WITC Superior

Charlotte Williams, Jones County Junior College

Bonnie Willy, Ivy Tech Community College of Indiana

Diane Wilson, J. Sargeant Reynolds Community College

James Wolfe, Metropolitan Community College

Marjory Wooten, Lanier Technical College

Mark Yanko, Hocking College

Alexis Yusov, Pace University

Naeem Zaman, San Joaquin Delta College

Kathleen Zimmerman, Des Moines Area Community College

We would also like to thank Lutz Ziob, Sanjay Advani, Jim DiIanni, Merrick Van Dongen, Jim LeValley, Bruce Curling, Joe Wilson, and Naman Kahn at Microsoft for their encouragement and support in making the Microsoft Official Academic Course programs the finest instructional materials for mastering the newest Microsoft technologies for both students and instructors.

Brief Contents

www.wiley.com/college/microsoft *or* call the MOAC Toll-Free Number: 1+(888) 764-7001

Contents

Lesson 15: Database Tools   376

FOR INSTRUCTORS

Wiley**PLUS** is built around the activities you perform in your class each day. With Wiley**PLUS** you can:

Prepare & Present
Create outstanding class presentations using a wealth of resources such as PowerPoint™ slides, image galleries, interactive simulations, and more. You can even add materials you have created yourself.

Create Assignments
Automate the assigning and grading of homework or quizzes by using the provided question banks, or by writing your own.

Track Student Progress
Keep track of your students' progress and analyze individual and overall class results.

Now Available with WebCT and Blackboard!

"It has been a great help, and I believe it has helped me to achieve a better grade."

Michael Morris,
Columbia Basin College

FOR STUDENTS

You have the potential to make a difference!

WileyPLUS is a powerful online system packed with features to help you make the most of your potential and get the best grade you can!

With Wiley**PLUS** you get:

A complete online version of your text and other study resources.

Problem-solving help, instant grading, and feedback on your homework and quizzes.

The ability to track your progress and grades throughout the term.

Access to Microsoft's Assessment, Learning Plan, and MCAS examination voucher.

For more information on what *WileyPLUS* can do to help you and your students reach their potential, please visit www.wiley.com/college/*wileyplus*.

76% of students surveyed said it made them better prepared for tests.*

*Based on a survey of 972 student users of *WileyPLUS*

---

www.wiley.com/college/microsoft *or* call the MOAC Toll-Free Number: 1+(888) 764-7001

Microsoft® Official Academic Course

Microsoft® Office Access® 2007

Database Essentials

LESSON SKILL MATRIX

SKILLS	MATRIX SKILL	SKILL NUMBER
Opening and Closing an Existing Database	Open databases	6.1.1
Defining Data Needs and Types	Define data needs and types	1.1
Defining Table Fields	Define table fields	1.1.1
Defining Data Types for Fields	Define appropriate table field data types for fields in each table	1.1.2
Defining Database Tables	Define tables in databases	1.1.3

The School of Fine Art in Poughkeepsie, New York, is the brainchild of two professional artists—Shaun Beasley, a printmaker, and Jane Clayton, a sculptor. Last year, the new private high school opened with an enrollment of 12 students and with Jane and Shaun as the only full-time instructors. All academic and business records were maintained manually by the founders. This year, however, you were hired as an executive assistant to help them manage an increasing amount of information. Enrollment is climbing, new full-time faculty members are being hired, and the school is receiving scholarship funds from local patrons. With the help of an Access database, you will organize the school's academic and business data. In this lesson, you will learn basic database concepts and how to define data needs and types.

KEY TERMS

badge
Connection Status menu
database
database management system (DBMS)
datasheet
data type
desktop
dialog box launcher
field
form
group
KeyTip
Microsoft Office Button
normal forms
normalization
object
primary key
query
Quick Access Toolbar
record
redundant data
relational database
report
Ribbon
tab
table

■ SOFTWARE ORIENTATION

Microsoft Access' Opening Screen

Before you begin working in Microsoft Access, you need to be familiar with the primary user interface. In the next section, you will be asked to open a new blank database in Access. When you do so, a screen will appear that will be similar to the one shown in Figure 1-1.

Figure 1-1

Opening screen for new blank Access database

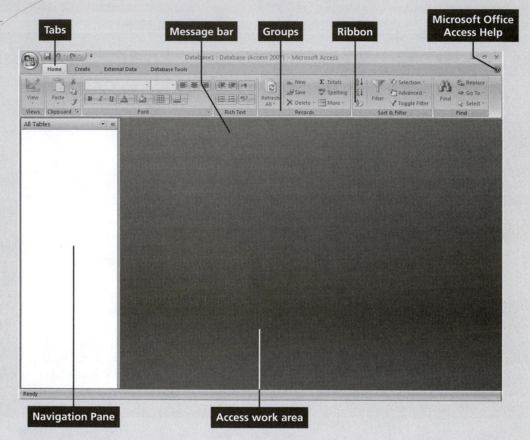

When you create a blank database in Microsoft Access, the opening screen provides you with a workspace in which to build a database. Understanding the screen elements helps orient you to important tools and information. The elements and features of your screen may vary if default settings have been changed or if other preferences have been set. Use this figure as a reference throughout this lesson as well as the rest of this book.

■ Getting Started

THE BOTTOM LINE

A database is a powerful tool for managing volumes of complex data. As with any program, however, the first tasks are the most basic. This section shows you how to start Access and open an existing database. It also details important elements of the Getting Started with Microsoft Office Access screen.

Starting Access

When you start Access, you can choose from among several options for creating a new database or opening an existing saved database.

START ACCESS

GET READY. Before you begin these steps, be sure to turn on and/or log on to your computer.

1. On the Windows taskbar, click the **Start** button and click **Programs.** A menu of installed programs appears.

2. Click **Microsoft Office**. Another menu appears.

3. Click **Microsoft Office Access 2007**. The Getting Started with Microsoft Office Access page appears, as shown in Figure 1-2. Your screen may look slightly different, depending on your system.

Figure 1-2

Getting Started with Microsoft Office Access page

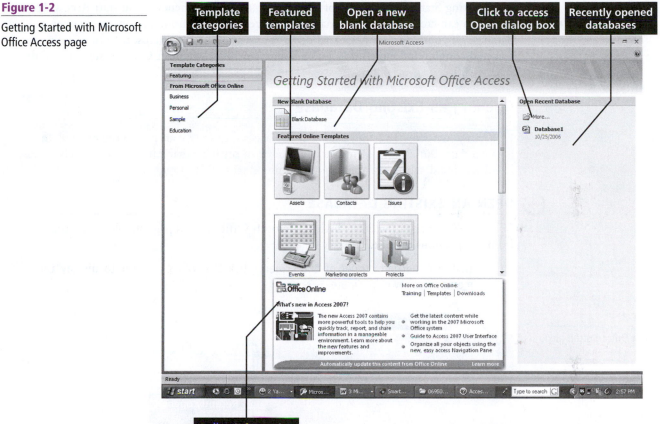

PAUSE. LEAVE the Getting Started with Microsoft Office Access page open to use in the next exercise.

ANOTHER WAY

When Office was installed on your computer, a shortcut icon might have been added to the Start menu or to your desktop. Click the shortcut to start Access without having to go through the Start menu.

Any list you make for a specific purpose can be considered a simple database, even a grocery list. A ***database*** is a tool for collecting and organizing information. Databases can store information about people, products, orders, or anything else. For example, a phone book contains names, addresses, and phone numbers. As a database, it organizes large amounts of data and enables you to access it in a predictable way—usually by name in alphabetic order.

As you collect more data and it becomes more complex, your need to manage the data increases. A computerized ***database management system (DBMS),*** such as Microsoft Office Access, enables you to easily collect large volumes of data organized into categories of related information. This type of database enables you to store, organize, and manage your data, no matter how complex it is, and then retrieve and present it in various formats and reports.

When you start your computer, the screen you see is called the Windows *desktop*. Click the Start button in the lower left corner of the taskbar to open the Start menu and then click (All) Programs. A popup menu will appear; then click Microsoft Office. Another popup menu appears; click Microsoft Office Access 2007.

When Access was installed on your computer, the program might have placed an icon on your desktop. If it did not, you can manually place the icon by creating a shortcut. Either way, double-clicking the program icon is an easy way to start Access.

The Getting Started with Microsoft Access screen appears whenever you start Access. From here, you can create a new blank database, create a database from a template, or open a recent database (if you have already created one). You can also access Microsoft Office Online for featured content and more information about the 2007 Microsoft Office system and Office Access 2007.

Opening an Existing Database

When you open an existing database, you access not only your previously entered and saved data, but also the elements you created to organize that data. In this exercise, you will open a database that is in the beginning stages of development.

⊘ OPEN AN EXISTING DATABASE

GET READY. The Getting Started with Microsoft Office Access page should be on the screen from the previous exercise.

1. In the upper-left corner of the screen, click the **Office Button** to display the menu, as shown in Figure 1-3.

Figure 1-3

Microsoft Office Button menu

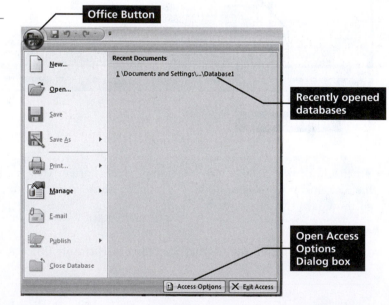

TAKE NOTE If the database you want to use is listed in the Recent Documents on the right of the menu, simply click to open it.

2. Click **Open**. The Open dialog box appears, as shown in Figure 1-4.

Figure 1-4

Open dialog box

 ANOTHER WAY

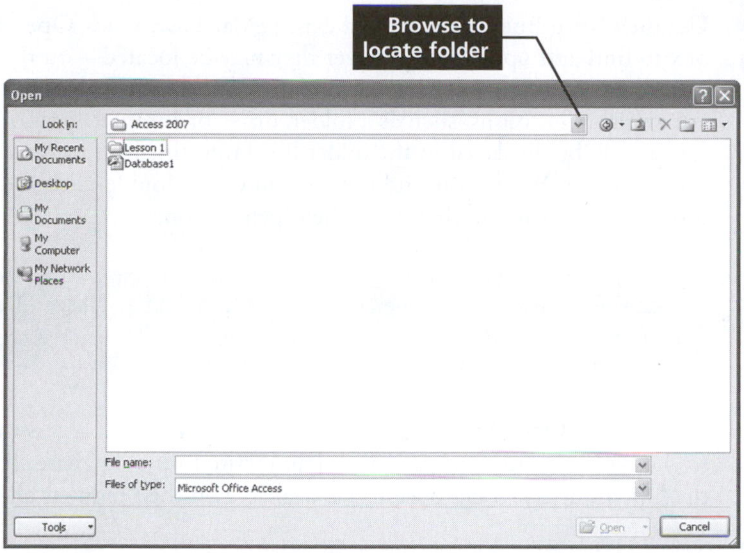

Press Ctrl+O to display the Open dialog box.

 CD

The *Student Information* database is available on the companion CD-ROM.

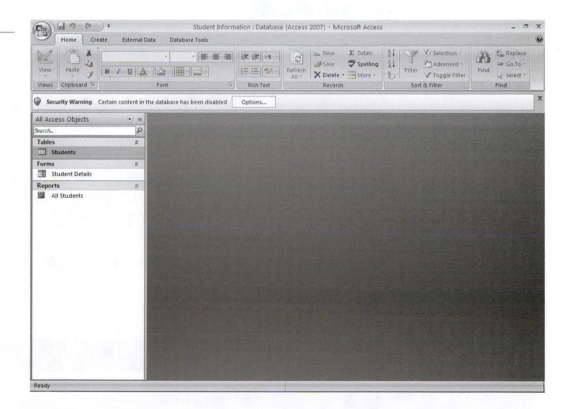

3. Navigate to the data files for this lesson and select **Student Information**.

4. Click the **Open** button. The existing database opens, as shown in Figure 1-5.

Figure 1-5

Existing database open in Access

TROUBLE**SHOOTING**

As part of the Office Access 2007 security model, when you open a database outside of a trusted location, a tool called the Message Bar will appear to warn you that certain content has been disabled. If you know you can trust the database, click Options and then choose to enable the content in the dialog box that appears.

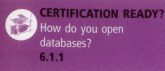

CERTIFICATION READY?
How do you open
databases?
6.1.1

PAUSE. LEAVE the database open to use in the next exercise.

Use the Office Button to open an existing database. Click Open to display the Open dialog box to find and open files wherever they may be located—on the desktop, in a folder on your computer, on a network drive, or on a CD or other removable media. The Look in box lists the available locations, such as a folder, drive, or Internet location. Click the location, and the folders will be displayed in the folder list. From this list, you can double-click the folder you want to open. When you find the file you want, double-click the filename to open it or click it once to select it and then click the Open button.

 **ANOTHER WAY**
You can also display the Open dialog box by clicking More in the Open Recent Database list on the Getting Started with Microsoft Office Access page.

Clicking the Open button opens the database for shared access in a multi-user environment so that you and other users can read and write to the database. If you click the arrow next to the Open button, other options are available on the menu, as shown in Figure 1-6.

Figure 1-6

Open button menu

The Open Read-Only option opens the database for read-only access so that you can view but not edit it—other users can still read and write to the database. The Open Exclusive option opens the database with exclusive access, which means that anyone else who tries to open the database receives a "file already in use" message. The Open Exclusive Read-Only option opens the database for read-only access—other users can still open the database, but they are limited to read-only mode.

 TAKE NOTE*
Each time you start Access, you open a new instance of Access. You can only have one database open at a time in a single instance of Access. In other words, you cannot start Access, open one database, and then open another database without closing the first database. However, you can open multiple databases at the same time by opening another instance of Access. For example, to have two Access databases open, start Access and open the first Access database, and then start a new instance of Access and open the second database.

■ Working in the Access Window

↓ THE BOTTOM LINE
The Access 2007 Window user interface was designed to help you find the commands you need quickly and successfully perform your tasks. You will start using the Navigation Pane and exploring the Ribbon across the top right away. Also in this lesson, you will practice using other on-screen tools and features, such as the Office Button and Access Help.

▪ SOFTWARE ORIENTATION

Navigation Pane

By default, the Navigation Pane, shown in Figure 1-7, appears on the left side of the Access screen each time you create or open a database.

Figure 1-7

Navigation Pane

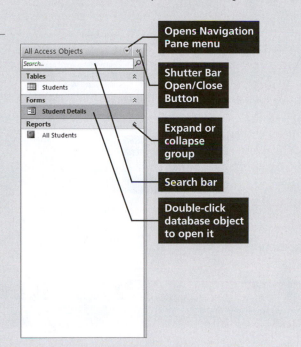

The Navigation Pane enables you to open, copy, and delete tables and other database objects. You will learn more about managing database objects such as forms, queries, and reports in later lessons of this book. For now, just familiarize yourself with the Navigation Pane. Use this figure as a reference throughout this lesson as well as the rest of this book.

Understanding Database Basics

Before you can create a database, you need to understand its most basic elements. This section introduces you to some of the elements in a database that help you organize data and navigate using the Navigation Pane, object tabs, and different views.

 USING THE NAVIGATION PANE

USE the database you used in the previous exercise.

1. In the Navigation Pane, double-click the **Students:Table** to display the table in the Access work area, as shown in Figure 1-8.

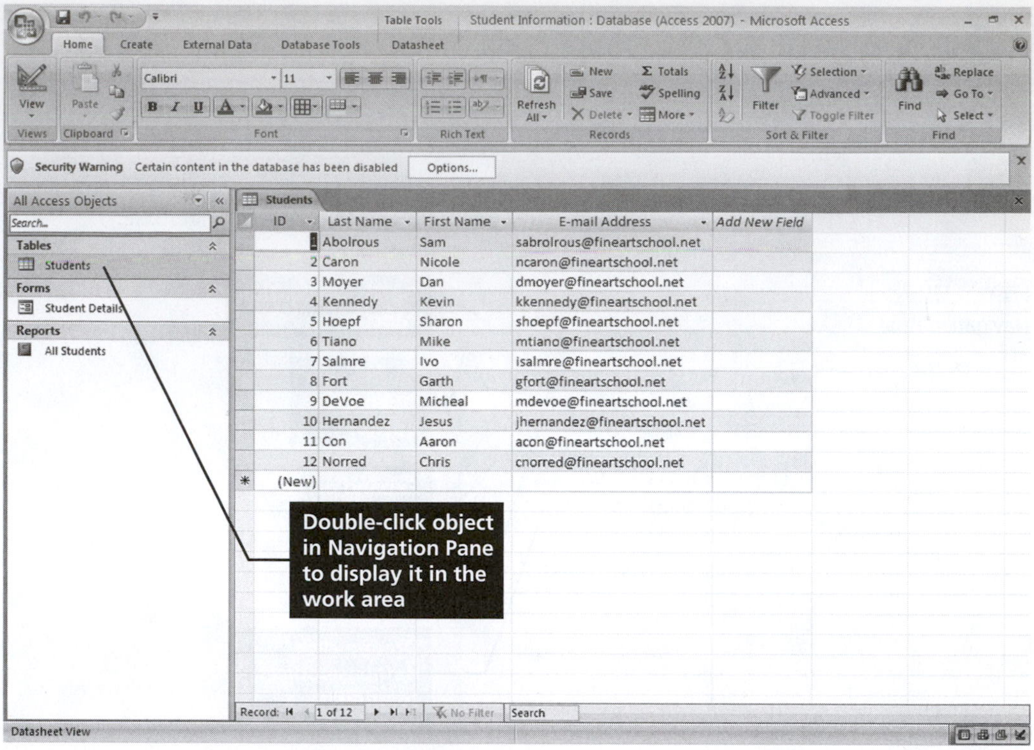

Figure 1-8

Table open in Access work area

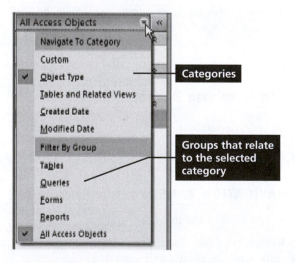

TAKE NOTE * The Navigation Pane replaces an older tool, the Database window, that appeared in earlier versions of Access.

2. Click the **down arrow** at the top of the Navigation Pane to display the menu, as shown in Figure 1-9.

Figure 1-9

Navigation Pane menu

3. Click **Tables and Related Views**. The default group in this category is All Tables, which appears in the menu at the top of the Navigation Pane.

4. Right-click in the white area of the Navigation Pane to display a shortcut menu. Click **View By** and then **Details**, as shown in Figure 1-10.

Figure 1-10

Navigation Pane shortcut menu

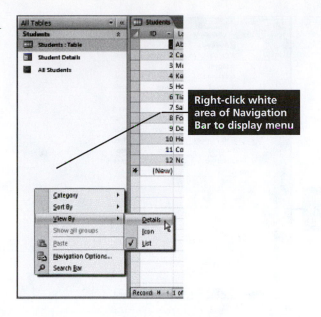

5. The database objects are displayed with details. Click the right side of the Navigation Pane and drag to make it wider so all the information can be read, as shown in Figure 1-11.

Figure 1-11

Widen the Navigation Pane

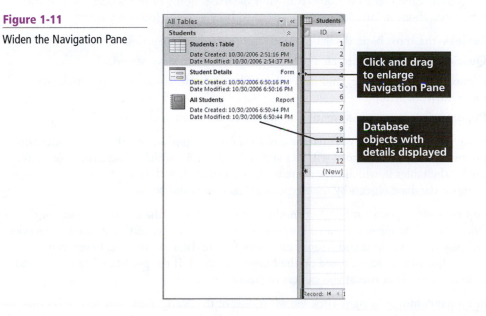

6. Right-click in the white area of the Navigation Pane. On the shortcut menu, click **Search Bar.** A search bar is displayed at the top of the Navigation Pane.

7. Display the Navigation Pane shortcut menu, click **View By** and then **List** to display the database objects in a list.

8. Click the **Shutter Bar Open/Close Button** to collapse the Navigation Pane. Notice it is not entirely hidden, as shown in Figure 1-12.

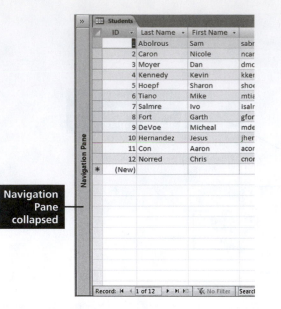

Navigation Pane collapsed

9. Click the **Shutter Bar Open/Close Button** to expand the Navigation Pane again.
   PAUSE. LEAVE the database open to use in the next exercise.

The Navigation Pane lists all the objects in your database. Some of the **objects,** which you will learn more about in later lessons, are described briefly in the following list:

- **Tables**—the most basic database object—store data in categories.
- **Queries** enable you to search and retrieve the data you have stored.
- **Forms** control data entry and data views. They provide visual cues that make data easier to work with.
- **Reports** present your information in ways that are most useful to you.

The Navigation Pane divides your database objects into categories, and those categories contain groups. The default category is Tables and Related Views, which groups the objects in a database by the tables to which they are related. You can change the category to Object Type, which groups database objects by their type—tables, forms, and so on.

To group your objects differently, select another category by using the menu at the top of the Navigation Pane. The menu is divided into two sections—the upper section contains categories, which display the predefined and custom categories for the database, and the lower section contains groups, which change based on the category selected. If the predefined categories and groups do not meet your needs, you can create custom ones.

For additional commands, right-click the white area of the Navigation Pane to display the shortcut menu to perform a variety of tasks. You can display the Search Bar to search for objects in large databases quickly. You can also change categories, sort the items in the pane, and show or hide the details for the objects in each group.

To expand or collapse the Navigation Pane, click the Shutter Bar Open/Close button. The pane is not entirely hidden when collapsed.

USING OBJECT TABS

USE the database you used in the previous exercise.

1. In the Navigation Pane, double-click **Details**. A new object tab opens to display the form, as shown in Figure 1-13.

Figure 1-13

Tab with form

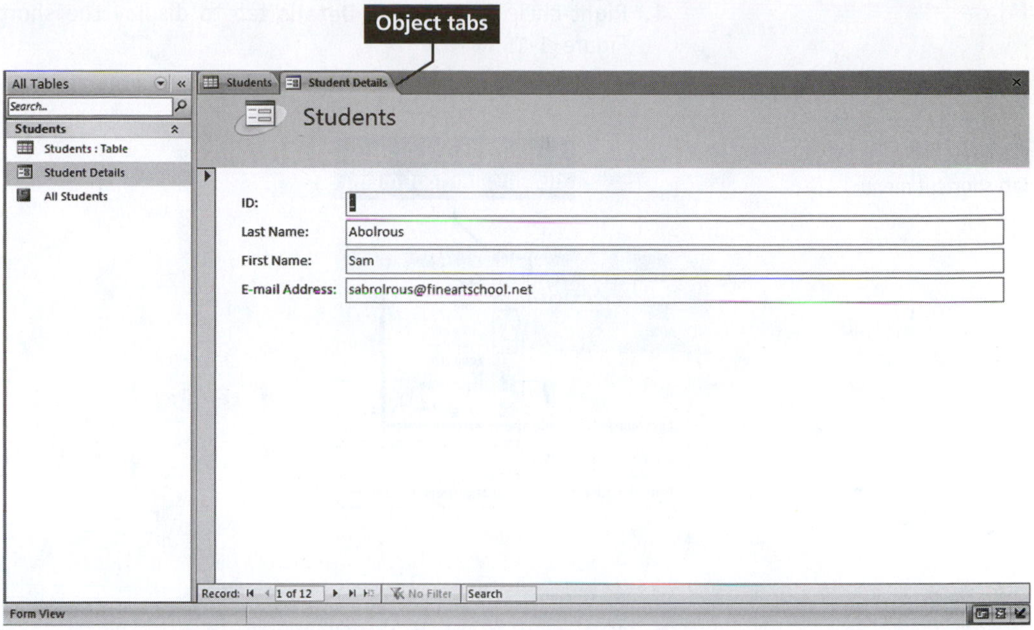

2. In the Navigation Pane, double-click **All Students**. A new object tab opens to display the report, as shown in Figure 1-14.

Figure 1-14

Tab with report

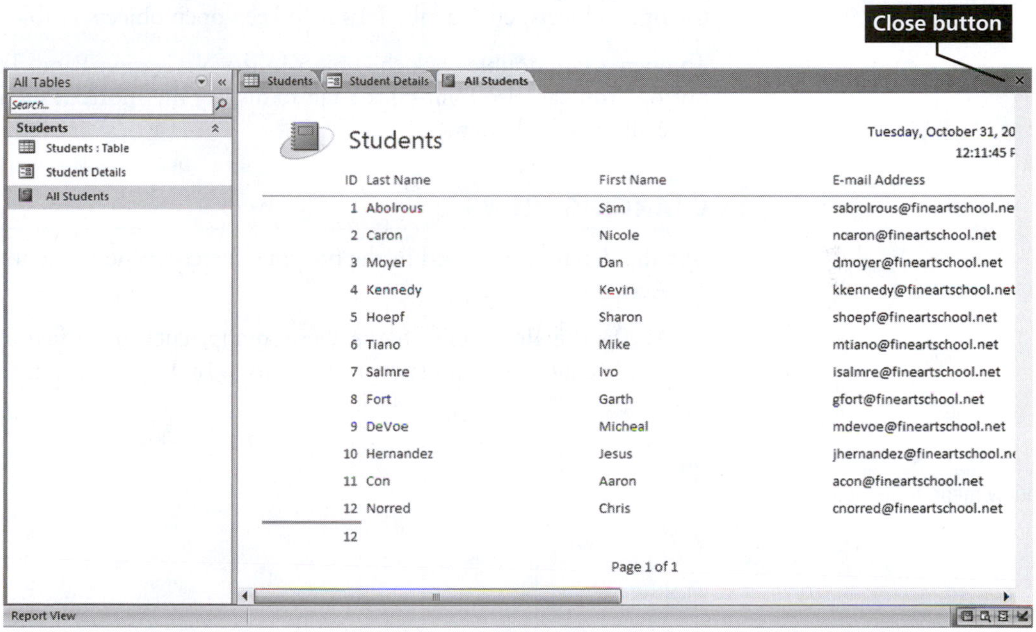

3. Click the **Close** button for the report tab to close it.

4. Right-click the **Student Details** tab to display the shortcut menu shown in Figure 1-15.

Figure 1-15

Tab shortcut menu

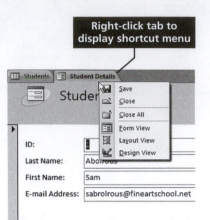

5. Click **Close** to close the form.

PAUSE. LEAVE the database open to use in the next exercise.

When you create a database in Access, all the objects in that database—including forms, tables, reports, queries—are displayed in a single window separated by tabs. To move among the open objects, click a tab. Tabs help keep open objects visible and accessible.

To open a tab, double-click the object in the Navigation Pane. To close a tab, click its Close button. You can also right-click a tab to display the shortcut menu where you can save, close, close all, or switch views.

⊕ CHANGING VIEWS

USE the database you used in the previous exercise. The Students table should be displayed in the Access work area.

1. On the Home tab, in the Views group, click the **View** button's down arrow to display the menu shown in Figure 1-16.

Figure 1-16

View menu for a table

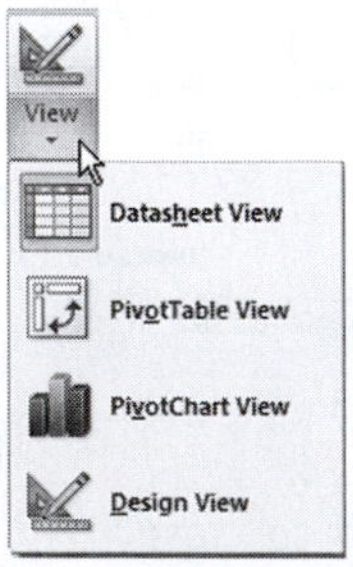

2. Click **Design View**. The table is displayed in Design View, as shown in Figure 1-17. Notice that the Design tab is now displayed on the Ribbon.

Figure 1-17

Table in Design View

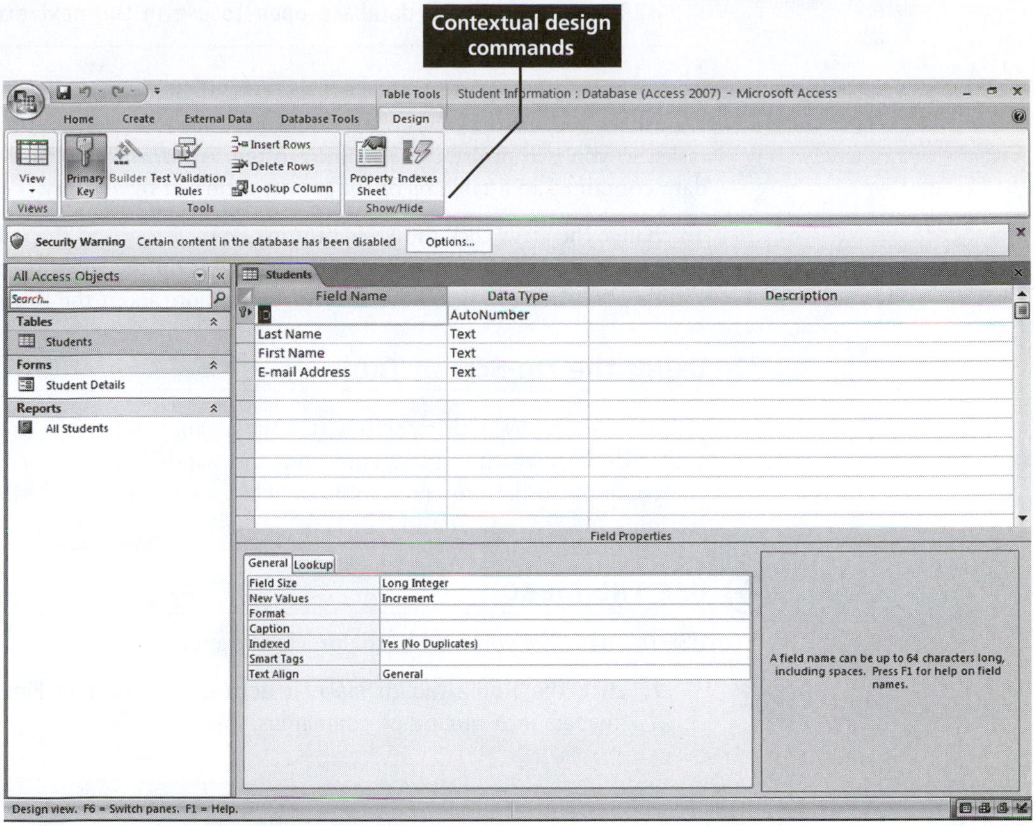

Contextual design commands

3. On the Design tab, in the Views group, click the View button's down arrow, and then click **Datasheet View**.

4. Click the **Datasheet** tab under the Table Tools tab on the Ribbon to display the contextual commands for that view, as shown in Figure 1-18.

Figure 1-18

Table in Datasheet View

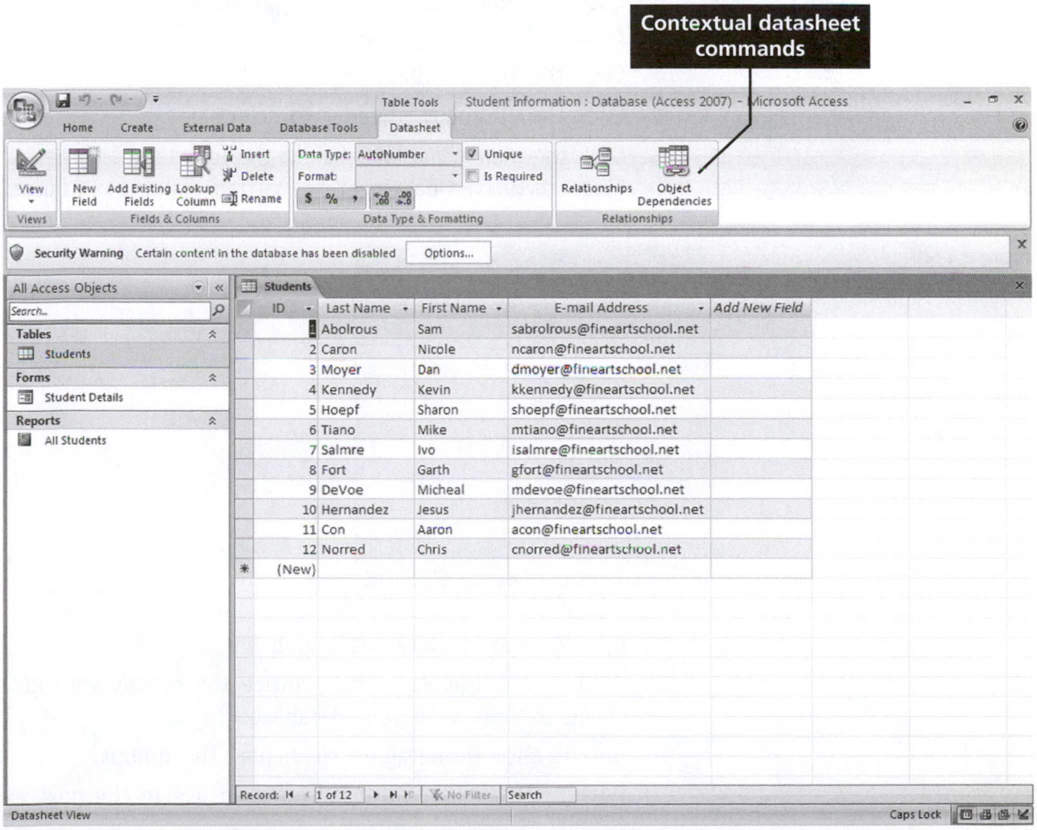

Contextual datasheet commands

PAUSE. LEAVE the database open to use in the next exercise.

Each database object can be viewed several different ways. The main views for a table are Datasheet View and Design View. Datasheet View can be used to perform most table design tasks, so you will probably use it most often. A *datasheet* is the visual representation of the data contained in a table or of the results returned by a query.

To change the view, click the View button's down arrow and then choose a view from the menu. When you change views, the commands available on the Ribbon change to match the tasks you will be performing in that view. You will learn more about the Ribbon in the next section.

Using the On-Screen Tools

Access has many tools to help with your database needs. In this section, you will explore the Ribbon, which displays common commands in groups arranged by tabs. You'll also learn about other on-screen tools to help you get your work done faster, such as the Quick Access Toolbar and KeyTips.

➡ USE THE RIBBON

USE the database you used in the previous exercise.

1. Click the **Home** tab to make it active. As shown in Figure 1-19, the Ribbon is divided into groups of commands.

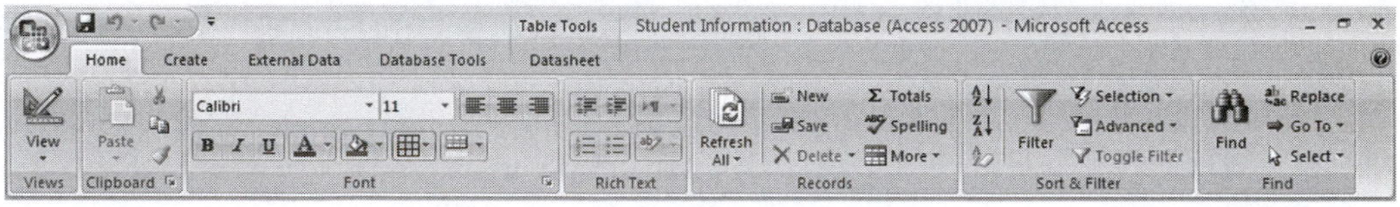

Figure 1-19

The Ribbon

2. Click **Create** to make it the active tab. Notice that the groups of commands change.
3. Click **External Data** and then **Database Tools** to see the commands available on those tabs.
4. Click the **Home** tab.
5. Click the ID column header to select it.
6. Click the dialog box launcher in the lower right corner of the Font group, as shown in Figure 1-19. The Datasheet Formatting dialog box appears, as shown in Figure 1-20.

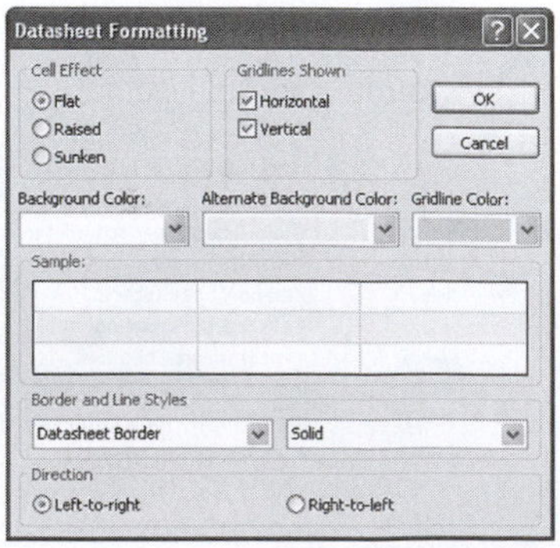

Figure 1-20

Datasheet Formatting dialog box

7. Click **Cancel** to close the dialog box.
8. Double-click the **Home** tab. Notice the groups are hidden to give you more screen space to work with your database.
9. Double-click **Home** again to display the groups.

PAUSE. LEAVE the database open to use in the next exercise.

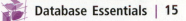

You have just practiced using the **Ribbon**, which is located across the top of the screen and contains tabs and groups of commands. It is divided into five **tabs**, or areas of activity. Each tab contains **groups** of related commands. The Ribbon is contextual, which means it offers you commands related to the object that you are working on or the task that you are performing.

Some groups have a **dialog box launcher**, which is a small arrow in the lower-right corner of the group that you click to launch a dialog box that displays additional options or information. Some commands on the Ribbon have small arrows pointing down. These arrows indicate that a menu is available that lists more options from which you can choose.

 USE THE QUICK ACCESS TOOLBAR NEW FEATURE

USE the database you used in the previous exercise.

1. Click the **Customize Quick Access Toolbar** button. A menu appears, as shown in Figure 1-21.

Figure 1-21

The Quick Access Toolbar

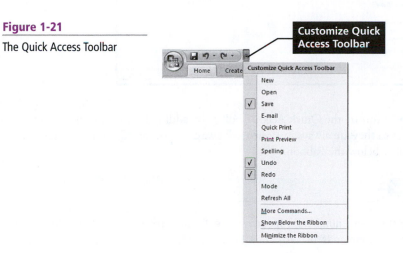

2. Click **Show Below the Ribbon**. The toolbar is moved.
3. Click the **Customize Quick Access Toolbar** button again. Click **Show Above the Ribbon**.

   PAUSE. LEAVE the database open to use in the next exercise.

The **Quick Access Toolbar** contains the commands that you use most often, such as Save, Undo, and Redo. On the menu, click More Commands to open the Customize screen in the Access Options dialog box, as shown in Figure 1-22.

Figure 1-22

Customize screen

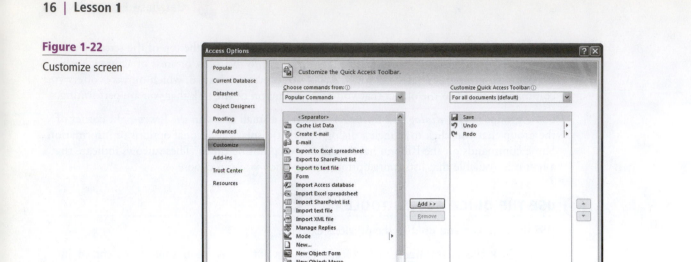

Use this dialog box to customize the Quick Access Toolbar by adding buttons for the commands that you need the most so they are always just one click away. As you practiced in the exercise, you can place the toolbar below the Ribbon.

 **USE KEYTIPS** NEW FEATURE

1. Press **ALT**. Letters and numbers appear on the Ribbon to let you know which key to use to access commands or tabs. See Figure 1-23.

Figure 1-23

KeyTips

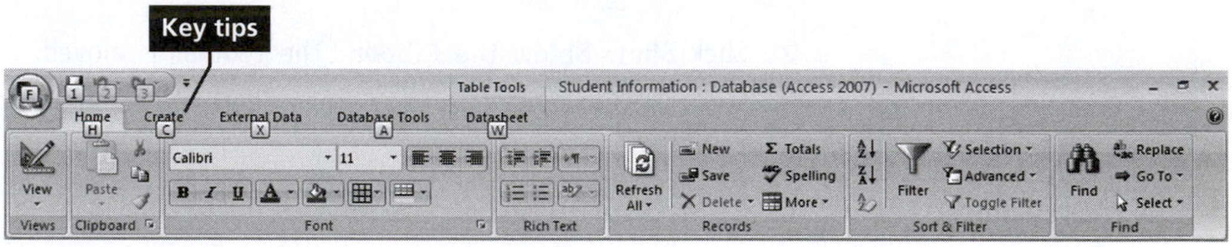

2. Press **C** to activate the Create tab.
3. Press **L** to display the Table Templates menu.
4. Press **ALT** to remove the KeyTips.

   PAUSE. LEAVE the database open to use in the next exercise.

When you press the ALT key, small letters and numbers called **KeyTips** appear on the Ribbon in small square labels, called **badges**. To execute a command using KeyTips, press the ALT key then press the KeyTip or sequence of KeyTips that corresponds to the command you want to use. Every command on the Ribbon has a KeyTip.

TAKE NOTE *

Shortcut keys are keys or combinations of keys pressed together to perform a command. Shortcut keys provide a quick way to give commands without having to move your hands off the keyboard and reach for a mouse. Keyboard shortcuts from previous versions of Access that begin with CTRL are the same. However, those that begin with ALT are different and require the use of KeyTips.

Using the Office Button

The Office Button is a menu of commands that you will use for the common tasks performed with your database files—such as opening, saving, and printing. It also contains commands for managing or publishing your database.

⊕ **USE OFFICE BUTTON**

USE the database you used in the previous exercise.

1. Click the **Office Button**. A menu appears, as shown in Figure 1-24.

Figure 1-24

Office Button and menu

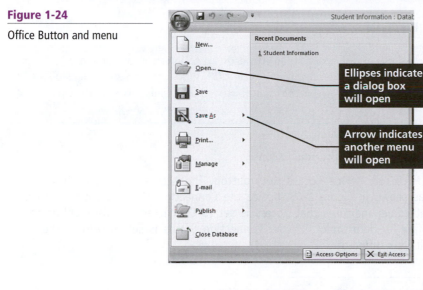

2. Point to the **Save As** command to view the options available.
3. Point to the **Print, Manage,** and **Publish** commands with the arrow to view more options.
4. Click the **Office Button** again to remove the menu.

   PAUSE. LEAVE the database open to use in the next exercise.

The *Office Button* is located in the upper-left corner of the screen. It opens a menu of basic commands for opening, saving, and printing files, as well as more advanced options. Some commands have arrows that indicate that another menu of options is available. You can click commands with an ellipsis to open a dialog box with more options.

The following is an overview of the commands on the Office Button:

- New: Create a new database.
- Open: Open an existing database.
- Save: Save the current document using the new Access format.
- Save As: Save the current database object as a new object or save the database in another format that is compatible with earlier versions of Access.
- Print: Quick print straight to the printer, open a dialog box from which to choose print options, or preview your document before printing.
- Manage: Perform maintenance on the database, back up the database to prevent data loss, or review and set the basic database properties.
- E-mail: E-mail the database.
- Publish: Save the database to a document management server for sharing or package the database and apply a digital signature.
- Close Database: Close the open database.

The Office Button also lists your Recent Documents for easy access. The Access Options button in the menu lets you customize Access. You can also exit the Access application by clicking the Exit Access button.

Using the Microsoft Office Access Help Button

If you have questions, Microsoft Access Help has answers. In fact, you can choose whether you want to use the help topics on your computer that were installed with Office, or if you are connected to the Internet, you can choose to use the help that is available online. Either way, you can key in search words, browse help topics, or choose a topic from the Table of Contents to get your answers.

⊕ USE THE HELP BUTTON

TAKE NOTE *

When you rest the mouse pointer over a command on the Ribbon, a ScreenTip will appear displaying the name of the command. Access 2007 also has Enhanced ScreenTips, which give more information about the command, as well as a Help button you can click to get more help.

USE the database you used in the previous exercise.

1. Click the **Microsoft Office Access Help** button. The Access Help dialog box appears, as shown in Figure 1-25. Notice the Connection Status command in the lower-right corner indicates that Access is set to Connected to Office Online to search online for help topics. If your Connection Status is set to Offline, the screen will look different.

Figure 1-25

Access Help dialog box when connected to Office Online

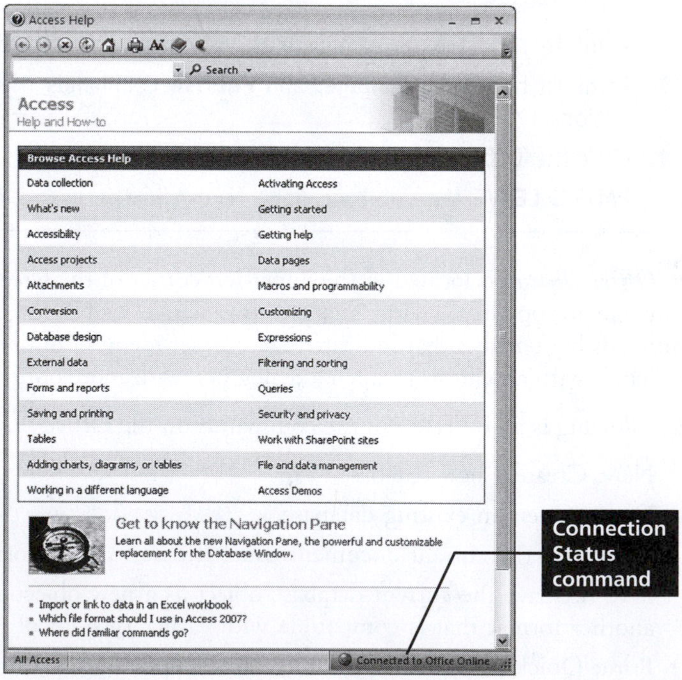

2. Click the **Connection Status** button. A menu appears, as shown in Figure 1-26.

Figure 1-26

Connection Status menu

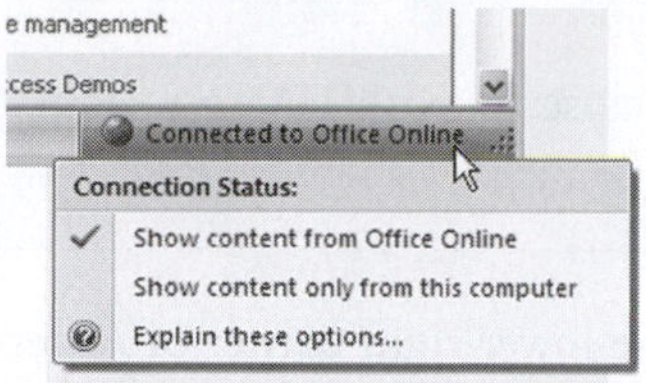

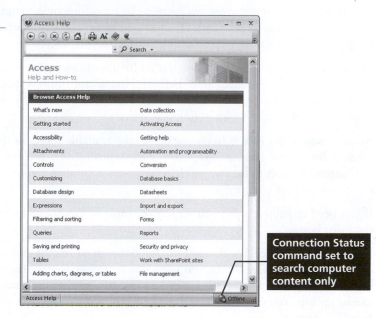

3. Click **Show content only from this computer**. Access Help appears, as shown in Figure 1-27.

Figure 1-27

Access Help dialog box when Offline

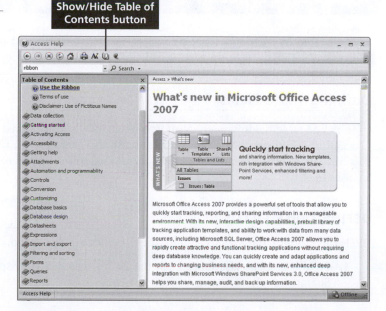

4. Key **ribbon** in the text box and click **Search**. A list of possible topics appears.
5. Click the **Use the Ribbon** link. The help topic appears.
6. Click the **Show Table of Contents** button.
7. Click the **What's new** link at the top.
8. Click **What's new in Microsoft Office Access 2007**. The text for the topic appears in the window, as shown in Figure 1-28.

Figure 1-28

Access Help with Table of Contents and topics displayed

9. Click the **Home** button.

10. Click the **Close** button to close Microsoft Access Help.

   STOP. CLOSE the database.

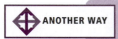

The **Connection Status menu** in the lower-right corner of Access Help lets you choose between the help topics that are available online and the help topics installed in your computer offline. If you are usually connected to the Internet, you might prefer to set the Connection Status to *Show content from Office Online* to get the most updated help available. But there may be times when you can't or don't want to be online; in those instances you can choose *Show content only from this computer* to get offline help topics. You can also click the Search menu to specify the scope of topics you want to search, such as All Access, Access Help, Access Templates, Access Training, or Developer References.

Microsoft Access Help works much like an Internet browser and has many of the same buttons, such as Back, Forward, Stop, Refresh, Home, and Print. A quick way to find what you need is to key a word or words into the text box and click the Search button. Access will display a list of related topics as links.

Another way to get help is to choose one of the available topics in the Browse Access Help list when online or the Browse Access 2007 Help when offline. You can also click the Show Table of Contents button to list Access Help categories. Choose a category to see a list of related topics within that category.

If you need to print a topic, just display the topic in the Access Help main window and click the Print button.

For your convenience, the Access Help window can be resized and moved to another location on the screen. The On Top button toggles to Keep On Top so that the window is always on top of the database you are editing or Not On Top, so that the database you are working on can be on top. You can also change the font size of the text in the window using the Change Font Size button.

ANOTHER WAY

The Access Help button is positioned in some dialog boxes and ScreenTips for quick access to context-related help. Click it wherever you see it to launch Access Help.

■ Defining Data Needs and Types

THE BOTTOM LINE

The first step in creating a database that achieves your goals and provides you with up-to-date, accurate information is to spend time planning and designing it.

Defining Table Fields

CERTIFICATION READY?
How do you define data needs and types?
1.1

To define table fields, you establish which data needs to be stored in the table. Planning is an important part of creating a database. In this exercise, you will open a database that is further along in the process of being developed to see what a more advanced database looks like.

The **Student Data** database is available on the companion CD-ROM.

DEFINE TABLE FIELDS

OPEN the **Student Data** database from the data files for this lesson.

1. On the Student List form, click the ID for record **5** to display the details for Sharon Hoepf, as shown in Figure 1-29.

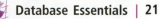

Figure 1-29

Student details

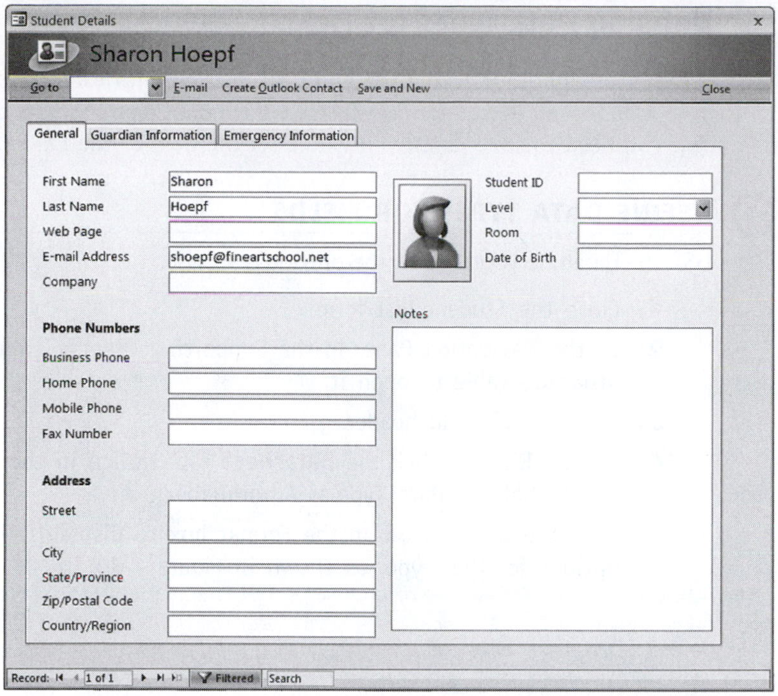

CERTIFICATION READY?
How do you define table fields?
1.1.1

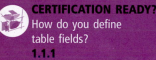

2. Click the **Guardian Information** tab and then the **Emergency Information** tab. Each of the fields on these tabs is an example of the type of information that could be contained in a database table.
3. Click **Close** to close the details.

PAUSE. LEAVE the database open to use in the next exercise.

When planning a database, the first step is to consider the purpose of your database. You need to design the database so that it accommodates all your data processing and reporting needs. You should gather and organize all the information that you want to include, starting with any existing forms or lists, and think about the reports and mailings you might want to create using the data.

Once you have decided how the information will be used, the next step is to categorize the information by dividing it into subjects such as Products or Orders, which become the tables in your database. Each table should only contain information that relates to that subject. If you find yourself adding extra information, create a new table.

In a database table, data is stored in rows and columns—similar in appearance to a spreadsheet. Each row in a table is called a ***record***. Each column in a table is called a ***field***. For example, if a table is named "Student List," each record (row) contains information about a different student and each field (column) contains a different type of information, such as last name or email address.

LOOKING AHEAD

You will learn more about defining and modifying a primary key in Lesson 3.

To create the columns within the table, you then need to determine what information you want to store in the table—such as Color, Year, or Cost. Break each piece of information into the smallest useful part—for example, use First Name and Last Name instead of just Name if you want to sort, search, calculate, or report using the separate pieces of information.

For each table, you will choose a primary key. A ***primary key*** is a column that uniquely identifies each row, such as Item Number.

Defining Data Types for Fields

When designing the database, you set a data type for each field (column) that you create to match the information it will store. Each data type has a specific purpose—for example, if you need to store dates, you would set the field to the Date/Time data type.

⊕ DEFINE DATA TYPES FOR FIELDS

USE the database you used in the previous exercise.

1. Close the Student List form.
2. In the Navigation Pane, in the Supporting Objects group, double-click the **Students** table to open it.
3. Click the **ID** field header.
4. On the Ribbon, click the **Datasheet** tab. Notice in the Data Type & Formatting group that the Data Type is AutoNumber.
5. Click the **down arrow** in the Format box to display the menu of formatting options for that type, as shown in Figure 1-30.

Figure 1-30

Format options for AutoNumber data type

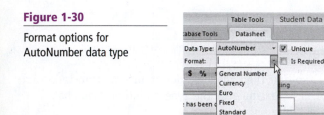

6. Click the **Last Name** header. Notice that the Data Type is Text and that no formatting options are available for that data type.
7. Scroll to the right and click the **Date of Birth** header.
8. Click the **down arrow** in the Format box to display the menu of formatting options for the Date/Time data type, as shown in Figure 1-31.

Figure 1-31

Format options for Date/Time data type

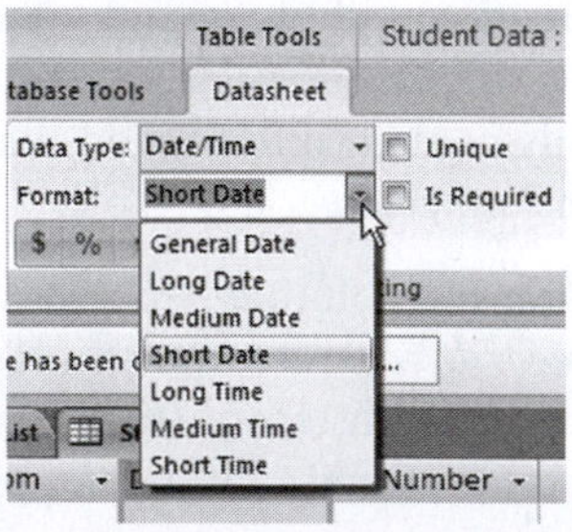

9. Scroll to the right and click the **Address** header.
10. In the Data Type box, click the **down arrow** and click **Text** to change the data type. When a warning message appears, click **Yes**.

TAKE NOTE ✱ Be aware that changing a data type might cut off some or all of the data in a field, and in some cases may remove the data entirely.

11. Scroll to the far right and click the **Add New Field header.** In the Data Type box, click **Yes/No**.

12. Click the **down arrow** in the Format box to display the menu of formatting options for the Yes/No data type, as shown in Figure 1-32.

Figure 1-32

Format options for Yes/No data type

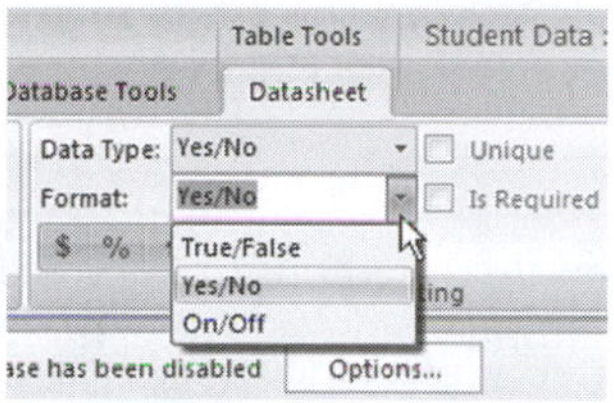

CERTIFICATION READY?

How do you define appropriate table field data types for fields in each table?

1.1.2

13. Click outside the menu to close it.

PAUSE. LEAVE the database open to use in the next exercise.

Each field in a table must be designated for a particular data type. A **data type** controls the type of data a field will contain—whether it is text, number, date/time, or some other type. Access provides ten different data types, each with its own purpose. The list in Table 1-1 describes the types of data that each field can be set to store.

Table 1-1

DATA TYPE	EXAMPLE	DESCRIPTION
Text	Last Name: Zimmerman Street: 6789 Walker Street	The most common data type for fields. Can store up to 255 characters of text, numbers, or a combination of both.
Memo	Comments: Student will make monthly payments on the 15th of each month of $247.	Allows you to store large amounts of text—up to 64,000 characters of text, numbers, or a combination (although if you use that much space, your database will run slowly).
Number	Age: 19	Stores numeric data that can be used in mathematical calculations.
Date/Time	Birthday: December 1, 1987	Stores date and/or time data.
Currency	Registration Fee: $50.00	Stores monetary data with precision to four decimal places. Use this data type to store financial data and when you don't want Access to round values.
AutoNumber	Student ID: 56	Unique values created by Access when you create a new record. Tables often contain an AutoNumber field used as the primary key.
Yes/No	Insurance? Yes	Stores Boolean (true or false) data. Access uses 1 for all Yes values and 0 for all No values.
OLE Object	Photo	Stores images, documents, graphs, and other objects from Office and Windows-based programs.
Hyperlink	Web addresses	Stores links to Web sites, sites or files on an intranet or Local Area Network (LAN), and sites or files on your computer.
Attachment	Any supported type of file	You can attach images, spreadsheet files, documents, charts, and other types of supported files to the records in your database, much like you attach files to email messages.

When you create a new field in a table and then enter data in it, Office Access 2007 automatically tries to detect the appropriate data type for the new column. For example, if you key a price, such as $10, Access recognizes the data as a price, and sets the data type for the field to Currency. If Access doesn't have enough information from what you enter to guess the data type, the data type is set to Text.

TAKE NOTE* The Number data type should only be used if the numbers will be used in mathematical calculations. For numbers such as phone numbers, use the Text data type.

LOOKING AHEAD

You will learn more about multivalued fields in Lesson 4.

When defining table fields, it will be important to define the appropriate data types for each. For example, if you are using a number, you should determine whether you need to use the Currency or Number data type. Or, if you need to store large amounts of text, you may need to use the Memo data type instead of Text. Most database management systems can store only a single value in a field, but with Microsoft Office Access 2007 you can create a field that holds multiple values, which may be appropriate in certain situations.

CERTIFICATION READY?
How do you define tables in databases?
1.1.3

Defining Database Tables

Tables are the most basic organizational element of a database. Not only is it important to plan the tables to hold the type of data you need, but also to plan how the tables and information will be connected.

⊕ DEFINE DATABASE TABLES

USE the database you used in the previous exercise.

1. On the Database Tools tab, in the Show/Hide section, click **Relationship** to display a visual representation of the relationship between the Students and Guardians tables, as shown in Figure 1-33.

Figure 1-33

Relationship between tables

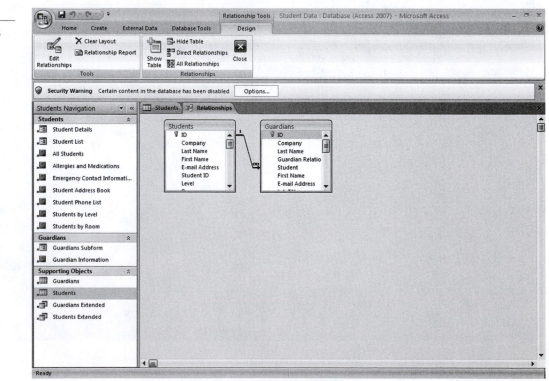

2. Close the Relationships tab.

3. Close the Students tab.

STOP. CLOSE the database.

In a simple database, you might only have one table, but most databases will have more. The tables you include in a database will be based on the data available. For example, a database of students might have a table for contact information, one for grades, and one for tuition and fees.

LOOKING AHEAD

You will learn more about table relationships in Lesson 3.

In database applications like Access, you can create a relational database. A ***relational database*** stores information in separate tables that are connected or linked by a defined relationship that ties the data together.

An important principle to consider when planning a database is to try to record each piece of information only once. Duplicate information, or ***redundant data,*** wastes space and increases the likelihood of errors. Relationships among database tables help ensure consistency and reduce repetitive data entry.

As you create each table, keep in mind how the data in the tables are related to each other. Enter test data and then add fields to tables or create new tables as necessary to refine the database. The last step is to apply data normalization rules to see if your tables are structured correctly and make adjustments as needed. ***Normalization*** is the process of applying rules to your database design to ensure that you have divided your information items into the appropriate tables.

Database design principles include standards and guidelines that can be used to determine if your database is structured correctly. These are referred to as ***normal forms***. There are five normal forms, but typically only the first three are applied, because that is usually all that is required. The following is a summary of the first three normal forms:

- **First Normal Form (1NF):** Break each field down into the smallest meaningful value, remove repeating groups of data, and create a separate table for each set of related data.
- **Second Normal Form (2NF):** Each nonkey column should be fully dependent on the entire primary key. Create new tables for data that applies to more than one record in a table and add a related field to the table.
- **Third Normal Form (3NF):** Remove fields that do not relate to, or provide a fact about, the primary key.

LOOKING AHEAD

You will learn more about importing data and linking to an external data source in Lesson 14.

Data can be brought into an Access database in a number of ways, including linking and importing. When defining tables, you will have to decide whether data should be linked to or imported from external sources. When you import data, Access creates a copy of the data or objects in the destination database without altering the source. Linking lets you connect to data from another source without importing it, so that you can view and modify the latest data in both the source and destination databases without creating and maintaining two copies of the same data. Any changes you make to the data in the source are reflected in the linked table in the destination database, and vice versa.

SUMMARY SKILL MATRIX

In this lesson you learned	Matrix Skill	Skill Number
To open and close an existing database	Open databases	6.1.1
To define data needs and types	Define data needs and types	1.1
To define table fields	Define table fields	1.1.1
To define data types for fields	Define appropriate table field data types for fields in each table	1.1.2
To define database tables	Define tables in databases	1.1.3

■ Knowledge Assessment

Matching

Match the term in Column 1 to its description in Column 2.

Column 1	Column 2

1. record

a. most basic database object; stores data in categories

2. field

b. database object that presents information in a format that is easy to read and print

3. redundant data

c. duplicate information in a database

4. primary key

d. row in a database table

5. database

e. database object that enables stored data to be searched and retrieved

6. table

f. column in a database that uniquely identifies each row

7. query

g. database object that simplifies the process of entering, editing, and displaying data

8. report

h. column in a database table

9. form

i. kind of information a field contains

10. data type

j. tool for collecting and organizing information

True / False

Circle T if the statement is true or F if the statement is false.

T | F **1.** Any list you make for a specific purpose can be considered a simple database, even a grocery list.

T | F **2.** By default, the Navigation Pane appears on the right side of the Access screen each time you create or open a database.

T | F **3.** Forms, queries, and reports are examples of database objects.

T | F **4.** The dialog box launcher contains the commands that you use most often, such as Save, Undo, and Redo.

T | F **5.** When you press the Shift key, small letters and numbers called KeyTips appear on the Ribbon.

T | F **6.** The Connection Status menu lets you choose between the help topics that are available online and the help topics installed in your computer offline.

T | F **7.** In a database table, data is stored in rows and columns—similar in appearance to a spreadsheet.

T | F **8.** Each field in a table must be designated for a particular data type.

T | F **9.** An important principal to consider when planning a database is to try to record each piece of information as many times as possible for easy access.

T | F **10.** Normalization is the process of applying rules to your database design to ensure that you have divided your information items into the appropriate tables.

■ Competency Assessment

Project 1-1: Personalizing Access

When working in Access or another Microsoft Office application, it is useful to personalize your copy of the software.

GET READY. Launch Access if it is not already running.

1. Click the **Office Button**.
2. Click the **Access Options** button to display the Access Options dialog box.
3. Click **Popular** on the left to display the screen where you can change the most popular options in Access.
4. In the *Personalize your copy of Microsoft Office* section, key **your name** in the User name and key **your initials** in the Initials box.
5. Click **OK** to close the dialog box.

   LEAVE Access open for the next project.

Project 1-2: Task List

As a busy editor at Lucerne Publishing, you use Access to organize and manage your task list.

The *task_list* database is available on the companion CD-ROM.

1. **OPEN** *Task_List* from the data files for this lesson.
2. Click the **Shutter Bar Open/Close Button** to display the Navigation Pane.
3. Click the **Contacts** group header in the Navigation Pane to display those database objects.
4. Click the **Supporting Objects** group header to display those database objects.
5. In the Supporting Objects group, double-click **Tasks** to open that table.
6. In the Tasks group, double-click **Tasks By Assigned To** to open that report.
7. In the Navigation Pane, click the **Tasks Navigation** header to display the menu and then click **Object Type**.
8. **CLOSE** the database.

   LEAVE Access open for the next project.

■ Proficiency Assessment

Project 1-3: Understanding Database Design

You work at Margie's Travel, a full-service travel agency that specializes in providing services to senior citizens. You plan to create a database of tours, cruises, adventure activities, group travel, and vacation packages geared toward seniors, but first you want to learn more about database design.

1. **OPEN** Access Help.
2. Search for **database design**.
3. Read the article about database design basics.
4. **OPEN** a new Word document.
5. List the steps that should be taken when designing a database with a short description of each.
6. **SAVE** the document as *database_design* and then **CLOSE** the file.

   LEAVE Access open for the next project.

Project 1-4: Planning Table Fields

You are a volunteer for the Tech Terrace Neighborhood Association that holds an annual March Madness 5K Run. In the past, all data has been kept on paper, but you decide it would be more efficient to create a database. Decide what fields would make sense for a table holding data about the runners.

1. Think about what fields would be useful in a database table that contains information about the runners in an annual 5K road race.
2. **OPEN** a new Word document.
3. In the document, key a list of the names of at least six possible field names.
4. **SAVE** the document as *race_fields* and keep the file open.

   LEAVE Access open for the next project.

■ Mastery Assessment

Project 1-5: Planning Data Types for Fields

Now that you have decided on what fields to use in a database table containing information about runners in an annual 5K road race, you need to determine what data type should be used for each field.

USE the document you used in the previous project.

1. Beneath the name of each possible field name for the table about runners in the annual 5K road race, key the data type that would be used with a short explanation of why you chose that type.
2. **SAVE** the document as *data_type* and then **CLOSE** the file.

   LEAVE Access open for the next project.

Project 1-6: Up to Speed with Access 2007

Your supervisor at Margie's Travel has suggested that you complete some additional training before you begin to create a database.

1. **OPEN** the Getting Started with Microsoft Office Access screen.
2. Use Access help to locate the demo training module called "Up to speed with Access 2007."
3. Watch the overview.

   CLOSE Access.

INTERNET READY

At the bottom of the Getting Started with Microsoft Office Access screen is an area called the Spotlight, as shown in Figure 1-34.

Figure 1-34

Spotlight

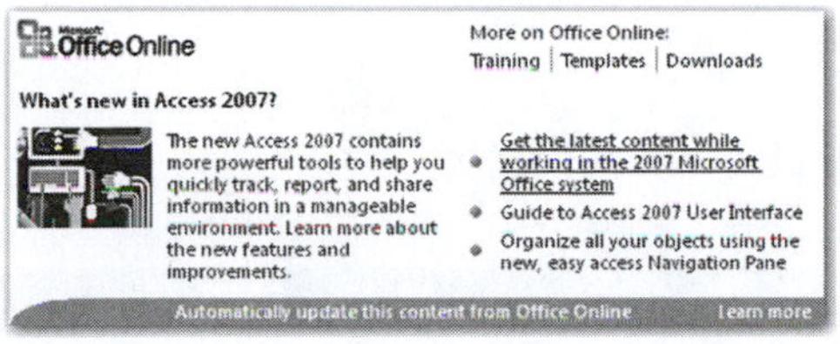

Use Access help to find out what this section offers and how to get the latest online content while working in Office 2007 by turning on automatic updates.

✳ **Workplace Ready**

Working with Templates in Access

In today's business world, it can be overwhelming to keep up with the different types of data that a company needs to collect, organize, and report. Sales invoices, client contacts, employee files, vendor information—the list seems endless. You can customize the templates available in Access to meet your business needs and save the time it would take to create database objects from scratch.

In your position as the technical support director for the A. Datum Corporation, you are responsible for coordinating technical support for the company. You can streamline your work by downloading an Access template to use as a starting point and then modifying it to track critical data. Using the Issues database, you can set up, organize, and track technical service requests submitted by people in your organization. You can then assign, prioritize, and follow the progress of issues from start to finish.

The database template contains various predefined tables—such as Issues and Contacts—that you can use to enter data. Such tables may be functional just as they are. But, as you work, chances are that you will need to create tables that are more specific to the needs of your company.

The Issues database template, like all others in Microsoft Office Access 2007, also includes pre-designed forms, reports, and queries that can be used as they are. This not only saves time, but also enables you to see a complete database system developed by professionals so you can be sure you are capturing essential business information in a logical and efficient manner.

Create Database Tables

LESSON SKILL MATRIX

Skills	Matrix Skill	Skill Number
Creating a Database	Create databases	2.1
Using a Template to Create a Database	Create databases using templates	2.1.1
Creating a Blank Database	Create blank databases	2.1.2
Creating a Database Table	Create tables	2.2
Creating a Table from Another Table	Create tables by copying the structure of other tables	2.2.2
Creating a Table from a Template	Create tables from templates	2.2.3

As an assistant curator at the Baldwin Museum of Science, you are responsible for the day-to-day management of the insect collection, including duties such as sorting and organizing specimens, as well as supervising the mounting and labeling of the insects. The insect collection catalog has never been transferred to an electronic database. Because you have experience with database management, part of your responsibility will be to create a database to store the information about the specimens and collections, as well as museum exhibits and events. In this lesson, you will learn how to create a blank database and how to use a template to create a database. You will also learn how to create a table from a template, how to create a table by copying the structure from another table, and how to save a database object.

KEY TERMS
template

■ SOFTWARE ORIENTATION

Getting Started with Microsoft Office Access

Part of the Getting Started with Microsoft Office Access page, shown in Figure 2-1, provides options for creating a database.

Figure 2-1

Getting Started with Microsoft Office Access

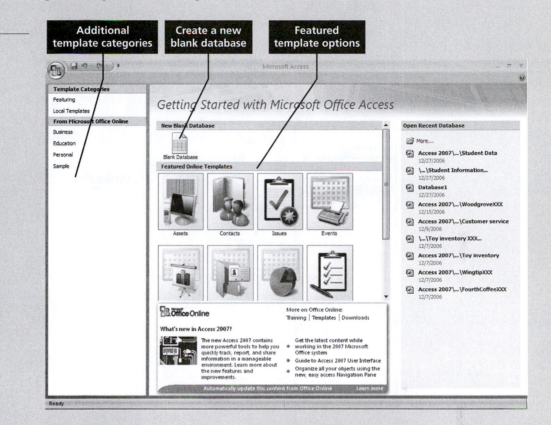

Several templates are displayed under Featured Online Templates, and more become available if you click one of the categories on the left. This is also where you can create a new, blank database. Use this figure as a reference throughout this lesson as well as the rest of this book.

■ Creating a Database

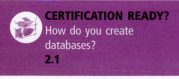

THE BOTTOM LINE

In Microsoft Office Access 2007, the process of creating a new database is easier than ever. You can create a database using one of the many templates available or by creating a new blank database.

Using a Template to Create a Database

CERTIFICATION READY?
How do you create databases?
2.1

If there is a template that fits your needs, that is usually the fastest way to create a database. Access offers a variety of templates to help get you started. Template databases can be used as is, or you can customize them to better suit your purposes.

→ **USE A TEMPLATE TO CREATE A DATABASE**

GET READY. Before you begin these steps, be sure that you are logged on to the Internet and launch Microsoft Access to display the Getting Started with Microsoft Office Access screen.

1. On the left of the Access window, in the From Microsoft Office Online section, click **Personal**.

2. In the list of Personal templates in the middle, click **Home inventory**. Your screen should look similar to Figure 2-2.

Figure 2-2

Personal templates

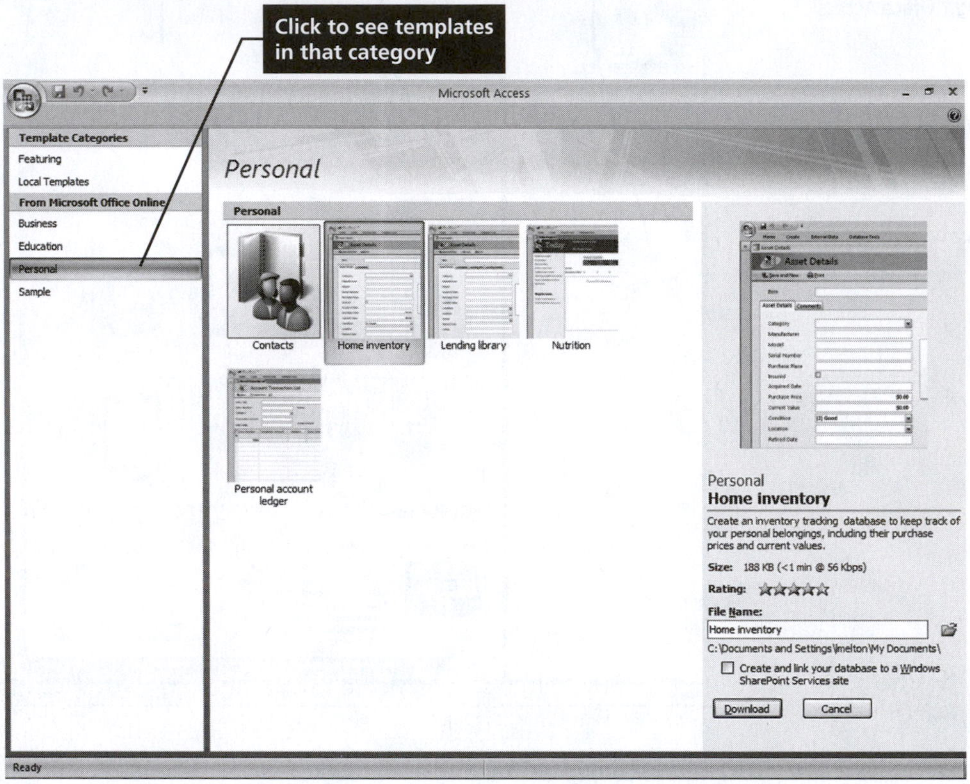

Click to see templates in that category

3. In the From Microsoft Office Online section on the left, click **Education**.

4. In the list of Education templates in the middle, click **Faculty**. Your screen should look similar to Figure 2-3.

Figure 2-3

Education templates

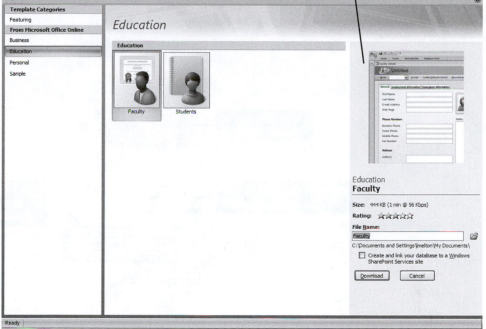

5. In the From Microsoft Office Online section on the left, click **Business**.

6. In the list of Business templates in the middle, click **Assets**. Your screen should look similar to Figure 2-4.

Figure 2-4

Business templates

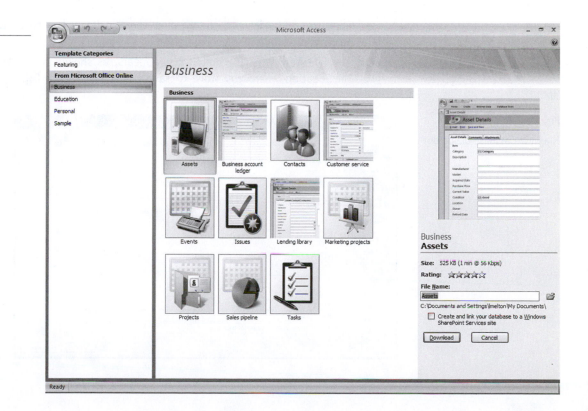

7. In the pane on the right, click in the File Name box and key your initials at the end of the suggested file name, so that the file name is now **AssetsXXX** (where XXX is your initials), as shown in Figure 2-5.

Figure 2-5

File Name box and folder icon

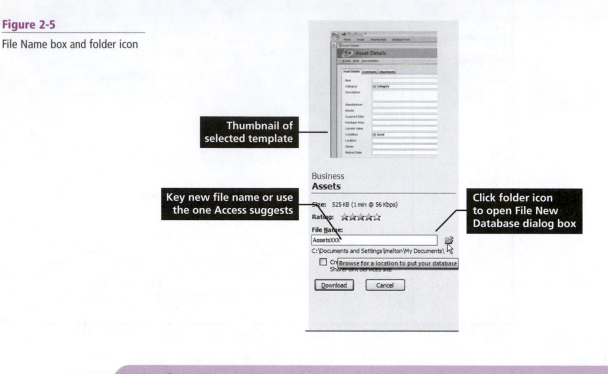

Thumbnail of selected template

Key new file name or use the one Access suggests

Click folder icon to open File New Database dialog box

TAKE NOTE * If you do not add an extension to your database file name, Access does it for you–for example, *AccessXXX.accdb.*

8. Click the folder icon to the right of the File Name box to browse for a location to store your database (see Figure 2-5).

9. The File New Database dialog box appears, as shown in Figure 2-6. Navigate to the location where you want to save the file and click **OK**.

Figure 2-6

File New Database dialog box

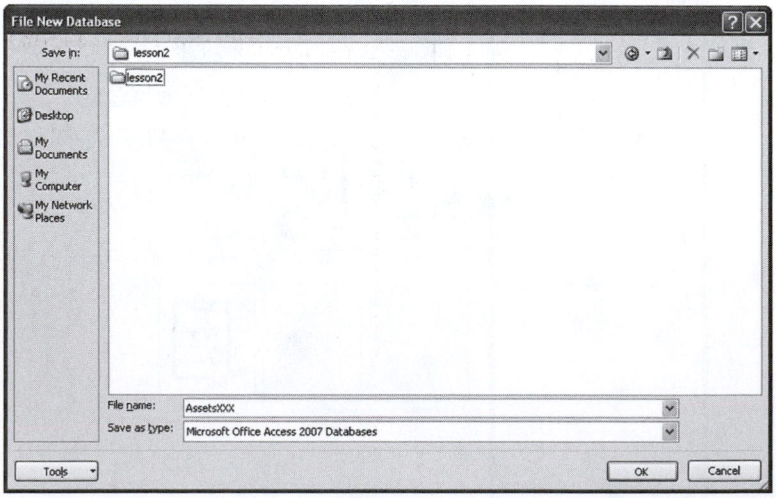

10. Click the **Download** button (see Figure 2-5). A dialog box shows that the template is being downloaded, as shown in Figure 2-7.

Figure 2-7

Downloading Template dialog box

11. Access creates and then opens the database. A form is displayed in which you can begin entering data, as shown in Figure 2-8. Click to place the insertion point in the first cell of the Item field and key **Canon EOS Rebel 300D**.

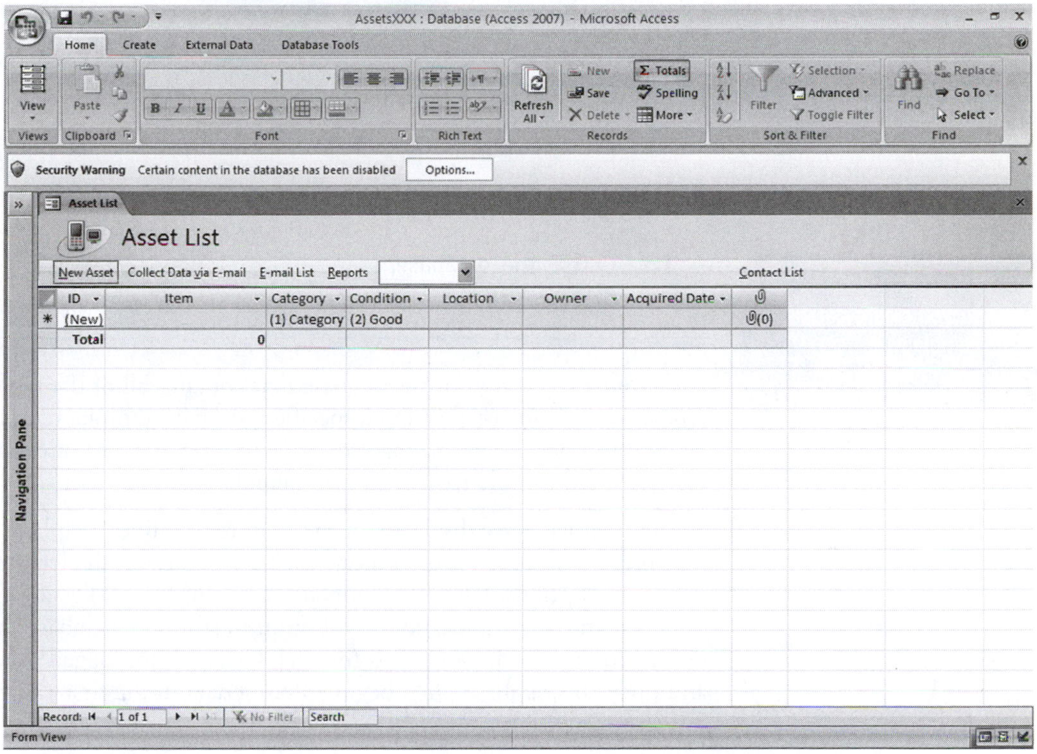

Figure 2-8

Assets template database

12. Click the **Shutter Bar Open/Close Button** to display the Navigation Pane, as shown in Figure 2-9, to see all the objects in the database.

Figure 2-9

Assets database with
Navigation Pane displayed

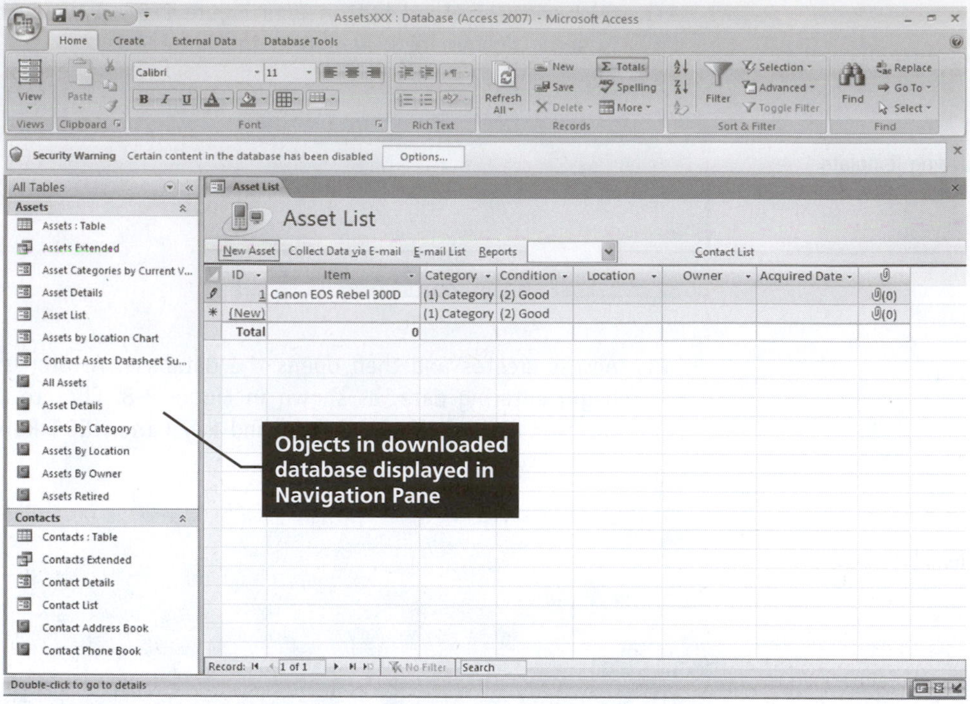

Objects in downloaded database displayed in Navigation Pane

CERTIFICATION READY?
How do you create databases using templates?
2.1.1

13. **CLOSE** the database.

PAUSE. LEAVE Access open to use in the next exercise.

A *template* is a ready-to-use database that contains all of the tables, queries, forms, and reports needed for performing a specific task. For example, templates are available that can be used to track issues, manage contacts, or keep a record of expenses. Some templates contain a few sample records to help demonstrate their use.

Several templates are displayed in the Featured Online Templates on the Getting Started with Microsoft Office Access or you can click a category on the left side of the Access window to view more options. Click the template you want to use, key a file name or use the one Access suggests, and select a location if you want to store the database in a location other than the default folder. Click Download (or click Create if not logged onto the Internet) to create and open the database, then begin entering data in the first empty cell on the form.

TAKE NOTE✱
Unless you choose a different folder, Access uses the following default locations to store your databases:
- Microsoft Windows Vista—*c:\Users\user name\Documents*
- Microsoft Windows Server 2003 or Microsoft Windows XP—*c:\Documents and Settings\user name\My Documents*

Creating a Blank Database

When you create a new blank database, Access opens a database that contains a table where you can enter data, but it creates no other database objects.

➔ CREATE A BLANK DATABASE

GET READY. The Getting Started with Microsoft Office Access page should be on the screen from the previous exercise.

1. In the New Blank Database section, click the **Blank Database** icon. A Blank Database pane appears, as shown in Figure 2-10.

Figure 2-10

Blank Database pane

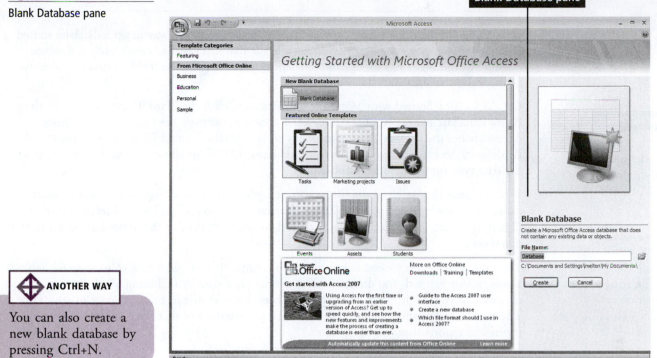

ANOTHER WAY

You can also create a new blank database by pressing Ctrl+N.

2. In the File Name box, key **BlankDatabaseXXX** (where XXX is your initials).

3. If you want to save the file in a location other than the one shown beneath the File Name box, click the folder icon and browse to a different location.

4. Click the **Create** button. A new blank database appears, as shown in Figure 2-11.

Figure 2-11

New blank database

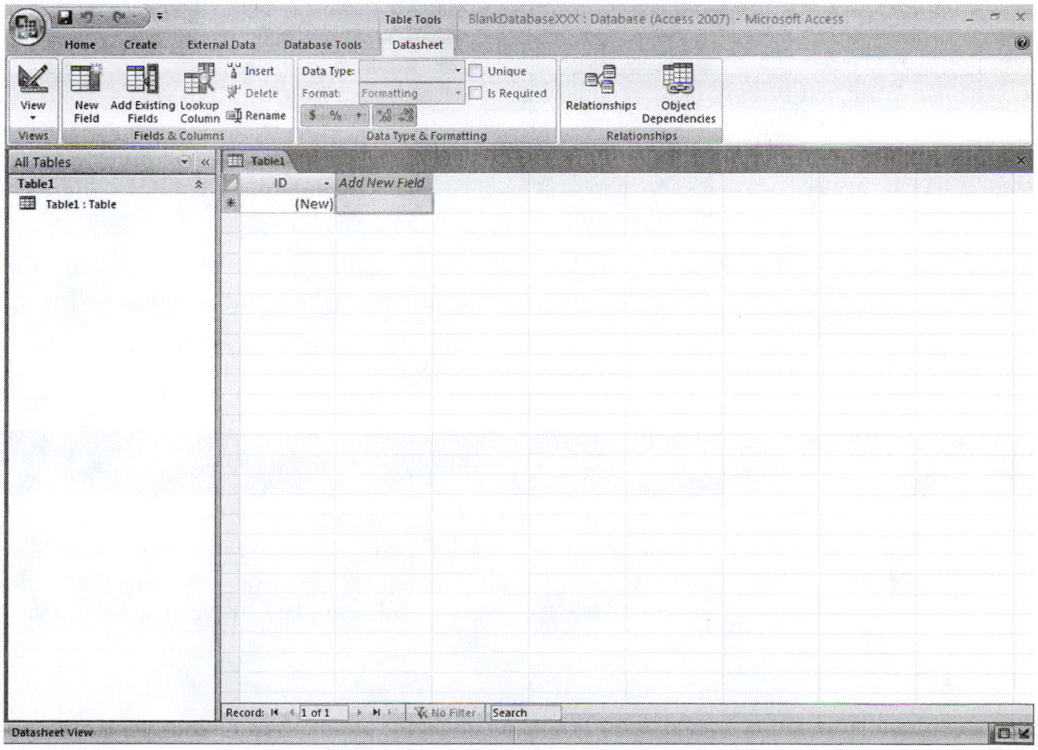

CERTIFICATION READY?
How do you create blank databases?
2.1.2

PAUSE. LEAVE the database open to use in the next exercise.

If there is a template that fits your needs, that is usually the fastest way to get a database started. However, if you have existing data, you may decide that it is easier to create a blank database because it would require a lot of work to adapt your existing data to the data structure already defined in the template.

On the Getting Started with Microsoft Office screen, click the Blank Database icon. In the Blank Database pane, key a file name, select a location to store the file, and click Create. Access creates the database, and then opens an empty table named Table1 in datasheet view. By default, Access creates a primary key field named "ID" for all new datasheets, and it sets the data type for the field to AutoNumber.

LOOKING AHEAD

You will learn more about defining and modifying a primary key in Lesson 3.

With the insertion point in the first empty cell, you can begin keying to add data. Entering data in Datasheet view is very similar to entering data into an Excel worksheet, except that data must be entered in contiguous rows and columns, starting at the upper-left corner of the datasheet.

LOOKING AHEAD

You will learn more about creating forms and reports in Lessons 5 and 6.

The table structure is created as you enter data. Anytime you add a new column to the table, a new field is defined. You do not need to format your data by including blank rows or columns, as you might do in an Excel worksheet, because that just wastes space in your table. The table merely contains your data. All visual presentation of that data will be done in the forms and reports that you design later.

◾ SOFTWARE ORIENTATION

Tables Group Commands

The Tables group on the Create tab provides several commands you can use to insert a new table.

Figure 2-12

Tables Group Commands

Use this figure as a reference throughout this lesson as well as the rest of this book.

◾ Creating a Database Table

↓ THE BOTTOM LINE

As you learned in the last exercise, when you create a new blank database, a new empty table is automatically inserted for you. You can also insert a new blank table into an existing database or use a table template to create a new table.

CERTIFICATION READY?
How do you create tables?
2.2

Creating a Table from a Template

It is easy to create a new table using a table template. Table templates are available for common subjects such as contacts, issues, and tasks.

⊕ **CREATE A TABLE FROM A TEMPLATE**

USE the database that is open from the previous exercise.

1. On the Create tab, in the Tables group, click the **Table Templates** button to display the menu shown in Figure 2-13.

Figure 2-13

Table Templates menu

2. Click **Contacts**. A new table is created with fields for contacts, as shown in Figure 2-14.

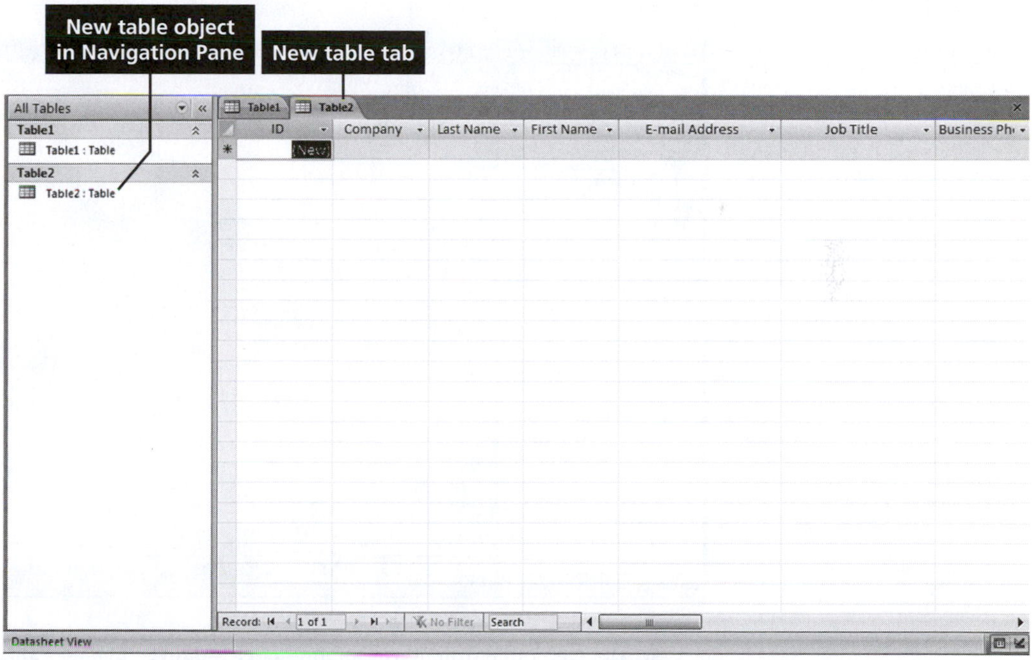

Figure 2-14

New table for contacts

New table object in Navigation Pane   **New table tab**

All Tables	ID	Company	Last Name	First Name	E-mail Address	Job Title	Business Ph
Table1	*						
Table1 : Table							
Table2							
Table2 : Table							

Record: I◄ ◄ 1 of 1 ► ►I ► No Filter Search

Datasheet View

3. On the Table Templates menu, click **Tasks**. A new table is created with fields for tasks, as shown in Figure 2-15.

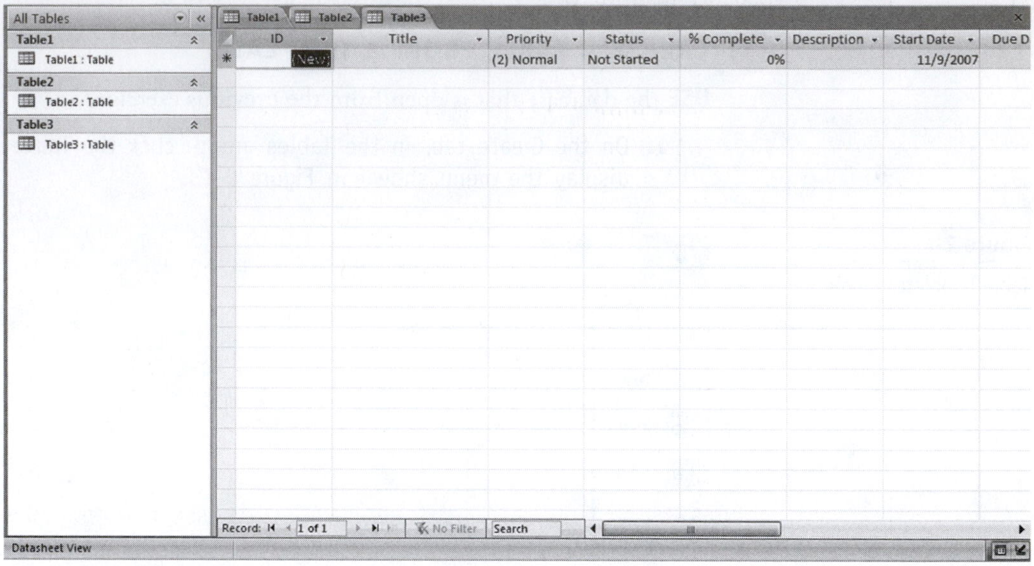

Figure 2-15

New table for tasks

4. On the Table Templates menu, click **Issues**. A new table is created with fields for issues, as shown in Figure 2-16.

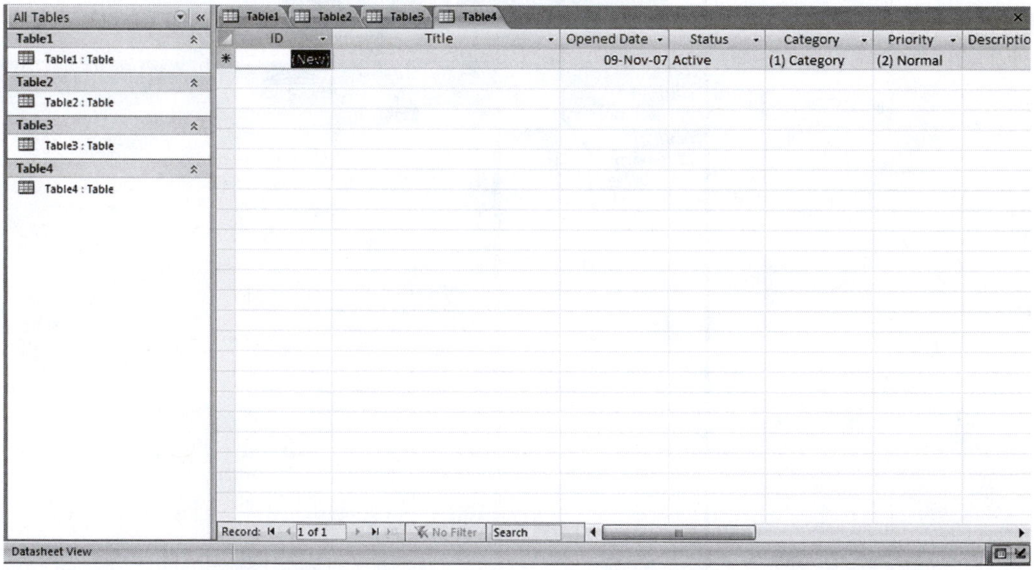

Figure 2-16

New table for issues

5. On the Table Templates menu, click **Events**. A new table is created with fields for events, as shown in Figure 2-17.

Figure 2-17

New table for events

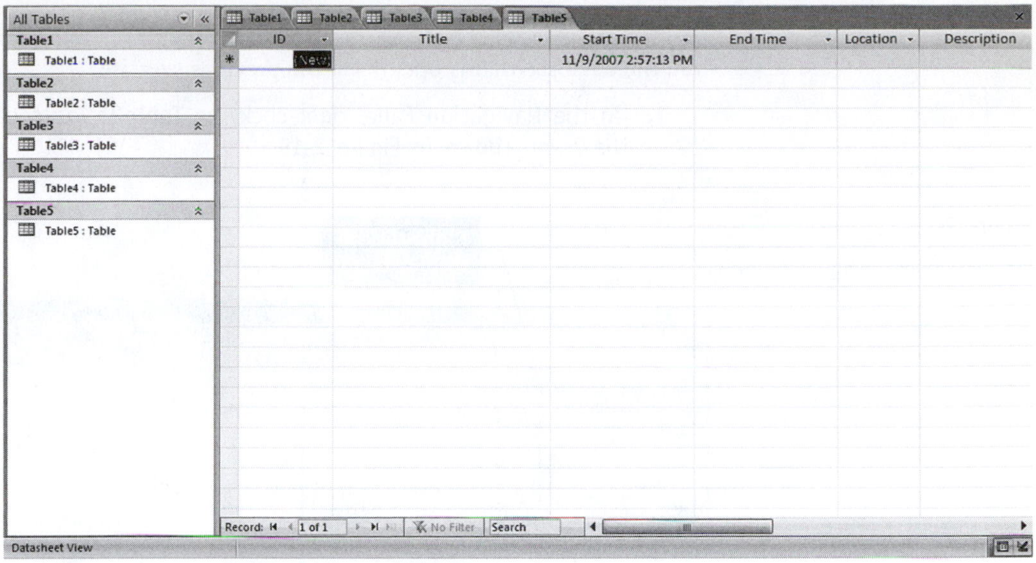

6. On the Table Templates menu, click **Assets**. A new table is created with fields for assets, as shown in Figure 2-18.

Figure 2-18

New table for assets

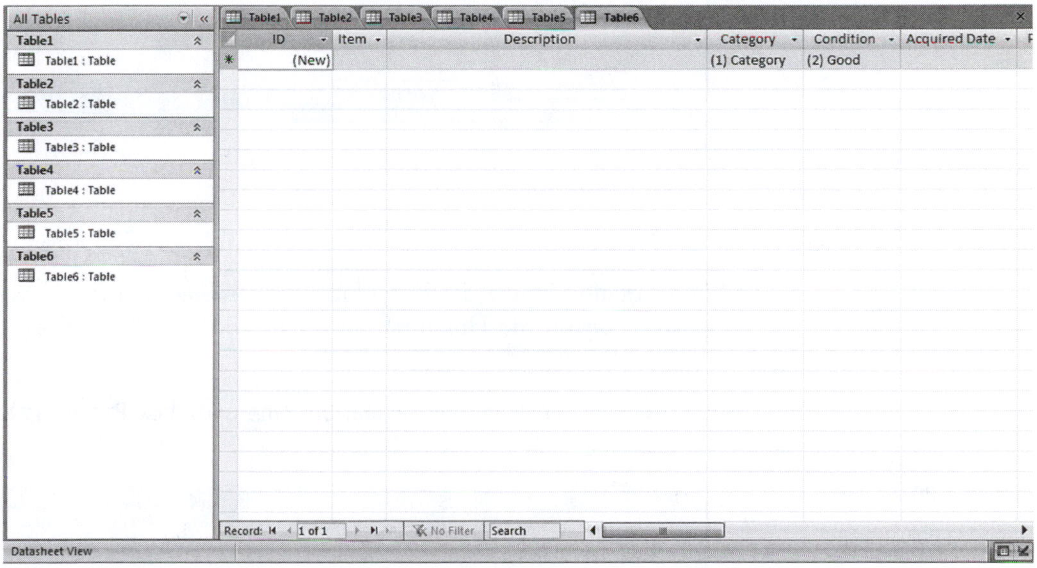

CERTIFICATION READY?
How do you create tables from templates?
2.2.3

PAUSE. LEAVE the database open to use in the next exercise.

LOOKING AHEAD

You will learn how to create a custom table in Lesson 9.

To create a table for common subjects such as contacts, issues, and tasks, you might want to start with a table template. Open the database to which you want to add a table. On the Create tab, in the Tables group, click the Table Template button and then select an available template from the menu. A new table is inserted in the database, based on the table template that you chose, and you can begin keying data.

Creating a Table from Another Table

Another way to create a table is to copy the structure of an existing table using the Copy and Paste commands.

→ CREATING A TABLE FROM ANOTHER TABLE

USE the database that is open from the previous exercise.

1. On the Navigation Pane, right-click the **Table2: Table** database object to display the menu shown in Figure 2-19.

Figure 2-19

Database object menu

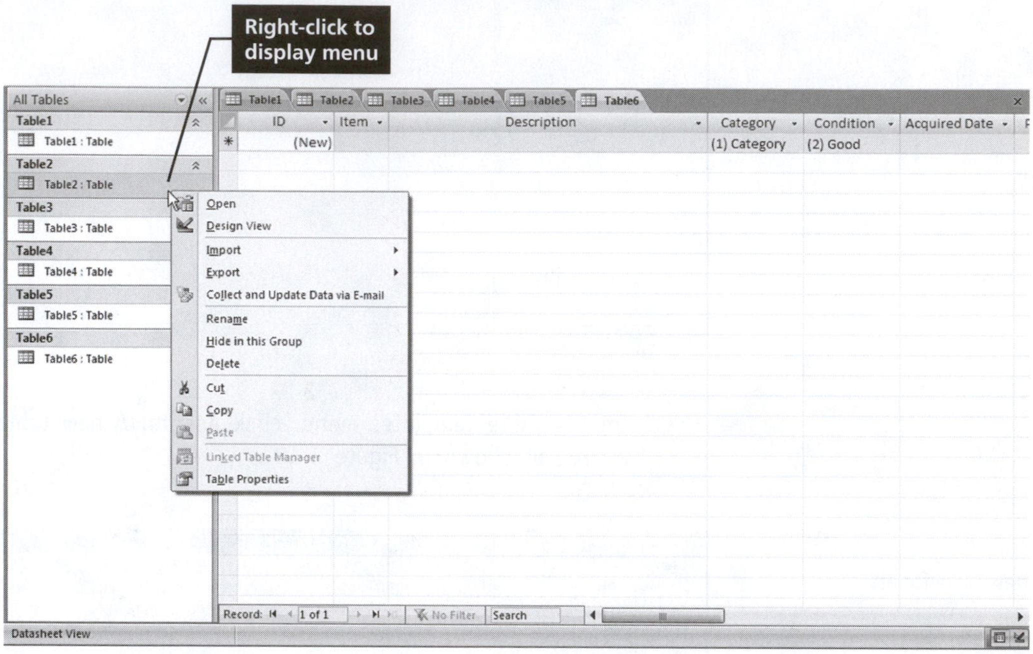

2. Click **Copy**.

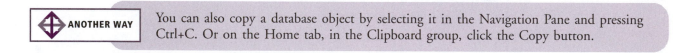

ANOTHER WAY You can also copy a database object by selecting it in the Navigation Pane and pressing Ctrl+C. Or on the Home tab, in the Clipboard group, click the Copy button.

3. Right-click in the Navigation Pane and click **Paste**, as shown in Figure 2-20.

Figure 2-20

Database object menu

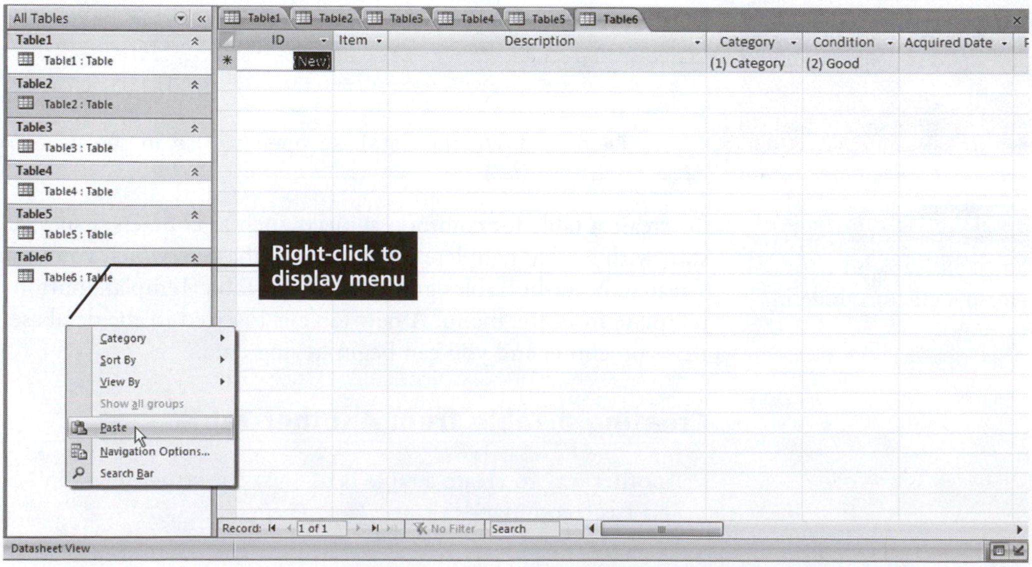

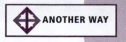 **ANOTHER WAY**

You can also paste a database object by selecting the destination location in the Navigation Pane and pressing Ctrl+V. Or on the Home tab, in the Clipboard group, click the Paste button.

4. The Paste Table As dialog box appears, as shown in Figure 2-21. In the Table Name box, key **Assets**.

Figure 2-21

Paste Table As dialog box

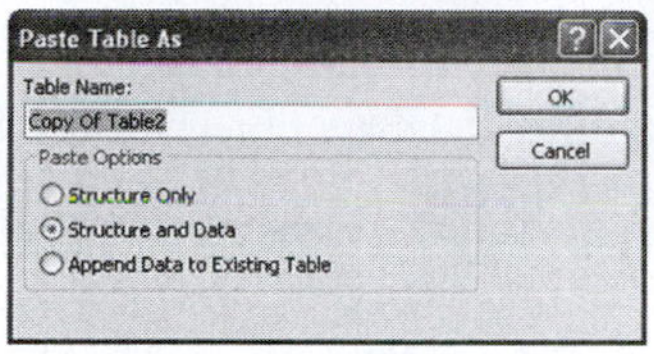

5. In the Paste Options section, select the **Structure Only** radio button.
6. Click **OK**.
7. The new table appears at the end of the list of database objects in the Navigation Pane, as shown in Figure 2-22.

Figure 2-22

New table copied from existing table

CERTIFICATION READY?
How do you create tables by copying the structure of other tables?
2.2.2

8. Double-click **Assets: Table** to open the new table. Notice that the structure of the new table is the same as the table from which it was copied.

   PAUSE. LEAVE the database open to use in the next exercise.

Another way to create a table is to copy the structure of an existing table and paste it into the database. You can copy a database object and paste it in the same database or into a different database that is open in another instance of Access.

Select the table in the Navigation Pane, right-click, and choose Copy. To paste, select the destination location, right-click, and choose Paste. In the Paste Table As dialog box, key a name for the new table. To paste just the structure of the table, click Structure Only. To also paste the data, click Structure and Data.

When you add a new table to an existing database, that new table stands alone until you relate it to your existing tables. For example, say you need to track orders placed by a distributor. To do that, you add a table named Distributor Contacts to a sales database. To take advantage of the power that a relational database can provide—to search for the orders placed by a given contact, for example—you must create a relationship between the new table and any tables that contain the order data.

LOOKING AHEAD

You will learn more about defining table relationships in Lesson 3.

■ Saving a Database Object

↓
THE BOTTOM LINE
Access automatically saves data that you have entered any time you move to a new record; close an object or database; or quit the application. But you will need to save the design of a table, or any other database object, after it is created.

Saving a Table

After you have created a table or other database object, you should save it with a descriptive name, such as Inventory Parts or Contacts.

⊕ SAVE A TABLE

USE the database that is open from the previous exercise.

1. Right-click on the **Table2 tab** to display the shortcut menu, as shown in Figure 2-23.

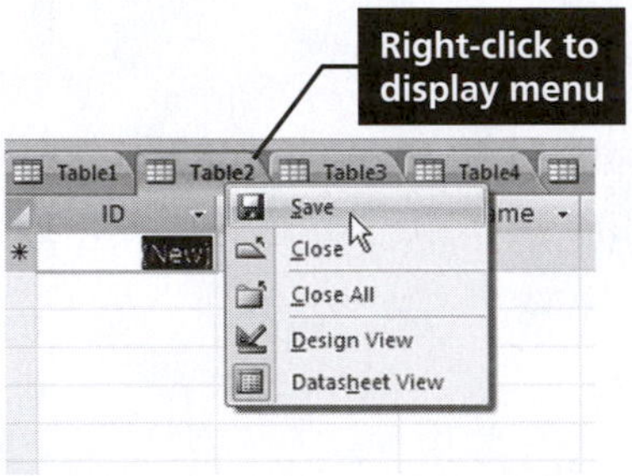

Figure 2-23

Shortcut menu

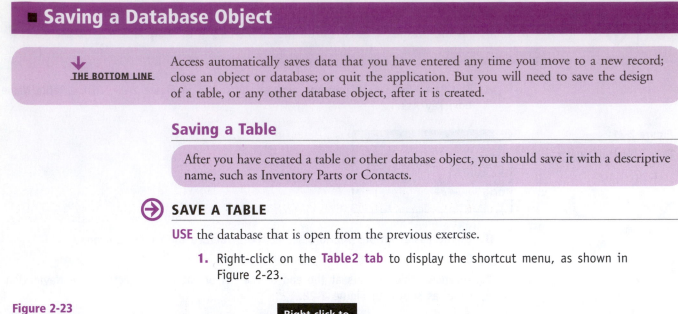

2. Click **Save**. The Save As dialog box appears, as shown in Figure 2-24.

Figure 2-24

Save As dialog box

3. In the Table Name box, key **Contacts**.
4. Click **OK**.
5. Click the **Table3 tab** to display that table.
6. Click the **Office Button** and click **Save** to display the Save As dialog box.
7. In the Table Name box, key **Tasks**.
8. Click **OK**.
9. Click the **Table4 tab** and save the table as **Issues**.
10. Click the **Table5 tab** and save the table as **Events.**
11. Click the **Table6 tab** and save the table as **Exhibits**.
12. **CLOSE** the database.

    CLOSE Access.

◆ **ANOTHER WAY**

You can also save a table by pressing Ctrl+S.

After you add fields to a table, you should save its design. When you save a new table for the first time, give it a name that describes the information it contains. You can use up to 64 characters (letters or numbers), including spaces. For example, you might name a table Orders 2007, Clients, or Tasks.

To save a table, click the Office Button and then click Save. Or you can right-click the table tab and then click Save on the shortcut menu. In the Save As dialog box, type a descriptive name for the table.

You do not need to save new data that you enter. Access automatically saves a record when you move to a different record or close the object or database.

Access also automatically saves changes to your data whenever you quit the program. However, if you have made changes to the design of any database objects since you last saved them, Access asks whether you want to save these changes before quitting.

SUMMARY SKILL MATRIX

IN THIS LESSON YOU LEARNED	MATRIX SKILL	SKILL NUMBER
To create a database	Create databases	2.1
To use a template to create a database	Create databases using templates	2.1.1
To create a blank database	Create blank databases	2.1.2
To create a database table	Create tables	2.2
To create a table from another table	Create tables by copying the structure of other tables	2.2.2
To create a table from a template	Create tables from templates	2.2.3

■ Knowledge Assessment

Fill in the Blank

Complete the following sentences by writing the correct word or words in the blanks provided.

1. You can create a database using one of the many templates available or by creating a new _____ database.

2. By default, Access creates a(n) _____ field named "ID" for all new datasheets.

3. Entering data in Datasheet view is very similar to entering data in a(n) _____.

4. Table _____ are available for common subjects such as contacts, issues, and tasks.

5. One way to create a table is to copy the _____ of an existing table and paste it into the database.

6. When you add a new table to an existing database, that new table stands alone until you _____ it to your existing tables.

7. You can use up to _____ characters (letters or numbers), including spaces, to name a database object.

8. Several options for creating a database are provided on the _____ page.

9. When you find a template that you want to use, click the _____ button for Access to create and open the database.

10. After you add _____ to a table, you should save its design.

Multiple Choice

Select the best response for the following statements.

1. A template is
   a. a database to manage contacts.
   b. where a database is stored.
   c. two tables linked together.
   d. a ready-to-use database.

2. When you create a new blank database, Access opens a database that contains
   a. one of each type of database object.
   b. a table.
   c. sample data.
   d. a template.

3. To save a database file in a location other than the default, click the
   a. folder icon.
   b. blank database icon.
   c. file name button.
   d. Help button.

4. The table structure is created when you
   a. format the data.
   b. enter data.
   c. insert blank rows and columns.
   d. switch to Design view.

5. The Tables group commands are located on which tab?
   a. Home
   b. Create
   c. Database Tools
   d. Datasheet

6. To copy a table, you must first select it in
   a. the Clipboard.
   b. Microsoft Office Online.
   c. the Navigation Pane.
   d. Datasheet view.

7. When you paste a table, which dialog box is displayed?
   a. Table Structure
   b. Copy Table
   c. Paste Data
   d. Paste Table As

8. After you have created a table or other database object, you should
   a. save it with a descriptive name.
   b. copy it to create a backup.
   c. link it to an external data source.
   d. insert a blank column at the end.

9. When you quit the program, Access automatically

    a. creates a link between all tables.

    b. leaves the Navigation Pane open.

    c. saves the data.

    d. renames the file.

10. Which is *not* a way to create a new database table?

    a. Use a table template.

    b. Choose Create on the Table menu.

    c. Copy the structure of another table.

    d. Create a new blank database.

■ Competency Assessment

Project 2-1: Contacts Database

You want to use Access to store, organize, and manage the contact information for the wholesale coffee suppliers used by Fourth Coffee, where you work as a buyer for the 15 stores in the northeast region. Use a template to create a database for the contacts.

GET READY. Launch Access if it is not already running.

1. In the Business template category, select the **Contacts** database.
2. Key *ContactsXXX* (where XXX is your initials) in the File Name box.
3. If necessary, click the folder icon and choose a different location for the file.
4. Click **Download** (or click **Create** if not logged onto the Internet) to create and open the database.
5. Click the **Shutter Bar Open/Close Button** to open the Navigation Pane.
6. Click the **Supporting Objects** header to display the database objects in that group.
7. Right-click the **Contacts** table to display the menu and click **Copy**.
8. Right-click in the white area of the Navigation Pane and click **Paste** on the menu.
9. In the Paste Table As dialog box, key **Suppliers**.
10. Click the **Structure Only** radio button.
11. Click **OK**.
12. **CLOSE** the database.

    LEAVE Access open for the next project.

Project 2-2: Database for Polling Sites

As a volunteer precinct captain, you are responsible for coordinating the polling sites for the upcoming general and special elections. You decide to create a database to store the necessary information.

1. On the Getting Started with Microsoft Office Access page, click the **Blank Database** icon.
2. In the Blank Database pane on the right, key **VotingXXX** (where xxx is your initials) in the File Name box.
3. If necessary, click the folder icon and choose a different location for the file.
4. Click the **Create** button.
5. Right-click the **Table1 tab** and click **Save**.
6. In the Save As dialog box, key **Locations**.
7. Click **OK**.

    LEAVE Access open for the next project.

■ Proficiency Assessment

Project 2-3: Adding Tables

You need to add some tables to the voting database that you just created for information about polling sites.

USE the database that is open from the previous project.

1. Use the Table Templates to create a table for contacts.
2. Name the table **Officials**.
3. Copy the structure of the Officials table to create a new table.
4. Name the new table **Volunteers**.
5. **CLOSE** the database.

   LEAVE Access open for the next project.

Project 2-4: Nutrition Tracker

You have become health conscious and want to track your activity, exercise, and food logs using Access.

1. If necessary, log on to the Internet.
2. In the Personal category, download the Nutrition template with the file name **Nutrition XXX** (where xxx is your initials).

TROUBLESHOOTING

If this template is not available, you may have to click "Automatically update this content from Office Online" on the Getting Started with Microsoft Office Access page.

TROUBLESHOOTING

If you are asked to enable the content, click the Options button on the Message Bar. In the dialog box, click Enable this content and then click OK.

3. Key your information in the My Profile form that is displayed to see your body mass index and recommended calorie consumption. (If the My Profile form is not displayed, open it first.)
4. Click **OK.**
5. Open the Tips table to view the tips stored in the database.
6. Explore the other useful forms and information available.
7. **CLOSE** the database.

   LEAVE Access open for the next project.

■ Mastery Assessment

Project 2-5: Northwind Traders

You have just joined the sales force at Northwind Traders. To familiarize yourself with the information available in the company database, open the file and browse through the objects.

1. In the Sample category, download the Northwind 2007 database using the name **Northwind 2007 XXX** (where XXX is your initials).
2. Enable the content.
3. Log in as a sales representative, Jan Kotas, by selecting that name from the Select Employee dropdown menu and clicking the Log In button.
4. Open the Navigation Pane and open each group to view all the objects that are part of the database.

5. CLOSE the database.

LEAVE Access open for the next project.

Project 2-6: Customer Service Database

Southridge Video has a large membership of customers that rent new release and film library movies, as well as video games. As the store manager, customer complaints are directed to you. Create an Access database for the purpose of tracking customer service issues.

1. Choose a template to create a database called **SouthridgeXXX** (where xxx is your initials) that will store information about customer service issues.

2. **CLOSE** the database.

LEAVE Access open for the next project.

INTERNET READY

If you can't find a template that fits your needs on the Getting Started with Microsoft Office Access page, you can explore the Office Online Web site for a larger selection. Near the bottom of the Getting Started with Microsoft Office Access page, under More on Office Online, click Templates to display the Templates Homepage, as shown in Figure 2-25.

Figure 2-25

Templates Homepage

Work with Tables/ Database Records

LESSON SKILL MATRIX

SKILLS	MATRIX SKILL	SKILL NUMBER
Navigating Among Records	Navigate among records	3.2
Entering, Editing, and Deleting Records	Enter, edit, and delete records	3.1
Creating and Modifying a Primary Key	Add, set, change, or remove primary keys	1.3
Defining and Modifying a Primary Key	Define and modify primary keys	1.3.1
Defining and Modifying a Multi-field Primary Key	Define and modify multi-field primary keys	1.3.2
Finding and Replacing Data	Find and replace data	3.3
Attaching and Detaching Documents	Attach documents to and detach from records	3.4
Sorting Data Within a Table	Sort data within tables	5.1.1
Filtering Data Within a Table	Filter data within tables	5.2.1
Removing a Filter	Remove a filter	5.2.5
Understanding Table Relationships	Define and print table relationships	1.2
Defining Table Relationships	Create relationships	1.2.1
Modifying Table Relationships	Modify relationships	1.2.2
Printing Table Relationships	Print table relationships	1.2.3

KEY TERMS

ascending
composite key
descending
filter
foreign key
innermost field
input mask
outermost field
referential integrity
sort
wildcard

Fourth Coffee is a national chain of coffee shops. A new store recently opened in your neighborhood. You were able to get a part-time job working in the office, helping the office manager organize data on the computer. In addition to being a traditional neighborhood coffee shop, the store has also started selling coffees to companies for use at their business sites. It is your job to manage the inventory, customers, and order tables in Access. In this lesson, you will learn to navigate among records; enter, edit, and delete records; find and replace data; sort and filter data; attach and detach documents; and define, modify, and print table relationships.

■ Navigating Among Records

↓
THE BOTTOM LINE

Database tables are usually large, which is why they are so useful. When a table contains many records and fields, it is important to be able to navigate among them.

Navigating Using the Keyboard

Access users who prefer using the keyboard to navigate records can press keys and key combinations to move among records in Datasheet view. If you prefer to use the mouse, you can move among records by clicking the navigation buttons.

  NAVIGATE AMONG RECORDS USING THE KEYBOARD

GET READY. Before you begin these steps, be sure to turn on and/or log on to your computer and start Access.

The Fourth Coffee database is available on the companion CD-ROM.

1. **OPEN** *Fourth Coffee* from the data files for this lesson.
2. Click the **Office Button**, point to Save As, and select **Access 2007 Database.**
3. Key **FourthCoffeeXXX** (where XXX is your initials) in the File name box. Find the location where you will save the solution files for this lesson and click **Save.**
4. In the Navigation Pane, double-click **Coffee Inventory: Table** to open the table.
5. Notice that the first cell of the first record is selected.
6. Press the Down Arrow key to move down to the next row. Notice that the cell is selected.
7. Press the Right Arrow key to move to the Product Name field.
8. Press the Tab key to move to the next cell.
9. Press the Tab key to move to the next cell.
10. Press the Tab key to move to the next row.
11. Press Ctrl + Down Arrow to move to the current field of the last record.
    PAUSE. LEAVE the database open to use in the next exercise.

In Datasheet view, you can navigate among records using the up, down, left, and right arrow keys to move to the field you want. You can also use the Tab key to move from field to field in a record and from the last field in a record to the first field of the next record.

Table 3-1 lists keys and key combinations for moving among records.

Table 3-1

Keyboard Commands for Navigating Records

PRESS	TO MOVE
Tab or Right Arrow	To the next field
End	To the last field in the current record
Shift + Tab or Left Arrow	To the previous field
Home	To the first field in the current record
Down Arrow	To the current field in the next record
Ctrl + Down Arrow	To the current field in the last record
Ctrl + End	To the last field in the last record
Up Arrow	To the current field in the previous record
Ctrl + Up Arrow	To the current field in the first record
Ctrl + Home	To the first field in the first record

CERTIFICATION READY?

How do you navigate among records?

3.2

Navigating Using Navigation Buttons

Access users who prefer to use the mouse can move among records by clicking the navigation buttons.

⊕ NAVIGATE AMONG RECORDS USING NAVIGATION BUTTONS

USE the database open from the previous exercise.

1. Click the **First record** button, shown in Figure 3-1. The selection moves to the first record.

Figure 3-1

Record navigation buttons

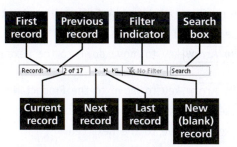

2. Click the **Next record** button. The selection moves to the next record.
3. Select the number *2* in the **Current Record** box. Key **5** and press Enter. The selection moves to the fifth record.
4. Click the **Search** box to position the insertion point. Key **sunrise** into the Search box. Notice that the selection moves to the first occurrence of the word *Sunrise*.
5. Press Enter. The selection moves to the next occurrence of the word *Sunrise*.
6. Click the **New (blank) record** button.

   PAUSE. LEAVE the database open to use in the next exercise.

The record navigation buttons are displayed at the bottom of the screen in Datasheet view. Click the First, Previous, Next, Last, and New (blank) Record buttons to go to those records. Key a record number into the Current Record box and press Enter to go to that record. Key data into the Search box to find a match in the table. The Filter Indicator shows whether a filter has been applied to the table.

■ Entering, Editing, and Deleting Records

↓
THE BOTTOM LINE
Databases are constantly changing. New data is added, and old data is updated or deleted. Keeping a database up-to-date and useful is an ongoing process. You can easily enter data by positioning the insertion point in the cell where you want to add data and begin keying. Select existing data to edit or delete it.

➔ ENTER, EDIT, AND DELETE RECORDS

USE the database you used in the previous exercise.

1. The insertion point should be positioned in the first field of the new, blank row at the bottom of the datasheet, as shown in Figure 3-2. Notice the asterisk in the record selector, which indicates that this is a new record, ready for data.

Figure 3-2

Blank record in Datasheet view

Product ID	Product Name	Pounds	Scheduled Order Date	Add New Field
20051	Cinnamon Vanilla Decaf	25	12/8/2007	
20056	Cinnamon Vanilla	30	12/29/2007	
20073	Fourth Blend Decaf	40	1/14/2008	
20077	Breakfast Blend Decaf	50	2/11/2008	
20078	Fourth Blend	25	12/29/2007	
20089	Morning Blend	40	12/29/2007	
20090	Morning Blend Decaf	35	1/14/2008	
21002	Columbian Decaf	25	1/14/2008	
21006	Breakfast Blend	50	1/14/2008	
21007	Morning Blend Decaf	40	2/11/2008	
21008	Colombian	30	1/14/2008	
21009	French Vanilla	30	1/14/2008	
21104	French Roast	25	12/8/2007	
21105	Sunrise Blend	40	2/11/2008	
21141	Sunrise Blend Decaf	40	2/11/2008	
21789	Kona	35	1/14/2008	
21890	Vanilla Nut	25	12/29/2007	
21901	Vanilla Nut Decaf	30	2/11/2008	

New record

Record selector

2. Key **21905** and press [Tab]. Notice that the asterisk has changed to a pencil icon, as shown in Figure 3-3, indicating that the record is being edited.

Figure 3-3

Enter data into a record

21141	Sunrise Blend Decaf	
21789	Kona	
21890	Vanilla Nut	
21901	Vanilla Nut Decaf	
21905		

Record selector indicates that the record is being edited

3. Key **Hazelnut** and press [Tab].

4. Key **30** and press [Tab].

5. Key **02112008** and press [Enter]. Notice that the input mask, shown in Figure 3-4, requires that the date be keyed exactly as formatted.

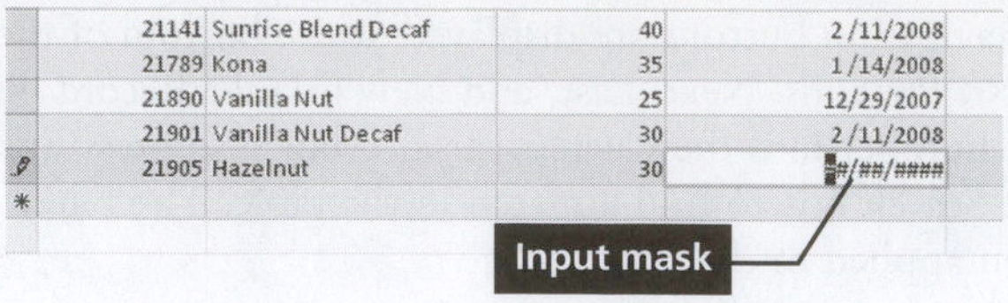

Figure 3-4

Input mask

6. Select **sunrise** in the Search box and key **Kona** to locate the Kona record.

7. Select **Kona** in the record to position the blinking insertion point there. Key **Hawaiian** and press **Tab**.

8. Click the **Undo** button on the Quick Access Toolbar.

9. Press **Tab**. Key **12292007** and press **Tab**.

10. Click the **Select All** button to the left of the Product ID field of the first record, *20051*.

11. On the Home tab, in the Records group, click the arrow beside the Delete button. Select **Delete Record** from the menu, as shown in Figure 3-5.

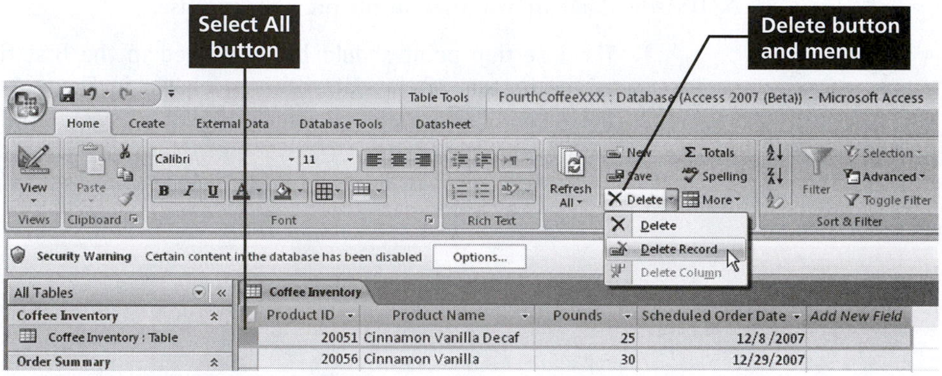

Figure 3-5

Delete menu

12. A dialog box appears, as shown in Figure 3-6, asking if you are sure you want to delete the record. Click **Yes**.

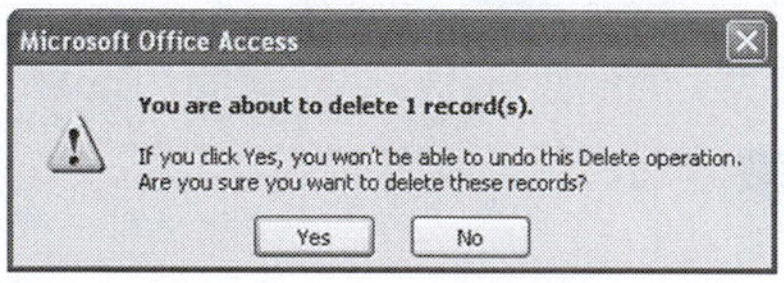

Figure 3-6

Microsoft Office Access Dialog box

13. Notice that the Undo button on the Quick Access Toolbar is not available because you cannot undo a deletion. **CLOSE** the table.

   PAUSE. LEAVE the database open to use in the next exercise.

In Datasheet view, position the insertion point in the first empty cell of a record and begin keying to add data. Continue entering data field by field and row by row. After you enter data and move to a new field, Access automatically saves the data in the table.

As you enter data, remember that each field in a table is formatted with a specific data type, so you must enter that kind of data in the field. If you do not, you will get an error message. For example, if a field is formatted to accept numbers, you cannot enter text.

Sometimes fields may contain an ***input mask***, which is a set of placeholder characters that force you to enter data in a specific format. For example, an input mask for a date might look like this: *xx/xx/xxxx*. All dates in that field must be entered in that format or you will get an error message. Input masks help maintain consistency and prevent users from entering invalid data.

To insert a new record, select any record in the table and click the New button on the Home tab in the Records group. You can also right-click a selected record and select New Record from the shortcut menu. A new record is added to the end of the table.

To delete information from a field, select it and press the Delete key or click the Delete button on the Home tab in the Records group. If you change your mind after you delete information from a field, you can undo the action by clicking the Undo button on the Quick Access Toolbar.

CERTIFICATION READY?
How do you enter, edit, and delete data?
3.1

You can also delete an entire record or several records at once from a database. Just select the row or rows and press the Delete key or click the Delete button on the Home tab in the Records group. You can also right-click and select Delete Record from the shortcut menu. After you delete a record, you cannot undo it.

ANOTHER WAY

An easy way to select an entire record is to click the Select All button, which is a square to the left of a record. If you need to select other records above or below it, you can drag the mouse up or down to include those in the selection. To delete one or more selected records, right-click the Select All button and choose Delete Record from the shortcut menu.

ANOTHER WAY

To delete a record without selecting it, place the cursor in one of the fields of a record and click the Delete menu on the Home tab in the Records group. Select Delete Record from the menu.

LOOKING AHEAD

As you become more advanced in your knowledge of Access, you may want to create a delete query that will delete multiple records at once. You will learn more about queries in Lesson 8.

■ Creating and Modifying Primary Keys

THE BOTTOM LINE

A primary key identifies a record or row in a table. Customer IDs, serial numbers, or product IDs usually make good primary keys. Each table should have a primary key, and some tables might have two or more. When you divide information into separate tables, the primary keys help Access bring the information back together again.

Defining and Modifying a Primary Key

A field designated as the primary key should uniquely identify each record, never be empty, and never change.

 DEFINE AND MODIFY A PRIMARY KEY

USE the database you used in the previous exercise.

1. **OPEN** the **Order Summary** table.
2. On the Home tab, in the Views group, click the arrow on the View menu. Select **Design View.**
3. Click the **Select All** box beside the Order ID row to select the row.

4. On the Design tab, in the Tools group, click the **Primary Key** button. The Primary Key button is pushed in and appears orange. A key icon is displayed on the Order ID row to designate the field as a primary key, as shown in Figure 3-7.

Figure 3-7

Primary key

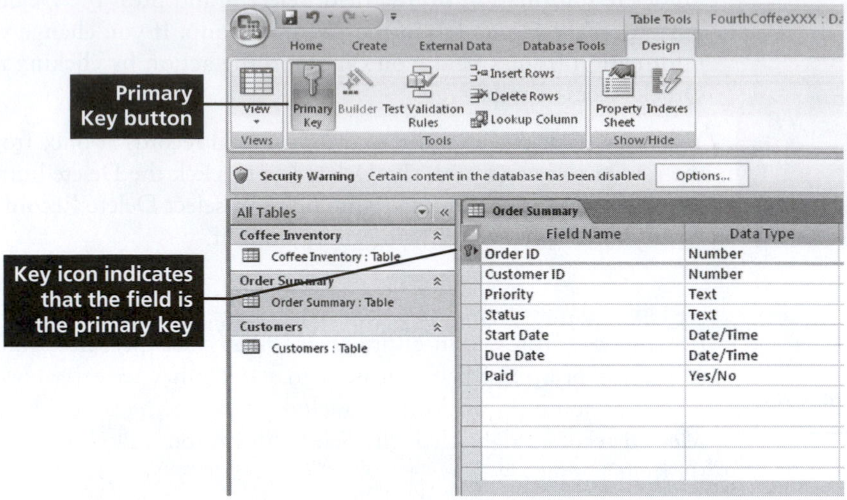

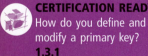

5. With the Order ID row still selected, click the **Primary Key** button. The button changes back to its original color, and the key icon in the Order ID row is removed.

ANOTHER WAY To add or remove the primary key from a field, you can also select the row, right-click, and select Primary Key from the shortcut menu.

PAUSE. LEAVE the table open to use in the next exercise.

As you learned in Lesson 1, a primary key is a column that uniquely identifies each row, such as Item Number.

You just defined a primary key in an existing table using Design view. Now that it is defined, you can use the primary key in other tables to refer back to the table with the primary key. When a primary key from one table is used in another table, it is called the *foreign key.* The foreign key is used to reference the data from the primary key to help avoid redundancy.

You can modify a primary key by deleting it from one field and adding it to another field. To delete a primary key in Design view, select the row and click the Primary Key button to remove it.

When you create a new database, Access creates a primary key field named "ID" by default and sets the data type for the field to AutoNumber. If you don't have a field in an existing database that you think will make a good primary key, you can use a field with the AutoNumber data type. It doesn't contain factual information (such as a telephone number) about a record and it is not likely to change.

CERTIFICATION READY?
How do you define and modify a primary key?
1.3.1

Defining and Modifying a Multi-field Primary Key

Some tables might have multiple primary keys.

DEFINE AND MODIFY A MULTI-FIELD PRIMARY KEY

USE the database open from the previous exercise.

1. Press and hold the CTRL key.

2. Click the **Select All** button beside the **Paid** row. Continue to hold down the **CTRL** key and click the **Order ID** selection button. Both fields should be selected, as shown in Figure 3-8. If not, continue to hold the **CTRL** key and click the **Paid** selection button again.

Figure 3-8

Primary key

Field Name	Data Type
Order ID	Number
Customer ID	Number
Priority	Text
Status	Text
Start Date	Date/Time
Due Date	Date/Time
Paid	Yes/No

Both fields are selected

3. On the Design tab, in the Tools group, click the **Primary Key** button. A key icon should be displayed beside each of the two fields.

4. With the rows still selected, click the **Primary Key** button again to remove the primary key designation from both the fields.

5. Click in any field to remove the selection.

6. Click the **Select All** button beside the **Order ID** row. Drag down to the next row, the **Customer ID** row, to select it as well.

7. On the Design tab, in the Tools group, click the **Primary Key** button. Both rows should have a key displayed beside them.

8. Click the **Save** button on the Quick Access Toolbar.

9. **CLOSE** the Design view.

PAUSE. LEAVE the database open to use in the next exercise.

CERTIFICATION READY?
How do you define and modify a multi-field primary key?
1.3.2

In some cases, you may want to use two or more fields that, together, provide the primary key of a table. For example, in the Order Summary table, you used the Order ID and the Customer ID as primary keys. Two or more primary keys in a table are called the *composite key.*

As you just practiced, you can modify the primary keys by changing which fields are defined as the primary keys. In Design view, select the rows you want to designate as primary keys and click the Primary Key button.

To remove multiple primary keys, select the rows and click the Primary Key button.

■ Finding and Replacing Data

THE BOTTOM LINE

A big advantage of using a computer database rather than paper and pencil for recordkeeping is the ability to quickly search for and/or replace data. These features may be accessed from the Find and Replace dialog box. The Find and Replace commands in Access work very much like those you've probably used in Word or other Office applications. You can use the Find command to search for specific text in a table or to move quickly to a particular word or number in the table. The Replace command can be used to automatically replace a word or number with another.

⊙ **FIND AND REPLACE DATA**

USE the database open from the previous exercise.

1. **OPEN** the **Customers** table.

2. On the Home tab, in the Find group, click the **Find** button. The Find and Replace dialog box appears with the Find tab displayed.

3. Click the **Replace** tab in the Find and Replace dialog box.

4. Key **Elm** into the Find What box.

5. Key **Little Elm** into the Replace With box.

6. Click the down arrow beside the Look in menu and select **customers**, so that the entire database will be searched instead of just the Customer ID field.

7. Click the down arrow beside the Match menu and select **Any Part of Field** to broaden the search. See Figure 3-9.

Figure 3-9

Find and Replace dialog box

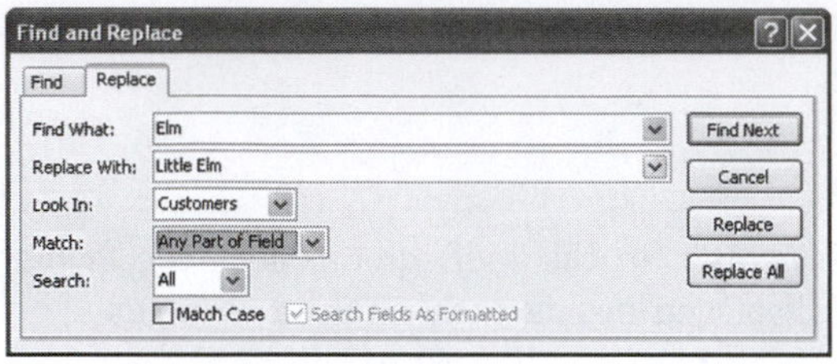

8. Click the **Find Next** button. Access searches the table and finds and selects the word *Elm*.

9. Click the **Replace** button. Access replaces *Elm* with *Little Elm*.

10. Click the **Find Next** button. Access finds *Elm* in the new text that was just inserted.

11. Click **Find Next** again. Access displays a message saying that no more occurrences of the word have been found. Click **OK**.

12. Click **Cancel** to close the dialog box.

13. Press Down Arrow to remove the selection and allow Access to save the change.

14. **CLOSE** the table.

   PAUSE. LEAVE the database open to use in the next exercise.

CERTIFICATION READY?
How do you find and replace data?
3.3

 ANOTHER WAY

To open the Find tab in the Find and Replace dialog box using the keyboard, press Ctrl+F. To open the Replace tab, press Ctrl+H.

In the Find and Replace dialog box, key the text or numbers that you want to search for into the Find What box and click Find Next to locate the record containing the data. If you want to replace the data, key the new data into the Replace With box and click Replace or Replace All.

TAKE NOTE ✱

When replacing data, it is usually a good practice to click Replace instead of Replace All so that you can confirm each replacement to make sure that it is correct.

The Find and Replace dialog box searches only one table at a time; it does not search the entire database. The Look In menu allows you to choose to search by field or to search the entire table. By default, Access searches the field that was selected when you opened the Find and Replace dialog box. If you want to search a different field, select the field while the dialog box is open; you don't have to close it first.

In the Match menu, you can specify where you want Access to look in a field. Select Any Part of Field for the broadest search.

Sometimes Access selects the Search Fields As Formatted checkbox. When it does, do not clear the checkbox, or your search probably will not return any results.

Click the Match Case box to search for text with the same uppercase and/or lowercase capitalization of text.

You can use *wildcard* characters to find words or phrases that contain specific letters or combinations of letters. Key a question mark (?) to represent a single character—for example, keying b?t will find *bat, bet, bit,* and *but*. Key an asterisk (*) to represent a string of characters—for example, m*t will find *mat, moment,* or even *medium format*.

If you key a wildcard character in the Replace With box, Access will insert that character just as you keyed it.

TAKE NOTE*

If you want to use the Find and Replace dialog box to search for characters that are used as wildcards, such as a question mark, you must enclose that character in brackets, for example, [?]. Follow this rule when searching for all wildcard characters except exclamation points (!) and closing brackets (]).

■ Attaching and Detaching Documents

↓
THE BOTTOM LINE

Access 2007 allows you to attach documents, such as Word documents or photo files, to records in a database. For example, the human resources department of a large company could keep a photo, a resume, and employee evaluation documents with each employee record. These attached files can also be easily detached, if necessary. The Attachments dialog box allows you to manage the documents attached to records.

→ **ATTACH AND DETACH DOCUMENTS**

USE the database open from the previous exercise.

1. **OPEN** the **Order Summary** table.
2. Click the header row of the Due Date field to select it.
3. On the Datasheet tab, in the Fields & Columns group, click the **New Field** button. The Field Templates menu appears.
4. Double-click **Attachment** under Basic Fields, as shown in Figure 3-10. The Attachment field is inserted in the table.

Figure 3-10

Field Templates menu

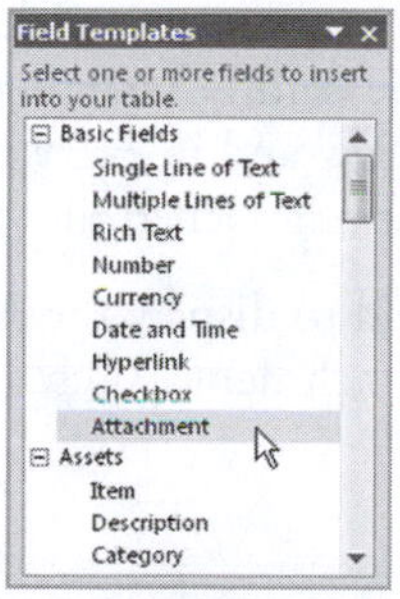

5. Click the **Close** button to close the Field Templates box.
6. Double-click the first row of the Attachments field. The Attachments dialog box appears.
7. Click the **Add** button. Navigate to the data files for this lesson and select *invoice100.docx.* Click **Open**. The document appears in the Attachments dialog box, as shown in Figure 3-11.

Figure 3-11

Attachments dialog box

```
Attachments                                    [X]
Attachments (Double-click to open)
 📎  invoice100.docx                          [ Add...   ]
                                              [ Remove   ]
                                              [ Open     ]
                                              [ Save As...]
                                              [ Save All...]

                                  [  OK  ]  [ Cancel ]
```

8. Click **OK**. The number of attachments in the first record changes to 1, as shown in Figure 3-12.

Figure 3-12

Attachments field

Attachments field

📎
📎(1)
📎(0)
📎(0)
📎(0)
📎(0)
📎(0)

Number of attachments

9. Double-click the attachment number. The Attachments dialog box appears.

10. Click the **Open** button. The attachment opens in Microsoft Word.

11. Click the **Close** button to close the invoice document.

12. Click the Access button on the taskbar to return to Access.

13. In the Attachments dialog box, click the **Remove** button and click **OK**. The attachment is removed from the record.

14. **CLOSE** the Order Summary table.

PAUSE. LEAVE the database open to use in the next exercise.

CERTIFICATION READY?
How do you attach and detach documents from a record?
3.4

TAKE NOTE * You can only attach files to databases created in Access 2007. You cannot share attachments with a database created in an earlier version of Access.

Before you can start attaching documents, you must create a field in a table and format it with the Attachment data type. You can add the field in Datasheet view or in Design view. Access displays a paper clip icon in the header row and in every record in the field along with a number in parentheses indicating the number of attached files in the field.

Double-click the record in the Attachments field to display the Attachments dialog box where you can add, remove, open, or save multiple attachments, such as images, documents, and spreadsheets, for a single record.

ANOTHER WAY You can also right-click in the Attachments field to display a shortcut menu. Select Manage Attachments from the menu to display the Attachments dialog box.

If the program that was used to create the attached file is installed on your computer, you can open and edit the file using that program. For example, if you open a Word resume that is attached to a record, the Word program starts and you view the document in Word. If you do not have the program that was used to create a file, Access prompts you to choose a program you do have to view the file.

You can save attached files to your hard disk or network drive so that you can save changes to documents there before saving them to the database.

■ Sorting and Filtering Data Within a Table

THE BOTTOM LINE

It is often helpful to display data in order or to display similar records. Sorting allows you to order records. For example, an office contact list that displays employees in alphabetical order by last name would help the user find information for a particular employee quickly. If you wanted to view only the records of employees in a particular department, you could create a filter to display only those records.

■ SOFTWARE ORIENTATION

Sort & Filter Group

The Sort & Filter group is located on the Home tab in the Ribbon.

Ascending button
Filter button
Selection menu
Descending button
Advanced menu
Clear All Sorts button
Toggle Filter button
Selection
Advanced
Filter
Toggle Filter
Sort & Filter

Figure 3-13

Sort & Filter Group

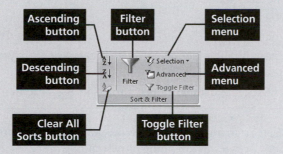

Use the Sort & Filter group of commands to sort and filter records in tables.

Sorting Data Within a Table

Sorting within a table displays all the records in the table in the order that you select. You can easily sort by one or more fields to achieve the order that you want.

SORT DATA WITHIN A TABLE

USE the database you used in the previous exercise.

1. **OPEN** the **Customers** table.
2. Click the header row of the Customer ID field to select it.
3. Right-click in the field to display the shortcut menu, shown in Figure 3-14. Select **Sort Largest to Smallest**.

Figure 3-14

Shortcut menu

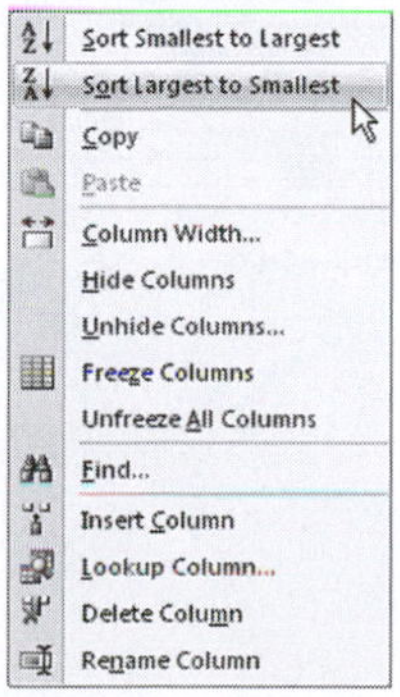

Sort Smallest to Largest
Sort Largest to Smallest
Copy
Paste
Column Width...
Hide Columns
Unhide Columns...
Freeze Columns
Unfreeze All Columns
Find...
Insert Column
Lookup Column...
Delete Column
Rename Column

4. The data is sorted and an arrow is inserted in the header row, as shown in Figure 3-15, indicating that the data is displayed in sort order.

Sort arrow

Customer ID	
109	B
108	V
107	V
106	H
105	T
104	C
103	S
102	P
101	A
*	

5. On the Home tab, in the Sort & Filter group, click the **Clear All Sorts** button. The sort is removed from the Customer ID field.

6. Select the First Name field. On the Home tab, in the Sort & Filter group, click the **Ascending** button.

7. Select the **Last Name** field. On the Home tab, in the Sort & Filter group, click the **Ascending** button.

8. On the Home tab, in the Sort & Filter group, click the **Clear All Sorts** button.

9. **CLOSE** the table. If a pop-up screen appears asking if you want to save changes to the table, click **No.**

PAUSE. LEAVE the database open to use in the next exercise.

CERTIFICATION READY?
How do you sort data within a table?
5.1.1

To *sort* data means to arrange it alphabetically, numerically, or chronologically. Access can sort text, numbers, or dates in ascending or descending order. *Ascending* order sorts data from beginning to end, such as from A to Z, 1 to 10, and January to December. *Descending* order sorts data from the end to the beginning, such as from Z to A, 10 to 1, and December to January.

To sort text, numbers, dates, or other data types in a column, you first need to select the column. Then click the Ascending or Descending button in the Sort & Filter group of the Home tab. You can also right-click a selected column and choose a Sort command from the shortcut menu. The available sort commands in the shortcut menu vary depending on the type of data in the column, as shown in Table 3-2.

Table 3-2

Sort Commands on the shortcut menu

TYPE OF DATA	SORT COMMAND ON THE SHORTCUT MENU
Number, Currency, or AutoNumber	Sort Smallest to Largest Sort Largest to Smallest
Text, Memo, or Hyperlink	Sort A to Z Sort Z to A
Yes/No	Sort Selected to Cleared Sort Cleared to Selected
Date/Time	Sort Oldest to Newest Sort Newest to Oldest

You can also sort records on multiple fields. When you are using multiple fields, determine which order you want them to be sorted in. The primary sort field is called the ***outermost field***. A secondary sort field is called an ***innermost field***. For example, if you want to sort a contact list so that each employee's last name is sorted primarily and first name is sorted secondarily, Last Name would be the outermost field and First Name would be the innermost field. In your completed sort, Wright, David, would be listed before Wright, Steven, in an A to Z sort. When designating the sort order, however, you select the innermost field first and choose the type of sort you want from the shortcut menu. Then select the outermost field and select the type of sort that you want.

After you sort one or more columns, Access inserts sort arrows in the header row to show that the field is sorted. These sort commands remain with the table until you remove them. When you want to remove a sort order, click the Clear All Sorts button from the Sort & Filter group on the Home tab. This removes the sorting commands from all the fields in the table. In a table with more than one sorted fields, you cannot remove just one sort.

Filtering Data Within a Table

> When you apply a filter, Access displays only the records that meet your filter criteria; the other records are hidden from view.

⊕ FILTER DATA

USE the database you used in the previous exercise.

1. **OPEN** the **Coffee Inventory** table. 
2. Select the **Product Name** field. On the Home tab, in the Sort & Filter group, click the **Filter** button. A menu appears.
3. Point to **Text Filters**. A second menu appears. Select **Contains**, as shown in Figure 3-16.

Figure 3-16

Filter menu

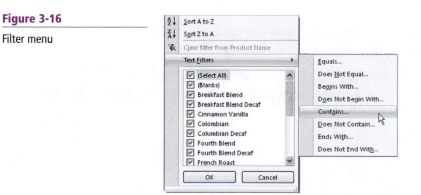

4. The Custom Filter box appears. Key **Decaf**, as shown in Figure 3-17, and click **OK**. Notice that only the records containing the word *Decaf* are displayed, and a filter icon is displayed in the header row of the field, as shown in Figure 3-18.

Figure 3-17

Custom filter box

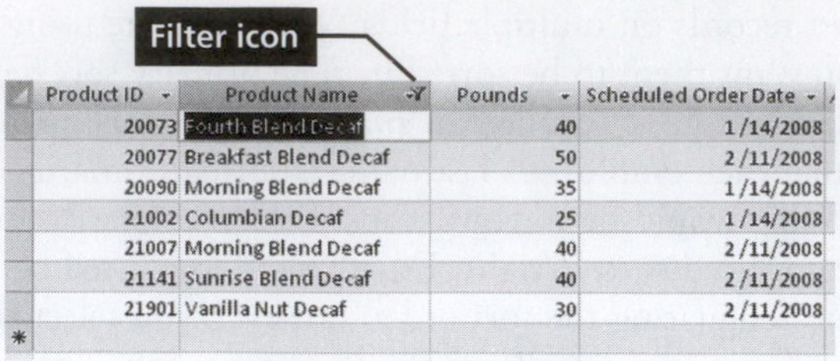
Filter icon
Product ID
Product Name
Pounds
Scheduled Order Date
20073 Fourth Blend Decaf 40 1/14/2008
20077 Breakfast Blend Decaf 50 2/11/2008
20090 Morning Blend Decaf 35 1/14/2008
21002 Columbian Decaf 25 1/14/2008
21007 Morning Blend Decaf 40 2/11/2008
21141 Sunrise Blend Decaf 40 2/11/2008
21901 Vanilla Nut Decaf 30 2/11/2008

Figure 3-18

Filtered records

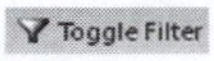
Toggle Filter

5. Click the **Toggle Filter** button to display the records without the filter.
6. In the second record in the Product Name field, double-click the word *Decaf* to select it.
7. Right-click to display the shortcut menu. Select **Does Not Contain "Decaf"**, as shown in Figure 3-19. Notice that the records are filtered to show only those that do not contain the word *Decaf*.

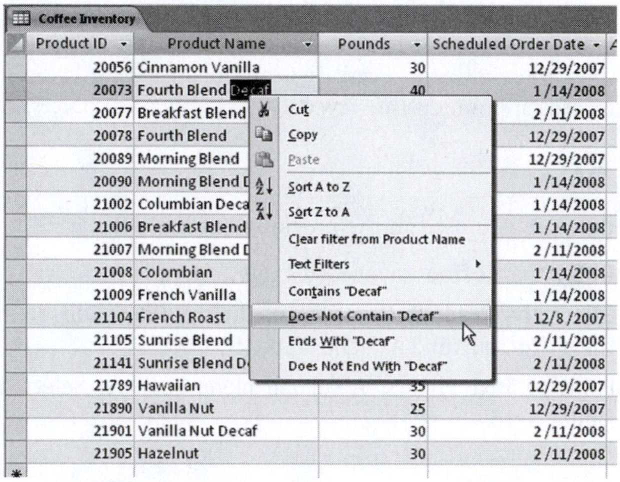
Coffee Inventory
Product ID
Product Name
Pounds
Scheduled Order Date
20056 Cinnamon Vanilla 30 12/29/2007
20073 Fourth Blend Decaf 40 1/14/2008
20077 Breakfast Blend 2/11/2008
20078 Fourth Blend 12/29/2007
20089 Morning Blend 12/29/2007
20090 Morning Blend 1/14/2008
21002 Columbian Deca 1/14/2008
21006 Breakfast Blend 1/14/2008
21007 Morning Blend 2/11/2008
21008 Colombian 1/14/2008
21009 French Vanilla 1/14/2008
21104 French Roast 12/8/2007
21105 Sunrise Blend 2/11/2008
21141 Sunrise Blend 2/11/2008
21789 Hawaiian 35 12/29/2007
21890 Vanilla Nut 25 12/29/2007
21901 Vanilla Nut Decaf 30 2/11/2008
21905 Hazelnut 30 2/11/2008
Cut
Copy
Paste
Sort A to Z
Sort Z to A
Clear filter from Product Name
Text Filters
Contains "Decaf"
Does Not Contain "Decaf"
Ends With "Decaf"
Does Not End With "Decaf"

Figure 3-19

Shortcut menu

8. Click the **Filtered** button on the Navigation button bar.
9. Click in the **Pounds** field of the first record.
10. On the Home tab, in the Sort & Filter group, click the **Filter** button.
11. Click the checkboxes to remove the checkmarks beside **30**, **35**, **40**, and **50**, as shown in Figure 3-20.

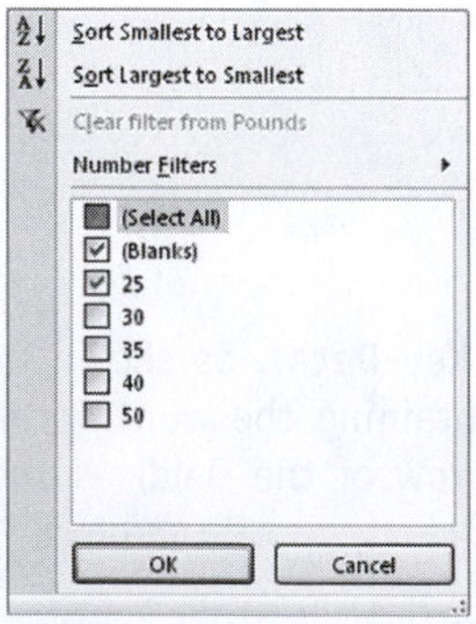
Sort Smallest to Largest
Sort Largest to Smallest
Clear filter from Pounds
Number Filters
(Select All)
(Blanks)
25
30
35
40
50
OK
Cancel

Figure 3-20

Filter menu

12. Click **OK**. Access filters the records to show only those containing the number 25.
13. Click the **Toggle Filter** button.
14. In the Date field of the second row, select **1/14/2008**.

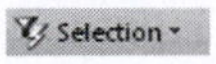
Selection

15. On the Home tab, in the Sort & Filter group, click the **Selection** button. A menu appears.

16. Select **On or After 1/14/2008**, as shown in Figure 3-21. The data is filtered.

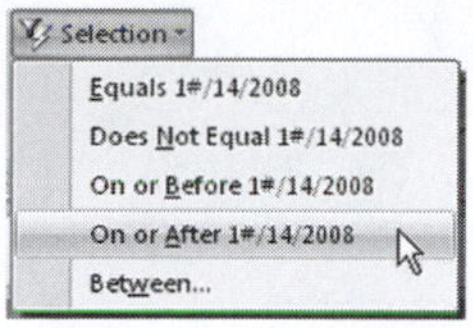

Figure 3-21

Selection menu

Figure 3-21

Selection menu

17. In the Pounds field of the seventh row, select **30**.

18. On the Home tab, in the Sort & Filter group, click the **Selection** button. Select **Less Than or Equal to 30**. The records are filtered.

PAUSE. LEAVE the database open to use in the next exercise.

A *filter* is a set of rules for determining which records will be displayed. Once the filtered records are displayed, you can edit and navigate the records just as you would without a filter applied.

You just practiced creating filters in several different ways.

You clicked the Filter button to view a menu of filtering choices, and you right-clicked fields to access context-related menus. The commands available on the menus vary, depending on the type of field or data selected. You also selected data and chose filters from the Selection menu.

TAKE NOTE★

Only one filter can be applied per column. When you apply a filter to a column that is already filtered, the previous filter is removed and the new filter is applied.

The Toggle Filter button in the Sort & Filter group on the Home tab lets you temporarily remove a filter and switches you back to the original view. Click the toggle button again to return to the filtered view. In the same way, you can click the Filtered/Unfiltered button on the navigator bar at the bottom of the page to switch between filtered and unfiltered views.

Filters remain in effect until you close the object. You can switch between views, and the filter settings will stay in effect. To make the filter available the next time you open the object, save the object before closing it.

Removing a Filter

After applying a filter, you may need to return to records not displayed by the filter. The Toggle Filter button lets you switch between viewing the filtered records and viewing the table without the filter. When you are finished using the filter, you can permanently remove it.

➔ **REMOVE A FILTER**

USE the table you used in the previous exercise.

1. Select the Pounds field. On the Home tab, in the Sort & Filter group, click the **Filter** button. A menu appears.

2. Select **Clear Filter from Pounds**, as shown in Figure 3-22.

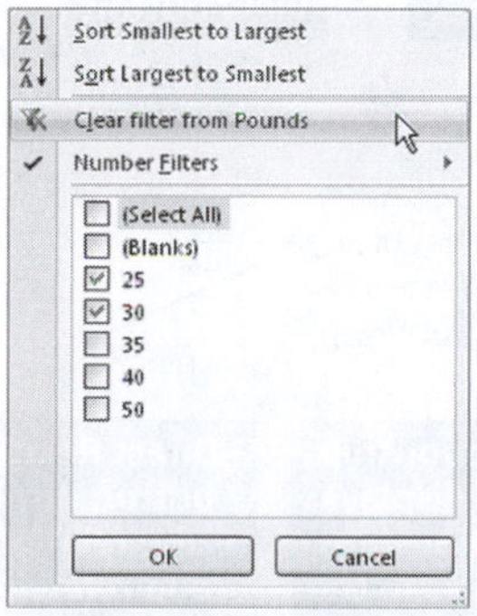

Figure 3-22

Filter menu

Advanced ▾

3. On the Home tab, in the Sort & Filter group, click the **Advanced** button. A menu appears.

4. Select **Clear All Filters** from the menu, as shown in Figure 3-23.

Figure 3-23

Advanced menu

Advanced
Clear All Filters
Filter By Form
Apply Filter/Sort
Advanced Filter/Sort...
Load from Query...
Save As Query
Delete Tab
Clear Grid
Close

CERTIFICATION READY?
How do you remove a filter?
5.2.5

5. **SAVE** and **CLOSE** the table.

PAUSE. LEAVE the database open to use in the next exercise.

If you want to permanently remove a filter from a single field, select the field and click the Filter button on the Sort & Filter group on the Home tab. From the menu, select Clear filter from field name.

To clear all filters from all fields, click the Advanced button from the Sort & Filter group on the Home tab. From the menu, select Clear All Filters. When you clear a filter, it is gone. You can no longer apply it again by clicking the Toggle Filter button.

■ Understanding Table Relationships

↓ **THE BOTTOM LINE**
As you have already learned, most databases have more than one table. Creating relationships among these tables allows Access to bring that information back together again so that you can display information from several tables at once. This is why it is a good idea to define table relationships before you start creating reports and queries.

■ SOFTWARE ORIENTATION

Relationship Tools on the Ribbon

When you click the Relationships button on the Datasheet tab, the Relationship window appears and the Relationship Tools are displayed in the Ribbon.

Figure 3-24

Relationship Tools

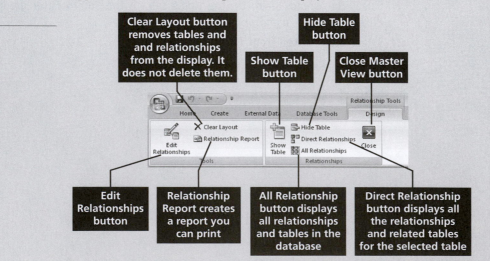

Use the Relationship Tools to define and modify table relationships.

Defining Table Relationships

In relational database applications like Access, you can store information in separate tables that are connected by a defined relationship that ties the data together. To create that relationship, you place common fields in tables and define the relationships between the tables.

⊕ **DEFINE TABLE RELATIONSHIPS**

USE the database you used in the previous exercise.

1. On the Database Tools tab in the Show/Hide group, click the **Relationships** button. The Relationships view appears with the Customers table represented.

2. Click the **Show Table** button. The Show Table dialog box appears, as shown in Figure 3-25.

Figure 3-25

Show Table dialog box

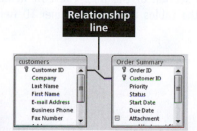

3. Select **Order Summary** and click **Add.**

4. Click **Close**. The two tables are represented in Relationship view.

5. Click the **Customer ID** field in the Customers table and drag it to the Customer ID field of the Order Summary table and release the mouse button. The Edit Relationship dialog box appears, as shown in Figure 3-26.

Figure 3-26

Edit Relationship dialog box

6. Click **Create**. The one-to-many table relationship of the Order Summary and the Customers Table is displayed, as shown in Figure 3-27.

Figure 3-27

One-to-many relationship

CERTIFICATION READY?
How do you define table relationships?
1.2.1

PAUSE. LEAVE the database open to use in the next exercise.

You can define a table relationship in the Relationships window.

Common fields used in different tables do not have to have the same names, but they usually do. They must have the same data type, though.

You can create three types of relationships: one-to-one, one-to-many, and many-to-many.

In a one-to-one relationship, both tables have a common field with the same data. Each record in the first table can only have one matching record in the second table, and each record in the second table can have only one matching record in the first table. This type of relationship is not common, because information related in this way is usually stored in the same table.

A one-to-many relationship is more common, because each record in the first table can have many records in the second table. For example, in a Customers table and an Orders table, one customer could have many orders. The Customer ID would be the primary key in the Customers table (the one) and the foreign key in the Orders table (the many).

In a third type of relationship, called a many-to-many relationship, many records in the first table can have many records in the second table.

Modifying Table Relationships

A table relationship is represented by the line that connects the tables in the Relationship window. To modify the relationship, you can double-click the line to display the Edit Relationships dialog box or delete the line to delete the relationship.

⊕ MODIFY TABLE RELATIONSHIPS

USE the database you used in the previous exercise.

1. Right-click the center section of the line connecting the two tables. A menu appears, as shown in Figure 3-28.

Figure 3-28

Edit/Delete menu

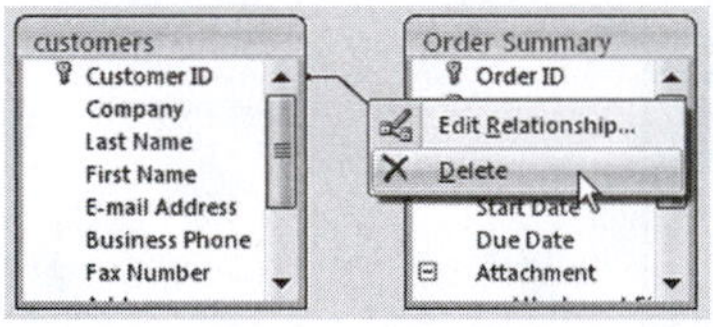

2. Select **Delete**. A message appears asking if you are sure you want to delete the relationship. Click **Yes**. The line disappears.

3. Select the **Customer ID** field in the first table. Drag the mouse to the Customer ID field in the second table and release the mouse button. The Edit Relationships dialog box appears.

4. Click the **Create** button. A line appears, creating the relationship.

5. Double-click the center section of the line. The Edit Relationships dialog box appears again, listing the tables and the Customer ID fields on each side.

6. Click the **Enforce Referential Integrity** box and click **OK.** The line appears thicker, with the number 1 beside the first table and the infinity symbol (∞) beside the second, as shown in Figure 3-29.

Figure 3-29

Relationship displaying enforced referential integrity

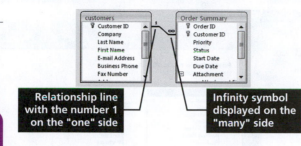

Relationship line with the number 1 on the "one" side

Infinity symbol displayed on the "many" side

PAUSE. LEAVE the database open to use in the next exercise.

When you want to change the table relationship, you can double-click the line connecting the tables or click the Edit Relationships command in the Tools group. The Edit Relationships dialog box allows you to change a table relationship. You can change the tables on either side of the relationship or the fields on either side. You can also set the join type or enforce referential integrity and choose a cascade option.

Referential integrity prevents orphan records. An orphan record is a record in one table that references records in another table that no longer exist. You can enforce referential integrity by clicking the Enforce Referential Integrity button in the Edit Relationships dialog box. Once this feature is turned on, Access will not allow any operation that violates referential integrity.

When you enforce referential integrity between tables, the line connecting the tables becomes thicker. The number 1 is also displayed on the line on the one side of the relationship and an infinity symbol (∞) appears on the other side.

To remove a table relationship, you must delete the relationship line. You can select the line by pointing to it and clicking it. When the relationship line is selected, it appears thicker. Press the Delete key to delete the line and remove the relationship or right-click the line to display the delete menu.

Printing Table Relationships

You may want to print out a table relationship to save for your records or to discuss with a colleague. The Relationship Report command makes this easy.

➔ PRINT TABLE RELATIONSHIPS

USE the database you used in the previous exercise.

1. Click the **Relationship Report** button. The report is created and the Print Preview tab appears, as shown in Figure 3-30.

Figure 3-30

Print preview of
Relationship Report

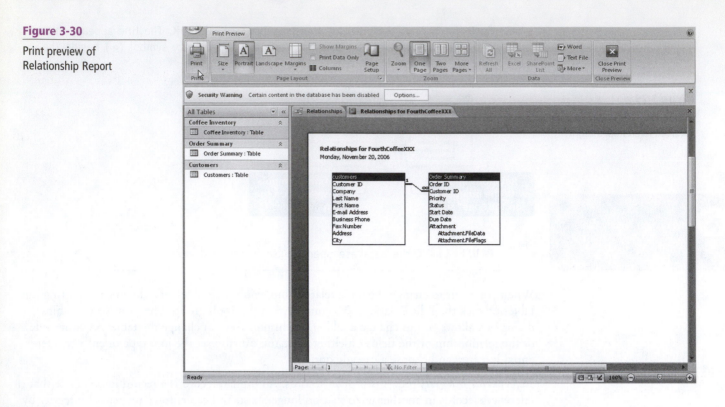

2. Click the **Print** button. The Print dialog box appears, allowing you to select the printer you want to use.

3. Click **OK**.

4. Click the **Close** button to close the Relationships for FourthCoffee tab. A message appears asking if you want to save changes to the report. Click **No**.

5. **CLOSE** the Relationships tab.

   STOP. **CLOSE** the database.

CERTIFICATION READY?
How do you print table relationships?
1.2.3

You printed a table relationship using the Relationship Report command. When you chose to print the report, the Print Preview tab appeared with options for viewing and printing the report. After you make any changes to the layout of the report, click the Print button to start printing. After printing the report, you can choose to save it.

SUMMARY SKILL MATRIX

IN THIS LESSON YOU LEARNED	MATRIX SKILL	SKILL NUMBER
To navigate among records	Navigate among records	3.2
To enter, edit, and delete records	Enter, edit, and delete records	3.1
To create and modify a primary key	Define and modify a primary key	1.3.1
To define and modify a primary key	Define and modify primary keys	1.3.1
To define and modify a multi-field primary key	Define and modify a multi-field primary keys	1.3.2
To find and replace data	Find and replace data	3.3
To attach and detach documents	Attach documents to and detach from records	3.4
To sort data within a table	Sort data within tables	5.1.1
To filter data within a table	Filter data within tables	5.2.1
To remove a filter	Remove filters	5.2.5
To understand table relationships	Define and print table relationships	1.2
To define table relationships	Create relationships	1.2.1
To modify table relationships	Modify relationships	1.2.2
To print table relationships	Print table relationships	1.2.3

■ Knowledge Assessment

Matching

Match the term in Column 1 to its description in Column 2.

Column 1

Column 2

1. foreign key

a. to prevent orphan records, to ensure that records do not reference other records that no longer exist

2. composite key

b. sorts data from beginning to end

3. input mask

c. sorts data from end to beginning

4. referential integrity

d. to arrange data alphabetically, numerically, or chronologically

5. wildcards

e. a primary key from one table that is used in another table

6. ascending order

f. a set of rules for determining which records will be displayed

7. descending order

g. the secondary sort field in a multi-field sort

8. filter

h. two or more primary keys in a table

9. sort

i. characters used to find words or phrases that contain specific letters or combinations of letters

10. innermost field

j. a set of placeholder characters that force you to enter data in a specific format

True / False

Circle T if the statement is true or F if the statement is false.

T | F **1.** You can use the Navigation buttons to search for data in a table.

T | F **2.** You can enter any kind of data into any field.

T | F **3.** After you enter data and move to a new field, Access automatically saves the data for you in the table.

T | F **4.** After you delete a record, you can click the Undo button to bring it back.

T | F **5.** The Find and Replace dialog box searches all the tables in a database at one time.

T | F **6.** An AutoNumber field will usually make a good primary key.

T | F **7.** Before you can attach a document, there must be a field in a table formatted with the Attachment data type.

T | F **8.** The outermost field is the primary sort field in a multi-field sort.

T | F **9.** The Toggle Filter button lets you permanently remove a filter and switches you back to the original view.

T | F **10.** In a one-to-many relationship, each record in the first table can have many records in the second table.

■ Competency Assessment

Project 3-1: Charity Event Contacts List

You are working as an intern for Woodgrove Bank. Part of your job is helping your supervisor organize a charity event. Use an Access table to create a contacts list that your supervisor will use to make calls to local businesses requesting sponsorships and donations for the event.

GET READY. Launch Access if it is not already running.

1. **OPEN** the *Charity Event* database.
2. Save the database as *Charity EventXXX* (where XXX is your initials).
3. Open the **Contacts** table.
4. Enter the records shown in the following table.

The *Charity Event* database is available on the companion CD-ROM.

ID	Company	Last Name	First Name	Business Phone
17	Trey Research	Tiano	Mike	469-555-0182
18	Fourth Coffee	Culp	Scott	469-555-0141
19	Wingtip Toys	Baker	Mary	972-555-0167
20	Margie's Travel	Nash	Mike	972-555-0189

5. Click the **View** menu and choose **Design** view.
6. Select the **ID** row. On the Design tab, on the Tools menu, click the **Primary Key** button.
7. Save the design of the table and return to Datasheet view.
8. On the Home tab, in the Find group, click the **Find** button. The Find and Replace dialog box appears. Key **0177** into the Find What box.
9. Select **Contents** from the Look In menu and select **Any Part of Field** in the Match menu.
10. Click the **Replace** tab. Key **0175** into the Replace With box.
11. Click **Find Next** and then click **Replace**.

12. Click **Cancel** to close the dialog box.

13. Select the **Lucern Publishing** record.

14. On the Home tab, in the Records group, click the **Delete** button. Click **Yes** to delete the record.

15. **CLOSE** the database.

LEAVE Access open for the next project.

Project 3-2: Angels Project Wish List

The four kindergarten classes at the School of Fine Art have adopted one boy and one girl "angel" from the community. Children from the classes may purchase holiday gifts for their angels. As an office assistant at the school, you are working with the Angel Project staff to organize information about each angel.

The *Angels* database is available on the companion CD-ROM.

1. **OPEN** *Angels* from the data files for this lesson.

2. **SAVE** the database as *AngelsXXX,* where XXX is your initials.

3. **OPEN** the List table.

4. Select the **Gender** field. On the Home tab, in the Sort & Filter group, click the **Ascending** button.

5. Select the **Age** field. On the Home tab, in the Sort & Filter group, click the **Descending** button.

6. On the Home tab, in the Sort & Filter group, click the **Clear All Sorts** button.

7. In the Gender field, select the **M** in the first record.

8. On the Home tab, in the Sort & Filter group, click the **Selection** button and select **Equals "M".**

9. On the Home tab, in the Sort & Filter group, click the **Toggle Filter** button.

10. Select the **Wants** field. On the Home tab, in the Sort & Filter group, click the **Filter** button. Select **Text Filters** from the menu, select **Contains** from the next menu, and key **Bike** in the Custom Filter dialog box.

11. On the Home tab, in the Sort & Filter group, click the **Advanced** button and select **Clear All Filters** from the menu.

LEAVE Access open for the next project.

■ Proficiency Assessment

Project 3-3: Angel Project Contact Information

1. The Angel database should be open on your screen.

2. **OPEN** the **Contact Information** table.

3. Enter the following new records.

ID	Last Name	First Name	Parent's Name	Address	City	State	Zip Code	Home Phone
15	Wright	Steven	Kevin	2309 Monroe Ct	Marietta	GA	34006	770-555-0142
16	Cook	Cathan	Patrick	1268 Oak Dr	Marietta	GA	34006	770-555-0128

4. Switch to Design view. Remove the primary key from the Home Phone field and define the ID field as the primary key.

5. Save the design and return to Datasheet view.

6. Select the ID field and sort it in ascending order.

7. On the Datasheet tab, in the Relationships group, click the **Relationships** button.

8. Create a one-to-one relationship between the ID field of the List table and the ID field of the Contact Information table.

8. **SAVE** the relationships view and **CLOSE** it.

9. **CLOSE** the tables and the database.

   LEAVE Access open for the next project.

Project 3-4: Wingtip Toys Inventory Table

Wingtip Toys, a small manufacturer of wooden toys, has kept most of its records on paper for the last 20 years. The business has recently expanded, and you have been hired to help the company transfer its entire inventory and other administrative data to Office 2007. Edit the table to include all the latest handwritten data you've found.

The *Wingtip Toys* database is available on the companion CD-ROM.

1. **OPEN** the *Wingtip Toys* database and save it as *WingtipXXX*, where XXX is your initials.

2. **OPEN** the **Inventory** table.

3. On the Home tab, in the Find group, click the **Replace** button to display the Find and Replace dialog box. Change the following prices:

   Find all **14.99** and replace with **29.99**

   Find all **16.99** and replace with **34.99**

   Find all **15.99** and replace with **30.99**

   Find all **24.99** and replace with **34.99**

4. Delete the following records from the database:

   ID = 13

   ID = 19

   ID = 16

5. Edit the following records:

   ID = 30, change the number of items in stock to 3

   ID = 28, change the number of items in stock to 6

   ID = 6, change the number of items in stock to 4

6. Select the **In Stock** field and create a filter to display all the records with a value less than or equal to 10 in the field.

7. Remove the filter.

8. **CLOSE** the table.

9. **CLOSE** the database.

   LEAVE Access open for the next project.

■ Mastery Assessment

Project 3-5: Soccer Roster

As coach of your son's soccer team, you have created a database in which to store information about the team. Enter, edit, and delete records to update it.

The *Soccer* database is available on the companion CD-ROM.

1. **OPEN** the *Soccer* database from the data files for this lesson.

2. **SAVE** the database as *SoccerXXX*, where XXX is your initials.

3. **OPEN** the **Roster** table.

4. Enter the following record for a new player:

   Eric Parkinson, 806-555-0170, uniform number 9

5. One player has quit the team, Russell King. Replace his data with the data for the following new player:

   George Jiang, 806-555-0123, uniform number 4

6. In the **Size** field, enter **XS** for each player, except for uniform numbers 4, 6, and 7, which should be size **S**.

7. Create an Attachment field and attach the Word document *medicalalert.docx* to the record for Garrett Young.

8. Define the Uniform field as the primary key.

9. **SAVE** the table design and **CLOSE** the database.

   LEAVE Access open for the next project.

The *medicalalert* document is available on the companion CD-ROM.

Project 3-6: Donations Table

Donations are starting to come in for Woodgrove Bank's charity event. Track the donation commitments received.

1. **OPEN** the *CharityEventXXX* database.

2. **OPEN** the **Donations** table.

3. Create a filter to display the items in the Needs field without Commitments from a company.

4. Clear the filter.

5. Use Find and Replace to find each occurrence of the word *Company* in the Needs field and replace it with the word *Volunteer*.

6. Create a relationship between the ID field in the Contacts table and the Committed Company ID in the Donations table.

7. Print the relationship.

8. **CLOSE** the relationship without saving.

9. **CLOSE** the tables.

10. **CLOSE** the database.

    CLOSE Access.

The *charity event* database is available on the companion CD-ROM.

INTERNET READY

Search the Internet for at least five coffee shops in your area or a favorite city of your choice. Draw a table on paper or in a Word document with fields for the Company Name, Location, Phone Number, and Hours of Operation. Insert data for the five coffee shops you found. If you feel ready for a challenge, create the table in a new database.

4 Modify Tables and Fields

Skills	Matrix Skill	Skill Number
Modifying a Database Table	Modify tables	2.3
Modifying Table Properties	Modify table properties	2.3.1
Renaming a Table	Rename tables	2.3.3
Deleting a Table	Delete tables	2.3.4
Creating Fields and Modifying Field Properties	Create fields and modify field properties	2.4
Modifying Field Properties	Modify field properties	2.4.2
Creating Fields	Create commonly used fields	2.4.1
Creating and Modifying Multi-value Fields	Create and modify multi-valued fields	2.4.3
Creating and Modifying Attachment Fields	Create and modify attachment fields	2.4.4

Margie's Travel is a full-service travel agency that specializes in sports-event travel packages. The company offers both individual and group travel packages to many of the leading sports events throughout the country. The travel packages can be customized to include plane tickets, event tickets, event transportation, hotel accommodations, official event souvenirs, and on-site staff assistance. As an assistant event coordinator, you are responsible for gathering information about a variety of events; you use Access to store the necessary data. In this lesson, you will learn how to modify table properties; rename a table; delete a table; modify field properties; and create and modify fields—including multi-value and attachment fields.

KEY TERMS
multi-valued field
validation rule
validation text
zero-length string

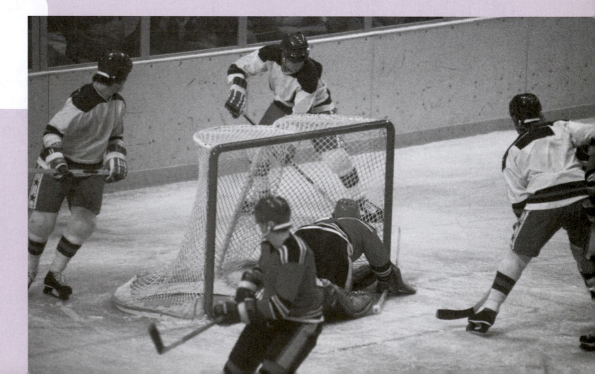

Modifying a Database Table

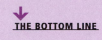

THE BOTTOM LINE

After a table has been created, you may need to modify it. You can make many changes to a table—or other database object—using its property sheet. You can also rename or delete a table, but keep in mind that such a change could possibly break the functionality of the database, because in a relational database the various components work together.

CERTIFICATION READY?
How do you modify a database table?
2.3

Modifying Table Properties

You can set properties that control the appearance or behavior characteristics for an entire table in the table's property sheet.

⊕ MODIFY TABLE PROPERTIES

GET READY. Before you begin these steps, be sure to launch Microsoft Access.

1. **OPEN** the *Events* database from the data files for this lesson.
2. **SAVE** the database as *EventsXXX* (where XXX is your initials).
3. Click the **Close 'Event List'** button to close that form.
4. In the Navigation Pane, double-click **Events** to open that table.
5. On the Home tab, in the Views group, click the **Views** button and then click **Design View**.
6. On the Design tab, in the Show/Hide group, click **Property Sheet**. The property sheet appears on the right of the Access window, as shown in Figure 4-1.

CD

The *Events* database is available on the companion CD-ROM.

Figure 4-1

Property sheet displayed

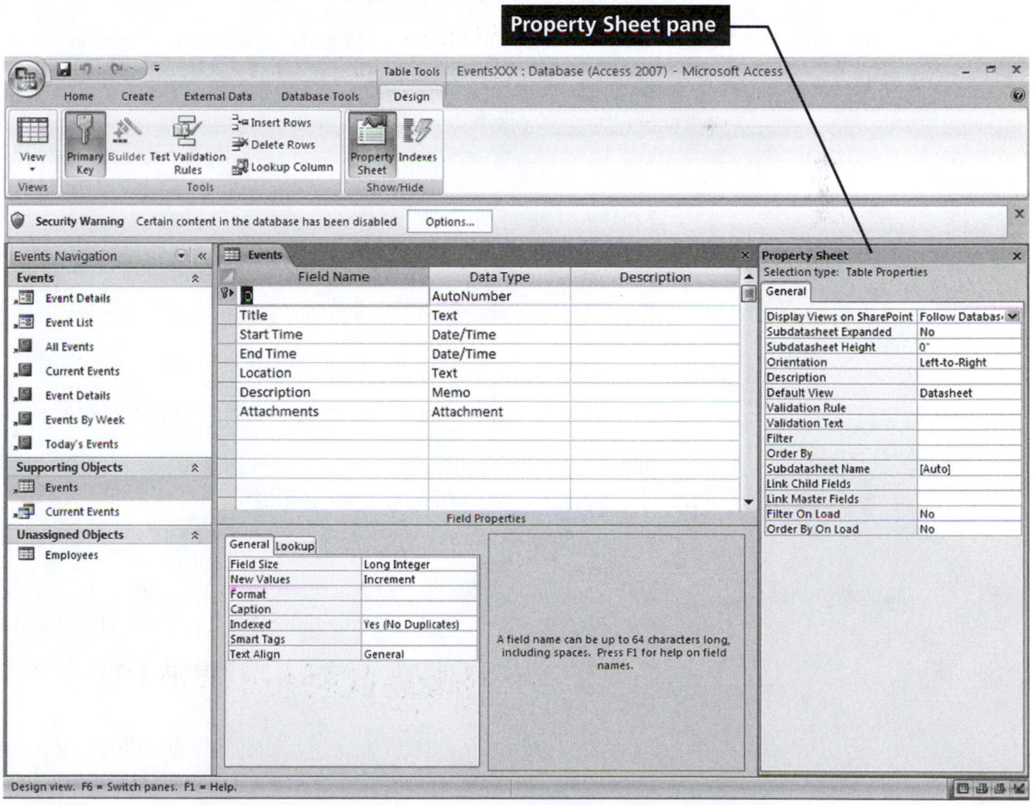

ANOTHER WAY

You can also press Alt+Enter to display the property sheet for an object.

7. Place the insertion point in the property box for Description.
8. Press **Shift** + **F2** to open the Zoom box, shown in Figure 4-2.

Figure 4-2

Zoom box

9. Key **Most popular events for 2008**.
10. Click **OK**.
11. Click the **Close** button on the property sheet to close it.
12. Click the **Office Button** and click **Save**.
13. **LEAVE** the database open.

    PAUSE. LEAVE Access open to use in the next exercise.

CERTIFICATION READY?
How do you modify table properties?
2.3.1

Table 4-1

Table Properties

To set the properties for a table, open the table in Design view. On the Design tab, in the Show/Hide group, click Property Sheet. Click the box for the property you want to set and key a setting for the property. Table 4-1 lists the available table properties and what they control.

USE THIS TABLE PROPERTY	TO
Display Views on SharePoint	Specify whether forms and reports associated with the table should be available on the View menu in Windows SharePoint Services if the database is published to a SharePoint site.
Subdatasheet Expanded	Set whether to expand all subdatasheets when you open the table.
Subdatasheet Height	Specify whether to expand to show all available subdatasheet rows (default) when opened or to set the height of the subdatasheet window to show when opened.
Orientation	Set the view orientation, according to whether your language is read left-to-right or right-to-left.
Description	Provide a description of the table.
Default View	Set Datasheet, PivotTable, or PivotChart as the default view when you open the table.
Validation Rule	Supply an expression that must be true whenever you add a record or change a record.
Validation Text	Enter text that appears when a record violates the Validation Rule expression.
Filter	Define criteria to display only matching rows in Datasheet view.
Order By	Select one or more fields to specify the default sort order of rows in Datasheet view.
Subdatasheet Name	Specify whether a subdatasheet should appear in Datasheet view, and, if so, which table or query should supply the rows in the subdatasheet.
Link Child Fields	List the fields in the table or query used for the subdatasheet that match this table's primary key field(s).
Link Master Fields	List the primary key field(s) in this table that match the child fields for the subdatasheet.
Filter On Load	Automatically apply the filter criteria in the Filter property (by setting to Yes) when the table is opened in Datasheet view.
Order By On Load	Automatically apply the sort criteria in the OrderBy property (by setting to Yes) when the table is opened in Datasheet view.

If you want more space to enter or edit a setting in the property box, press Shift+F2 to display the Zoom box. Because you have made changes to the design of the table, you will need to save the changes before closing the database.

Renaming a Table

Think carefully before you rename a table. If existing database objects, such as queries or reports, use data from that table, the name modification might break the functionality of the database.

RENAME A TABLE

USE the database that is open from the previous exercise.

1. On the Create tab, in the Tables group, click the **Table Templates** button and click **Events** to create a new table.
2. Click **Table1** in the Navigation Pane and press **F2**. A message appears that states that you cannot name the table while it is open, as shown in Figure 4-3.

Figure 4-3

Can't rename table message

3. Click the **Close 'Table1'** button. A message appears asking if you want to save the design changes, as shown in Figure 4-4.

Figure 4-4

Save design changes message

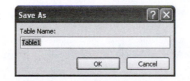

4. Click **Yes**. The Save As dialog box appears, as shown in Figure 4-5.

Figure 4-5

Save As dialog box

5. Click **OK** to save the table as Table1.
6. Right-click **Table1** in the Navigation Pane to display the menu shown in Figure 4-6.

Figure 4-6

Rename command on table shortcut menu

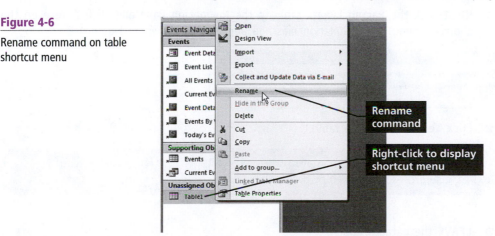

7. Click **Rename**. The table name is now selected for renaming, as shown in Figure 4-7.

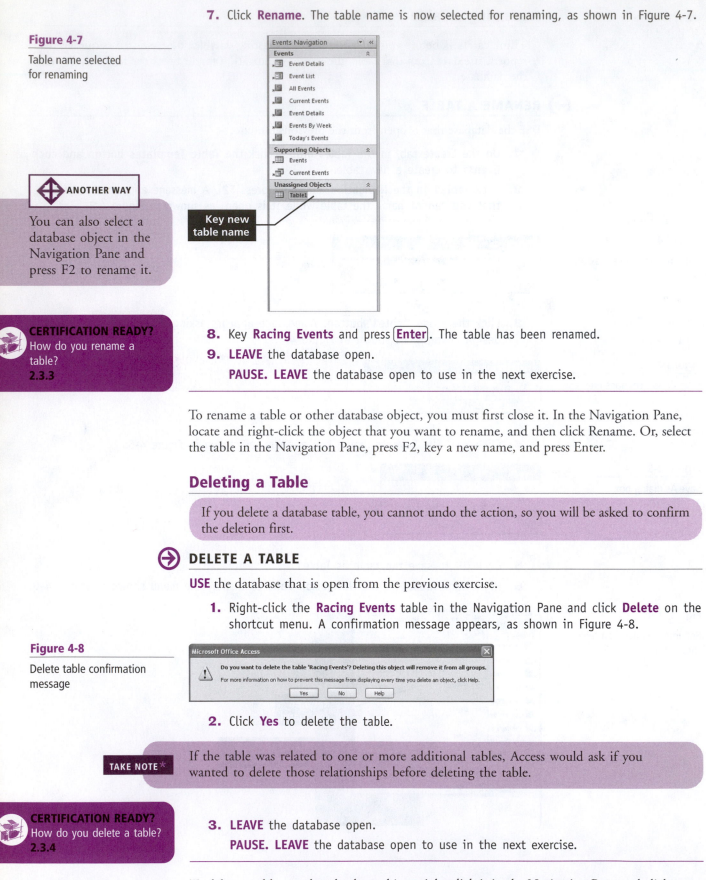

Key new
table name

8. Key **Racing Events** and press **Enter**. The table has been renamed.
9. **LEAVE** the database open.

   PAUSE. LEAVE the database open to use in the next exercise.

To rename a table or other database object, you must first close it. In the Navigation Pane,
locate and right-click the object that you want to rename, and then click Rename. Or, select
the table in the Navigation Pane, press F2, key a new name, and press Enter.

Deleting a Table

If you delete a database table, you cannot undo the action, so you will be asked to confirm
the deletion first.

⊕ DELETE A TABLE

USE the database that is open from the previous exercise.

1. Right-click the **Racing Events** table in the Navigation Pane and click **Delete** on the
   shortcut menu. A confirmation message appears, as shown in Figure 4-8.

Microsoft Office Access

⚠ Do you want to delete the table 'Racing Events'? Deleting this object will remove it from all groups.

For more information on how to prevent this message from displaying every time you delete an object, click Help.

[Yes]　[No]　[Help]

2. Click **Yes** to delete the table.

TAKE NOTE＊ If the table was related to one or more additional tables, Access would ask if you
wanted to delete those relationships before deleting the table.

3. **LEAVE** the database open.

   PAUSE. LEAVE the database open to use in the next exercise.

To delete a table or other database object, right-click it in the Navigation Pane and click
Delete. Or, select the table in the Navigation Pane and press Delete.

LOOKING AHED

You will learn more about backing up a database in Lesson 15.

Deleting an entire table is not a complex process; however, remember that when you delete an entire table you might break the functionality of your database. In addition, you lose all the data in the deleted table permanently. For those reasons, you should always back up your database before you delete a table.

X REF

Another way to remove data is to delete information from individual records or delete entire records from a table, as you learned in Lesson 3.

■ SOFTWARE ORIENTATION

Field Properties

Some field properties are available in Datasheet view, but to access the complete list of field properties you must use Design view. An example of field properties for a table in Design view is shown in Figure 4-9.

Figure 4-9

Field properties

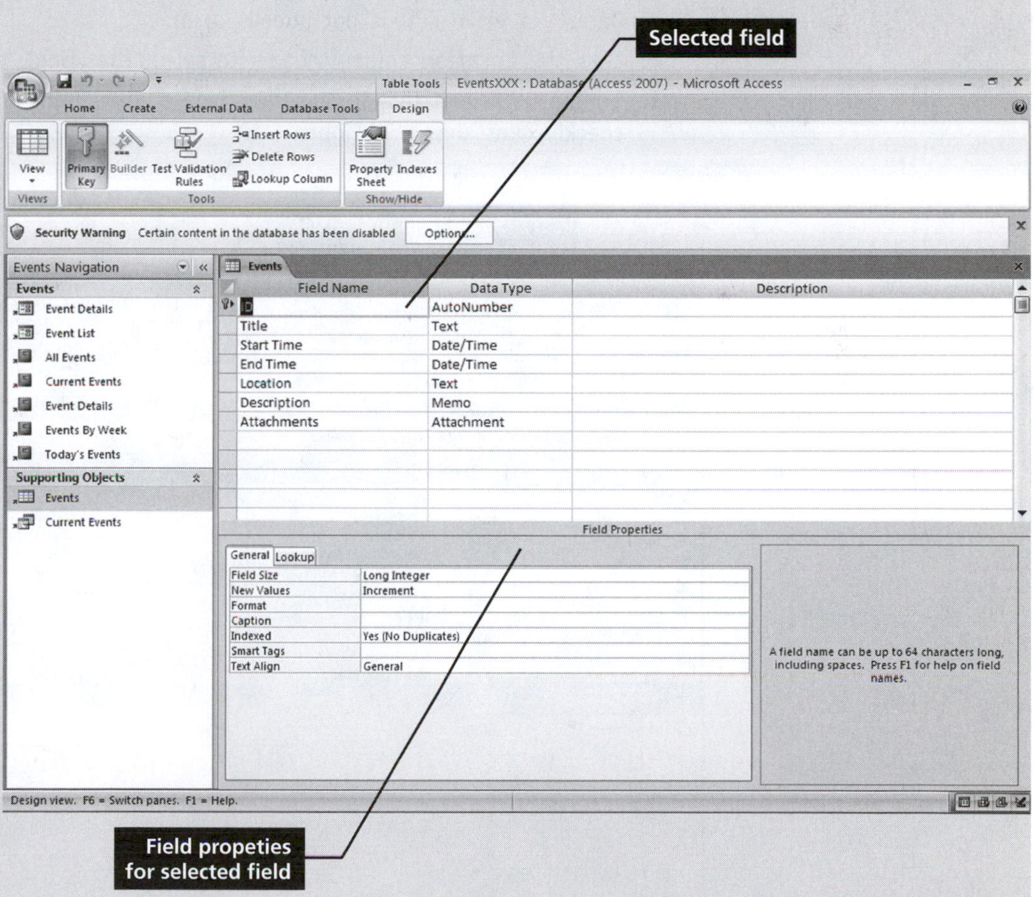

Use this Figure as a reference throughout this lesson as well as the rest of this book.

■ Creating Fields and Modifying Field Properties

THE BOTTOM LINE

A field has certain defining characteristics, such as a name that uniquely identifies the field within a table and a data type that's chosen to match the information to be stored. Every field also has an associated group of settings called *properties* that define the appearance or behavior of the field. In this section, you will learn how to create fields and modify field properties.

CERTIFICATION READY?
How do you create fields and modify field properties?
2.4

Modifying Field Properties

You can control the appearance of information, prevent incorrect entries, specify default values, speed up searching and sorting, and control other appearance or behavior characteristics by setting or modifying field properties. For example, you can format numbers to make them easier to read or you can define a validation rule that must be satisfied for information to be entered in a field.

➔ SET A FIELD PROPERTY IN DATASHEET VIEW

USE the database that is open from the previous exercise.

1. Double-click the **Events** table in the Navigation Pane to open the table in Datasheet view, if it is not already open.
2. Click the **Location** column header to select that field.
3. On the Datasheet tab, in the Data Type & Formatting group, click the **Is Required** checkbox, as shown in Figure 4-10.

Figure 4-10

Set field property in Datasheet view

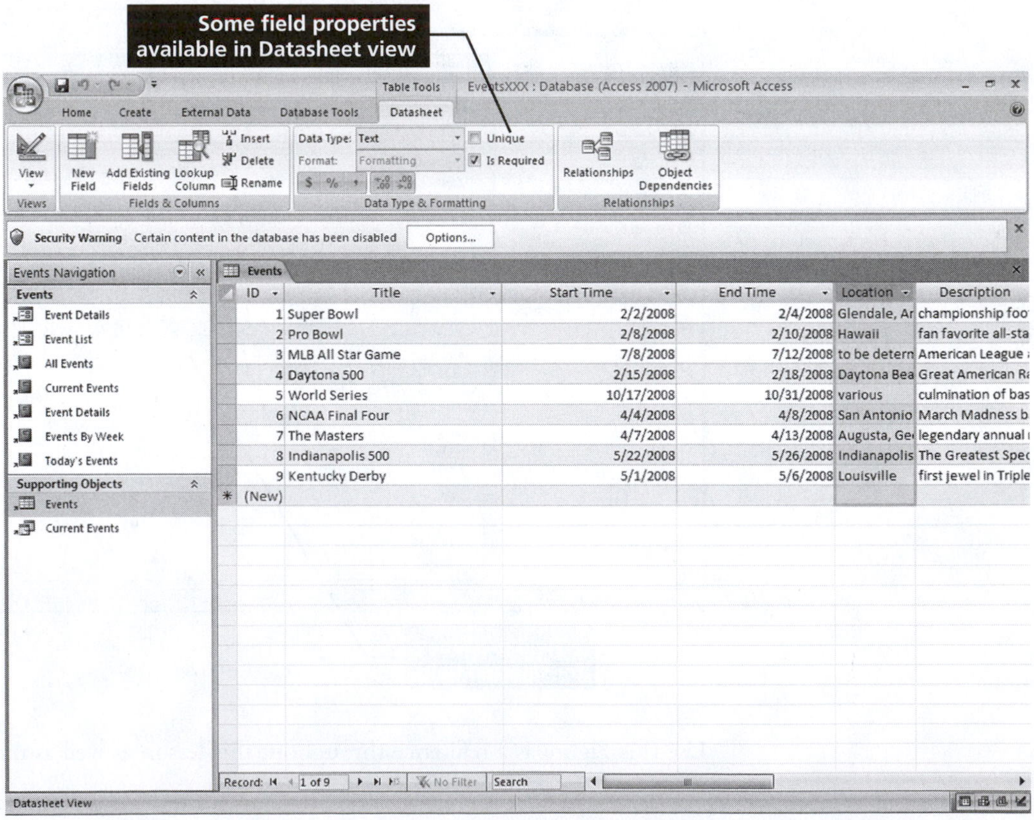

PAUSE. LEAVE the database open to use in the next exercise.

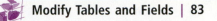

Access uses the field property settings when you view and edit data. For example, the Format, Input Mask, and Caption properties affect how your information appears in table and query datasheets. In addition, any controls on new forms and reports that are based on the fields in the table inherit these same property settings by default.

To set a field property in Datasheet view, open the table in Datasheet view. Click in the field for which you want to set the property. On the Datasheet tab, in the Data Type & Formatting group, select the Unique checkbox to require the values in the field to be unique for all the records in the table. Or, select the Is Required checkbox to make this a required field where all instances of this field must contain a value.

You can set only a few of the available field properties in Datasheet view. To set additional field properties, you must open the table in Design view.

➔ DEFINE TEXT LENGTH

USE the database that is open from the previous exercise.

1. On the Home tab, in the Views group, click the **View** button and click **Design View**.

2. In the Field Name column in the upper portion of the table design grid, click in the **Title** cell.

3. In the Field Size row in the lower portion of the table design grid, select **150** in the property box and key **175** to change the maximum number of characters you can enter.

TAKE NOTE *

To define the text length for a field, modify the Field Size property. The maximum number of characters you can enter into a field is 255.

PAUSE. LEAVE the database open to use in the next exercise.

To set field properties in Design view, open the table in Design view. In the upper portion of the table design grid, click the field for which you want to set properties. The properties for this field are displayed in the lower portion of the table design grid.

Click the box for the field property you want to set. Alternatively, you can press F6 and then move to the property by using the arrow keys. Type a setting for the property or, if an arrow appears at the right side of the property box, click the arrow to choose from a list of settings for the property.

Table 4-2 lists the available field properties.

USE THIS FIELD PROPERTY	TO
Field Size	Set the maximum size for data stored as a Text, Number, or AutoNumber data type.
Format	Customize the way the field appears when displayed or printed.
Decimal Places	Specify the number of decimal places to use when displaying numbers.
New Values	Set whether an AutoNumber field is incremented or assigned a random value.
Input Mask	Display editing characters to guide data entry.
Caption	Set the text displayed by default in labels for forms, reports, and queries.
Default Value	Automatically assign a default value to a field when new records are added.
Validation Rule	Supply an expression that must be true whenever you add or change the value in this field.
Validation Text	Enter text that appears when a value violates the Validation Rule expression.
Required	Require that data be entered in a field.
Allow Zero Length	Allow entry (by setting to Yes) of a zero-length string ("") in a Text or Memo field.
Indexed	Speed up access to data in this field by creating and using an index.
Unicode Compression	Compress text stored in this field when a large amount of text is stored (> 4,096 characters).
IME Mode	Specify an Input Method Editor, a tool for using English versions of Access with files created in Japanese or Korean versions of Access.
IME Sentence Mode	Specify the type of data you can enter by using an Input Method Editor.
SmartTags	Attach a smart tag to this field.
Append Only	Allow versioning (by setting to Yes) of a Memo field.
Text Format	Choose Rich Text to store text as HTML and allow rich formatting. Choose Plain Text to store only text.
Text Align	Specify the default alignment of text within a control.
Precision	Specify the total number of digits allowed, including those both to the right and the left of the decimal point.
Scale	Specify the maximum number of digits that can be stored to the right of the decimal separator.

DEFINE INPUT MASKS FOR FIELDS

USE the database that is open from the previous exercise.

1. In the Field Name column in the upper portion of the table design grid, click in the **Start Time** cell.

2. Click the **Input Mask** property box in the lower portion of the table design grid to display the Input Mask Wizard button on the far right of the cell, as shown in Figure 4-11.

Figure 4-11

Input Mask Wizard button

Click to open
Input Mask Wizard

Field Properties

General	Lookup
Format	General Date
Input Mask	
Caption	
Default Value	
Validation Rule	>=#1/1/1900#
Validation Text	Value must be greater than 1/1/1900.
Required	No
Indexed	Yes (Duplicates OK)
IME Mode	Off
IME Sentence Mode	None
Smart Tags	
Text Align	General
Show Date Picker	For dates

Help.

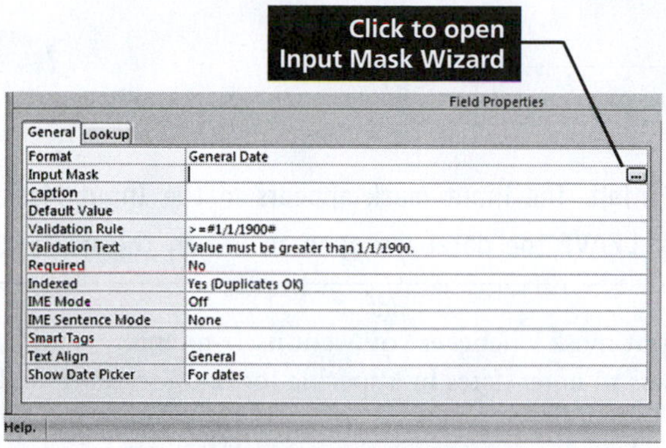

3. Click the **Input Mask Wizard button**. A message appears asking if you want to save the table now, as shown in Figure 4-12.

Figure 4-12

Input Mask Wizard message

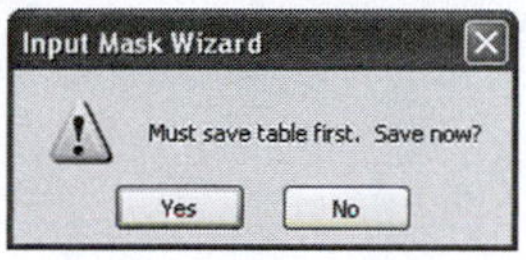

Input Mask Wizard

⚠ Must save table first. Save now?

Yes   No

4. Click **Yes** to display the Input Mask Wizard, as shown in Figure 4-13.

Figure 4-13

Input Mask Wizard

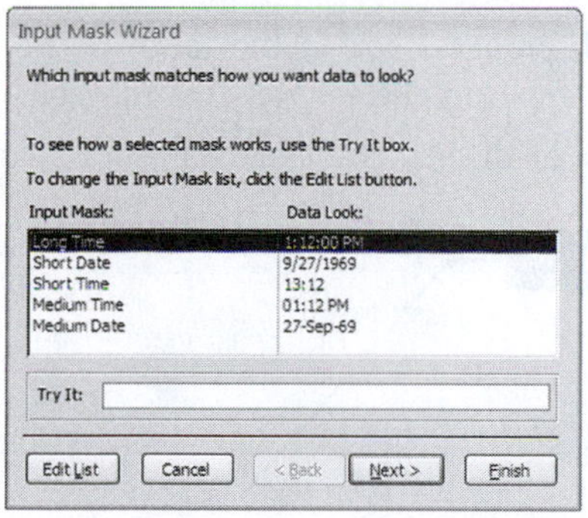

Input Mask Wizard

Which input mask matches how you want data to look?

To see how a selected mask works, use the Try It box.

To change the Input Mask list, click the Edit List button.

Input Mask:	Data Look:
Long Time	1:12:00 PM
Short Date	9/27/1969
Short Time	13:12
Medium Time	01:12 PM
Medium Date	27-Sep-69

Try It:

Edit List   Cancel   < Back   Next >   Finish

5. Click **Medium Date** and then click **Next>**. The next screen in the Input Mask Wizard appears, as shown in Figure 4-14.

Figure 4-14

Input Mask Wizard, next screen

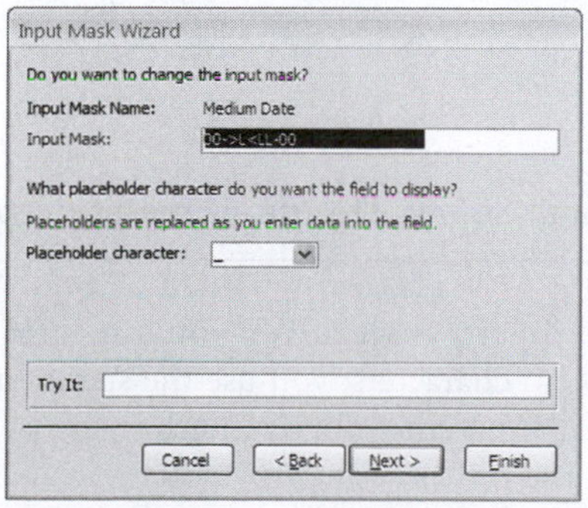

Input Mask Wizard

Do you want to change the input mask?

Input Mask Name: Medium Date

Input Mask: 00->L<LL-00

What placeholder character do you want the field to display?

Placeholders are replaced as you enter data into the field.

Placeholder character: _

Try It:

Cancel   < Back   Next >   Finish

6. Click **Next** to display the final Input Mask Wizard screen, as shown in Figure 4-15.

Figure 4-15

Input Mask Wizard, final screen

7. Click **Finish**. The input mask appears in the Input Mask row.

PAUSE. LEAVE the database open to use in the next exercise.

You use an input mask whenever you want users to enter data in a specific way. An input mask can require users to enter dates in a specific format, for example, DD-MM-YYYY, or telephone numbers that follow the conventions for a specific country or region. An input mask is helpful because it can prevent users from entering invalid data (such as a phone number in a date field). In addition, input masks can ensure that users enter data in a consistent way.

You can add input masks to table fields by running the Input Mask Wizard or by manually entering masks in the Input Mask field property. In this exercise, you specified that dates in the Start Time field be entered in Medium Date format, following the required pattern, *24-Sep-69*.

⊕ ALLOW ZERO LENGTH

USE the database that is open from the previous exercise.

1. In the Field Name column in the upper portion of the table design grid, click in the **Description** cell.

2. Click the **Zero Length** property box in the lower portion of the table design grid to display the down arrow on the far right of the cell.

3. Click the **down arrow** to display the menu, as shown in Figure 4-16.

Figure 4-16

Zero Length property menu

Click to display menu

Field Properties	
General	Lookup
Format	
Caption	
Default Value	
Validation Rule	
Validation Text	
Required	No
Allow Zero Length	No
Indexed	Yes
Unicode Compression	No
IME Mode	No Control
IME Sentence Mode	Phrase Predict
Smart Tags	
Text Format	Rich Text
Text Align	General

Help.

4. Click **Yes**.

PAUSE. LEAVE the database open to use in the next exercise.

When the Zero Length field property is set to Yes, you can enter zero-length strings in a field. A *zero-length string* contains no characters; you use the string to indicate that you know no value exists for a particular field. You enter a zero-length string by typing two double quotation marks with no space between them ("").

SET MEMO FIELD AS APPEND ONLY

USE the database that is open from the previous exercise.

1. In the Field Name column in the upper portion of the table design grid, the **Description** cell should be selected.

2. Click the **Append Only** property box in the lower portion of the table design grid to display the down arrow on the far right of the cell.

3. Click the **down arrow** to display the menu and click **Yes**.

   PAUSE. LEAVE the database open to use in the next exercise.

TAKE NOTE*

By default, when you try to position the pointer in a Memo field with the Append Only property enabled, Access hides the text.

A field's data type determines the properties you can set. For example, the Append Only property applies only to a field that is set to the Memo data type. You cannot set this property on a field with any other data type.

You use a Memo field when you need to store large amounts of text in a database. When the Append Only field is enabled, users can add data to the Memo field, but they cannot change or remove existing data.

 SET DATA VALIDATION RULES

USE the database that is open from the previous exercise.

1. In the Field Name column in the upper portion of the table design grid, click the **End Time** cell.

2. Click the **Validation Rule** property box in the lower portion of the table design grid to display the Expression Builder button on the far right of the cell, as shown in Figure 4-17.

Figure 4-17

Expression Builder button

```
                                          Click to open the
                                          Expression Builder

                                              Field Properties

General | Lookup |
Format                General Date
Input Mask
Caption
Default Value
Validation Rule       >=#1/1/1900#|                                    [...]
Validation Text       Value must be greater than 1/1/1900.
Required              No
Indexed              Yes (Duplicates OK)
IME Mode             Off
IME Sentence Mode    None
Smart Tags
Text Align           General
Show Date Picker     For dates

Help.
```

3. Click the **Expression Builder button** to display the Expression Builder dialog box, as shown in Figure 4-18.

Figure 4-18

Expression Builder dialog box

```
Expression Builder                              [?][X]
 >=#1/1/1900#|                                   OK
                                                 Cancel
                                                 Undo

 + - / * | & | = > < <> | And Or Not Like | ( ) | Paste | Help

 [+] Functions
 [ ] Constants
 [ ] Operators
```

4. Select the number **1900** and replace it by keying **2006**.

5. Click **OK**.

6. Click the **Validation Text** property box in the lower portion of the table design grid.

7. Select the number **1900** and replace it by keying **2006**. The property boxes should look like those shown in Figure 4-19.

Figure 4-19

Modified Validation field properties

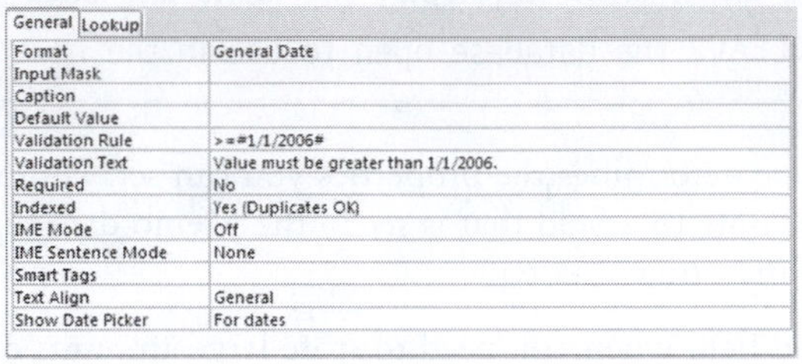

General	Lookup
Format	General Date
Input Mask	
Caption	
Default Value	
Validation Rule	>=#1/1/2006#
Validation Text	Value must be greater than 1/1/2006.
Required	No
Indexed	Yes (Duplicates OK)
IME Mode	Off
IME Sentence Mode	None
Smart Tags	
Text Align	General
Show Date Picker	For dates

PAUSE. LEAVE the database open to use in the next exercise.

Validation rules restrict what users can enter into a given field and also help to ensure that your database users enter the proper types or amounts of data. A ***validation rule*** is an expression that limits the values that can be entered in the field. The maximum length for the Validation Rule property is 2,048 characters. For example, if the field contains a date, you can require that the date entered in the field be later than January 1, 1964.

When data is entered that violates the rule defined for the field, you can use the Validation Text property to specify the resulting error message. ***Validation text*** specifies the text in the error message that appears when a user violates a validation rule. For example, the error message could say "Please enter a date that is later than January 1, 1964." The maximum length for the Validation Text property is 255 characters.

Data can be validated in several ways, and you will often use multiple methods to define a validation rule. Each of the following can be used to ensure that your users enter data properly:

- **Data types**—When you design a database table, you define a data type for each field in the table, and that data type restricts what users can enter. For example, a Date/Time field accepts only dates and times, a Currency field accepts only monetary values, and so on.

- **Field sizes**—Field sizes provide another way to validate text. For example, if you create a field that stores first names, you can set it to accept a maximum of 15 characters. This can prevent a malicious user from pasting in large amounts of text into the field. It could also prevent an inexperienced user from mistakenly entering a first, middle, and last name in a field designed only to hold a first name.

- **Table properties**—Table properties provide very specific types of validation. For example, you can set the Required property to Yes, and, as a result, force users to enter a value in a field.

- **Field properties**—You can also use field properties, such as the Validation Rule property, to require specific values, and the Validation Text property, to alert your users to any mistakes. For example, entering a rule such as >1 and <100 in the Validation Rule property forces users to enter values between 1 and 100. Entering text such as "Enter values between 1 and 100" in the Validation Text property tells users when they have made a mistake and how to fix the error.

As you already learned in this lesson, the Input Mask field property is another way to validate data by forcing users to enter values in a specific way. For example, an input mask can force users to enter dates in a European format, such as 2008.07.10.

ENTER CAPTIONS

USE the database that is open from the previous exercise.

1. In the Field Name column in the upper portion of the table design grid, click the **Location** cell.
2. Click the **Caption** property box in the lower portion of the table design grid.
3. Key **To be announced**.

PAUSE. LEAVE the database open to use in the next exercise.

> **CERTIFICATION READY?**
> How do you modify field properties?
> **2.4.2**

The Caption property field specifies the text displayed by default in labels for forms, reports, and queries. This property is used in the Text field. The maximum length for the Caption property is 255 characters. If you don't specify a caption to be displayed, the field name is used as the label.

■ SOFTWARE ORIENTATION

Fields & Columns Group

When creating fields, you will use the Fields & Columns group on the Datasheet tab, which is shown in Figure 4-20. You can use these commands to create a new field, add an existing field, or insert a lookup column, as well as insert, delete, or rename columns.

Figure 4-20

Fields & Column group

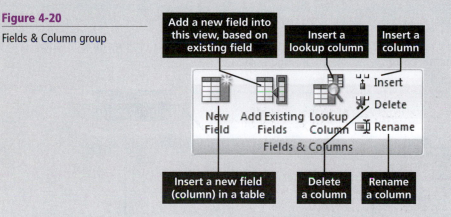

Use this figure as a reference throughout this lesson as well as the rest of this book.

Creating and Deleting Fields

Fields can be created in several different ways. You can add fields to a table in Datasheet view, add fields with a field template, or add a field from another table.

 CREATE FIELDS

USE the database that is open from the previous exercise.

1. On the Home tab, in the Views group, click the **View** button and click **Datasheet View**. Save the table, if required. If you get a message about data integrity, click **OK**.

2. Scroll to the right of the Events table to display the last column and click in the first cell below the Add New Field header, as shown in Figure 4-21.

Figure 4-21

Add New Field column

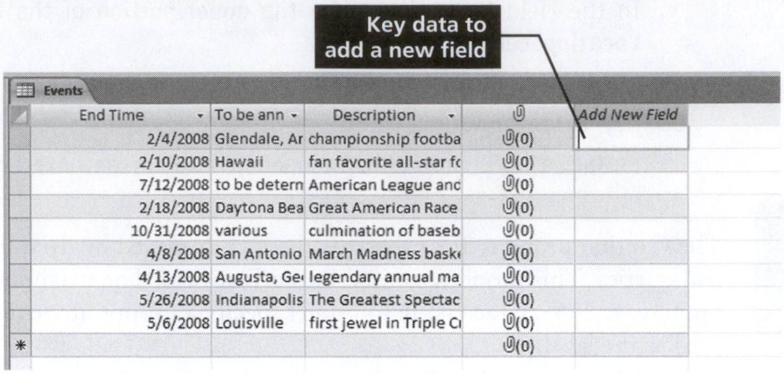

3. Key **Yes** and press [Enter]. A new field named *Field1* is added, and the Add New Field column becomes the last column in the table, as shown in Figure 4-22.

Figure 4-22

New field created

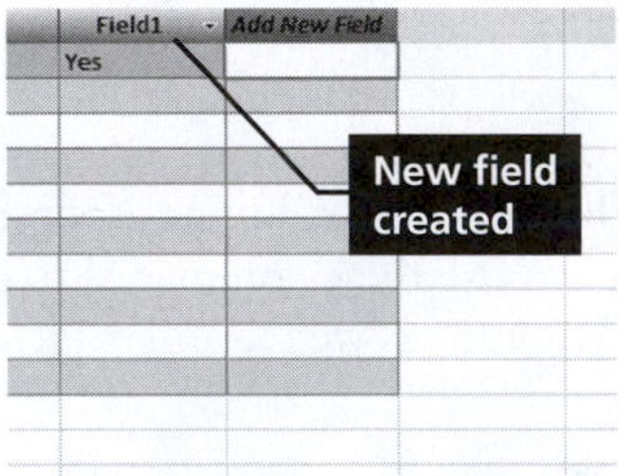

4. Right-click the **Field1** column header to display the shortcut menu and click **Rename Column**, as shown in Figure 4-23.

Figure 4-23

Column shortcut menu

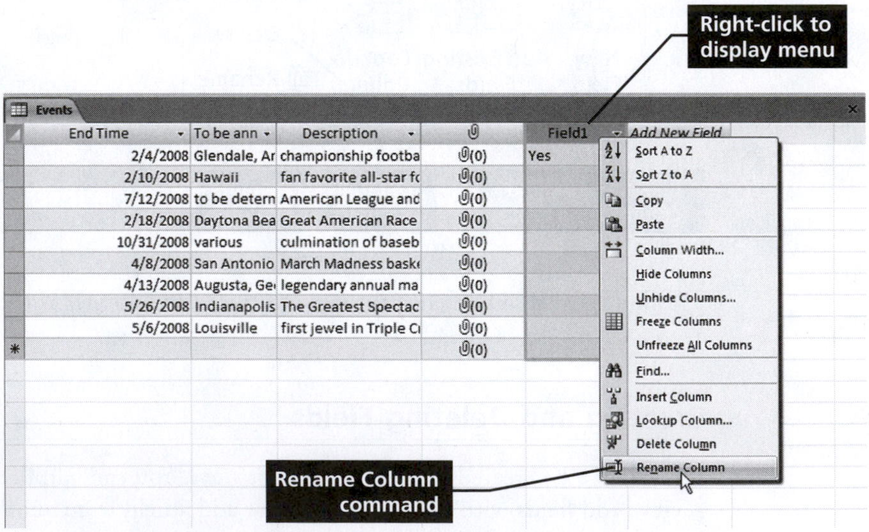

5. Key **On-site staff?** as the column name.
6. On the Datasheet tab, in the Fields & Columns group, click **New Field** to display the Field Templates pane, which is shown in Figure 4-24.

Figure 4-24

Field Templates pane

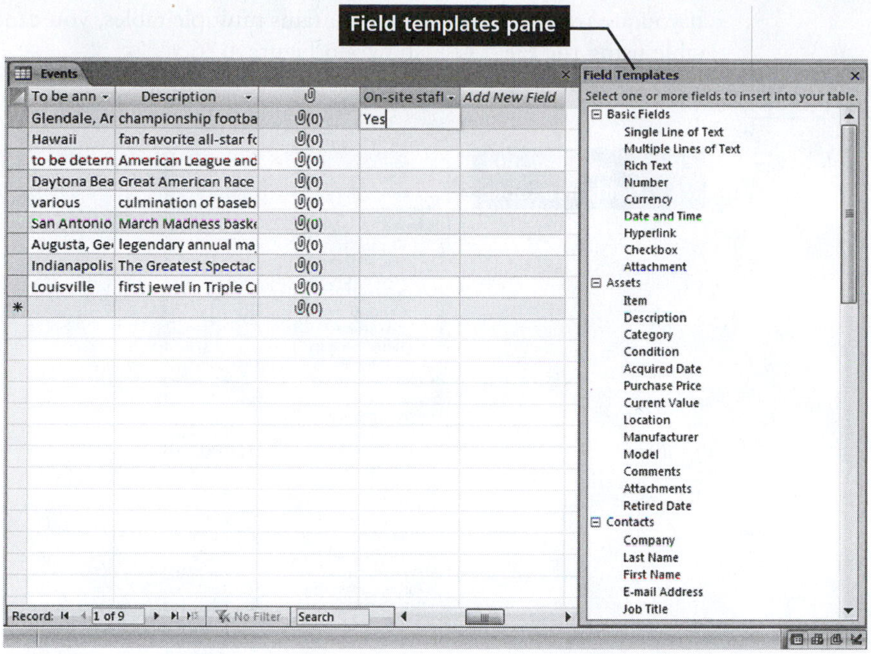

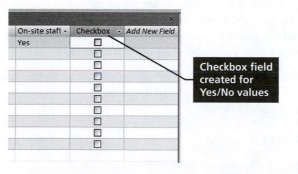

7. In the Basic Fields category, double-click **Checkbox**. A new field with checkboxes is created in the table, as shown in Figure 4-25.

Figure 4-25

Checkbox field created

Checkbox field created for Yes/No values

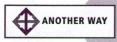
ANOTHER WAY

You can select more than one field in the Field Templates pane and then drag them to the table. When the insertion line appears, drop the fields into position.

CERTIFICATION READY?
How do you create commonly used fields?
2.4.1

8. On the Datasheet tab, in the Fields & Columns group, click the **Rename** button.
9. Key **Souvenirs** and press **Enter**.
10. Click **Close** to close the Field Templates pane.

PAUSE. LEAVE the database open to use in the next exercise.

The last column in a table in Datasheet view has an Add New Field column in which you can add a field simply by keying information in that column. Rename the field by right-clicking the column head, choosing Rename Column from the menu, and keying a new name.

Sometimes it is easier to choose from a predefined list of fields than to manually create a field. Access comes with a set of built-in field templates that can save you considerable time when creating fields. A field template is a predefined set of characteristics and properties that describes a field, including a field name, a data type, and a number of other field properties.

To create a new field using a field template, display the Field Templates pane, and then double-click a field template or drag and drop one or more templates to the table that is opened in Datasheet view.

If you are using a database that contains multiple tables, you can add a field from an existing table using the Field List, shown in Figure 4-26.

Figure 4-26

Field list

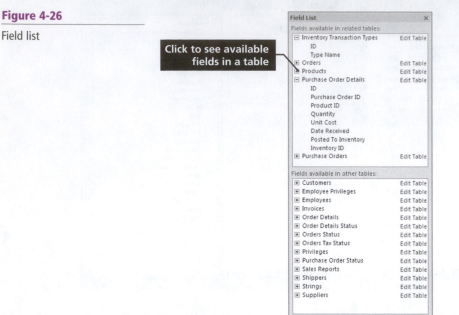

On the Datasheet tab, in the Fields & Columns group, click Add Existing Fields. The Field List pane appears; it lists all of the other tables in your database in two categories: fields available in related tables and fields available in other tables. The first category lists all of the tables with which the table you have open has a relationship. The second category lists all of the tables with which your table does not have a relationship.

Click the plus sign (+) next to a table to see a list of all of the fields available in that table. To add a field to your table, drag and drop the field you want from the Field List pane to the table in Datasheet view.

 **DELETE A FIELD**

USE the database that is open from the previous exercise.

1. Click the column header for the **Attachment** field, located between the *Description* field and the *On-site staff?* field.
2. Right-click in the column to display the shortcut menu and click **Delete Column**, as shown in Figure 4-27.

Figure 4-27

Delete Column command on field shortcut menu

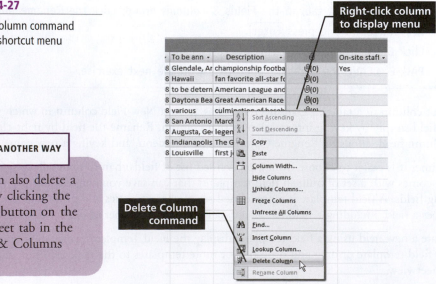

ANOTHER WAY

You can also delete a field by clicking the Delete button on the Datasheet tab in the Fields & Columns group.

3. A message appears, as shown in Figure 4-28. Click **Yes**.

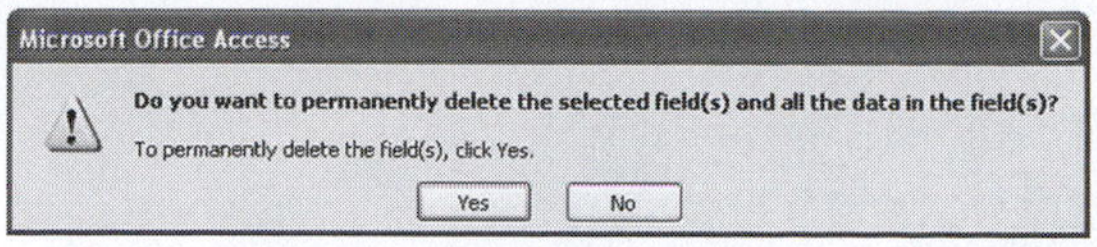

Figure 4-28

Delete field message

> **Microsoft Office Access**
>
> ⚠ Do you want to permanently delete the selected field(s) and all the data in the field(s)?
>
> To permanently delete the field(s), click Yes.
>
> [Yes]   [No]

4. A confirmation message appears, as shown in Figure 4-29. Click **Yes**. The field is deleted.

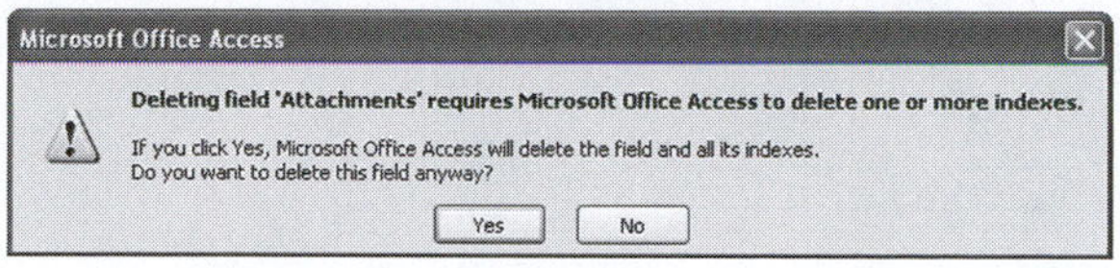

Figure 4-29

Delete field confirmation message

> **Microsoft Office Access**
>
> ⚠ Deleting field 'Attachments' requires Microsoft Office Access to delete one or more indexes.
>
> If you click Yes, Microsoft Office Access will delete the field and all its indexes. Do you want to delete this field anyway?
>
> [Yes]   [No]

PAUSE. LEAVE the database open to use in the next exercise.

Before you delete a column from a datasheet, remember that doing so deletes all the data in the column and that the action cannot be undone. For that reason, you should back up the table before you delete the column. Before you can delete a primary key or a lookup field, you must first delete the relationships for those fields.

To delete a field in Datasheet view, select the column, right-click, and then click Delete Column from the shortcut menu. Or, on the Datasheet tab in the Fields & Columns group, click the Delete button. You will see a confirmation message asking if you are sure you want to delete the column and all the data.

⬥ **ANOTHER WAY** You can also delete a field in Design view by selecting the field (row) that you want to delete and clicking Delete Rows on the Design tab, in the Tools group.

Creating and Modifying Multi-valued Fields

In Office Access 2007, it is possible to create a multi-valued field that lets you select more than one choice from a list, without having to create a more advanced database design.

➔ CREATE A MULTI-VALUED FIELD

USE the database that is open from the previous exercise.

1. Place the insertion point in the first cell of the table. On the Datasheet tab, in the Field & Column group, click the **Lookup Column** button. The Lookup Wizard appears, as shown in Figure 4-30.

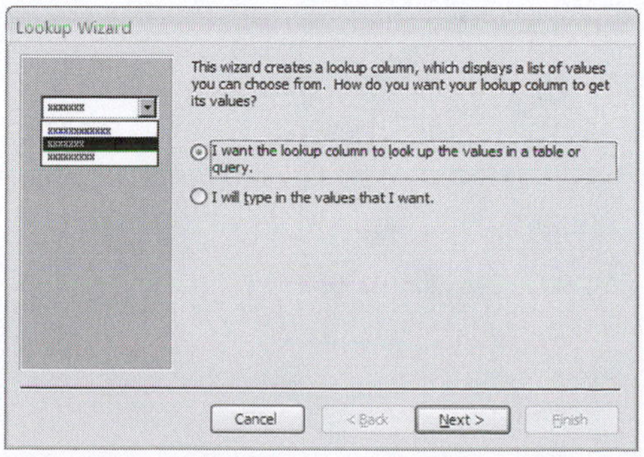

Figure 4-30

Lookup Wizard

> **Lookup Wizard**
>
> This wizard creates a lookup column, which displays a list of values you can choose from. How do you want your lookup column to get its values?
>
> ◉ I want the lookup column to look up the values in a table or query.
>
> ○ I will type in the values that I want.
>
> [Cancel]   [< Back]   [Next >]   [Finish]

2. Click **Next>** to display the next screen in the Lookup Wizard, as shown in Figure 4-31.

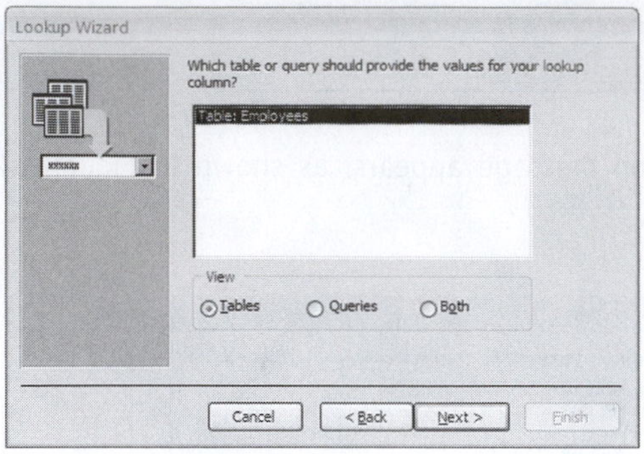

Figure 4-31

Lookup Wizard, second screen

3. Click **Next>** to display the next screen in the Lookup Wizard, as shown in Figure 4-32.

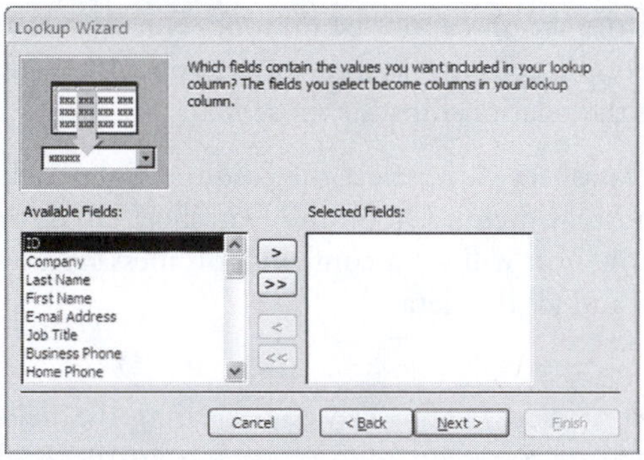

Figure 4-32

Lookup Wizard, third screen

4. In the Available Fields list, select **Last Name**, then click the **>** button to move it to the Selected Fields box.

5. In the Available Fields list, select **First Name**, then click the **>** button to move it to the Selected Fields box.

6. Click **Next>** to display the next screen in the Lookup Wizard.

7. Click the down arrow in the first box and click **Last Name**, as shown in Figure 4-33.

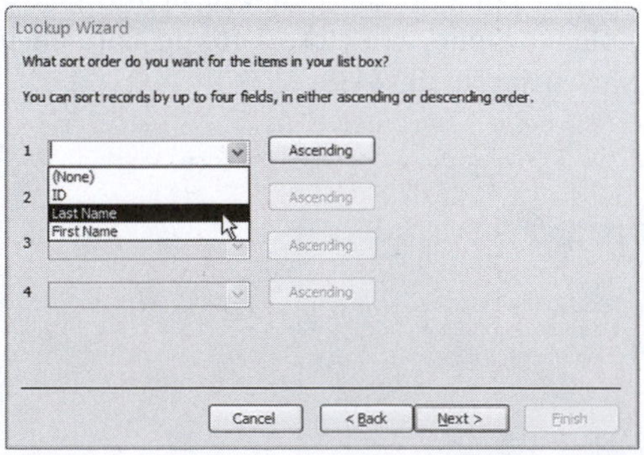

Figure 4-33

Lookup Wizard, fourth screen

8. Click **Next>** to display the next screen in the Lookup Wizard, as shown in Figure 4-34.

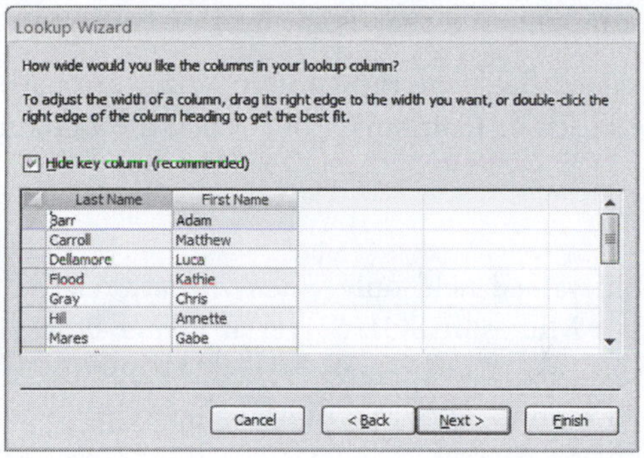

9. Click **Next>** to display the final screen in the Lookup Wizard, as shown in Figure 4-35.

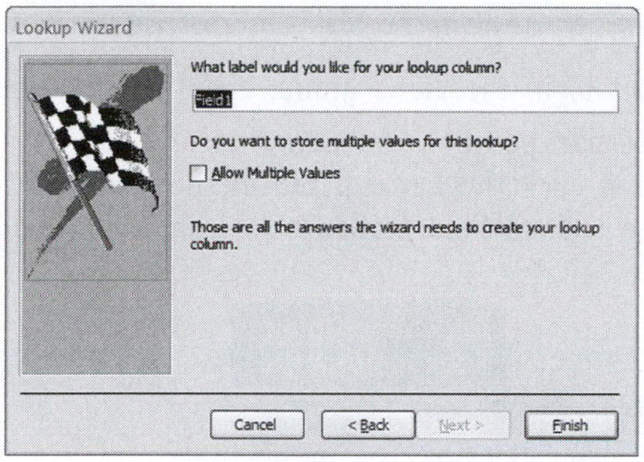

Figure 4-35

Lookup Wizard, final screen

10. In the *What label would you like for your lookup column?* box, key **Coordinator**.

11. Click the **Finish** button. A new column named Coordinator appears at the beginning of the table. Click the down arrow to display the list of names, as shown in Figure 4-36.

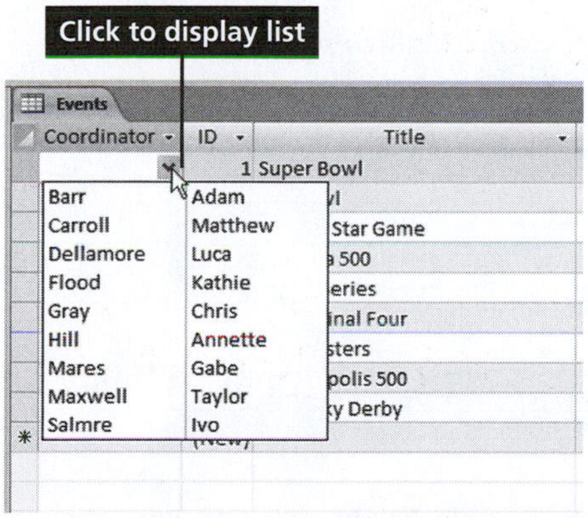

Figure 4-36

Lookup column

12. Click **Flood/Kathie** on the list to choose that value for the field.

PAUSE. LEAVE the database open to use in the next exercise.

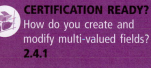

CERTIFICATION READY?
How do you create and modify multi-valued fields?
2.4.1

In most database management systems, including earlier versions of Microsoft Access, a field can store only a single value. But in Microsoft Office Access 2007, you can create a field that holds multiple values, such as a list of employees that you have assigned to a particular event. You can use a ***multi-valued field*** to select more than one value from a list.

Use a multi-valued field when you want to store multiple selections from a list of choices that is relatively small. It is also appropriate to use a multi-valued field when you will be integrating your database with Windows SharePoint Services—for example, by exporting an Access table to a SharePoint site or linking to a SharePoint list that contains a multi-valued field type.

To create the multi-valued field, use the Lookup Wizard in table Design view. On the Datasheet tab, in the Fields & Columns group, click the Lookup Column button to start the Lookup Wizard.

TROUBLESHOOTING Consider using a multi-valued field only when you are relatively sure that your database will not be moved to a Microsoft SQL Server at a later date. An Access multi-valued field is upsized to SQL Server as a memo field that contains a delimited set of values. Because SQL Server does not support a multi-valued data type, additional design and conversion work might be needed.

→ **MODIFY A MULTI-VALUED FIELD**

USE the database that is open from the previous exercise.

1. On the Home tab, in the Views group, click the **View** button and click **Design View**.

2. Place the insertion point in the **Coordinator** cell in the upper portion of the table design grid and click the **Lookup** tab in the lower portion of the table design grid to display the Lookup field properties, as shown in Figure 4-37.

Figure 4-37

Lookup field properties

Click and display Lookup properties

Field Name	Data Type
Coordinator	Number
ID	AutoNumber
Title	Text
Start Time	Date/Time
End Time	Date/Time
Location	Text
Description	Memo
Attachments	Attachment
On-site staff?	Text
Souvenirs	Yes/No

Field Properties

General | Lookup

Display Control	Combo Box
Row Source Type	Table/Query
Row Source	SELECT [Employees].[ID], [Employees].[Last Name], [Employees].[First Name] F
Bound Column	1
Column Count	3
Column Heads	No
Column Widths	0";1";1"
List Rows	16
List Width	2"
Limit To List	Yes
Allow Multiple Values	No
Allow Value List Edits	Yes
List Items Edit Form	
Show Only Row Source V	No

Help.

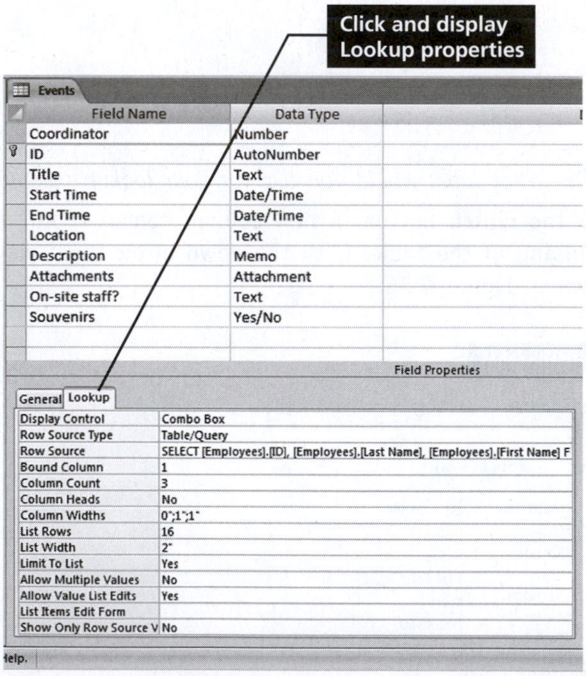

3. Click in the Allow Multiple Values property box, then click the **down arrow** on the right side, and click **Yes**. A message appears, as shown in Figure 4-38.

Modify Tables and Fields | 97

Figure 4-38

Change lookup column message

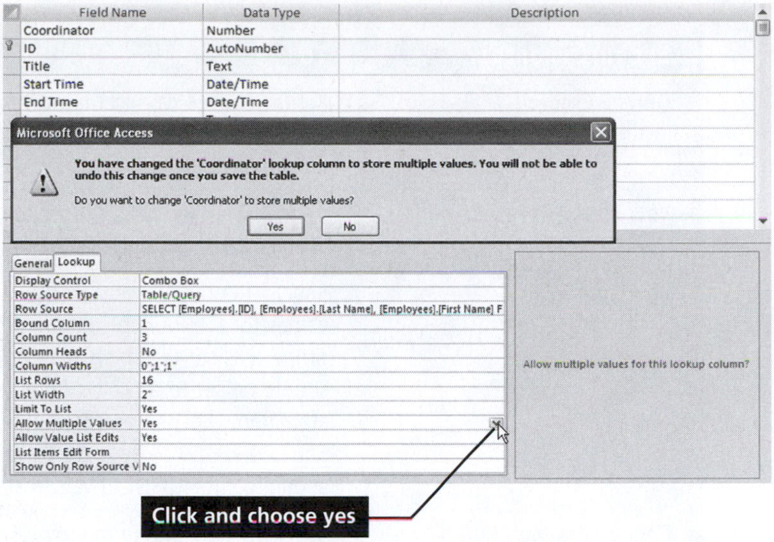

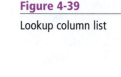

4. Click **Yes**.

5. On the Home tab, in the Views group, click the **View** button and click **Datasheet View**.

6. Click **Yes** to save the table.

7. Click the down arrow in the second cell of the Coordinator column to display the list, as shown in Figure 4-39.

Figure 4-39

Lookup column list

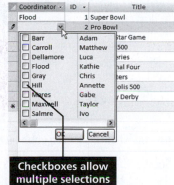

8. Notice the list now allows multiple values by providing checkboxes. Click to select the checkboxes for **Adam Barr** and **Annette Hill**.

9. Click **OK**.

PAUSE. LEAVE the database open to use in the next exercise.

To modify the lookup field properties, you can view and change them in the bottom pane of Design view under Field Properties. To see the properties specifically related to the lookup column, click the Lookup tab. Table 4-3 shows the properties you can set for the Lookup field properties.

Table 4-3

Lookup Field Properties

SET THIS PROPERTY	TO
Display Control	Set the control type to Check Box, Text Box, List Box, or Combo Box. Combo Box is the most common choice for a lookup column.
Row Source Type	Choose whether to fill the lookup column with values from another table or query or from a list of values that you specify.
Row Source	Specify the table, query, or list of values that provides the values for the lookup column. When the Row Source Type property is set to Table/Query or Field List, this property should be set to a table or query name or to a SQL statement that represents the query. When the Row Source Type property is set to Value List, this property should contain a list of values separated by semicolons.
Bound Column	Specify the column in the row source that supplies the value stored by the lookup column. This value can range from 1 to the number of columns in the row source.
Column Count	Specify the number of columns in the row source that can be displayed in the lookup column. To select which columns to display, provide a column width in the Column Widths property.
Column Heads	Specify whether to display column headings.
Column Widths	Enter the column width for each column. If you don't want to display a column, such as an ID column, specify 0 for the width.
List Rows	Specify the number of rows that appear when you display the lookup column.
List Width	Specify the width of the control that appears when you display the lookup column.
Limit To List	Choose whether you can enter a value that isn't in the list.
Allow Multiple Values	Specify whether the lookup column employs a multi-valued field and allows multiple values to be selected.
Allow Value List Edits	Specify whether you can edit the items in a lookup column that is based on a value list. When this property is set to Yes and you right-click a Lookup field that is based on a single column value list, you will see the Edit List Items menu option. If the lookup field has more than one column, this property is ignored.
List Items Edit Form	Name an existing form to use to edit the list items in a lookup column that is based on a table or query.
Show Only Row Source Values	Show only values that match the current row source when Allow Multiple Values is set to Yes.

Creating and Modifying Attachment Fields

Attachment fields are used to add one or more pieces of data, such as files or graphics, to the records in your database.

→ CREATE AND MODIFY ATTACHMENT FIELDS

USE the database that is open from the previous exercise.

1. Scroll to the end of the table and click the **Add New Field** header.
2. On the Datasheet tab, in the Data Type & Formatting group, click the **down arrow** in the Data Type box to display the menu.
3. Click **Attachment**. A new column is inserted with a paper clip icon in the header, as shown in Figure 4-40.

Figure 4-40

Attachments field created

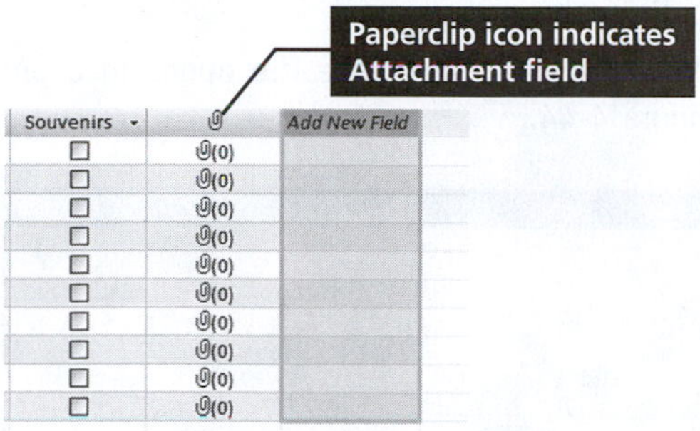

Paperclip icon indicates Attachment field

> **TAKE NOTE** *
>
> Once a field has been set to the Attachment data type, it cannot be converted to another data type.

4. Double-click on the first cell in the Attachment column to open the Attachments dialog box, as shown in Figure 4-41.

Figure 4-41

Attachment dialog box

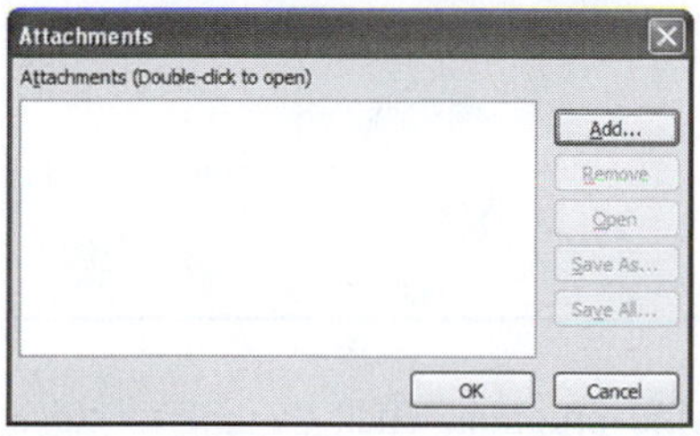

5. Click the **Add** button. The Choose File dialog box opens, as shown in Figure 4-42.

Figure 4-42

Choose File dialog box

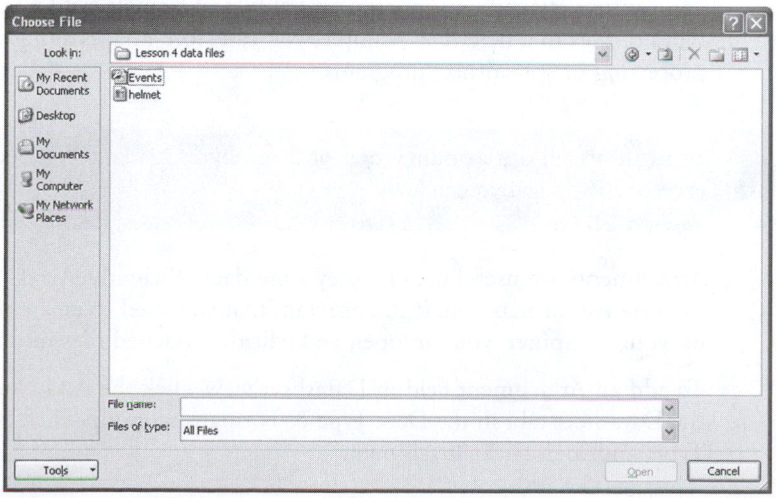

6. Navigate to the data files for this lesson and select the helmet image file. Click **Open**. The file is added to the Attachment dialog box.

7. Click **OK** to close the Attachment dialog box and attach the file to the record, as shown in Figure 4-43.

Figure 4-43

Record with file attached

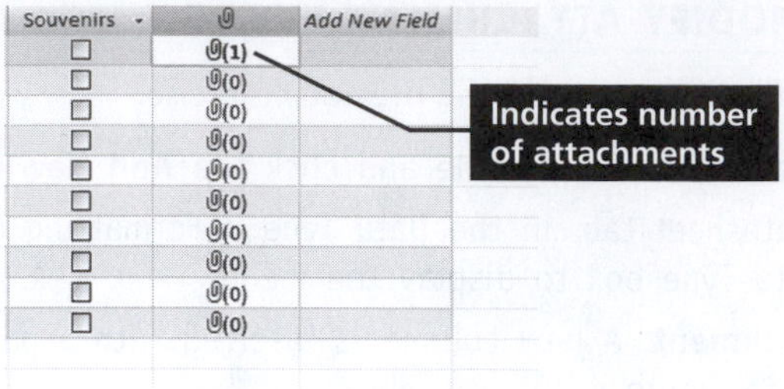

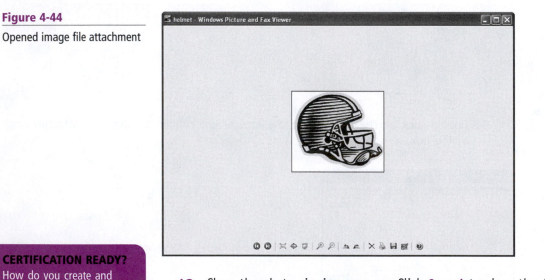

The **helmet.jpg** image file is available on the companion CD-ROM.

8. Double-click the attachment field in the record that has the file attachment. The Attachment dialog box opens.

9. Double-click *helmet.jpg*. The image file opens in a program that will display it, as shown in Figure 4-44.

Figure 4-44

Opened image file attachment

CERTIFICATION READY?
How do you create and modify attachment fields?
2.4.4

10. Close the photo-viewing program. Click **Cancel** to close the Attachments dialog box. **STOP. CLOSE** the database.

You can use attachments to store several files in a single field, and you can even store multiple types of files in a field. For example, you can store images along with files created with word processing or spreadsheet programs.

TAKE NOTE ✱

You can attach a maximum total of 2 gigabytes of data, but each individual file cannot exceed 256 megabytes in size.

Attachments are useful because they store data efficiently. Access stores the attached files in their native formats and, if the program that was used to create the attached file is installed on your computer, you can open and edit the attached files in that program.

To add an Attachment field in Datasheet view, click the Add New Field column header. On the Datasheet tab, in the Data Type & Formatting group, click the down arrow next to Data Type, and then click Attachment.

ANOTHER WAY

You can also add an Attachment field in Design view by selecting a blank row, keying a name for the Attachment field, and clicking Attachment under Data Type in the same row.

Access sets the data type for the field to Attachment and places a paperclip icon in the header row of the field. By default, you cannot enter text into the header row of Attachment fields. Use the Attachments dialog box to add, edit, and manage attachments. You can open the dialog box directly from the attachment field in a table by double-clicking the field.

By default, each field in a relational database contains only one piece of data. However, even though you can attach more than one file to a field, this does not break the rules of database design, because as you attach files to a record Access 2007 creates one or more system tables and uses those tables behind the scenes to normalize your data. You cannot view or work with those tables.

SUMMARY SKILL MATRIX

IN THIS LESSON YOU LEARNED	MATRIX SKILL	SKILL NUMBER
To modify a database table	Modify tables	2.3
To modify table properties	Modify table properties	2.3.1
To rename a table	Rename tables	2.3.3
To delete a table	Delete tables	2.3.4
To create fields and modify field properties	Create fields and modify field properties	2.4
To modify field properties	Modify field properties	2.4.2
To create fields	Create commonly used fields	2.4.1
To create and modify multi-value fields	Create and modify multi-valued fields	2.4.3
To create and modify attachment fields	Create and modify attachment fields	2.4.4

■ Knowledge Assessment

Fill in the Blank

Complete the following sentences by writing the correct word or words in the blanks provided.

1. _____ or _____ a table could possibly break the functionality of the database.

2. If you want more space to enter or edit a setting in the property box, press Shift+F2 to display the _____ box.

3. A(n) _____ contains no characters, and you use it to indicate that you know no value exists for a field.

4. _____ specifies the text in the error message that appears when users violate a validation rule.

5. The _____ property field specifies the text displayed by default in labels for forms, reports, and queries.

6. When creating fields, use the commands in the _____ group on the Datasheet tab.

7. A(n) _____ is a predefined set of characteristics and properties that describes a field.

8. To add a field to your table, drag and drop the field you want from the _____ pane to the table in Datasheet view.

9. You can use _____ to store several files in a single field.

10. By default, each field in a(n) _____ database contains only one piece of data.

Multiple Choice

Select the best response for the following statements or questions.

1. To rename a table or other database object, first
   a. save it.
   b. close it.
   c. rename it.
   d. open it.

2. If you delete a database table,
   a. you cannot undo the action.
   b. click Undo to restore the table.
   c. it is still available in the Navigation Pane.
   d. the data is transferred to the Clipboard.

3. A complete list of field properties is available in
   a. the Navigation Pane.
   b. Datasheet view.
   c. Design view.
   d. all of the above.

4. Which of the following is *not* a field property?
   a. Column Template
   b. Field Size
   c. Caption
   d. Allow Zero Length

5. Which field property requires users to enter data in a specific format?
   a. Validation Text
   b. Default Value
   c. Required
   d. Input Mask

6. The Append Only property applies only to a field that is set to
   a. Memo.
   b. Number.
   c. Currency.
   d. Text.

7. Which of the following is *not* a way to validate data?
   a. Data type
   b. Field sizes
   c. Filtering
   d. Field properties

8. The Caption field property is used for which field?
   a. Text
   b. Attachment
   c. Date/Time
   d. Hyperlink

9. Which type of field allows you to select more than one choice from a list?
   a. Attachment
   b. Multi-valued
   c. Caption
   d. Validation

10. A paperclip icon in the header row indicates what type of field?
    a. Attachment
    b. Input mask
    c. Caption
    d. Memo

■ Competency Assessment

Project 4-1: Home Inventory

You decide to use Access to create a home inventory database for insurance purposes. To include all the information you want, you need to add several fields to the existing table.

GET READY. Launch Access if it is not already running.

The *Home inventory* database file is available on the companion CD-ROM.

1. **OPEN** *Home inventory* from the data files for this lesson.
2. **SAVE** the database as *Home inventory XXX* (where XXX is your initials).
3. Close the Home Inventory List form that is open.
4. In the Navigation Pane, double-click the **Assets** table to open it.
5. Scroll to the end of the table and click in the cell below the Add New Field header.
6. On the Datasheet tab, in the Data Type & Formatting group, click the down arrow in the Data Type box and click **Yes/No**. A column named **Field1** is created.
7. On the Datasheet tab, in the Fields & Columns group, click the **Rename** button.
8. Key **Insured** to rename the Field1 column.
9. Click in the cell below the Add New Field header.
10. On the Datasheet tab, in the Data Type & Formatting group, click the down arrow in the Data Type box and click **Attachment** to create an attachment field.
11. **CLOSE** the database.

    LEAVE Access open for the next project.

Project 4-2: Customer Service

You are employed in the customer service department at City Power & Light. Each call that is received is recorded in an Access database. Because you know how to modify tables and fields, your supervisor asks you to add a lookup column to the Calls table to record the customer service representative who receives the call.

The *Customer service* database file is available on the companion CD-ROM.

1. OPEN *Customer service* from the data files for this lesson.
2. SAVE the database as *Customer serviceXXX* (where XXX is your initials).
3. Close the Case List form that is open.
4. In the Navigation Pane, open the Supporting Objects group and double-click the **Calls** table to open it. Place the insertion point in the first cell of the table.
5. On the Datasheet tab, in the Field & Column group, click the **Lookup Column** button. The Lookup Wizard appears.
6. Click **Next>** to display the next screen in the Lookup Wizard.
7. Select **Table: Employees** and click **Next>**.
8. In the Available Fields list, select **First Name**, then click the **>** button to move it to the Selected Fields box.
9. In the Available Fields list, select **Last Name**, then click the **>** button to move it to the Selected Fields box.
10. Click **Next>** to display the next screen in the Lookup Wizard.
11. Click the down arrow in the first box and click **Last Name**.
12. Click **Next>** to display the next screen in the Lookup Wizard.
13. Click **Next>** again to display the final screen in the Lookup Wizard.
14. In the *What label would you like for your lookup column?* box, key **Service Rep**.
15. Click the **Finish** button. A new column named Service Rep appears at the beginning of the table.
16. Click the down arrow and choose **Clair/Hector** from the list.
17. LEAVE the database open for the next project.

    LEAVE Access open for the next project.

■ Proficiency Assessment

Project 4-3: Modify Field Properties

Your supervisor at City Power & Light asks you to make some modifications to the field properties in the Calls table of the customer service database.

USE the database that is open from the previous project.

1. Switch to **Design View**.
2. Display the Lookup field properties for the **Service Rep** field.
3. Change the Allow Multiple Values property to **Yes** and confirm the change.
4. Display the General field properties for the **Call Time** field.
5. Change the Validation Rule property so that the value must be greater than **1/1/2000**.
6. Change the Validation Text property to say "Please enter a value that is greater than 1/1/2000."
7. Display the General field properties for the **Caller** field.
8. Change the Field Size property to **60**.
9. Display the General field properties for the **Notes** field.

10. Change the Allow Zero Length property to **Yes**.

11. Change the Append Only property to **Yes**.

12. Save the table. If a data integrity message appears, click **No**.

13. **CLOSE** the database.

LEAVE Access open for the next project.

Project 4-4: Modify Database Tables

You work as the operations manager at Alpine Ski House and decide to increase your efficiency by using Access to plan the annual race events. You have started to create a database to manage the events sponsored by the company, but need to modify the tables.

The *Alpine* database file is available on the companion CD-ROM.

1. **OPEN** *Alpine* from the data files for this lesson.

2. Save the database as *AlpineXXX* (where XXX is your initials).

3. Close the Event List form that is open.

4. Delete the Nordic Events table and confirm the action.

5. Rename the World Cup table to **Championships**.

6. Open the Events table and switch to Design view.

7. Display the property sheet.

8. In the Description property box, key **Annual events**.

9. **CLOSE** the database.

LEAVE Access open for the next project.

■ Mastery Assessment

Project 4-5: Changing List Items

You are the owner of Coho Vineyard & Winery, a growing company that is converting all of its data from spreadsheets to Access. You created a table using the Assets table template, but need to make some modifications before you enter information in the database. Because you have not made changes to list items before, you might need to use Access Help.

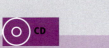

The *Coho* database file is available on the companion CD-ROM.

1. **OPEN** *Coho* from the data files for this lesson.

2. Save the database as *Coho XXX* (where XXX is your initials).

3. Open the **Red Wine** table and switch to Design view.

4. Display the Lookup properties for the Category field.

5. Change the **Allow Value List Edits** property to **Yes**.

6. Place the insertion point in the Row Source property box and click the button on the right side to display the Edit List Items dialog box.

7. Set the list items as follows:

(1) **Merlot**

(2) **Cabernet**

(3) **Shiraz**

(4) **Zinfandel**

8. Change the default value to (1) **Merlot**.

9. Change the name of the Category column to **Type**.

10. Change the name of the Condition column to **Country**.

11. Display the Lookup properties for the Country field.

12. Change the **Allow Value List Edits** property to **Yes**.

13. Display the Edit List Items dialog box for the Country field and set them as follows:

    (1) **Chile**

    (2) **France**

    (3) **South Africa**

    (4) **Spain**

    (5) **United States**

14. Change the default value to **(1) Chile**.

15. **SAVE** the table and switch to Datasheet view.

16. **CLOSE** the database.

    LEAVE Access open for the next project.

Project 4-6: Lending Library

You have an extensive personal library that friends and family frequently ask to share. To keep track of all your books, you decide to use Access to create a lending library database.

1. **OPEN** *Lending library* from the data files for this lesson.

2. SAVE the database as *Lending library XXX* (where XXX is your initials).

3. Use the skills you have learned in this lesson to make any changes that you think would be useful to the tables or field properties.

4. **CLOSE** the database.

   CLOSE Access.

The *Lending library* database is available on the companion CD-ROM.

INTERNET READY

A number of online resources can provide solutions to challenges that you might face during a typical workday. Search the Microsoft site for Work Essentials, shown in Figure 4-45.

Figure 4-45

Work Essentials site

Work Essentials is a place where you can find information on how to use Microsoft Access efficiently to perform typical business tasks and activities. Explore the resources and content that Work Essentials offers to discover tools or solutions that could be useful on the job and ways you could use the site to be more productive.

5 Create Forms

SKILLS	MATRIX SKILL	SKILL NUMBER
Creating Forms	Create forms	2.5
Creating a Simple Form	Create simple forms	2.5.8
Creating a Form in Design View	Create forms using Design view	2.5.1
Creating a Form in Layout View	Create forms using Layout view	2.5.7
Creating a Datasheet Form	Create datasheet forms	2.5.2
Applying AutoFormat	Apply AutoFormats to forms and reports	2.7.7
Sorting Data Within a Form	Sort data within forms	5.1.4
Filtering Data Within a Form	Filter data within forms	5.2.4

You are the owner of the Graphic Art Institute, a small fine-arts gallery dedicated to presenting challenging and contemporary visual arts and educational programs. The current exhibition is successfully underway; you are now calling for submissions for the next exhibition—a juried art show featuring photographic work from the local region. The competition is open to all regional artists who use photographic processes in their work. This particular event will be open to digital submissions. As each submission is received, you will enter the artist and image information into an Access database for easy retrieval. In this lesson, you will learn how to create forms using a variety of methods; how to apply an AutoFormat to a form; and how to sort and filter data within a form.

KEY TERMS
AutoFormat
Blank Form tool
common filter
filter by form
Form Design button
Form tool
Form Wizard

SOFTWARE ORIENTATION

Forms Group

The Forms group is located on the Create tab in the Ribbon and can be used to create a variety of forms.

Figure 5-1

Forms group

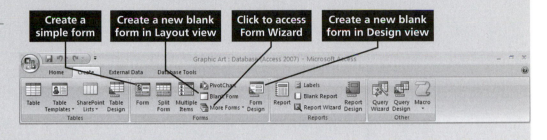

Use this figure as a reference throughout this lesson as well as the rest of this book.

Creating Forms

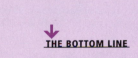

THE BOTTOM LINE

A form is a database object that you can use to enter, edit, or display data from a table or query. Forms can be used to control access to data by limiting which fields or rows of data are displayed to users. For example, certain users might need to see only certain fields in a table. Providing those users with a form that contains just those fields makes it easier for them to use the database. Think of forms as windows through which people see and reach your database in a more visually attractive and efficient way.

CERTIFICATION READY?
How do you create forms?
2.5

Creating a Simple Form

You can use the Form tool to create a form with a single mouse-click.

CREATE A SIMPLE FORM

GET READY. Before you begin these steps, be sure to launch Microsoft Access.

CD

The *Graphic Art* database file is available on the companion CD-ROM.

1. **OPEN** the *Graphic Art* database from the data files for this lesson.
2. **SAVE** the database as *Graphic Art XXX* (where XXX is your initials).
3. In the Navigation Pane, click the **Photo Exhibit** table.
4. On the Create tab, in the Forms group, click the **Form** button. Access creates the form and displays it in Layout view, as shown in Figure 5-2. Your form may be slightly different.

Figure 5-2

Simple form

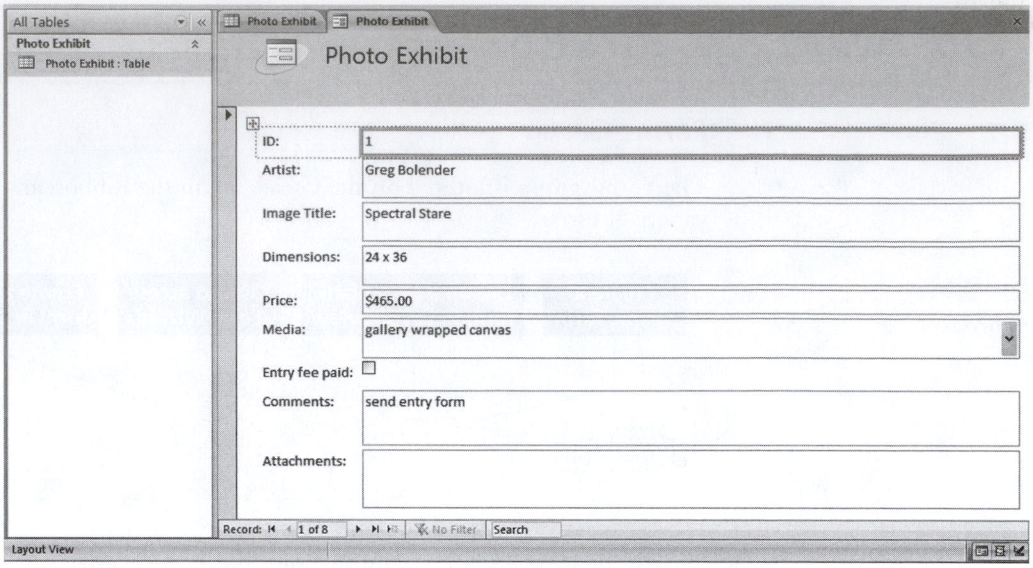

5. Click the **Office Button** and click **Save**. The Save As dialog box appears, as shown in Figure 5-3.

Figure 5-3

Save As dialog box

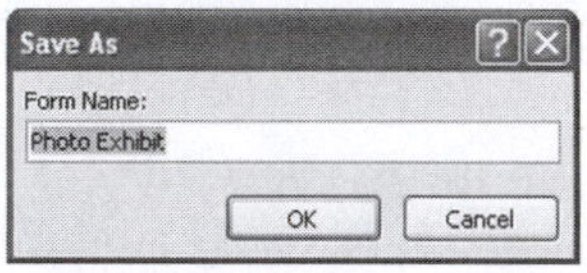

TAKE NOTE *

You can use the record navigation buttons at the bottom of a form to navigate among the form's records, just as you used them to navigate among records in a table in Lesson 3.

---

6. Click **OK** to accept the *Photo Exhibit* form name suggested by Access. The form name appears in the Navigation Pane.

CERTIFICATION READY?
How do you create simple forms?
2.5.8

7. Click the **Close 'Photo Exhibit'** button to close the form.

8. **LEAVE** the database open.

PAUSE. LEAVE Access open to use in the next exercise.

To use the ***Form tool*** to create a simple form, first click the table in the Navigation Pane that contains the data you want to see on the form. On the Create tab, in the Forms group, click Form. When you use this tool, all the fields from the underlying data source are placed on the form.

Access creates the form and displays it in Layout view. You can begin using the new form immediately, or you can modify it in Layout view or Design view to better suit your needs.

To save your form design, click the Office Button and click Save. Key a name in the Form Name box and click OK. After you save your form design, you can run the form as often as you want. The design stays the same, but you see current data every time you view the form. If your needs change, you can modify the form design or create a new form that is based on the original.

Creating a Form in Design View

Click the Form Design button to quickly create a new blank form in Design view where you can view a detailed structure of the form.

→ CREATE A FORM IN DESIGN VIEW

USE the database that is open from the previous exercise.

1. On the Create tab, in the Forms group, click the **Form Design** button. A new blank form is created in Design view, as shown in Figure 5-4.

Figure 5-4

New blank form in Design view

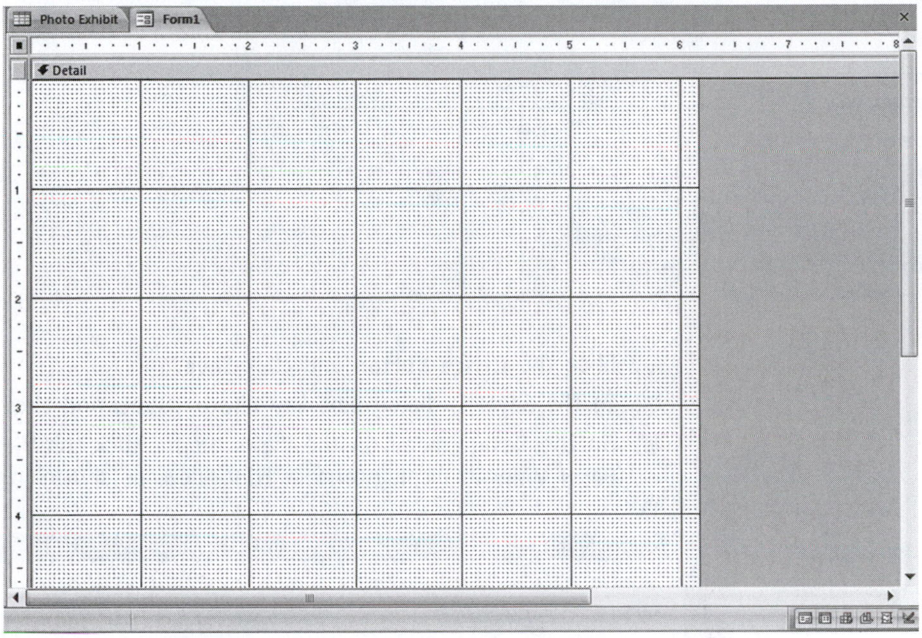

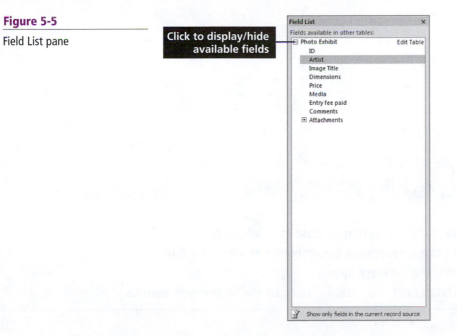

ANOTHER WAY

You can also display the Field List pane by clicking Alt+F8.

2. On the Design tab, in the Tools group, click the **Add Existing Fields** button. The Field List pane appears, as shown in Figure 5-5.

Figure 5-5

Field List pane

3. In the list of fields, double-click **Artist** to add it to the form.

4. Double-click **Image Title** to add it to the form.

5. Double-click **Price** to add it to the form. Your form should look similar to Figure 5-6.

Figure 5-6

Fields inserted in Design view

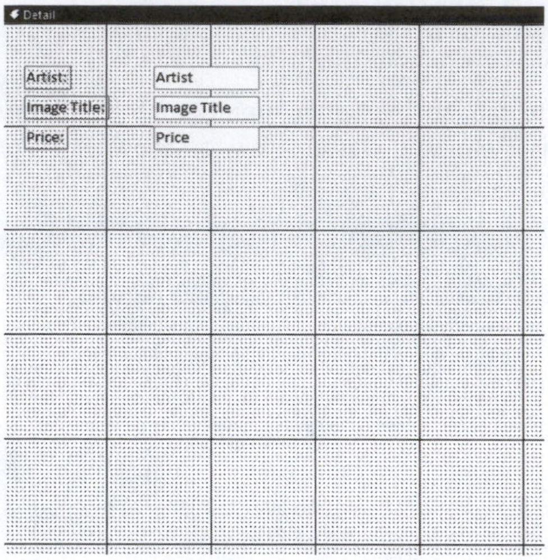

ANOTHER WAY

You can also click the field name and drag it onto the form to add a field.

6. Click the **Office Button** and click **Save**.

7. In the Save As dialog box, key **Photo Label**, and click **OK**.

8. On the Design menu, in the Views group, click the **View** button and click **Form View** to display form in Form view, as shown in Figure 5-7.

Figure 5-7

Form view

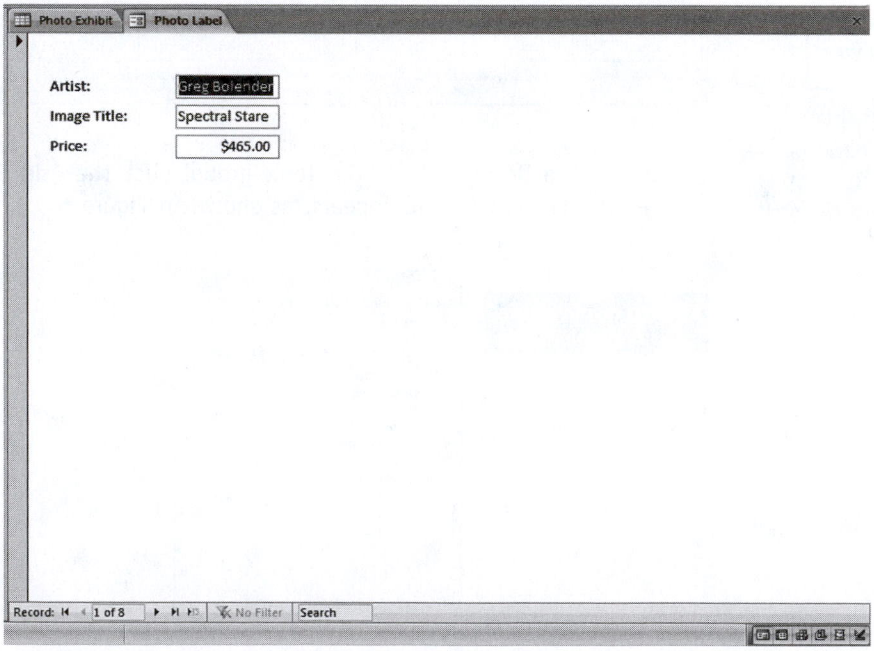

9. Click the **Close** button to close the Field List.

10. Click the **Close 'Photo Label'** button to close the form.

11. **LEAVE** the database open.

   PAUSE. LEAVE the database open to use in the next exercise.

CERTIFICATION READY?

How do you create forms using Design view?

2.5.1

When you click the *Form Design button*, a new blank form is created in Design view. Design view gives you a more detailed view of the structure of your form than Layout view. The form is not actually running when it is shown in Design view, so you cannot see the underlying data while you are making design changes.

You can fine-tune your form's design by working in Design view. To switch to Design view, right-click the form name in the Navigation Pane and then click Design View. You can add new controls and fields to the form by adding them to the design grid, plus the property sheet gives you access to a large number of properties that you can set to customize your form.

LOOKING AHEAD   In Lesson 7, you will learn how to use the commands in the Controls group that can help you enhance and format a form.

Creating a Form in Layout View

Click the Blank Form button to quickly create a new blank form in Layout view with which you can make design changes to the form while viewing the underlying data.

⊕ CREATE A FORM IN LAYOUT VIEW

USE the database that is open from the previous exercise.

1. On the Create tab, in the Forms group, click the **Blank Form** button. A new blank form is created in Layout view, with the Field List displayed, as shown in Figure 5-8.

Figure 5-8

New blank form in Layout view

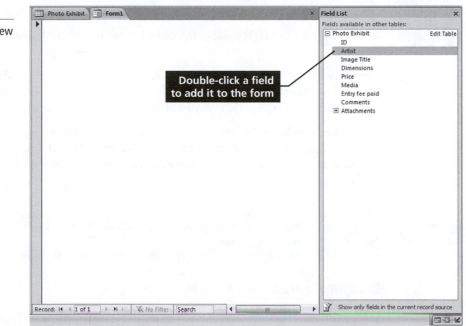

2. In the list of fields, double-click **Image Title** to add it to the form.
3. Double-click **Dimensions** to add it to the form.
4. Double-click **Media** to add it to the form. Your form should look similar to Figure 5-9.

Figure 5-9

Fields inserted in Layout view

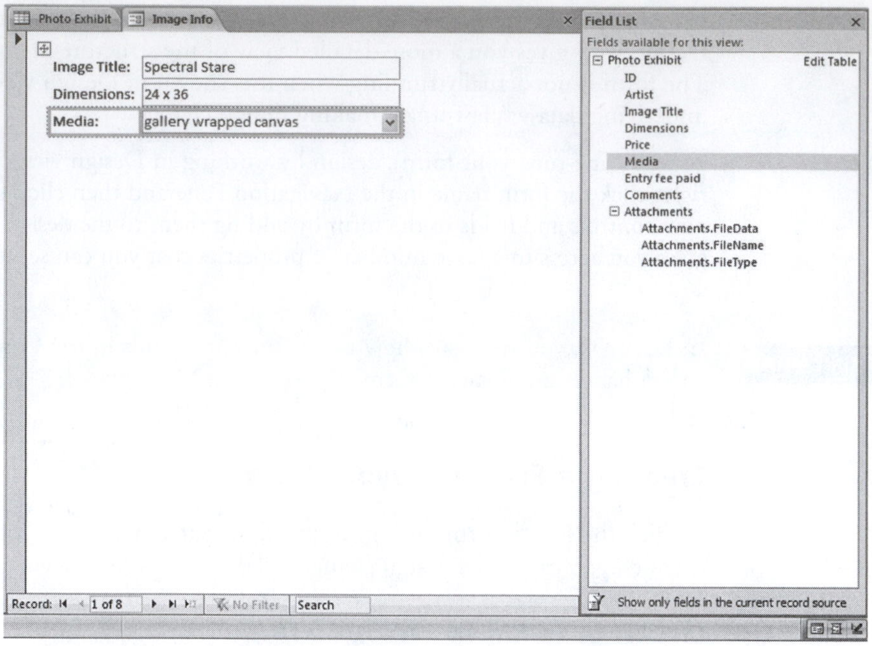

5. Click the **Office Button** and click **Save**.

6. In the Save As dialog box, key **Image Info**, and click **OK**.

7. Click the **Close** button to close the Field List.

8. Click the **Close 'Image Info'** button to close the form.

9. **LEAVE** the database open.

   PAUSE. LEAVE the database open to use in the next exercise.

CERTIFICATION READY?
How do you create forms using Layout view?
5.1.4

If other form-building tools do not fit your needs, you can use the Blank Form tool to create a form. The **Blank Form tool** creates a new form in Layout view. This can be a very quick way to build a form, especially if you plan to put only a few fields on your form.

On the Create tab, in the Forms group, click the Blank Form button. Access opens a blank form in Layout view, and displays the Field List pane. To add a field to the form, double-click it or drag it onto the form. In Layout view, you can make design changes to the form while it is displaying data.

TAKE NOTE*

To add more than one field at a time, press CTRL and click several fields; then, drag them all onto the form at once.

Creating a Datasheet Form

A datasheet form looks very similar to the table upon which it is based and provides a way to enter data using columns and rows.

CREATE A DATASHEET FORM

USE the database that is open from the previous exercise.

1. On the Create tab, in the Forms group, click the **More Forms** button to display the menu shown in Figure 5-10.

Figure 5-10

More Forms menu

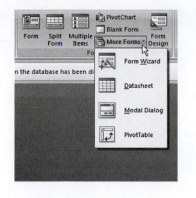

2. Click **Form Wizard** to display the Form Wizard, as shown in Figure 5-11.

Figure 5-11

Form Wizard

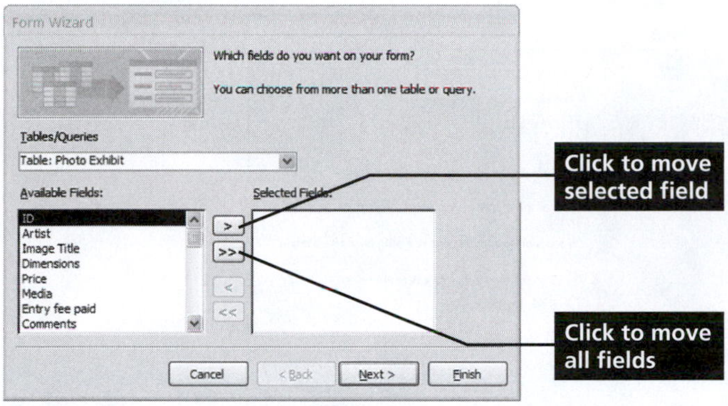

Click to move
selected field

Click to move
all fields

3. Click the **>>** button to move all the fields from the Available Fields box to the Selected Fields box.

4. Click the **Next>** button to move to the next page in the Form Wizard, shown in Figure 5-12.

Figure 5-12

Form Wizard, page 2

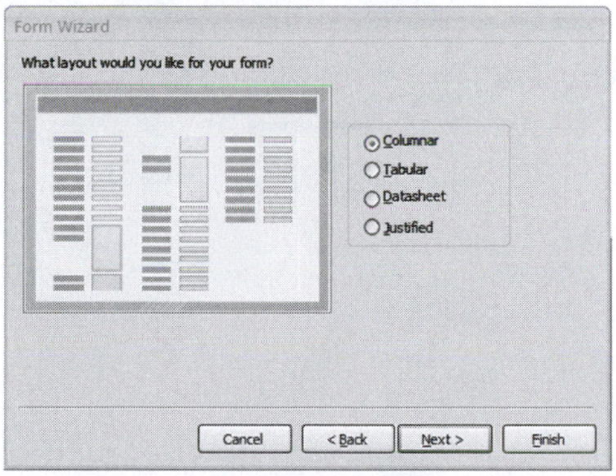

5. Click **Datasheet** as the layout for the form.

6. Click the **Next>** button to move to the next page in the Form Wizard, as shown in Figure 5-13.

Figure 5-13

Form Wizard, page 3

Form Wizard
What style would you like?
Label
Data
Access 2003
Access 2007
Apex
Aspect
Civic
Concourse
Equity
Flow
Foundry
Median
Metro
Module
None
Northwind
Cancel
< Back
Next >
Finish

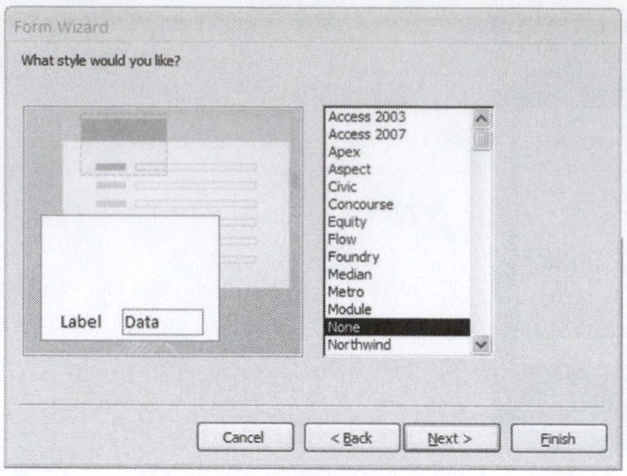

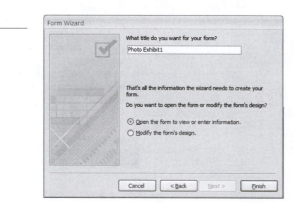

7. Click **None** as the style.
8. Click the **Next>** button to move to the final page in the Form Wizard, as shown in Figure 5-14.

Figure 5-14

Form Wizard, final page

Form Wizard
What title do you want for your form?
Photo Exhibit1
That's all the information the wizard needs to create your form.
Do you want to open the form or modify the form's design?
Open the form to view or enter information.
Modify the form's design.
Cancel
< Back
Next >
Finish

9. Key **Photo Details** as the title of the form.
10. Click the **Finish** button. A datasheet form appears, as shown in Figure 5-15.

Figure 5-15

Datasheet form

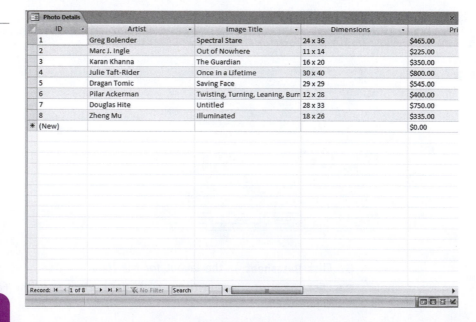

Photo Details
ID
Artist
Image Title
Dimensions
Pri
1 Greg Bolender Spectral Stare 24 x 36 $465.00
2 Marc J. Ingle Out of Nowhere 11 x 14 $225.00
3 Karan Khanna The Guardian 16 x 20 $350.00
4 Julie Taft-Rider Once in a Lifetime 30 x 40 $800.00
5 Dragan Tomic Saving Face 29 x 29 $545.00
6 Pilar Ackerman Twisting, Turning, Leaning, Burr 12 x 28 $400.00
7 Douglas Hite Untitled 28 x 33 $750.00
8 Zheng Mu Illuminated 18 x 26 $335.00
(New) $0.00
Record: 1 of 8
No Filter
Search

CERTIFICATION READY?
How do you create datasheet forms?
2.5.2

11. Click the **Close 'Photo Details'** button to close the form.

PAUSE. LEAVE the database open to use in the next exercise.

Another method of building a form is to use the **Form Wizard** tool. On the Create tab, in the Forms group, click More Forms, and then click Form Wizard. The Form Wizard allows you to select the fields that will appear on the form, choose the form layout, and also choose a predefined style, if desired.

In this exercise, you used the Form Wizard to create a datasheet form. Another way to quickly create a datasheet form that includes all the fields from the selected table is to click Datasheet on the More Forms menu.

TAKE NOTE*

To include fields from more than one table on your form, do not click Next or Finish after you select the fields from the first table on the first page of the Form Wizard. Instead, repeat the steps to select another table, and click any additional fields that you want to include on the form before continuing.

Applying AutoFormat

The AutoFormat command applies a predefined format to a form or report.

 APPLY AUTOFORMAT

USE the database that is open from the previous exercise.

1. Double-click the **Image Info** form in the Navigation Pane to open it.
2. On the Home tab, in the Views group, click the **View** button, and click **Layout View**.
3. On the Formatting tab, in the AutoFormat group, click the **More** button, shown in Figure 5-16.

Figure 5-16

AutoFormat group

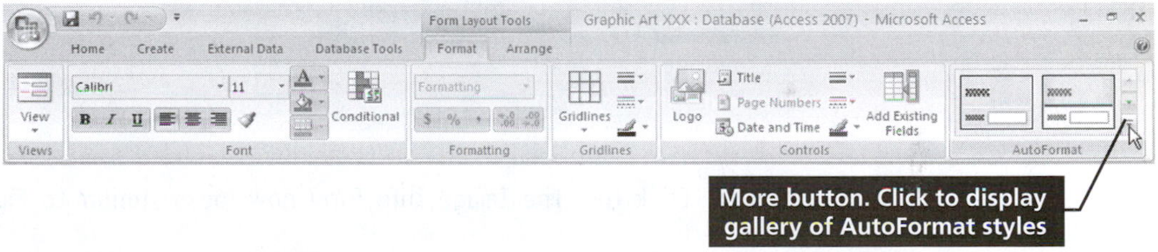

![AutoFormat group ribbon]

More button. Click to display gallery of AutoFormat styles

4. A gallery of format options appears, as shown in Figure 5-17.

Figure 5-17

AutoFormat options

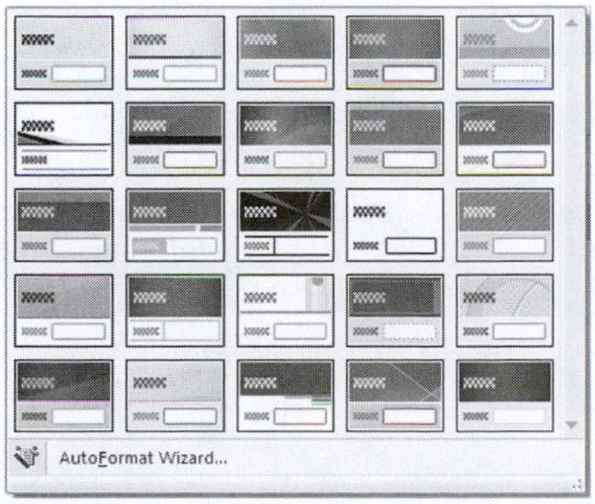

![AutoFormat options gallery]

5. Click **AutoFormat Wizard...** at the bottom of the gallery to display the AutoFormat dialog box, shown in Figure 5-18.

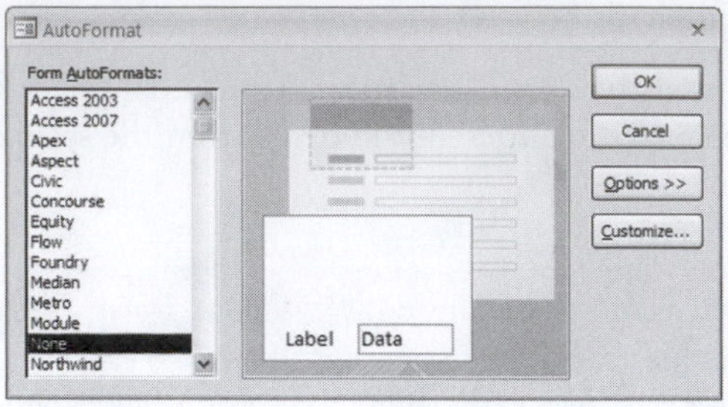

Figure 5-18

AutoFormat dialog box

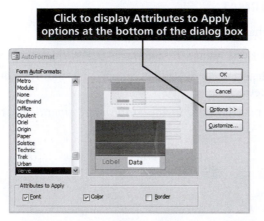

6. In the Form AutoFormats list, scroll down and click **Verve**.

7. Click the **Options>>** button. The Attributes to Apply box appears at the bottom of the dialog box.

8. Click the **Borders** checkbox to deselect it. The dialog box should look similar to Figure 5-19.

Figure 5-19

AutoFormat Attributes to Apply

9. Click **OK**. The Image Info form now looks similar to Figure 5-20.

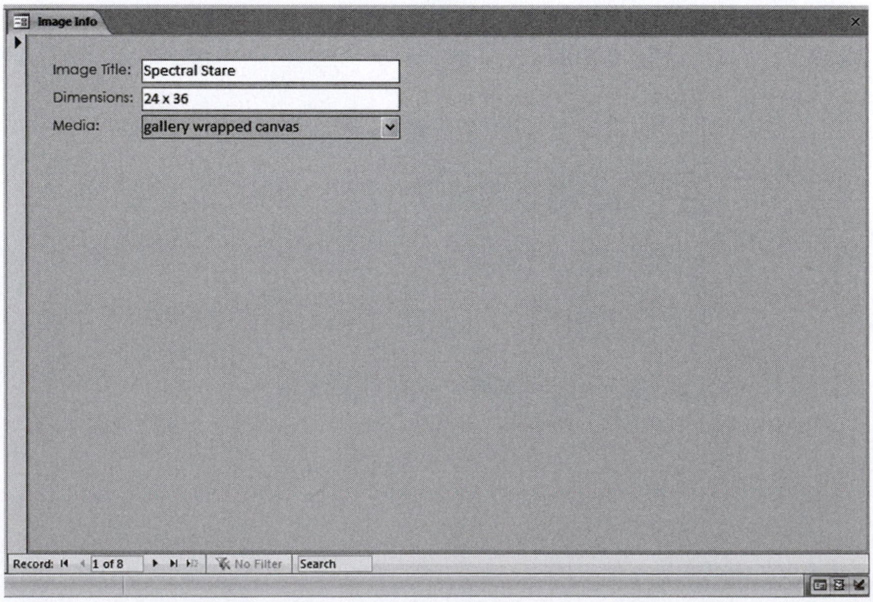

Figure 5-20

Form with AutoFormat applied

CERTIFICATION READY?
How do you apply AutoFormats to forms and reports?
2.7.7

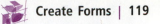

10. Click **Close 'Image Info'** to close the form. When asked if you want to save the changes, click **Yes**.

PAUSE. LEAVE the database open to use in the next exercise.

The ***AutoFormat*** command applies a predefined format that you select to a form or report. To access the AutoFormat options, first switch to Layout view. On the Formatting tab, in the AutoFormat group, click the More button to see a gallery of format styles from which to choose. You can point to each option to see the name of that format.

To manage the AutoFormats, click the AutoFormat Wizard at the bottom of the gallery to open the AutoFormats dialog box. Click the Options button to select which attributes—font, color, and border—that you want to apply. Click the Customize button to display options shown in Figure 5-21 that allow you to create, update, or delete an AutoFormat.

Figure 5-21
Customize AutoFormat dialog box

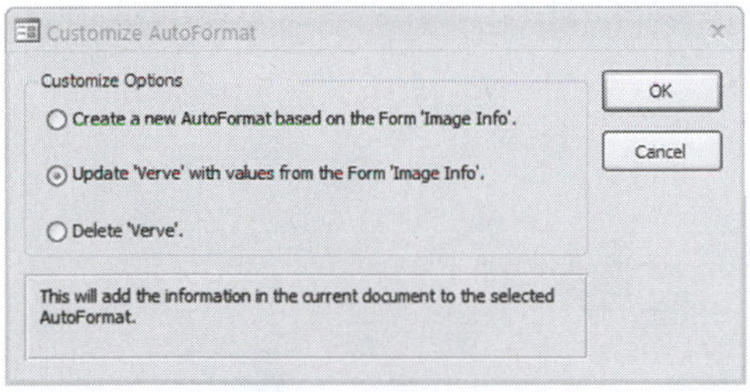
Customize AutoFormat
Customize Options
Create a new AutoFormat based on the Form 'Image Info'.
Update 'Verve' with values from the Form 'Image Info'.
Delete 'Verve'.
OK
Cancel
This will add the information in the current document to the selected AutoFormat.

Sorting Data Within a Form

Sorting data in a form can help make it much more effective and easy to use. Sorting helps users review and locate the records they want without having to browse the data.

SORT DATA WITHIN A FORM

USE the database that is open from the previous exercise.

1. Double-click the **Photo Label** form in the Navigation Pane to open it in Form view.
2. Right-click the **Price** field to display the shortcut menu shown in Figure 5-22.

Figure 5-22
Price field shortcut menu

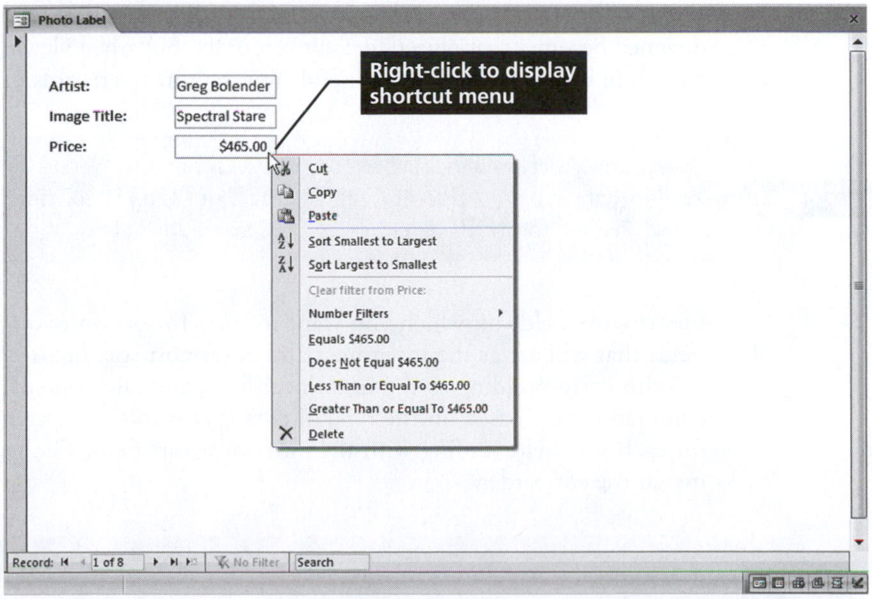
Photo Label
Artist:
Greg Bolender
Image Title:
Spectral Stare
Price:
$465.00
Right-click to display shortcut menu
Cut
Copy
Paste
Sort Smallest to Largest
Sort Largest to Smallest
Clear filter from Price:
Number Filters
Equals $465.00
Does Not Equal $465.00
Less Than or Equal To $465.00
Greater Than or Equal To $465.00
Delete
Record: 1 of 8
No Filter
Search

3. Click **Sort Smallest to Largest**. The form is sorted by price from smallest to largest. The record with the smallest price is displayed first, as shown in Figure 5-23.

Figure 5-23

Form sorted by price

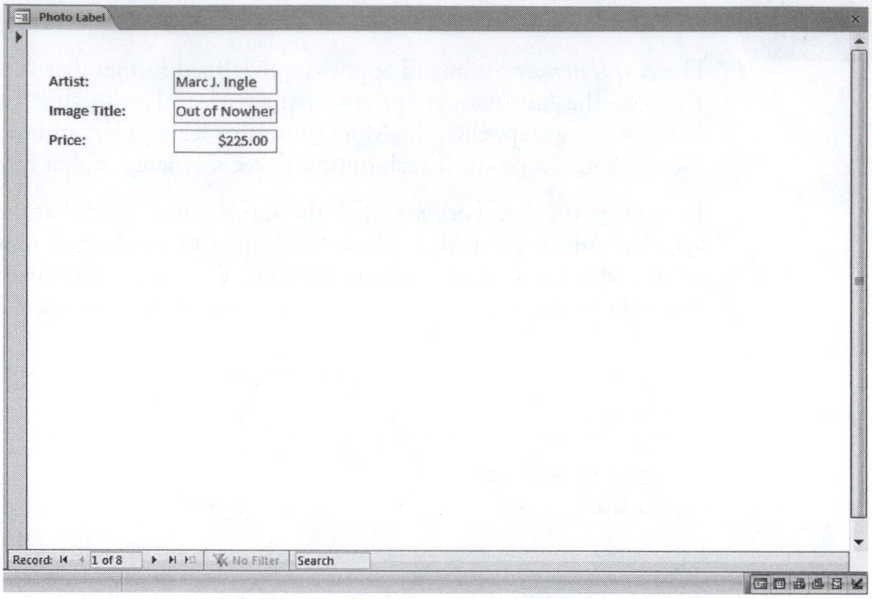

ANOTHER WAY

You can also sort on a field by selecting it and clicking the Ascending or Descending button on the Home tab in the Sort & Filter group.

4. Click the **Next record** button on the record navigator at the bottom of the form. Continue clicking through all the records to see the records in order according to price.

5. On the Home tab, in the Sort & Filter group, click the **Clear All Sorts** button.

6. Click **Close 'Photo Label'** to close the form.

PAUSE. LEAVE the database open to use in the next exercise.

CERTIFICATION READY?

How do you sort data within forms?

2.4.1

Data can be sorted in the Form view of a form. The order that is chosen when a form is designed becomes that object's default sort order. But when viewing the form, users can sort the records in whatever way is most useful. You can sort the records in a form on one or more fields.

TAKE NOTE*

You cannot sort on a field that contains attachments. When sorting on a field with the Yes/No data type, a value of "Yes," "True," or "On" is considered "Selected"; a value of "No," "False," or "Off" is considered "Cleared."

Identify the fields on which you want to sort. To sort on two or more fields, identify the fields that will act as the innermost and outermost sort fields. Right-click anywhere in the column corresponding to the innermost field, and click one of the sort commands. The commands vary based on the type of data that is in the selected field. Repeat the process for each sort field, ending with the outermost sort field. The records are rearranged to match the sort order.

X REF

You already learned how to sort data within a table in Lesson 3. Sorting in a form is very similar.

The last-applied sort order is automatically saved with the form. If you want it automatically applied the next time you open the form, make sure the Order By On Load property of the form is set to Yes. Remember that you cannot remove a sort order from just a single field. To remove sorting from all sort fields, on the Home tab, in the Sort & Filter group, click Clear All Sorts.

Filtering Data Within a Form

To find one or more specific records in a form, you can use a filter. A filter limits a view of data to specific records without requiring you to alter the design of the form.

⊙ **FILTER DATA WITH COMMON FILTERS**

USE the database that is open from the previous exercise.

1. Double-click the **Photo Exhibit** form in the Navigation Pane to open it in Form view.
2. Right-click the **Media** field to display the shortcut menu and click **Text Filters**, as shown in Figure 5-24.

Figure 5-24

Media field text filters

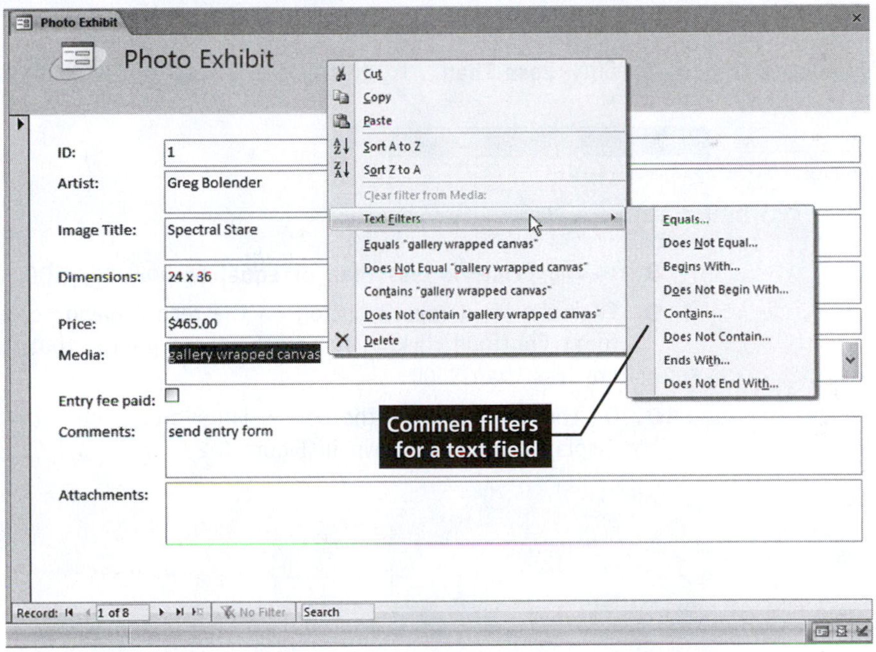

3. Click **Contains...** to display the Custom Filter dialog box, as shown in Figure 5-25.

Figure 5-25

Custom Filter dialog box

4. In the **Media: contains** box, key **print**, and click **OK**.
5. Click the **Next record** button on the record navigator at the bottom of the form. Continue clicking to see the five records that contain the word "print" in the Media field.
6. Right-click the **Price** field to display the shortcut menu and click **Number Filters**, as shown in Figure 5-26.

Figure 5-26

Price field number filters

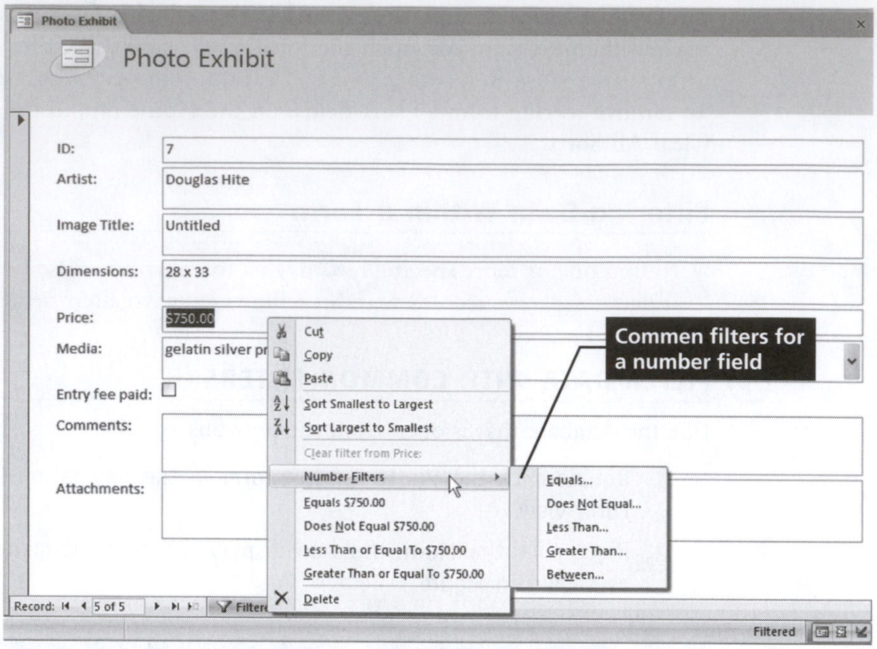

(Screenshot of Photo Exhibit form showing a record with ID: 7, Artist: Douglas Hite, Image Title: Untitled, Dimensions: 28 x 33, Price: $750.00, Media: gelatin silver print, and a right-click context menu displaying options: Cut, Copy, Paste, Sort Smallest to Largest, Sort Largest to Smallest, Clear filter from Price:, Number Filters, Equals $750.00, Does Not Equal $750.00, Less Than or Equal To $750.00, Greater Than or Equal To $750.00, Delete. A submenu for Number Filters shows: Equals..., Does Not Equal..., Less Than..., Greater Than..., Between... A callout reads "Commen filters for a number field.")

7. Click **Less Than...** to display the Custom Filter dialog box shown in Figure 5-27.

Figure 5-27

Custom Filter dialog box

(Screenshot of Custom Filter dialog box with label "Price: is less than or equal to" and an input field, with OK and Cancel buttons.)

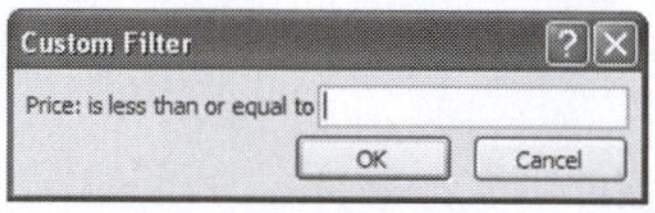

8. In the **Price: is less than or equal to** box, key **500**, and click **OK**.

9. Click the **Next record** button on the record navigator at the bottom of the form. Continue clicking to see the three photos that use print media and are less than $500.

10. On the Home tab, in the Sort & Filter group, click the **Advanced** button to display the menu shown in Figure 5-28.

Figure 5-28

Advanced button menu

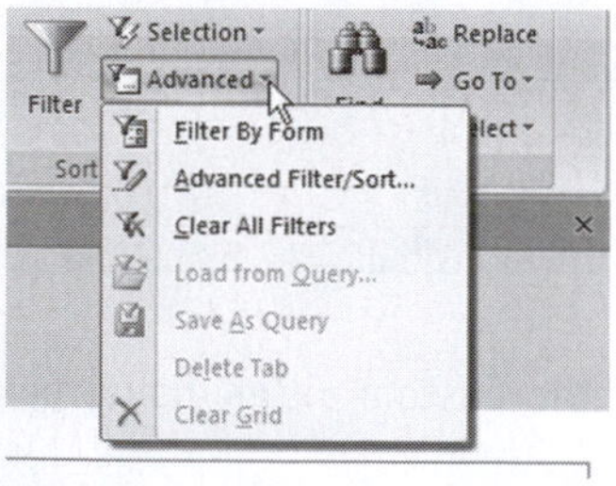

(Screenshot of Advanced button menu showing: Selection, Advanced, Replace, Go To, Filter By Form, Advanced Filter/Sort..., Clear All Filters, Load from Query..., Save As Query, Delete Tab, Clear Grid.)

CERTIFICATION READY?
How do you filter data within forms?
5.2.4

11. Click **Clear All Filters**.

PAUSE. LEAVE the database open to use in the next exercise.

X REF

You already learned how to filter data within a table in Lesson 3. Filtering in a form using common filters is very similar.

Filters are easy to apply and remove. ***Common filters*** are built into every view that displays data. The filters available depend on the type and values of the field. When you apply the filter, only records that contain the values that you are interested in are included in the view. The rest are hidden until you remove the filter.

Filter settings remain in effect until you close the form, even if you switch to another view. If you save the form while the filter is applied, it will be available the next time that you open the form. To permanently remove a filter, on the Home tab, in the Sort & Filter group, click the Advanced button and click Clear All Filters.

Although only a single filter can be in effect for any one field at any one time, you can specify a different filter for each field that is present in the view. In addition to the ready-to-use filters for each data type, you can also filter a form by completing a form called Filter by Form.

 FILTER BY FORM

USE the database that is open from the previous exercise.

1. On the Home tab, in the Sort & Filter group, click the **Advanced** button and click **Filter by Form**. A form filter appears, as shown in Figure 5-29.

Figure 5-29

Form filter

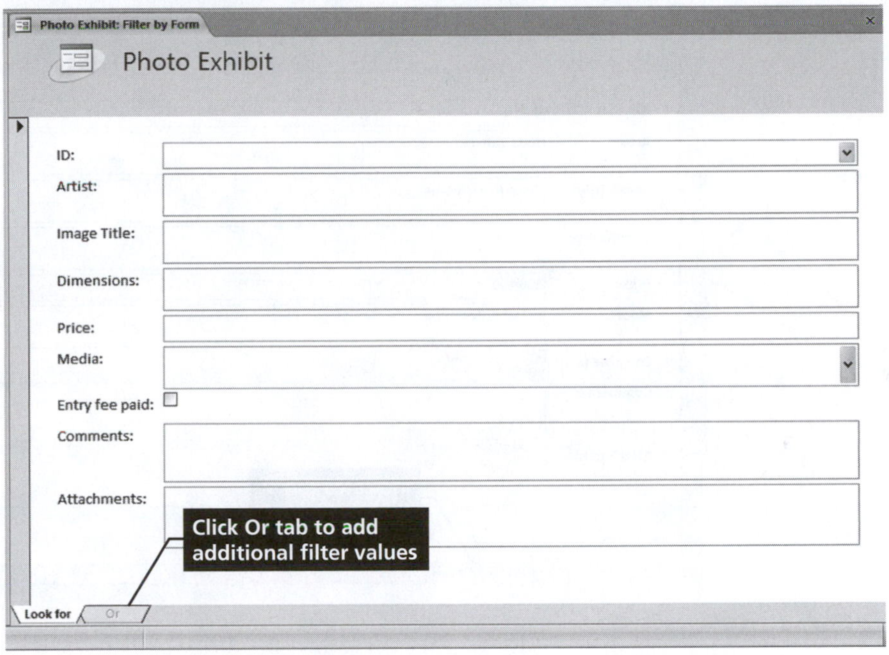

> Photo Exhibit: Filter by Form
>
> Photo Exhibit
>
> ID:
> Artist:
> Image Title:
> Dimensions:
> Price:
> Media:
> Entry fee paid: ☐
> Comments:
> Attachments:
>
> **Click Or tab to add additional filter values**
>
> Look for / Or

2. Place the insertion point in the **Dimensions** box and click the **down arrow** on the right to display the list of options shown in Figure 5-30.

Figure 5-30

Form filter field options

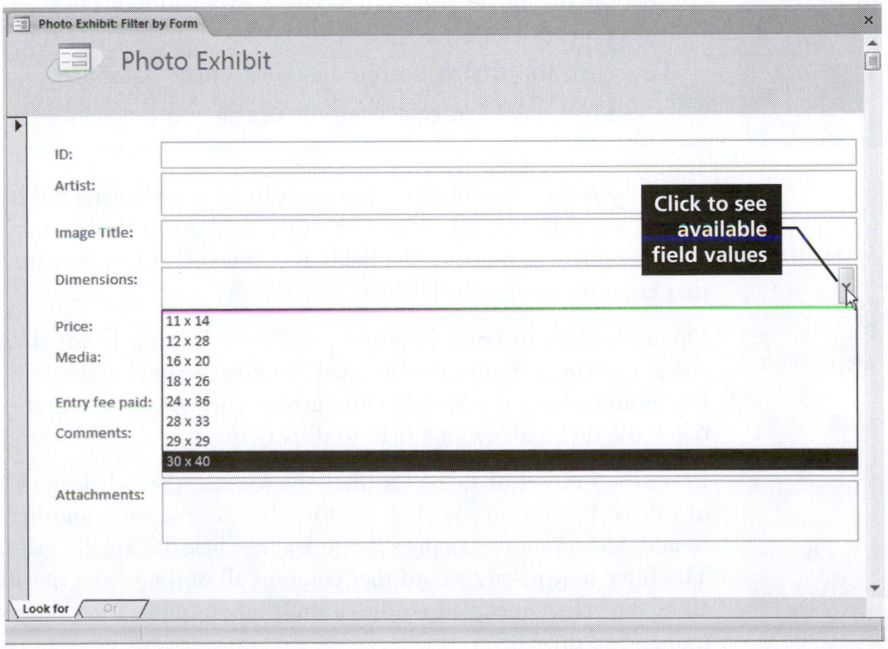

> Photo Exhibit: Filter by Form
>
> Photo Exhibit
>
> ID:
> Artist:
> Image Title:
> Dimensions:
>
> **Click to see available field values**
>
> Price: 11 x 14
>   12 x 28
> Media: 16 x 20
>   18 x 26
> Entry fee paid: 24 x 36
>   28 x 33
> Comments: 29 x 29
>   30 x 40
>
> Attachments:
>
> Look for / Or

3. Click **30 × 40**.

4. Click the **Or** tab at the bottom of the form.

5. Place the insertion point in the **Dimensions** box, click the **down arrow**, and then click **12 × 28**.

6. On the Home tab, in the Sort & Filter group, click the **Toggle Filter** button to apply the filter. The records containing either the dimensions 30 × 40 or 12 × 28 are displayed, as shown in Figure 5-31.

Figure 5-31

Form filter results

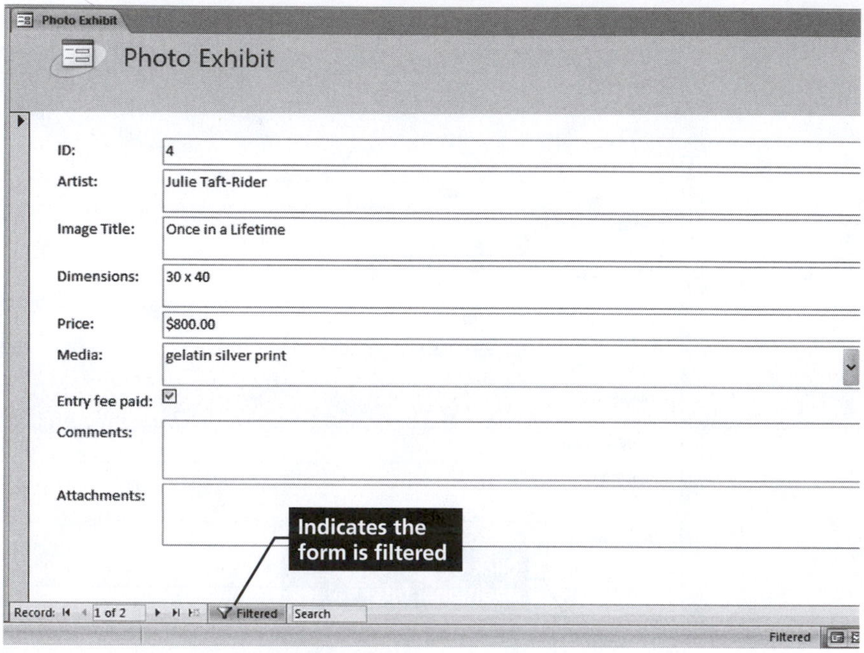

7. Click the **Next record** button on the record navigator at the bottom of the form to see the second record in the form filter results.

8. On the Home tab, in the Sort & Filter group, click the **Toggle Filter** button again to remove the filter.

9. On the Home tab, in the Sort & Filter group, click the **Advanced** button and click **Clear All Filters**.

10. Click the **Office Button** and click **Close Database**.

   STOP. LEAVE Access open for use in the projects.

CERTIFICATION READY?
How do you filter data within forms?
5.2.4

Filter by form is useful when you want to filter on several fields in a form or if you are trying to find a specific record. Access creates a blank form that is similar to the original form, you then complete as many of the fields as you want. When you are done, Access finds the records that contain the specified values.

Open the form in Form view and make sure the view is not already filtered by verifying that either the Unfiltered or the dimmed No Filter icon is present on the record selector bar. On the Home tab, in the Sort & Filter group, click Advanced, and then click Filter by Form. Click the down arrow in a field to display the available values.

TAKE NOTE *

If you want a field value to operate as a filter that is independent of other field values, you must enter that value on the Look for tab and each Or tab. In other words, the Look for tab and each Or tab represents an alternate set of filter values.

Enter the first set of values on the Look for tab, then click the Or tab and enter the next set of values. Each time you click the Or tab, Access creates another Or tab so you can continue to add additional filter values if you want. Click the Toggle Field button to apply the filter. The filter returns any record that contains all of the values specified on the Look for tab, or all of the values specified on the first Or tab, or all of the values specified on the second Or tab, and so on.

SUMMARY SKILL MATRIX

IN THIS LESSON YOU LEARNED	MATRIX SKILL	SKILL NUMBER
To create forms	Create forms	2.5
To create a simple form	Create simple forms	2.5.8
To create a form in Design view	Create forms using Design view	2.5.1
To create a form in Layout view	Create forms using Layout view	2.5.7
To create a datasheet form	Create datasheet forms	2.5.2
To apply AutoFormat	Apply AutoFormats to forms and reports	2.7.7
To sort data within a form	Sort data within forms	5.1.4
To filter data within a form	Filter data within forms	5.2.4

■ Knowledge Assessment

Matching

Match the term in Column 1 to its description in Column 2.

Column 1	Column 2
1. Form Wizard	a. useful when you want to filter on several fields in a form or if you are trying to find a specific record
2. Form Design button	b. creates a simple form with a single mouse-click
3. AutoFormat command	c. applies a predefined format that you select to a form or report
4. Blank Form button	d. quickly creates a new blank form in Design view
5. form	e. allows you to select fields for the form, choose the form layout, and also choose a predefined style
6. Filter by Form	f. limits a view of data to specific records without requiring you to alter the design of the form
7. sorting	g. built into every view that displays data
8. Form tool	h. database object that you can use to enter, edit, or display data from a table or a query
9. common filters	i. helps users review and locate records without having to browse the data
10. filter	j. quickly creates a new blank form in Layout view

True / False

Circle T if the statement is true or F if the statement is false.

T | F **1.** The Forms group is located on the Home tab in the Ribbon.

T | F **2.** Forms can be used to control access to data, such as which fields or rows of data are displayed.

T | F   3. After you save your form design, you can run the form as often as you want.

T | F   4. Layout view gives you a more detailed view of the structure of your form than Design view.

T | F   5. Using the Blank Form tool is a very quick way to build a form, especially if you plan to put only a few fields on your form.

T | F   6. To access the AutoFormat options, first switch to Form view.

T | F   7. You cannot remove a sort order from just a single field.

T | F   8. The filters available depend on the field's data type and values.

T | F   9. To filter by form, first switch to Design view.

T | F   10. When using the Form Wizard, you can only include fields from one table.

■ Competency Assessment

Project 5-1: Form Wizard

As a travel agent at Margie's Travel, you need an easy way to input data about events into the database. You decide to use the Form Wizard to create a datasheet form that has a preformatted style.

GET READY. Launch Access if it is not already running.

1. **OPEN** *Travel Events* from the data files for this lesson.
2. **SAVE** the database as *Travel Events XXX* (where XXX is your initials).
3. On the Create tab, in the Forms group, click the **More Forms** button, and click **Form Wizard.**
4. Click the **>>** button to move all the fields from the Available Fields box to the Selected Fields box.
5. Click the **Next>** button to move to the next page in the Form Wizard.
6. Click **Datasheet** as the layout for the form.
7. Click the **Next>** button to move to the next page in the Form Wizard.
8. Click **Module** as the style.
9. Click the **Next>** button to move to the final page in the Form Wizard.
10. Key **Event Details** as the title of the form.
11. Click the **Finish** button to create a datasheet form.
12. On the Home tab, in the Views group, click the **View** button, and click **Form View**.
13. Click the **'Close Event Details'** button to close the form.
14. **CLOSE** the database.

    LEAVE Access open for the next project.

The *Travel Events* database file is available on the companion CD-ROM.

Project 5-2: Used Games Forms

You are the manager at Southridge Video. To expand the store, you have recently started taking used games in trade. You store information about each title in an Access database. You decide to create some forms to help you use the database more efficiently.

1. **OPEN** *Games inventory* from the data files for this lesson.
2. SAVE the database as *Games inventory XXX* (where XXX is your initials).
3. In the Navigation Pane, double-click **Games: Table** to open the table.

The *Games inventory* database file is available on the companion CD-ROM.

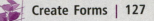

4. On the Create tab, in the Forms group, click the **Form** button to create a simple form and display it in Layout view.

5. Click the **Office Button** and click **Save**.

6. In the Save As dialog box, click **OK** to accept the *Games* form name suggested by Access.

7. Click the **Close 'Games'** button to close the form.

8. On the Create tab, in the Forms group, click the **Form Design** button to create a new blank form in Design view.

9. On the Design tab, in the Tools group, click the **Add Existing Fields** button to display the Field List pane.

10. Click the **+** next to Games to list the available fields.

11. Double-click **Title** to add it to the form.

12. Double-click **Rating** to add it to the form.

13. Double-click **Platform** to add it to the form.

14. Click the **Office Button** and click **Save**.

15. In the Save As dialog box, key **Game Rating**, and click **OK**.

16. Click the **Close** button to close the Field List.

17. On the Design menu, in the Views group, click the **View button** and click **Form View** to display form in Form view.

18. Click the **Close 'Game Rating'** button to close the form.

19. **LEAVE** the database open for the next project.

LEAVE Access open for the next project.

■ Proficiency Assessment

Project 5-3: Sort and Filter Games

A customer comes into Southridge Video and asks about game publishers and the availability of a particular game. Sort and filter data in the forms you created to get the information that you need.

USE the database that is open from the previous project.

1. In the Navigation Pane, double-click the **Games** form to open it.

2. Right-click the **Publisher** field to display the shortcut menu.

3. Click **Sort A to Z** to sort the form by publisher name in alphabetic order.

4. Navigate to **record 3**, titled *Marvel: Ultimate Alliance*.

5. Right-click the **Title** field and click **Equals "Marvel: Ultimate Alliance"**.

6. Click the **Next record** button on the record navigator at the bottom of the form to see all the versions of the game with that name.

7. On the Home tab, in the Sort & Filter group, click the **Clear All Sorts** button.

8. **CLOSE** the database.

LEAVE Access open for the next project.

Project 5-4: Toy Inventory

Your brother owns Wingtip Toys and recently started keeping a list of the store inventory in an Access database. He wants to add a form to the database and asks for your help. Add a simple form and then show him how to sort and apply filters.

The *Toy inventory* database file is available on the companion CD-ROM.

1. **OPEN** *Toy inventory* from the data files for this lesson.
2. Save the database as *Toy inventory XXX* (where XXX is your initials).
3. Open **Inventory: Table**.
4. Use the **Form** tool to create a simple form.
5. Format it using the **Trek** style AutoFormat option.
6. Save the form as **Inventory**.
7. Sort the **In Stock** field from **Largest to Smallest**.
8. Sort the **Description** field from **A to Z**.
9. Run a filter that finds all the records where the **Price** field is **between $50 and $100**.
10. Clear all sorts and filters.
11. Create a filter by form to find all the records that have two items in stock.
12. **CLOSE** the form and close the database.

    LEAVE Access open for the next project.

■ Mastery Assessment

Project 5-5: Red Wines

The Coho Vineyard has started a monthly wine club. Each month features a red wine hand-picked for its unique label and diverse style. Information about the monthly club selections is stored in an Access database; you will create forms so that you can retrieve the data in a useful way.

The *Red Wine* database file is available on the companion CD-ROM.

1. Open the *Red Wine* database from the data files for this lesson.
2. Save the database as *Red Wine XXX* (where XXX is your initials).
3. Create a simple form that contains all the fields in the Club Selections table and name it **Club Wines**.
4. Use the Form Design button to create a form named **Wine Details** that looks like the one shown in Figure 5-32 when displayed in Form view.

Figure 5-32

Wine Details form

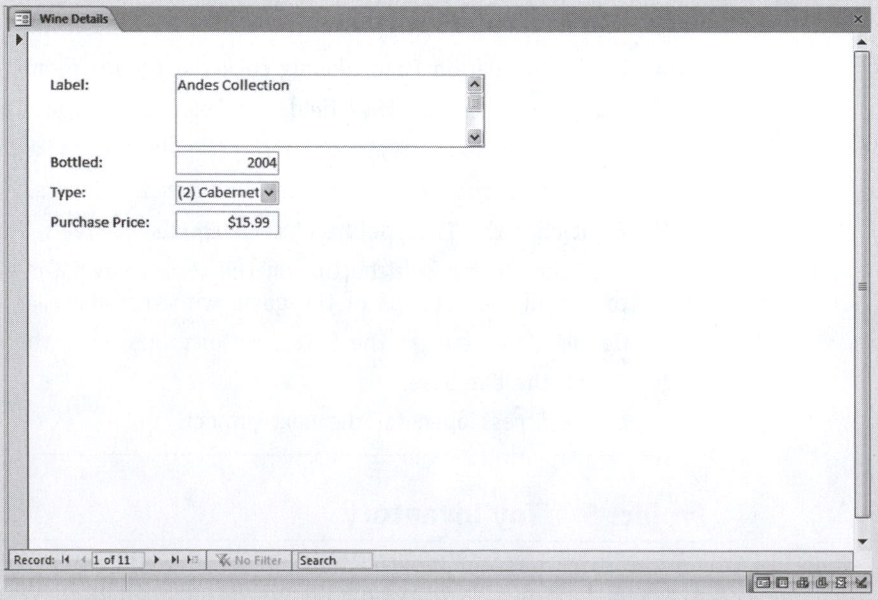

Wine Details		×
Label:	Andes Collection	
Bottled:	2004	
Type:	(2) Cabernet	
Purchase Price:	$15.99	

Record: 1 of 11   No Filter   Search

5. **CLOSE** the database.

   LEAVE Access open for the next project.

Project 5-6: Personal Contacts

Your address book is becoming outdated, and you decide to transfer all the current information about friends and family to an Access database. Input the data and then create forms to manage it efficiently.

The *Personal Contacts* database file is available on the companion CD-ROM.

1. **OPEN** *Personal Contacts* from the data files for this lesson.
2. **SAVE** the database as *Personal Contacts XXX* (where XXX is your initials).
3. Input as much contact information as you have about at least five friends or family members.
4. Create at least two forms that help you input, sort, or filter the data in a useful way. Use AutoFormats to improve the look of the forms.
5. **CLOSE** the database.

   STOP. CLOSE Access.

INTERNET READY

Microsoft has numerous online resources available to provide solutions, services, and support for whatever business needs you may have. If you are in small business, a helpful site is the Microsoft Small Business Center. Here, you can find advice, products, tools, and information tailored to small businesses. Search the Microsoft site for the Small Business Center, shown in Figure 5-33.

Figure 5-33

Microsoft Small Business Center

Explore the resources offered on the site. In the Articles & Research section, choose a topic about which you would like to know more, and read an article that interests you.

↻ Circling Back

You are a real estate agent and have recently opened your own office—Woodgrove Real Estate—with several other licensed agents. Because you are the one who is most knowledgeable about computers, you will be responsible for keeping track of the listings and other relevant information. You will use Access to begin developing the database that will be used by everyone in the office.

➜ Project 1: Create a Database and Tables

After sketching out a plan on paper, you are ready to begin creating the database and tables.

GET READY. Launch Access if it is not already running.

1. In the New Blank Database section, click the **Blank Database icon.** A Blank Database pane appears.
2. In the File Name box, key **WoodgroveXXX** (where XXX is your initials).
3. Click the folder icon and browse to the location where you want to store the file.
4. Click the **Create** button to create a new blank database.
5. Right-click **Add New Field** and click **Rename Column** on the shortcut menu.
6. Key **Address** and press ⎡Enter⎤.
7. Add new columns named **Bedrooms**, **Bathrooms**, **Square Feet**, and **Price**.
8. Click the **Microsoft Office Button** and click **Save**.
9. In the Save As dialog box, key **Listings** as the table name and click **OK**.
10. On the Create tab, in the Tables group, click the **Table Templates** button, and click **Contacts** to create a new table.
11. Right-click the **Company** field header and click **Delete Column** on the shortcut menu.
12. Delete the Job Title, Business Phone, Fax Number, Address, City, State/Province, ZIP/Postal Code, Country/Region, Web Page, Notes, and Attachment columns. (If you get a message asking if you want to delete all indexes for the ZIP column, click **Yes**.)
13. Save the table as **Agents**.

    PAUSE. LEAVE the database open to use in the next project.

➜ Project 2: Modify Tables and Fields

Now that you have created the tables for your database, you need to modify them to suit your needs.

USE the database that is open from the previous project. The Agents table should be displayed.

1. On the Home tab, in the Views group, click **Design** view.
2. On the Home tab, in the Show/Hide group, click **Property Sheet**.
3. In the Description property box, key **Agent contact information**.
4. Click **Close** to close the property sheet.
5. In the upper portion of the table design grid, click the **E-mail Address field.** In the field properties on the bottom, click in the Required property box and set it to **Yes**.
6. **SAVE** the table and switch back to **Datasheet** view.
7. Click the **Listings** table tab to switch to that table. Place the insertion point in the **Price** column.

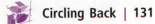

8. On the Datasheet tab, in the Data Type & Formatting group, click the **down arrow** in the Data Type box and click **Number**.

9. In the Format box, click the **down arrow** and choose **Currency**.

10. Change the data type/format on the Bedrooms, Bathrooms, and Square Feet fields to **Number/General Number**.

11. Click the **Add New Field** column. Choose **Attachment** as the data type to create an attachment column.

12. **SAVE** the table.

   PAUSE. LEAVE the database open for the next project.

Project 3: Create Forms and Enter Data

Now it is time to enter data into your database. First you create a form to make this task easier.

USE the database that is open from the previous project. The Listings table should be displayed.

1. On the Create tab, in the Forms group, click the **More Forms** button.

2. Click **Datasheet** to create a datasheet form.

3. Click the **Microsoft Office Button** and click **Save**.

4. In the Save As dialog box, key **Listings** as the form name and click **OK**.

5. Use the form to enter data into the Listings table, as shown in Figure 1.

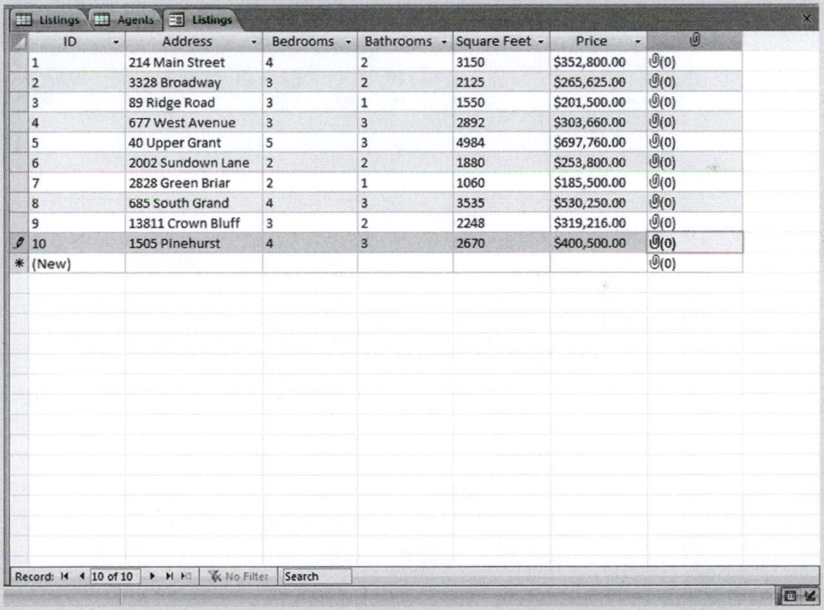

Figure 1

Listings data

ID	Address	Bedrooms	Bathrooms	Square Feet	Price	📎
1	214 Main Street	4	2	3150	$352,800.00	(0)
2	3328 Broadway	3	2	2125	$265,625.00	(0)
3	89 Ridge Road	3	1	1550	$201,500.00	(0)
4	677 West Avenue	3	3	2892	$303,660.00	(0)
5	40 Upper Grant	5	3	4984	$697,760.00	(0)
6	2002 Sundown Lane	2	2	1880	$253,800.00	(0)
7	2828 Green Briar	2	1	1060	$185,500.00	(0)
8	685 South Grand	4	3	3535	$530,250.00	(0)
9	13811 Crown Bluff	3	2	2248	$319,216.00	(0)
10	1505 Pinehurst	4	3	2670	$400,500.00	(0)
(New)						(0)

Record: ◄ ◄ 10 of 10 ► ►► No Filter   Search

6. Display the **Agents** table.

7. On the Create tab, in the Forms group, click the **Form** button.

8. Save the form as **Agents**.

9. Switch to Form view and use the form to enter the data shown in Figure 2.

Figure 2

Agents data, record 1

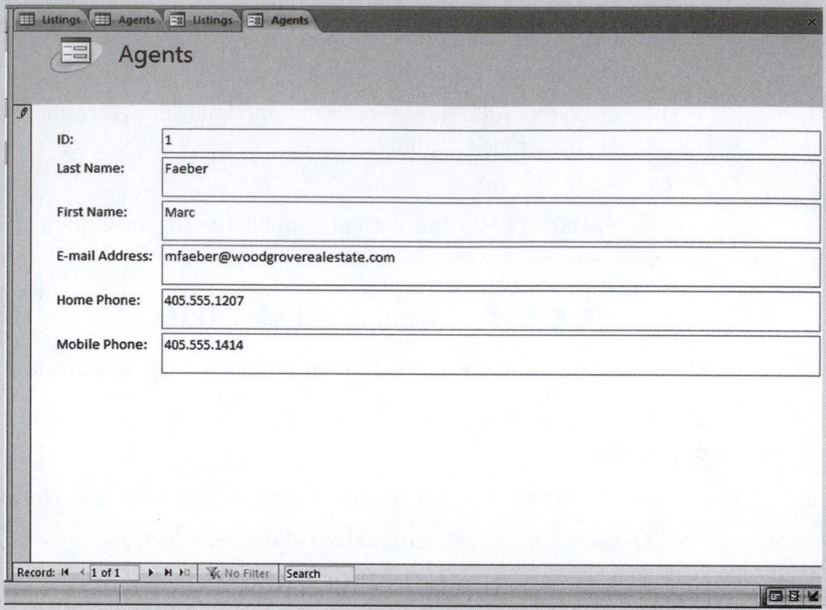

10. Click the **Next record** button on the record navigator.

11. Enter the data shown in Figure 3 as the second record.

Figure 3

Agents data, record 2

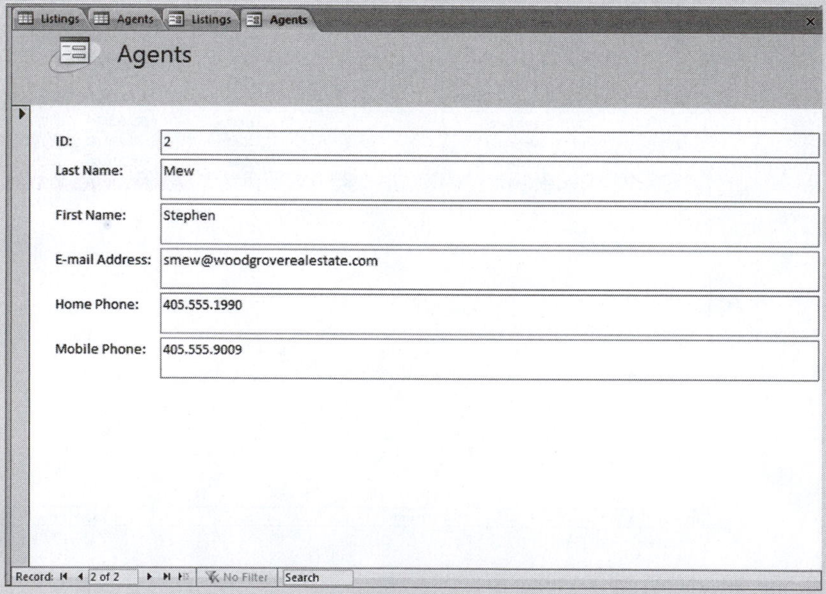

12. Enter the data shown in Figure 4 as the third record.

Figure 4

Agents data, record 3

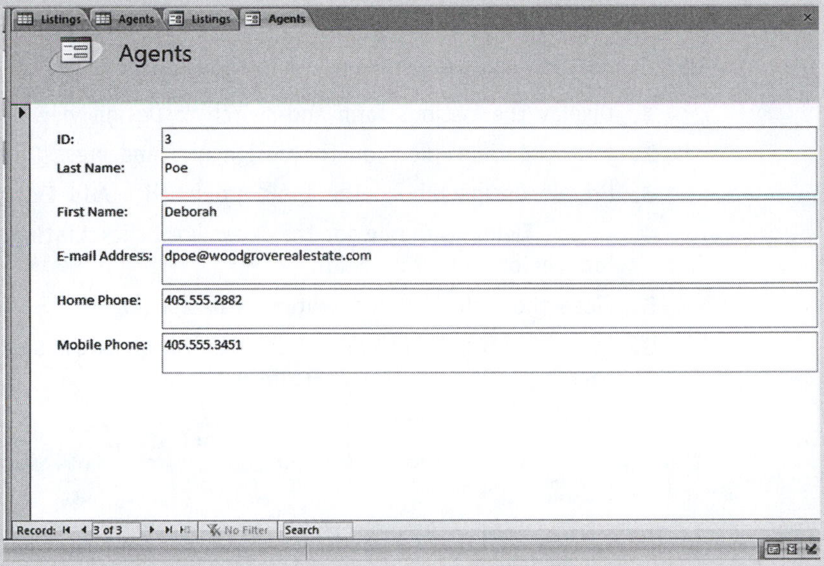

13. CLOSE the Agents form and the Listings form.

PAUSE. LEAVE the database open for the next project.

Project 4: **Add Attachments and Create a Lookup Field**

You have begun to use the database and realize it would be helpful for the Listings table to include the listing agent. Create a lookup field with this information and attach photos for some of the houses.

USE the database that is open from the previous project

1. In the Listings table, double-click the **Attachment field for the fourth record** (677 West Avenue).
2. In the Attachments dialog box, click **Add**.
3. Navigate to the data files for this lesson, select *677_West_Avenue*, and click **Open**.
4. In the Attachments dialog box, click **OK**.
5. Attach the photo named **2002_Sundown_Lane** to the sixth record.
6. **CLOSE** the Listings form.
7. Display the Listings table and place the insertion point in the Add New Field column.
8. On the Datasheet tab, in the Fields & Columns group, click the **Lookup Column** button.
9. Click **Next>** twice.
10. Click **Last Name** and then click the **>** button to move it to the Selected Fields box.
11. Click **Next>** three times.
12. Key **Listing Agent** as the title for your lookup column.
13. Click **Finish**.
14. **SAVE** the **Listings** table.

PAUSE. LEAVE the database open for the next project.

The *677_West_Avenue* file is available on the companion CD-ROM.

The *2002_Sundown_Lane* file is available on the companion CD-ROM.

Project 5: Modify a Form

Now that you have a lookup field, you want to add it to your form and use it to enter additional information.

USE the database that is open from the previous project.

1. Display the Listings form and switch to Design view.
2. Click the Field1 field on the design grid and press Delete.
3. On the Design tab, in the Tools group, click **Add Existing Fields**.
4. In the Fields available for this view box, click **Listing Agent** and drag it to the form below the Price field.
5. Close the Field List and switch to Datasheet view.
6. In the Listing Agent column click the down arrow and select the last name for each record, as shown in Figure 5.

Figure 5

Listing agents

ID	Address	Bedrooms	Bathrooms	Square Feet	Price	Listing Agent
1	214 Main Street	4	2	3150	$352,800.00	Faeber
2	3328 Broadway	3	2	2125	$265,625.00	Faeber
3	89 Ridge Road	3	1	1550	$201,500.00	Poe
4	677 West Avenue	3	3	2892	$303,660.00	Mew
5	40 Upper Grant	5	3	4984	$697,760.00	Faeber
6	2002 Sundown Lane	2	2	1880	$253,800.00	Poe
7	2828 Green Briar	2	1	1060	$185,500.00	Poe
8	685 South Grand	4	3	3535	$530,250.00	Faeber
9	13811 Crown Bluff	3	2	2248	$319,216.00	Mew
10	1505 Pinehurst	4	3	2670	$435,210.00	Faeber
*	(New)					

7. **CLOSE** the form.

STOP. CLOSE the database.

Create Reports

LESSON SKILL MATRIX

Skills	Matrix Skill	Skill Number
Creating a Simple Report	Create reports as a simple report	2.6.1
Using the Report Wizard	Create reports by using the Report Wizard	2.6.2
Creating a Report in Design View	Create reports by using Design view	2.6.3
Applying AutoFormat	Apply AutoFormats to forms and reports	2.7.7
Sorting Data Within a Report	Sort data within reports	5.1.3
Filtering Data Within a Report	Filter data within reports	5.2.3

Alpine Ski House is a small mountain lodge that features cross-country skiing in the winter and hiking in the summer. As an administrative assistant for Alpine Ski House, you take care of many of the administrative duties for the innkeepers, including reservations, billing, and recordkeeping. You have recently started using Access to keep track of customers and reservations at the lodge. In this lesson, you will learn three different ways to create reports for the lodge. You will also learn to apply Auto Formats to reports as well as sort and filter report data.

KEY TERMS
record source
report

■ SOFTWARE ORIENTATION

Reports Group

The Reports group is located on the Create tab in the Ribbon.

Figure 6-1

Reports group

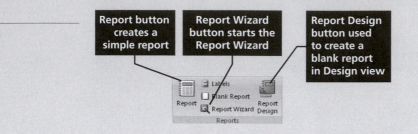

Use the Reports group of commands to create reports.

■ Creating Reports

THE BOTTOM LINE

Reports display data pulled from tables and queries. You can create a report using the Report button, the Report Wizard, or Design view, depending on the amount of customization desired. After creating a report, you can apply an AutoFormat to create an instant professional look. You can also sort and filter data in a report to display the records to suit your needs.

Creating a Simple Report

You can use Access 2007 to create simple or complex reports. When creating a complex report, you might spend quite a bit of time choosing which fields you want to include from various tables or queries. That is fine when you need such a report, but when you need a simple display of all the fields in a table or query you can use the Report button to create a simple report.

⊕ CREATE A REPORT

GET READY. Before you begin these steps, be sure to turn on and/or log on to your computer and start Access.

The **AlpineSkiHouse** database is available on the companion CD-ROM.

1. **OPEN** *AlpineSkiHouse* from the data files for this lesson.

2. Save the database as *AlpineSkiHouseXXX* (where XXX is your initials).

3. In the Navigation Pane, click the **Rooms** table to select it. This is your record source.

4. On the Create tab, in the Reports group, click the **Report** button. The report appears in Layout view, as shown in Figure 6-2. Notice the Report Layout tools that appear in the Ribbon.

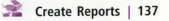

Figure 6-2

Simple report

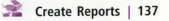

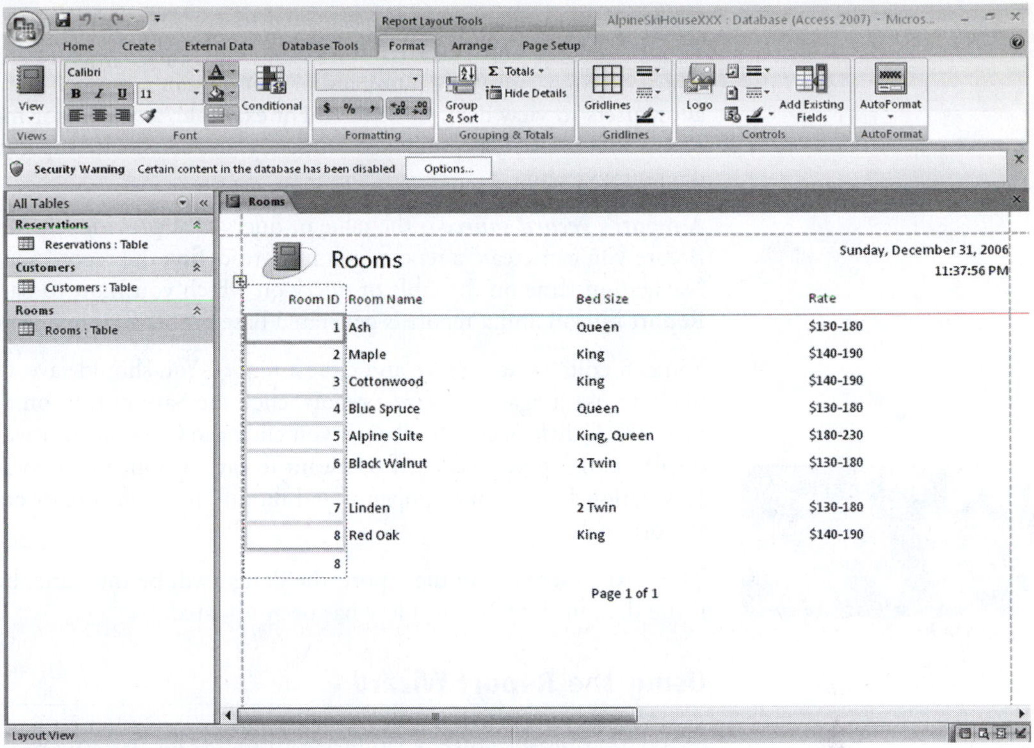

5. Click the **Room ID** header to select it. Position the pointer over the right border until you see a double-sided arrow. Click and drag to the left, resizing the column to remove excess white space.

6. Resize the other columns until your screen looks similar to Figure 6-3.

Figure 6-3

Report with resized columns

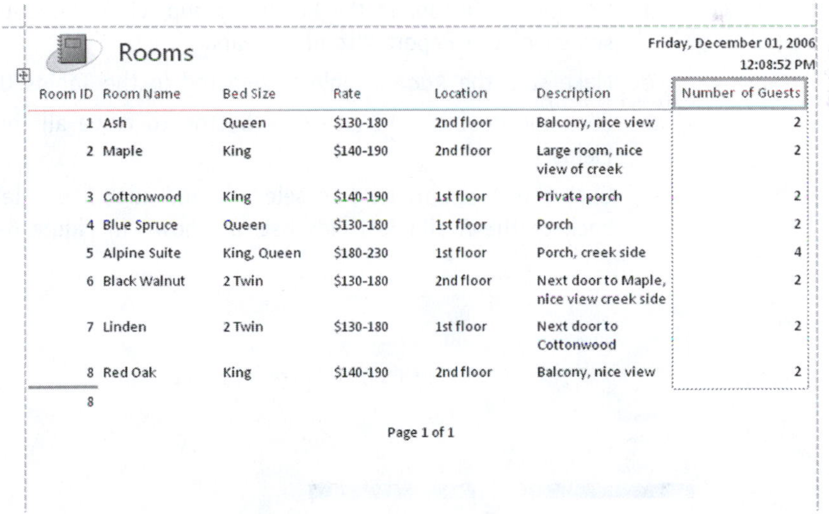

7. Click the **Save** button on the Quick Access Toolbar. The Save As dialog box appears with *Rooms* in the Report Name box. Click **OK.** Notice that the Rooms report is listed in the Navigation Pane.

8. Click the **Close** button to close the Rooms report.

PAUSE. LEAVE the database open to use in the next exercise.

A *report* is a database object that is used to organize and display data from tables and queries. Reports are commonly used as formatted hard copies of table or query data. You can modify a report's design, but you cannot add or edit data in a report. The purpose of a report is to allow users to view data, not edit it. For example, a supervisor might ask you to create a sales report that is filtered to show only one region's sales. The supervisor does not need to edit the data, just view it.

A report's *record source* is the table or query that provides the data used to generate a report. Before you can create a report, you need to define the record source by clicking in the Navigation Pane on the table or query on which you want to base the report. Then, click the Report button and a report is generated based on the table or query you selected.

You can edit, print, or save and close a report. You should save a report's design if you are likely to use it again. To save a report, click the Save button on the Microsoft Office Button or in the Quick Access Toolbar. If you click the Close button without saving, Access will display a dialog box asking if you want to save it. Once it is saved, the report is listed in the Navigation Pane. You can open it and modify in the future or create a new report based on the original.

The next time you run the report, the design will be the same, but the data will be different if the data in the table or query has been updated.

CERTIFICATION READY?
How do you create a simple report?
2.6.1

Using the Report Wizard

You are probably already familiar with the way a "wizard" works. The Report Wizard displays a series of questions about the report you want and then it creates the report for you based on your answers. The Report Wizard knows what makes a good report, so the questions are designed to help you create a professional report with little effort.

➔ USE THE REPORT WIZARD

USE the database you used in the previous exercise.

1. On the Create tab, in the Reports group, click the **Report Wizard** button. The first screen of the Report Wizard appears.

2. Make sure the **Rooms** table is selected in the Tables/Queries menu.

3. Click the double right arrow **>>** button to move all the fields into the Selected Fields list.

4. Click the **Room ID** field to select it and click the **<** left arrow button to move it back to the Available Fields list, as shown in Figure 6-4. Click the **Next** button.

Figure 6-4

The Report Wizard Fields screen

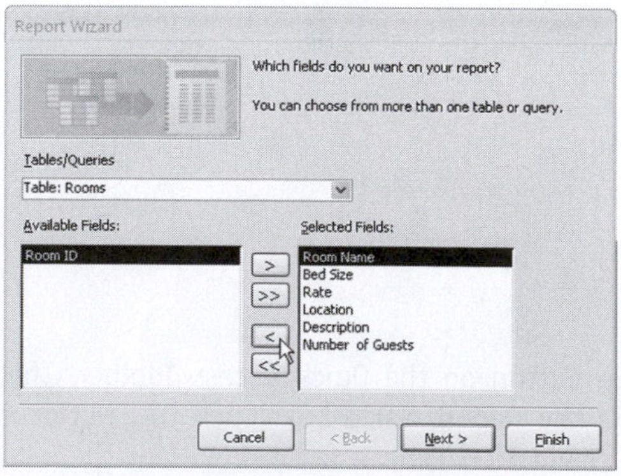

5. Click the **Location** field to select it and click the **>** right arrow button to add it as a grouping level, as shown in Figure 6-5.

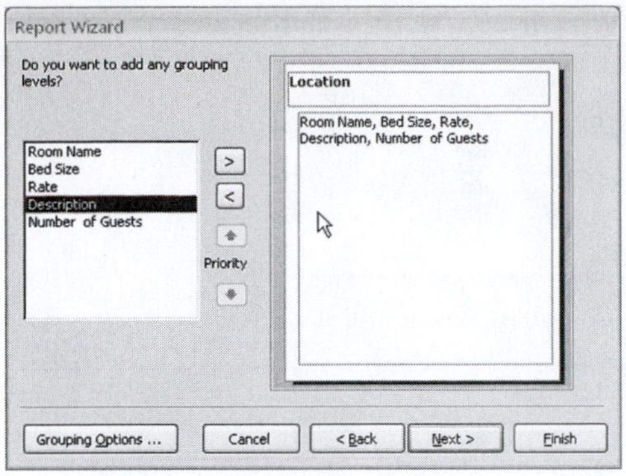

Figure 6-5

The Report Wizard
Grouping screen

6. Click the **Next** button.

7. Select **Room Name** from the fields menu to sort in ascending order, as shown in Figure 6-6, and click the **Next** button.

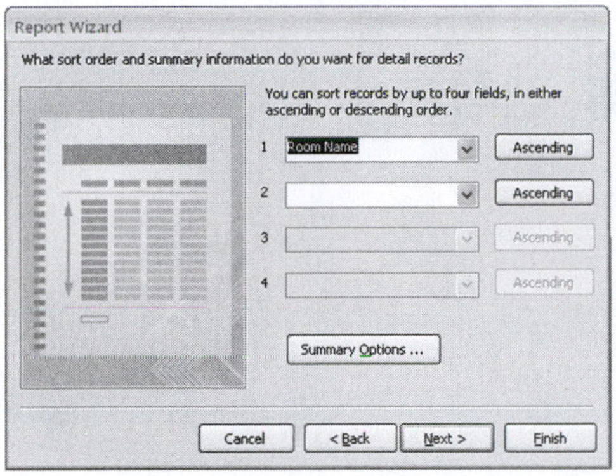

Figure 6-6

The Report Wizard Sort screen

8. In the Layout section, click the **Outline** button. In the Orientation section, click the **Landscape** button, as shown in Figure 6-7. Click **Next**.

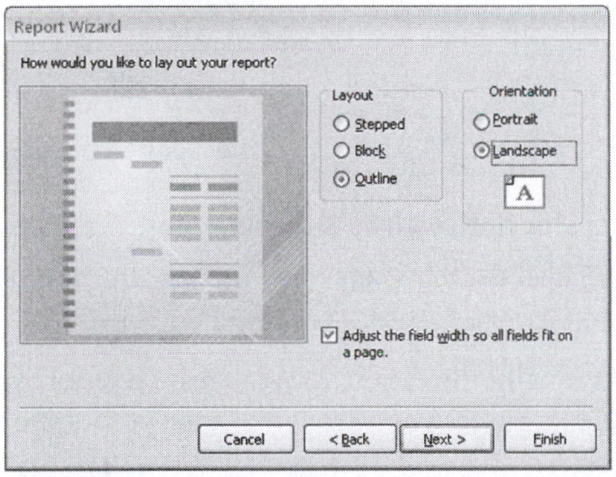

Figure 6-7

The Report Wizard
Layout screen

9. Click **Flow** in the styles list, as shown in Figure 6-8, and click **Next**.

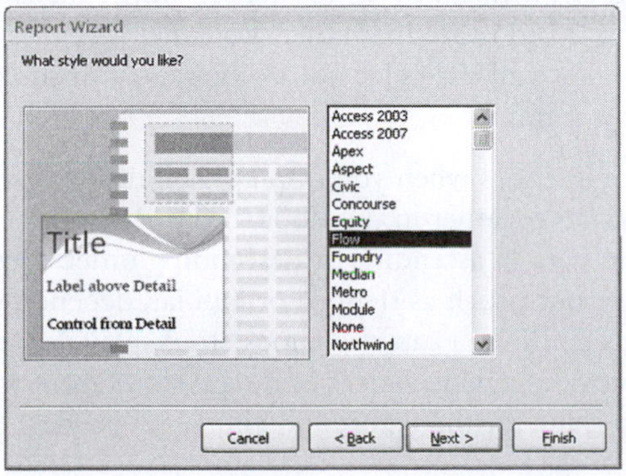

Figure 6-8

The Report Wizard Style screen

10. Key **Rooms Wizard** as the title of the report, as shown in Figure 6-9.

Figure 6-9

The Report Wizard Title screen

11. Click **Finish**. The Rooms Wizard report appears on the screen, as shown in Figure 6-10.

Figure 6-10

The Rooms Wizard report

Rooms Wizard

Location	1st floor				
Room Name	Bed Size		Rate	Description	Number
Alpine Suite	King, Queen		180-230	Porch, creek side	
Blue Spruce	Queen		130-180	Porch	
Cottonwood	King		140-190	Private porch	
Linden	2 Twin		130-180	Next door to Cottonwood	

Location	2nd floor				
Room Name	Bed Size		Rate	Description	Number
Ash	Queen		130-180	Balcony, nice view	
Black Walnut	2 Twin		130-180	Next door to Maple, nice view creek	
Maple	King		140-190	Large room, nice view of creek	
Red Oak	King		140-190	Balcony, nice view	

Page: 1   No Filter

12. **CLOSE** the report. Notice that the new report is listed in the Navigation Pane.

PAUSE. LEAVE the database open to use in the next exercise.

The Report Wizard is usually the easiest way to create a report when you want to choose which fields to include. It guides you through a series of questions and then generates a report based on your answers.

The Report Wizard allows you to include fields from more than one table or query. You can click the double right arrow button (>>) to include all the fields in the report or click the single right arrow button (>) to move them one at a time. Likewise, you can click the double left arrow button (<<) to move all the fields out of the report or the single left arrow button (<) to move them one at a time.

You can specify group levels, as when you displayed all of the first floor rooms together and all of the second floor rooms together in the Room Wizard report. You can also choose up to four fields on which to sort data in ascending or descending order. On the layout screen, you can choose from various layouts, such as stepped or tabular, depending on the data and the choices you have made to this point. You can also choose to display the report in portrait or landscape orientation. Access provides a wide variety of design styles from which to choose. On the last screen, you can key a name for the report and choose to preview or modify the report.

LOOKING AHEAD

You will learn more about grouping in Lesson 11.

If you want to skip steps such as Sorting or Grouping, click the Next button to go to the next screen. You can click the Finish button anytime it is available to create the report with the choices you have specified.

Creating a Report in Design View

When you want a customized report, you can create it in Design view, which offers you many options for creating the report exactly the way you want it.

→ CREATE A REPORT IN DESIGN VIEW

USE the database you used in the previous exercise.

1. If necessary, click the Rooms table in the Navigation Pane to select it.

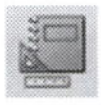

2. On the Create tab, in the Reports group, click the **Report Design** button. A new blank report is displayed in Design view, as shown in Figure 6-11.

CERTIFICATION READY?
How do you use the Report Wizard to create a report?
2.6.2

Figure 6-11

New blank report in Design view

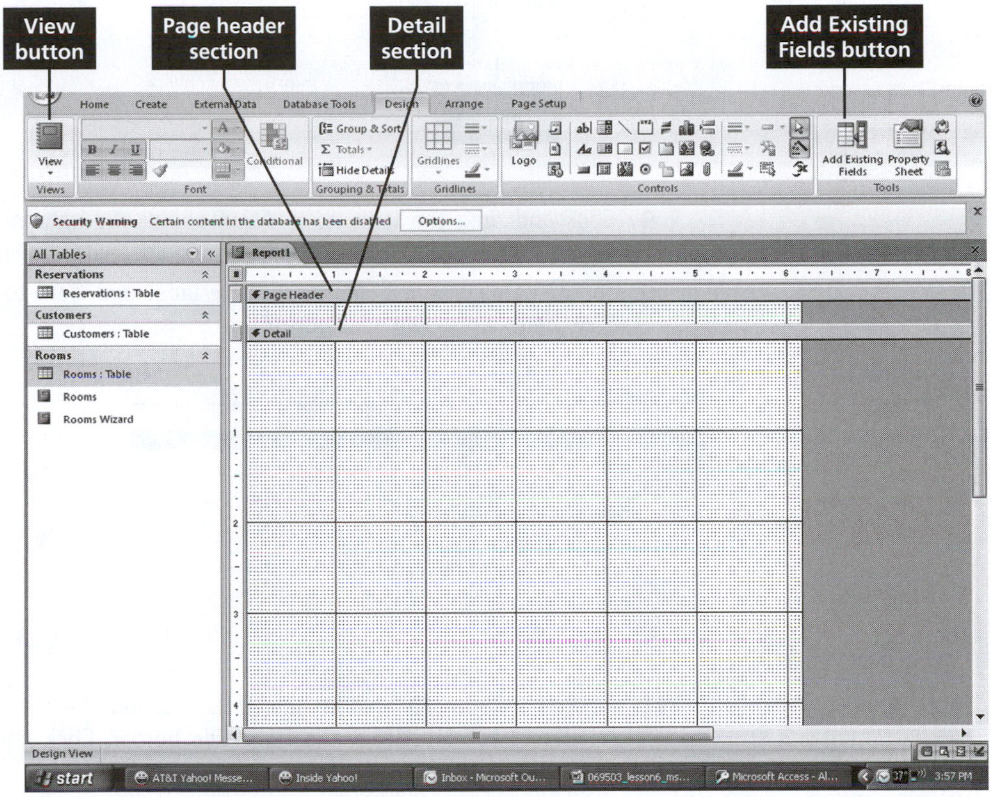

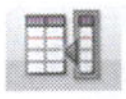

3. If the Fields List is not already displayed, on the Design tab, in the Tools group, click the **Add Existing Fields** button. The Fields List appears.

4. Click the plus (+) box beside **Rooms** to display the fields in the table, as shown in Figure 6-12.

Figure 6-12

Fields List pane

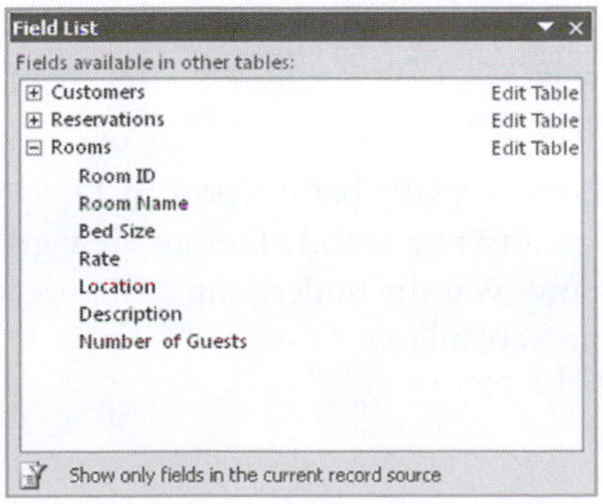

Field List	▼ ×
Fields available in other tables:	
⊞ Customers	Edit Table
⊞ Reservations	Edit Table
⊟ Rooms	Edit Table
Room ID	
Room Name	
Bed Size	
Rate	
Location	
Description	
Number of Guests	
Show only fields in the current record source	

5. Double-click **Room ID**. The field is inserted onto the design grid.

6. Double-click **Room Name**, **Bed Size**, and **Rate**.

7. Click the **Close** button on the Field List pane.

8. Click the **Bed Size** label. The border around the label changes to orange, indicating it is selected. Position the insertion point over the top orange border until the pointer changes to a four-sided arrow, as shown in Figure 6-13.

Figure 6-13

Move pointer

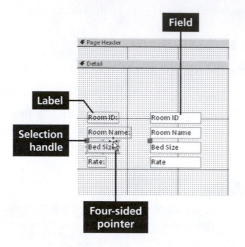

9. Click and drag the label to position about one-half inch to the right of the Room ID field and release the mouse button. The field moved along with the label.

10. In the same manner, move the **Rate** label and field to position below the Bed Size field, as shown in Figure 6-14.

Figure 6-14

Moved fields

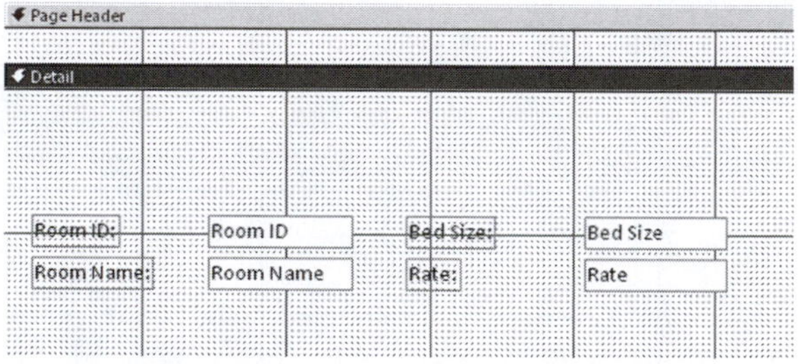

11. Click the **Room ID** field to select it. Position the mouse pointer on the square handle in the middle of the right-side border. Click and drag the field to the left to decrease the size by about one-quarter inch.

12. On the Home tab, in the Views group, click the **View** button and select **Report View** from the menu. The report is shown in Report View. Scroll down to see all the records.

13. Click the **Save** button on the Quick Access Toolbar.

14. Key **Report Design** in the Report Name box and click **OK.**

15. **CLOSE** the report.

PAUSE. LEAVE the table open to use in the next exercise.

In the previous exercise, you created a very basic report in Design view. In Lesson 7, you will learn how to add more functionality to a report. Design view gives you the most options for creating a report, because it shows you the underlying structure of the report. It also provides you with more design tools and capabilities.

In Design view, a report is displayed on a design grid with sections. The sections include the following:

- Report Header: This section is printed once at the beginning of every report. This is a good place to include a logo, a date, or information that might normally appear on a cover page.
- Page Header: This section is printed at the top of every page of a report, so it would be good place to include the report title.
- Group Header: This section is printed at the beginning of a group. It is a good place to include the group name.
- Detail: This section includes the body of the report. It is printed once for every row in a record source.
- Group Footer: This section is printed at the end of a group. It may include summary information for the group.
- Page Footer: This section is printed at the bottom of every page of a report, so it would be a good place to include information such as a page number.
- Report Footer: This section is printed once at the end of every report. This is a good place for report totals.

To add fields to the report design, you can display the Field List pane by clicking the Add Existing Fields button. Double-click a field in the Field List to add it to the design grid, or you can drag the field to a location on the grid.

TAKE NOTE You can add more than one field to a report design at once. Hold down the **CTRL** key and click the fields you want, and then drag the selected fields onto the report.

LOOKING AHEAD

In Lesson 7, you will learn how to add controls to reports in Design view.

If you need to move a field on the grid, click the field to select it and then position the pointer on the border until you see a four-sided arrow. Then, drag to the new location. To change the size of a field, click and drag a selection handle.

To see what your report will look like, click the View button on the Views group and select Report from the menu.

CERTIFICATION READY?
How do you create a report in Design view?
2.6.3

Applying AutoFormat

An AutoFormat applies a set of predefined fonts, colors, and design to a report. The instant formatting can quickly give your report the professional look you want.

→ APPLY AUTOFORMAT

USE the database open from the previous exercise.

1. **OPEN** the **Rooms** report.
2. On the Home tab, in the Views group, click the **View** button. Select **Layout view** from the menu.
3. On the Format tab, in the AutoFormat group, click the **AutoFormat** button. A menu of predefined report formats appears.
4. Click the **Metro** design, as shown in Figure 6-15. The format is applied to the report.

Figure 6-15

AutoFormat menu

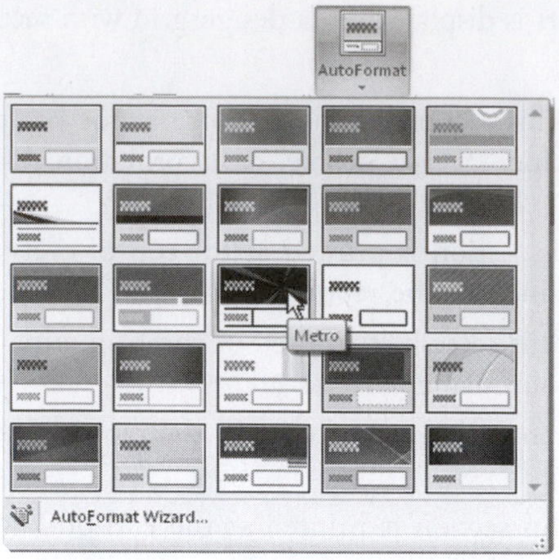

5. On the Format tab, in the AutoFormat group, click the **AutoFormat** button. Select **AutoFormat Wizard** from the menu. The AutoFormat dialog box appears.

6. Click **Module** in the Report AutoFormats list, as shown in Figure 6-16, and click **OK.** The new format is applied.

Figure 6-16

AutoFormat dialog box

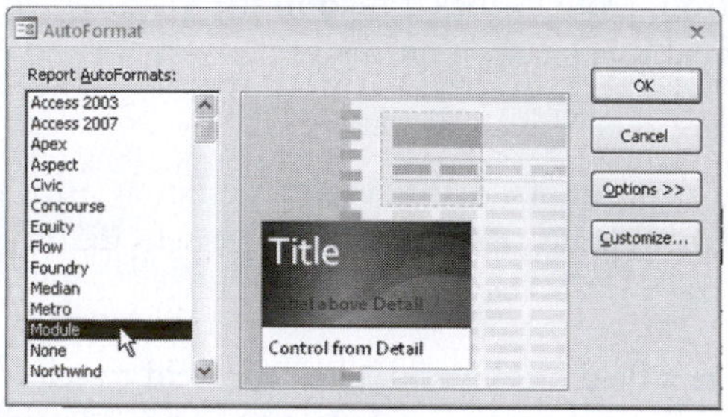

CERTIFICATION READY?

How do you apply AutoFormat to a report?

2.7.7

7. **SAVE** the report.

   PAUSE. LEAVE the report open to use in the next exercise.

An AutoFormat is a predefined format that you can apply to any report in Layout view. The AutoFormat menu displays a variety of designs. After you click the design you want, it is applied to the report.

Select the AutoFormat Wizard command to display the AutoFormat dialog box. You can select a design from the list displayed. You can also format options and customize an AutoFormat. You can create a new AutoFormat based on the current report, update the AutoFormat design with values from the current report, or delete the AutoFormat design.

Sorting Data Within a Report

Sorting organizes data in a particular order, such as alphabetic order or from smallest to largest numbers. For example, you can sort a customer list in alphabetic order by last name or by customer ID number. You can sort data by clicking the buttons on the Ribbon, right-clicking and choosing commands from the shortcut menu, or by using the Group, Sort, and Total pane.

SORT DATA WITHIN A REPORT

USE the report open from the previous exercise.

1. On the Home tab in the Views group, click the **View** button. Select **Layout** from the menu.

2. Click the **Room Name** header.

3. On the Home tab, in the Sort & Filter group, click the **Ascending** button. The column is sorted in ascending alphabetic order.

4. On the Home tab, in the Sort & Filter group, click the **Clear All Sorts** button. The Sort is cleared.

5. Right-click the **Room Name** header. The shortcut menu appears.

6. Select **Sort Z to A**, as shown in Figure 6-17. The column is sorted.

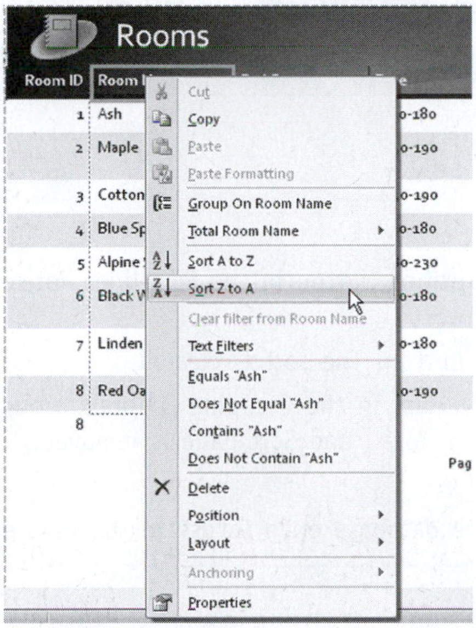

Figure 6-17

Shortcut menu

7. On the Home tab, in the Sort & Filter group, click the **Clear All Sorts** button. The Sort is cleared.

8. On the Formatting tab, in the Grouping & Totals group, click the **Group & Sort** button. The Group, Sort, and Total pane appears at the bottom of the screen, as shown in Figure 6-18.

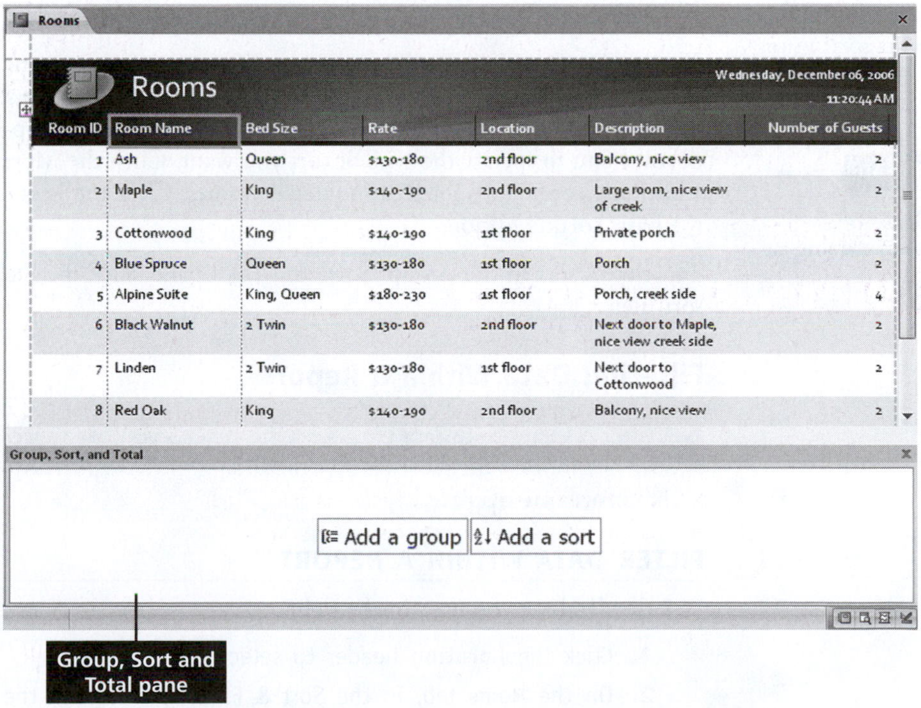

Figure 6-18

Group, Sort, and Total pane

9. Click the **Add a Sort** button in the Group, Sort, and Total pane.

10. Click the **Room Name** field in the fields list. Notice that the field was sorted in ascending order by default and a line was added describing the sort.

11. Click the down arrow beside **with A on top** and select **with Z on top** from the menu, as shown in Figure 6-19. The field is sorted in descending order.

Figure 6-19

Sort displayed in the Group, Sort, and Total pane

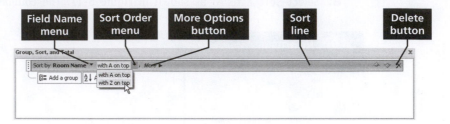

12. Click the **More Options** button in the Sort line. Notice the options available for customizing a sort.

13. Click the **Delete** button. The sort is cleared.

14. On the Formatting tab, in the Grouping & Totals group, click the **Group & Sort** button. The Group, Total, and Sort pane is removed.

15. **SAVE** the table.

PAUSE. LEAVE the database open to use in the next exercise.

CERTIFICATION READY?

How do you sort data within a report?

5.1.3

X REF

Lesson 3 has more information about sorting in a table.

X REF

Lesson 5 has more information about sorting in a form.

LOOKING AHEAD

Lesson 8 has more information about sorting in a query.

Sorting data in a report is similar to sorting in a table. In Layout view, select the field you want to sort and click the Ascending or Descending button on the Home tab, in the Sort & Filter group. Click the Clear All Sorts button to remove the sort orders. You can sort as many fields as you like one at a time.

You can also easily sort data by right-clicking in a field and choosing the type of sort you want from the shortcut menu. The sort commands in the shortcut menu vary depending on the type of data in the field. For text, you will choose Sort A to Z or Sort Z to A; for numbers, you will choose Sort Smallest to Largest or Sort Largest to Smallest; and for dates, you will choose Sort Oldest to Newest or Sort Newest to Oldest.

The Group, Sort, and Total pane gives you more sorting options. You can use the pane to specify the sort order or to view the results of sorting using the shortcut menu. To specify a sort, click the Add a Sort button and select a field from the pop-up menu. Click the drop-down menu to specify the type of sort you want. Click the More Options button to display additional commands for creating detailed sorts. Click the Less Options button to return to the basic sorting options.

To delete a sort in the Group, Sort, and Total pane, click the Delete button at the end of the sort line.

Filtering Data Within a Report

A filter displays only data that meet the criteria you have specified and hides the rest. It does not modify the table data or the design of the report. After you remove a filter, all the records are displayed again.

FILTER DATA WITHIN A REPORT

USE the database you used in the previous exercise.

1. Click the **Location** header to select it.

2. On the Home tab, in the Sort & Filter group, click the **Filter** button. A menu appears.

3. Point to **Text Filters**. A second menu appears. Select **Begins with. . .**, as shown in Figure 6-20.

Figure 6-20

Shortcut menu

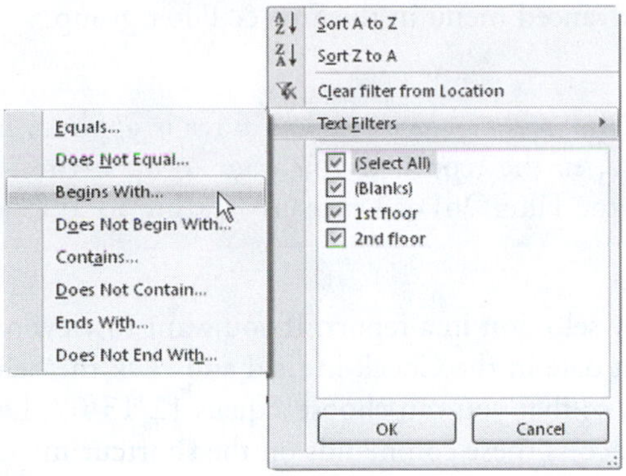

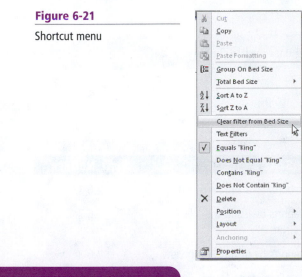

4. Key **1** into the Custom Filter box and click **OK.** The data is filtered to show only the rooms on the first floor.
5. Click the **Toggle Filter** button.
6. In the Bed Size field, click **King** in the second row.
7. On the Home tab, in the Sort & Filter group, click the **Selection** button. Select **Equals "King"** from the menu. The data is filtered to show only the rooms with King size beds.
8. Right-click the **Bed Size** header. A shortcut menu appears. Notice that the Equals "King" filter and the other filters from the Selection menu are also available in the shortcut menu, shown in Figure 6-21.

Figure 6-21

Shortcut menu

CERTIFICATION READY?
How do you filter data within a report?
5.2.3

9. Select **Clear filter from Bed Size** from the menu. The filter is cleared.
10. **SAVE** and **CLOSE** the table. **CLOSE** the database.

STOP. CLOSE Access.

Filtering data in Layout view of a report is very similar to filtering data in a table. You can apply common filters using the commands on the Sort & Filter group or by right-clicking a field and choosing a filter from the shortcut menu. The filters available on the shortcut menu vary depending on the type of data in the field.

Only one filter can be applied to a field at a time. However, you can specify a different filter for each field.

You can toggle between filtered and unfiltered views using the Toggle Filter button. You just practiced removing a filter from a field by right-clicking in the field and selecting the *Clear filter from field name* command. To remove all filters permanently, select the Clear All Filters command on the Advanced menu in the Sort & Filter group.

TAKE NOTE＊ If you save a report (or other object) while a filter is applied, it will be available the next time that you open the report. If you want to open the report and see the filter already applied, set the FilterOnLoad property setting to Yes.

You can also filter by selection in a report. If you want to view only the reservations for 12/13/07, select that date in the Check-in field and click the Selection button. That date will appear in the menu, so that you can choose Equals 12/13/07, Does Not Equal 12/13/07, and so on. You can also access these commands on the shortcut menu by right-clicking the value.

TAKE NOTE＊ If you need to apply a filter that is not in the common filters list, you can write an advanced filter using the Advanced Filter/Sort command on the Advanced menu. You will need to be familiar with writing expressions, which are similar to formulas, and be familiar with the criteria that you specify when designing a query.

X REF Lesson 3 has more information about filtering records in a table.

X REF Lesson 5 has more information about filtering data within a form.

LOOKING AHEAD Lesson 8 has more information about filtering data within a query.

SUMMARY SKILL MATRIX

IN THIS LESSON YOU LEARNED	MATRIX SKILL	SKILL NUMBER
To create a simple report	Create reports as a simple report	2.6.1
To use the Report Wizard	Create reports by using the Report Wizard	2.6.2
To create a report in Design view	Create reports by using Design view	2.6.3
To apply AutoFormat	Apply AutoFormats to forms and reports	2.7.7
To sort data within a report	Sort data within reports	5.1.3
To filter data within a report	Filter data within reports	5.2.3

Knowledge Assessment

Matching

Match the term in Column 1 to its description in Column 2.

Column 1	Column 2
1. report	**a.** organizes data in a particular order
2. record source	**b.** displays data that meets the criteria you have specified and hides the rest
3. Report Wizard	**c.** a list of available fields for adding to a report
4. Field List pane	**d.** a database object that is used to organize and display data from tables and queries
5. Detail	**e.** removes all sort orders
6. AutoFormat	**f.** the table or query that provides the data used to generate a report
7. Sort	**g.** the way a report is displayed in Design view
8. Filter	**h.** guides you through a series of questions and then generates a report based on your answers
9. design grid	**i.** the section of a report that includes the body of the report
10. Clear All Sorts	**j.** a predefined format that you can apply to any report in Layout view

True / False

Circle T if the statement is true or F if the statement is false.

T F 1. A simple report contains all the records in a table or query.

T F 2. You can edit the data in a report.

T F 3. Click the Report button to define a record source.

T F 4. In the Report Wizard, you can skip steps such as Sorting or Grouping by clicking the Next button.

T F 5. You can drag a field from the Field List pane to the design grid to add it to the report.

T F 6. Layout view gives you the most options for creating a report, because it shows you the underlying structure of the report.

T F 7. AutoFormat resizes column widths for you.

T F 8. You can save a filter with a report.

T F 9. You can use the Group, Sort, and Total pane to specify sort order or view the results of sorting using the shortcut menu.

T F 10. The Toggle Filter button removes a filter permanently.

■ Competency Assessment

Project 6-1: Soccer Team Report

You need a copy of the soccer team's roster that you can print and take with you to work. Create a simple report and apply an AutoFormat.

GET READY. Launch Access if it is not already running.

The *Soccer Team* database is available on the companion CD-ROM.

1. Open the *SoccerTeam* database.
2. Save the database as *SoccerTeamXXX* (where XXX is your initials).
3. Click the **Roster** table to select it.
4. On the Create tab, in the Reports group, click the **Report** button. A new report is created.
5. Resize each field so that all fields fit on one page.
6. On the Format tab, in the AutoFormat group, click the **AutoFormat** button.
7. Select the purple format in the fourth row named **Opulent.**
8. Click the **Save** button on the Quick Access Toolbar. The Save As dialog box appears with the name *Roster* in it. Click **OK** to accept that name for the report.
9. **CLOSE** the report.
10. **CLOSE** the database.

    LEAVE Access open for the next project.

Project 6-2: Fourth Coffee Inventory Report

In your job at Fourth Coffee, you are responsible for maintaining the coffee inventory. Create a report to view the inventory and prepare for the next order.

The *Coffee* database is available on the companion CD-ROM.

1. **OPEN** *Coffee* from the data files for this lesson.
2. **SAVE** the database as *CoffeeXXX* (where XXX is your initials).
3. Click the **Coffee Inventory Table** in the Navigation Pane to select it.
4. On the Create tab, in the Reports group, click the **Report Wizard** button. The first Report Wizard screen appears.
5. Click the double arrow **>>** to move all the fields to the Selected Fields list and click **Next**.
6. On the grouping screen, click the **Scheduled Order Date** field, click the **>** arrow, and click **Next**.
7. On the sorting screen, click the down arrow on the menu, select **Pounds**, and click **Next**.
8. Keep the defaults as is on the layout screen and click **Next**.
9. On the style screen, click **Paper**, and click **Next**.
10. Click **Finish**. The report is created.
11. **CLOSE** the report.
12. **CLOSE** the database.

    LEAVE Access open for the next project.

■ Proficiency Assessment

Project 6-3: Alpine Ski House Reservations Report

Every week is different at the Alpine Ski House. Sometimes the lodge is full of guests, and sometimes only a few rooms are occupied. Create a report to show the innkeepers what to expect in the coming weeks.

The *AlpineHouse* database is available on the companion CD-ROM.

1. **OPEN** the *AlpineHouse* database.
2. **SAVE** it as *AlpineHouseXXX* (where XXX is your initials).
3. Use the Report Wizard to create a report using the Room, Check-in Date, and Check-out Date fields.
4. Group the report by Room and sort it in ascending order by Check-in Date.
5. Use stepped and portrait layout and apply the Foundry format.
6. Name the report **December Reservations** and finish the wizard.
7. Switch to Layout view and increase the width of the Room field.
8. **SAVE** and **CLOSE** the table.
9. **CLOSE** the database.

    LEAVE Access open for the next project.

Project 6-4: Wingtip Toys Design View Report

The manufacturing department at Wingtip Toys needs summary information about each toy in inventory. Create a report in Design view that will display the requested information.

The *Wingtip Toys* database is available on the companion CD-ROM.

1. **OPEN** *Wingtip Toys* and save it as *WingtipToysXXX* (where XXX is your initials).
2. Click the **Inventory** table in the Navigation Pane to select it.
3. On the Create tab, in the Reports group, click the **Report Design** button.
4. On the Design tab, in the Tools group, click the **Add Existing Fields** button. The Field List pane appears.
5. Position the fields onto the design grid, as shown in Figure 6-22. Adjust field widths as shown.

Figure 6-22

Wingtip Toys report in Design view

Page Header			
Detail			
Description:	Description	Price:	Price
In Stock:	In Stock		

6. Save the report as **Toy Summary.**
7. **CLOSE** the report.

    LEAVE the database open for the next project.

■ Mastery Assessment

Project 6-5: Filter and Sort a Wingtip Toys Report

A large order was recently filled, and now the inventory at Wingtip Toys is quite low on some items. Create a report that displays this information.

The *WingtipToysXXX* database should be open.

1. Define the **Inventory** table as the record source for a new report.
2. Create a simple report.
3. Apply the **Equity** AutoFormat to the new report.
4. Sort the report in ascending order by the Description field.
5. Click the first row of the **In Stock** field, which contains the number 10.
6. Filter by selection to display the toys with 10 or fewer items in stock.
7. Click the **In Stock** field header and sort the field in ascending order.
8. Clear all sorts.
9. Clear all filters.
10. **SAVE** the report as **Inventory**.
11. **CLOSE** the report.
12. **CLOSE** the database.

    LEAVE Access open for the next project.

Project 6-6: Angel Project Report

The school Angel Project has begun. Information for the boy angels needs to be distributed to the boys in the kindergarten classes, and the girl angels' information needs to be distributed to the girls. Create a report with filters that displays the boy and girl information separately.

The *AngelProject* database is available on the companion CD-ROM.

1. **OPEN** the *AngelProject* database.
2. Save the database as **AngelProjectXXX** (where XXX is your initials).
3. Define the List table as the record source for a new report.
4. Use the Report Wizard to create a report with all the fields.
5. Skip the grouping and sorting screens, and choose a tabular, portrait layout and the Trek format.
6. Name the report **Angel Needs and Wants.**
7. Switch to Layout view and adjust field widths as necessary so that all data fits on the screen and on one page.
8. Display the Group, Sort, and Total pane.
9. Sort the report in ascending order by Age.
10. Create a filter to show only the information for the males.
11. Toggle the filter and create a new filter to show only the information for the females.
12. **SAVE** and **CLOSE** the report.
13. **CLOSE** the database.

    CLOSE Access.

INTERNET READY

Search the Internet for at least five dream vacation packages and create a database table that lists each hotel's location, name, cost, and favorite amenities or activities. After creating the table, use the Report Wizard to create a professional looking report that displays your data.

Use Controls in Reports and Forms

7

LESSON SKILL MATRIX

SKILLS	MATRIX SKILL	SKILL NUMBER
Adding Controls	Add controls	2.7.1
Adding Unbound Controls	Add controls	2.7.1
Adding Bound Controls	Add controls, Bind controls to fields	2.7.1, 2.7.2
Adding Calculated Controls	Add controls	2.7.1
Adding Controls Using a Wizard	Add controls	2.7.1
Formatting Controls	Format controls	2.7.4
Creating Conditional Formatting on Controls	Apply and change conditional formatting on controls	2.7.6
Arranging Control Layout	Arrange controls	2.7.5
Arranging Control Alignment, Size, and Position	Arrange controls	2.7.5
Defining Control Tab Order	Define the tab order of controls	2.7.3

Wingtip Toys is a mom-and-pop operation with fewer than 25 employees, many of whom craft the heirloom-style wooden toys that the company has sold successfully for more than 20 years. As the newly hired marketing coordinator, you are learning every aspect of the business in order to market its products effectively. In this lesson, you will learn to add, format, and arrange controls on forms and reports that you can use to evaluate sales and inventory for the company.

KEY TERMS
bound control
calculated control
conditional formatting
control
control layouts
control tab order
Control Wizard
Expression Builder
stacked layout
tabular layout
unbound control

▪ SOFTWARE ORIENTATION

Controls Group in Reports and Forms

When you view a report in Design view, the Report Design Tools are displayed in the Ribbon. The Controls group is located on the Design tab. When you position the mouse pointer over a tool, Access will display the tool's name in a ScreenTip.

Figure 7-1

Controls group on the Design tab for reports

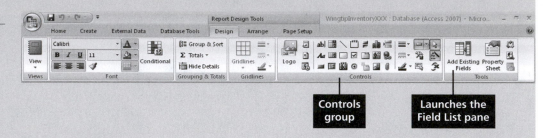

Controls group

Launches the Field List pane

Use the Controls group on the Design tab to add controls to a report.

The Controls group located on the Design tab in the Forms Ribbon, shown in Figure 7-2, is very similar to the one for reports. The procedure for adding controls to a form and a report are similar as well.

Figure 7-2

Controls group on the Design tab for forms

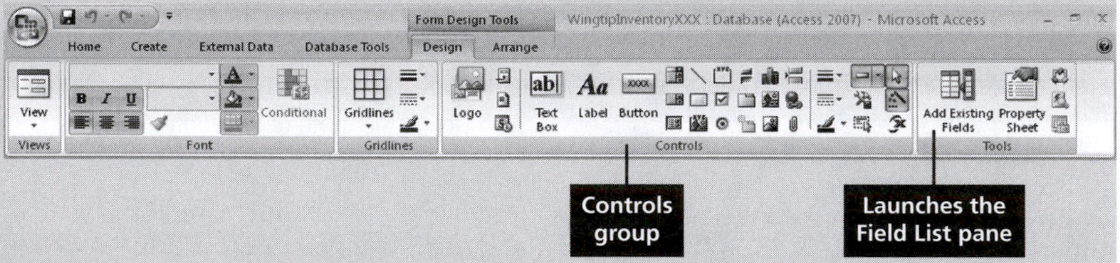

Controls group

Launches the Field List pane

Use the Controls group on a form's Design tab to add controls to a form.

▪ Adding Controls

THE BOTTOM LINE

Controls add functionality to a report or form. For example, you can add a logo control to a report to enhance the look of the report or a list box control to allow users to choose from a list of items. You can insert bound, unbound, and calculated controls using the tools on the Controls group. The Control Wizard is helpful when creating some of the more complicated controls.

Adding Unbound Controls

Unbound controls are not connected to a field, but they display information that is important for reports and forms, such as titles, dates, and page numbers.

⊙ ADD UNBOUND CONTROLS

CD

The *WingtipInventory* database is available on the companion CD-ROM.

GET READY. Before you begin these steps, be sure to turn on and/or log on to your computer and start Access.

1. **OPEN** *WingtipInventory* from the data files for this lesson.
2. Save the database as *WingtipInventoryXXX* (where XXX is your initials).

3. Double-click the **Toy Summary** report in the Navigation pane.

4. On the Home tab, in the Views group, click the **View** button and select **Design View** from the menu.

5. On the Design tab, in the Controls group, click the **Logo** button. The Insert Picture dialog box appears.

6. Double-click the **Sample Pictures** folder. Click **Sunset** in the list and click **OK**. The picture is inserted in the Report Header section.

7. On the Design tab, in the Controls group, click the **Title** button. The title control with the title Toy Summary is inserted in the Report Header section. The text in the title is selected.

8. Key **Inventory Summary by Toy** and press the Enter key.

9. On the Design tab, in the Controls group, click the **Date & Time** button. The Date & Time dialog box appears, as shown in Figure 7-3.

Figure 7-3

Date & Time dialog box

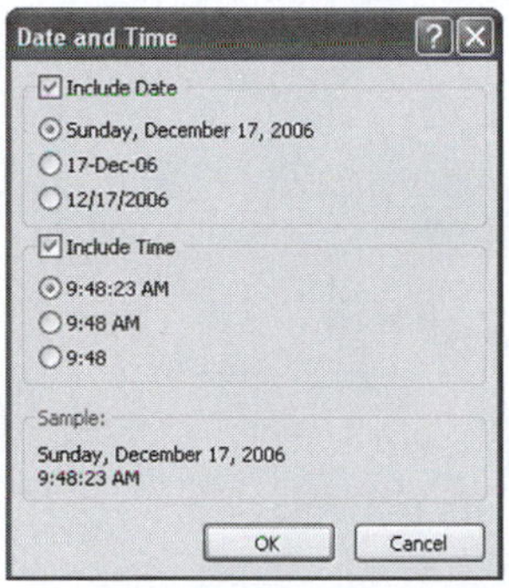

> **Date and Time** ? X
> ☑ Include Date
> ⦿ Sunday, December 17, 2006
> ○ 17-Dec-06
> ○ 12/17/2006
> ☑ Include Time
> ⦿ 9:48:23 AM
> ○ 9:48 AM
> ○ 9:48
>
> Sample:
> Sunday, December 17, 2006
> 9:48:23 AM
>
> [OK] [Cancel]

10. Click **OK** to accept the default date and time formats. The Date and Time controls are inserted in the Report Header section of the report, as shown in Figure 7-4.

Figure 7-4

Report shown in Design view

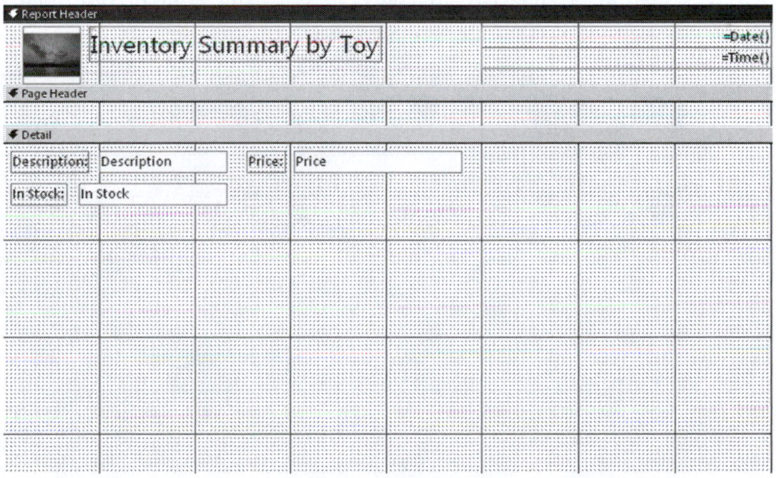

> Report Header
> Inventory Summary by Toy   =Date()
>   =Time()
> Page Header
>
> Detail
> Description: Description   Price: Price
> In Stock: In Stock

11. Click the **Save** button on the Quick Access Toolbar.

PAUSE. LEAVE the report open to use in the next exercise.

A ***control*** is an object that displays data, performs actions, and lets you improve the look and usability of a form or report. Access uses three different types of controls: bound, unbound, and calculated.

An ***unbound control*** does not have a data source; it displays information such as lines, shapes, or pictures. You just added unbound controls to the report in the previous exercise. Titles, page numbers, and logos are examples of unbound controls.

CERTIFICATION READY?
How do you add a control to a report or form?
2.7.1

You can add controls to a form or report using the tools on the Controls group. When you added the title label in the previous exercise, you only had to click the Title tool and the report's name was inserted in the Report Header section as the title. The title was inserted with the text in it already selected. If you want to change the title, you can key the new text and press Enter.

Adding Bound Controls

Bound controls display data from a field in a table. You can bind a control to a field by moving it from the Field List pane or by using the Property Sheet.

BIND A CONTROL TO A FIELD

USE the database open from the previous exercise.

1. On the Design tab, in the Tools group, click the **Add Existing Fields** button. The Field List pane appears, as shown in Figure 7-5.

Figure 7-5

Field List pane

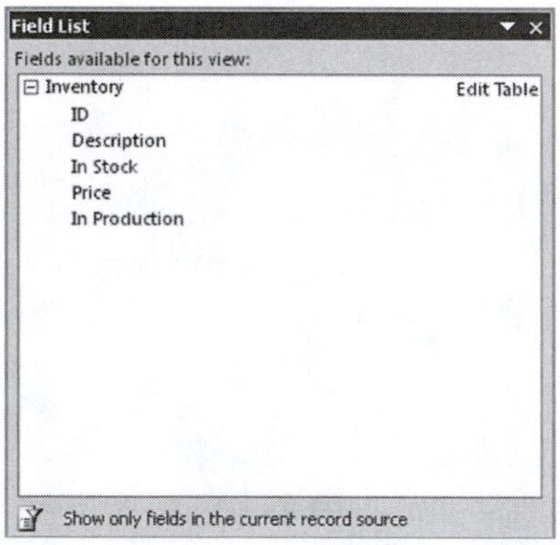

2. Click the **ID** field and drag it to the right of the Price field, as shown in Figure 7-6.

Figure 7-6

Bound control dragged from the Field List pane

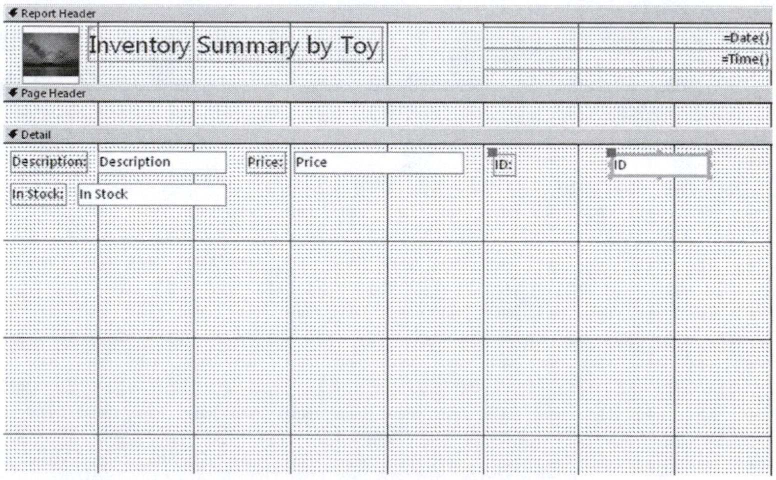

3. Drag the **In Production** field to the design grid below the **ID** field.
4. Click the close box on the Field List pane.
5. Click the **ID** field control until you see the orange border with selection handles on the borders and corners.
6. Right-click in the control to display the shortcut menu.
7. Select **Delete** from the menu, as shown in Figure 7-7. The control and label are removed from the design grid.

Figure 7-7

Shortcut menu

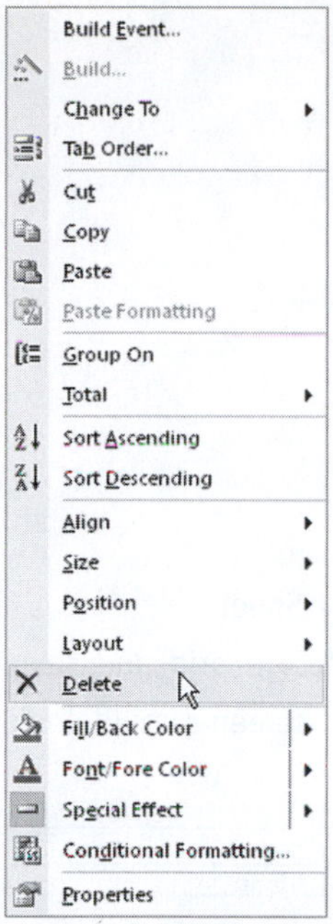

	Build Event...
	Build...
	Change To ▸
	Tab Order...
✂	Cut
	Copy
	Paste
	Paste Formatting
	Group On
	Total ▸
A↓	Sort Ascending
Z↓	Sort Descending
	Align ▸
	Size ▸
	Position ▸
	Layout ▸
✕	Delete
	Fill/Back Color ▸
A	Font/Fore Color ▸
	Special Effect ▸
	Conditional Formatting...
	Properties

8. Select the **In Production** control, right-click and select **Delete** from the menu.

9. On the Design tab, in the Controls group, click the **Text Box** button. The mouse pointer changes to a move pointer.

10. Position the pointer at approximately the same location of the deleted **ID** field control and click to create the text box control as shown in Figure 7-8. Notice that the word Unbound is shown in the control and the word Text and a number (depending on the number of controls you have created in this session) appear in the label.

Figure 7-8

Unbound control

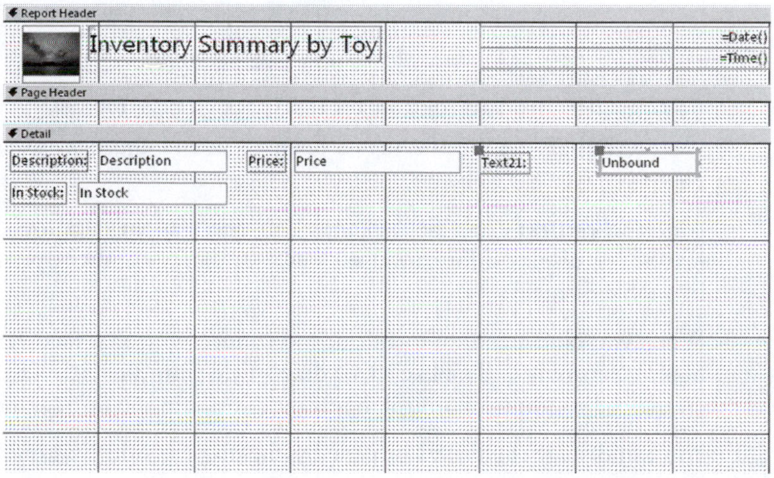

Report Header				
Inventory Summary by Toy				=Date() =Time()
Page Header				
Detail				
Description: Description	Price: Price	Text21:	Unbound	
In Stock: In Stock				

11. Select the control if it isn't selected already.

12. On the Design tab, in the Tools group, click the **Property Sheet** button. The Property Sheet appears.

13. In the Data tab, click the down arrow on the **Control Source** row and click the **ID** field, as shown in Figure 7-9. Notice the control now displays the field name ID, which means that it is now bound to the control.

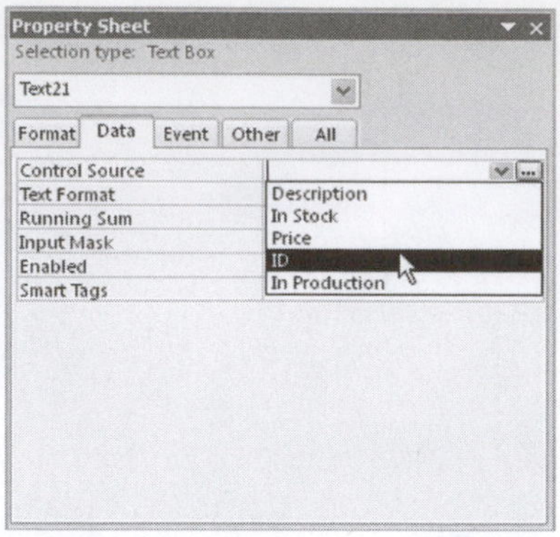

Figure 7-9

Property Sheet

14. Click the close box on the Property Sheet.
15. Click the **ID** control label on the design grid and select the text in the label.
16. Key **ID** and then press Enter. Your screen should look similar to Figure 7-10.

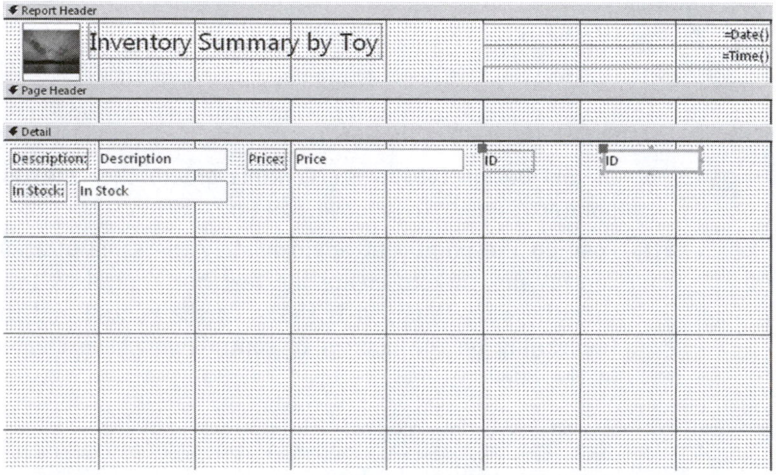

Figure 7-10

Bound control

17. Click the **Save** button on the Quick Access Toolbar.

    PAUSE. LEAVE the report open to use in the next exercise.

ANOTHER WAY

You can also display the Field List pane by pressing ALT+F8.

ANOTHER WAY

You can also display the property sheet by clicking control and pressing F4.

CERTIFICATION READY?

How do you add a control to a report or form?

2.7.1

A **bound control** uses a field in a table or query as the data source. Bound controls, such as text boxes, display information such as text, dates, numbers, pictures, or graphs from a field in a table or query.

When you bind a control to a field, you connect it to that field. The easiest way to create a bound control is to double-click or drag a field from the Field List pane to the report. Access creates the appropriate control, binds the control to the field, and creates a label for the control.

You can display the Field List pane by clicking the Add Existing Fields button on the Tools group.

Another way to bind a control to a field is to first add an unbound text box to a report or form. Then, open its Property Sheet either by right-clicking and choosing Properties from the shortcut menu or by clicking the Property Sheet button on the Tools group in the Design tab. On the Property Sheet, in the Data tab, click the down arrow beside the Control Source property and select the field you want to display in the control.

When you click the button in the Control group, the pointer changes to the move pointer with a plus sign (+). Click where you want the upper-left portion of the control to start. Remember that a label will also be inserted, so leave enough space for the label. Click once to create a default-sized control, or click the tool and then drag it into the design grid to create the size that you want.

CERTIFICATION READY?
How do you bind a control to a field?
2.7.2

To delete a control from the grid, select it, display the shortcut menu, and choose Delete.

Adding Calculated Controls

Calculated controls can display calculations that are vital to the usefulness of a report or form. When your company needs to know the amount of sales dollars generated by each toy in a product line, you can multiply the number of toys sold by the price and display the value in a report or form.

ADD A CALCULATED CONTROL

USE the database open from the previous exercise.

1. On the Design tab, in the Controls group, click the **Text Box** button.
2. Position the mouse pointer on the design grid and drag down and to the right to create a control the size of the one shown in Figure 7-11.

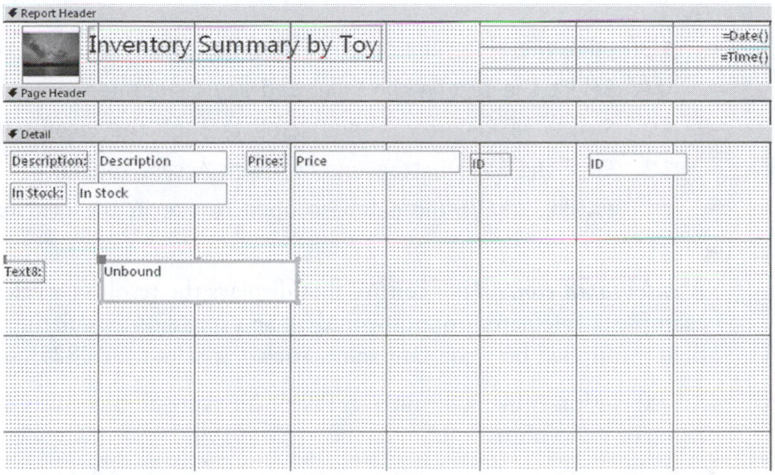

Figure 7-11
Text box control

3. With the control selected, right-click to display the shortcut menu.
4. Select **Properties** from the menu. The Property Sheet appears.
5. On the Data tab, in the Control Source row, click the **Build** button. The Expression Builder dialog box appears.
6. In the <Report> list, scroll down and double-click **In Stock**, as shown in Figure 7-12. The In Stock field is inserted in the expression box.

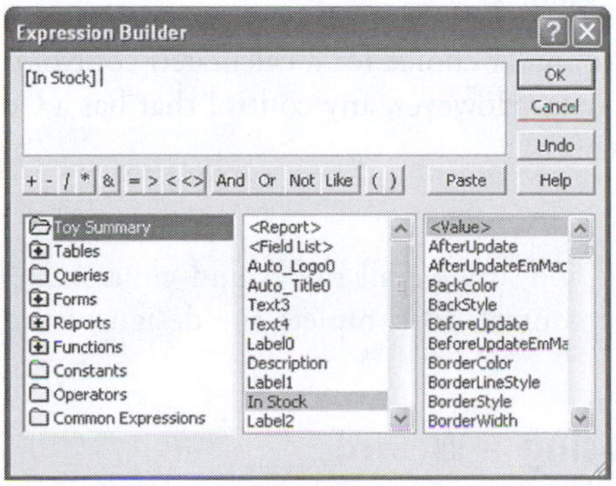

Figure 7-12
Expression Builder

7. Click the * asterisk button to select the multiplication operator.
8. Double-click the **Price** field in the <Report> list.

9. Click **OK.** The expression appears in the Control Source row of the Property Sheet, as shown in Figure 7-13. Notice that Access added the equal sign (=) that starts an expression.

Figure 7-13

Expression in the
Property Sheet

Property Sheet		▼ ×
Selection type: Text Box		
Text8	⌄	

Format	Data	Event	Other	All

Control Source	= [In Stock]*[Price]	⌄ ...
Text Format	Plain Text	
Running Sum	No	
Input Mask		
Enabled	Yes	
Smart Tags		

10. Click the close box on the Properties Sheet.
11. Select the text in the label and key **Investment.**
12. Switch to Report view and scroll through the records to view the calculated totals.
13. Click the **Save** button on the Quick Access toolbar.

    PAUSE. LEAVE the database open to use in the next exercise.

A *calculated control* is a control that displays the result of a calculation or expression. For example, a calculated control would be an expression calculating the price of an item in a field multiplied by a constant value, such as a sales tax (.0825).

An expression is like a formula in Excel. An expression consists of the following elements used alone or in combination:

- Identifiers, which are the names or properties of fields or controls
- Operators such as + (plus), − (minus), or * (multiply)
- Functions, such as SUM or AVG
- Constants, which are values that do not change, such as numbers that are not calculated

To create a calculated control, you can either key an expression in the Control Source property box or use the *Expression Builder*, which is a feature that provides names of the fields and controls in a database, lists the operators available, and has built-in functions to help you create an expression.

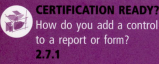

CERTIFICATION READY?
How do you add a control
to a report or form?
2.7.1

Text boxes are the most popular choice for a calculated control because they can display so many different types of data. However, any control that has a Control Source property can be used as a calculated control.

TAKE NOTE✱ It is often easiest to add and arrange all the bound controls first, and then add the unbound and calculated controls to complete the design of the report.

Adding Controls Using a Wizard

It could take quite a bit of time to figure out how to set all the properties necessary to create option groups and list boxes for a report or form. To speed up this task, Access 2007 includes wizards that help you create some of the more complicated controls, such as option groups and list boxes.

➔ USE THE CONTROL WIZARD

USE the database open from the previous exercise.

1. Switch to Design view, if necessary.
2. On the Design tab, in the Controls group, locate the **Wizards** button and make sure it is turned on. It should be displayed in orange.
3. On the Design tab, in the Controls group, click the **Option Group** button.
4. Position the mouse pointer and drag to draw a rectangle, as shown in Figure 7-14.

Figure 7-14

Drag to draw a custom control

◄ Report Header				
Inventory Summary by Toy				=Date() =Time()
◄ Page Header				
◄ Detail				
Description: Description	Price: Price	ID	ID	
In Stock: In Stock				
Investment: =[In Stock]*[Price]				

5. When you release the mouse button, the Option Group Wizard appears. In the Label Names list, key **Yes** and press the Tab key.
6. On the next row, key **No**, as shown in Figure 7-15, and press the Tab key.

Figure 7-15

Option Group Wizard label names screen

Option Group Wizard

An option group contains a set of option buttons, check boxes, or toggle buttons. You can choose only one option.

What label do you want for each option?

Label Names
Yes
No

Cancel   < Back   Next >   Finish

7. Click **Next**.
8. On the next screen, click the button beside **No, I don't want a default**, as shown in Figure 7-16.

Figure 7-16

Option Group Wizard default screen

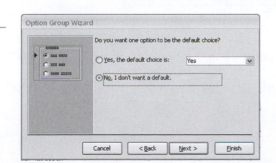

Option Group Wizard

Do you want one option to be the default choice?

○ Yes, the default choice is: Yes

⦿ No, I don't want a default.

Cancel   < Back   Next >   Finish

9. Click **Next**.

10. In the first row of the Values column, the number *1* is selected. Key **-1** and press the [Tab] key.

11. In the second row of the Value column, the number *2* is selected. Key **0**, as shown in Figure 7-17, and press the [Tab] key.

Figure 7-17

Option Group Wizard values screen

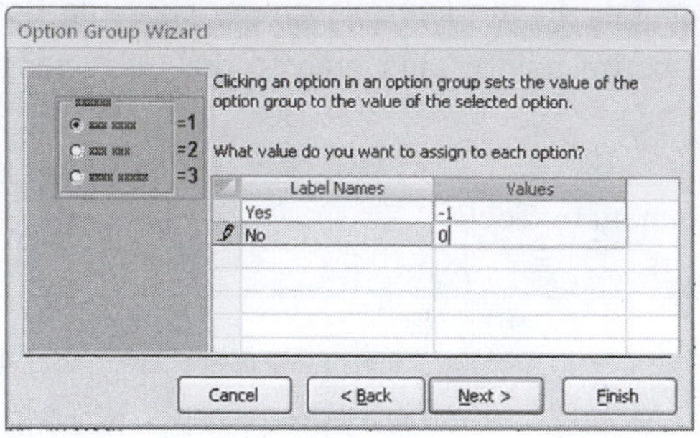

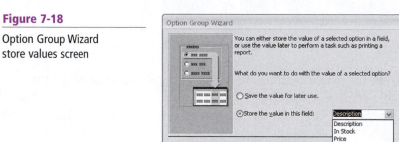

12. Click **Next**.

13. Click the button beside **Store the value in this field** and click the down arrow to display the menu. Select **In Production** from the menu, as shown in Figure 7-18.

Figure 7-18

Option Group Wizard store values screen

14. Click **Next**.

15. Click the **Check boxes** check box, as shown in Figure 7-19.

Figure 7-19

Option Group Wizard options screen

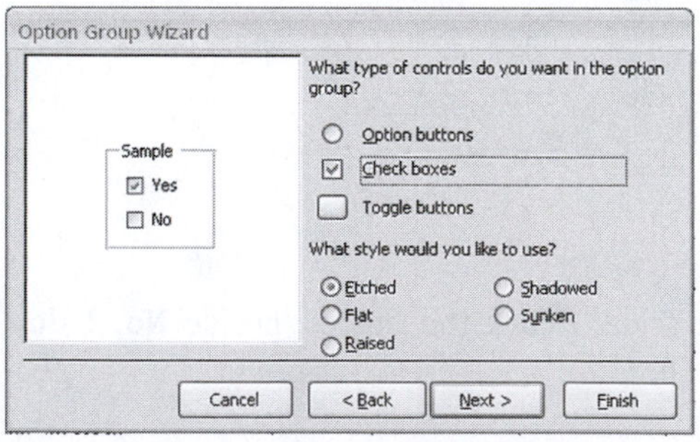

16. Click **Next**.

17. Key **In Production** in the text box, as shown in Figure 7-20.

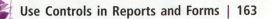

Figure 7-20

Option Group Wizard caption screen

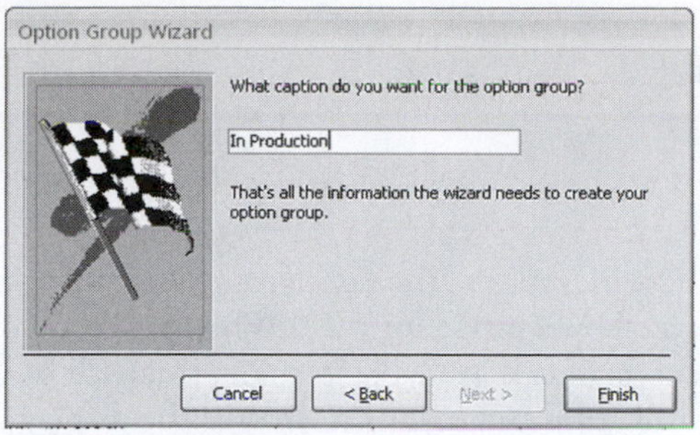

Option Group Wizard
What caption do you want for the option group?
In Production
That's all the information the wizard needs to create your option group.
Cancel
< Back
Next >
Finish

18. Click **Finish**. Your screen should look similar to Figure 7-21.

Figure 7-21

Report with option group control

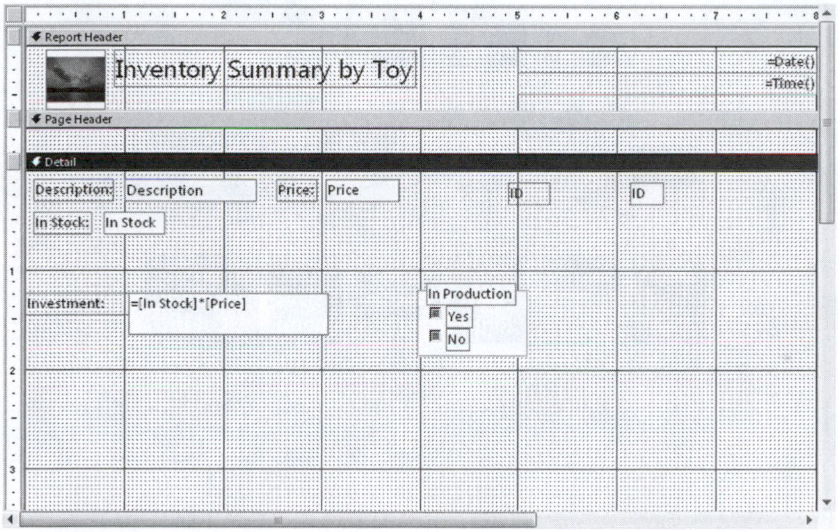

Report Header
Inventory Summary by Toy
=Date()
=Time()
Page Header
Detail
Description:
Description
Price:
Price
ID
ID
In Stock:
In Stock
Investment:
=[In Stock]*[Price]
In Production
Yes
No

19. Switch to Report view and scroll through the records to see the check boxes work.

20. **SAVE** the report.

PAUSE. LEAVE the database open to use in the next exercise.

CERTIFICATION READY?
How do you add a control to a report or form?
2.7.1

Control Wizards can help you create controls such as command buttons, list boxes, combo boxes, and option groups. Like other wizards you have used, a Control Wizard asks you questions about how you want the control to look and operate, and then it creates the control based on your answers. The Control Wizard's button is a toggle button that you can click to activate and deactivate wizards on controls that use them.

■ SOFTWARE ORIENTATION

Font Group

When you are working with reports, the Font group is located on the Design tab in the Report Design Tools, as shown in Figure 7-22. When you are working with forms, the same Font group of commands is available in the Format tab of the Form Layout Tools. Use these common formatting commands to change the display of controls and their labels in forms and reports.

Figure 7-22

Font Group on the Design tab in Report Design Tools

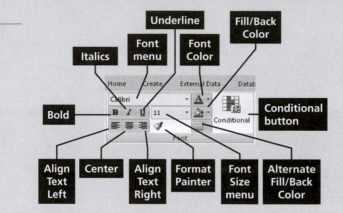

Refer to this figure in the following section and throughout the book.

■ Controls

THE BOTTOM LINE

Formatting professional-looking reports and forms not only projects high quality, but it also improves the form or report's readability. Display formatting allows you to refine the look of your reports and forms. You can change the font, font size, font color, alignment, and other attributes of text and numbers in controls and their associated labels. You can even use conditional formatting to change the look of data when certain conditions are met.

Formatting Controls

To format the display of a control, you can use many of the formatting tools that you have probably used before to format text, numbers, and objects in other Office programs, such as Word.

⊙ FORMAT THE DISPLAY OF CONTROLS

USE the database open from the previous exercise.

1. Switch to Design view.
2. Click the **In Stock** control. Position the mouse pointer over the resize handle on the right border. The mouse pointer changes to a double-sided arrow. Drag to the left to resize the control, as shown in Figure 7-23.

Figure 7-23

Resize a control

3. In the same manner, reduce the size of the **Price** and **ID** controls.

4. Click the **Description** control to select it.

5. On the Design tab, in the Font group, click the **Bold** button.

6. Click the arrow on the **Font Size** menu and select **12** from the menu.

7. Click the **In Stock** control to select it.

8. On the Design tab, in the Font group, click the **Left Align** button.

9. **SAVE** the report. Your report should look similar to Figure 7-24.

Figure 7-24

Report with display
formatting applied

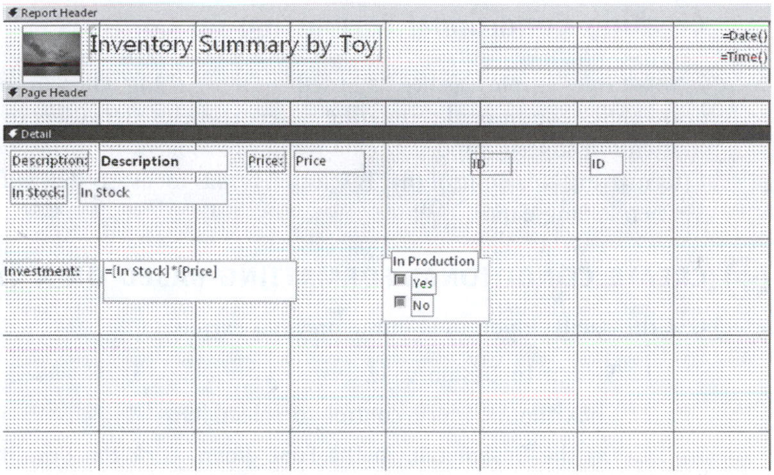

Inventory Summary by Toy

| Description: | Description | Price: | Price | | ID | | ID |

In Stock: In Stock

Investment: =[In Stock]*[Price]

In Production
Yes
No

CERTIFICATION READY?

How do you format
controls?

2.7.4

10. Switch to Report view to see the changes you made.

PAUSE. LEAVE the database open to use in the next exercise.

You can resize controls and their labels by clicking the resize handles, which are tiny squares located on the borders and corners of a selected control or label. Position the mouse pointer over a handle to get a two-sided arrow, then drag to increase or decrease the width or height of a label. To move a control and its label, select the control and position the mouse pointer over the selection until you see a four-sided arrow, then drag to the new position.

As you remember from previous lessons, forms and reports are divided into sections, including the Report Header, Page Header, Detail, Page Footer, and Report Footer. You can change the amount of space between sections to eliminate extra space and to accommodate the controls in the report or form. To increase or decrease the height of the section, position the mouse pointer over the top edge of the section border until you see a double-sided resizing arrow and drag up or down.

TAKE NOTE ✱

Double-click a section bar or any blank space within a section to display the Property Sheet for that section.

Controls on forms and reports display the format applied to the source table. However, you can change the display formatting for each control and label on a form or report. Your changes will only affect each control and the way the data appears. It does not change how users enter data or how data is stored.

TAKE NOTE You cannot apply visual formats to controls bound to Attachment and OLE Object fields. However, you can change the format of the label associated with the control.

You can format a control in Design view or Layout view using the commands in the Font group. You can change the font as well as the size, color, alignment, and background color of text. You can also add bold, underline, and italics. The Format Painter button copies formats so that you can easily apply the same formatting to another control.

TAKE NOTE By default, text does not automatically wrap when it reaches the edge of a field or box. It remains on a single line and extends beyond the edges of the control. To enable text wrapping in a form or report, set the height to a nondefault size and change the CanGrow and CanShrink properties for the control to Yes.

Creating Conditional Formatting on Controls

Sometimes employees need a little help recognizing when inventory is low or when sales are high. Conditional formatting in reports helps alert users to text or numbers that need attention so that important data is not overlooked. In forms, you can apply conditional formatting to a control that is selected or has focus, so that you don't lose your place when keying data.

→ **CREATE CONDITIONAL FORMATTING BASED ON A VALUE**

USE the database you used in the previous exercise.

1. Switch to Design view.
2. Click the **In Stock** control to select it.
3. On the Design tab, in the Font group, click the **Conditional** button. The Conditional Formatting dialog box appears.
4. In the Condition 1 section, keep the **Field Value Is** in the first menu. Click the dropdown arrow next to **between** and scroll to the bottom of the list to select **less than or equal to**. Click in the empty text box and key **10**.
5. Click the **Bold** button in the Condition 1 section.
6. Click the down arrow on the **Fill/Back Color** button. A menu of colors appears. Click **Red**, as shown in Figure 7-25.

Figure 7-25

Fill Color menu on Conditional Formatting dialog box

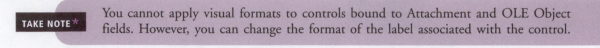

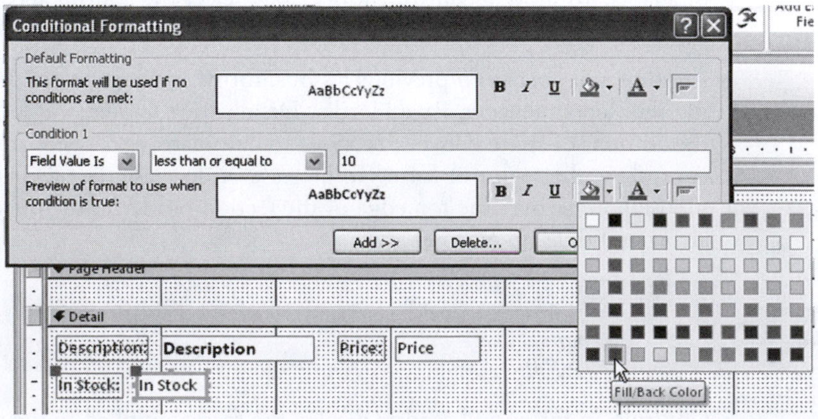

7. Click the **Add** button. A Condition 2 section is added to the dialog box, as shown in Figure 7-26.

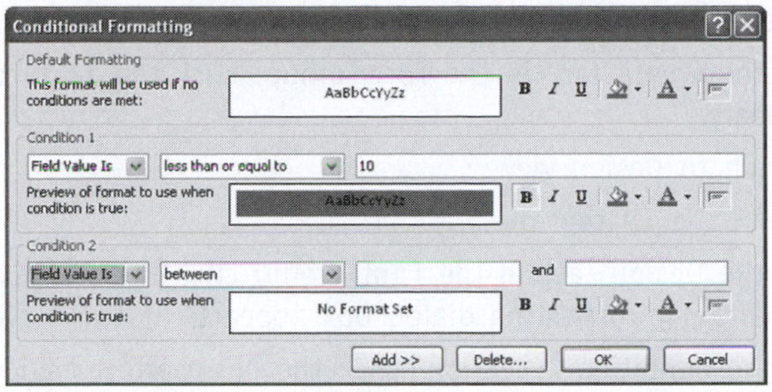

Figure 7-26

Condition 2 section on Conditional Formatting dialog box

8. Click the **Delete** button. The Delete Conditional Formatting dialog box appears, as shown in Figure 7-27.

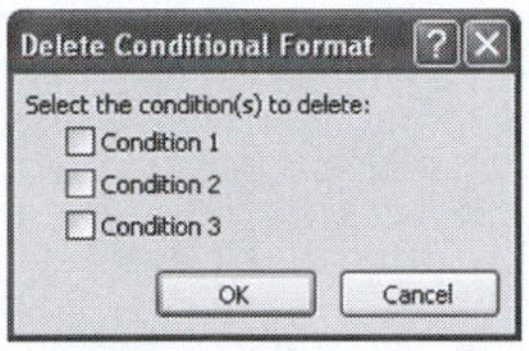

Figure 7-27

Delete Conditional Formatting dialog box

9. Click the **Condition 2** check box and click **OK.** The Condition 2 section is deleted from the dialog box.

10. Click **OK.**

11. **SAVE** the report.

12. Switch to Report view and scroll through the records to see the conditional formatting at work.

13. **CLOSE** the report.

PAUSE. LEAVE the database open to use in the next exercise.

CERTIFICATION READY?
How do you create conditional formatting on controls?
2.7.6

Conditional formatting changes the appearance of a control or the value in a control when certain conditions are met. You can change the color of text or numbers in the control or the background color.

You can create conditional formatting based on a value or expression. For example, when the number of products in an inventory falls below 10 for a single product, you can set the conditional formatting so that Access will display that number in red or with a red background so that you and others will notice the low inventory number.

The easiest way to add conditional formatting to a form or report is by using the Conditional Formatting dialog box. In Design view, select the control you want to add conditional formatting to, and click the Conditional button in the Font group. The Conditional Formatting dialog box appears, showing the current default formatting for the control. You can change the default formatting or create a condition using the dropdown menus and formatting options.

Click the Add button to add a new condition. You can specify up to three conditions for each control. If you need to delete a condition, click the Delete button to display the Delete Conditional Formatting dialog box. Click the checkbox beside the condition you want to delete and click OK.

CREATE CONDITIONAL FORMATTING WHEN A CONTROL HAS FOCUS

USE the database you used in the previous exercise.

1. Select the Inventory Table.
2. On the Create tab, in the Form group, click the **Form** button. A simple form appears.
3. Switch to Design view.
4. Select the **ID** control.
5. On the Design tab, in the Font group, click the **Conditional** button. The Conditional Formatting dialog box appears.
6. In the Condition 1 section, click the down arrow beside **Field Value Is** and select **Field Has Focus.**
7. Click the down arrow on the **Fill/Back Color** button to display the color menu. Select a light gray, as shown in Figure 7-28. The preview box displays the format.

Figure 7-28

Color menu

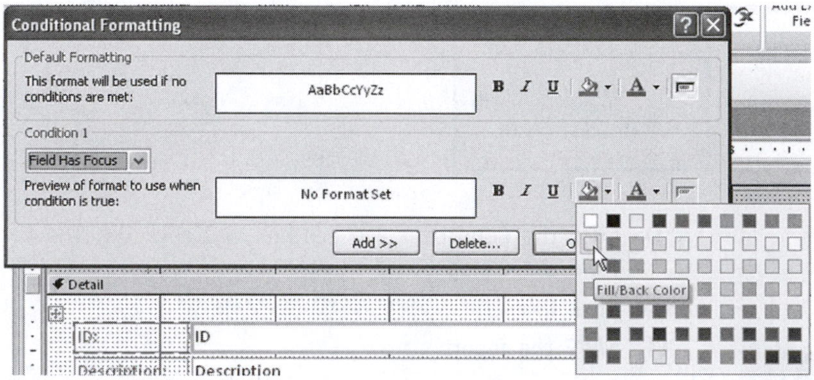

8. Click **OK.**
9. Click the **Description** control to select it.
10. Press and hold the [Shift] key. Click the **In Stock** and **Price** controls. The three controls should be selected.
11. On the Design tab, in the Font group, select **Conditional Formatting.** The Conditional Formatting dialog box appears.
12. In the Condition 1 section, click the down arrow beside **Field Value Is** and select **Field Has Focus.**
13. Click the **Fill/Back Color** button to apply the same gray color and click **OK.**
14. **SAVE** the form as **Inventory Form.**
15. Switch to Form view and press the [Tab] key to move from control to control to see the conditional formatting at work.

    PAUSE. LEAVE the form open to use in the next exercise.

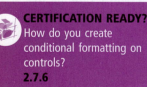

CERTIFICATION READY?
How do you create conditional formatting on controls?
2.7.6

You just created conditional formatting on a control in a form that has focus. The control that has focus is the active control, or the control that is visually highlighted. When you have a form with many controls on it, you can set conditional formatting so that Access will display the control that is selected with a different color background. This visual clue lets users know where they are in the form, which is especially helpful when entering data.

■ SOFTWARE ORIENTATION

Arrange Tab

The Arrange tab, shown in Figure 7-29, is located in the Report Design Tools. It contains groups of commands for arranging the layout, alignment, size, and position of controls on a report.

Figure 7-29

Arrange tab in the Report Design Tools Ribbon

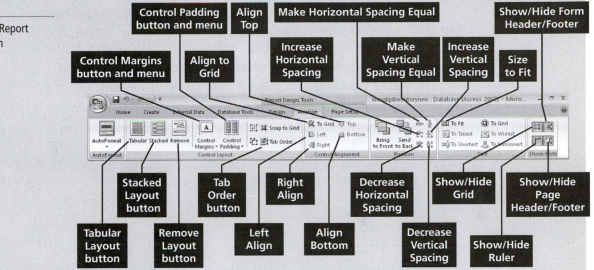

Use the commands in the Arrange tab to arrange controls on a report.

Similar to a report, the Arrange tab is displayed in the Form Design Tools area of the Ribbon. The Arrange tab, shown in Figure 7-30, contains groups of commands for arranging the layout, alignment, size, and position of controls on a form.

Figure 7-30

Arrange tab in the Forms Design Tools Ribbon

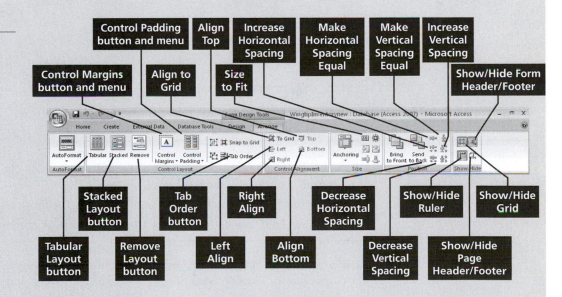

Use the commands in the Arrange tab to arrange controls on a form.

Arranging Control Layout

After you have created a form or report, you can arrange the controls on it to fit the data or to best display the data. Access provides commands for arranging the layout, alignment, position, and size of controls.

⊕ ARRANGE CONTROL LAYOUT

USE the database open from the previous exercise.

1. Click the **Inventory** table in the Navigation pane to select it.
2. On the Create tab, in the Forms group, click the **Form Design** button. A new, blank form is created, and the Field List pane is displayed. (If it isn't, click the Add Existing Fields button.)
3. Double-click the **Description** field to add it to the form.
4. Double-click the **In Stock** field to add it to the form.
5. Double-click the **Price** field to add it to the form.
6. Press and hold the [Shift] key and click each of the three controls to select them all.
7. On the Arrange tab, in the Control Layout group, click the **Stacked** button. The controls and labels are arranged in a stacked layout, as shown in Figure 7-31.

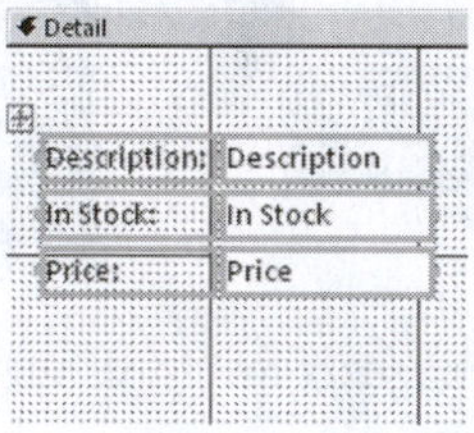

Figure 7-31

Stacked control layout

8. On the Arrange tab, in the Control Layout group, click the **Tabular** button. The controls and labels are arranged in a tabular layout, as shown in Figure 7-32.

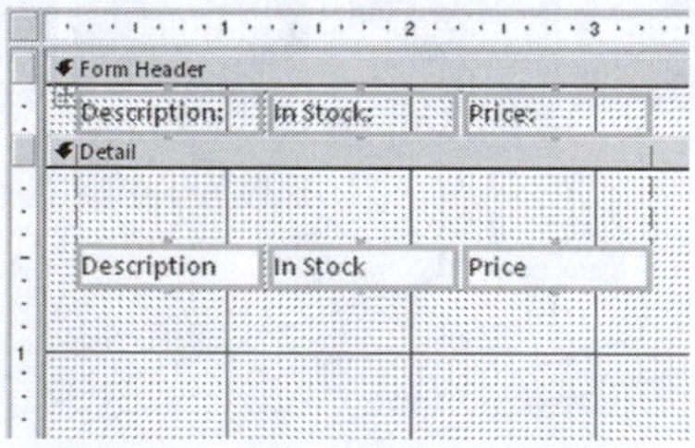

Figure 7-32

Tabular control layout

9. On the **Arrange** tab, in the **Control Layout** group, click the **Stacked** button to switch it back to a stacked layout.
10. **SAVE** the form as **Stacked Form** and leave it open for use in the next exercise.

PAUSE. LEAVE the database open to use in the next exercise.

Control layouts align your controls horizontally and vertically to give your report or form a uniform appearance. The two types of control layouts are tabular and stacked.

Controls are arranged vertically in a ***stacked layout***, with a label on the left and the control on the right, as shown in Figure 7-31. Stacked layouts are contained in one report or form section.

In a ***tabular layout***, the controls are arranged in rows and columns like a spreadsheet, with labels across the top, as shown in Figure 7-32. Tabular layouts use two sections of a report or form. The labels are displayed in one section and the fields are arranged in the section below.

You can have more than one layout on a report. For example, you could have a tabular layout to create a row of data for each record, then a stacked layout underneath with more information about the same record.

Access automatically creates tabular control layouts when you create a new report using the Report button or the Blank Report button in the Create tab. When you create a new form using the Form button or the Blank Form button, Access creates stacked control layouts.

On an existing blank report, you can create a new control layout by holding down the Shift key and selecting the fields you want to include in the form or report from the Field List pane. On the Arrange tab, in the control Layout group, click the Tabular button or the Stacked button.

You can switch the entire layout of a report or form to the other by selecting all the cells in the layout and then clicking the layout button you want, either Stacked or Tabular.

You can split a control layout into two different layouts. Hold down the Shift key and click the controls you want to move to the new control layout and click the Tabular or Stacked button.

➔ ADD AND REMOVE A CONTROL FROM A LAYOUT

USE the database open from the previous exercise.

1. Select all three controls, if they aren't selected already.
2. Click on the selection and move the group of fields down about half an inch.
3. Click the **In Production** field from the Field List pane. Drag it to the grid and place it to the right of the **Description** field.
4. Drag the **ID** field to the grid and place it above the **Description** field.
5. Press and hold the [Shift] key and select the **ID** field control, if necessary. Select the **Description**, **In Stock**, and **Price** fields so that all four are selected.
6. On the Arrange tab, in the Control Layout group, click the **Stacked** button. The **ID** control is added to the stacked layout.
7. On the Arrange tab, in the Control Layout group, click the **Control Margins** button and select **Narrow** from the menu, as shown in Figure 7-33.

Figure 7-33

Control Margins button and menu

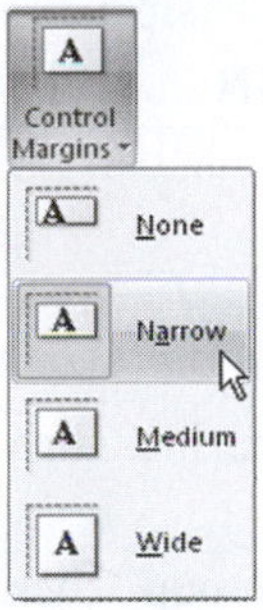

8. On the Arrange tab, in the Control Layout group, click the **Control Padding** button and select **Wide** from the menu, as shown in Figure 7-34.

Figure 7-34

Control Padding button and menu

9. Select the **Price** control and move it to the top of the layout. You should see a horizontal bar indicating where the field is being moved. When you see the horizontal bar at the top of the **ID** control, release the mouse button.

10. Move the **Price** control back to the bottom of the layout.

11. Try to move the **Price** control into place under the **In Production** field. It won't move out of the layout.

12. Select the **Price** control if it isn't selected already.

13. On the Arrange tab, in the Control Layout group, click the **Remove** button.

14. Drag the **Price** control into place under the **In Production** control.

15. **SAVE** the form.

   PAUSE. LEAVE the form open to use in the next exercise.

CERTIFICATION READY?
How do you arrange controls?
2.7.5

When you want to add a new field from the Field List to an existing control layout, just drag the field from the Field List pane to the grid. To add it to the layout, select all the controls in the layout and the new control and click the Stacked or Tabular button.

Removing a control from a control layout allows you to place it anywhere on the report without affecting the positioning of any other controls. Select the control you want to remove and click the Remove button on the Control Layout group.

You can adjust the location of information displayed in a control with the Control Margins button in the Control Layout group. You can choose None, Narrow, Medium, or Wide settings in the Control Margins menu.

 The Control Padding button adjusts the amount of space between a control and the gridlines of a layout. The Control Padding menu contains choices for None, Narrow, Medium, or Wide padding.

TAKE NOTE*

To select multiple controls, hold down the **Shift** key and then click the controls.

Arranging Control Alignment, Size, and Position

Aligning, sizing, and positioning commands on the Arrange tab gives you more options for improving the look of controls and labels in forms and reports.

➔ ARRANGE ALIGNMENT, SIZE, AND POSITION

USE the database open from the previous exercise.

1. Select the **Price** label and control.

2. On the Arrange tab, in the Size group, click the **Size to Fit** button.

3. Select all the controls in the stacked layout, including the labels and controls for the **ID**, **Description**, and **In Stock** controls.

4. On the Arrange tab, in the Control Layout group, click the **Remove** button.

5. All the controls and labels should be still selected. On the Arrange tab, in the Size group, click the **Size to Fit** button.

6. With the controls and labels still selected, on the Arrange tab, in the Control Alignment group, click the **Right** button. The labels are right-aligned to the controls.

7. Select the **Price** label and control.

8. On the Arrange tab, in the Control Position group, click the **Decrease Horizontal Spacing** button until your screen looks similar to Figure 7-35.

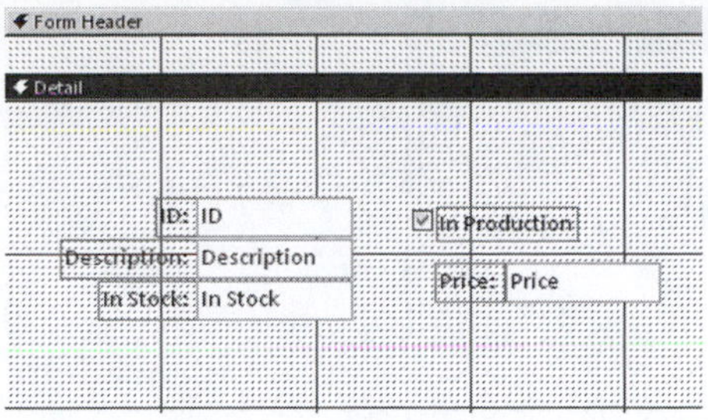

Figure 7-35

Form with arranged controls

9. Click on a blank space on the design grid.

10. On the Arrange tab, in the Show/Hide group, click the **Grid** button. The design grid disappears.

11. Click the **Grid** button again. The design grid appears.

12. On the Arrange tab, in the Show/Hide group, click the **Ruler** button. The rulers disappear.

13. Click the **Ruler** button again. The rulers reappear.

14. **SAVE** the form.

   PAUSE. LEAVE the form open to use in the next exercise.

As you just practiced, you can change the alignment, size, or position of controls and associated labels. The Control Alignment group has commands for aligning labels and controls to the grid as well as aligning left, right, top, and bottom.

The Size group contains the Anchoring command, which ties a control to another control or section so that it resizes or moves with the parent. Also in the Size group, you can use the commands to adjust the size of controls and labels to Size to Fit, Size to Grid, Size to Tallest, Size to Widest, Size to Shortest, or Size to Narrowest.

The Position group has Bring to Front and Send to Back commands to move objects in front or to the back of other objects. Also in the position group, you can use the commands to increase or decrease horizontal or vertical spacing using the Make Horizontal Spacing Equal, Make Vertical Spacing Equal, Increase Horizontal Spacing, Decrease Horizontal Spacing, Increase Vertical Spacing, and Decrease Horizontal Spacing commands.

The Show/Hide group contains toggle commands for showing or hiding the Grid, Report or Form Header/Footer sections, the Ruler, or Page Header/Footers.

Defining Control Tab Order

Control tab order refers to the order in which the selection, or focus, moves from field to field in a form or report. When entering data in a form, it is helpful to set the control tab order to a sequence that matches the order of the data you are entering.

DEFINE CONTROL TAB ORDER

USE the database you used in the previous exercise.

1. Switch to Form view.

2. Press the Tab key several times to see the order in which the controls are selected each time you press it. Notice that the tab order begins with the **Description** control and moves to the **In Stock**, **Price**, **In Production**, and **ID** controls.

3. Switch back to Design view.

4. On the Arrange tab, on the Control Layout group, click the **Tab Order** button. The Tab Order dialog box appears, as shown in Figure 7-36, displaying the tab order in the Custom Order list.

Figure 7-36

Tab Order dialog box

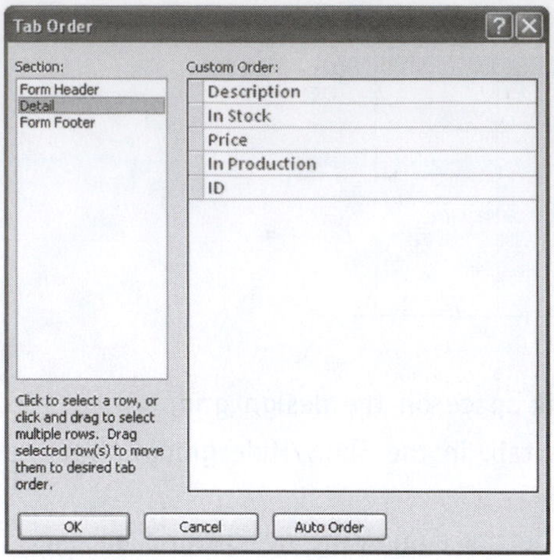

Tab Order

Section:
Form Header
Detail
Form Footer

Custom Order:
Description
In Stock
Price
In Production
ID

Click to select a row, or click and drag to select multiple rows. Drag selected row(s) to move them to desired tab order.

OK   Cancel   Auto Order

5. Click the **Auto Order** button. The order is changed.

6. Click the row selector to the left of the **Description** field to select it.

7. Click and hold the row selector. The mouse pointer changes to a move pointer with an empty rectangle. Drag up a row and notice the black horizontal line moves with you. Drag up until the black horizontal line is in place at the bottom of the **ID** field; release the mouse button. The **Description** field should be second, right below the **ID** field.

8. In the same manner, select the **In Stock** row and move it up in place below the **Description** row, as shown in Figure 7-37.

Figure 7-37

New Order on the Tab Order dialog box

Tab Order

Section:
Form Header
Detail
Form Footer

Custom Order:
ID
Description
In Stock
In Production
Price

Click to select a row, or click and drag to select multiple rows. Drag selected row(s) to move them to desired tab order.

OK   Cancel   Auto Order

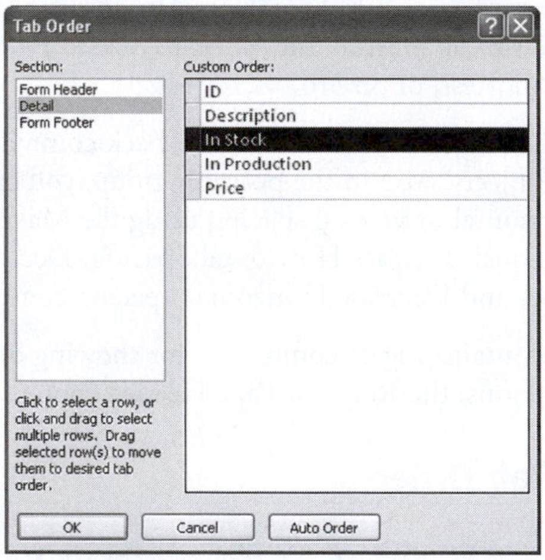

9. Click **OK**.

10. Save the form design.

11. Switch to Form view.

12. Press the [Tab] key several times to see the new tab order.

13. **CLOSE** the form.

PAUSE. CLOSE the database.

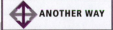

ANOTHER WAY

You can also right-click the design grid in Design view to access the Tab Order dialog box.

When you are in Form or Report view, pressing the Tab key moves the selection, or focus, to the next field. The order in which the selection moves from field to field is called the ***control tab order.*** To provide better usability, you may often need to change the tab order using the Tab Order dialog box.

CERTIFICATION READY?
How do you define control tab order?
2.7.3

The Tab Order dialog box lists each section of the report or form and the tab order of the fields in each section. Click the selection button to the left of each row in the Custom Order list to select the row. You can drag the rows into the tab order you want, from top to bottom. The AutoOrder button places the fields in the order that they appear on the form or report, from top to bottom, left to right.

SUMMARY SKILL MATRIX

IN THIS LESSON YOU LEARNED	MATRIX SKILL	SKILL NUMBER
To add an unbound control	Add controls	2.7.1
To add bound controls	Add controls, Bind controls to fields	2.7.1, 2.7.2
To add calculated controls	Add controls	2.7.1
To add controls using a Wizard	Add controls	2.7.1
To format controls	Format controls	2.7.4
To create conditional formatting on controls	Apply and change conditional formatting on controls	2.7.6
To arrange control layouts	Arrange controls	2.7.5
To arrange control alignment, size, and position	Arrange controls	2.7.5
To define control tab order	Define the tab order of controls	2.7.3

■ Knowledge Assessment

Matching

Match the term in Column 1 to its description in Column 2.

Column 1

1. control
2. unbound control
3. bound control
4. calculated control
5. Expression Builder
6. Control Wizards
7. conditional formatting

Column 2

a. a control that displays the result of a calculation or expression

b. helps you create controls such as command buttons, list boxes, combo boxes, and option groups

c. a layout in which the controls are arranged in rows and columns, with labels across the top

d. a control that doesn't have a source; it displays information such as lines, shapes, or pictures

e. controls that are arranged vertically with a label on the left and the control on the right

f. layouts that align controls horizontally and vertically to give your report or form a unique appearance

g. an object that displays data, performs actions, and lets you improve the look and usability of a form or report

8. control layouts

    h. a control that uses a field in a table or query as the data source

9. tabular layout

    i. means to change the appearance of a control or the value in a control when certain conditions are met

10. stacked layout

    j. provides the names of the fields and controls in a database, lists the operators available, and has built-in functions to help you create an expression

True / False

Circle T if the statement is true or F if the statement is false.

T F 1. The easiest way to create a bound control is to double-click or drag a field from the Property Sheet to the report.

T F 2. You can bind a control to a field using the Property Sheet.

T F 3. You can turn off Control Wizards.

T F 4. Display formatting can be applied to controls and labels in a form or report.

T F 5. You can specify an unlimited number of conditions for conditional formatting.

T F 6. You can switch an entire control layout of a report or form from one type to the other.

T F 7. Control padding adjusts the amount of space between a control and the gridlines of a layout.

T F 8. The Remove command in the Control Layout group removes a control from a form or report.

T F 9. You can set a tab order for each section of a form or report.

T F 10. Tab order refers to the order of tabs displayed in a dialog box.

■ Competency Assessment

Project 7-1: Refine the Alpine Ski House Report

You have learned a great deal about reports and forms while working as an administrative assistant at the Alpine Ski House. Refine the basic report you created previously so you can display it proudly at the front desk.

GET READY. Launch Access if it is not already running.

The *Alpine* database is available on the companion CD-ROM.

1. Open the *Alpine* database.
2. Save the database as *AlpineXXX* (where XXX is your initials).
3. Open the **Report Design** report.
4. Switch to Design view.
5. Select all four controls in the report.
6. On the Arrange tab, in the Control Layout group, click the **Tabular** button.
7. On the Arrange tab, in the Control Layout group, click the **Control Margins** button and select **Narrow** from the menu.
8. On the Arrange tab, in the Control Layout group, click the **Control Padding** button and select **Medium** from the menu.

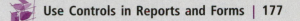

9. On the Design tab, in the Controls group, click the **Title** button. A title is inserted in the report header.

10. Key **Alpine Ski House Rooms Report** and press **Enter**.

11. On the Design tab, in the Controls group, click the **Logo** button. Open the Sample Pictures folder and select **Winter.** Click **OK.**

12. Press and hold the **Shift** key and click on all four labels and controls to select them.

13. On the Design tab in the Font group, click the **Font Color** button. Select the dark blue color called **Title Text** in the upper-left corner of the Access Theme Colors section.

14. Make sure all the controls are still selected. On the Arrange tab, in the Control Layout group, click **Remove.**

15. With the controls still selected, click and drag them together up to position just below the Detail section bar.

16. Scroll down and position the mouse pointer over the Page Footer section bar. Drag the section bar up to position just below the controls. Your screen should look similar to Figure 7-38.

Figure 7-38

Report design report

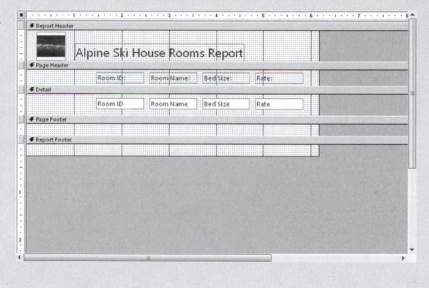

17. **SAVE** and **CLOSE** the report.

CLOSE the database.

Project 7-2: Format the Soccer Roster

Since you have increased your Access skills, you decide to improve on the soccer roster you created at the beginning of the season. There have been a few changes anyway, so you need an updated version.

The *SoccerData* database is available on the companion CD-ROM.

1. **OPEN** *SoccerData* from the data files for this lesson.

2. **SAVE** the database as *SoccerDataXXX* (where XXX is your initials).

3. **OPEN** the Roster report.

4. Switch to Design view.

5. Press and hold the **Shift** key and click on all the labels in the Page Header section to select them.

6. On the Design tab, in the Font group, click the **Bold** button.

7. Select the title, Roster, and key **Soccer Roster.**

8. On the Design tab, in the Font group, click the **Font** menu and select **Arial Black.**

CD

The *soccer.jpg* image is available on the companion CD-ROM.

9. On the Design tab, in the Font group, click the **Font Size** menu and select **22.**
10. On the Arrange tab, in the Size group, click the **To Fit** button.
11. Delete the report image.
12. On the Design tab, in the Controls group, click the **Logo** button.
13. Locate the data files for this lesson and select **soccer.jpg.**
14. **SAVE** the report and view it in Report view.
    CLOSE the database.

■ Proficiency Assessment

Project 7-3: Create the Fourth Coffee Order Summary Form

In your part-time job at Fourth Coffee, you are often involved in taking and filling orders. Create a summary table to help make your job easier.

CD

The *Coffee Data* database is available on the companion CD-ROM.

1. **OPEN** *Coffee Data* from the data files for this lesson.
2. **SAVE** the database as *CoffeeDataXXX* (where XXX is your initials).
3. Select the **Order Summary** table in the Navigation pane.
4. Create a simple form using the **Form** button.
5. Insert a **Date and Time** control with the format 00/00/0000.
6. Delete the **Paid** control and create a Yes/No **Option Group** control using check boxes with **Paid** as the caption. Remember that the value for Yes is **-1** and the value for No is **0.**
7. Delete the **Attachment** field.
8. Resize and arrange the controls to look similar to the form in Figure 7-39. Remember to remove the control layout formatting so that you can move individual controls.

Figure 7-39

Order Summary form

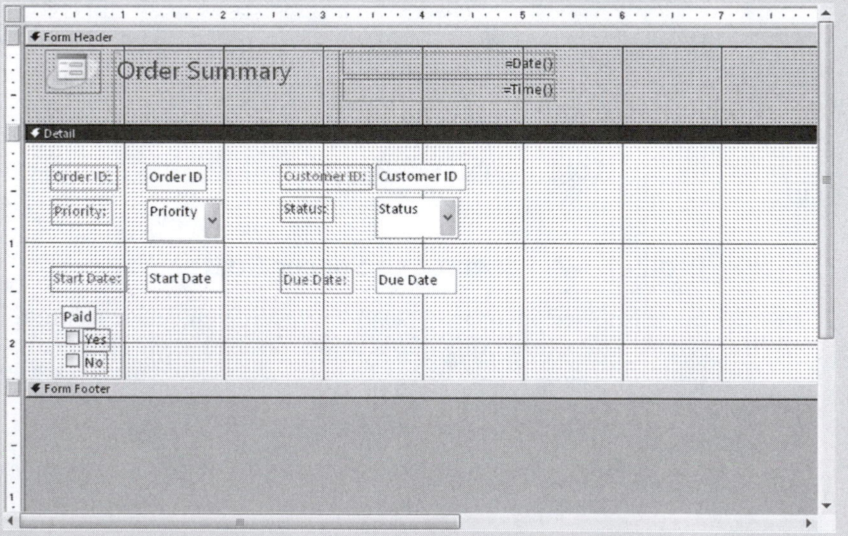

9. Save the form as **Order Summary.**
10. Check your work in Form view.
11. **CLOSE** the form.
    CLOSE the database.

Project 7-4: Create the Alpine Ski House Reservations Form

Entering data in the table is becoming cumbersome, so you decide to create a form you can use to enter reservation data.

USE *AlpineXXX*, which you saved in a previous exercise.

1. Click the **Reservations** table in the Navigation pane to select it.
2. Create a new form using Design View.
3. Insert a title control. Change the title to **Alpine Ski House Reservations Form.**
4. Insert a logo control using the **Winter** picture from the Sample Pictures folder.
5. Add the following bound controls to the design grid: **Customer ID, Room, Rate, Check-In Date, Check-Out Date,** and **Notes.**
6. Select all the controls and apply the **Stacked** control layout.
7. Position the controls in the upper-left corner of the Details section, as shown in Figure 7-40.

Figure 7-40

Reservations form

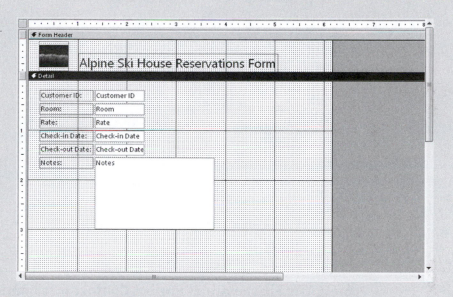

8. Remove the stacked layout and resize the **Notes** control, as shown in Figure 7-40.
9. Save the form as **Reservations Form** and leave it open for use in the next exercise.

   LEAVE the database open for the next project.

■ Mastery Assessment

Project 7-5: Refine the Alpine Ski House Reservations Form

The reservations form you created is very helpful; however, you need to add more functionality to the form using calculated controls and Control Wizards.

USE the form open from the previous exercise.

1. Add an Option box control on the right side of the form. Use the Control Wizard to create the option box for the **Credit Card on File** field. Remember that the value for Yes is **-1** and the value for No is 0. Use option buttons, and label the control **Credit Card on File.**
2. Add an unbound text box control below the Credit Card on File field.
3. Open the Property Sheet and click the **Build** button in the Control Source property.

4. Create an expression to subtract the **Check-In Date** from the **Check-Out date.**
5. Key **Number of Nights** as the label. (Note the default label number, such as Text##.)
6. Add an unbound text box control beside the **Notes** control.
7. Open the Property Sheet and click the **Build** button in the Control Source property.
8. Create an expression to multiply the **Number of Nights** (or Text##) by the **Rate.**
9. Key **Rate Subtotal** as the label.
10. Change all the controls and labels you added with black text to the blue Title Text color.
11. Your screen should look similar to Figure 7-41.

Figure 7-41

Revised reservations form

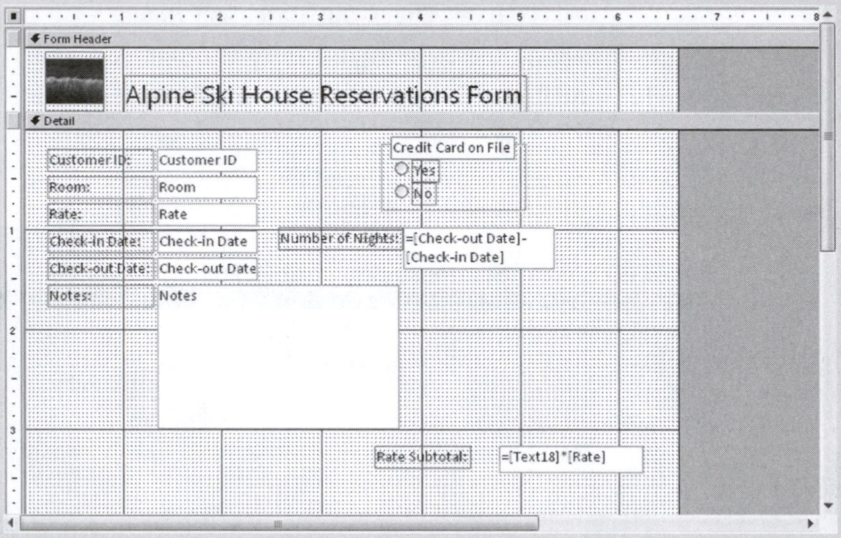

12. Save the form and switch to Form view.
13. **CLOSE** the database.

Project 7-6: Fix the Angel Project Contact Information Form

A volunteer did some work on the Angel Project database while you were on vacation. The Contact Information form has a few problems that you need to fix.

CD

The *AngelData* database is available on the companion CD-ROM.

1. **OPEN** *AngelData* from the data files for this lesson.
2. Save the database as **AngelDataXXX** (where XXX is your initials).
3. Open the **Contact Information Form.**
4. Change the layout from tabular to stacked.
5. Bind the unbound control to the **City** field.
6. Fix the control tab order.
7. **SAVE** and close the form.
   CLOSE Access.

INTERNET READY

What are your favorite toys? Maybe you have some favorites from childhood or perhaps you have some favorite grown-up toys, such as electronic gadgets. Search online stores for details about the toys. Create a database table with fields like Name, Description, Store, and Price. Use what you've learned in this lesson to create a form with controls for each field. Enter the data for five toys into your form. For extra practice, create a report that displays a summary of all your data.

Create and Modify Queries

Skills	Matrix Skill	Skill Number
Creating a Query	Create queries	4.1
Creating a Query from a Table	Create queries based on a single table	4.1.1
Creating a Query from Multiple Tables	Create queries based on more than one table	4.1.2
Modifying a Query	Modify queries	4.2
Adding a Table to a Query	Add tables to and remove tables from queries	4.2.1
Removing a Table from a Query	Add tables to and remove tables from queries	4.2.1
Adding Criteria to a Query	Add criteria to queries	4.2.2
Sorting Data Within a Query	Sort data within queries	5.1.2
Filtering Data Within a Query	Filter data within queries	5.2.2

You work for Northwind Traders, a mountain-climbing apparel company dedicated to producing high-quality and technically innovative products. The company has a program called Industry Friends that offers discount purchasing privileges for employees and other outdoor professionals and friends who qualify. As operations coordinator, you are responsible for approving applications for the program and entering related information into the database. You often need to pull specific data from the database. In this lesson, you will learn how to create queries from a single table—including a simple query and a find duplicates query—and how to create queries from multiple tables, including a find unmatched query. You will learn how to modify a query by adding a table, removing a table, and adding criteria to a query. You will also learn how to sort and filter data within a query.

KEY TERMS
field list
parameter query
query criterion
recordsource
select query

▪ SOFTWARE ORIENTATION

Other Group

The Other group on the Create tab contains the commands used to create queries. The Query Wizard button launches the Query Wizard, which helps you to create a simple query, a crosstab query, a find duplicates query, or a find unmatched query. The Query Design button creates a new, blank query in Design view.

Figure 8-1

Other group

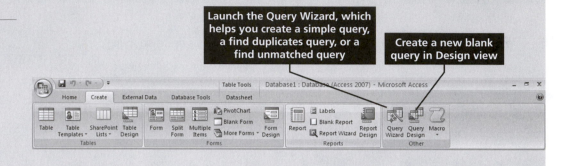

Launch the Query Wizard, which helps you create a simple query, a find duplicates query, or a find unmatched query

Create a new blank query in Design view

Use this figure as a reference throughout this lesson as well as the rest of this book.

▪ Creating a Query

THE BOTTOM LINE

A query is a set of instructions used for working with data. Creating a query is like asking the database a question. Running a query performs these instructions and provides the answers. The results that a query returns can be sorted, grouped, or filtered. A query can also create, copy, delete, or change data.

Creating a Query from a Table

CERTIFICATION READY?
How do you create queries?
4.1

When one table will provide the information that you need, you can create a simple select query using the Query Wizard. You can also use a query to find records with duplicate field values in a single table.

⊙ **CREATE A SIMPLE QUERY**

CD

The *Northwind* database file is available on the companion CD-ROM.

GET READY. Before you begin these steps, be sure to launch Microsoft Access.

1. **OPEN** the *Northwind* database from the data files for this lesson.
2. **SAVE** the database as *Northwind XXX* (where XXX is your initials).
3. On the Create tab, in the Other group, click the **Query Wizard** button. The New Query dialog box appears, as shown in Figure 8-2.

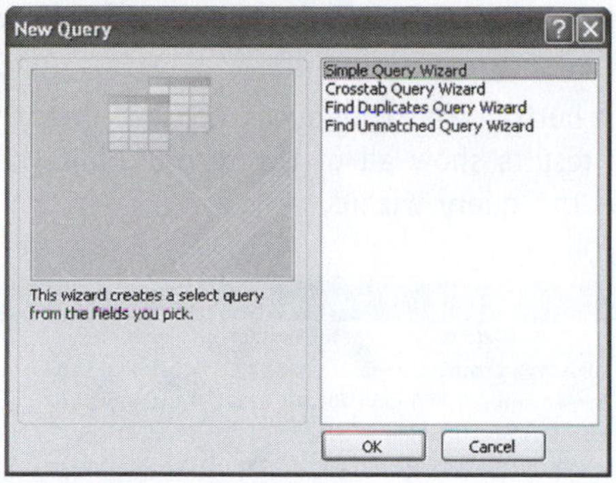

Figure 8-2

New Query dialog box

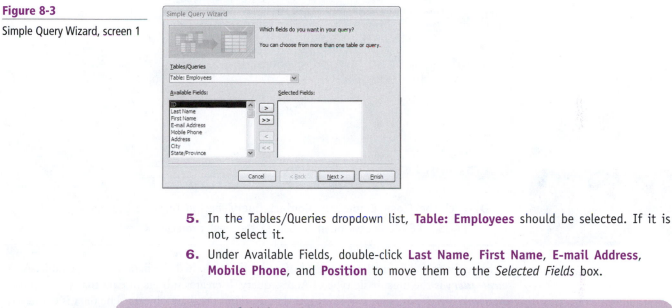

4. Click **Simple Query Wizard** and then click **OK.** The Simple Query Wizard appears, as shown in Figure 8-3.

Figure 8-3

Simple Query Wizard, screen 1

5. In the Tables/Queries dropdown list, **Table: Employees** should be selected. If it is not, select it.

6. Under Available Fields, double-click **Last Name**, **First Name**, **E-mail Address**, **Mobile Phone**, and **Position** to move them to the *Selected Fields* box.

TAKE NOTE To remove a field from the Selected Fields box, double-click the field. This moves it back to the Available Fields box.

7. Click the **Next >** button. The second screen in the Simple Query Wizard appears, as shown in Figure 8-4.

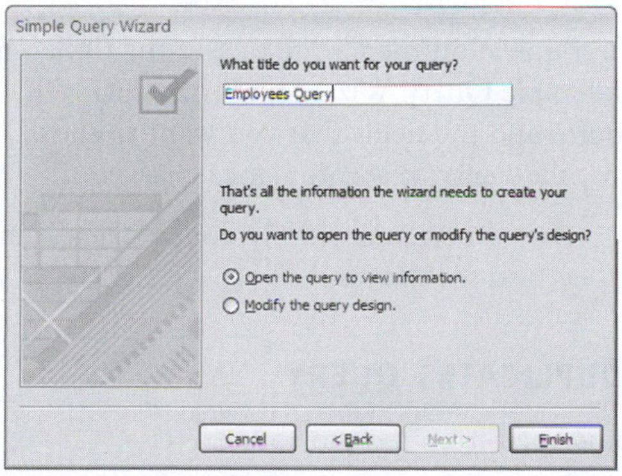

Figure 8-4

Simple Query Wizard, screen 2

8. Name the query **Employees Contact Query**. *Open the query to view information* should be selected.

9. Click the **Finish** button. The Employees Contact Query is displayed, as shown in Figure 8-5. The results show all of the records, but show only the five fields that you specified in the query wizard.

Figure 8-5

Simple select query

Last Name	First Name	E-mail Address	Mobile Phor	Position
Busch	Patricia	pbusch@northwindtrade	203.555.1455	Customer Serv
Coleman	Pat	pcoleman@northwindtra	203.555.4312	Customer Serv
Daniels	David	ddaniels@northwindtrad	203.555.0979	Product Line Di
DeOliveira	Jose	jdeoliveira@northwindtr	430.555.7542	Graphic Design
Fatima	Suroor	sfatima@northwindtrade	203.555.8652	Product Line M
Hanson	Mark	mhanson@northwindtra	406.555.2333	Sales Associate
Holliday	Nicole	nholliday@northwindtra	203.555.7319	Assistant Sales
Johnson	Willis	wjohnson@northwindtra	203.555.0034	Director of Sale
Laszlo	Rebecca	rlaszlo@northwindtrader	918.555.3488	Marketing Coo
Lee	Frank	flee@northwindtraders.c	203.555.2831	Director of Mar
Lee	Mark	mlee@northwindtraders	203.555.5632	Marketing Man
Reiter	Tsvi	treiter@northwindtrader	203.555.7535	Sales Operatio
Su	Min	smin@northwindtraders.	203.555.2341	Business Opera

Record: 1 of 13 | No Filter | Search

CERTIFICATION READY?
How do you create queries based on single tables?
4.1.1

10. Click the **Close 'Employees Contact Query'** button to close the query.

PAUSE. LEAVE Access open to use in the next exercise.

In this activity, you created a simple select query that searched the data in a single table. A *select query* is the most basic type of Access query. It creates subsets of data that you can use to answer specific questions or to supply data to other database objects. The data is displayed in Datasheet view without being changed.

A query is a powerful and versatile database tool. Queries differ from sort or filter commands because they can be saved for future use and can extract data from multiple tables or queries.

A query can get its data from one or more tables, from existing queries, or from a combination of the two. The tables or queries from which a query gets its data are referred to as its *recordsource*.

To create a simple select query, on the Create tab, in the Other group, click the Query Wizard button. Click Simple Query Wizard and then click OK. Specify the table you want to use as the recordsource and the fields that you want to show. Name the query and click Finish. When you close the query, it is automatically saved.

To run a query after it has been created, simply double-click it in the Navigation pane to open it in Datasheet view and see the results.

CREATE A FIND DUPLICATES QUERY

USE the database that is open from the previous exercise.

1. On the Create tab, in the Other group, click the **Query Wizard** button. The New Query dialog box appears.

2. Click **Find Duplicates Query Wizard** and then click **OK**. The Find Duplicates Query Wizard appears, as shown in Figure 8-6.

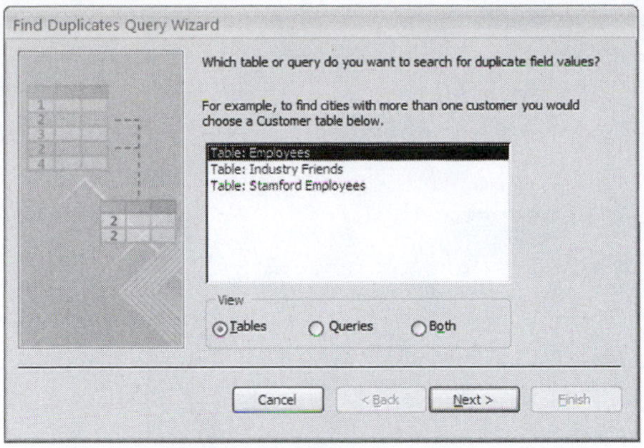

Figure 8-6

Find Duplicates Query
Wizard, screen 1

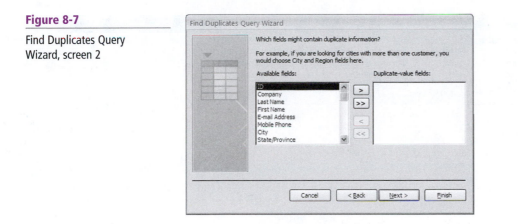

3. Click **Table: Industry Friends** and then click **Next>**. The next screen in the Find Duplicates Query Wizard appears, as shown in Figure 8-7.

Figure 8-7

Find Duplicates Query
Wizard, screen 2

4. Double-click **Last Name**, **First Name**, and **E-mail Address** to move them to the *Duplicate-value fields* box.

5. Click **Next >** to display the next screen in the Find Duplicate Query Wizard, shown in Figure 8-8.

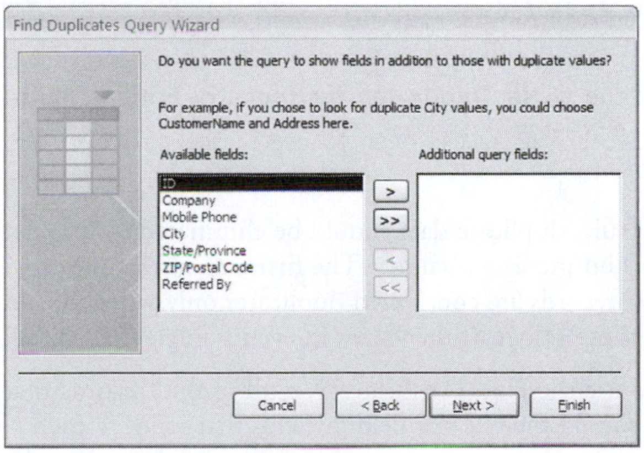

Figure 8-8

Find Duplicates Query
Wizard, screen 3

6. Double-click **Company** and **Referred By** to move them to the *Additional query fields* box.

7. Click **Next >** to display the final screen in the Find Duplicate Query Wizard, shown in Figure 8-9.

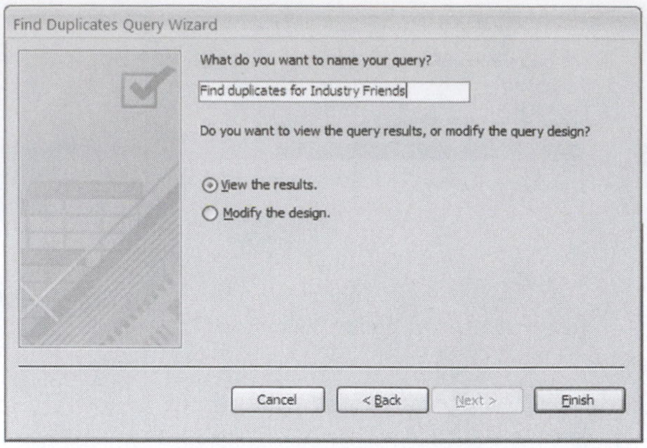

Figure 8-9

Find Duplicates Query
Wizard, final screen

Find Duplicates Query Wizard

What do you want to name your query?

Find duplicates for Industry Friends

Do you want to view the query results, or modify the query design?

◉ View the results.

○ Modify the design.

| Cancel | < Back | Next > | Finish |

8. Name the query **Duplicates for Industry Friends** and click **Finish**. The query showing duplicate records in the table is displayed, as shown in Figure 8-10.

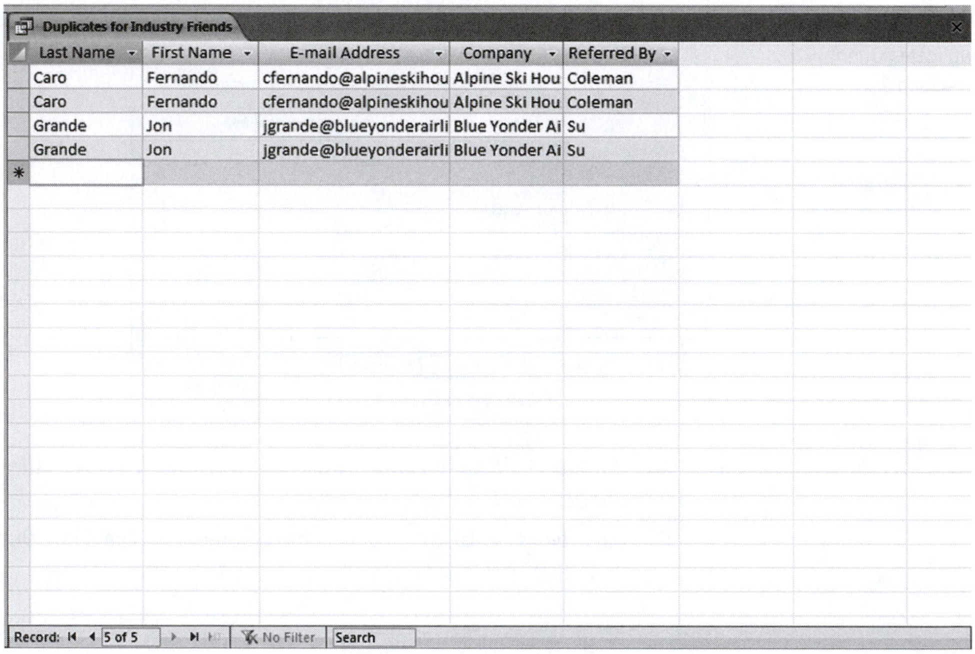

Figure 8-10

Duplicates for Industry
Friends query

Duplicates for Industry Friends

Last Name	First Name	E-mail Address	Company	Referred By
Caro	Fernando	cfernando@alpineskihou	Alpine Ski Hou	Coleman
Caro	Fernando	cfernando@alpineskihou	Alpine Ski Hou	Coleman
Grande	Jon	jgrande@blueyonderairli	Blue Yonder Ai	Su
Grande	Jon	jgrande@blueyonderairli	Blue Yonder Ai	Su

Record: I◀ ◀ 5 of 5 ▶ ▶I ▶☐ No Filter Search

CERTIFICATION READY?
How do you create queries based on single tables?
4.1.1

9. Click the **Close 'Duplicates for Industry Friends'** button to close the query.

PAUSE. LEAVE Access open to use in the next exercise.

As a general rule, duplicate data should be eliminated from a database whenever possible to reduce costs and increase accuracy. The first step in this process is finding duplicate data. Two or more records are considered duplicates only when all the fields in your query results contain the same values. If the values in even a single field differ, each record is unique.

You can also use the Find Duplicates Wizard to find records that contain *some* matching field values. You should include the field or fields that identify each record uniquely, typically the primary key. The query returns matching records where the values in the specified fields match character for character.

Creating a Query from Multiple Tables

If the data you need is spread out in more than one table, you can build a query that combines information from multiple sources. You can also create a query that finds records in one table that have no related records in another table.

➔ CREATE A QUERY FROM MULTIPLE TABLES

USE the database that is open from the previous exercise.

1. In the Navigation pane, double-click **Employees: Table** to open the table.

2. On the Datasheet tab, in the Relationships group, click the **Relationships** button to display the table relationship, as shown in Figure 8-11.

Figure 8-11

Relationships for Employees table

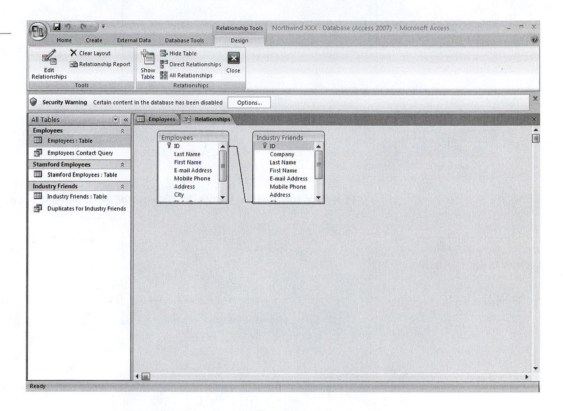

3. Click the **Close 'Relationships'** button to close the Relationship window and click the **Close 'Employees'** button to close the Employees table.

4. On the Create tab, in the Other group, click the **Query Wizard** button to display the New Query dialog box.

5. Click **Simple Query Wizard** and then click **OK** to display the Simple Query Wizard.

6. In the Tables/Queries dropdown list, click **Table: Industry Friends.**

7. Under Available Fields, double-click **Last Name**, **First Name**, and **Referred By** to move them to the *Selected Fields* box.

8. In the Tables/Queries dropdown list, click **Table: Employees.**

9. Under Available Fields, double-click **Position** and then **E-mail Address** to move them to the *Selected Fields* box.

10. Click the **Next >** button to display the next screen, shown in Figure 8-12. Detail query should be selected.

Figure 8-12

Simple Query Wizard for multiple tables

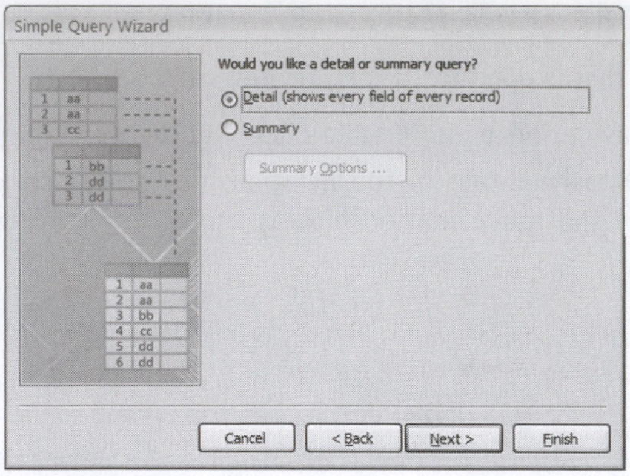

LOOKING AHEAD If you want your query to perform aggregate functions, you would choose a summary query. You will learn about aggregated functions in Lesson 12.

11. Click the **Next >** button to display the final screen, shown in Figure 8-13.

Figure 8-13

Simple Query Wizard for multiple tables, final screen

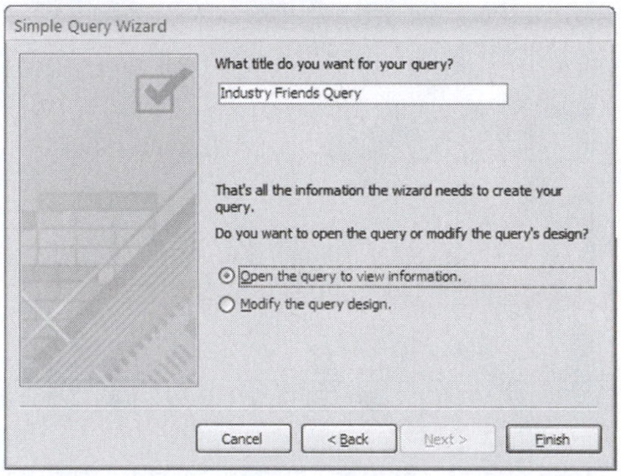

12. Click the **Finish** button to accept the suggested name and display the query, shown in Figure 8-14. This query shows the position and e-mail address of the employee who referred each industry friend.

Figure 8-14

Industry Friends query

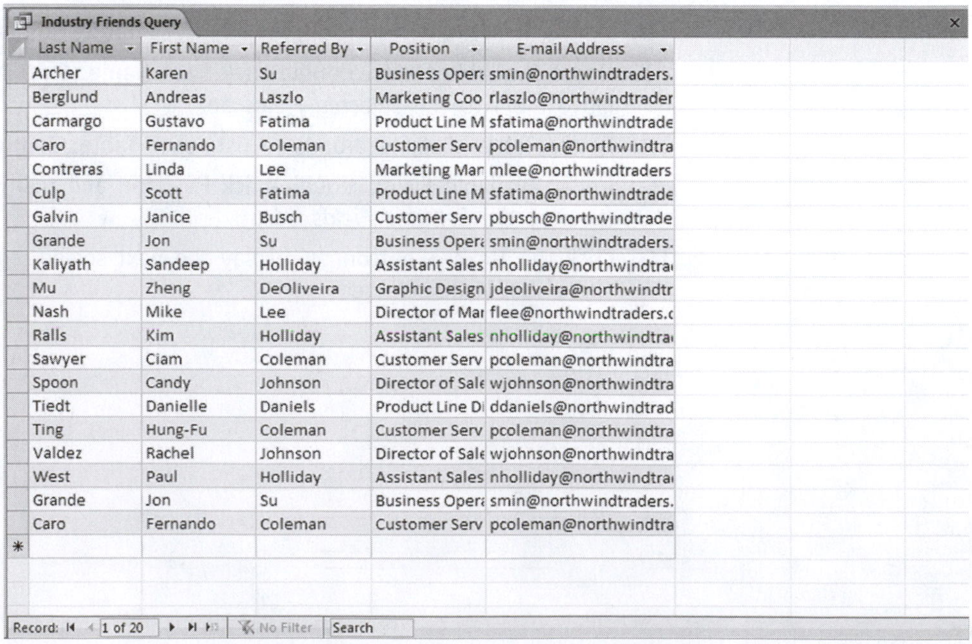

Last Name	First Name	Referred By	Position	E-mail Address
Archer	Karen	Su	Business Opera	smin@northwindtraders.
Berglund	Andreas	Laszlo	Marketing Coo	rlaszlo@northwindtrader
Carmargo	Gustavo	Fatima	Product Line M	sfatima@northwindtrade
Caro	Fernando	Coleman	Customer Serv	pcoleman@northwindtra
Contreras	Linda	Lee	Marketing Man	mlee@northwindtraders
Culp	Scott	Fatima	Product Line M	sfatima@northwindtrade
Galvin	Janice	Busch	Customer Serv	pbusch@northwindtrade
Grande	Jon	Su	Business Opera	smin@northwindtraders.
Kaliyath	Sandeep	Holliday	Assistant Sales	nholliday@northwindtra
Mu	Zheng	DeOliveira	Graphic Design	jdeoliveira@northwindtr
Nash	Mike	Lee	Director of Mar	flee@northwindtraders.c
Ralls	Kim	Holliday	Assistant Sales	nholliday@northwindtra
Sawyer	Ciam	Coleman	Customer Serv	pcoleman@northwindtra
Spoon	Candy	Johnson	Director of Sale	wjohnson@northwindtra
Tiedt	Danielle	Daniels	Product Line Di	ddaniels@northwindtrad
Ting	Hung-Fu	Coleman	Customer Serv	pcoleman@northwindtra
Valdez	Rachel	Johnson	Director of Sale	wjohnson@northwindtra
West	Paul	Holliday	Assistant Sales	nholliday@northwindtra
Grande	Jon	Su	Business Opera	smin@northwindtraders.
Caro	Fernando	Coleman	Customer Serv	pcoleman@northwindtra

Record: 1 of 20 | No Filter | Search

13. Click the **Close 'Industry Friends Query'** button to close the query.

PAUSE. LEAVE the database open to use in the next exercise.

CERTIFICATION READY?
How do you create queries based on more than one table?
4.1.2

Sometimes using data from a related table would help make the query results clearer and more useful. For example, in this activity, you could pull the name of the industry friends and the employee who referred them from one table. But to get additional information about the referring employees, you need to pull data from the related Employee table.

When you need to include multiple tables in your query, you can use the Simple Query Wizard to build a query from a primary table and a related table. The process is similar to creating a query from a single table, except that you include fields from additional tables.

REF

You learned about defining and modifying table relationships in Lesson 3.

Before creating a query from multiple tables, you must first ensure that the tables have a defined relationship in the Relationships window. A relationship appears as a line connecting the two tables on a common field. You can double-click a relationship line to see which fields in the tables are connected by the relationship.

FIND UNMATCHED RECORDS

USE the database that is open from the previous exercise.

1. On the Create tab, in the Other group, click the **Query Wizard** button. The New Query dialog box appears.

2. Click **Find Unmatched Query Wizard** and then click **OK**. The Find Unmatched Query Wizard appears, as shown in Figure 8-15.

Figure 8-15

Find Unmatched Query Wizard, screen 1

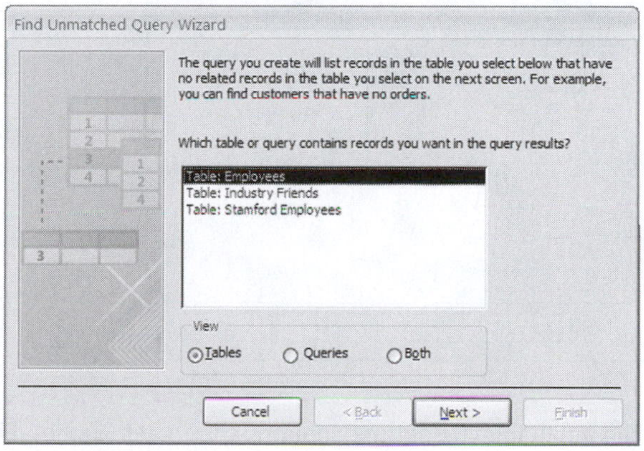

> Find Unmatched Query Wizard
>
> The query you create will list records in the table you select below that have no related records in the table you select on the next screen. For example, you can find customers that have no orders.
>
> Which table or query contains records you want in the query results?
>
> Table: Employees
> Table: Industry Friends
> Table: Stamford Employees
>
> View
> ⦿ Tables   ○ Queries   ○ Both
>
> Cancel   < Back   Next >   Finish

3. **Table: Employees** should be selected. Click the **Next >** button to display the next screen in the Find Unmatched Query Wizard, shown in Figure 8-16.

Figure 8-16

Find Unmatched Query Wizard, screen 2

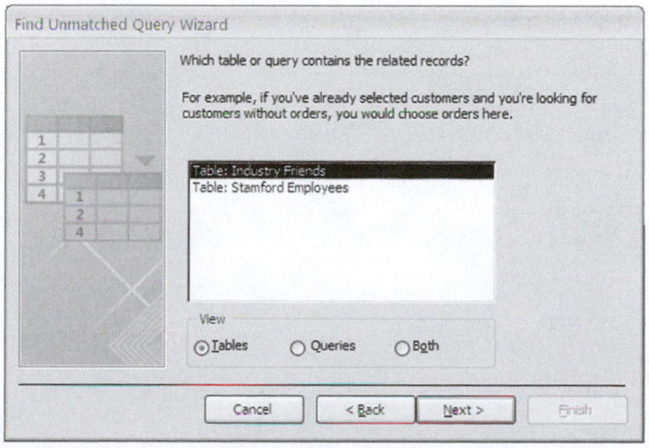

> Find Unmatched Query Wizard
>
> Which table or query contains the related records?
>
> For example, if you've already selected customers and you're looking for customers without orders, you would choose orders here.
>
> Table: Industry Friends
> Table: Stamford Employees
>
> View
> ⦿ Tables   ○ Queries   ○ Both
>
> Cancel   < Back   Next >   Finish

4. Select **Table: Stamford Employees**. Click the **Next >** button to display the next screen in the Find Unmatched Query Wizard, shown in Figure 8-17.

Figure 8-17

Find Unmatched Query
Wizard, screen 3

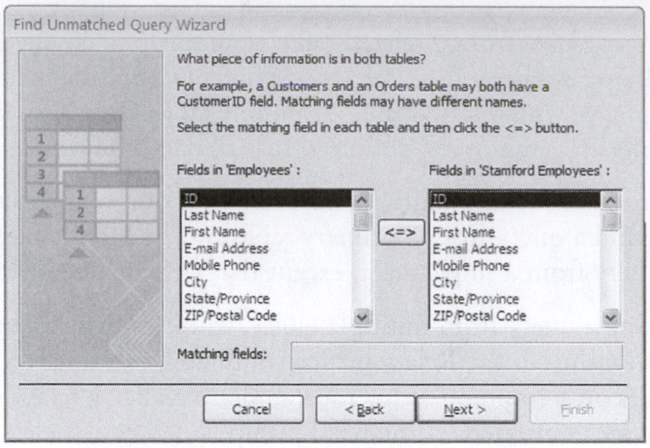

5. Click **E-mail Address** in the Fields in 'Employees' list. Click **E-mail Address** in the Fields in 'Stamford Employees' list. Click the **<=>** button to display them in the Matching fields box.

6. Click the **Next >** button to display the next screen in the Find Unmatched Query Wizard, shown in Figure 8-18.

Figure 8-18

Find Unmatched Query
Wizard, screen 4

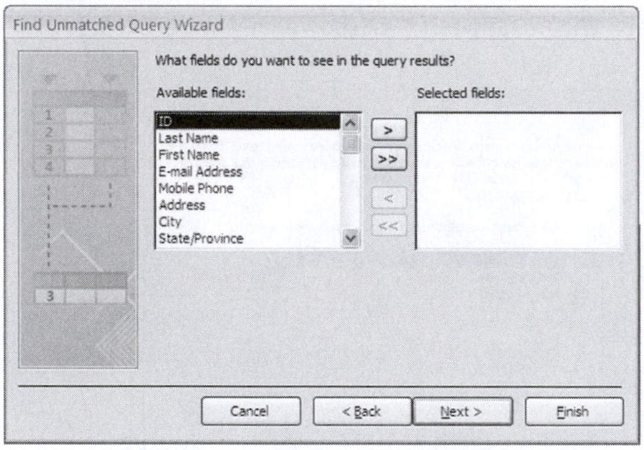

7. In the Available fields box, double-click **Last Name**, **First Name**, **Position**, and **City** to move them to the *Selected fields* box.

8. Click the **Next >** button to display the final screen in the Find Unmatched Query Wizard, shown in Figure 8-19.

Figure 8-19

Find Unmatched Query
Wizard, final screen

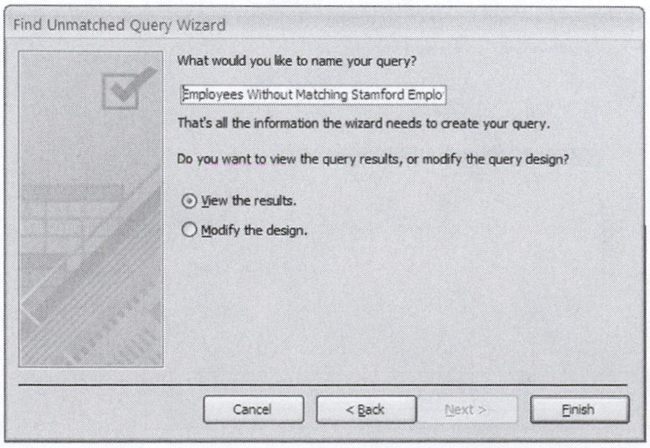

9. Name the query **Non-Stamford Employees** and click the **Finish** button. The query is displayed, as shown in Figure 8-20.

Figure 8-20

Non-Stamford Employees query

Last Name	First Name	Position	City
Daniels	David	Product Line Di	New Canaan
Holliday	Nicole	Assistant Sales	Darien
Laszlo	Rebecca	Marketing Coo	Darien
Reiter	Tsvi	Sales Operatio	Norwalk

Record: ⏮ ◀ 1 of 4 ▶ ⏭ ▷ ✖ No Filter Search

CERTIFICATION READY?
How do you create queries based on more than one table?
4.1.2

10. Click the **Close 'Non-Stamford Employees'** button to close the query.

PAUSE. LEAVE the database open to use in the next exercise.

To view only the records in one table that do not have a matching record in another table, you can create a Find Unmatched query. In the activity above, you created a query that displayed all the employees who do not live in Stamford.

On the Create tab, in the Other group, click Query Wizard and then click Find Unmatched Query Wizard to start the wizard. In this activity, once you have created a find unmatched query, it returns four records in the Employees table that do not have overlapping records in the Stamford Employees table.

Design Tab

By switching to Design view, you can access all the tools needed to modify your query on the Design tab, shown in Figure 8-21.

Figure 8-21

Design tab

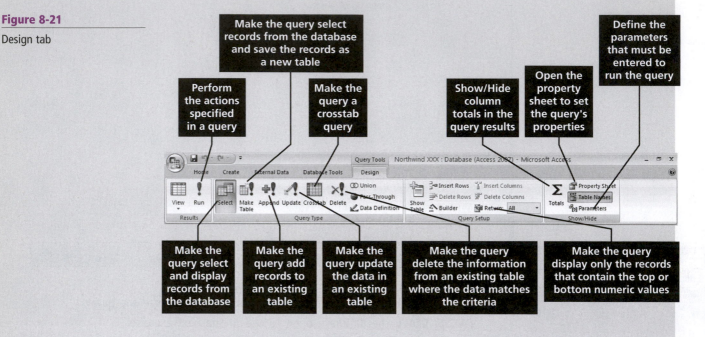

Use this figure as a reference throughout this lesson as well as the rest of this book.

■ Modifying a Query

THE BOTTOM LINE  A query can be modified in Design view, regardless of how it was created. You can add or remove a table, add or remove fields, or add criteria to refine query results.

CERTIFICATION READY?
How do you modify queries?
4.2

Adding a Table to a Query

The Show Table dialog box is used to add a table to a query in Design view.

⊕ **ADD A TABLE TO A QUERY**

USE the database that is open from the previous exercise.

1. Double-click the **Industry Friends** query in the Navigation pane to open it.
2. On the Home tab, in the Views menu, click the **View** button and then click **Design View**. The query appears in Design view, as shown in Figure 8-22.

Figure 8-22

Query in Design view

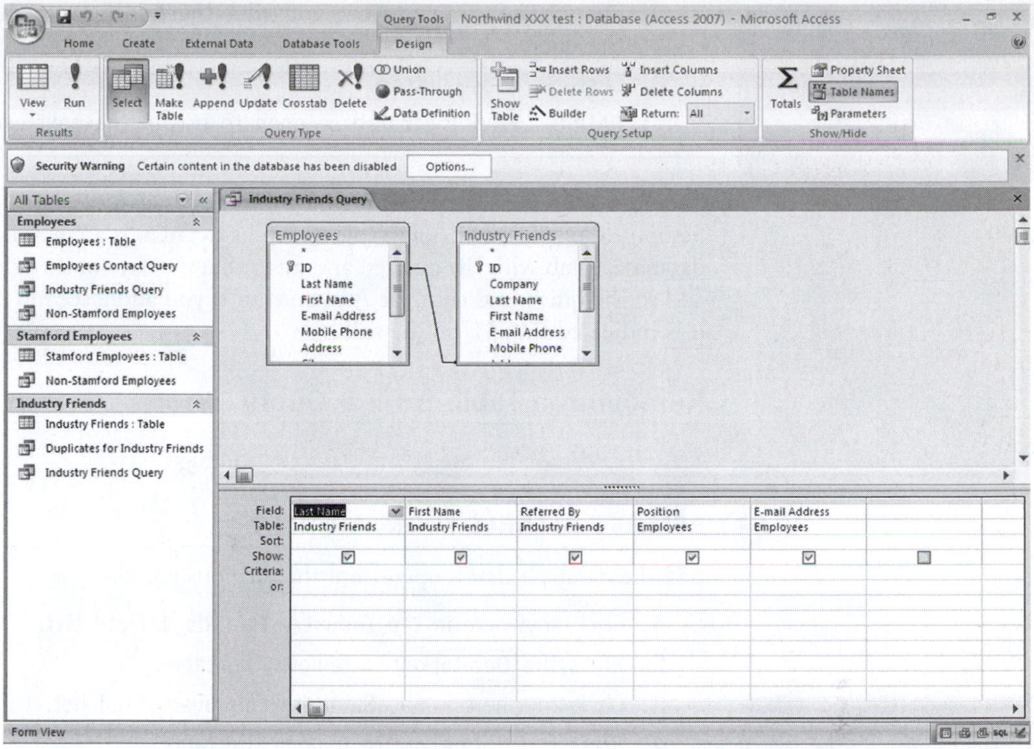

3. On the Design tab, in the Query Setup group, click the **Show Table** button to display the Show Table dialog box, shown in Figure 8-23.

Figure 8-23

Show Table dialog box

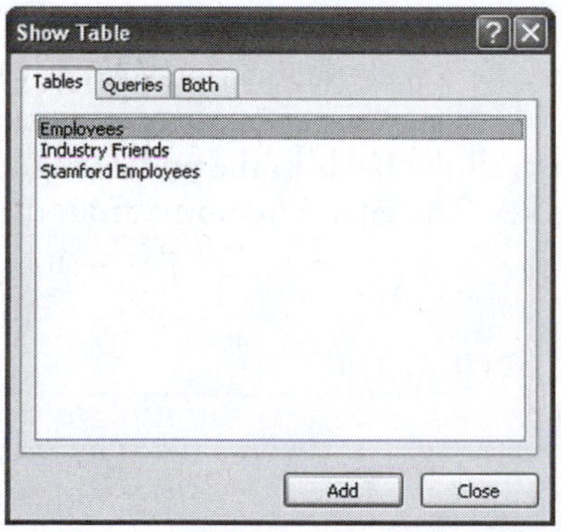

4. Click **Industry Friends** and click the **Add** button. A second copy of the Industry Friends table is added to the query, as indicated by the "1" in the title, as shown in Figure 8-24.

Figure 8-24

Second copy of table in a query

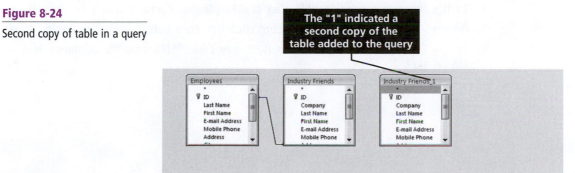

The "1" indicated a second copy of the table added to the query

CERTIFICATION READY?
How do you add tables to and remove tables from queries?
4.2.1

5. Click **Stamford Employees** and click the **Add** button. The table is added to the query.

6. Click the **Close** button.

PAUSE. LEAVE the database open to use in the next exercise.

To add a table to a query, you must be in Design view. On the Design tab, in the Query Setup group, click the Show Table dialog box. There is a tab that contains the tables in the database, a tab with the queries, and a tab that displays both. Select the object you want to add to the query and click the Add button. If you add a second copy of a table to the query, it is indicated by a "1" in the title.

Removing a Table from a Query

A table can be removed from a query in Design view.

➔ REMOVE A TABLE FROM A QUERY

USE the database that is open from the previous exercise.

1. Click anywhere in the **Industry Friends_1 field list**.
2. Press the [Delete] key to remove the table.
3. Click anywhere in the Stamford Employees field list.
4. Press the [Delete] key to remove the table.
5. Click the **Close 'Industry Friends'** button to close the query. If a message asks you if you want to save the changes, click **Yes**.

PAUSE. LEAVE the database open to use in the next exercise.

To remove a table from a query, first open the query in Design view. In the upper part of query Design view, select the table you want to remove by clicking anywhere in its field list—a **field list** is a window that lists all the fields in the underlying record source or database object—then press the Delete key. The table is removed from the query, but it is not deleted from the database.

Adding Criteria to a Query

Not all queries must include criteria, but if you are not interested in seeing all the records that are stored in the underlying recordsource, you can add criteria to a query when designing it.

➔ ADD CRITERIA TO A QUERY

USE the database that is open from the previous exercise.

1. In the Navigation pane, double-click the **Employees Contact Query** to open it.
2. On the Home tab, in the Views group, click the **View** button and click **Design View**.
3. In the Criteria row of the Position field, key **Like "*Manager*"**, as shown in Figure 8-25.

CERTIFICATION READY?
How do you add tables to and remove tables from queries?
4.2.1

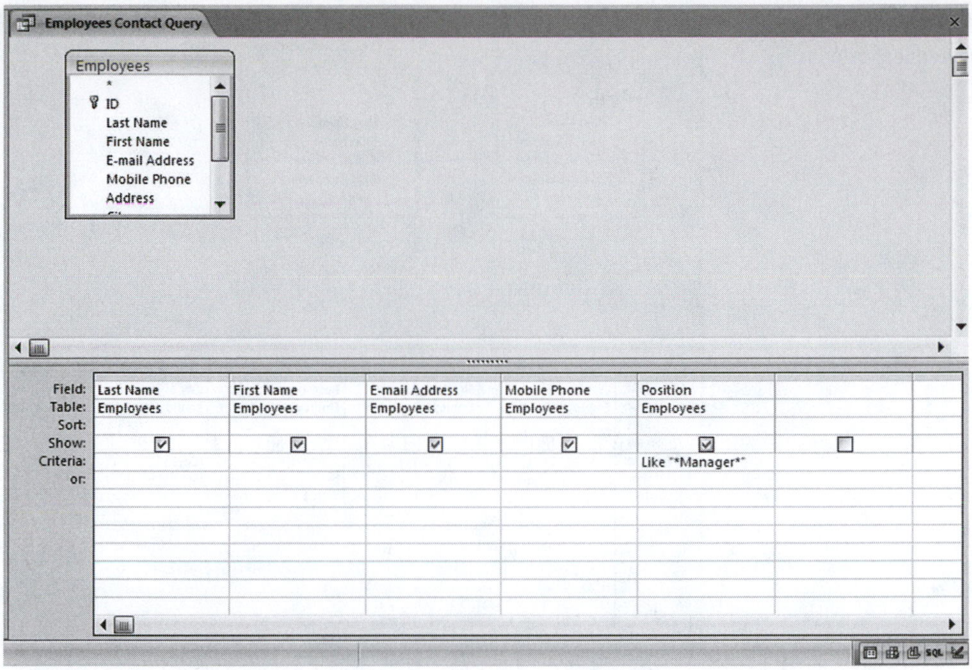

Figure 8-25

Query criterion

4. On the Design tab, in the Results group, click the **View** button and click **Datasheet View**. The query results display all records with "Manager" in the position field, as shown in Figure 8-26.

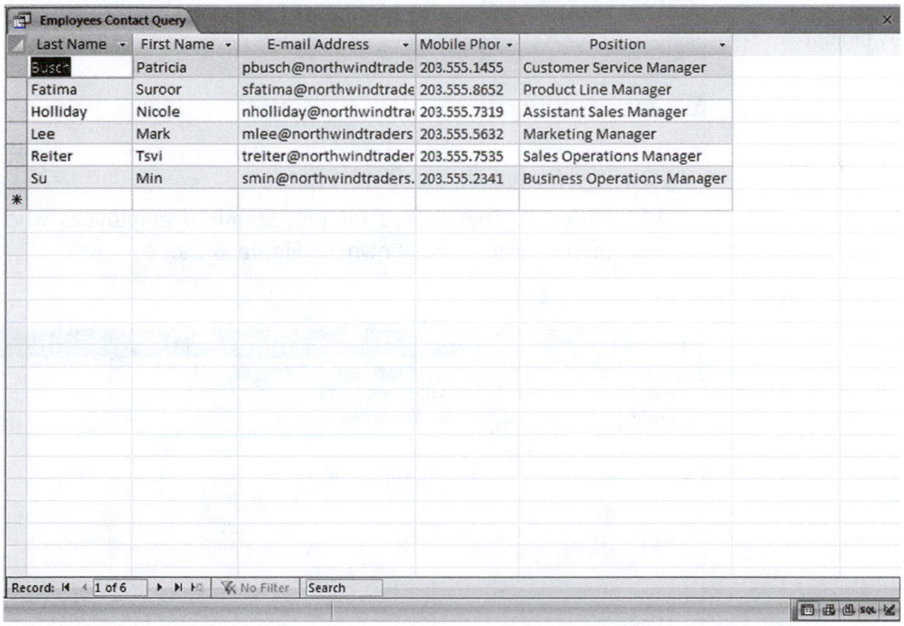

Figure 8-26

Results with query criteria applied

5. Click the **Close 'Employees Contact Query'** button to close the query. When prompted to save, click **Yes**.

6. In the Navigation pane, double-click the **Non-Stamford Employees Query** to open it.

7. On the Home tab, in the Views group, click the **View** button and click **Design View**.

8. In the Criteria row of the Position field, key **[City?]**, as shown in Figure 8-27.

Figure 8-27

Parameter query criteria

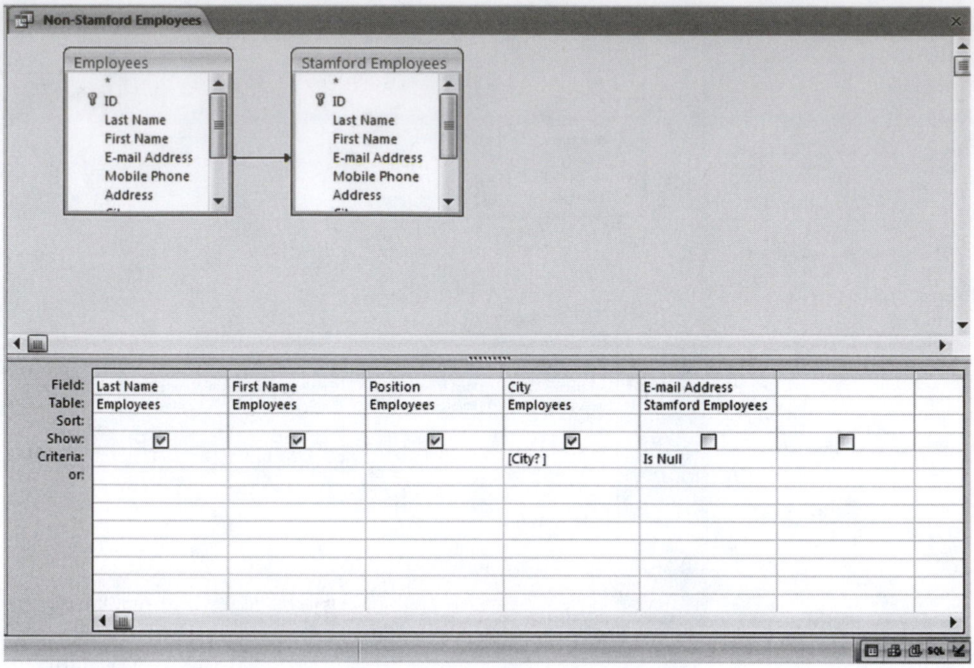

9. On the Home tab, in the Views group, click the **View** button and click **Datasheet View**. The prompt appears in the Enter Parameter Value dialog box, as shown in Figure 8-28.

Figure 8-28

Parameter query prompt dialog box

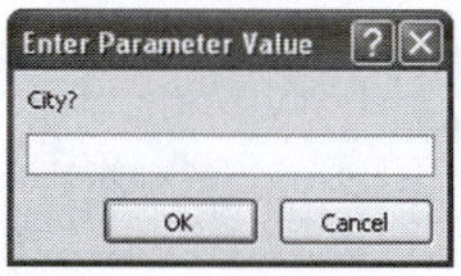

10. Key **Darien** in the City? box.

11. Click **OK**. The records for non-Stamford employees who live in Darien are displayed in the results, as shown in Figure 8-29.

Figure 8-29

Parameter query results

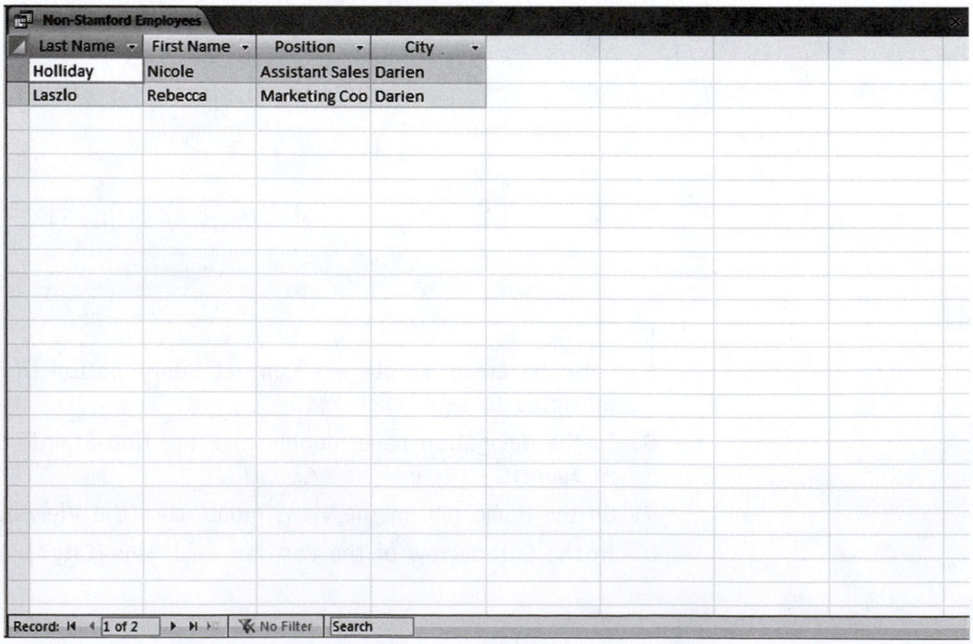

CERTIFICATION READY?
How do you add criteria to queries?
4.2.2

12. Click the **Close 'Non-Stamford Employees'** button to close the query. When prompted to save, click **Yes**.

PAUSE. LEAVE the database open to use in the next exercise.

A *query criterion* is a rule that identifies the records that you want to include in the query result. To specify one or more criteria to restrict the records returned in the query results, open the query in Design view. Select the field and type the condition that you want to specify in the Criteria row. To see the results, switch to Datasheet view.

A criterion is similar to a formula. Some criteria are simple and use basic operators and constants. Others are complex and use functions, special operators, and include field references. Criteria can look very different from each other, depending on the data type of the field to which they apply and your specific requirements.

Table 8-1 shows some sample criteria and explains how they work. Table 8-2 shows the query results that are returned when specific criterion is used.

Table 8-1

Criteria examples

CRITERIA	DESCRIPTION
>25 and <50	This criterion applies to a Number field, such as Inventory. It includes only those records where the Inventory field contains a value greater than 25 and less than 50.
DateDiff ("yyyy", [BirthDate], Date()) > 21	This criterion applies to a Date/Time field, such as BirthDate. Only records where the number of years between a person's birth date and today's date is greater than 21 are included in the query result.
Is Null	This criterion can be applied to any type of field to show records where the field value is null.

Table 8-2

Query result examples

TO INCLUDE RECORDS THAT...	USE THIS CRITERION	QUERY RESULT
Exactly match a value, such as Manager	"Manager"	Returns records where the given field is set to Manager.
Do not match a value, such as Chicago	Not "Chicago"	Returns records where the given field is set to a value other than Chicago.
Begin with the specified string, such as B	Like B*	Returns records for the given field where the value starts with "B," such as Boston, Bakersfield, and so on.
Do not begin with the specified string, such as B	Not Like B*	Returns records for the given field where the value starts with a character other than "B."
Contain the specified string, such as Sales	Like "*Sales*"	Returns records for the given field that contain the string "Sales."
Do not contain the specified string, such as Sales	Not Like "*Sales*"	Returns records for the given field that do not contain the string "Sales."

You can also run a *parameter query*, in which the user interactively specifies one or more criteria values. This is not a separate query; it extends the flexibility of another type of query, such as a select query, by prompting the user for a value when it is run.

■ Sorting and Filtering Data Within a Query

 THE BOTTOM LINE Sorting and filtering data within a query allows you to display only the records you want and/or only in a particular order.

Sorting Data Within a Query

Sorting data in a query can help organize data efficiently and make it easier for users to review and locate the records they want without having to browse the data.

X REF You learned about sorting data within a table in Lesson 3, sorting data within a form in Lesson 5, and sorting data within a report in Lesson 6.

➡ SORT DATA WITHIN A QUERY

USE the database that is open from the previous exercise.

1. In the Navigation pane, double-click the **Industry Friends Query** to open it.
2. Right-click the **Referred by** field to display the shortcut menu shown in Figure 8-30.

Figure 8-30

Shortcut menu

Last Name	First Name	Referred By	Position	E-mail Address
Archer	Karen	Su		@northwindtraders.
Berglund	Andreas	Laszlo		@northwindtrader
Carmargo	Gustavo	Fatima		a@northwindtrade
Caro	Fernando	Coleman		man@northwindtra
Contreras	Linda	Lee		@northwindtraders
Culp	Scott	Fatima		a@northwindtrade
Galvin	Janice	Busch		h@northwindtrade
Grande	Jon	Su		@northwindtraders.
Kaliyath	Sandeep	Holliday		day@northwindtra
Mu	Zheng	DeOliveira		veira@northwindtr
Nash	Mike	Lee	Director of Mar	@northwindtraders.c
Ralls	Kim	Holliday	Assistant Sales	nholliday@northwindtra
Sawyer	Ciam	Coleman	Customer Serv	pcoleman@northwindtra
Spoon	Candy	Johnson	Director of Sale	wjohnson@northwindtra
Tiedt	Danielle	Daniels	Product Line Di	ddaniels@northwindtrad
Ting	Hung-Fu	Coleman	Customer Serv	pcoleman@northwindtra
Valdez	Rachel	Johnson	Director of Sale	wjohnson@northwindtra
West	Paul	Holliday	Assistant Sales	nholliday@northwindtra
Grande	Jon	Su	Business Opera	smin@northwindtraders.
Caro	Fernando	Coleman	Customer Serv	pcoleman@northwindtra

Shortcut menu items shown over the query:
- Sort A to Z
- Sort Z to A
- Copy
- Paste
- Column Width...
- Hide Columns
- Unhide Columns...
- Freeze Columns
- Unfreeze All Columns

Record: ◄ ◄ 1 of 20 ► ►► ►* | No Filter | Search

3. Click **Sort A to Z**. The field is sorted in alphabetic order from A to Z, as shown in Figure 8-31.

Figure 8-31

Sorted query

Last Name	First Name	Referred By	Position	E-mail Address
Galvin	Janice	Busch	Customer Serv	pbusch@northwindtrade
Caro	Fernando	Coleman	Customer Serv	pcoleman@northwindtra
Sawyer	Ciam	Coleman	Customer Serv	pcoleman@northwindtra
Ting	Hung-Fu	Coleman	Customer Serv	pcoleman@northwindtra
Caro	Fernando	Coleman	Customer Serv	pcoleman@northwindtra
Tiedt	Danielle	Daniels	Product Line Di	ddaniels@northwindtrad
Mu	Zheng	DeOliveira	Graphic Design	jdeoliveira@northwindtr
Culp	Scott	Fatima	Product Line M	sfatima@northwindtrade
Carmargo	Gustavo	Fatima	Product Line M	sfatima@northwindtrade
Ralls	Kim	Holliday	Assistant Sales	nholliday@northwindtra
West	Paul	Holliday	Assistant Sales	nholliday@northwindtra
Kaliyath	Sandeep	Holliday	Assistant Sales	nholliday@northwindtra
Spoon	Candy	Johnson	Director of Sale	wjohnson@northwindtra
Valdez	Rachel	Johnson	Director of Sale	wjohnson@northwindtra
Berglund	Andreas	Laszlo	Marketing Coo	rlaszlo@northwindtrader
Nash	Mike	Lee	Director of Mar	flee@northwindtraders.c
Contreras	Linda	Lee	Marketing Mar	mlee@northwindtraders
Grande	Jon	Su	Business Opera	smin@northwindtraders.
Archer	Karen	Su	Business Opera	smin@northwindtraders.
Grande	Jon	Su	Business Opera	smin@northwindtraders.

Industry Friends Query

Record: I◄ ◄ 1 of 20 ► ►I ►※ | ※ No Filter | Search

4. On the Home tab, in the Sort & Filter group, click the **Clear All Sorts** button.

5. On the Home tab, in the Sort & Filter group, click the **Advanced** button to display the menu shown in Figure 8-32.

Figure 8-32

Advanced menu

Selection ▾ Replace
Advanced ▾ Go To ▾
Filter   ←elect ▾
Sort

- Clear All Filters
- Filter By Form
- Apply Filter/Sort
- Advanced Filter/Sort...
- Load from Query...
- Save As Query
- Delete Tab
- × Clear Grid
- Close

6. Click **Advanced Filter/Sort**. An Industry Friends QueryFilter1 tab appears, as shown in Figure 8-33.

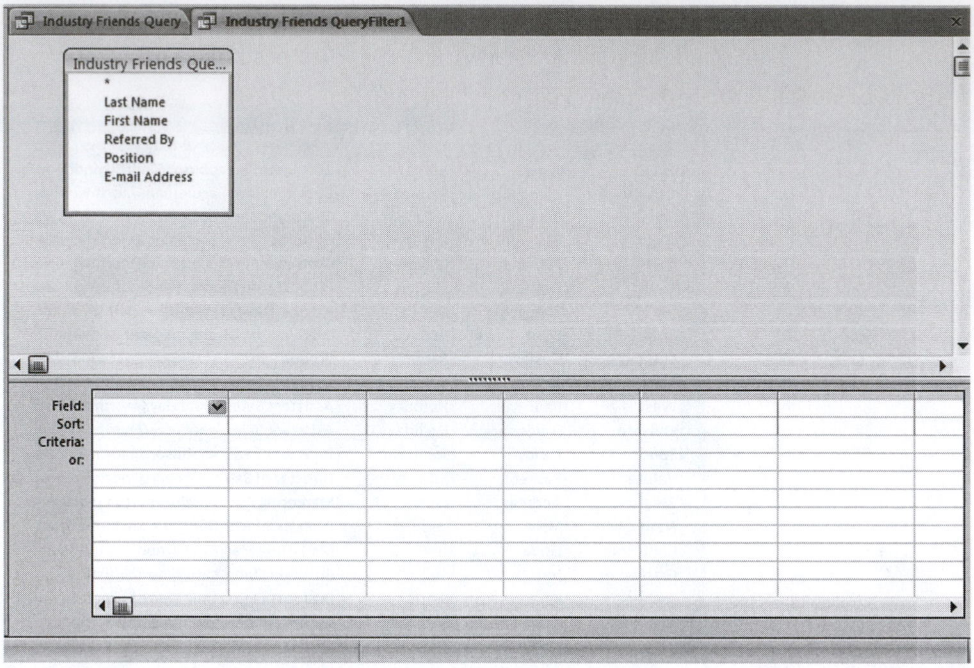

Figure 8-33

Industry Friends
QueryFilter1 tab

7. Click the **Field cell** in the first column, click the **down arrow**, and click **Referred by** on the dropdown menu.

8. Click the **Sort cell** in the first column, click the **down arrow**, and click **Ascending** on the dropdown menu.

9. Click the **Field cell** in the second column, click the **down arrow**, and click **Last Name** on the dropdown menu.

10. Click the **Sort cell** in the second column, click the **down arrow**, and click **Ascending** on the dropdown menu. Your screen should look similar to Figure 8-34.

Figure 8-34

Advanced sort criteria

11. On the Home tab, in the Sort & Filter group, click the **Advanced** button and click **Apply Filter/Sort**. The query is sorted by the Referred by field in ascending order and then by the Last Name field in ascending order, as shown in Figure 8-35.

Figure 8-35

Sorted query

Last Name	First Name	Referred By	Position	E-mail Address
Galvin	Janice	Busch	Customer Serv	pbusch@northwindtrade
Caro	Fernando	Coleman	Customer Serv	pcoleman@northwindtra
Caro	Fernando	Coleman	Customer Serv	pcoleman@northwindtra
Sawyer	Ciam	Coleman	Customer Serv	pcoleman@northwindtra
Ting	Hung-Fu	Coleman	Customer Serv	pcoleman@northwindtra
Tiedt	Danielle	Daniels	Product Line Di	ddaniels@northwindtrad
Mu	Zheng	DeOliveira	Graphic Design	jdeoliveira@northwindtr
Carmargo	Gustavo	Fatima	Product Line M	sfatima@northwindtrade
Culp	Scott	Fatima	Product Line M	sfatima@northwindtrade
Kaliyath	Sandeep	Holliday	Assistant Sales	nholliday@northwindtra
Ralls	Kim	Holliday	Assistant Sales	nholliday@northwindtra
West	Paul	Holliday	Assistant Sales	nholliday@northwindtra
Spoon	Candy	Johnson	Director of Sale	wjohnson@northwindtra
Valdez	Rachel	Johnson	Director of Sale	wjohnson@northwindtra
Berglund	Andreas	Laszlo	Marketing Coo	rlaszlo@northwindtrader
Nash	Mike	Lee	Director of Mar	flee@northwindtraders.c
Contreras	Linda	Lee	Marketing Mar	mlee@northwindtraders
Archer	Karen	Su	Business Opera	smin@northwindtraders.
Grande	Jon	Su	Business Opera	smin@northwindtraders.
Grande	Jon	Su	Business Opera	smin@northwindtraders.

Record: 1 of 20   No Filter   Search

CERTIFICATION READY?
How do you sort data within queries?
5.1.2

12. On the Home tab, in the Sort & Filter group, click the **Clear All Sorts** button.
PAUSE. LEAVE the database open to use in the next exercise.

Data can be sorted in the Datasheet view of a query. Right-click the field on which you want to sort and click the sort order you want—ascending or descending—from the shortcut menu. The records are rearranged to match the sort order.

TAKE NOTE *

The same tab is used to perform an advanced filter for the query.

To sort by more than one field, on the Home tab, in the Sort & Filter group, click the Advanced button and click Advanced Filter/Sort to open up a tab where you can specify more than one field to sort by and the sort order.

Filtering Data Within a Query

A filter limits a view of data to specific records without requiring you to alter the design of the underlying query.

 REF

You learned about filtering data within a table in Lesson 3, filtering data within a form in Lesson 5, and filtering data within a report in Lesson 6.

→ FILTER DATA WITHIN A QUERY

USE the database that is open from the previous exercise. The Industry Friends Query should be open.

1. Click the **Position header** to select the field.
2. On the Home tab, in the Sort & Filter group, click the **Filter** button. A menu appears on the field, as shown in Figure 8-36.

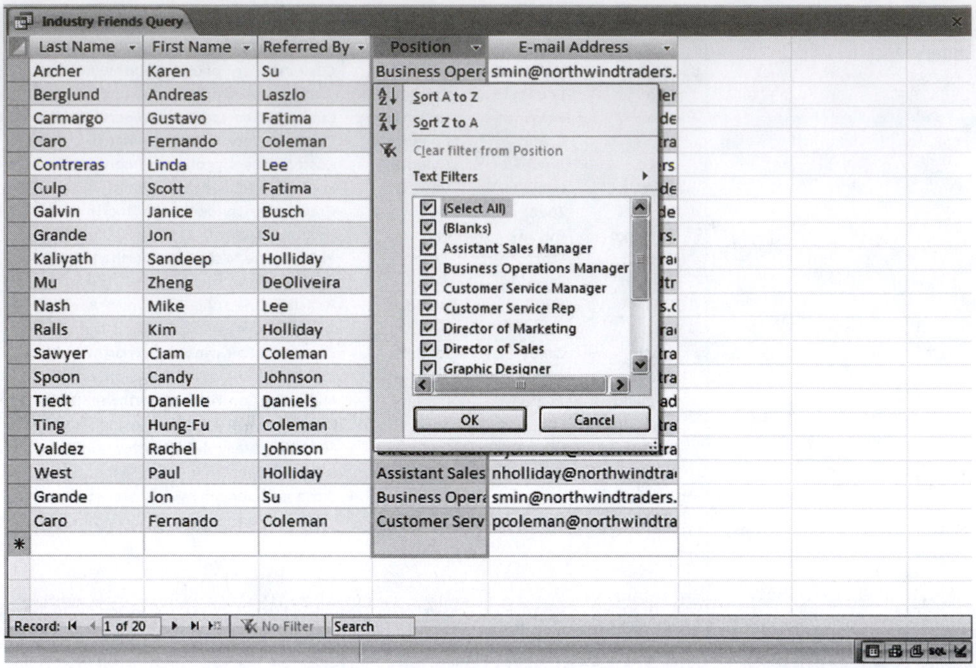

Figure 8-36

Filter menu

3. Click **Text Filters** and click **Contains** on the submenu. A Custom Filter dialog box appears, as shown in Figure 8-37.

Figure 8-37

Custom Filter dialog box

4. In the Position contains box, key **Marketing** and click **OK**. The records are filtered to show only those containing the word "Marketing" in the Position field, as shown in Figure 8-38.

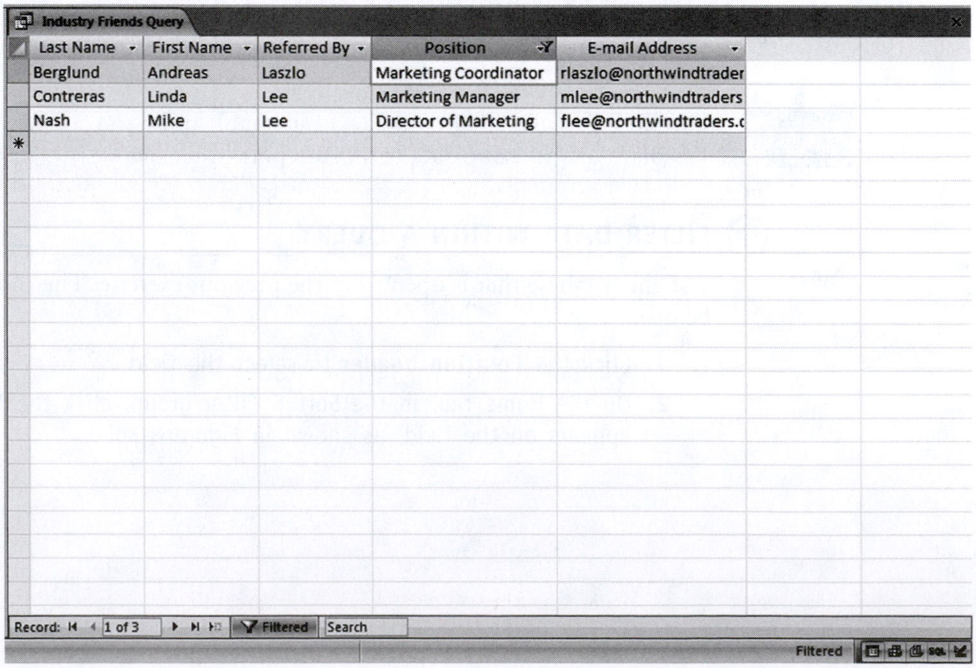

Figure 8-38

Filtered query

5. On the Home tab, in the Sort & Filter group, click the **Toggle Filter** button to remove the filter.

6. Click the **Close 'Industry Friends Query'** to close the query and click **Yes** to save changes when prompted.
   CLOSE the database.

If the criteria are temporary or change often, you can filter the query result instead of frequently modifying the query criteria. A filter is a temporary criterion that changes the query result without altering the design of the query.

Click the field you want to filter. On the Home tab, in the Sort & Filter group, click the Filter button. The filters available depend on the type and values of the field. When you apply the filter, only records that contain the values that you are interested in are included in the view. The rest are hidden until you remove the filter by clicking the Toggle Filter button.

SUMMARY SKILL MATRIX

In this lesson you learned	Matrix Skill	Skill Number
To create a query	Create queries	4.1
To create a query from a table	Create queries based on a single table	4.1.1
To create a query from multiple tables	Create queries based on more than one table	4.1.2
To modify a query	Modify queries	4.2
To add a table to a query	Add tables to and remove tables from queries	4.2.1
To remove a table from a query	Add tables to and remove tables from queries	4.2.1
To add criteria to a table	Add criteria to queries	4.2.2
To sort data within a query	Sort data within queries	5.1.2
To filter data within a query	Filter data within queries	5.2.2

■ Knowledge Assessment

Fill in the Blank

Complete the following sentences by writing the correct word or words in the blanks provided.

1. The Other group on the _____ tab contains the commands used to create queries.

2. The _____ button creates a new, blank query in Design view.

3. A(n) _____ is the most basic type of Access query.

4. The tables or queries from which a query gets its data are referred to as its _____.

5. To run a query after it has been created, double-click it in the Navigation pane to open it in _____ view and see the results.

6. Two or more records are considered _____ only when all the fields in your query results contain the same values.

7. When you need to include multiple tables in your query, use the _____ Wizard to build a query from a primary table and a related table.

8. To view only the records in one table that don't have a matching record in another table, you can create a _____ query.

9. By switching to _____ view, you can access all the tools needed to modify your query.

10. A(n) _____ is a window that lists all the fields in the underlying record source or database object.

Multiple Choice

Select the best response for the following statements or questions.

1. Creating a query is like
   a. sorting the data.
   b. asking the database a question.
   c. creating a new table.
   d. opening an existing database.

2. The results that a query returns can be
   a. sorted.
   b. grouped.
   c. filtered.
   d. all of the above.
   e. none of the above.

3. When one table will provide the information that you need, you can create a
   a. recordsource.
   b. simple select query.
   c. query criterion.
   d. parameter query.

4. Which query cannot be created using the Query Wizard?
   a. Parameter query
   b. Simple query
   c. Find duplicates query
   d. Find unmatched query

5. Queries are different from sort or filter commands because they can be
   a. applied to multiple fields.
   b. saved.
   c. modified.
   d. used on forms.

6. A query can get its data from
   a. one or more tables.
   b. existing queries.
   c. a combination of a and b.
   d. all of the above
   e. none of the above.

7. To find records that contain matching field values, you can create a query using which wizard?

   a. Find Matching

   b. Matching Fields

   c. Duplicate Records

   d. Find Duplicates

8. Before creating a query from multiple tables, you must first ensure that the tables have

   a. unmatched records.

   b. a defined relationship.

   c. a filter applied.

   d. no related records.

9. To add a table to a query, you must be in what view?

   a. SQL

   b. Datasheet

   c. PivotTable

   d. Design

10. A rule that identifies the records that you want to include in the query result is called a

    a. parameter query.

    b. query criterion.

    c. select query.

    d. field list.

■ Competency Assessment

Project 8-1: Games Select Query

As the manager at Southridge Video, you have stored information in an Access database about each used game that the store has taken in trade. Now that you know how to create queries, you decide to create a select query to list the title, rating, and category, which are the fields that you most often need to view.

GET READY. Launch Access if it is not already running.

The *Games* database file is available on the companion CD-ROM.

1. **OPEN** *Games* from the data files for this lesson.

2. **SAVE** the database as *GamesXXX* (where XXX is your initials).

3. On the Create tab, in the Other group, click the **Query Wizard** button to display the New Query dialog box.

4. Click **Simple Query Wizard** and then click **OK**.

5. In the Tables/Queries dropdown list, **Table: Games** should be selected.

6. Under Available Fields, double-click **Title**, **Rating**, and **Category** to move them to the *Selected Fields* box.

7. Click the **Next >** button. The second screen in the Simple Query Wizard appears.

8. Name the query **Games Query**. *Open the query to view information* should be selected.

9. Click the **Finish** button.

10. Click the **Close 'Games Query'** button to close the query.
11. **LEAVE** the database open for the next project.

    LEAVE Access open for the next project.

Project 8-2: Find Duplicates Query

You have taught the night manager at Southridge Video how to enter used game information into the database, but you have not yet developed a reliable system for determining if the game has already been entered. You are concerned there may be duplicate records. Create a find duplicates query to determine if there are duplicates.

USE the database that is open from the previous project.

1. On the Create tab, in the Other group, click the **Query Wizard** button.
2. In the New Query dialog box, click **Find Duplicates Query Wizard** and then click **OK**.
3. Click **Table: Games** and then click **Next >**. The next screen in the Find Duplicates Query Wizard appears.
4. Double-click **Title**, **Platform**, and **Publisher** to move them to the *Duplicate-value fields* box.
5. Click **Next >** to display the next screen in the Find Duplicates Query Wizard.
6. Double-click **Category** to move it to the *Additional query fields* box.
7. Click **Next >** to display the final screen in the Find Duplicates Query Wizard.
8. Name the query **Duplicates for Games** and click **Finish** to display the query showing duplicate records in the table.
9. Click the **Close 'Duplicates for Games'** button to close the query.
10. **CLOSE** the database.

    LEAVE Access open for the next project.

■ Proficiency Assessment

Project 8-3: Create a Query from Multiple Tables

Information about each selection for the Coho Vineyard monthly wine club is stored in an Access database. Information about red wine and white wine is stored in separate tables. In your position as customer service rep, it would be useful to be able to query information from both tables.

CD

The ***Club Wines*** database file is available on the companion CD-ROM.

1. **OPEN** *Club Wines* from the data files for this lesson.
2. **SAVE** the database as *Club WinesXXX* (where XXX is your initials).
3. Open the **Red Wines: Table**.
4. Open the Relationships window to ensure there is a relationship between the red and white wine tables. **CLOSE** the Relationships window.
5. Start the Query Wizard and choose **Simple Query Wizard**.
6. In the Tables/Queries dropdown list, click **Table: Red Wines**.
7. Move the **Bottled**, **Label**, and **Type** fields to the **Selected Fields** box.
8. In the Tables/Queries dropdown list, click **Table: White Wines**.
9. Move the **Bottled**, **Label**, and **Type** fields to the **Selected Fields** box.
10. Click the **Next >** button.
11. Click the **Next >** button and name the query **Wines Query**.
12. Click the **Finish** button.

13. Review the information in the query and then close it.

14. **LEAVE** the database open for the next project.

LEAVE Access open for the next project.

Project 8-4: Find Unmatched Query

A red wine and a white wine should be selected for each month. To determine if there are any records in the red wine table that don't have a matching record in the white wine table, you decide to create a find unmatched query.

USE the database that is open from the previous project.

1. Start the **Query Wizard** and choose **Find Unmatched Query Wizard.**

2. **Table: Red Wines** should be selected. Click the **Next >**.

4. Select **Table: White Wines** and click the **Next >** button.

5. Click **ID** in the Fields in 'Red Wines' list. Click **ID** in the Fields in 'White Wines' list. Click the **<=>** button to display them in the **Matching fields** box.

6. Click the **Next >** button.

7. Move the **Month?**, **Bottled**, **Label**, and **Type** fields to the **Selected fields** box.

8. Click the **Next>** button and name the query.

9. Name the query **Unmatched Month** and click the **Finish** button to display the query.

10. **CLOSE** the query.

11. **CLOSE** the database.

LEAVE Access open for the next project.

■ Mastery Assessment

Project 8-5: Query

The *Sports Events* database file is available on the companion CD-ROM.

In your job as a travel agent at Margie's Travel, a client has asked you to provide a list of all the travel packages available to sporting events that start in the month of April or May. You will add criteria to a query to get this information from the database.

1. Open *Sports Events* from the data files for this lesson.

2. Save the database as *Sports EventsXXX* (where XXX is your initials).

3. Open the **Events** query and switch to Design view.

4. Add criteria that will query the database for all events that start between 4/1/2008 and 5/31/2008.

5. Run the query.

6. **CLOSE** the query and save the design when prompted.

7. **CLOSE** the database.

LEAVE Access open for the next project.

Project 8-6: Parameter Query

The *Toys* database file is available on the companion CD-ROM.

Your brother, who owns Wingtip Toys, wants to be able to pull data from his toy inventory and asks for your help in creating a query. He wants to be able to query the database for toys for specific ages when prompted, so you show him how to create a parameter query.

1. **OPEN** *Toys* from the data files for this lesson.

2. **SAVE** the database as *ToysXXX* (where XXX is your initials).

3. Create a simple query named **Inventory Query** that contains all the available fields, except the ID field.

4. Create a parameter query on the For Ages field that gives you the prompt shown in Figure 8-39 when the query is run.

Figure 8-39

Enter Parameter Value prompt

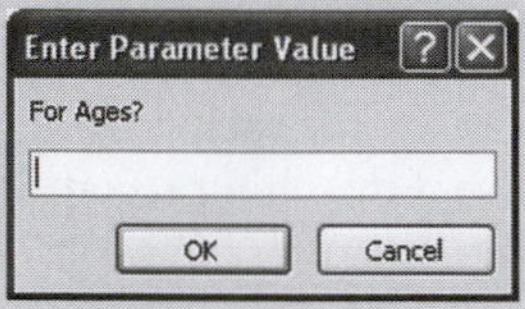

5. Query the database for all the toys for ages 10-14 years.

6. **CLOSE** the query and save when prompted.

7. **CLOSE** the database.

   CLOSE Access.

INTERNET READY

Blogs can be a fun way to pass time, but they can also be a great source of business information. If you enjoy blogs, check out some of the business-related blogs available, such as The Microsoft Connections Blog, shown in Figure 8-40. The URL for this blog is: *http://blogs.msdn.com/conblog/default.aspx.* Search for information on mail merges or another topic of interest to you and see what you can find.

Figure 8-40

The Microsoft Connections Blog

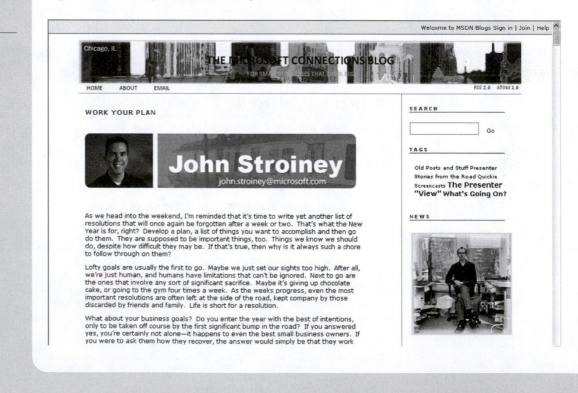

Advanced Tables

LESSON SKILL MATRIX

SKILLS	MATRIX SKILL	SKILL NUMBER
Creating a Custom Table	Create custom tables in Design view	2.2.1
Using the Table Analyzer	Evaluate table design by using the Table Analyzer	2.3.2
Summarizing Table Data	Summarize table data by adding a Totals row	2.3.5

Lucerne Publishing is a large publisher with a variety of products. You have just been hired as sales manager for the Business Books division. You will be responsible for working with the sales people in your division to increase sales. The previous sales manager used Access 2007 to track sales, so some data is already available. In this lesson, you will create a new custom table, use the Table Analyzer to divide one table into two tables, and add a Totals row to a table.

KEY TERMS
aggregate functions
Table Analyzer
Totals row

Creating a Custom Table

THE BOTTOM LINE

When a table template doesn't suit your needs, you can create a custom table in Design view. In Design view, you can insert fields, set data types, and perform other advanced table design tasks.

Creating a Custom Table

Creating a table from scratch in Design view gives you maximum flexibility. You can do everything you need to do to create the table in Design view, including adding fields, setting data types, defining field properties, and defining a primary key. As you create a table, you can also easily insert and delete rows in your table design.

CREATE A CUSTOM TABLE IN DESIGN VIEW

GET READY. Before you begin these steps, be sure to turn on and/or log on to your computer and start Access.

1. **OPEN** *Lucerne Publishing* from the data files for this lesson.
2. **SAVE** the database as *Lucerne PublishingXXX* (where XXX is your initials).
3. On the Create tab, in the Tables group, click the **Table Design** button. A new blank table is created in Design view, as shown in Figure 9-1.

Figure 9-1

Blank table in Design view

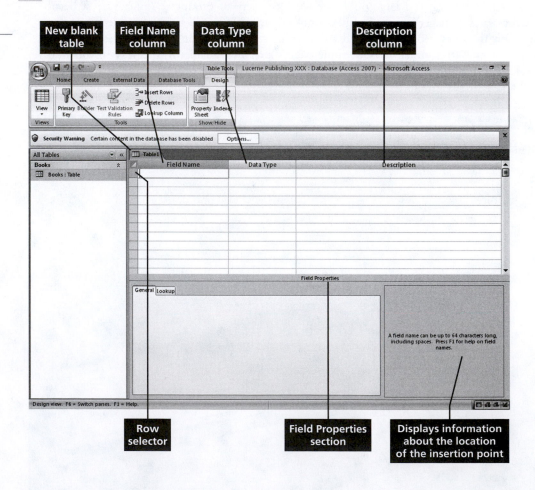

New blank table | Field Name column | Data Type column | Description column

Row selector | Field Properties section | Displays information about the location of the insertion point

4. Key **ID** in the Field Name column, as shown in Figure 9-2.

Figure 9-2

Field Name in Design view

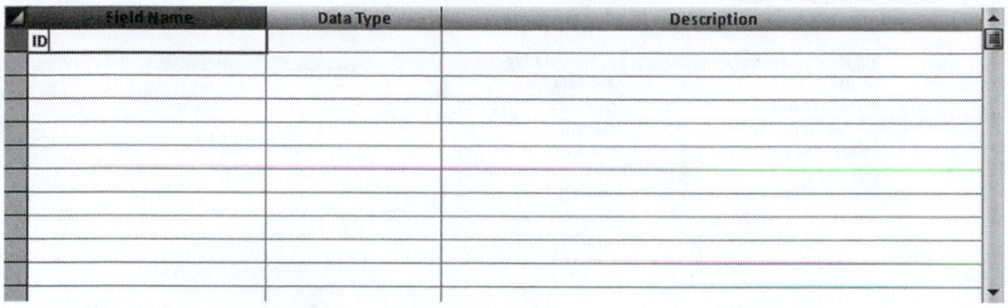

5. Press the [Tab] key to move to the Data Type column.
6. Click the **down arrow** in the Data Type column and select **AutoNumber** from the menu, as shown in Figure 9-3.

Figure 9-3

Data Types menu
in Design view

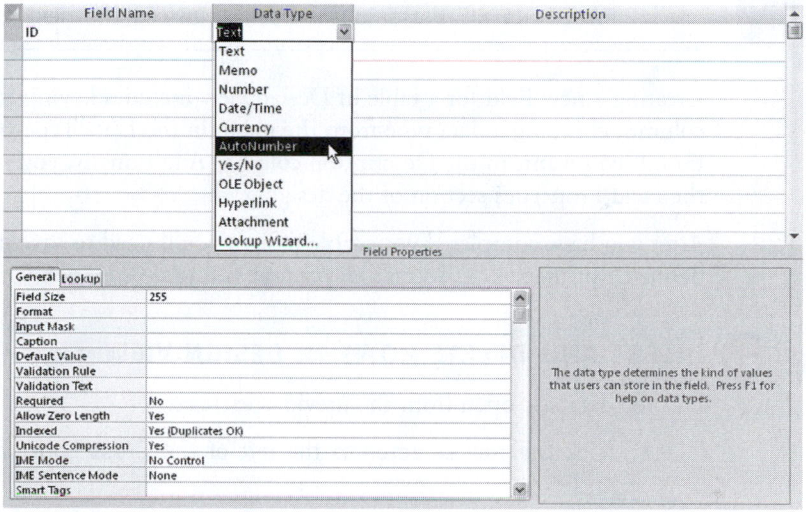

7. Press the [Tab] key to move to the Description field.
8. Leave the Description field blank and press [Tab] again to move to the next blank field row.
9. Key **Gross Sales** and press the [Tab] key.
10. Click the **down arrow** on the Data Type column and select **Currency** from the menu.
11. Click in the **Decimal Places** row in the Field Properties section. Click the **down arrow** and select **0** from the menu, as shown in Figure 9-4.

Figure 9-4

Field Properties in Design view

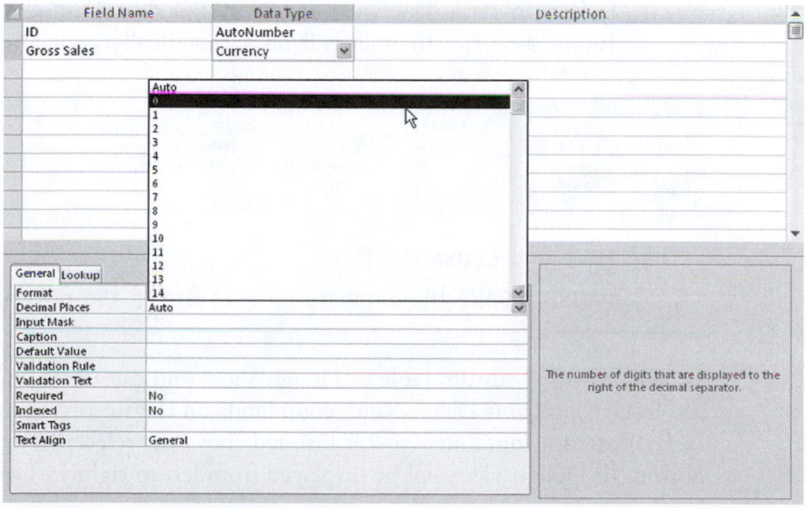

12. Enter the remaining fields, as shown in Figure 9-5, formatting each with the **Currency** data type and **0** decimal places.

Figure 9-5

Custom Table in Design view

Field Name	Data Type	Description
ID	AutoNumber	
Gross Sales	Currency	
Cost of Goods	Currency	
Net Sales	Currency	

13. Click the **row selector** to the left of the **ID** field to select the row.

14. On the Design tab, in the Tools group, click the **Primary Key** button.

15. Click the **Save** button on the Quick Access Toolbar. The Save As dialog box appears.

16. Key **Sales** and click **OK**.

> PAUSE. LEAVE the database open to use in the next exercise.

CERTIFICATION READY?
How do you create a custom table?
2.2.1

Creating a new field for a table in Design view includes keying the name in the Field Name column; choosing a data type from the menu in the Data Type column; and keying a description, if you want, in the Description column. Additionally, you can modify field properties in the Field Properties section of the design grid.

After you have completed your table design, you'll need to save it. If you haven't already defined a primary key, Access will prompt you to do so when you save the table.

⊙ INSERT AND DELETE ROWS IN DESIGN VIEW

USE the database open from the previous exercise.

1. Click the **row selector** to the left of the **Gross Sales** field to select the entire row.

⇥✕ Delete Rows

2. On the Design tab, in the Tools group, click the **Delete Rows** button. The field row is deleted from the table.

3. Click the **Undo** button on the Quick Access Toolbar. The field row reappears.

⇥⊏ Insert Rows

4. On the Design tab, in the Tools group, click the **Insert Rows** button. A blank row is inserted.

5. In the Field Name column, key **Area** and press the [Tab] key.

6. Press the [Tab] key again to accept the **Text** data type.

7. Leave the Description field blank and press [Tab] again to move to the next field.

8. Click the **Save** button on the Quick Access Toolbar.

9. Switch to Datasheet view and enter the records in the table as shown in Figure 9-6. The **ID** field will be automatically generated, so just tab past it.

Figure 9-6

Sales table

ID	Area	Gross Sales	Cost of Goods	Net Sales
1	East	$423,098	$69,039	$354,059
2	West	$434,432	$75,987	$358,445
3	North	$533,424	$66,765	$466,659
4	South	$516,323	$86,876	$429,447
*	(New)			

10. **SAVE** and **CLOSE** the table.

> PAUSE. LEAVE the database open to use in the next exercise.

When creating a custom table in Design View, you can insert and delete rows as needed using the Insert Rows and Delete Rows commands on the Records group. When you click the Insert Rows button, a new row is inserted above the selected row. The field order from top to bottom in Design view will be displayed from left to right in Datasheet view.

 **ANOTHER WAY** You can also right-click a selected row and choose Insert Rows or Delete Rows from the shortcut menu.

■ Using the Table Analyzer

↓ THE BOTTOM LINE The Table Analyzer helps you design efficient tables. If it determines that a table has duplicate information, it can split a table into two more efficient tables for you, or you can choose to do it yourself.

Using the Table Analyzer

The Table Analyzer is a wizard that examines a table and asks you a series of questions about the table to determine whether it should be divided into two or more tables.

⊕ USE THE TABLE ANALYZER

USE the database open from the previous exercise.

1. Open the **Books** table.
2. Scroll through the table to become familiar with the fields in the table.
3. On the Database Tools tab, in the Analyze group, click the **Analyze Table** button. The first Table Analyzer Wizard dialog box appears, as shown in Figure 9-7.

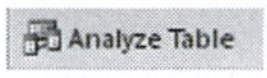

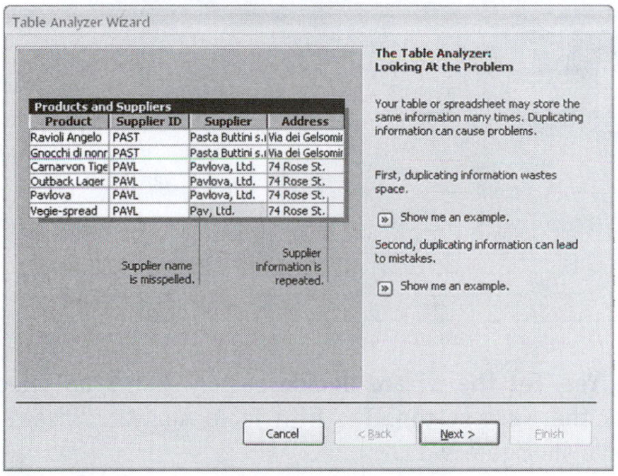

Figure 9-7

First Table Analyzer dialog box

4. Click the **Next** button. The second Table Analyzer Wizard dialog box appears, as shown in Figure 9-8.

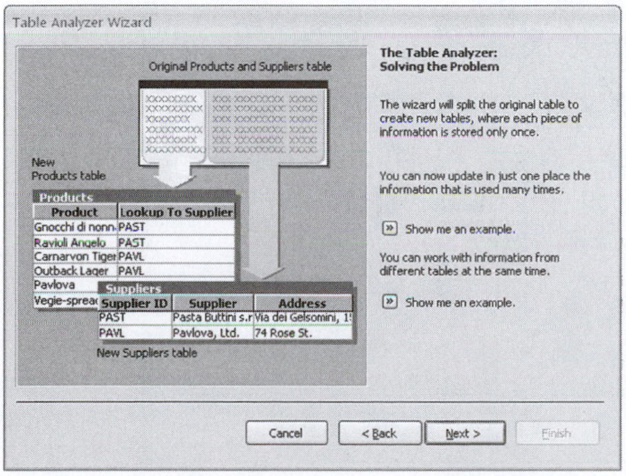

Figure 9-8

Second Table Analyzer dialog box

5. Click the **Next** button. The third Table Analyzer Wizard dialog box appears, as shown in Figure 9-9.

Figure 9-9

Third Table Analyzer Wizard dialog box

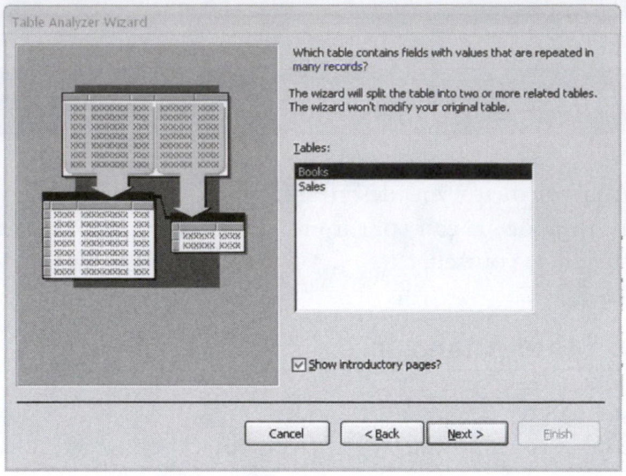

6. The **Books** table should be selected in the list; if it is not, select it. Click the **Next** button. The fourth Table Analyzer Wizard dialog box appears, as shown in Figure 9-10.

Figure 9-10

Fourth Table Analyzer Wizard dialog box

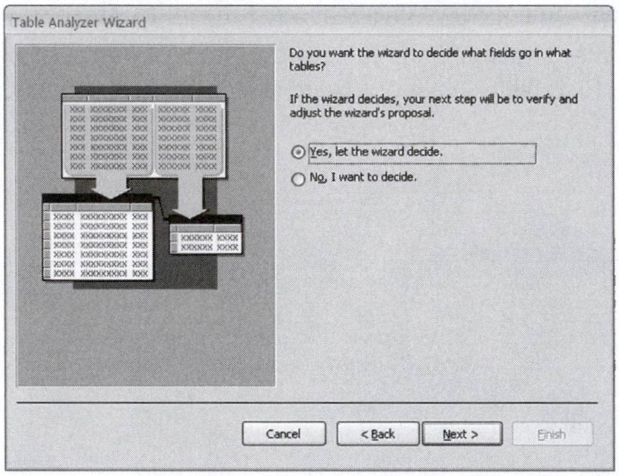

7. The **Yes, let the wizard decide** button should be selected; if it is not, select it. Click the **Next** button. The fifth Table Analyzer Wizard dialog box appears, as shown in Figure 9-11.

Figure 9-11

Fifth Table Analyzer Wizard dialog box

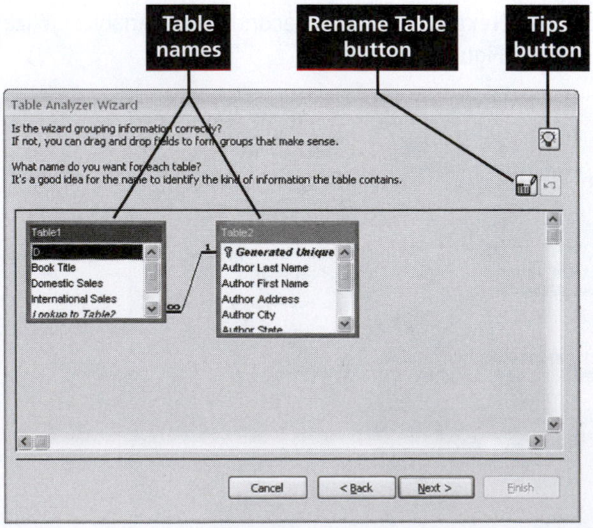

8. Scroll to the bottom of the Table2 box and click the **Year** field to select it. Notice that the wizard has placed it in the wrong table.

9. Drag the selected field to the Table1 box. Position the horizontal black line below the **Book Title** field and release the mouse button to place the **Year** field in its new location.

10. Click the **Table1** name to select it. Click the **Rename Table** button. The Table Analyzer Wizard dialog box appears, as shown in Figure 9-12.

Figure 9-12

Rename Table dialog box

11. Key **Book Sales** and click **OK.**

12. Click the **Table2** name and click the **Rename Table** button. The Table Analyzer Wizard dialog box appears.

13. Key **Author Contact Information** and click **OK.**

14. Scroll down to the bottom of the Book Sales table. Notice that the *Lookup to Author Contact Information* field was added.

15. Scroll through the Author Contact Information table. Notice that the *Generated Unique Id* field was added as a primary key. Click the **Next** button. The sixth Table Analyzer Wizard dialog box appears, as shown in Figure 9-13.

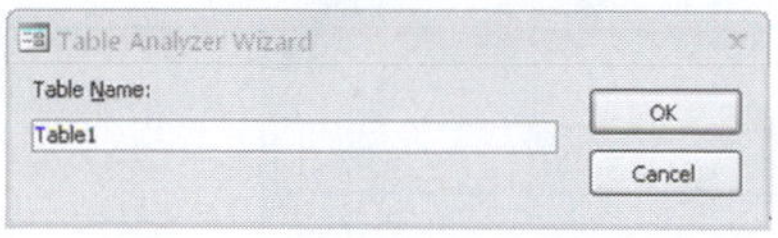

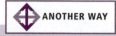
ANOTHER WAY

You can also double-click a table name to launch the Table Analyzer Wizard Rename Table dialog box.

Figure 9-13

Sixth Table Analyzer Wizard dialog box

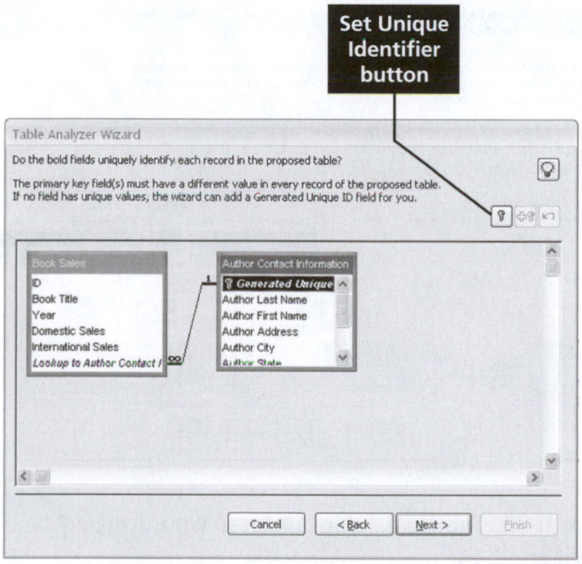

16. Click the **ID** field in the Book Sales table to select it. Click the **Set Unique Identifier** button. A primary key is inserted.

17. Click **Next.** The seventh Table Analyzer Wizard dialog box appears, as shown in Figure 9-14.

Figure 9-14

Seventh Table Analyzer
Wizard dialog box

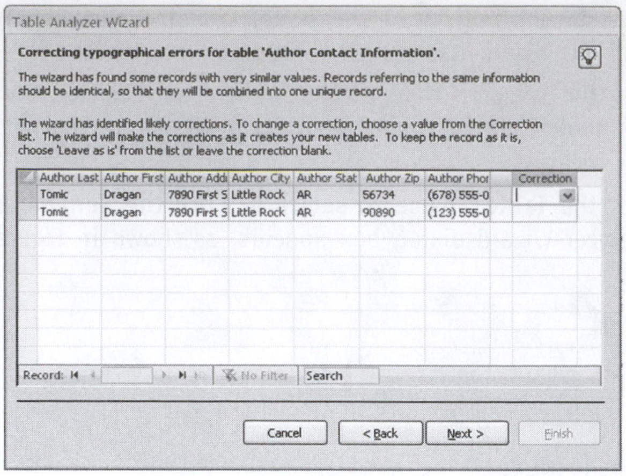

18. Notice that the Table Analyzer Wizard has detected two similar records, one with an incorrect zip code and phone number. Click the **down arrow** in the first row of the Correction field and select **Leave as is. This is the correct field.**

19. Click the **down arrow** on the second row of the Correction field and select the **Tomic** correction from the menu, as shown in Figure 9-15, to replace the incorrect record.

Figure 9-15

Corrections to the new tables

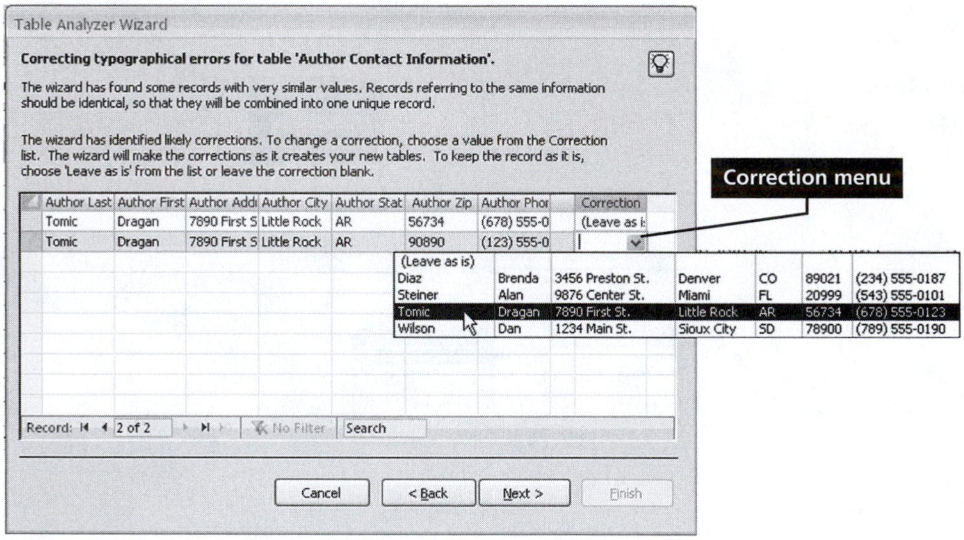

20. Click **Next**. The final Table Analyzer Wizard dialog box appears, as shown in Figure 9-16.

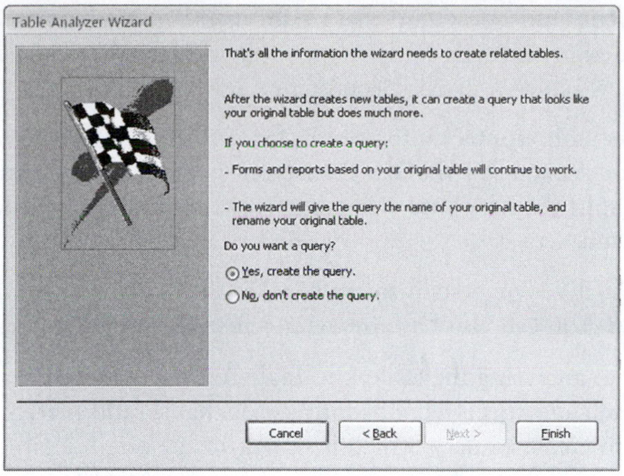

Figure 9-16

Final Table Analyzer Wizard dialog box

21. The **Yes, create the query** option button should be selected. Click the **Finish** button.

22. A message saying that the new query will be saved as **Books_NEW** appears. Click **OK.**

23. If Access Help appears on your screen, close it. Your screen should look similar to Figure 9-17.

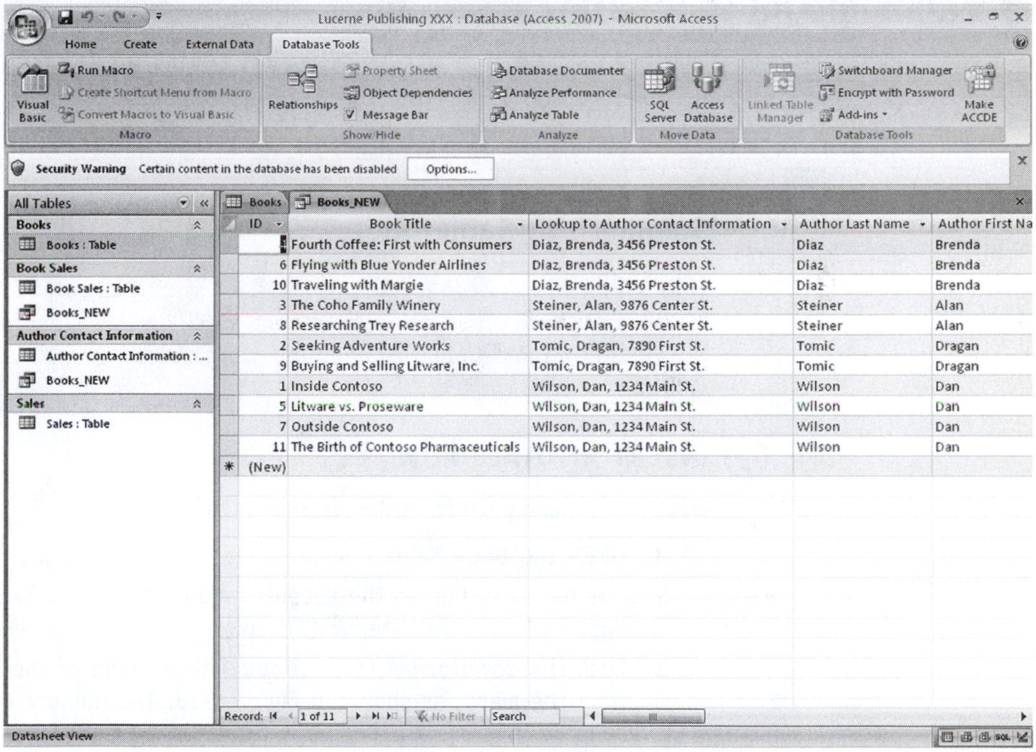

Figure 9-17

New tables and queries created by the Table Analyzer Wizard

24. CLOSE all tables and queries.

PAUSE. LEAVE the database open to use in the next exercise.

CERTIFICATION READY?

How do you use the Table Analyzer?

2.3.2

Well-designed databases do not store data in more than one place. Redundant data storage takes more disk space and increases the likelihood for data entry errors. In Lesson 1, you were introduced to the concept of normalization, which is the process of applying rules to a database design to ensure that you have divided your data into the appropriate tables.

X REF

Lesson 1 contains more information about normalization.

The *Table Analyzer* is a wizard that performs the normalization process for you by examining a table design and suggesting a way to divide the table for maximum efficiency. You can create the new tables yourself if you prefer.

In the Books table, contact information for authors had to be entered for each book the author wrote. As you saw the Table Analyzer work, it determined that a more efficient database would split the table into two tables—one with author contact information and one with book sales data.

The Table Analyzer suggests primary keys for the new tables or allows you to determine the primary keys. You can also have the wizard insert a unique identifier field.

In addition to analyzing the table, the Table Analyzer Wizard also analyzes the redundant data in a table and suggests corrections for records that should match. It also gives you the choice of whether to create a query, which is similar to the original table. Creating the query allows forms and reports that were created with the original table to continue to function properly. The original table may be renamed, but it will not be removed or altered.

TROUBLESHOOTING

If you run the Table Analyzer before entering records in the table, you may get a message stating that you need to enter at least two records in the table to get a meaningful analysis.

■ Summarizing Table Data

↓ THE BOTTOM LINE

It is often necessary to count or summarize data in a table, column by column. Tables that contain columns of sales figures or other numbers need to summed, averaged, or counted to be more useful. The Totals row makes these tasks easy.

Summarizing Table Data

Much like the bottom row of a spreadsheet, the Totals row is a new feature in Access 2007 that makes it easy to sum, average, or count the values in a datasheet column. You can also find maximum or minimum values and use statistical functions such as Standard Deviation and Variance.

⊕ INSERT A TOTALS ROW

USE the database open from the previous exercise.

1. **OPEN** the **Book Sales** table.

2. On the Home tab, in the Records group, click the **Totals** button. The Totals Row appears below the asterisk (*) row.

3. Click the **down arrow** in the **Book Title** column of the Totals row. Select **Count** from the menu, as shown in Figure 9-18. The number of records in the column is counted, and the number *11* is displayed.

Figure 9-18

Totals row

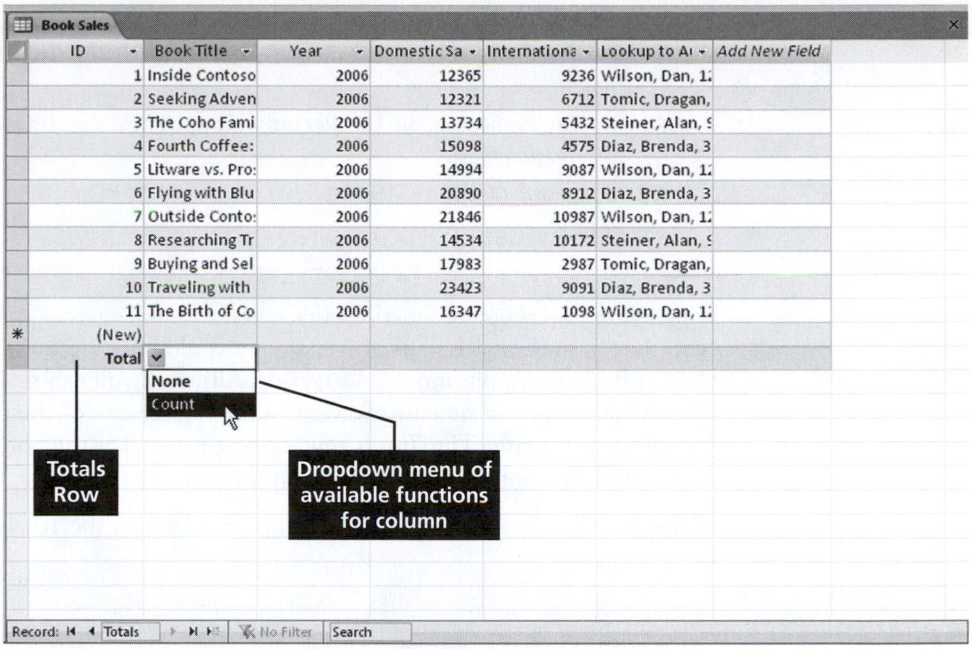

4. Click the **down arrow** in the **Domestic Sales** column of the Totals row and select **Sum** from the menu.

5. Click the **down arrow** in the **International Sales** column of the Totals row and select **Sum** from the menu. Your screen should look similar to Figure 9-19.

Figure 9-19

Totals row in the Book Sales table

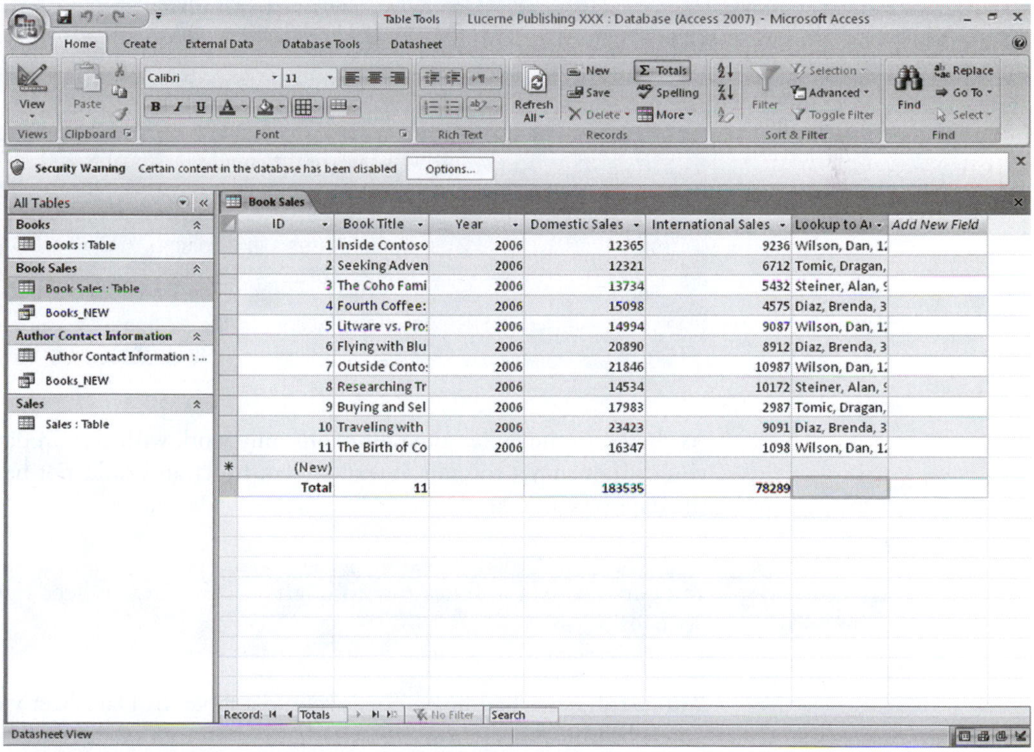

6. **SAVE** the table.

7. On the Home tab, in the Records group, click the **Totals** button. The Totals row is hidden.

8. On the Home tab, in the Records group, click the **Totals** button again. The Totals row reappears.

9. **SAVE** and **CLOSE** the table.

CLOSE Access.

Aggregate functions are functions that calculate values across a range of data, such as in a column. In previous versions of Access, you could only use these functions in queries or in Visual Basic for Applications (VBA) code. Although you can still use those methods, the Totals row saves you time by allowing you to choose one of these functions from a menu, applying it instantly. The *Totals row* is a row inserted at the bottom of a table that provides a menu of functions for each column in the row.

Table 9-1 describes the aggregate functions available in the Totals row and the data types that they work with.

Table 9-1

Aggregate functions in the Totals row

AGGREGATE FUNCTION	DESCRIPTION	DATA TYPES
Average	Calculates the average value for a column.	Number, Decimal, Currency, Date/Time
Count	Counts the number of items in a column.	All (except multi-valued list)
Maximum	Returns the item with the highest value.	Number, Decimal, Currency, Date/Time
Minimum	Returns the item with the lowest value.	Number, Decimal, Currency, Date/Time
Standard Deviation	Measures how widely values are dispersed from an average value.	Number, Decimal, Currency
Sum	Adds items in a column.	Number, Decimal, Currency
Variance	Measures the statistical variance of all values in the column.	Number, Decimal, Currency

As shown in the table, some functions only work with certain data types. For example, you cannot sum a column of text, so that function would not be available for a column with the data type of text.

TAKE NOTE *

You can also add a Totals row to queries open in Datasheet view and to a split form open in Form view.

You just practiced adding a Totals row to a table. In Datasheet view, you can click the Totals button and the row is inserted at the bottom of the datasheet below the row with the asterisk (*). The word *Totals* is inserted in the first column, but you can choose a function from its menu to change it if you want. Each column of the Totals row contains a dropdown menu from which you can choose the aggregate function you want to use.

If you want to sort or filter data, Access will exclude the Totals row by default.

TAKE NOTE ✲ You cannot add a Totals row to a report, but you can use aggregate functions in reports using other methods.

You cannot delete a Totals row, but you can hide it by clicking the Totals button again.

CERTIFICATION READY?
How do you summarize table data?
2.3.5

SUMMARY SKILL MATRIX

IN THIS LESSON YOU LEARNED	MATRIX SKILL	SKILL NUMBER
To create a custom table	Create custom tables in Design view	2.2.1
To use the Table Analyzer	Evaluate table design by using the Table Analyzer	2.3.2
To summarize table data	Summarize table data by adding a Totals row	2.3.5

■ Knowledge Assessment

Matching

Match the term in Column 1 to its description in Column 2.

Column 1

1. aggregate function
2. Table Analyzer
3. Totals row
4. row selector
5. Insert Rows button
6. Delete Rows button
7. normalization
8. count
9. currency
10. description

Column 2

a. square to the left of a field in Design view

b. inserts a blank row above a selected row in Design view

c. the process of applying rules to a database design to ensure that you have divided your information into the appropriate tables

d. a wizard that performs the normalization process by examining a table design and suggesting a way to divide the table for maximum efficiency

e. an aggregate function that counts the records in a column

f. an optional part of Design view where you can enter a field description

g. a data type

h. function that calculates values across a range of data

i. a row inserted at the bottom of a table that provides a menu of functions for each column in the row

j. deletes a selected field row in Design view

True / False

Circle T if the statement is true or F if the statement is false.

T F **1.** If you haven't already defined a primary key, Access will prompt you to do so when you save the table in Design view.

T F **2.** Well-designed databases store data in more than one place.

T F **3.** The row selector is located at the bottom of the table.

T F **4.** The Table Analyzer does not remove the original table.

T F **5.** The Table Analyzer gives you the choice of whether to create a query.

T F **6.** The Table Analyzer does not add new fields.

T F **7.** Average is an example of an aggregate function.

T F **8.** The Totals row is inserted above the asterisk row.

T F **9.** Certain functions only work with certain data types.

T F **10.** You cannot delete a Totals row, but you can hide it.

■ Competency Assessment

Project 9-1: Summarize the Sales Table

The Sales table you created at Lucerne Publishing seems incomplete. Add a Totals row to summarize the data.

USE Lucerne Publishing XXX that you saved in a previous exercise.

1. Open the **Sales** table.

2. On the Home tab, in the Records group, click the **Totals** button. The Totals row appears.

3. Click the **down arrow** in the Totals row of the **Gross Sales** column. Select **Sum** from the menu.

4. Click the **down arrow** in the Totals row of the **Cost of Goods** column. Select **Sum** from the menu.

5. Click the **down arrow** in the Totals row of the **Net Sales** column. Select **Sum** from the menu.

6. **SAVE** and **CLOSE** the table.

   CLOSE the database.

Project 9-2: Analyze the Fourth Coffee Customers Table

In your part-time job as an office assistant at Fourth Coffee, you have been taking on most of the database responsibilities. As you learn more and more about Access, you decide to use the Table Analyzer to check a table you created previously to make sure it is efficient.

The *Fourth Coffee Inventory* database is available on the companion CD-ROM.

1. **OPEN Fourth Coffee Inventory** from the data files for this lesson.

2. **SAVE** the database as *Fourth Coffee InventoryXXX* (where XXX is your initials).

3. Open the **Customers** table.

4. On the Database Tools tab, in the Analyze group, click the **Analyze Table** button. The Analyze Table Wizard dialog box appears.

5. Click **Next** to display the next Analyze Table Wizard dialog box.

6. Click **Next** to display the next Analyze Table Wizard dialog box.

7. The **Customers** table should be selected. Click **Next**.

8. The **Yes, let the Wizard decide** option button should be selected. Click **Next**.

9. A message is displayed that says the wizard does not recommend dividing the table. Click **OK.**

10. Click **Cancel** to close the Analyze Table Wizard.

11. **CLOSE** the table.

    LEAVE the database open for use in the next project.

■ Proficiency Assessment

Project 9-3: Design the Fourth Coffee Sales Table

Sales data for Fourth Coffee has just come in for the first quarter. The manager asks you to create a table that displays the sales for each of the five stores in your division. Note: Each store is known by a three-digit number, such as 656.

USE the *Fourth Coffee InventoryXXX* database that you saved in a previous exercise.

1. Create a new table in Design View.

2. Key **ID** as the first field name and press the [Tab] key. Set the data type to **AutoNumber.**

3. Key **Month** as the second field name and press the [Tab] key. A message appears stating that the word *month* is a reserved word. Click **OK**. Change the field name to **Mon** and set its data type to **Text**.

4. Enter the remaining field names and data types, as shown in Figure 9-20. Set the primary key as shown.

Figure 9-20

Monthly Sales by Store in Design view

Field Name	Data Type	Description
🔑 ID	AutoNumber	
Mon	Text	
Store	Text	
Sales	Currency	

5. **SAVE** the table as **Monthly Sales by Store**.

6. Switch to Datasheet view.

7. Enter the data in the table as shown in Figure 9-21.

Figure 9-21

Monthly Sales by Store table

ID	Mon	Store	Sales	Add New Field
1	January	651	$88,432.00	
2	February	651	$97,798.00	
3	March	651	$67,890.00	
4	April	651	$59,098.00	
5	January	656	$105,890.00	
6	February	656	$96,789.00	
7	March	656	$96,789.00	
8	April	656	$87,890.00	
9	January	660	$106,098.00	
10	February	660	$77,998.00	
11	March	660	$94,927.00	
12	April	660	$84,123.00	
13	January	662	$90,890.00	
14	February	662	$67,223.00	
15	March	662	$87,010.00	
16	April	662	$74,280.00	
*	(New)			

8. Insert a Totals row.
9. **Count** the **Mon** field and **sum** the **Sales** field.
10. **SAVE** and **CLOSE** the table.

   CLOSE the database.

Project 9-4: Summarize the Wingtip Toys Table

As marketing coordinator at Wingtip Toys, you are constantly examining sales data and trying to think of ways to increase sales. Total the inventory table to get a clear picture of the current inventory.

The *Wingtip Toys Inventory* database is available on the companion CD-ROM.

1. **OPEN** *Wingtip Toys Inventory* from the data files for this lesson.
2. **SAVE** the database as *Wingtip Toys InventoryXXX* (where XXX is your initials).
3. **OPEN** the **Inventory** table.
4. Insert a Totals row.
5. Count the **Description** field, sum the **In Stock** field, and sum the **Price** field.
6. **SAVE** and **CLOSE** the table.

   LEAVE the database open for use in the next project.

■ Mastery Assessment

Project 9-5: Design the Wingtip Toys Yearly Sales Table

The owner of Wingtip Toys has given you yearly sales data for each of the company's sales channels. Create a table in which to store and total the data.

USE the *Wingtip Toys InventoryXXX* that you saved in a previous exercise.

1. Create a new table in Design View.
2. Create the table as shown in Figure 9-22.

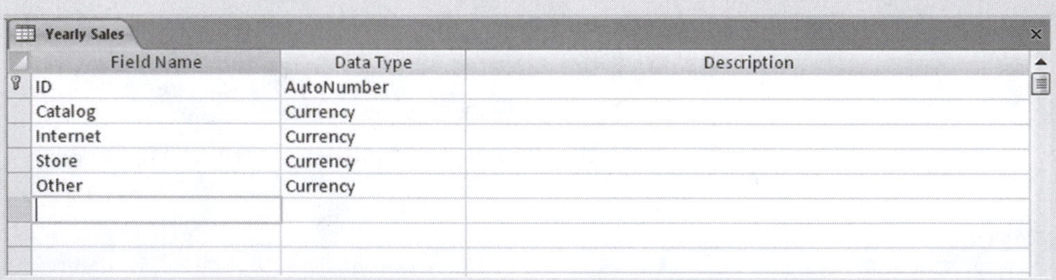

Figure 9-22

Yearly Sales Table in Design view

Field Name	Data Type	Description
ID	AutoNumber	
Catalog	Currency	
Internet	Currency	
Store	Currency	
Other	Currency	

3. **SAVE** the table and switch to Datasheet view.
4. Switch back to Design view.
5. Insert a blank row above the **Catalog** field.
6. Key **Yr** as a new field with the Text data type.
7. Select the **Yr** field and click the **Primary Key** button to designate the **Yr** field as the new primary key.
8. Delete the **ID** field.
9. **SAVE** the table and switch to Datasheet view.
10. Enter data in the table as shown in Figure 9-23.

Figure 9-23

Yearly Sales table

Yr	Catalog	Internet	Stores	Other	Add New Field
2008	$87,987.00	$109,897.00	$208,767.00	$23,987.00	
2009	$57,984.00	$98,789.00	$197,098.00	$10,761.00	
2010	$61,089.00	$78,907.00	$168,234.00	$9,125.00	
*					

11. **SAVE** the table.

12. Insert a Totals row.

13. Sum the **Catalog**, **Internet**, **Stores**, and **Other** columns.

14. **SAVE** and **CLOSE** the table.

    CLOSE the database.

Project 9-6: Analyze the Alpine Reservations Table

As administrative assistant for Alpine Ski House, you have noticed that one of the tables you use on a regular basis seems large and cumbersome and you have to enter some of the same data again and again. You decide to run the Table Analyzer to see if the table needs to be split.

The *Alpine Reservations* database is available on the companion CD-ROM.

1. **OPEN** *Alpine Reservations* from the data files for this lesson.

2. **SAVE** the database as *Alpine ReservationsXXX* (where XXX is your initials).

3. Select the **Reservations** table in the Navigation pane.

4. Run the Table Analyzer, letting the wizard decide how to split the table.

5. Rename Table1 to **Reservation Details** and rename Table2 to **Room Details.**

6. Select the **ID** field in the Reservation Details table and designate it as the primary key.

7. Create the query and finish the wizard.

8. **SAVE** and **CLOSE** the database.

    CLOSE Access.

INTERNET READY

The *New York Times* best sellers list is watched closely by readers, writers, and publishers around the world. Categories of best sellers include fiction, nonfiction, advice, and children's books. Search the www.nytimes.com Web site for the *New York Times* best sellers list of your choice. Create a new table in Design view that includes information about the top five best sellers in your favorite category. Include relevant fields such as the title, author, description, and price.

Advanced Forms

10

LESSON SKILL MATRIX

SKILLS	MATRIX SKILL	SKILL NUMBER
Creating Advanced Forms	Create forms	2.5
Creating a Multi-Item Form	Create multiple item forms	2.5.3
Creating a Split Form	Create split forms	2.5.4
Creating a Subform	Create subforms	2.5.5
Creating a PivotTable Form	Create PivotTable forms	2.5.6

As a regional manager for Contoso Pharmaceuticals, you are in charge of overseeing the sales reps in your division. The sales people you supervise call on doctors to promote Contoso medications and to leave samples. You use Access to put the sales information together and pull data from a variety of sources. In this lesson, you will learn how to create a multi-item form, a split form, a subform, and a PivotTable form.

KEY TERMS
hierarchical form
main form
Multiple Items tool
PivotTable
split form
subform

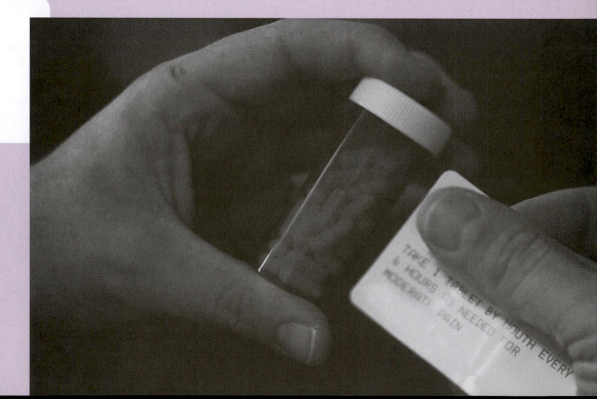

SOFTWARE ORIENTATION

Forms Group

The Forms group, located on the Create tab, contains commands for creating all types of forms—some of which you have already learned about. Figure 10-1 shows the commands you will use to create advanced forms.

Figure 10-1

Forms group

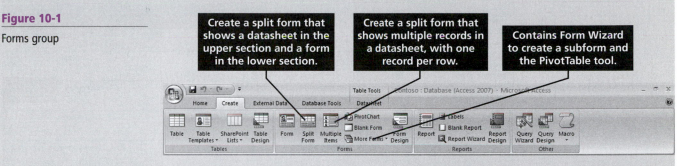

> **Create a split form that shows a datasheet in the upper section and a form in the lower section.**

> **Create a split form that shows multiple records in a datasheet, with one record per row.**

> **Contains Form Wizard to create a subform and the PivotTable tool.**

Use this figure as a reference throughout this lesson as well as the rest of this book.

X REF

In Lesson 5, you learned how to use some of the commands in the Forms group to create several basic forms.

Creating Advanced Forms

↓ **THE BOTTOM LINE**

Access provides tools to help you create forms quickly—including advanced forms with features that can improve the usability of your database.

Creating a Multi-Item Form

Use the Multiple Items tool to create a customizable form that displays multiple records.

 CREATE A MULTI-ITEM FORM

GET READY. Before you begin these steps, be sure to launch Microsoft Access.

The *Contoso* database file is available on the companion CD-ROM.

1. **OPEN** the *Contoso* database from the data files for this lesson.
2. **SAVE** the database as *Contoso XXX* (where XXX is your initials).
3. In the Navigation pane, double-click the **Doctors** table to open it.

4. On the Create tab, in the Forms group, click the **Multiple Items** button. Access creates the form and displays it in Layout view, as shown in Figure 10-2.

Figure 10-2

Multiple Items form in Layout view

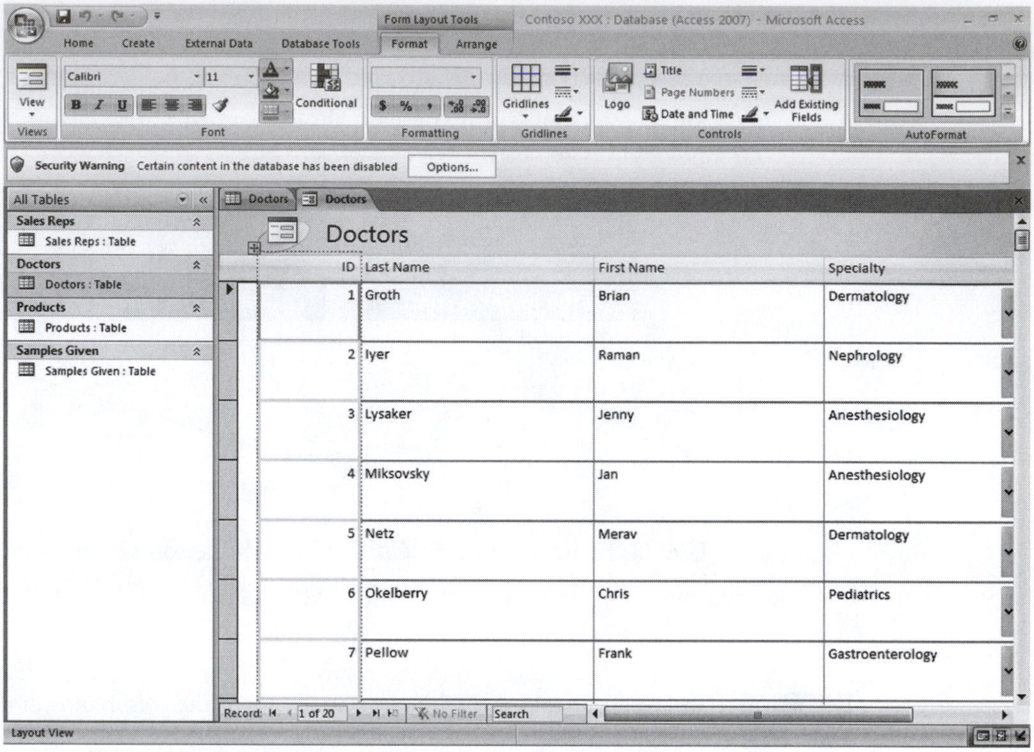

5. Scroll down and to the right to view the multiple records on the form.

6. Click the **Office Button** and click **Save**.

7. In the Save As dialog box, key **Doctors Multiple** and click **OK**.

8. Click the **Close 'Doctors Multiple'** button to close the form.

9. Click the **Close 'Doctors'** button to close the table.

10. **LEAVE** the database open.

> **PAUSE. LEAVE** Access open to use in the next exercise.

CERTIFICATION READY?

How do you create multiple-item forms?

2.5.3

When you create a simple form by using the Form tool, Access creates a form that displays a single record at a time. To create a form that displays multiple records but that is more customizable than a datasheet, you can use the Multiple Items tool. The *Multiple Items tool* creates a customizable form that displays multiple records.

In the Navigation pane, click the table that contains the data you want on your form. On the Create tab, in the Forms group, click Multiple Items. Access creates the form and displays it in Layout view.

X REF

You learned about using controls to format your forms in Lesson 7.

When you use the Multiple Items tool, the form that Access creates resembles a datasheet. The data is arranged in rows and columns, and you see more than one record at a time. However, a Multiple Items form gives you more customization options than a datasheet, such as the ability to add graphical elements, buttons, and other controls.

Creating a Split Form

Creating a split form allows you to see two views of your data at the same time—in Form view and in Datasheet view.

CREATE A SPLIT FORM

USE the database that is open from the previous exercise.

1. In the Navigation pane, double-click the **Sales Rep** table to open it.

2. On the Create tab, in the Forms group, click the **Split Form** button. Access creates the form and displays it in Form view and Datasheet view at the same time, as shown in Figure 10-3.

Figure 10-3

Split form

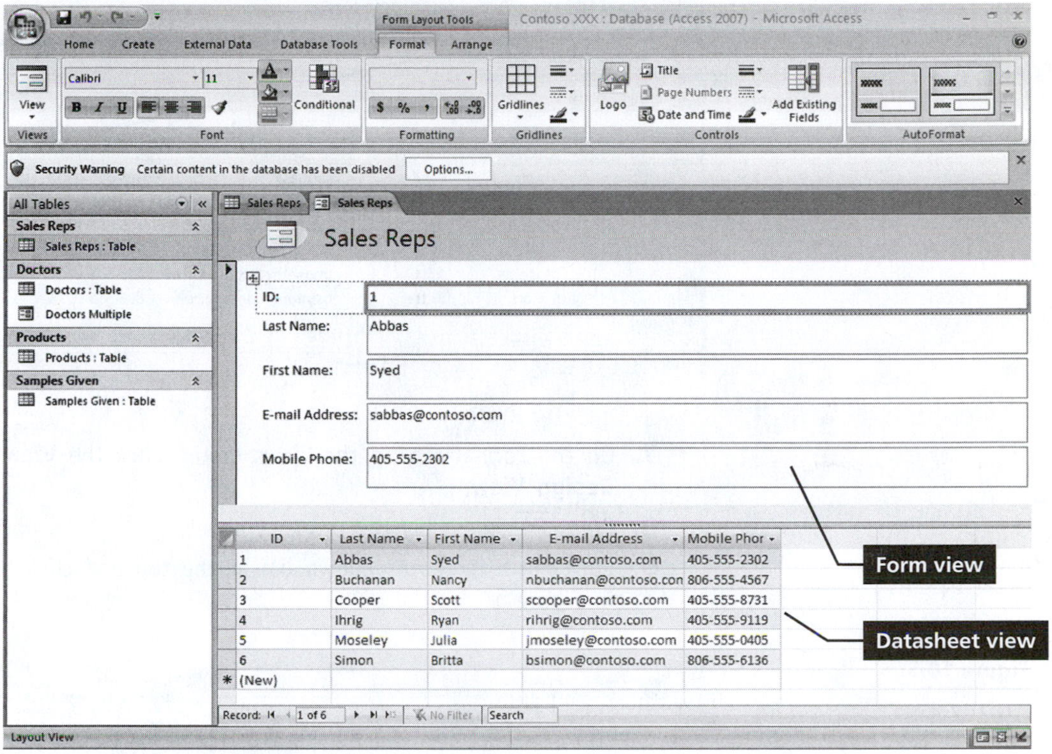

3. Click the **Next Record** navigation button to display the next record in Form view.

4. In the datasheet part on the bottom, place the insertion point in the **Mobile Phone** field for Nancy Buchanan. Notice that the same field is selected in the form part at the top.

5. Change the number for Nancy Buchanan in the **Mobile Phone** field to **806-555-4489**.

6. Click on the form part at the top and notice that the mobile phone number has been changed there as well, as shown in Figure 10-4.

Figure 10-4

Editing a split form

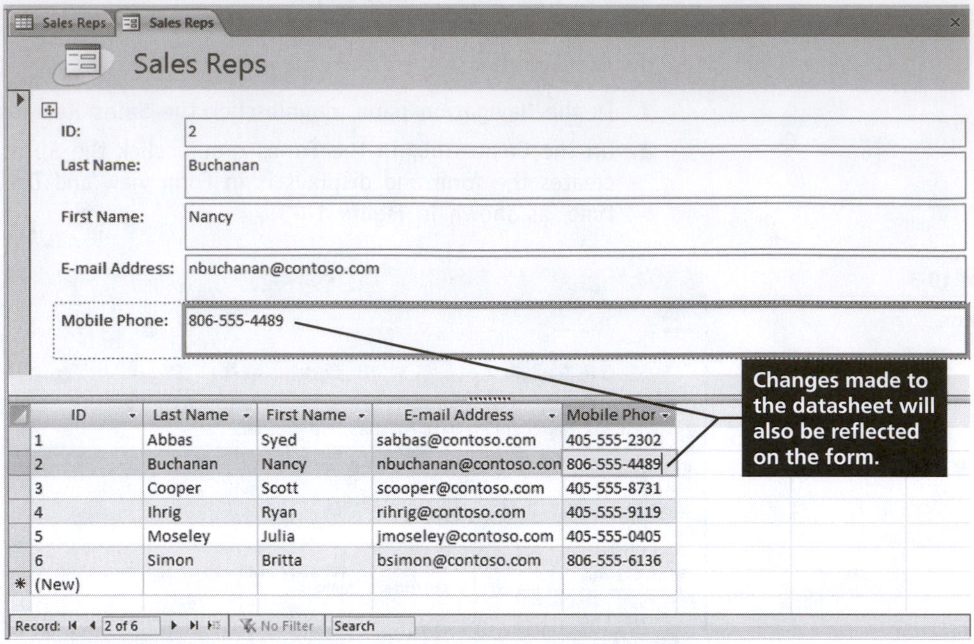

Sales Reps

Sales Reps

ID:	2
Last Name:	Buchanan
First Name:	Nancy
E-mail Address:	nbuchanan@contoso.com
Mobile Phone:	806-555-4489

Changes made to the datasheet will also be reflected on the form.

ID	Last Name	First Name	E-mail Address	Mobile Phor
1	Abbas	Syed	sabbas@contoso.com	405-555-2302
2	Buchanan	Nancy	nbuchanan@contoso.con	806-555-4489
3	Cooper	Scott	scooper@contoso.com	405-555-8731
4	Ihrig	Ryan	rihrig@contoso.com	405-555-9119
5	Moseley	Julia	jmoseley@contoso.com	405-555-0405
6	Simon	Britta	bsimon@contoso.com	806-555-6136
*	(New)			

Record: I◄ ◄ 2 of 6 ► ►I ►⧗ No Filter Search

7. On the Format tab, in the Views group, click the **View** button and click **Design View**.

8. Press F4 to display the property sheet.

9. Click **Form** in the dropdown list at the top and click the **Format** tab, as shown in Figure 10-5.

Figure 10-5

Property sheet

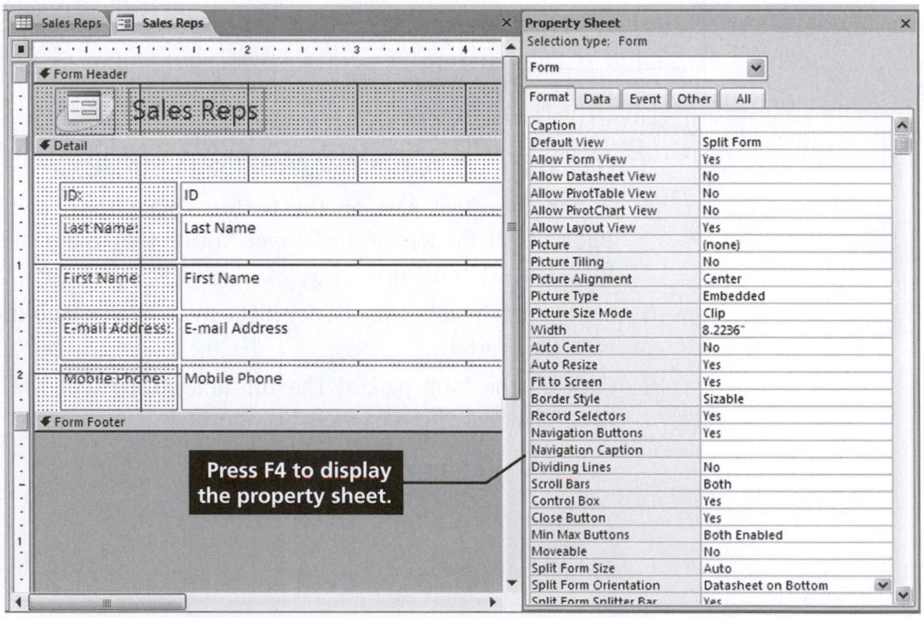

Sales Reps   Sales Reps

Form Header

Sales Reps

Detail

ID:	ID
Last Name:	Last Name
First Name:	First Name
E-mail Address:	E-mail Address
Mobile Phone:	Mobile Phone

Form Footer

Press F4 to display the property sheet.

Property Sheet

Selection type: Form

Form

Format | Data | Event | Other | All

Caption	
Default View	Split Form
Allow Form View	Yes
Allow Datasheet View	No
Allow PivotTable View	No
Allow PivotChart View	No
Allow Layout View	Yes
Picture	(none)
Picture Tiling	No
Picture Alignment	Center
Picture Type	Embedded
Picture Size Mode	Clip
Width	8.2236"
Auto Center	No
Auto Resize	Yes
Fit to Screen	Yes
Border Style	Sizable
Record Selectors	Yes
Navigation Buttons	Yes
Navigation Caption	
Dividing Lines	No
Scroll Bars	Both
Control Box	Yes
Close Button	Yes
Min Max Buttons	Both Enabled
Moveable	No
Split Form Size	Auto
Split Form Orientation	Datasheet on Bottom
Split Form Splitter Bar	Yes

10. Scroll down to the Split Form Orientation property, click the **down arrow**, and click **Datasheet on Top**, as shown in Figure 10-6.

Figure 10-6

Changing a property

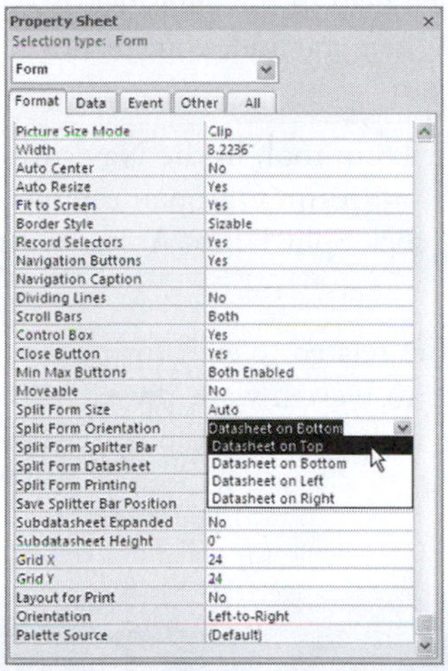

> **TAKE NOTE***
>
> If all text for the properties is not visible, click the left border of the property sheet and drag to widen it.

11. Click the **Close** button to close the property sheet.

12. On the Format tab, in the Views group, click the **View** button and click **Layout View**. The split form is displayed with the datasheet on top, as shown in Figure 10-7.

Figure 10-7

Split form with datasheet on top

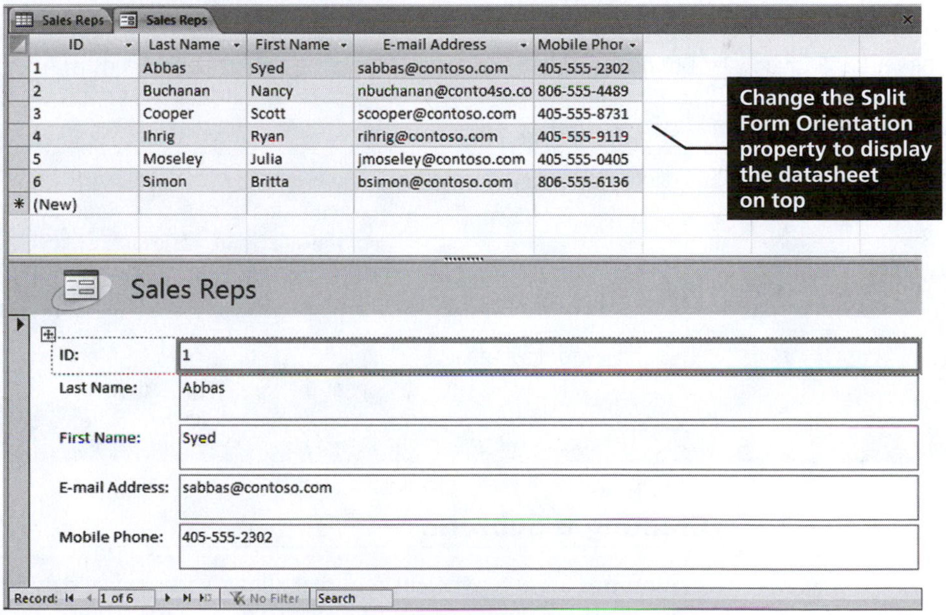

13. Click the **Office Button** and click **Save**.

14. In the Save As dialog box, key **Sales Reps Split** and click **OK**.

15. Click the **Close 'Sales Reps Split'** button to close the form.

16. Click the **Close 'Sales Reps'** button to close the table.

17. **LEAVE** the database open.

PAUSE. LEAVE the database open to use in the next exercise.

CERTIFICATION READY?
How do you create split forms?
2.5.4

X REF

You learned how to set properties using the property sheet in Lesson 4.

A *split form* gives you two views of your data at the same time—in both Form view and Datasheet view. Working with split forms gives you the benefits of both types of forms in a single form. The two views are connected to the same data source and are completely synchronized with each other. Selecting a field in the datasheet part of the form selects the same field in the form part of the form. When you add, edit, or delete data in the datasheet part, the change is reflected in the form part.

To create a split form using the Split Form tool, in the Navigation pane click the table that contains the data that you want on your form. Or, open the table in Datasheet view and on the Create tab, in the Forms group, click Split Form. Access creates the form and displays it in Layout view.

Table 10-1 lists some of the properties related to split forms that you can set on the property sheet to fine-tune your form. Switch to Design view, press F4 to display the property sheet, select Form from the dropdown list at the top of the property sheet, and click the Format tab.

Table 10-1

PROPERTY	VIEW(S) IN WHICH YOU CAN SET THE PROPERTY	DESCRIPTION
Split Form Orientation	Design view	Allows you to define whether the datasheet appears above, below, to the left, or to the right of the form.
Split Form Datasheet	Design view or Layout view	If set to *Allow Edits* (and the form's record source is updateable), Access allows edits to be made on the datasheet. If set to *Read Only*, Access prevents edits from being made on the datasheet.
Split Form Splitter Bar	Design view	If set to *Yes*, Access allows you to resize the form and datasheet by moving the splitter bar that separates the two parts. If set to *No*, the splitter bar is hidden, and the form and datasheet cannot be resized.
Save Splitter Bar Position	Design view	If set to *Yes*, the form opens with the splitter bar in the same position in which you last left it. If set to *No*, the form and datasheet cannot be resized, and the splitter bar is hidden.
Split Form Size	Design view or Layout view	Allows you to specify an exact height or width (depending on whether the form is split vertically or horizontally) for the form part of the split form. For example, key *1"* to set the form to a height or width of 1 inch. Key *Auto* to set the dimension by other means, such as dragging the splitter bar in Layout view.
Split Form Printing	Design view or Layout view	Allows you to define which portion of the form is printed when you print the form. If set to *Form Only*, only the form portion is printed. If set to *Datasheet Only*, only the datasheet portion is printed.

Creating a Subform

Subforms are a convenient tool that allows you to view data from more than one table or query on the same form.

➔ CREATE A SUBFORM

USE the database that is open from the previous exercise.

1. On the Create tab, in the Forms group, click the **More Forms** button and click **Form Wizard**.
2. In the first screen on the Form Wizard, click the **down arrow** in the Tables/Queries box and click **Table: Samples Given**.

3. In the Available Fields box, double-click the **Week Name**, **Sales Rep**, **Product**, and **Quantity** fields to move them to the Selected Fields box.

4. Click the **down arrow** in the Tables/Queries box and click **Table: Doctors**.

5. In the Available Fields box, double-click the **Last Name**, **First Name**, **Specialty**, and **Hospital** fields to move them to the Selected Fields box. The screen should look like Figure 10-8.

Figure 10-8

Form Wizard, screen 1

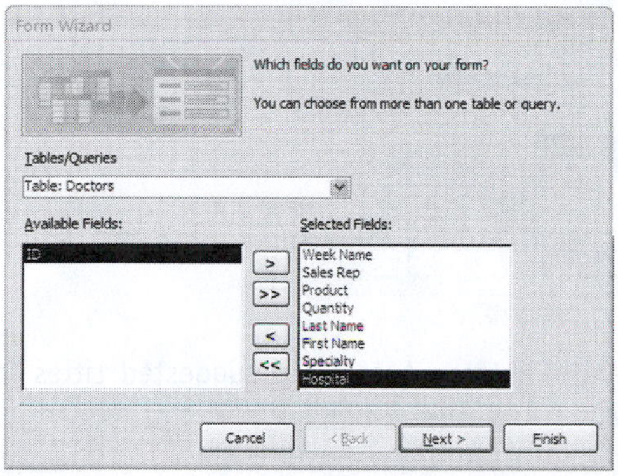

Form Wizard

Which fields do you want on your form?

You can choose from more than one table or query.

Tables/Queries

Table: Doctors

Available Fields:

ID

Selected Fields:

Week Name
Sales Rep
Product
Quantity
Last Name
First Name
Specialty
Hospital

Cancel | < Back | Next > | Finish

6. Click the **Next >** button.

7. In the *How do you want to view your data?* box, click **by Doctors**. The *Form with subform(s)* radio button should be selected, and the Form Wizard should look like Figure 10-9.

Figure 10-9

Form Wizard, screen 2

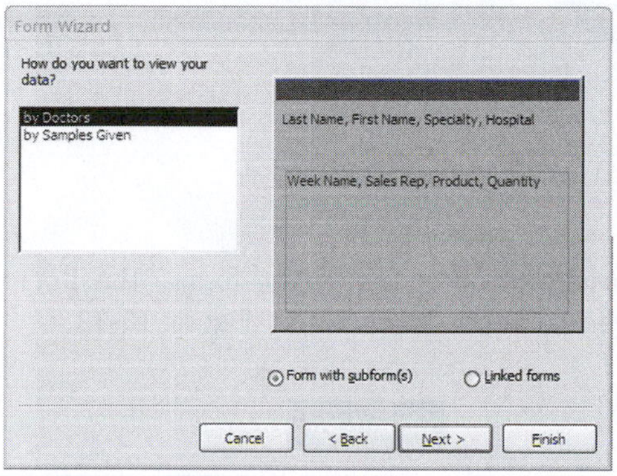

Form Wizard

How do you want to view your data?

by Doctors
by Samples Given

Last Name, First Name, Specialty, Hospital

Week Name, Sales Rep, Product, Quantity

⦿ Form with subform(s)   ○ Linked forms

Cancel | < Back | Next > | Finish

8. Click the **Next >** button.

9. Click the **Tabular** radio button to select that as the layout for your subform, as shown in Figure 10-10.

Figure 10-10

Form Wizard, screen 3

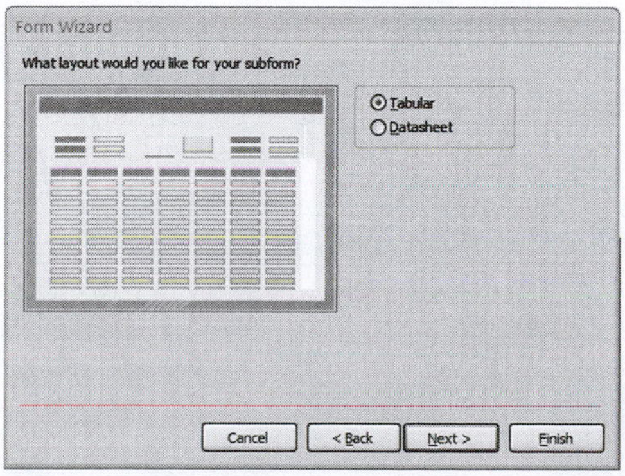

Form Wizard

What layout would you like for your subform?

⦿ Tabular
○ Datasheet

Cancel | < Back | Next > | Finish

10. Click the **Next** > button.

11. Click **Solstice** for the style, as shown in Figure 10-11.

Figure 10-11

Form Wizard, screen 4

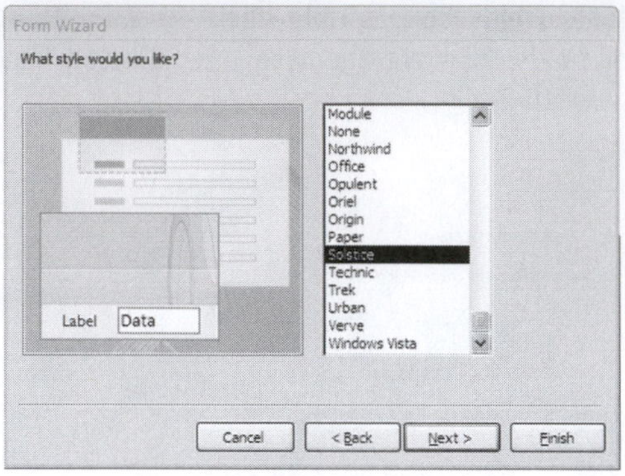

12. Click the **Next** > button. Access has suggested titles for the forms, as shown in Figure 10-12.

Figure 10-12

Form Wizard, screen 5

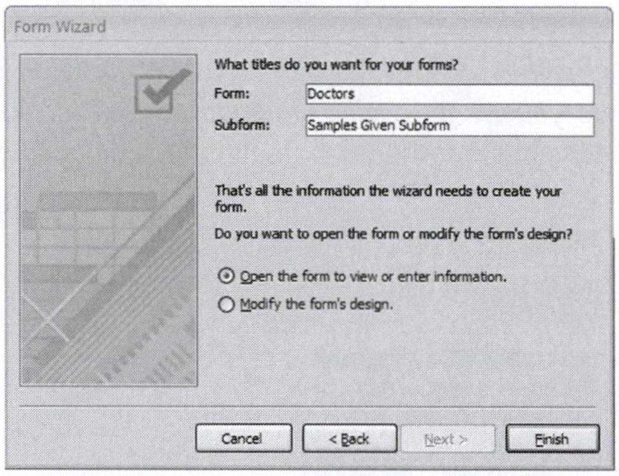

13. Click the **Finish** button to create the forms. The Doctors form appears with the Samples Given subform, as shown in Figure 10-13.

Figure 10-13

Doctors form with subform

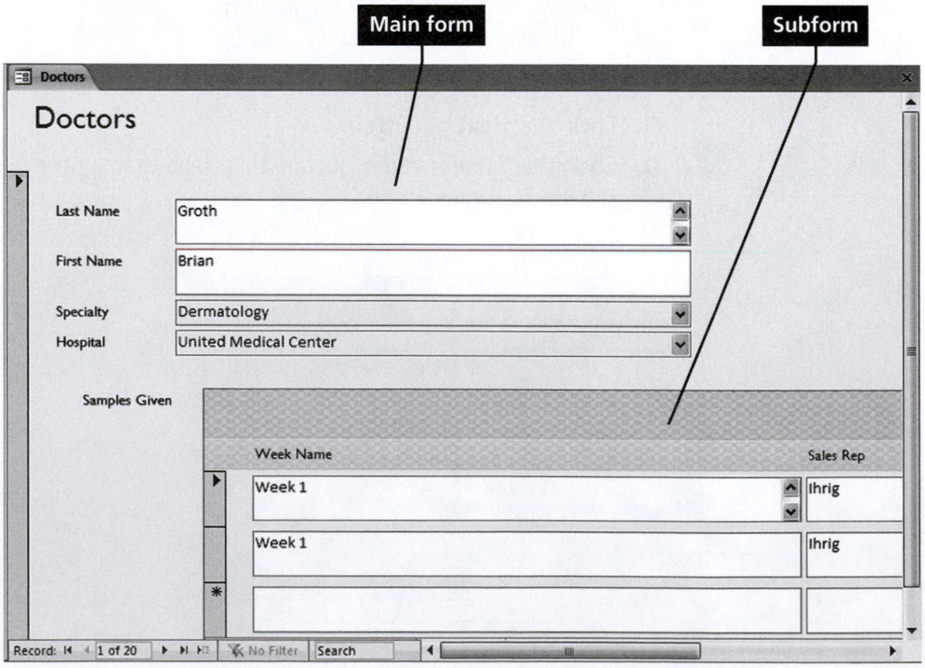

14. In the Navigation pane, double-click the **Samples Given Subform** to open it, as shown in Figure 10-14.

Figure 10-14

Samples Given subform

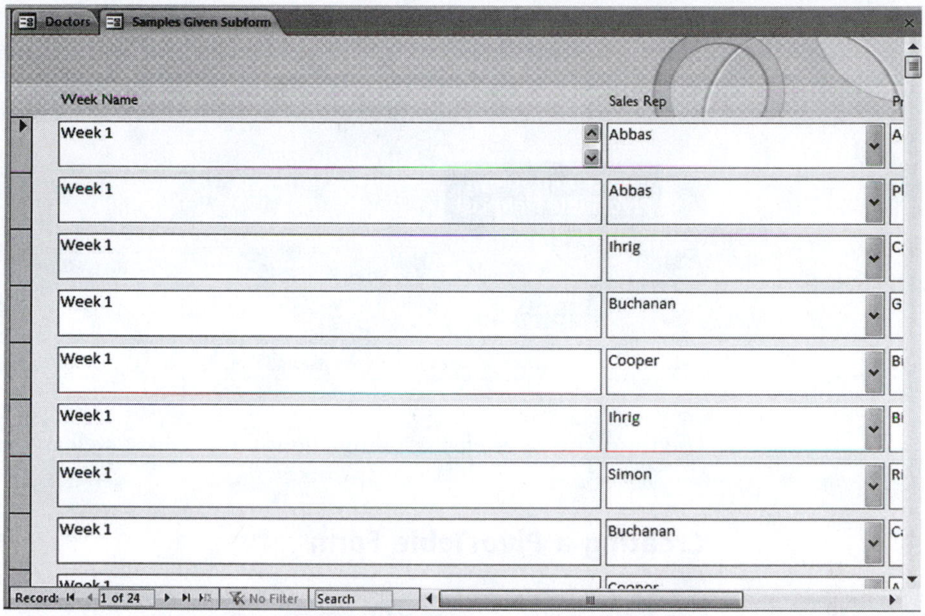

Week Name		Sales Rep		Pr
Week 1		Abbas		A
Week 1		Abbas		Pl
Week 1		Ihrig		Ca
Week 1		Buchanan		G
Week 1		Cooper		Bi
Week 1		Ihrig		Bi
Week 1		Simon		Ri
Week 1		Buchanan		Ca
Week 1		Cooper		A

Record: I◄ ◄ 1 of 24 ► ►I ►⃰ No Filter Search

15. Scroll down and to the right to see the data contained in the records and then click the **Close 'Samples Given Subform'** button to close the subform.

16. Click the **Close 'Doctors'** button to close the form.

17. **LEAVE** the database open.

PAUSE. LEAVE the database open to use in the next exercise.

CERTIFICATION READY?
How do you create subforms?
2.5.5

When working with a relational database, you often need to view data from more than one table or query on the same form. For example, you want to see customer data, but you also want to see information about the customer's orders at the same time. Subforms are a convenient tool for doing this, and you can use the Form Wizard to help you create subforms quickly. For best results, all relationships should be established first. This enables Access to automatically create the links between subforms and main forms.

A ***subform*** is a form that is inserted into another form. The primary form is called the ***main form***, and the form within the form is called the subform. A form/subform combination is sometimes referred to as a ***hierarchical form***, a *master/detail form*, or a *parent/child form*. Subforms are especially effective when you want to show data from tables or queries that have a one-to-many relationship—the main form shows data from the "one" side of the relationship and the subform shows the data from the "many" side of the relationship.

■ SOFTWARE ORIENTATION

PivotTable Tools

When you create a PivotTable form, tools for working with the PivotTable are displayed on the Design tab. Figure 10-15 shows the commands that are available.

Figure 10-15

PivotTable tools

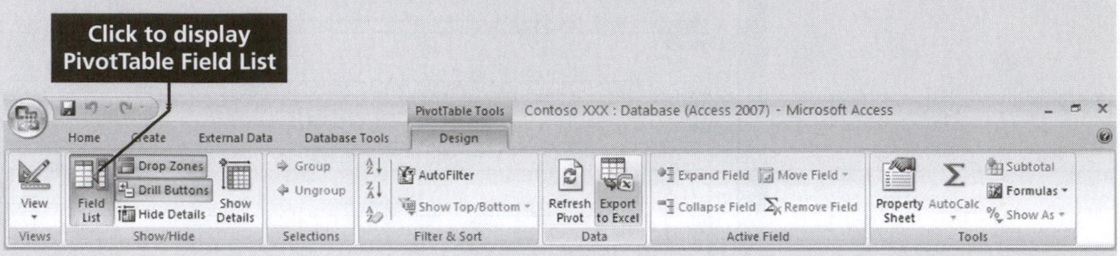

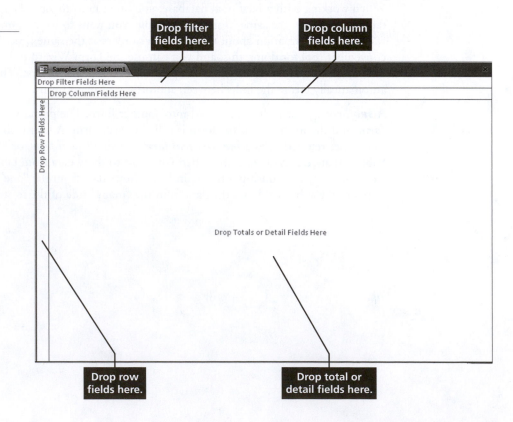

Use this figure as a reference throughout this lesson as well as the rest of this book.

Creating a PivotTable Form

A PivotTable is a special type of form that allows you to analyze data from different perspectives by quickly changing the alignment of columns and rows.

 **CREATE A PIVOTTABLE FORM**

USE the database that is open from the previous exercise.

1. In the Navigation Pane, click the **Samples Given Subform** to select it.
2. On the Create tab, in the Forms group, click the **More Forms** button and click **PivotTable**. A PivotTable form appears, as shown in Figure 10-16.

Figure 10-16

PivotTable form

3. On the Design tab, in the Show/Hide group, click the **Field List** button to display the PivotTable Field List, as shown in Figure 10-17.

Figure 10-17

PivotTable Field List

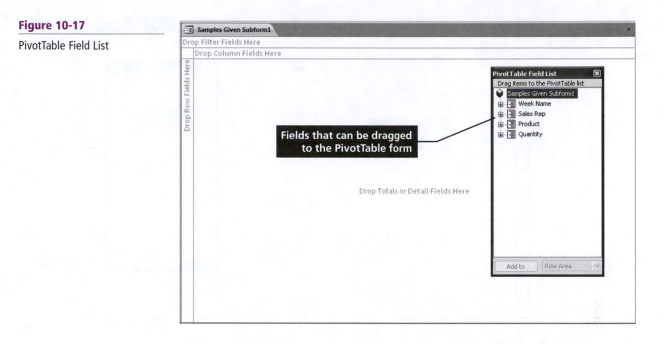

4. Click **Sales Rep** in the PivotTable Field List and drag it to the *Drop Column Fields Here* area of the PivotTable form, as shown in Figure 10-18.

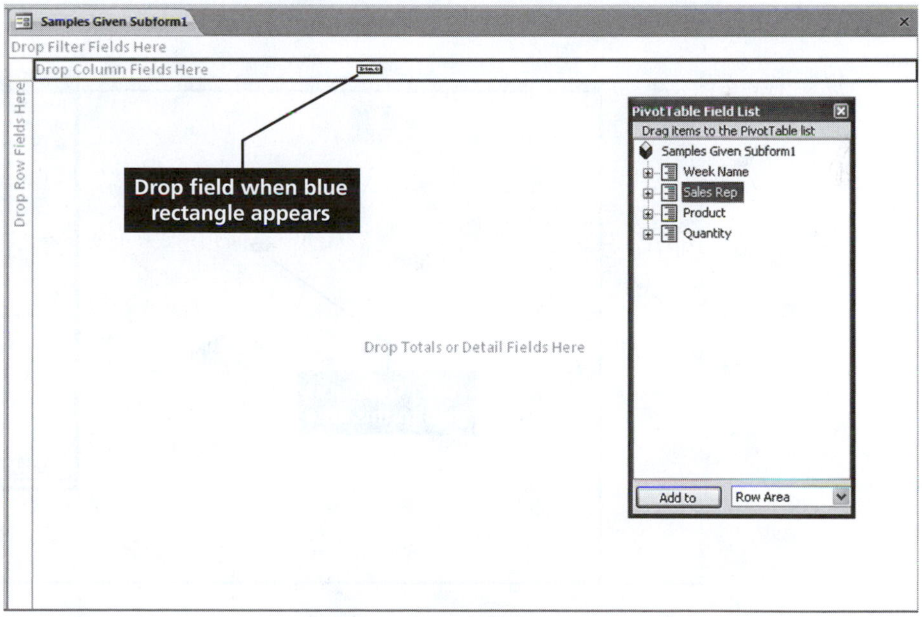

Figure 10-18

Drag column field to the PivotTable form

5. Click **Product** in the PivotTable Field List and drag it to the *Drop Row Fields Here* area of the PivotTable form, as shown in Figure 10-19.

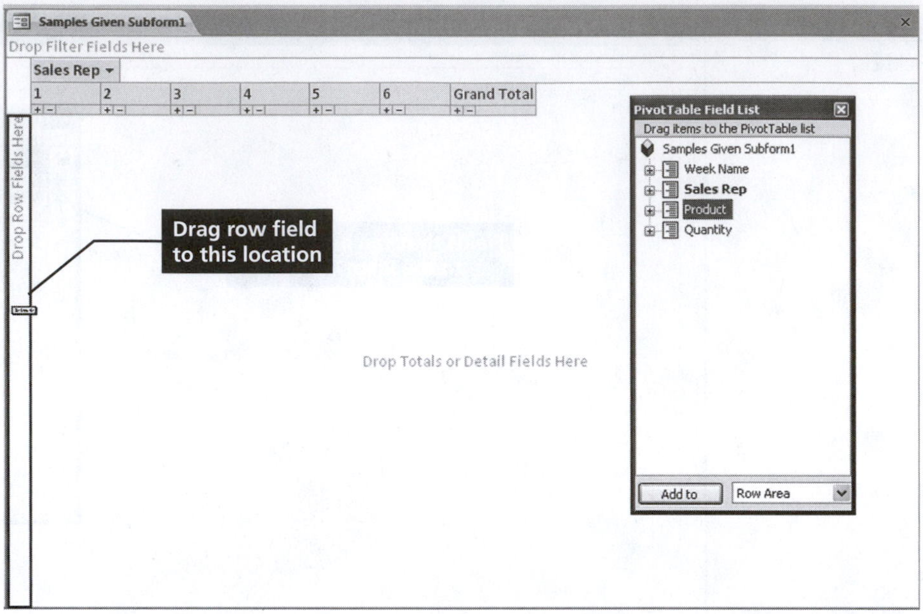

Figure 10-19

Drag row field to the PivotTable form

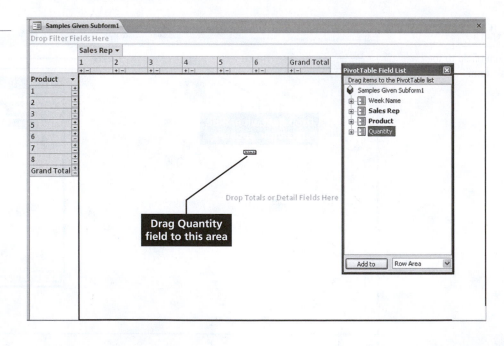

6. Click **Quantity** in the PivotTable Field List and drag it to the *Drop Totals or Detail Fields Here* area of the PivotTable form, as shown in Figure 10-20.

Figure 10-20

Drag detail field to the PivotTable form

7. Click the **Close** button to close the PivotTable Field List.

8. Click one of the **Quantity** headers to select the quantity data, as shown in Figure 10-21.

Figure 10-21

Select quantity data

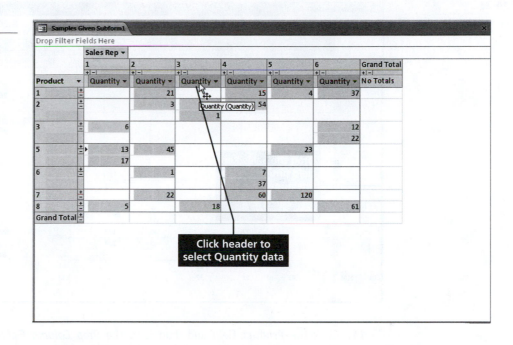

Click header to
select Quantity data

9. On the Design tab, in the Tools group, click the **AutoCalc** button and click **Sum**, as shown in Figure 10-22, to display the totals.

Figure 10-22

AutoCalc menu

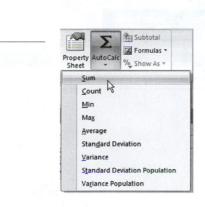

10. Click the **Sales Rep** field and drag it to the left until a blue line appears before the Product field, as shown in Figure 10-23, then drop the field.

Figure 10-23

Drag fields to reorganize data

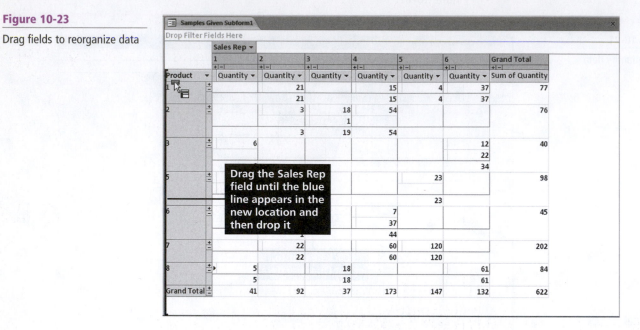

11. Click the **Product** field and drag it to the *Drop Column Fields Here* area of the PivotTable form, as shown in Figure 10-24.

Figure 10-24

Drag fields to a new location

12. The new arrangement of the PivotTable form, shown in Figure 10-25, displays the data in a different format.

Figure 10-25

PivotTable in a new arrangement

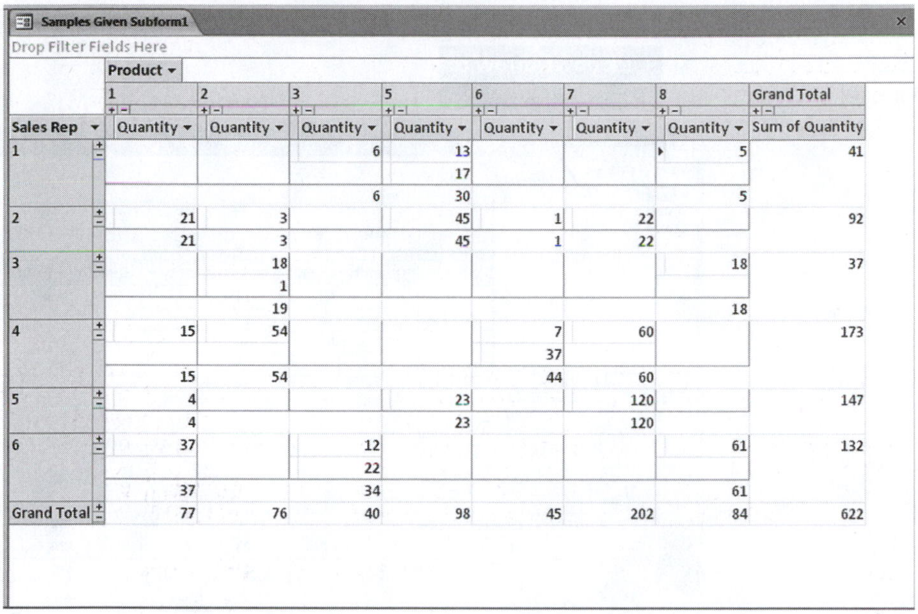

Samples Given Subform1								✕

Drop Filter Fields Here

	Product ▾							
	1	2	3	5	6	7	8	Grand Total
	+ −	+ −	+ −	+ −	+ −	+ −	+ −	+ −
Sales Rep ▾	Quantity ▾	Quantity ▾	Quantity ▾	Quantity ▾	Quantity ▾	Quantity ▾	Quantity ▾	Sum of Quantity
1 + −				6	13		▸ 5	41
					17			
				6	30		5	
2 + −	21	3			45	1	22	92
	21	3			45	1	22	
3 + −			18				18	37
			1					
			19				18	
4 + −	15	54			7		60	173
					37			
	15	54			44		60	
5 + −	4			23		120		147
	4			23		120		
6 + −	37		12				61	132
			22					
	37		34				61	
Grand Total + −	77	76	40	98	45	202	84	622

13. On the Design tab, in the Show/Hide group, click the **Field List** button to display the PivotTable Field List.

14. Click the **Week Name** field and drag it to the *Drop Filter Fields Here* area of the PivotTable, as shown in Figure 10-26.

Figure 10-26

Drag filter field to the PivotTable form

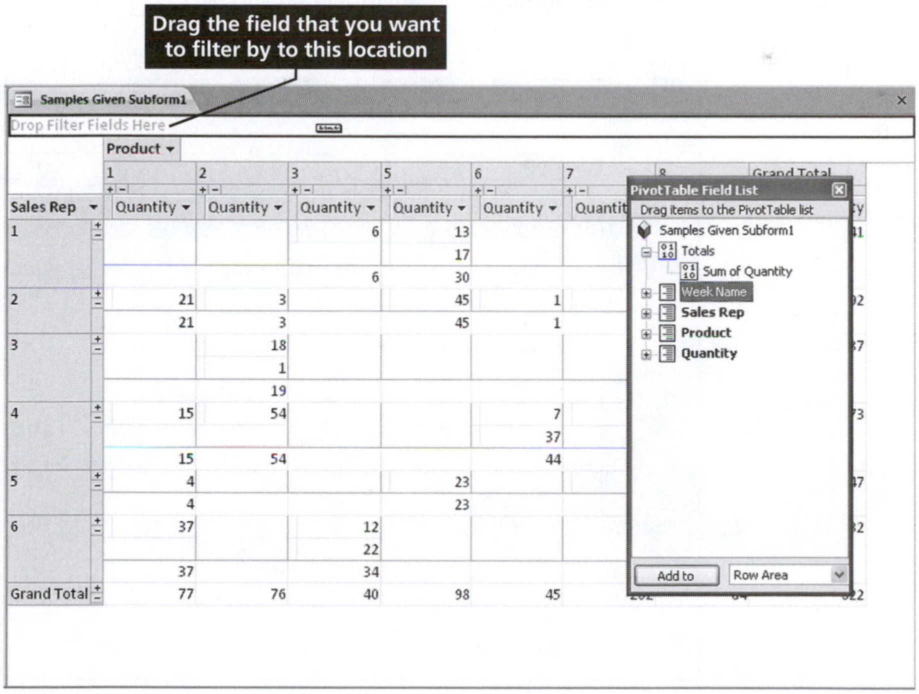

> **Drag the field that you want to filter by to this location**

Samples Given Subform1								✕

Drop Filter Fields Here

	Product ▾							
	1	2	3	5	6	7	8	Grand Total
	+ −	+ −	+ −	+ −	+ −			
Sales Rep ▾	Quantity ▾	Quantity ▾	Quantity ▾	Quantity ▾	Quantity ▾	Quantit		ty ▾
1 + −				6	13			41
					17			
				6	30			
2 + −	21	3			45	1		92
	21	3			45	1		
3 + −			18					37
			1					
			19					
4 + −	15	54			7			73
					37			
	15	54			44			
5 + −	4			23				47
	4			23				
6 + −	37		12					
			22					
	37		34					
Grand Total + −	77	76	40	98	45	202	84	622

PivotTable Field List ✕

Drag items to the PivotTable list

- 🔖 Samples Given Subform1
  - ⊟ Totals
    - Sum of Quantity
  - ⊞ Week Name
  - ⊞ **Sales Rep**
  - ⊞ **Product**
  - ⊞ **Quantity**

[Add to] [Row Area ▾]

15. Click the **Close** button to close the PivotTable Field List.

16. Click the **down arrow** next to the Week Name header to display the menu shown in Figure 10-27.

Figure 10-27

Week Name menu

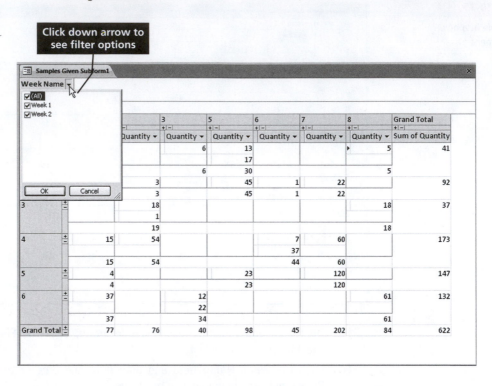

17. Click to deselect the **Week 1 checkbox** and click **OK**. Only the data for Week 2 is displayed, as shown in Figure 10-28.

Figure 10-28

PivotTable filtered

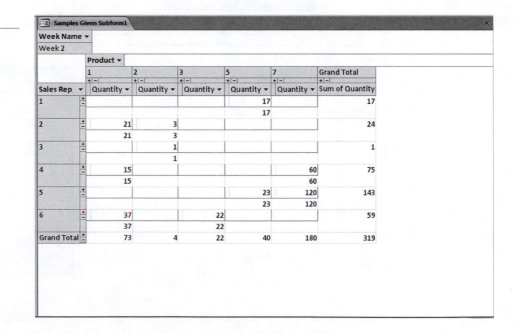

18. Click the **Office Button** and click **Save**.

19. In the Save As dialog box, key **Samples Given PivotTable** and click **OK**.

20. Click the **Close 'Samples Given PivotTable'** button to close the form.
STOP. CLOSE the database.

A *PivotTable* is a type of form that allows you to reorganize columns and rows to analyze data. It is a powerful tool because you can quickly change the format dynamically to emphasize different aspects of the data simply by dragging the form elements to a new location.

To create a PivotTable form, first select the table or query in the Navigation pane. On the Create tab, click the More Forms button and then click PivotTable. Display the Field List and drag fields to the desired location on the PivotTable. When you drag the field to an area, a blue rectangle appears. Release the mouse button to drop the field into that area.

To change the format, simply click the field header and drag to a new location. The data is rearranged and recalculated dynamically. You can also filter the whole PivotTable by a specific field. In this exercise, you used the Week Name field to have the PivotTable show records for only one week at a time.

SUMMARY SKILL MATRIX

IN THIS LESSON YOU LEARNED	MATRIX SKILL	SKILL NUMBER
To create advanced forms	Create forms	2.5
To create a multi-item form	Create multiple-item forms	2.5.3
To create a split form	Create split forms	2.5.4
To create a subform	Create subforms	2.5.5
To create a PivotTable form	Create PivotTable forms	2.5.6

■ Knowledge Assessment

Fill in the Blank

Complete the following sentences by writing the correct word or words in the blanks provided.

1. The Forms group, located on the _____ tab, contains commands for creating all types of forms.

2. When Access creates a Multiple Items form, it is displayed in _____ view.

3. Creating a(n) _____ form allows you to see two views of your data at the same time.

4. To set properties for a split form, first switch to _____ view.

5. For best results, all _____ should be established before creating a subform.

6. When creating a subform, the primary form is called the _____ form.

7. To create a PivotTable form, first select the table or query in _____.

8. A(n) _____ form resembles a datasheet, but it gives you more customization options.

9. The views in a split form are connected to the same data _____ and are completely synchronized with each other.

10. Subforms are especially effective when you want to show data from tables or queries that have a(n) _____ relationship.

Multiple Choice

Select the best response for the following statements or questions.

1. Which tool creates a customizable form that displays multiple records?
   a. PivotTable
   b. Subform
   c. Split Form
   d. Multiple Items

2. When you use the Multiple Items tool, the form that Access creates resembles a
   a. control.
   b. datasheet.
   c. filter.
   d. query.

3. A split form shows your data in which views?
   a. Form view and Datasheet view
   b. Layout view and Design view
   c. Form view and Design view
   d. Layout view and Datasheet view

4. Which split form property allows you to define whether the datasheet appears above, below, to the left, or to the right of the form?
   a. Split Form Orientation
   b. Split Form Datasheet
   c. Split Form Splitter Bar
   d. Split Form Size

5. Which type of form allows you to view data from more than one table or query on the same form?
   a. Multi-item form
   b. Split form
   c. Subform
   d. PivotTable form

6. Which tool would you use to create a subform?
   a. Form Design
   b. Blank Form
   c. Form
   d. Form Wizard

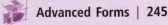

7. A form/subform combination is sometimes referred to as a
   a. hierarchical form.
   b. master/detail form.
   c. parent/child form.
   d. all of the above.

8. Which type of form allows you to reorganize columns and rows to analyze data?
   a. Multi-item form
   b. Split form
   c. Subform
   d. PivotTable

9. What appears when you drag the field to an area of a PivotTable?
   a. Blue rectangle
   b. Hourglass icon
   c. Dotted line
   d. Blinking insertion point

10. To change the format of a PivotTable, click the field header and
    a. choose Cut on the Edit menu.
    b. click the Move button.
    c. drag it to a new location.
    d. press Enter.

■ Competency Assessment

Project 10-1: Create Multi-Item Form

In your job as a travel agent at Margie's Travel, you want to create a form that displays multiple database records but that is more customizable than a datasheet. You will use the Multiple Items tool to create the form.

GET READY. Launch Access if it is not already running.

The *Margie's Events* database file is available on the companion CD-ROM.

1. **OPEN** the *Margie's Events* database from the data files for this lesson.
2. **SAVE** the database as *Margie's Events XXX* (where XXX is your initials).
3. In the Navigation pane, double-click the **Events** table to open it.
4. On the Create tab, in the Forms group, click the **Multiple Items** button.
5. Scroll down and to the right to view the multiple records on the form.
6. Click the **Office Button** and click **Save**.
7. In the Save As dialog box, key **Events Multiple** and click **OK**.
8. Click the **Close 'Events Multiple'** button to close the form.
9. Click the **Close 'Events'** button to close the table.
10. **CLOSE** the database.

   LEAVE Access open for the next project.

Project 10-2: Create a Split Form

Your brother, who owns Wingtip Toys, wants to be able to see two views of his inventory data at the same time—in Form view and in Datasheet view. He asks you to help him create a split form and to modify it so that the datasheet is on top.

The *Toy Stock* database file is available on the companion CD-ROM.

1. **OPEN** *Toy Stock* from the data files for this lesson.
2. **SAVE** the database as *Toy Stock XXX* (where XXX is your initials).
3. In the Navigation pane, double-click the **Inventory** table to open it.
4. On the Create tab, in the Forms group, click the **Split Form** button to create the form and display it in Form view and Datasheet view at the same time.
5. On the Format tab, in the Views group, click the **View** button and click **Design View**.
6. Press **F4** to display the property sheet.
7. Click **Form** in the dropdown list at the top and click the **Format** tab.
8. Scroll down to the Split Form Orientation property, click the **down arrow**, and click **Datasheet on Top**.
9. Click the **Close** button to close the property sheet.
10. On the Format tab, in the Views group, click the **View** button and click **Layout View** to display the split form with the datasheet on top.
11. Click the **Office Button** and click **Save**.
12. In the Save As dialog box, key **Inventory Split** and click **OK**.
13. Click the **Close 'Inventory Split'** button to close the form.
14. Click the **Close 'Inventory'** button to close the table.
15. **CLOSE** the database.

    LEAVE Access open for the next project.

■ Proficiency Assessment

Project 10-3: Forms for Wine Club Database

Information about each selection for the Coho Vineyard monthly wine club is stored in an Access database. As purchasing manager, you use the database frequently and need to have several types of forms available to work with the data. Create a multi-item form and a split form.

The *Wines* database file is available on the companion CD-ROM.

1. **OPEN** *Wines* from the data files for this lesson.
2. **SAVE** the database as *Wines XXX* (where XXX is your initials).
3. Create a multi-item form for the red wine table.
4. Name the form **Red Wines Multi** and close it.
5. Create a multi-item form for the white wine table.
6. Name the form **White Wines Multi** and close it.
7. Create a split form for the red wine table.
8. Name the form **Red Wines Split** and close it.
9. Create a split form for the white wine table.
10. Name the form **White Wines Split** and close it.
11. **LEAVE** the database open for the next project.

    LEAVE Access open for the next project.

Project 10-4: Create a Subform

As purchasing manager for Coho Winery, it would be helpful to view data about wines by distributor. Create a subform that shows the red wines in the monthly club by distributor.

1. On the Create tab, in the Forms group, click the **More Forms** button and click **Form Wizard**.

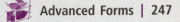

2. In the first screen on the Form Wizard, select **Table: Red Wines** in the Tables/Queries box.

3. Move the **Bottled**, **Label**, and **Type** fields to the Selected Fields box.

4. Select **Table: Distributors** in the Tables/Queries box.

5. Move the **Company** field to the Selected Fields box.

6. In the second screen of the Form Wizard, choose to view your data **by distributors**.

7. In the third screen of the Form Wizard, choose to view your data in **tabular** layout.

8. In the fourth screen of the Form Wizard, choose the **Flow** style.

9. In the final screen of the Form Wizard, accept the default form names and click **Finish**.

10. Navigate to the third record to see which red wines in your monthly club are distributed by Northwind Traders.

11. **CLOSE** the form.

12. **CLOSE** the database.

LEAVE Access open for the next project.

■ Mastery Assessment

Project 10-5: Modifying a Split Form

As the manager at Southridge Video, you created a split form to work with the used game information in the Access database. However, when you open the form, it appears that someone has made changes because the datasheet is on the right and the splitter bar is not visible. Change the form properties back to the way you want them.

The *Used Games* database file is available on the companion CD-ROM.

1. **OPEN** *Used Games* from the data files for this lesson.

2. **SAVE** the database as *Used Games XXX* (where XXX is initials).

3. Open the split form *Games*.

4. Switch to Design view and open the form properties.

5. Change the property to make the datasheet to appear on the top.

6. Change the property to make the splitter bar visible, thus allowing the form and datasheet to be resized.

7. Change the form property so the form will open with the splitter bar in the same position in which you last left it.

8. Change the property to allow edits to be made on the datasheet.

9. Change the property to print only the datasheet portion of the form.

10. Switch to Layout view.

11. **CLOSE** the form and save the changes to the design when prompted.

12. **CLOSE** the database.

LEAVE Access open for the next project.

Project 10-6: PivotTable Form

Your son plays on a recreational league basketball team, and you have volunteered to keep the statistics for the season. In order to be able to dynamically rearrange data as needed to see the information from different perspectives, you decide to create a PivotTable form.

CD

The ***Stats*** database file is available on the companion CD-ROM.

1. **OPEN** ***Stats*** from the data files for this lesson.
2. **SAVE** the database as ***Stats XXX*** (where XXX is your initials).
3. Use the **Stats: Table** and the skills you have learned in this lesson to create the PivotTable shown in Figure 10-29.

Figure 10-29

PivotTable form

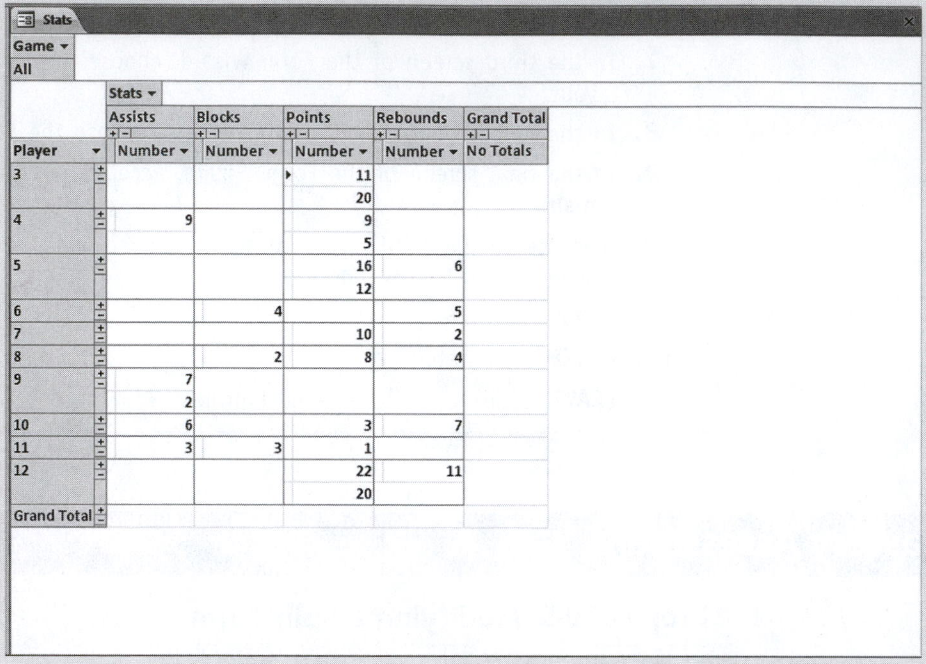

4. To gain even more specific information, use the AutoCalc tool to sum the number field and then filter the data to show only the figures for Game 2, as shown in Figure 10-30.

Figure 10-30

PivotTable form filtered and summed

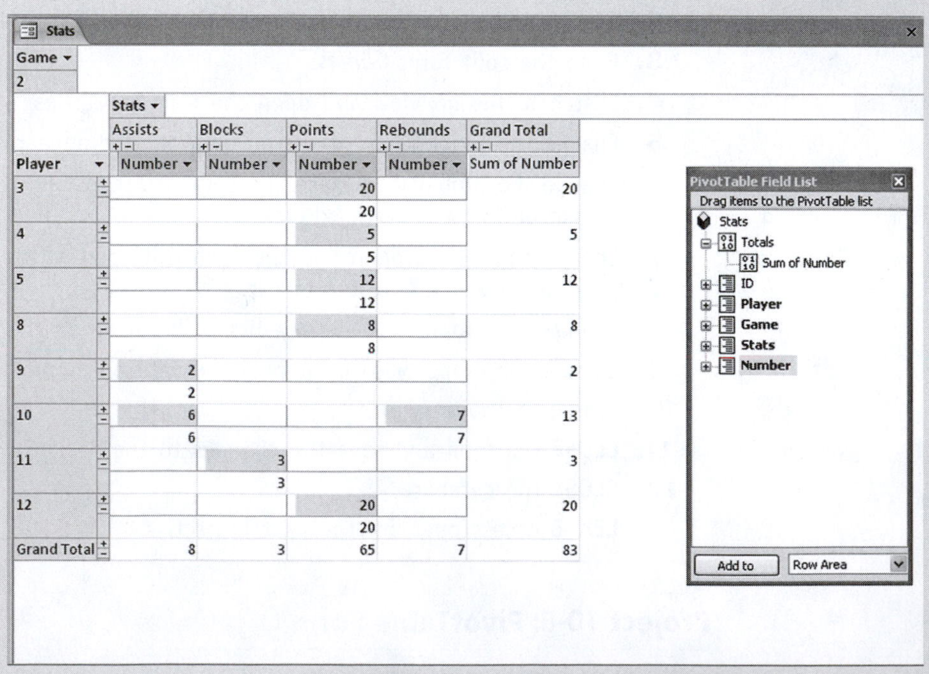

5. **SAVE** the form as **Stats PivotTable** and close.

6. **CLOSE** the database.

   CLOSE Access.

INTERNET READY

Get help learning Access or other Microsoft Office applications with self-paced training courses and more. Click the *Training* link located near the bottom of the Getting Started with Microsoft Office Access page, under More on Office Online. On the Help and How-to page, shown in Figure 10-31, you can find demos, Webcasts, skill assessments, and certification information. Online resources don't have to be dull. For some solid advice—with an attitude—click *Get advice from the Crabby Office Lady* under Quick Links.

Figure 10-31

Help and How-to

Circling Back

Woodgrove Real Estate is growing and adding more listings. Your office has added another real estate agent and has begun listing commercial properties as well as residential ones. The database you created has been a great way to keep track of all the listings and other relevant information. As you learn more about Access, you begin using it for a wider variety of tasks.

Project 1: Create and Format a Report

You want to create a report to display data about each agent's listings. Use the Report Wizard and then switch to Design view to make changes to the format and add a control.

CD

The *Real Estate* file is available on the companion CD-ROM.

GET READY. Launch Access if it is not already running.

1. **OPEN** the *Real Estate* database from the data files for this lesson.
2. **SAVE** the database as *Real Estate XXX* (where XXX is your initials).
3. On the Create tab, in the Reports group, click the **Report Wizard** button.
4. In the Tables/Queries menu, choose **Table: Listings**.
5. Click the **double right arrow >>** button to move all the fields into the Selected Fields list.
6. Click the **ID** field to select it and click the **left arrow <** button to move it back to the Available Fields list.
7. Click the **Next** button.
8. Click the **Listing Agent** field to select it and click the **right arrow >** button to add it as a grouping level.
9. Click the **Next** button.
10. Select **Price** from the fields menu to sort in Ascending order and click the **Next** button.
11. In the Layout section, click the **Outline** button. In the Orientation section, click the **Landscape** button. Click **Next**.
12. Click **Paper** in the styles list and click **Next**.
13. Key **Listings Report** as the title of the report.
14. Click **Finish** to display the Listings Report.
15. On the Print Preview tab, in the Close Preview group, click the **Close Print Preview** button to display the report in Design view.
16. In the Listing Agent Header section, click and drag the **right border of the Listing Agent** field to make it smaller.
17. Click and drag the **right border of the Price** field to make it larger.
18. Click and drag the **right border of the Price** field to make it smaller.
19. On the Design tab, in the Views group, click the **View** button and click **Report View**. Your report should look similar to Figure 1.

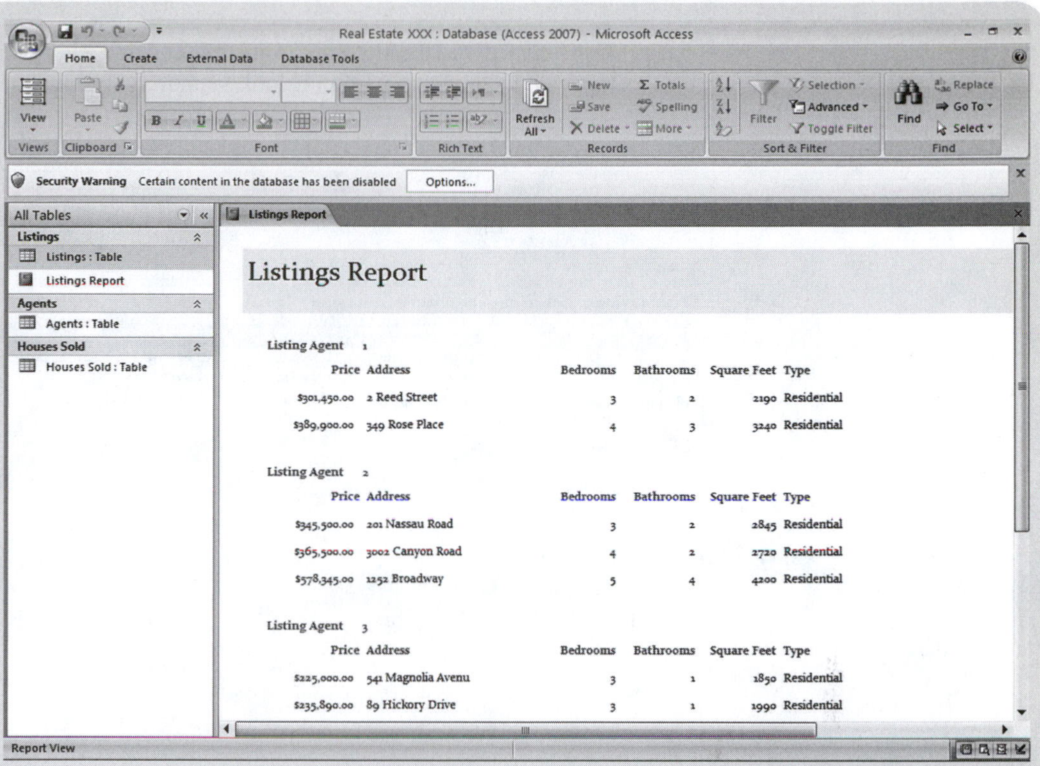

Figure 1

Listings report

20. Click the **Close 'Listings Report'** button to close the report and save the changes when prompted.

   PAUSE. LEAVE the database open to use in the next project.

Project 2: Create and Modify Queries

You want to query the database to find all the houses that closed in June. Create a query using the Query Wizard and then add criteria to get the information you need.

USE the database that is open from the previous project.

1. On the Create tab, in the Other group, click the **Query Wizard** button to display the New Query dialog box.

2. Click **Simple Query Wizard** and then click **OK** to display the Simple Query Wizard.

3. In the Tables/Queries dropdown list, click **Table: Houses Sold.**

4. Under Available Fields, double-click **Listing Agent**, **Address**, **Selling Price**, and **Closing Date** to move them to the Selected Fields box.

5. Click the **Next** > button to display the next screen. Detail query should be selected.

6. Click the **Next** > button to display the final screen.

7. Click the **Finish** button to display the query.

8. On the Home tab, in the Views group, click the **View** button and click **Design View**.

9. In the Criteria row of the Closing Date field, key **Between #6/1/2008# And #6/30/2008#**.

10. On the Design tab, in the Results group, click the **View** button and click **Datasheet View** to display the query results of all records for houses that closed in June.

11. Right-click the **Closing Date field header** and choose **Sort Oldest to Newest** on the menu. Your query should look similar to Figure 2.

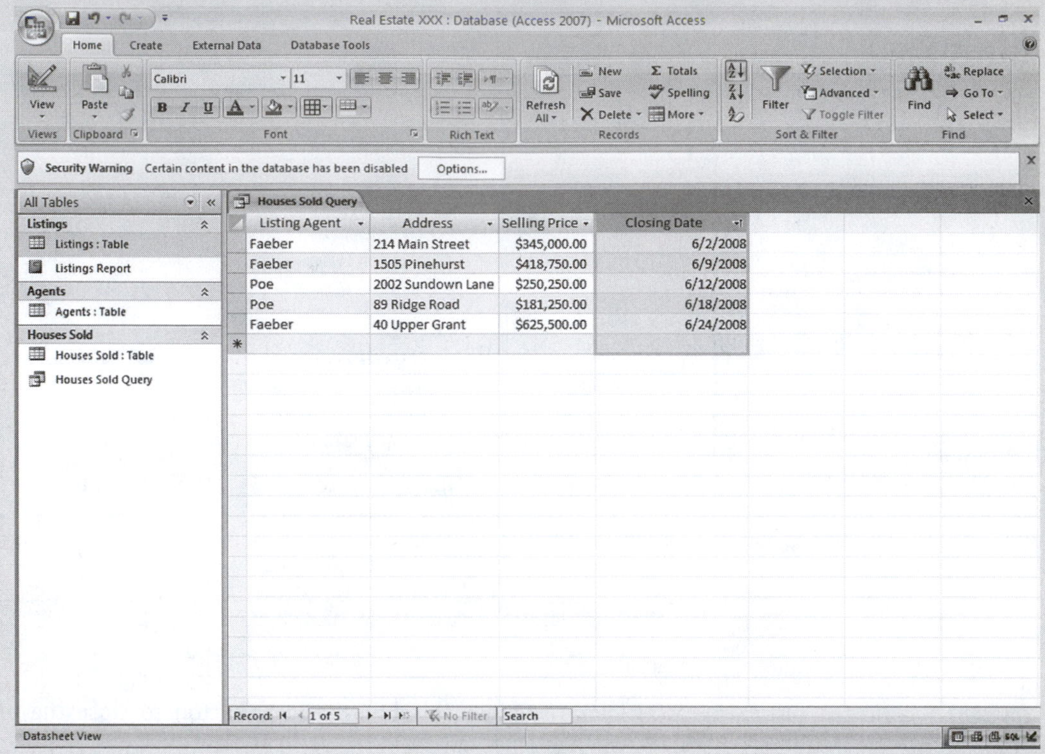

12. Click the **Close 'Houses Sold Query'** button to close the query. When prompted to save, click **Yes**.

PAUSE. LEAVE the database open for the next project.

Project 3: Sum Table Data

You want to know the total value of the current listings. Open the table and add a Totals Row to get this information.

USE the database that is open from the previous project.

1. **OPEN** the **Listings** table.

2. On the Home tab, in the Records group, click the **Totals** button. The Totals Row appears below the asterisk (*) row.

3. Click the **down arrow** in the Price column of the Totals Row. Select **Sum** from the menu. Your screen should look similar to Figure 3.

Figure 3

Totals row

ID	Address	Bedrooms	Bathrooms	Square Feet	Price	Listing Agent	Type
1	541 Magnolia Avenue	3	1	1850	$225,000.00	Poe	Resident
2	3002 Canyon Road	4	2	2720	$365,500.00	Mew	Resident
3	309 Wall Street	2	2	1475	$179,250.00	Friske	Resident
4	23 Austin Lane	0	0	9050	$875,000.00	Friske	Commer
5	4500 Monroe Avenue	4	3	3675	$459,200.00	Poe	Resident
6	2 Reed Street	3	2	2190	$301,450.00	Faeber	Resident
7	111 Sundown Highway	0	0	8990	$1,250,000.00	Poe	Commer
8	1252 Broadway	5	4	4200	$578,345.00	Mew	Resident
9	201 Nassau Road	3	2	2845	$345,500.00	Mew	Resident
10	66 Maple Street	3	3	3100	$415,400.00	Friske	Resident
11	349 Rose Place	4	3	3240	$389,900.00	Faeber	Resident
12	89 Hickory Drive	3	1	1990	$235,890.00	Poe	Resident
13	1502 Main Street	0	0	9750	$1,550,000.00	Friske	Commer
(New)							
Total					$7,170,435.00		

4. On the Home tab, in the Records group, click the **Totals** button to hide the Totals Row.

5. On the Home tab, in the Records group, click the **Totals** button again. The Totals Row reappears.

6. **SAVE** and **CLOSE** the table.

   PAUSE. LEAVE the database open for the next project.

Project 4: Creating a Subform

You want to see the real estate agent's contact information along with the listings. Use the Form Wizard to create a subform that will show all the data in the same place.

USE the database that is open from the previous project.

1. On the Create tab, in the Forms group, click the **More Forms** button and click **Form Wizard**.

2. In the first screen on the Form Wizard, click the **down arrow** in the Tables/Queries box and click **Table: Agents**.

3. In the Available Fields box, double-click the **First Name**, **Last Name**, and **Mobile Phone** fields to move them to the Selected Fields box.

4. Click the **down arrow** in the Tables/Queries box and click **Table: Listings**.

5. In the Available Fields box, double-click the **Address**, **Square Feet**, and **Price** fields to move them to the Selected Fields box.

6. Click **Next >**.

7. In the *How do you want to view your data?* box, click **by Agents**. The *Form with subform(s)* radio button should be selected.

8. Click **Next >**.

9. Click the **Tabular** radio button to select that as the layout for your subform.

10. Click **Next >**.

11. Click **Civic** for the style and click **Next >**.

12. Click the **Finish** button to create Agents form with the Listings Subform. Your form should look similar to Figure 4.

Figure 4

Subform

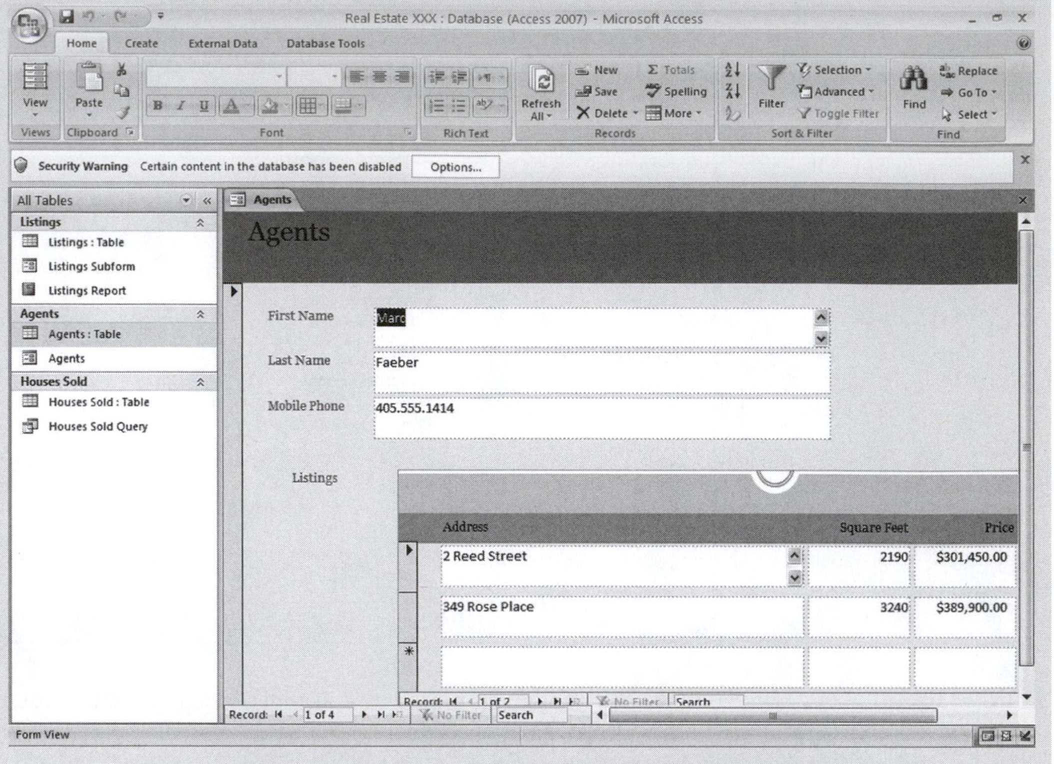

13. In the Navigation pane, double-click the **Listings Subform** to open it.

14. Scroll down to see the data contained in the records and then click the **Close 'Listings Subform'** button to close the subform.

15. Click the **Close 'Agents'** button to close the form.

STOP. CLOSE the database.

✳ **Workplace Ready**

Collaborating using Windows SharePoint Services

As a purchase order manager for Coho Vineyard and Winery, you use Access to organize and manage all purchase-related data, such as purchase status, vendor and supplier information, and activity logs. You use the database to quickly track activities, print purchase orders, and create summary reports.

Microsoft Office Access 2007 also allows you to share this information with colleagues by moving Access files to a Windows SharePoint Services Web site. In this way, your team can communicate, share documents, and work together on projects by interacting with published files through a browser. Using Windows SharePoint Services, you can easily transfer your local data to a server where it can be managed, kept secure, and backed up at regular intervals. You can track records and view when data was created, edited, and deleted, and by whom. You can set data access permissions for various users and also recover deleted information using the Recycle Bin feature.

Advanced Reports

LESSON SKILL MATRIX

SKILLS	MATRIX SKILL	SKILL NUMBER
Defining Group Headers	Define group headers	2.6.4
Creating Aggregate Fields	Create aggregate fields	2.6.5
Creating the Print Layout	Set the print layout	2.6.6
Using the Label Wizard	Create labels by using the Label Wizard	2.6.7

Consolidated Messenger is a New York City–based company that provides quick and reliable pick-up and delivery services to area businesses. The company provides courier service by foot, bike, or truck. The company has a sales force that negotiates contracts with some of its larger corporate clients. As sales manager, you have created a database with tables and reports to keep track of this data. In this lesson, you will generate reports that group data, create aggregate fields to total data in reports, use Print Preview to adjust reports before printing, and use the Label Wizard to create labels for customer mailings.

KEY TERMS
aggregate fields
group
group footer
group header
grouping fields
grouping intervals
grouping levels
Label Wizard
Print Preview

■ Defining Group Headers

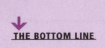

THE BOTTOM LINE

When data is arranged in groups, it is often easier to comprehend and more meaningful. For example, if you want to see the sales performance for each region, it is easier to review this data if each region's sales are grouped together. You can go a step further and specify another group level, such as sales person. This allows you to group a report by region and by sales person within each region. In this way, Access allows you to specify as many as 10 groups in a report. Groups can be nested so that that you can easily see the group structure.

Using the Report Wizard

The Report Wizard lets you specify how you would like data to be grouped as you create the report. You can also add grouping to an existing report using the Group, Sort, and Total pane. Grouping options let you further specify how you want the groups to appear in your report.

⊙ USE THE REPORT WIZARD

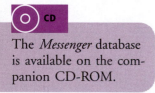

The *Messenger* database is available on the companion CD-ROM.

🔍 Report Wizard

GET READY. Before you begin these steps, be sure to turn on and/or log on to your computer and start Access.

1. **OPEN** *Messenger* from the data files for this lesson.
2. Save the database as *Messenger XXX* (where XXX is your initials).
3. Open the **Corporate Sales** table. 
4. On the Create tab, in the Reports group, click the **Report Wizard** button. The first Report Wizard dialog box appears.
5. Select the **Region (Borough)** field and click the **single right arrow (>)** to move the field to the Selected Fields list.
6. Using the same method, move the **Sales Person Last Name**, **Company Name**, and **Contract Amount** fields from the Available Fields list to the Selected Fields list, as shown in Figure 11-1.

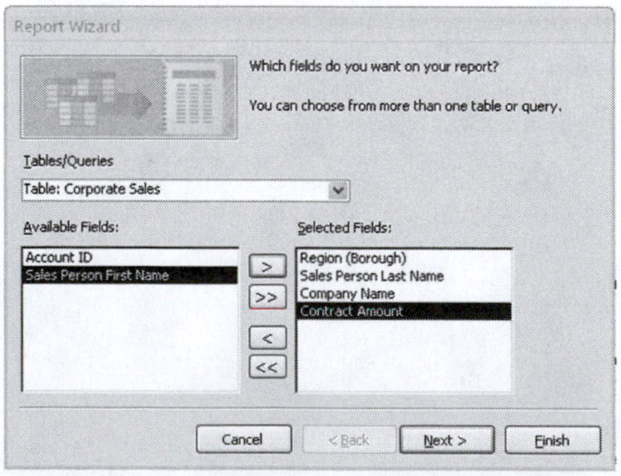

Figure 11-1

First Report Wizard screen

![Report Wizard dialog box. Which fields do you want on your report? You can choose from more than one table or query. Tables/Queries: Table: Corporate Sales. Available Fields: Account ID, Sales Person First Name. Selected Fields: Region (Borough), Sales Person Last Name, Company Name, Contract Amount. Buttons: Cancel, < Back, Next >, Finish.]

7. Click the **Next** button. The second Report Wizard dialog box appears.
8. Select the **Region (Borough)** field and click the **single right arrow (>)** to move it to the grouping levels box.
9. Select the **Contract Amount** field and click the **single right arrow (>)** to move it to the grouping levels box.
10. Select the **Sales Person Last Name** field and click the **single right arrow (>)** to move it to the grouping levels box.

11. Notice that the Sales Person Last Name field is the active field in bold type. Click the **Priority up arrow** to move the **Sales Person Last Name** field to the second level of grouping. Your screen should look similar to Figure 11-2.

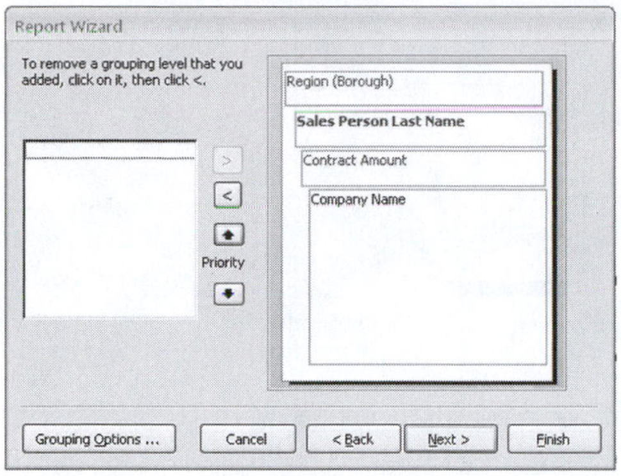

Figure 11-2

Second Report Wizard screen

12. Click the **Grouping Options** button. The Grouping Intervals dialog box appears, as shown in Figure 11-3.

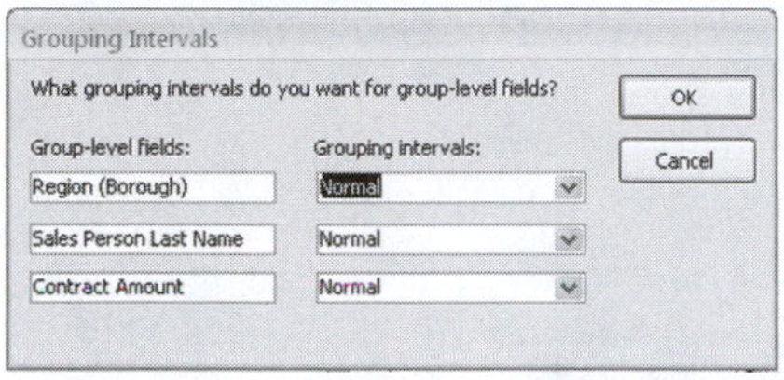

Figure 11-3

Grouping Intervals dialog box

13. Click the **down arrow** on the first Grouping intervals menu to see the choices available. Select **Normal** from the menu and click **OK**.

14. Click the **Next** button. The third Report Wizard screen appears.

15. Click the **down arrow** on the Sort menu and select **Company Name**, as shown in Figure 11-4.

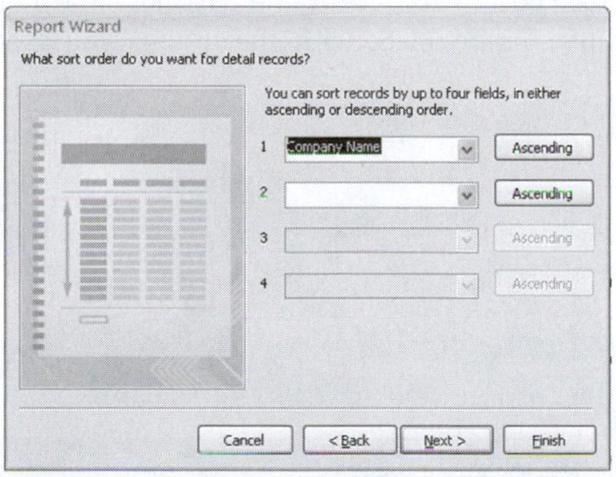

Figure 11-4

Third Report Wizard dialog box

16. Click the **Next** button. The fourth Report Wizard screen appears.

17. In the Layout section, click the **Block** option button, as shown in Figure 11-5.

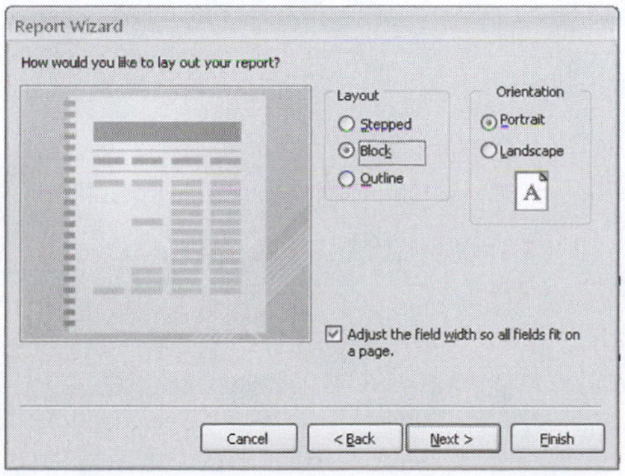

Figure 11-5

Fourth Report Wizard dialog box

18. Click the **Next** button. The Fifth Report Wizard dialog box appears.

19. Select the **Module** style, as shown in Figure 11-6.

Figure 11-6

Fifth Report Wizard dialog box

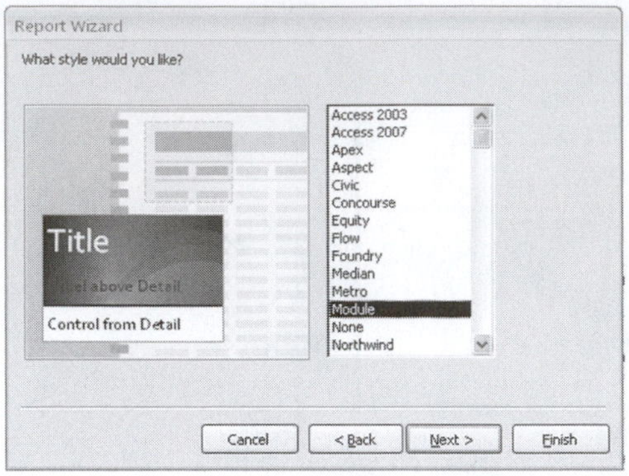

20. Click the **Next** button. The Sixth Report Wizard dialog box appears, as shown in Figure 11-7.

Figure 11-7

Sixth Report Wizard dialog box

21. Click the **Finish** button to accept the settings. The Report Wizard creates the report, shown in Figure 11-8, with the groups you specified.

Figure 11-8

Corporate Sales report

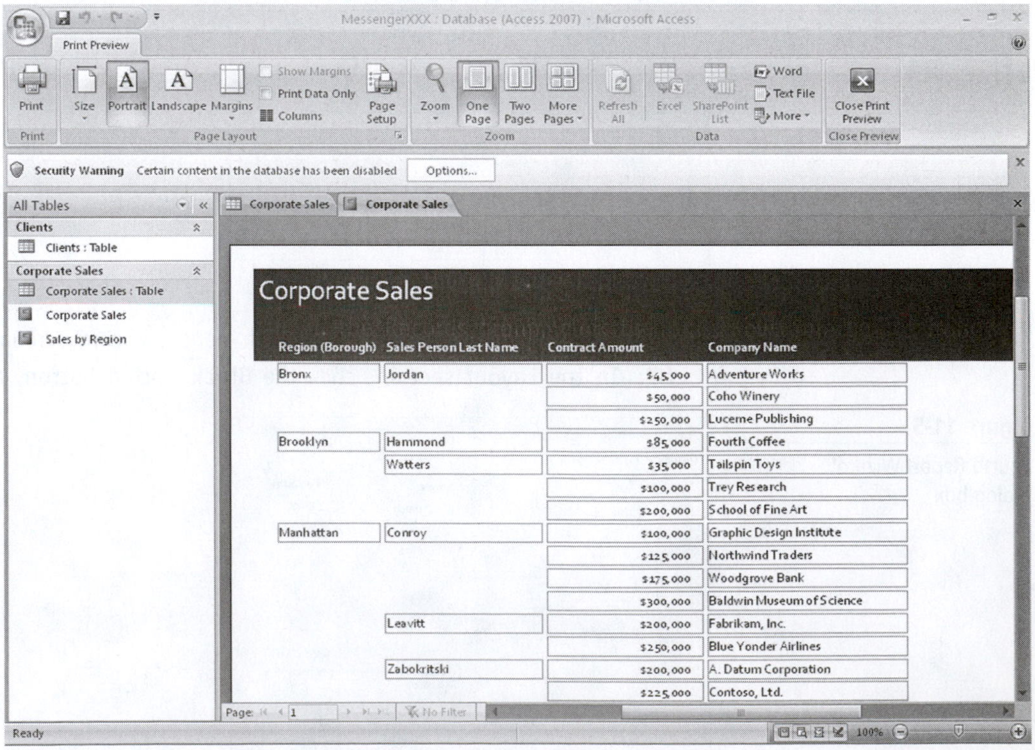

22. CLOSE the report and **CLOSE** the table.

PAUSE. LEAVE the database open to use in the next exercise.

A *group* is a collection of records separated visually with any introductory or summary information displayed with it. Reports can be grouped on fields or expressions. A *grouping field* is a field by which data is grouped.

You can easily specify groups with the Report Wizard when creating a new report. This is an easy and fast way to create a report with groups.

Grouping levels are the nested arrangement of the groups in a report. Access creates indented levels to show the groups from highest to lowest priority. You can change a group's level in the Report Wizard by using the priority up and down arrows.

You can specify grouping intervals by using the Grouping Options button. *Grouping intervals* establish the way that records are grouped together. They can be very useful in arranging a large number of records in a group. You can group on the first character of a text field so that all of the records are visually separated alphabetically. You can specify a group interval of a day, week, month, or quarter on a date field. This is useful if you want to view the sales for each week in a report. You can also specify a custom interval.

⊕ USE THE GROUP, SORT, AND TOTAL PANE

USE the database open from the previous exercise.

1. OPEN the **Sales by Region** report. Notice that the report is not arranged by groups.

2. Switch to Layout view and close the Field List pane if it opens.

3. On the Format tab, in the Grouping & Totals group, click the **Group & Sort** button. The Group, Sort, and Total pane appears at the bottom of the screen, as shown in Figure 11-9.

Figure 11-9

Group, Sort, and Total Pane

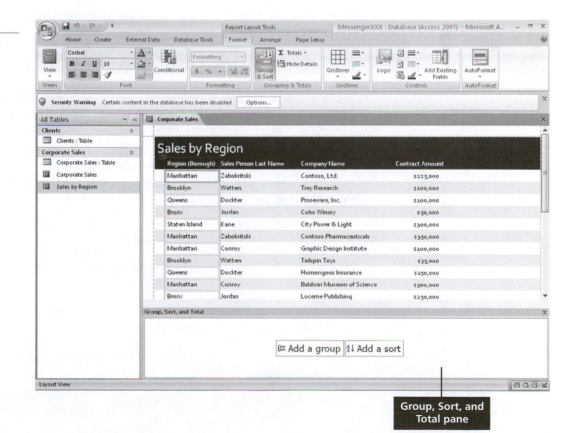

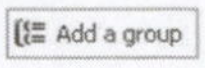

4. Click the **Add a group** button. Select **Region (Borough)** from the Group on menu, as shown in Figure 11-10. The report is now grouped on the **Region (Borough)** field.

Figure 11-10

Group on menu

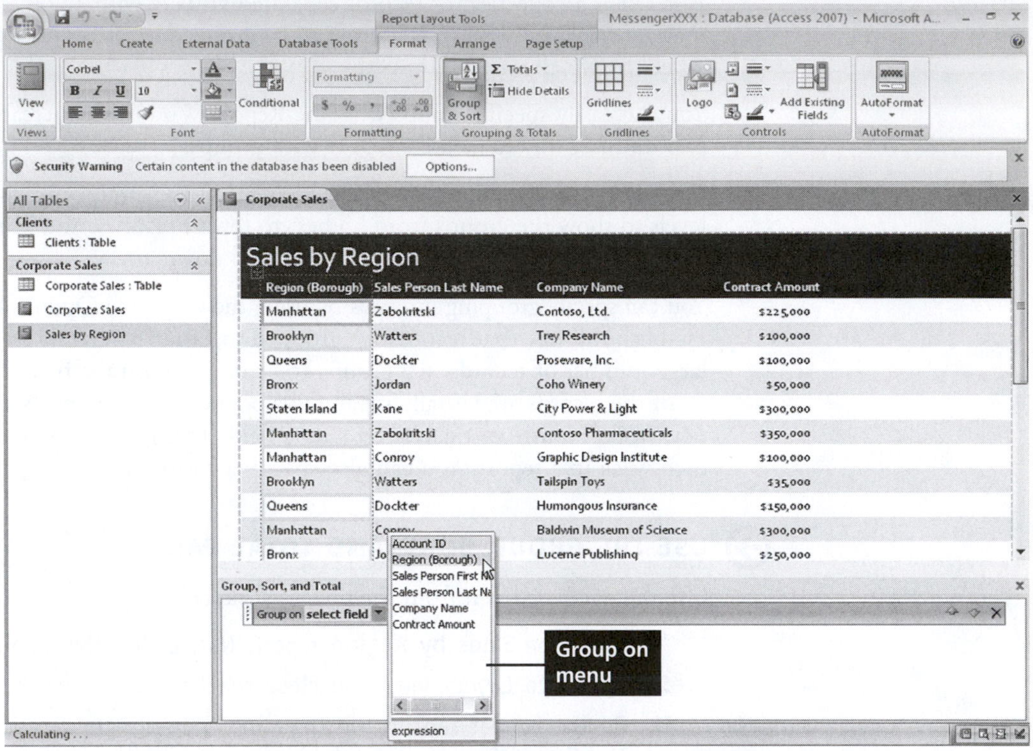

ANOTHER WAY You can also right-click a field header in Layout view and select Group on Fieldname from the shortcut menu to define a group header.

5. Click the **Add a group** button on the Group, Sort, and Total pane. Select **Sales Person Last Name** from the Group on menu. The report is now also grouped on the **Sales Person Last Name** field.

6. Switch to Design view. Your screen should look similar to Figure 11-11. Notice that there is a Region (Borough) Header for that group and a Sales Person Last Name header for that group. The Company Name and Contract Amount fields are arranged in the Detail section.

Figure 11-11

Group headers in Design view

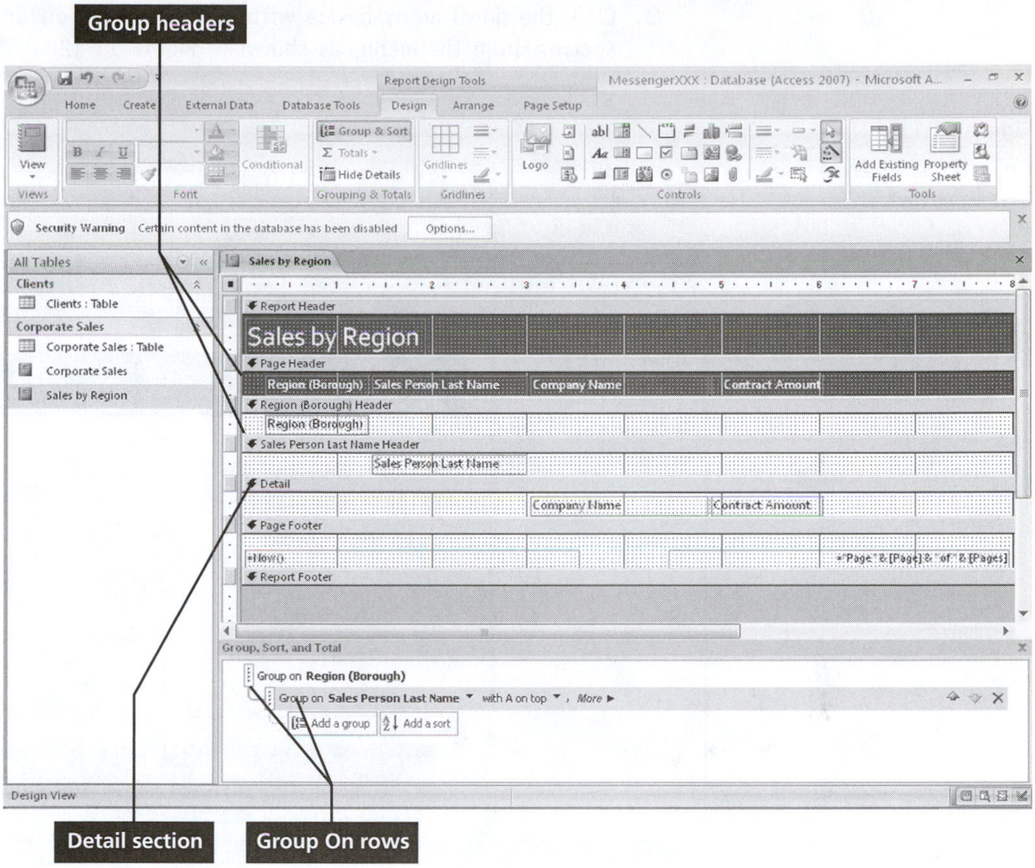

7. **SAVE** the report.

PAUSE. LEAVE the database open to use in the next exercise.

As you may remember from Lesson 6, a report is organized into sections. You can view sections of a report in Design view. The **group header** is the section of a report where the name of a grouped field is displayed and printed. Group headers take on the name of the group, so instead of seeing a group header named *Group Header* you will see *[Fieldname] Header,* as shown in Figure 11-11.

You can add group headers to a report using the Group, Sort, and Total pane. When you select a field from the Group on menu, the group header is added to the report.

A **group footer** is the section of the report where the data in the group is summarized. It is optional. If you do not have any summary data, such as a total, you don't need a group footer.

CERTIFICATION READY?
How do you define group headers?
2.6.4

CHANGE GROUPING OPTIONS

USE the database and report open from the previous exercise.

1. Switch to Layout view.
2. Click the **Group On *Sales Person Last Name*** row in the Group, Sort, and Total Pane and then click the **More** button to view the available grouping options.

3. Click the down arrow beside **with a header section** and select **without a header section** from the menu, as shown in Figure 11-12.

Figure 11-12

Group On *Sales Person Last Name* row

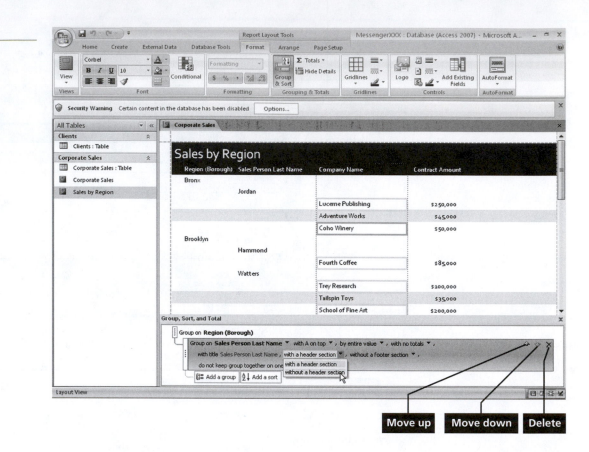

4. Switch to Design view. Note that the Sales Person Last Name Header has been deleted.

5. Switch to Layout view.

6. Click the down arrow beside the **without a header section** and select **with a header section**.

7. Click the **Move up** arrow at the end of the Group On Sales Person Last Name row. Notice that the Sales Person Last Name group is now the top level group in the report.

8. Click the **Add a group** button and select **Company Name** from the menu. A new group level is added to the report.

9. On the Format tab, in the Grouping & Totals group, click the **Hide Details** button. The data in the Contract Amount field is hidden.

10. On the Format tab, in the Grouping & Totals group, click the **Hide Details** button. The data in the Amount field is displayed.

11. Click the **More** button.

12. Click the down arrow beside **with A on top** on the Group On Company Name row in the Group, Sort, and Total Pane and select **with Z on top**. The sort order is changed from ascending to descending order.

13. Click the down arrow beside **with Z on top** and select **with A on top.**

14. Click the **Delete** button on the right side of the Group On Company Name row in the Group, Sort, and Total pane. The row is deleted, as is the Company Name header section.

15. Switch to Report view to see the report.

16. **SAVE** the report.

PAUSE. LEAVE the database open to use in the next exercise.

After grouping data, Access gives you options for displaying grouped data. To display the grouping options in the Group, Sort, and Total pane, click More on the group level that you want to change. If you want to hide the grouping options, click Less.

Grouping options include:

- Sort order—choose ascending or descending
- Group interval—change the way records are grouped together
- Totals—add totals to fields
- Title—change the label of a column heading or summary field
- With/without header—add or remove the header section
- With/without footer—add or remove footer section
- Keep group together—decide how or if you want to keep grouped data together on the same page
    - Do not keep group together on one page—groups can be broken up by page breaks
    - Keep whole group together on one page—minimizes the number of page breaks in a group
    - Keep header and first record together on one page—makes sure a group header is not printed by itself at the bottom of a page

You can also click the Move up and Move down arrows at the end of the Group On row to change the priority of grouping levels. To delete a grouping level, click the Delete button at the end of its Group On row and Access will move the data to the Detail section of the report. However, if other controls are in the header Access will warn you that these could be deleted.

The Hide Details command is a toggle button that hides data in the Details section of the report. Click it again to display the data.

■ Creating Aggregate Fields

THE BOTTOM LINE

Report data often contains numbers, such as sales figures, that need to be totaled. A report that lists sales for each month in a quarter but does not total all the sales for the quarter is incomplete. Aggregate fields use functions to provide summary information of such data.

Access 2007 provides a Totals command that lets you create an aggregate field that can not only provide grand totals, but totals for groups in a report as well. You can also use the Group, Sort, and Total pane to add aggregate functions to fields.

⊙ CREATE AGGREGATE FIELDS

USE the database and report open from the previous exercise.

1. Switch to Layout view.

2. Click the **Group On** *Sales Person Last Name* row and click **More**.

3. Click the down arrow beside **with no totals**. The Totals menu appears, as shown in Figure 11-13.

Figure 11-13

Totals menu

4. Click the down arrow on the **Total On** menu and select **Contract Amount.**

5. Click the down arrow on the **Type** menu and select **Sum** if it isn't selected already.

6. Click the **Show Grand Total** box and click the **Show in Group Footer** box.

7. Click outside the menu to close it and apply the settings.

8. Select the **Sales Person Last Name** field header.

Σ Totals ▾

9. On the Format tab, in the Grouping & Totals group, click the **Totals** button and select **Count Records** from the menu.

10. Switch to Report view. The total appears at the bottom of the report.

> ◆ **ANOTHER WAY**
>
> You can also right-click a field in Layout view and select Total from the shortcut menu to apply an aggregate function to a field.

CERTIFICATION READY?
How do you create aggregate fields?
2.6.5

11. **SAVE** the report and **CLOSE** it.

PAUSE. LEAVE the database open to use in the next exercise.

In previous lessons, you learned how to use aggregate functions such as Sum, Count, and Average to total columns of data in a table. In a similar way, you can create an *aggregate field* by using aggregate functions to calculate data in a field. The aggregate functions you can use are Sum, Average, Count Records, Count Values, Max, Min, Standard Deviation, or Variance.

You can create aggregate fields using the Totals command or by using the Group, Sort, and Total pane.

X REF

For more information about aggregate functions, see Lesson 9.

The Totals command is located on the Format tab, in the Grouping & Totals group, but you can also access it on the shortcut menu. In Layout view, just right-click the field you want to total and select Totals from the shortcut menu. The Totals command adds a calculated control in the report footer where it displays the grand total. If you don't already have group footers in your report, the Totals command adds group footers and calculated controls to calculate the totals for each group.

You have a few more options when using the Group, Sort, and Total pane to create an aggregate field in a report. The Totals menu gives you options for choosing the field and type of function as well as options on how you want to display totals. You can display a grand total or a group total as a percentage of the grand total. You can also choose to show the totals in the group header or footer.

SOFTWARE ORIENTATION

Print Preview tab

The Print Preview tab has commands for viewing a report in a variety of ways and for adjusting its layout. You can display the Print Preview tab by choosing Print Preview from the Views menu.

Figure 11-14

Print Preview tab

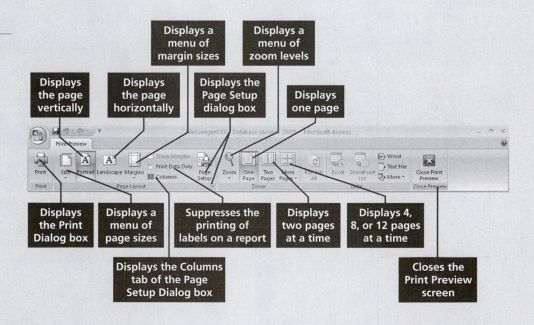

Use the Print Preview tab to view and adjust page layout before printing.

■ Creating the Print Layout

THE BOTTOM LINE

Reports are often created so that they can be printed and displayed or shared with colleagues. You can print a report from any view: Report, Layout, Design, or Print Preview. You can even print a report from the Navigation pane. But before you print a report, you should check settings such as margins and page orientation to make sure the report will print correctly.

Print Preview allows you to view a report on the screen as it will look when printed. This allows you to make adjustments to the layout before clicking the Print button. The settings that you choose will be saved with the report, so you won't have to select the same settings each time you print.

➔ **CREATE THE PRINT LAYOUT**

USE the database open from the previous exercise.

1. Right-click the Sales by Region report in the Navigation pane and select **Rename** from the menu.

2. Key **Sales by Sales Person**.

3. Open the report in Design view and click the Report title. Select **Region** and key **Sales Person,** because the report no longer shows sales by region, but sales by sales person.

4. On the Home tab, in the Views group, click the **View** button and select **Print Preview** from the menu. The report is displayed in Print Preview, as shown in Figure 11-15.

Figure 11-15

Report in Print Preview

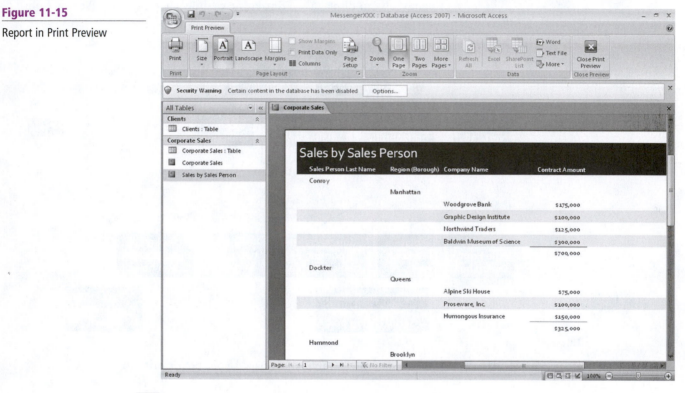

5. On the Print Preview tab, in the Zoom group, click the **Two Pages** button. Both pages of the report are displayed on the screen.

6. On the Print Preview tab, in the Page Layout group, click the **Landscape** button. The report is displayed in landscape orientation.

7. On the Print Preview tab, in the Page Layout group, click the **Portrait** button. The report is displayed in portrait orientation again. The margins need adjustment.

8. Click the **Margins** button and select **Narrow** from the menu.

9. On the Print Preview tab, in the Page Layout group, click the **Page Setup** button. The Page Setup dialog box appears, as shown in Figure 11-16. Notice it has many of the same options that are available in the Page Layout group, but more options and details to choose from.

Figure 11-16

Page Setup dialog box

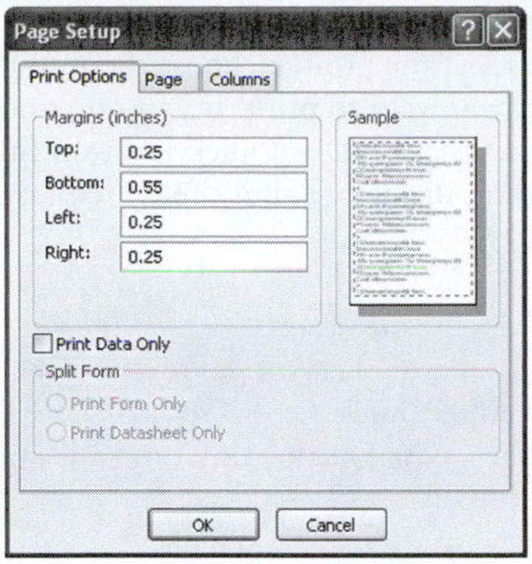

Page Setup

Print Options | Page | Columns

Margins (inches)

Top: 0.25

Bottom: 0.55

Left: 0.25

Right: 0.25

Sample

☐ Print Data Only

Split Form

○ Print Form Only

○ Print Datasheet Only

OK | Cancel

10. Click the **Page** tab. Click the down arrow in the Size box and select **Legal (8½ x 14 in)** from the menu to see if all data will fit on one page.

11. Click **OK.**

12. On the Print Preview tab, in the Zoom group, click the **Zoom** button and select **50%** from the menu. Notice that all data does not fit on one page.

13. On the Print Preview tab, in the Page Layout group, click the **Size** button and select **Letter (8 1/2 x 11 in)** from the menu. Notice that the group at the bottom of the first page is split and continues on the second page.

14. Click the **Close Print Preview** button.

15. Switch to Layout view.

16. On the Group, Sort, and Total pane, on the **Group On Sales Person Last Name** row, click the **More** button. Click the down arrow beside **do not keep group together on one page** and select **keep whole group together on one page** from the menu.

17. **SAVE** the report design.

18. Right-click in a blank area of the report and select **Print Preview** from the shortcut menu, as shown in Figure 11-17. Notice that the group is no longer split across two pages.

Figure 11-17

Shortcut menu

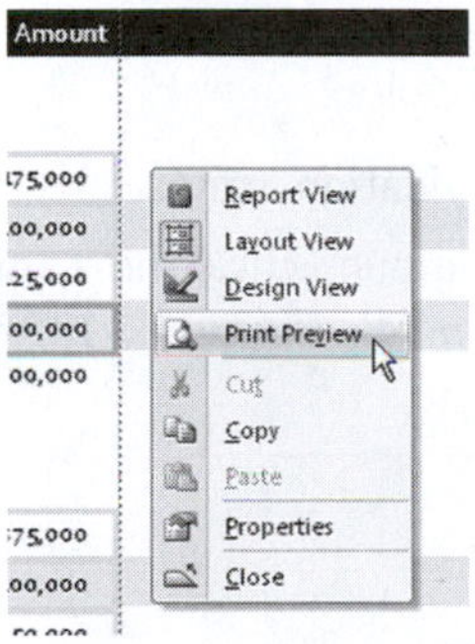

Amount

| 75,000 |
| 00,000 |
| 25,000 |
| 00,000 |
| 00,000 |

📊 **R**eport View

🖳 La**y**out View

📐 **D**esign View

🔍 Print Preview

✂ Cut

📋 **C**opy

📋 **P**aste

| 75,000 |
| 00,000 |

📑 **P**roperties

📄 **C**lose

19. Click the **Print** button. The Print dialog box appears. Click **OK**.

20. **CLOSE** the report.

PAUSE. LEAVE the database open to use in the next exercise.

Print Preview displays a report as it will look when printed. It is helpful to preview a report before printing it so that you can make sure the report prints the way that you want.

The Print Preview tab has commands for printing, changing the page layout, and zooming in or out to view the pages. When you are finished previewing a report, you can click the Close Print Preview button to leave the view.

When you are confident your report will print correctly, you can click the Print button. The Print dialog box lets you select the printer, choose the number of copies you want to print, and specify which pages you want to print. If you don't need to preview a report, you can skip Print Preview and select Print or Quick Print on the Office button. The Print command displays the Print dialog box, but the Quick Print command sends the report directly to the printer.

TAKE NOTE * You can add the Print Preview and/or the Quick Print command to the Quick Access Toolbar by clicking the Customize Quick Access Toolbar down arrow at the end of the toolbar and selecting Print Preview or Quick Print from the menu.

ANOTHER WAY Start Print Preview by clicking the Office button, pointing to Print, and clicking Print Preview.

ANOTHER WAY Right-click the report you want to preview in the Navigation pane and select Print Preview from the shortcut menu.

■ Using the Label Wizard

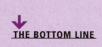

THE BOTTOM LINE

You can create labels for mailing, or other purposes, using the data in your Access databases. The Label Wizard helps you create a label-sized report that you can use to print labels. You can choose from a wide variety of sizes, including sizes to fit label sheets that you purchase at the office supply store or custom created labels.

The Label Wizard asks you a series of questions about the labels you want and then creates the labels based on your answers.

⊙ **USE THE LABEL WIZARD**

USE the database open from the previous exercise.

1. Select the **Clients** table in the Navigation pane.

 2. On the Create tab, in the Reports group, click the **Labels** button. The first Label Wizard dialog box appears, as shown in Figure 11-18.

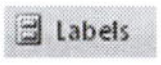

Figure 11-18

First Label Wizard dialog box

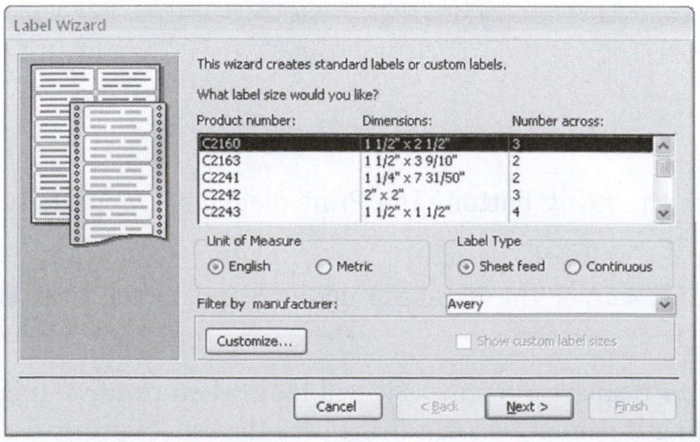

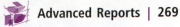

3. Scroll down in the Product number box and select **Avery USA 5160** and click the **Next** button. The second Label Wizard dialog box appears, as shown in Figure 11-19.

Figure 11-19

Second Label Wizard dialog box

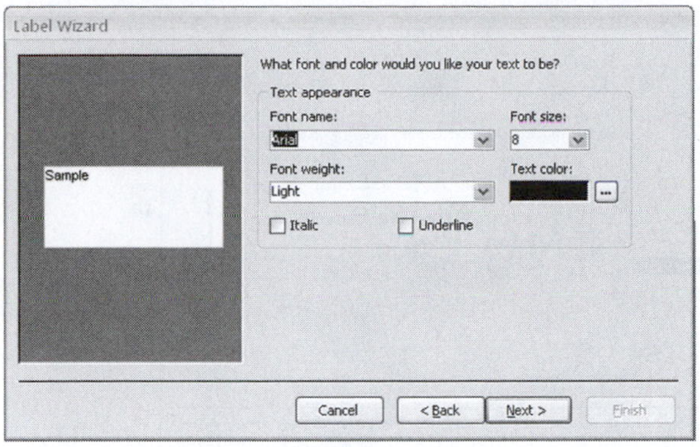

4. Click the **Font name** menu and scroll down to select **Times New Roman**. Notice the preview sample displays the new font.

5. Click the **Font size** menu and select **9.**

6. Click the **Font weight** menu and select **Normal**.

7. In the Text color section, click the **Ellipses** button to display the Color menu. Notice the options available, then click **Cancel** to close it.

8. Click the **Next** button. The third Label Wizard dialog box appears, as shown in Figure 11-20.

Figure 11-20

Third Label Wizard dialog box

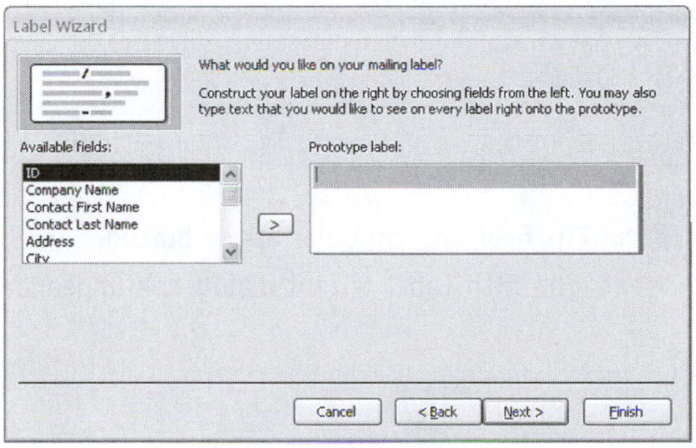

9. Select the **Company Name** field in the Available Fields list and click the **arrow** button to place it on the Prototype label.

10. Press **Enter**.

11. Key **ATTN:** and press the **Spacebar**.

12. Select the **Contact First Name** field and click the **arrow** button.

13. Press the **Spacebar** to insert a blank space between fields.

14. Select the **Contact Last Name** field and click the **arrow** button.

15. Press **Enter**.

16. Select the **Address** field and click the **arrow** button. Press **Enter**.

17. Select the **City** field and click the **arrow** button. Key a **comma** and press the **Spacebar**.

18. Select the **State** field and click the **arrow** button. Press the **Spacebar**.

19. Select the **Zip** field and click the **arrow** button. Your screen should look similar to Figure 11-21.

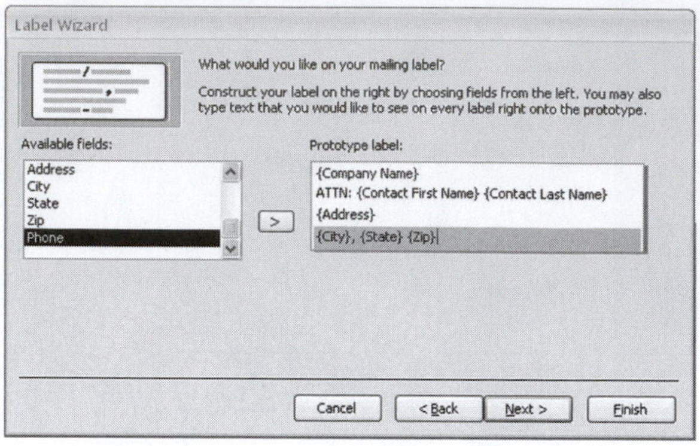

Figure 11-21

Completed Prototype label

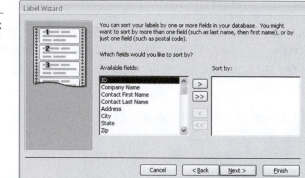

20. Click **Next**. The fourth Label Wizard dialog box appears, as shown in Figure 11-22.

Figure 11-22

Fourth Label Wizard dialog box

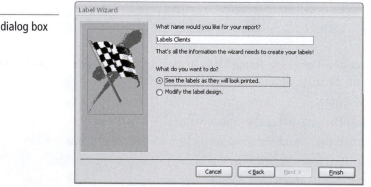

21. Select the **Zip** field and click the **arrow** button.

22. Click **Next**. The fifth Label Wizard dialog box appears, as shown in Figure 11-23.

Figure 11-23

Fifth Label Wizard dialog box

23. Click the **Modify the label design** button and click **Finish.** Your screen should look similar to Figure 11-24.

Figure 11-24

Label report

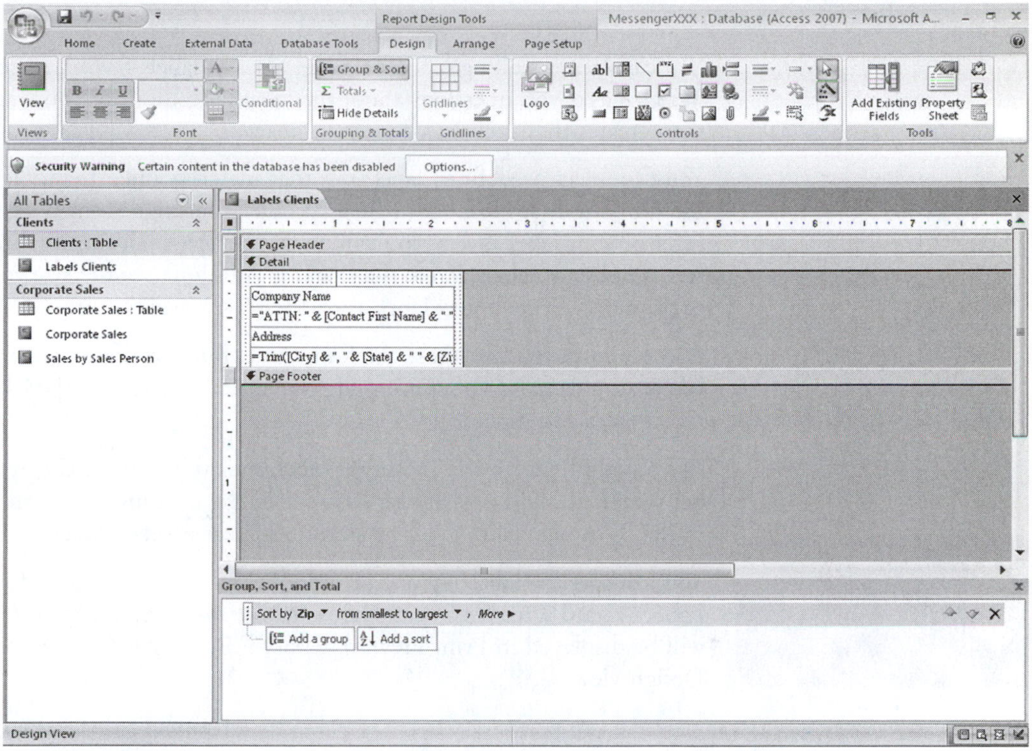

24. On the Home tab, in the Views group, click the **View** menu and select **Print Preview** from the menu. Your screen should look similar to Figure 11-25.

Figure 11-25

Report in Print Preview

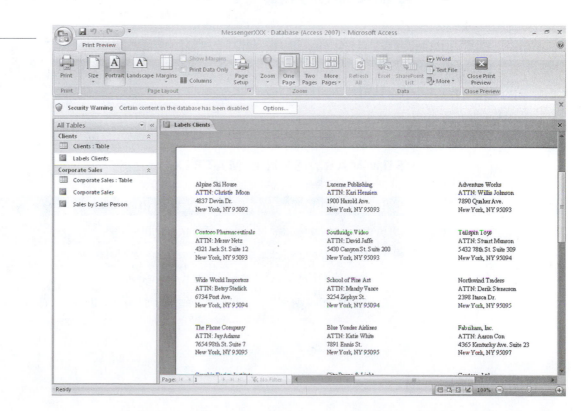

25. Click the **Print** button. The Print dialog box appears. Click **OK**.

26. **CLOSE** the report.

CLOSE the database.

You can create mailing labels or other types of labels from an Access table or query. The **Label Wizard** asks you questions about the labels and the data you want to display on them and then creates the labels based on your answers.

You can select predefined label sizes that match popular manufacturer's label sheets. These are listed by Product Number in the first Label Wizard screen. If you don't know the manufacturer of your label sheets, you can choose a sheet with similar dimensions and with the correct number of labels across the sheet. If you don't see the size you need, you can customize the size and create a new label using the Customize button.

Access allows you to choose the font name, font size, font weight, and text color for your labels. You can also choose to underline or italicize text in the label. The Sample box displays the choices you make.

As you add fields to the Prototype label, remember to use the Spacebar to add a space between fields and press Enter to move to the next line. You can also key text directly in the Prototype label that you want to appear on each label.

CERTIFICATION READY?
How do you create labels using the Label Wizard?
2.6.7

You can sort the labels by one or more fields, such as zip code for bulk mailings. On the last Label Wizard screen, you can choose to *See the labels as they will look when printed* and they will be displayed in Print Preview. Choose *Modify the label design* to view the label report in Design view.

TROUBLESHOOTING

If Access displays a message warning you that some of your data may not be displayed, this means the controls on the label are too wide for the allotted space. If this happens, try reducing the size of the controls in Design view so that they fit in the space available for a single label or try reducing the page margins using Page Setup.

TAKE NOTE*

As an alternative to printing labels, you can print addresses directly onto envelopes. To do this, you will need to create a custom label instead of a predefined label and set the Label Type setting to Sheet Feed.

SUMMARY SKILL MATRIX

In this lesson you learned	Matrix Skill	Skill Number
To define group headers	Define group headers	2.6.4
To create aggregate fields	Create aggregate fields	2.6.5
To create the print layout	Set the print layout	2.6.6
To use the Label Wizard	Create labels by using the Label Wizard	2.6.7

Knowledge Assessment

Matching

Match the term in Column 1 to its description in Column 2.

Column 1	Column 2

1. group   **a.** asks you questions about the labels and data you want to display and then creates labels based on your answers

2. group header   **b.** field that contains an aggregate function to calculate data

3. group footer   **c.** a field by which data is grouped

4. Hide Details command   **d.** the nested arrangement of the groups in a report

5. grouping field   **e.** a collection of records separated visually with any introductory or summary information displayed with it

6. aggregate field   **f.** the section of a report where the name of a grouped field is displayed and printed

7. Print Preview   **g.** the sample in the Label Wizard where you create the label design

8. grouping levels   **h.** hides the data in the Details section of a report

9. Label Wizard   **i.** the section of a report where the data in a group is summarized

10. Prototype label   **j.** displays a report as it will look when printed

True / False

Circle T if the statement is true or F if the statement is false.

T F **1.** Grouping intervals establish the way that records are grouped together.
T F **2.** You cannot group data in the Report Wizard.
T F **3.** Group headers take on the name of the group.
T F **4.** Group footers are optional in a report.
T F **5.** The arrows at the end of a Group On row determine sort order.
T F **6.** Average is an aggregate function.
T F **7.** The Totals command adds group footers and calculated controls for you.
T F **8.** You must preview a report before you can print.
T F **9.** You can modify labels in Design view.
T F **10.** Labels are small reports.

■ Competency Assessment

Project 11-1: Create Address Labels for Authors

You need to send out confidential contract information to the authors in the Business Books division. Create labels for the authors using the Author Contact Information table.

GET READY. Launch Access if it is not already running.

The *Lucerne* database is available on the companion CD-ROM.

1. Open the *Lucerne* database.
2. Save the database as *LucerneXXX* (where XXX is your initials).
3. Select the **Author Contact Information** table in the Navigation pane.
4. On the Create tab, in the Reports group, click the **Labels** button.
5. Select the **C2242** label in the Product name box and click **Next**.
6. Select **Arial** from the Font name menu and select **9** from the Font size menu.
7. Click the **Italic** button and click **Next**.
8. Key **CONFIDENTIAL** in all caps and press [Enter].
9. Key **For Addressee Only** and press [Enter].
10. Select the **Author First Name** field and click the **arrow** button. Press the [Spacebar].
11. Select the **Author Last Name** field and click the **arrow** button. Press [Enter].
12. Select the **Author Address** field and click the **arrow** button. Press [Enter].
13. Select the **Author City** field and click the **arrow** button. Key a [comma] and press the [Spacebar].
14. Select the **Author State** field and click the **arrow** button. Press the [Spacebar].
15. Select the **Author Zip** field and click the **arrow** button.
16. Click **Finish**.
17. **CLOSE** the report.

    LEAVE the database open for the next project.

Project 11-2: Total and Preview the Book Sales Report

Finish the Book Sales report to show totals for Domestic and International Sales. You also need to make some adjustments in Print Preview before printing.

USE the database open from the previous project.

1. **OPEN** the *Book Sales* report.
2. In Layout view, select the **Domestic Sales** field header.
3. On the Format tab, in the Grouping & Totals group, click the **Totals** button and select **Sum** from the menu.
4. Select the **International Sales** field header.
5. On the Format tab, in the Grouping & Totals group, click the **Totals** button and select **Sum** from the menu.
6. Select the **Book Title** field header.
7. On the Format tab, in the Grouping & Totals group, click the **Totals** button and select **Count Records** from the menu.
8. On the Format tab, in the Views group, click the **View** menu and select **Print Preview** from the menu.
9. On the Print Preview tab, in the Page Layout group, click the **Margins** button and select **Wide** from the menu.
10. On the Print Preview tab, in the Zoom group, click the **Zoom** button and select **Fit to Window**.

11. **SAVE** the report.

12. On the Print Preview tab, in the Print group, click the **Print** button. Click **OK.**

13. **CLOSE** the report.

   CLOSE the database.

■ Proficiency Assessment

Project 11-3: **Create a Grouped Report with Aggregate Fields**

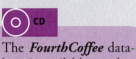

The *FourthCoffee* database is available on the companion CD-ROM.

Your supervisor asks you to create a report using the Monthly Sales by Store table that shows monthly sales by store.

1. **OPEN** *FourthCoffee* from the data files for this lesson.

2. **SAVE** the database as *FourthCoffeeXXX* (where XXX is your initials).

3. Select the **Monthly Sales by Store** table.

4. Use the Report Wizard to create a report that includes the Mon, Store, and Sales fields.

5. Group by Store and create a Stepped layout with the Office style.

6. Close Print Preview and switch to Layout view to decrease the width of the Mon and Sales columns.

7. Click the **Group & Sort** button to open the Group, Sort, and Total pane.

8. Click the **Add a Sort** button and select **Sales** from the menu. Sort from smallest to largest.

9. Select the **Sales** field header.

10. Click the **Totals** button and select **Sum** from the menu.

11. **SAVE** the report.

   LEAVE the report open for use in the next project.

Project 11-4: **Preview and Print the Monthly Sales Report**

You need to print the Monthly Sales by Store report. View the report in Print Preview to make sure the report is centered on the page before printing.

USE the *FourthCoffeeXXX* database that you saved in a previous exercise.

1. Switch to Print Preview.

2. Click the **Zoom** button and select **Fit to Window.**

3. Click the **Margins** button and select **Wide** from the menu.

4. Click the **Page Setup** button.

5. Click the **Print Options** tab. In the Margins section, key **2** in the Top box and key **2** in the Bottom box.

6. Key **2.5** in the left box and key **2.5** in the right box.

7. Click **OK.**

8. Click the **Print** button and click **OK.**

9. **SAVE** the report.

10. Click the **Close Print Preview** button.

11. **CLOSE** the report.

   CLOSE the database.

■ Mastery Assessment

Project 11-5: Group and Total the Inventory Report

As marketing manager at Wingtip Toys, you review Inventory information regularly with other employees. Add groups and totals to the Inventory report before your meeting with the production manager.

The *Wingtip* database is available on the companion CD-ROM.

1. Open *Wingtip* from the data files for this lesson.
2. Save the database as *WingtipXXX* (where XXX is your initials).
3. Open the **Inventory** report.
4. Switch to Layout view and open the Group, Sort, and Total pane.
5. Group the report by the **In Stock** field.
6. Sort the **Description** column from A to Z.
7. Sum the **Price** field. Show a grand total and totals in the group footers.
8. **SAVE** and **CLOSE** the report.

   CLOSE the database.

Project 11-6: Create Labels for Alpine Ski House Customers

In your position as Administrative Assistant for Alpine Ski House, you are involved in a variety of projects. The owners want to send a special thank you letter and promotion to previous customers. Create labels for the mailing.

The *Alpine* database is available on the companion CD-ROM.

1. **OPEN** *Alpine* from the data files for this lesson.
2. Save the database as *AlpineXXX* (where XXX is your initials).
3. Open the **Customers** table.
4. Use the Label Wizard to create address labels for all the customers in the table.
5. Select the **C2160** labels.
6. Arrange the customers' last name, first name, address, city, state, and zip code fields appropriately on the mailing label.
7. Name the labels **Customers Labels**.
8. **SAVE**, **PRINT** and **CLOSE** the report.
9. **CLOSE** the database.

   CLOSE Access.

INTERNET READY

Delivery service companies are used extensively in business. As a result, comparing service and prices can be very important for a company to make sure that it is using a reliable and economical delivery service. Search the Internet for three companies that pick up and deliver packages. Find out information such as services offered and prices charged for common services such as overnight delivery or two-day service. Create a database table and report that displays the data grouped by company with group totals for like services. Preview your report, make sure it looks attractive on the page, and then print it.

Advanced Queries

LESSON SKILL MATRIX

SKILLS	MATRIX SKILL	SKILL NUMBER
Creating Crosstab Queries	Create crosstab queries	4.1.4
Creating a Subquery	Create subqueries	4.1.5
Saving a Filter as a Query	Save filters as queries	4.1.6
Creating Action Queries	Create action queries	4.1.3
Creating a Join	Create joins	4.2.3
Creating a Calculated Query Field	Create calculated fields in queries	4.2.4
Adding an Alias to a Query Field	Add aliases to query fields	4.2.5
Creating Aggregated Queries	Create sum, average, min/max, and count queries	4.2.6

World Wide Importers is a car dealership that specializes in imported luxury cars. The company has recently opened a used car division in order to be able to sell vehicles acquired in trade and expand the buyer's purchasing options. As the office manager for the new division, you have started using Access to track inventory and sales. In this lesson, you will learn how to create an action query, a crosstab query, a subquery, and how to save filters as a query. You will also learn how to create joins, include calculated fields in a query, add aliases to query fields, and create aggregated queries.

KEY TERMS

action query
aggregate function
alias
append query
calculated field
cross join
crosstab query
delete query
inner join
join
left outer join
make table query
outer join
right outer join
SELECT statement
subquery
unequal join
update query

■ Creating Advanced Queries

↓ **THE BOTTOM LINE**

Queries are a powerful tool that can be used to retrieve exactly the data you need from your database, showing only the relevant records. Depending on the information you want to display, these advanced queries can help refine the results of your search or perform the actions you want.

X REF

In Lesson 8, you learned how to create and modify several types of queries.

Creating Crosstab Queries

A crosstab query is a special type of query that displays its results in a grid similar to an Excel worksheet. Crosstab queries summarize your values and then group them by two sets of facts—a set of row headers down the side and a set of column headers across the top.

→ CREATE CROSSTAB QUERIES

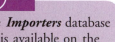

The *Importers* database file is available on the companion CD-ROM.

GET READY. Before you begin these steps, be sure to launch Microsoft Access.

1. **OPEN** the *Importers* database from the data files for this lesson.
2. **SAVE** the database as *ImportersXXX* (where XXX is your initials).
3. On the Message Bar, click **Options**. The Microsoft Office Security Options dialog box appears, as shown in Figure 12-1.

Figure 12-1

Microsoft Office Security Options dialog box

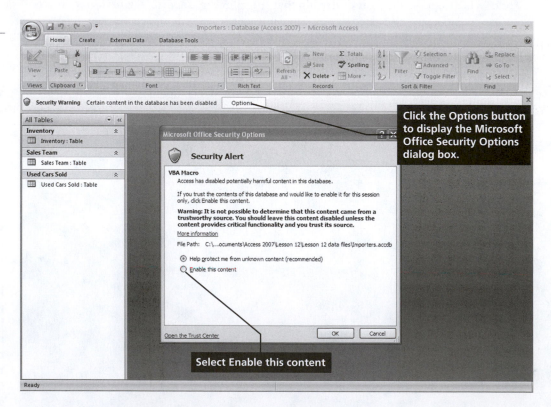

4. Click **Enable this content**, and then click **OK**.

5. On the Create tab, in the Other group, click the **Query Wizard** button to display the New Query dialog box, shown in Figure 12-2.

Figure 12-2

Figure 12-2

New Query dialog box

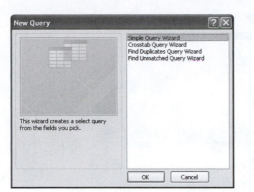

6. Click **Crosstab Query Wizard** and click **OK** to display the Crosstab Query Wizard, shown in Figure 12-3.

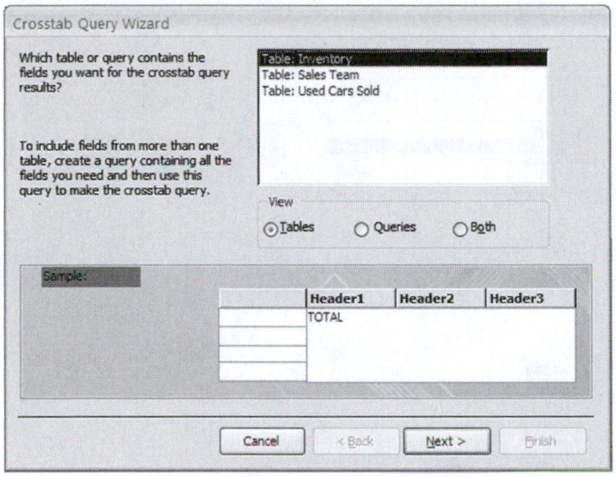

Figure 12-3

Crosstab Query Wizard, first screen

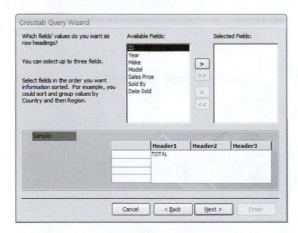

7. Click **Table: Used Cars Sold** and then click **Next >** to display the next screen, shown in Figure 12-4.

Figure 12-4

Crosstab Query Wizard, second screen

8. In the Available Fields box, double-click **Sold By** to move it to the Selected Fields box and then click **Next >**. The next screen appears, as shown in Figure 12-5.

Figure 12-5

Crosstab Query Wizard, third screen

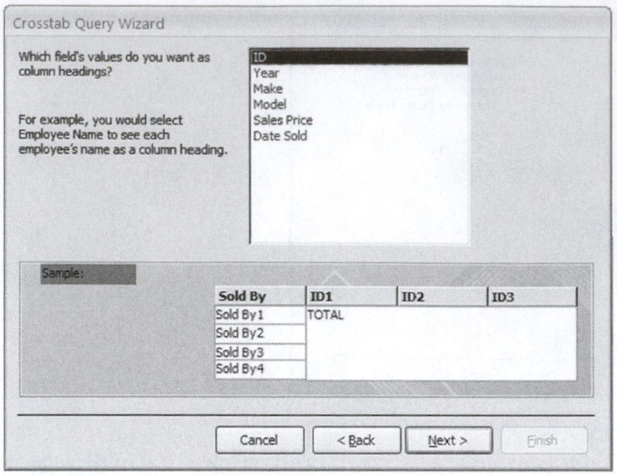

9. Click **Date Sold** and then click **Next >** to display the next screen, shown in Figure 12-6.

Figure 12-6

Crosstab Query Wizard, fourth screen

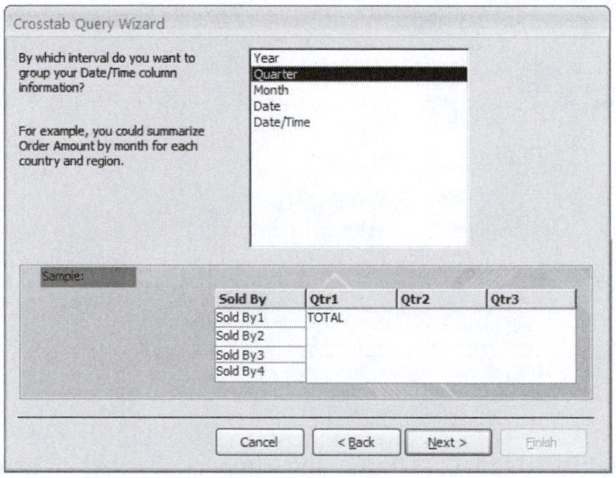

10. Click **Month** and then click **Next >** to display the next screen, shown in Figure 12-7.

Figure 12-7

Crosstab Query Wizard, fifth screen

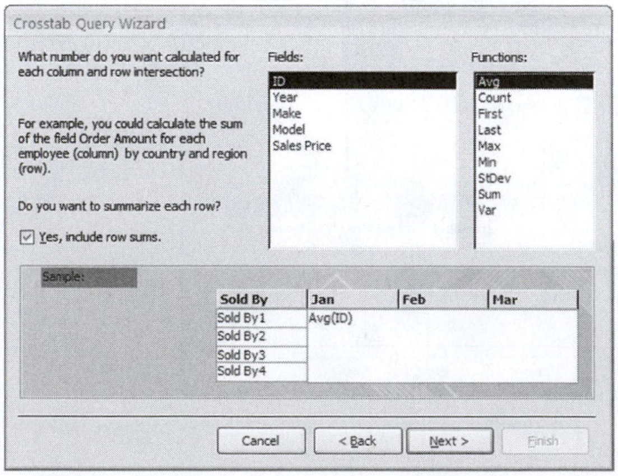

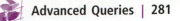

11. In the Fields box, click **Sales Price**, and in the Function box, click **Sum**. Click **Next >** to display the final screen, as shown in Figure 12-8.

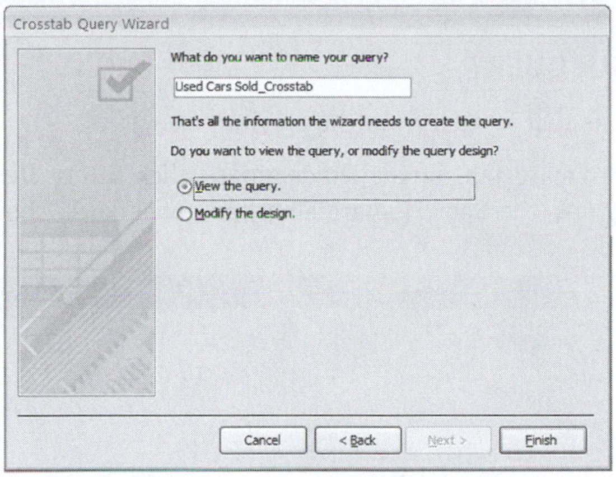

Figure 12-8

Crosstab Query Wizard, final screen

> **Crosstab Query Wizard**
>
> What do you want to name your query?
>
> Used Cars Sold_Crosstab
>
> That's all the information the wizard needs to create the query.
>
> Do you want to view the query, or modify the query design?
>
> ⊙ View the query.
> ○ Modify the design.
>
> Cancel   < Back   Next >   Finish

12. Click **Finish** to display the results of the crosstab query, as shown in Figure 12-9.

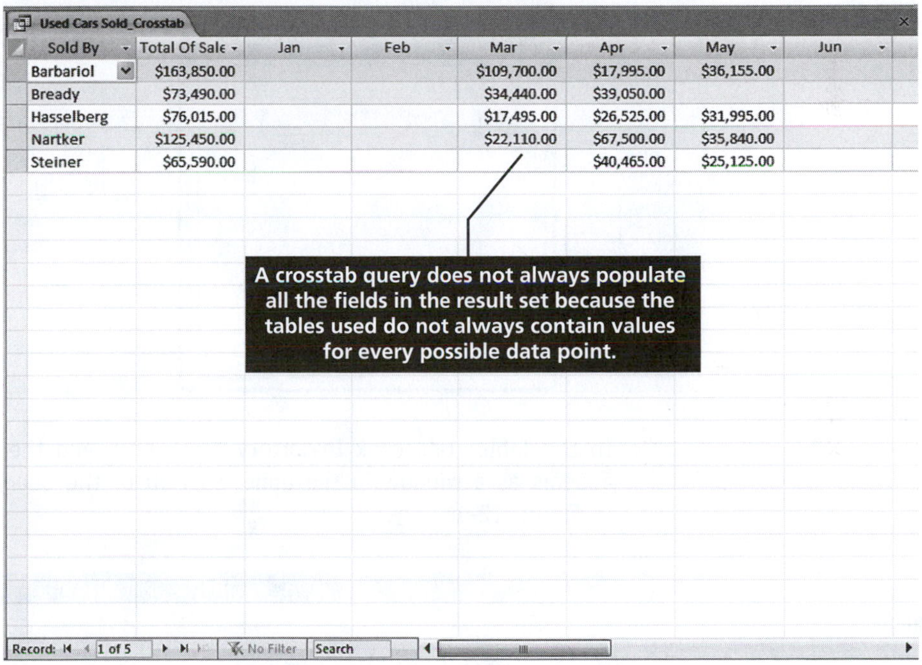

Figure 12-9

Crosstab query results

Sold By	Total Of Sale	Jan	Feb	Mar	Apr	May	Jun
Barbariol	$163,850.00			$109,700.00	$17,995.00	$36,155.00	
Bready	$73,490.00			$34,440.00	$39,050.00		
Hasselberg	$76,015.00			$17,495.00	$26,525.00	$31,995.00	
Nartker	$125,450.00			$22,110.00	$67,500.00	$35,840.00	
Steiner	$65,590.00				$40,465.00	$25,125.00	

Used Cars Sold_Crosstab

> A crosstab query does not always populate all the fields in the result set because the tables used do not always contain values for every possible data point.

Record: 1 of 5   No Filter   Search

13. Click the **Close 'Used Cars Sold_Crosstab'** button to close the query.

PAUSE. LEAVE the database open to use in the next exercise.

CERTIFICATION READY?

How do you create crosstab queries?

4.1.4

A *crosstab query* calculates a sum, average, count, or other type of total on records and then groups the results by two types of information: one down the left side of the datasheet and the other across the top. When you summarize data using a crosstab query, you select values from specified fields or expressions as column headings so you can view data in a more compact format than with a select query.

A crosstab query typically includes data from more than one table and always includes three types of data: the data used as row headings, the data used as column headings, and the values that you want to sum or otherwise compute. A crosstab query does not always populate all the fields in the result set because the tables that you use in the query do not always contain values for every possible data point.

The easiest way to create a crosstab query is to use the Crosstab Query Wizard. To run a crosstab query, double-click it in the Navigation pane, or click it and then press Enter. When you run a crosstab query, the results are displayed in Datasheet view.

Creating a Subquery

You can use a subquery to limit the amount of data returned by a query.

➔ CREATE A SUBQUERY

USE the database that is open from the previous exercise.

1. On the Create tab, in the Other group, click **Query Design**. The query designer opens, and the Show Table dialog box appears, as shown in Figure 12-10.

Figure 12-10

Show Table dialog box

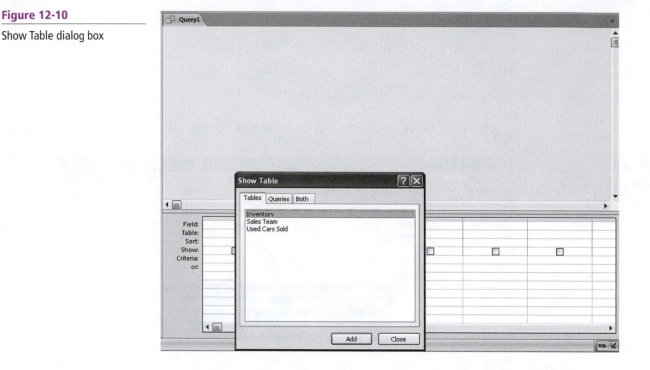

2. In the Tables tab, click **Inventory**, click **Add**, and then click **Close**. The table appears as a window in the upper section of the query design grid, as shown in Figure 12-11.

Figure 12-11

Query design grid

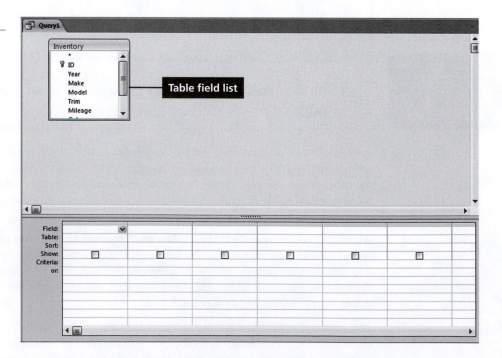

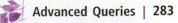

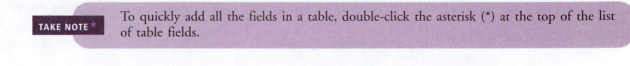

TAKE NOTE To quickly add all the fields in a table, double-click the asterisk (*) at the top of the list of table fields.

3. In the list of table fields, double-click **Year, Make, Model,** and **AskingPrice** to add those fields to the design grid, as shown in Figure 12-12.

Figure 12-12

Fields added to design grid

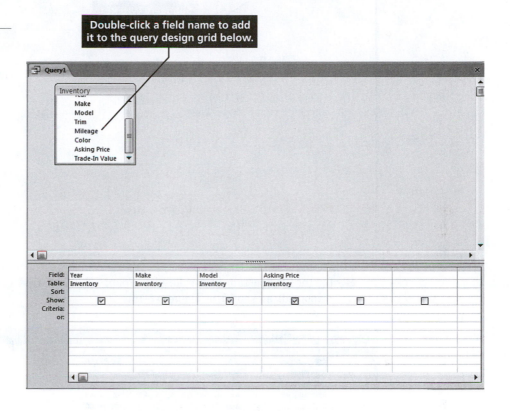

4. Place the insertion point in the Criteria row of the AskingPrice field and press [Shift]+[F2] to display the Zoom dialog box.
5. Key the following expression in the Zoom dialog box, as shown in Figure 12-13:

   >=(SELECT Avg(AskingPrice) FROM Inventory WHERE Make = Inventory.Make)

Figure 12-13

Zoom dialog box with expression

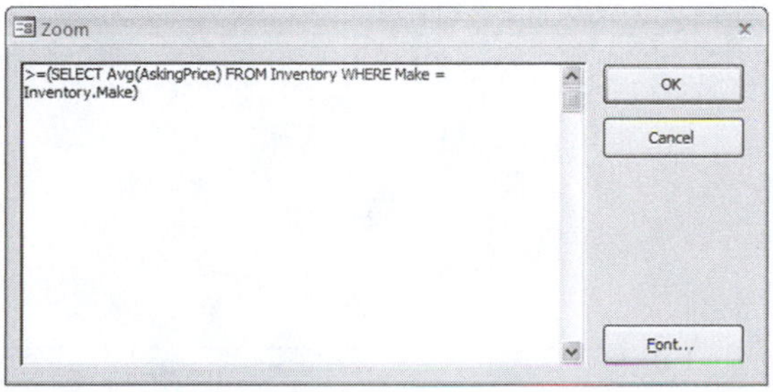

6. Click **OK** to insert the expression in the Criteria row of the **Asking Price** field.

7. On the Design tab, in the Results group, click the **View** tab, and click **SQL View** to see the entire expression, as shown in Figure 12-14.

Figure 12-14

SQL View

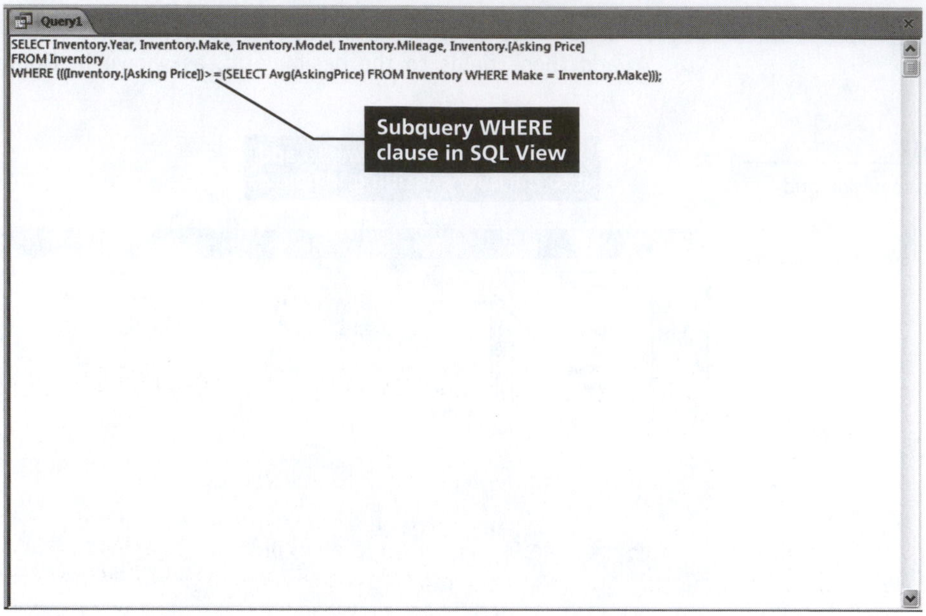

```
SELECT Inventory.Year, Inventory.Make, Inventory.Model, Inventory.Mileage, Inventory.[Asking Price]
FROM Inventory
WHERE (((Inventory.[Asking Price])>=(SELECT Avg(AskingPrice) FROM Inventory WHERE Make = Inventory.Make)));
```

Subquery WHERE clause in SQL View

8. On the Design tab, in the Results group, click **Run**. The query results are displayed, as shown in Figure 12-15.

Figure 12-15

Subquery results

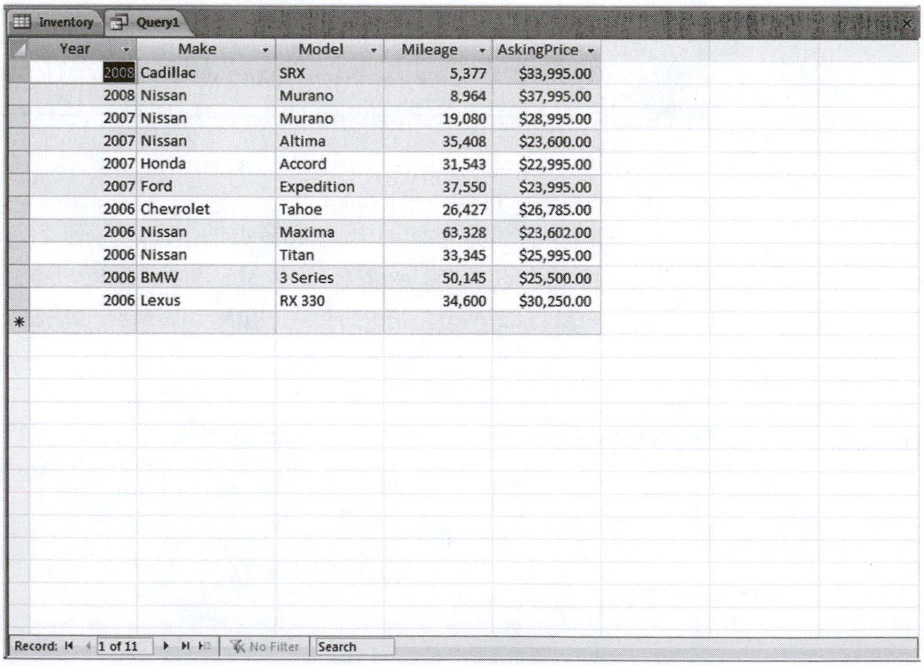

Year	Make	Model	Mileage	AskingPrice
2008	Cadillac	SRX	5,377	$33,995.00
2008	Nissan	Murano	8,964	$37,995.00
2007	Nissan	Murano	19,080	$28,995.00
2007	Nissan	Altima	35,408	$23,600.00
2007	Honda	Accord	31,543	$22,995.00
2007	Ford	Expedition	37,550	$23,995.00
2006	Chevrolet	Tahoe	26,427	$26,785.00
2006	Nissan	Maxima	63,328	$23,602.00
2006	Nissan	Titan	33,345	$25,995.00
2006	BMW	3 Series	50,145	$25,500.00
2006	Lexus	RX 330	34,600	$30,250.00

Record: 1 of 11   No Filter   Search

9. Click the **Office Button** and click **Save**.

10. In the Save As dialog box, key **Subquery** as the query name and click **OK**.

11. Click the **Close 'Subquery'** button to close the query.

PAUSE. LEAVE the database open to use in the next exercise.

CERTIFICATION READY?
How do you create a subquery?
4.1.5

A *subquery* is a SELECT statement that is inside another select or action query. A **SELECT statement** is a SQL command that instructs the Microsoft Access database engine to return information from the database as a set of records. At a minimum, the syntax for a SELECT statement is:

SELECT *fields* FROM *table*

An asterisk (*) can be used to select all the fields in a table. The following example selects all the fields in the Inventory table:

SELECT * FROM Inventory

Clauses such as WHERE and ORDER BY can be used in a SELECT statement to restrict and organize your returned data. Table 12-1 shows some SELECT statements and the results that are returned.

Table 12-1

SELECT STATEMENT	RESULT
SELECT [FirstName], [LastName] FROM [Employees] WHERE [LastName] = "Cooper";	Displays the values in the FirstName and LastName fields for employees whose last name is Cooper.
SELECT [ProductID], [ProductName] FROM [Products] WHERE [CategoryID] = Forms![New Products]![CategoryID];	Displays the values in the ProductID and ProductName fields in the Products table for records in which the CategoryID value matches the CategoryID value specified in an open New Products form.
SELECT Avg([ExtendedPrice]) AS [Average Extended Price] FROM [Order Details Extended] WHERE [ExtendedPrice] > 1000;	Displays in a field named Average Extended Price the average extended price of orders for which the value in the ExtendedPrice field is more than 1,000.
SELECT [CategoryID], Count([ProductID]) AS [CountOfProductID] FROM [Products] GROUP BY [CategoryID] HAVING Count([ProductID]) > 10;	Displays in a field named CountOfProductID the total number of products for categories with more than 10 products.

A SELECT statement can be entered in a field or criteria cell in Design view. If you need more space in which to enter the SELECT statement in a field or criteria cell, press SHIFT + F2 and enter the statement in the Zoom box. You can see the entire SQL statement by switching to SQL view.

In a subquery, you use a SELECT statement to provide a set of one or more specific values to evaluate in the WHERE or HAVING clause expression. A subquery has three parts:

- *comparison*—an expression and a comparison operator that compares the expression with the results of the subquery
- *expression*—an expression for which the result set of the subquery is searched
- *sqlstatement*—a SELECT statement, following the same format and rules as any other SELECT statement. It must be enclosed in parentheses.

The subquery used in the activity you just did returns results that select only the records from the Inventory table whose asking price is equal to or greater than the average asking price.

Saving a Filter as a Query

A filter can be saved as a query so it can be run again anytime you want.

⊕ SAVE A FILTER AS A QUERY

USE the database that is open from the previous exercise.

1. On the Create tab, in the Other group, click the **Query Wizard** button.
2. In the New Query dialog box, click **Simple Query Wizard** and click **OK**.
3. In the Tables/Queries dropdown list, click **Table: Used Cars Sold**.
4. Click the **>>** button to move all the fields from the Available Fields to the Selected Fields box and then click **Next >**.
5. Click **Next >** again and then click **Finish** to display a simple select query.
6. On the Home tab, in the Sort & Filter dialog box, click the **Advanced** button and then click **Filter by Form**.
7. In the Filter by Form, click the **down arrow** in the Year field and click **2006**, as shown in Figure 12-16.

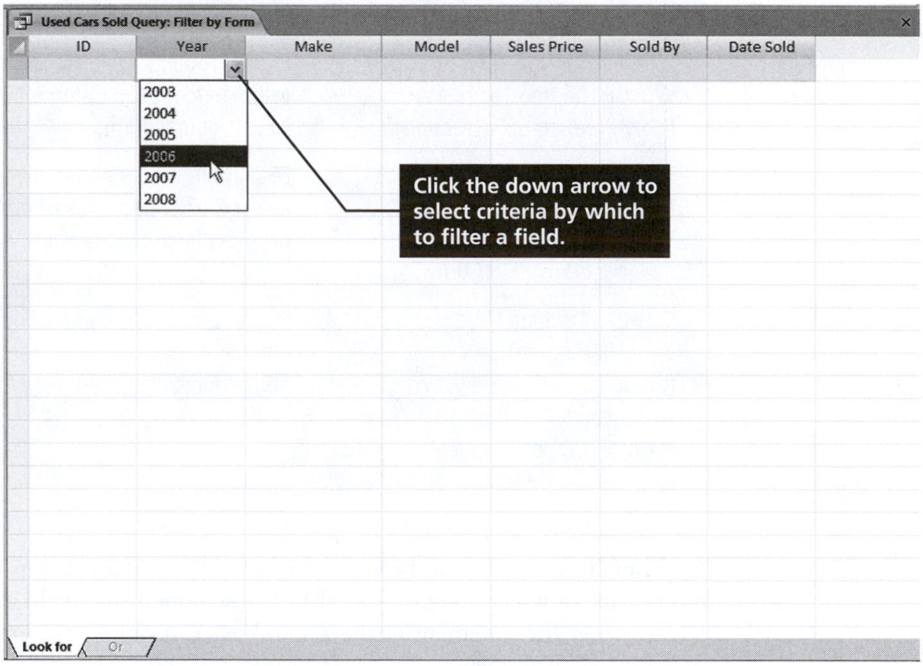

Figure 12-16

Filter by Form

8. On the Home tab, in the Sort & Filter dialog box, click the **Toggle Filter** button to apply the filter. The results are displayed, as shown in Figure 12-17.

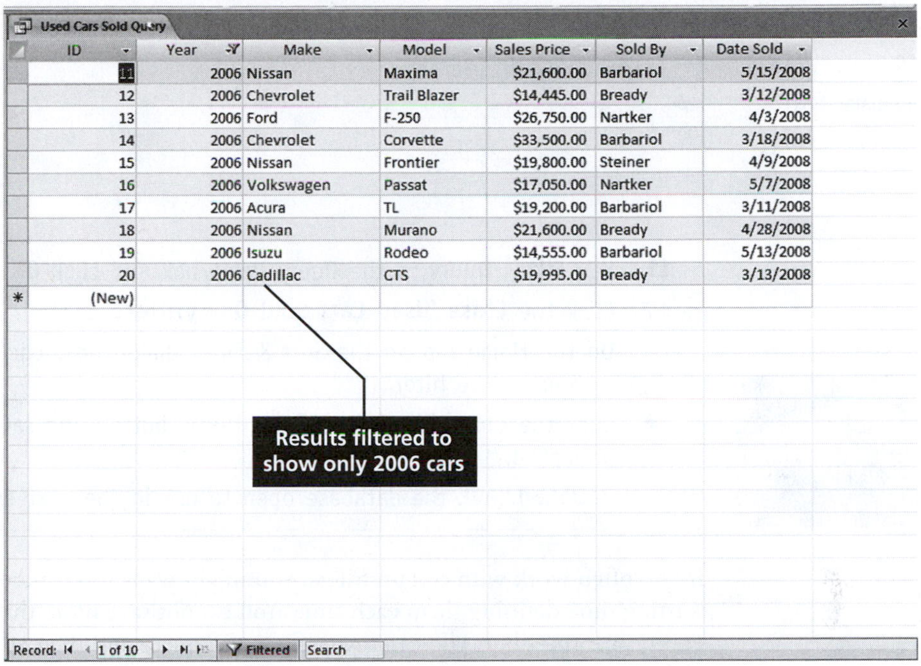

Figure 12-17

Filter by Form results

ID	Year	Make	Model	Sales Price	Sold By	Date Sold
11	2006	Nissan	Maxima	$21,600.00	Barbariol	5/15/2008
12	2006	Chevrolet	Trail Blazer	$14,445.00	Bready	3/12/2008
13	2006	Ford	F-250	$26,750.00	Nartker	4/3/2008
14	2006	Chevrolet	Corvette	$33,500.00	Barbariol	3/18/2008
15	2006	Nissan	Frontier	$19,800.00	Steiner	4/9/2008
16	2006	Volkswagen	Passat	$17,050.00	Nartker	5/7/2008
17	2006	Acura	TL	$19,200.00	Barbariol	3/11/2008
18	2006	Nissan	Murano	$21,600.00	Bready	4/28/2008
19	2006	Isuzu	Rodeo	$14,555.00	Barbariol	5/13/2008
20	2006	Cadillac	CTS	$19,995.00	Bready	3/13/2008
*	(New)					

Results filtered to show only 2006 cars

Record: 1 of 10   Filtered   Search

9. On the Home tab, in the Sort & Filter dialog box, click the **Advanced** button and then click **Advanced Filter/Sort** to display the new query design grid, shown in Figure 12-18.

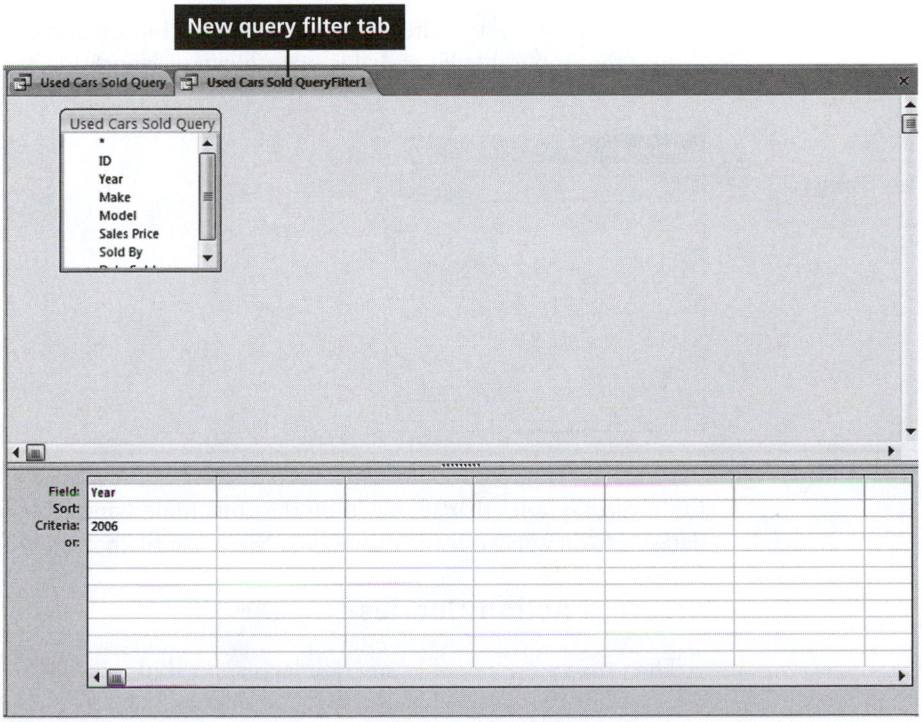

Figure 12-18

New query design grid

New query filter tab

Used Cars Sold Query   Used Cars Sold QueryFilter1

Used Cars Sold Query
*
ID
Year
Make
Model
Sales Price
Sold By

Field:	Year					
Sort:						
Criteria:	2006					
or:						

10. On the Home tab, in the Sort & Filter dialog box, click the **Advanced** button and then click **Save As Query**. The Save As Query dialog box appears, as shown in Figure 12-19.

Figure 12-19

Save As Query dialog box

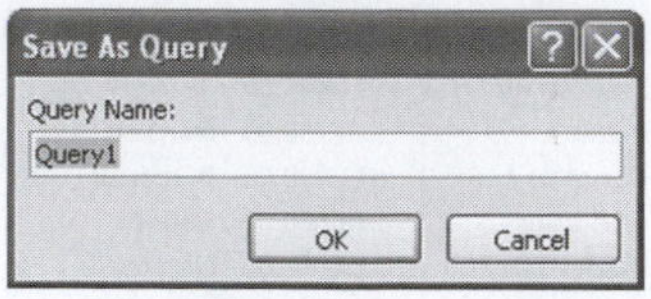

11. Key **Filter Query** in the Query Name box and click **OK**.

12. Click the **Close 'Used Cars Sold Queryfilter1'** button.

13. On the Home tab, in the Sort & Filter dialog box, click the **Toggle Filter** button to remove the filter.

14. Click the **Close 'Used Cars Sold Query'** button and save the changes when prompted.

PAUSE. LEAVE the database open to use in the next exercise.

CERTIFICATION READY?
How do you save a filter as a query?
4.1.6

If you often work with certain filters, you might want to save these filters so that you are not wasting time defining them each time. You cannot save more than one filter for each table, query, or form—but, you can save a filter as a query and then apply the query as a filter when and where you want.

Create a filter by form and apply it to the query. On the Home tab, in the Sort & Filter group, click the Advanced button and click Advanced Filter/Sort. The new query appears in the Database window. It automatically includes all the fields from the underlying view. On the Home tab, in the Sort & Filter group, click the Advanced button and click Save As Query. Key a name for the query and click OK.

To apply the query as a filter, click the Advanced button and click Load from Query to display the Applicable Filter dialog box, shown in Figure 12-20.

Figure 12-20

Applicable Filter dialog box

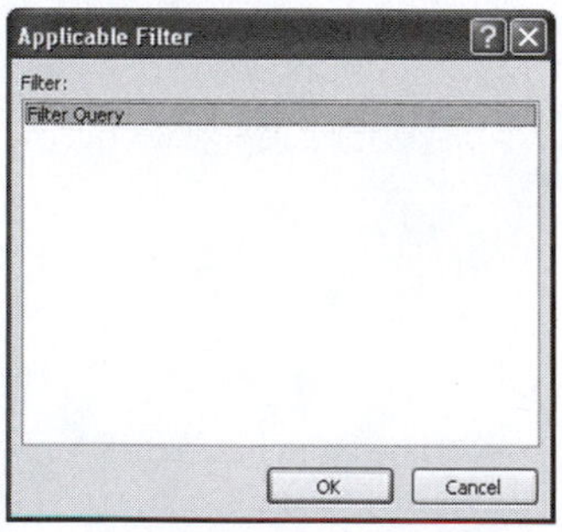

Only select queries that are based on the same underlying table or query as the form or datasheet will appear in the dialog box. Select the filter, click OK, and then apply the filter.

Creating Action Queries

There are four types of action queries—append, delete, update, and make table—and except for the make table query, action queries make changes to the data in the tables that they are based on.

CREATE AN APPEND QUERY

USE the database that is open from the previous exercise.

1. On the Create tab, in the Other group, click the **Query Design** button.

2. In the Show Table dialog box, double-click **Inventory** to add it to the upper section of the query design grid.

3. Click **Close** to close the Show Table dialog box.

4. In the list of table fields, double-click **Year, Make, Model,** and **Asking Price** to add those fields to the design grid. Your screen should look similar to Figure 12-21.

Figure 12-21

Design grid

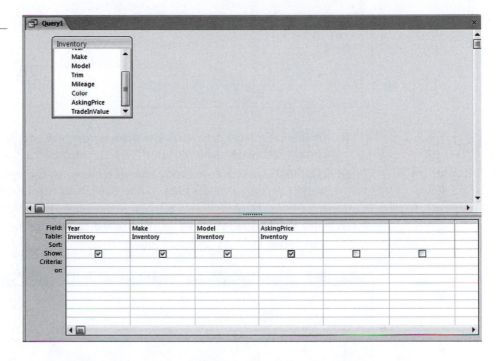

5. On the Design tab, in the Results group, click **Run.** Verify that the query returned the records that you want to append, as shown in Figure 12-22.

Figure 12-22

Records to be appended

Year	Make	Model	AskingPrice
2008	Toyota	Corolla	$18,495.00
2008	Chevrolet	Equinox	$21,995.00
2008	Nissan	Altima	$20,995.00
2008	Cadillac	SRX	$33,995.00
2008	Ford	Mustang	$18,995.00
2008	Nissan	Murano	$37,995.00
2007	Mitsubishi	Outlander	$19,111.00
2007	Nissan	Murano	$28,995.00
2007	Nissan	Altima	$23,600.00
2007	Chevrolet	Impala	$19,555.00
2007	Ford	Explorer	$18,495.00
2007	Honda	Accord	$22,995.00
2007	Ford	Expedition	$23,995.00
2007	Honda	Civic	$18,495.00
2006	Nissan	Sentra	$14,495.00
2006	Saturn	ION	$15,400.00
2006	Chevrolet	Tahoe	$26,785.00
2006	Nissan	Maxima	$23,602.00
2006	Toyota	Camry	$19,887.00
2006	Nissan	Titan	$25,995.00
2006	BMW	3 Series	$25,500.00
2006	Buick	Rendezvous	$17,995.00
2006	Lexus	RX 330	$30,250.00
2005	Honda	Pilot	$22,680.00
2005	GMC	Envoy	$19,495.00
2005	Lincoln	Town Car	$19,995.00

Record: 1 of 26   No Filter   Search

TAKE NOTE* If you need to add or remove fields from the query, switch back to Design view and double-click to add fields or select the fields that you don't want and press Delete to remove them from the query.

6. Right-click the document tab for the open query and click **Design View** on the shortcut menu.

7. On the Design tab, in the Query Type group, click **Append**. The Append dialog box appears, as shown in Figure 12-23.

Figure 12-23

Append dialog box

```
Append                                    [?][X]
┌─ Append To ──────────────────────────┐  ┌──────┐
│ Table Name:  [              ▼]        │  │  OK  │
│                                       │  └──────┘
│ ◉ Current Database                    │  ┌──────┐
│ ○ Another Database:                   │  │Cancel│
│ File Name: [                    ]     │  └──────┘
│                          [Browse...]  │
└───────────────────────────────────────┘
```

8. In the Table Name box, click the **down arrow** and click **Used Cars Sold**. The **Current Database** radio button should be selected.

9. Click **OK**. Access automatically adds the names of the destination fields that match the source field names to the Append to row in the design grid. Because the **Asking Price** field doesn't have a match, Access leaves that field blank.

10. Click the **Asking Price** cell in the Append to row and select **Sales Price** as the destination field, as shown in Figure 12-24.

Figure 12-24

Source and destination fields matched

[Figure showing Query1 design view with Inventory table field list (ID, Year, Make, Model, Trim, Mileage, Color, Asking Price) and the design grid below. A callout box reads: "Click the down arrow to manually choose SalesPrice as the destination field for the AskingPrice source field"]

Field:	Year	Make	Model	Asking Price		
Table:	Inventory	Inventory	Inventory	Inventory		
Sort:						
Append To:	Year	Make	Model	[▼]		
Criteria:						
or:						

Drop-down list showing: Used Cars Sold.*, ID, Year, Make, Model, Sales Price, Sold By, Date Sold

11. Right-click the document tab for the query, and then click **Datasheet View** to preview your changes.

12. Right-click the document tab for the query, and then click **Design View**.

13. On the Design tab, in the Results group, click **Run**. An alert message appears, as shown in Figure 12-25.

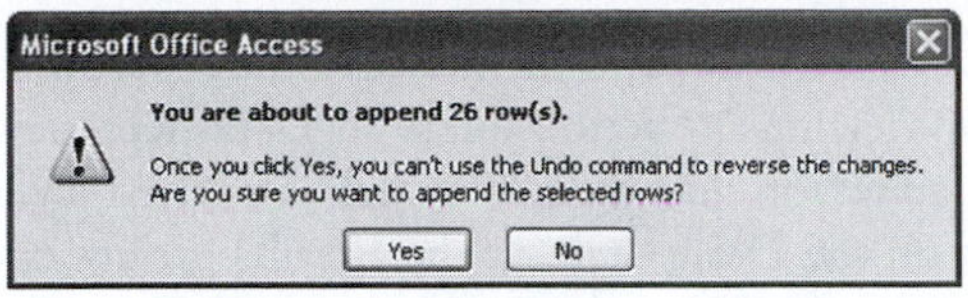

14. Click **Yes**.

15. Open the **Used Cars Sold** table and scroll down to see that the records from the Inventory table have been appended to the end, as shown in Figure 12-26.

Figure 12-26

Results of append query

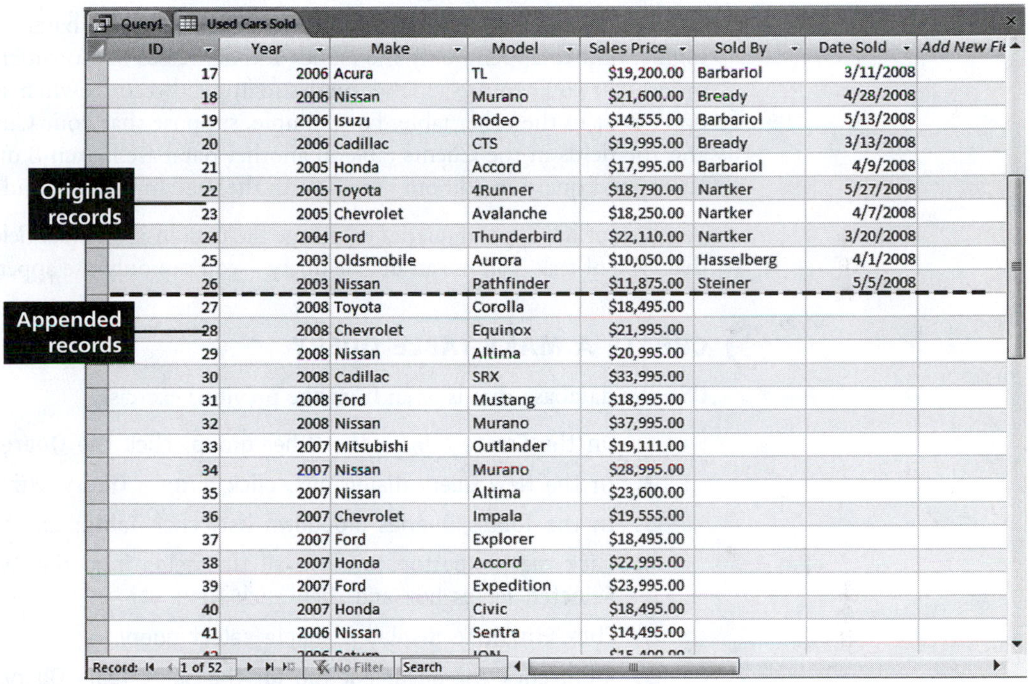

ID	Year	Make	Model	Sales Price	Sold By	Date Sold
17	2006	Acura	TL	$19,200.00	Barbariol	3/11/2008
18	2006	Nissan	Murano	$21,600.00	Bready	4/28/2008
19	2006	Isuzu	Rodeo	$14,555.00	Barbariol	5/13/2008
20	2006	Cadillac	CTS	$19,995.00	Bready	3/13/2008
21	2005	Honda	Accord	$17,995.00	Barbariol	4/9/2008
22	2005	Toyota	4Runner	$18,790.00	Nartker	5/27/2008
23	2005	Chevrolet	Avalanche	$18,250.00	Nartker	4/7/2008
24	2004	Ford	Thunderbird	$22,110.00	Nartker	3/20/2008
25	2003	Oldsmobile	Aurora	$10,050.00	Hasselberg	4/1/2008
26	2003	Nissan	Pathfinder	$11,875.00	Steiner	5/5/2008
27	2008	Toyota	Corolla	$18,495.00		
28	2008	Chevrolet	Equinox	$21,995.00		
29	2008	Nissan	Altima	$20,995.00		
30	2008	Cadillac	SRX	$33,995.00		
31	2008	Ford	Mustang	$18,995.00		
32	2008	Nissan	Murano	$37,995.00		
33	2007	Mitsubishi	Outlander	$19,111.00		
34	2007	Nissan	Murano	$28,995.00		
35	2007	Nissan	Altima	$23,600.00		
36	2007	Chevrolet	Impala	$19,555.00		
37	2007	Ford	Explorer	$18,495.00		
38	2007	Honda	Accord	$22,995.00		
39	2007	Ford	Expedition	$23,995.00		
40	2007	Honda	Civic	$18,495.00		
41	2006	Nissan	Sentra	$14,495.00		

Original records

Appended records

Record: 1 of 52   No Filter   Search

16. Click the **Close 'Used Cars Sold'** button to close the table.

17. Click the **Office Button** and click **Save**.

18. In the Save As dialog box, key **Append Query** as the query name and click **OK**.

19. Click the **Close 'Append Query'** button to close the query.

PAUSE. LEAVE Access open to use in the next exercise.

CERTIFICATION READY?
How do you create action queries?
4.1.3

An *action query* changes the data in its datasource or creates a new table. There are four types of action queries:

- *Append query*: adds the records in the query's result set to the end of an existing table
- *Delete query*: removes rows matching the criteria that you specify from one or more tables
- *Update query*: changes a set of records according to criteria that you specify
- *Make table query*: creates a new table and then creates records in it by copying records from an existing table

As their name suggests, action queries make changes to the data in the tables they are based on (except for make table queries, which create new tables). Changes made by action queries cannot be easily undone, so if you later decide you didn't want to make those changes, usually you will have to restore the data from a backup copy. For this reason, you should always make sure you have a current backup of the underlying data before running an action query.

To minimize the risk involved in running an action query, you can first preview the data that will be acted upon by viewing the action query in Datasheet view before running it. When you are ready to run an action query, double-click it in the Navigation pane or click it and then press Enter. Or, on the Design tab, in the Results group, click Run.

An **append query** adds a set of records from one or more source tables (or queries) to one or more destination tables. Typically, the source and destination tables reside in the same database, but they don't have to. For example, suppose that you acquire some new customers and a database that contains a table of information about those customers. To avoid entering that new data manually, you can append it to the appropriate table in your database.

You can also use append queries to append fields that are based on criteria. For example, you might want to append only the names and addresses of customers who have outstanding orders. Or you can use append queries to append records when some of the fields in one table don't exist in the other table. For example, suppose that your Customers table has 10 fields, and the fields in the Clients table in another database match 8 of your 10 fields. You can use an append query to add only the data in the matching fields and ignore the others.

You cannot use append queries to change the data in individual fields in existing records. To do that type of task, you use an update query—you can only use append queries to add rows of data.

CREATE A MAKE TABLE QUERY

USE the database that is open from the previous exercise.

1. On the Create tab, in the Other group, click the **Query Wizard** button.
2. In the New Query dialog box, click **Simple Query Wizard** and click **OK**.
3. In the Tables/Queries dropdown list, click **Table: Sales Team**.
4. Click the **>>** button to move all the fields from the Available Fields to the Selected Fields box and then click **Next >**.
5. Click **Finish** to display a simple select query.
6. Right-click the document tab for the Sales Team Query and click **Design View** to display the query in design view, as shown in Figure 12-27.

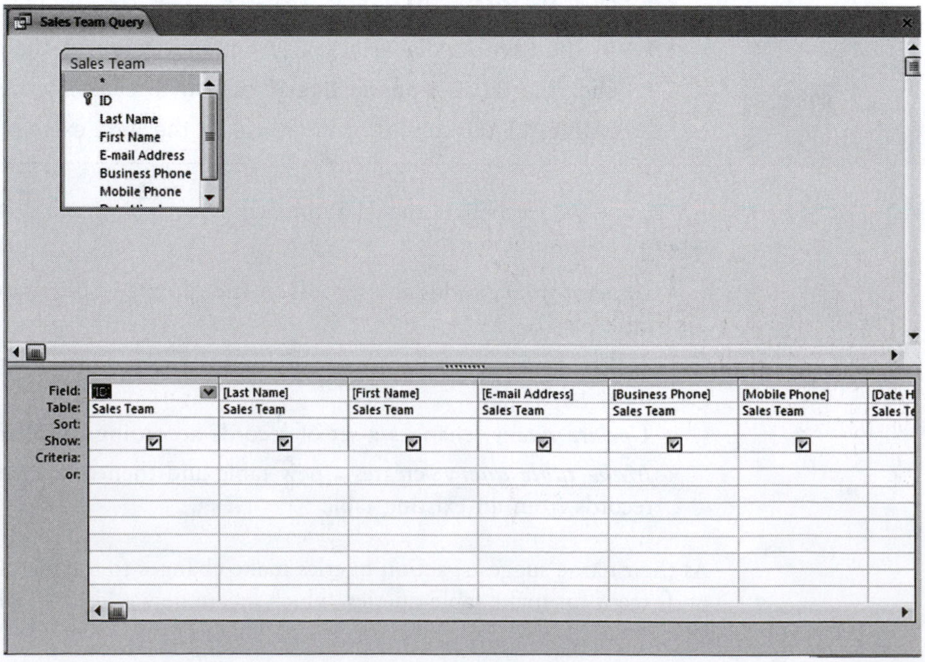

Figure 12-27

Query in Design view

7. On the Design tab, in the Query Type group, click **Make Table**. The Make Table dialog box appears, as shown in Figure 12-28.

Figure 12-28

Make Table dialog box

8. In the Table Name box, key **Sales Team Backup**. If it isn't already selected, click **Current Database**, and then click **OK**.

9. On the Design tab, in the Results group, click **Run**. An alert message appears, as shown in Figure 12-29.

Figure 12-29

Make table alert message

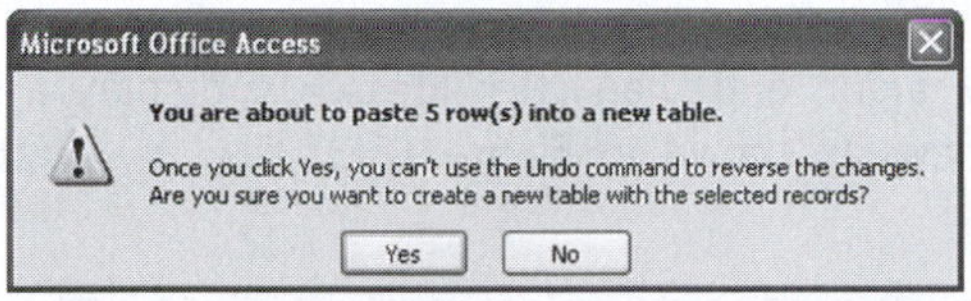

10. Click **Yes**. A new table appears in the Navigation pane.

11. Double-click **Sales Team Backup: Table** in the Navigation pane to open the new table, as shown in Figure 12-30.

Figure 12-30

New table

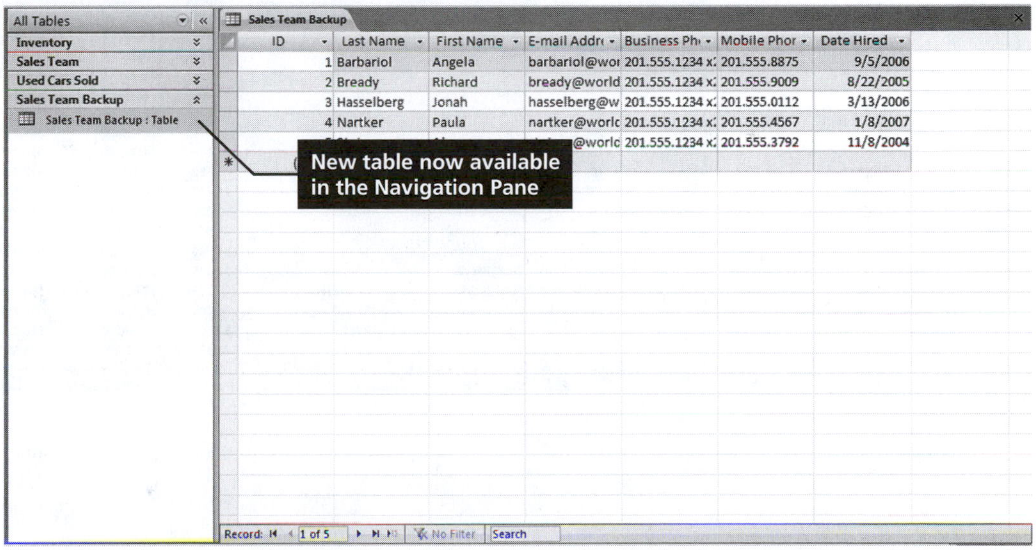

New table now available in the Navigation Pane

12. Click the **Close 'Sales Team Backup'** button to close the table.

13. Click the **Close 'Sales Team Query'** button to close the query. Save the changes when prompted.

14. **LEAVE** the database open.

PAUSE. LEAVE Access open to use in the next exercise.

CERTIFICATION READY?
How do you create action queries?
4.1.3

A *make table query* is an action query that creates a new table and then creates records in it by copying records from an existing table. You use a make table query when you need to copy the data in a table or to archive data.

You create a make table query by first creating a select query with the data that you need, and then converting it to a make table query. On the Design tab, in the Query Type group, click

Make Table. Key a name for the new table, choose whether to place the new table in the existing database or in another database, and click OK. Click Run and then Yes to perform the action and create the new table.

⊙ CREATE AN UPDATE QUERY

USE the database that is open from the previous exercise.

1. On the Create tab, in the Other group, click the **Query Wizard** button.
2. In the New Query dialog box, click **Simple Query Wizard** and click **OK**.
3. In the Tables/Queries drop-down list, click **Table: Inventory**.
4. Click the **>>** button to move all the fields from the Available Fields to the Selected Fields box.
5. Click **Trim** and then the **<** button to move it back to the Selected Fields box. Click **Color** and then the **<** button button to move it back to the Selected Fields box. Click **Next >**.
6. Click **Next >** again and then click **Finish** to display a simple select query in Datasheet view, as shown in Figure 12-31.

Figure 12-31

Select query in Datasheet view

ID	Year	Make	Model	Mileage	AskingPrice	TradeInValue
1	2008	Toyota	Corolla	5,686	$18,495.00	$15,995.00
2	2008	Chevrolet	Equinox	21,804	$21,995.00	$19,000.00
3	2008	Nissan	Altima	11,071	$20,995.00	$16,995.00
4	2008	Cadillac	SRX	5,377	$33,995.00	$27,500.00
5	2008	Ford	Mustang	12,033	$18,995.00	$15,500.00
6	2008	Nissan	Murano	8,964	$39,495.00	$32,750.00
7	2007	Mitsubishi	Outlander	25,951	$19,111.00	$16,675.00
8	2007	Nissan	Murano	19,080	$28,995.00	$25,900.00
9	2007	Nissan	Altima	35,408	$23,600.00	$19,400.00
10	2007	Chevrolet	Impala	17,962	$19,555.00	$15,250.00
11	2007	Ford	Explorer	49,997	$18,495.00	$14,880.00
12	2007	Honda	Accord	31,543	$22,995.00	$18,430.00
13	2007	Ford	Expedition	37,550	$23,995.00	$19,700.00
14	2007	Honda	Civic	24,925	$18,495.00	$14,975.00
15	2006	Nissan	Sentra	42,344	$14,495.00	$10,980.00
16	2006	Saturn	ION	45,682	$15,400.00	$12,000.00
17	2006	Chevrolet	Tahoe	26,427	$26,785.00	$22,500.00
18	2006	Nissan	Maxima	63,328	$23,602.00	$19,999.00
19	2006	Toyota	Camry	33,986	$19,887.00	$16,600.00
20	2006	Nissan	Titan	33,345	$25,995.00	$20,450.00
21	2006	BMW	3 Series	50,145	$25,500.00	$21,000.00
22	2006	Buick	Rendezvous	28,135	$17,995.00	$14,775.00
23	2006	Lexus	RX 330	34,600	$30,250.00	$26,990.00
24	2005	Honda	Pilot	57,606	$22,680.00	$18,220.00
25	2005	GMC	Envoy	31,135	$19,495.00	$15,500.00

Record: 1 of 26   No Filter   Search

7. Right-click the document tab for the Inventory Query and click **Design View** to display the query in Design view, as shown in Figure 12-32.

Figure 12-32

Select query in Design view

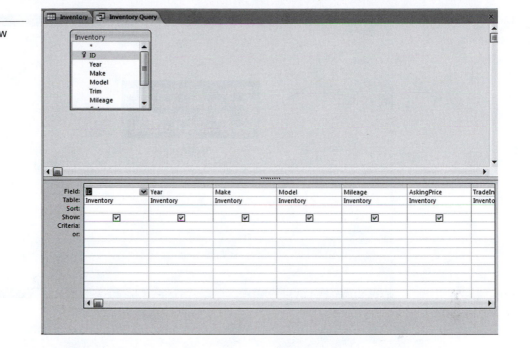

8. Key **2008** in the Criteria row of the **Year** field.

9. On the Design tab, in the Query Type group, click **Update**. Access adds the Update to row in the query design grid.

10. In the Update to row of the **AskingPrice** field, key **[AskingPrice] + 500**. The design grid should look similar to Figure 12-33.

Figure 12-33

Select and update criterion

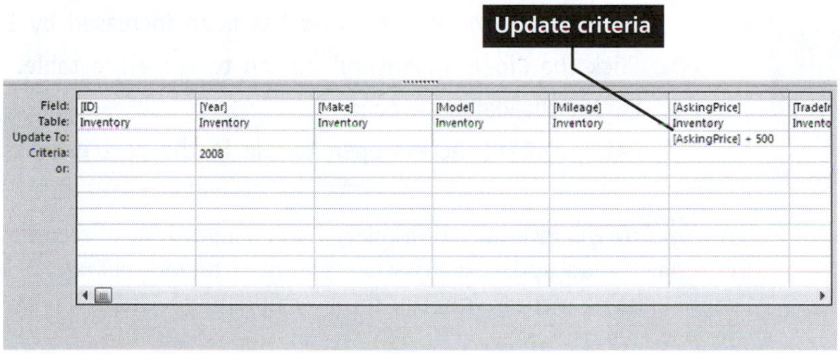

					Update criteria	
Field: [ID]	[Year]	[Make]	[Model]	[Mileage]	[AskingPrice]	[TradeIn
Table: Inventory	Inventory	Inventory	Inventory	Inventory	Inventory	Invento
Update To:					[AskingPrice] + 500	
Criteria:	2008					
or:						

11. On the Design tab, in the Results group, click **Run**. An alert message appears, as shown in Figure 12-34.

Figure 12-34

Update alert message

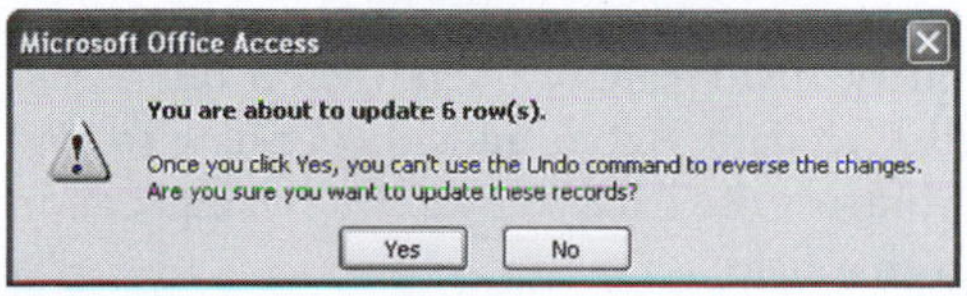

Microsoft Office Access

⚠ You are about to update 6 row(s).

Once you click Yes, you can't use the Undo command to reverse the changes.
Are you sure you want to update these records?

[Yes] [No]

12. Click **Yes**.

13. Right-click the document tab for the Inventory Query and click **Datasheet View** to display the update query results, as shown in Figure 12-35.

Figure 12-35

Update query results

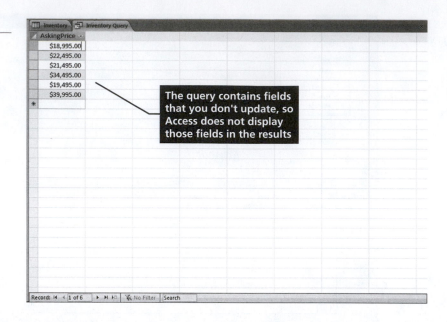

The query contains fields that you don't update, so Access does not display those fields in the results

TAKE NOTE*

When you run the query, you will notice that some fields are missing from your result set. If the query contains fields that you don't update, Access does not display those fields in the results.

14. Click the **Close 'Inventory Query'** button to close the query. Save the changes when prompted.

15. Double-click **Inventory: Table** in the Navigation pane to open it. Notice that the asking price for all 2008 cars has been increased by $500.

16. Click the **Close 'Inventory'** button to close the table.

17. **LEAVE** the database open.

PAUSE. LEAVE Access open to use in the next exercise.

CERTIFICATION READY?
How do you create action queries?
4.1.3

An ***update query*** is an action query that changes a set of records according to specified criteria. Use an update query when you need to add, change, or delete the data in one or more existing records. You can think of update queries as a powerful form of the Find and Replace dialog box.

You enter a select criterion and an update criterion. Unlike the Find and Replace dialog box, update queries can accept multiple criteria. You can use them to update a large number of records in one pass and to change records in more than one table at one time. You can also update the data in one table with data from another—as long as the data types for the source and destination fields match or are compatible.

To create an update query, first create or open a select query. On the Design tab, in the Query Type group, click Update. Access adds the Update to row in the query design grid. Locate the field that contains the data you want to change, and type your change criteria in the Update to row for that field.

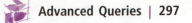

You can use any valid expression in the Update to row. Table 12-2 shows some example expressions and explains how they change data.

Table 12-2

EXPRESSION	RESULT
"Chicago"	In a Text field, changes a text value to Chicago.
#9/25/08#	In a Date/Time field, changes a date value to 25-Sept-08.
Yes	In a Yes/No field, changes a No value to Yes.
"PN" & [PartNumber]	Adds "PN" to the beginning of each specified part number.
[UnitPrice] * [Quantity]	Multiplies the values in fields named UnitPrice and Quantity.
[Shipping] * 1.5	Increases the values in a field named Shipping by 50 percent.
DSum("[Quantity] * [UnitPrice]", "Order Details", "[ProductID] =" & [ProductID])	Where the ProductID values in the current table match the ProductID values in table named Order Details, this expression updates sales totals by multiplying the values in a field named Quantity by the values in a field named UnitPrice. The expression uses the DSum function because it can operate against more than one table and table field.
Right([PostalCode], 5)	Removes the leftmost characters in a text or numeric string and leaves the 5 rightmost characters.
IIf(IsNull([SalesPrice]), 0, [SalesPrice])	Changes a null (unknown or undefined) value to a zero (0) value in a field named SalesPrice.

On the Design tab, in the Results group, click Run. When an alert message appears, click Yes to run the query and update the data. You may notice that some fields are missing from the query results, because Access only displays the fields that have been updated.

CREATE A DELETE QUERY

USE the database that is open from the previous exercise.

1. On the Create tab, in the Other group, click **Query Wizard**.
2. In the New Query dialog box, click **Simple Query Wizard** and click **OK**.
3. In the Tables/Queries dropdown list, click **Table: Used Cars Sold**.
4. Click the **>>** button to move all the fields from the Available Fields to the Selected Fields box and then click **Next >**.
5. Click **Next >** again.
6. Key **Delete Query** as the title and then click **Finish** displaying a simple select query.
7. Right-click the document tab for the Delete Query and click **Design View** to display the query in Design view.
8. Key **<#3/31/2008#.** in the Criteria row of the **Date Sold** field, as shown in Figure 12-36.

Figure 12-36

Date Sold criteria

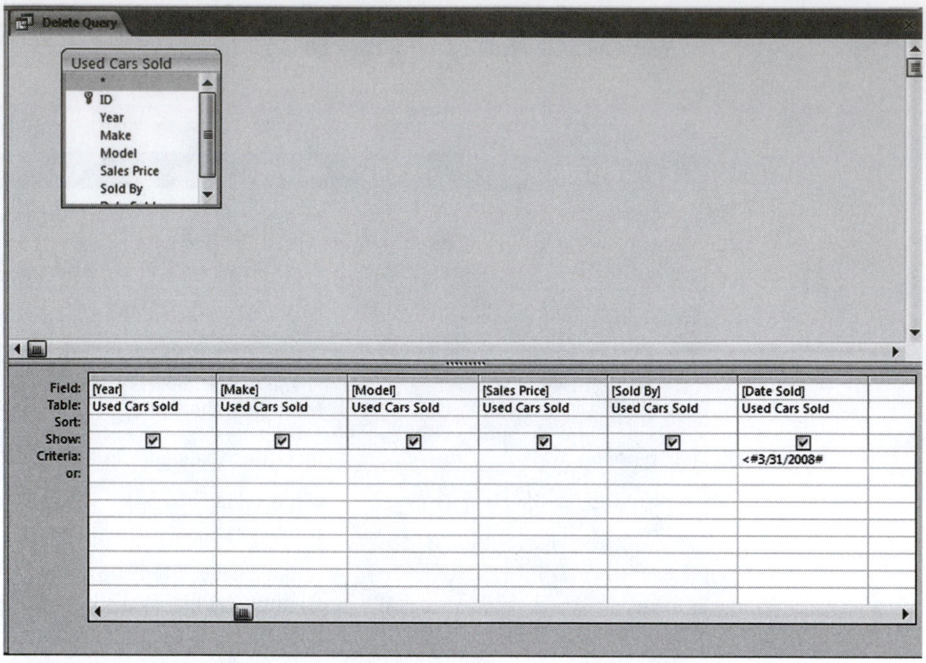

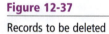

9. On the Design tab, in the Results group, click **Run** to display the records to be deleted, as shown in Figure 12-37.

Figure 12-37

Records to be deleted

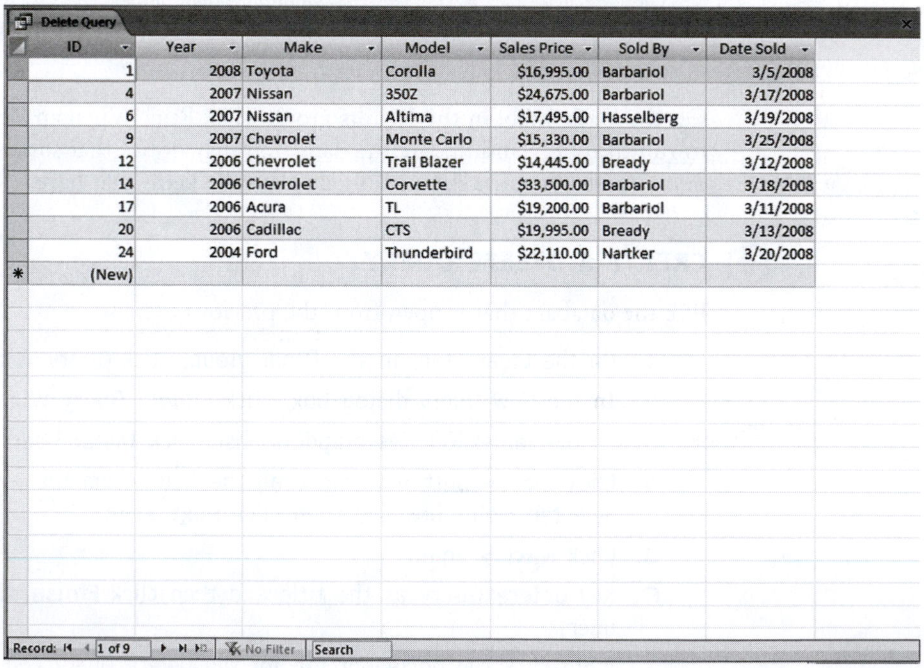

ID	Year	Make	Model	Sales Price	Sold By	Date Sold
1	2008	Toyota	Corolla	$16,995.00	Barbariol	3/5/2008
4	2007	Nissan	350Z	$24,675.00	Barbariol	3/17/2008
6	2007	Nissan	Altima	$17,495.00	Hasselberg	3/19/2008
9	2007	Chevrolet	Monte Carlo	$15,330.00	Barbariol	3/25/2008
12	2006	Chevrolet	Trail Blazer	$14,445.00	Bready	3/12/2008
14	2006	Chevrolet	Corvette	$33,500.00	Barbariol	3/18/2008
17	2006	Acura	TL	$19,200.00	Barbariol	3/11/2008
20	2006	Cadillac	CTS	$19,995.00	Bready	3/13/2008
24	2004	Ford	Thunderbird	$22,110.00	Nartker	3/20/2008
*	(New)					

Record: 1 of 9 — No Filter — Search

10. Right-click the document tab for the Delete Query and click **Design View** to display the query in Design view.

11. On the Design tab, in the Query Type group, click **Delete**. Access hides the Show row in the lower section of the design grid and adds the Delete row, as shown in Figure 12-38.

Figure 12-38

Delete row in design grid

Figure 12-38

Delete row in design grid

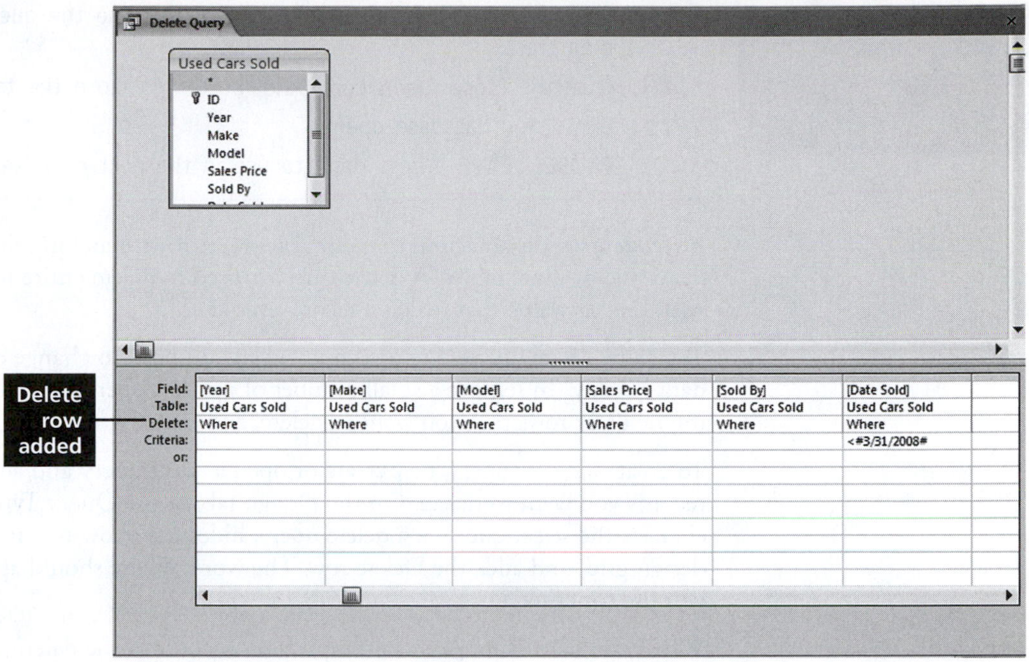

12. On the Design tab, in the Results group, click **Run**. An alert message appears, as shown in Figure 12-39.

Figure 12-39

Delete alert message

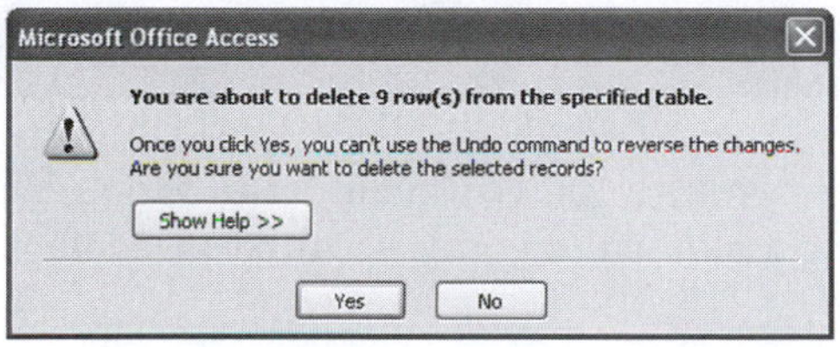

13. Click **Yes**.

14. Double-click **Used Cars Sold: Table** in the Navigation pane to open it. Notice that all the records for cars sold before March 31, 2008 have been deleted, as shown in Figure 12-40.

Figure 12-40

Table with records deleted

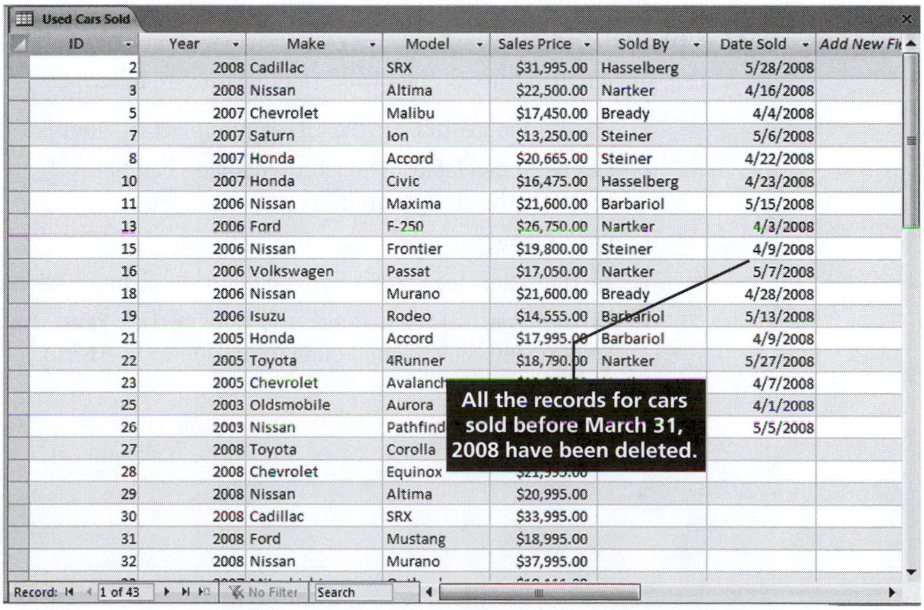

15. Click the **Close 'Delete Query'** button to close the query. Save the changes when prompted.

16. Click the **Close 'Used Cars Sold'** button to close the table.

17. **LEAVE** the database open.

PAUSE. LEAVE Access open to use in the next exercise.

A **delete query** is an action query that removes rows matching the criteria that you specify from one or more tables. A delete query is used to delete entire records from a table, along with the key value that makes a record unique.

Typically, delete queries are used only when you need to change or remove large amounts of data quickly. To remove a small number of records, open the table in Datasheet view, select the fields or rows that you want to delete, and press Delete.

To create a delete query, first create or open a select query and add criteria to return the records you want to delete. On the Design tab, in the Query Type group, click Delete. Access changes the select query to a delete query, hides the Show row in the lower section of the design grid, and adds the Delete row. The word Where should appear in any columns that you use for criteria.

When you click Run, Access prompts you to confirm the deletion. Click Yes to delete the data and then open the table to see that the records have been deleted.

■ Advanced Query Modification

THE BOTTOM LINE

After a query has been created, you can modify it in various ways to suit your purposes—by creating a join, creating calculated fields, adding aliases, or using aggregated functions.

Creating a Join

When you include multiple tables in a query, you use joins to help you get the results you are looking for. A join helps a query return only the records from each table you want to see, based on how those tables are related to other tables in the query.

⊙ CREATE A JOIN

USE the database that is open from the previous exercise.

1. On the Create tab, in the Other group, click **Query Design**.

2. In the Show Table dialog box, double-click **Sales Team** and **Used Cars Sold** to add them to the design grid.

3. Click **Close**.

4. In the Sales Team field list, double-click **E-mail Address**.

5. In the Used Cars Sold field list, double-click **Year**, **Make**, **Model**, and **Sales Price**. Your screen should look similar to Figure 12-41.

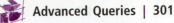

Figure 12-41

New query

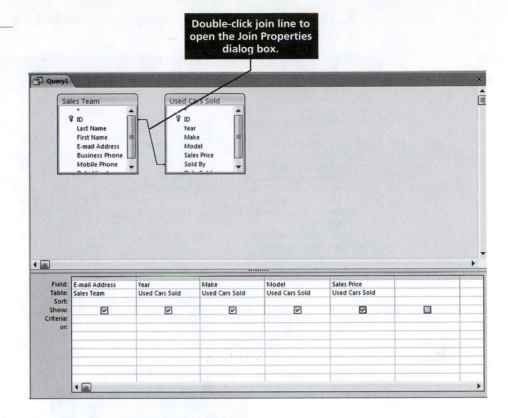

6. Double-click the **join line** between the tables, indicating which fields are joined. The Join Properties dialog box opens, as shown in Figure 12-42.

Figure 12-42

Join Properties dialog box

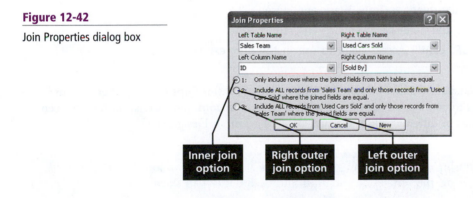

7. Click option **2** and then click **OK** to create a left outer join.
8. On the Design tab, in the Results group, click **Run**.

9. The results of the query are displayed, as shown in Figure 12-43.

Figure 12-43

Left outer join

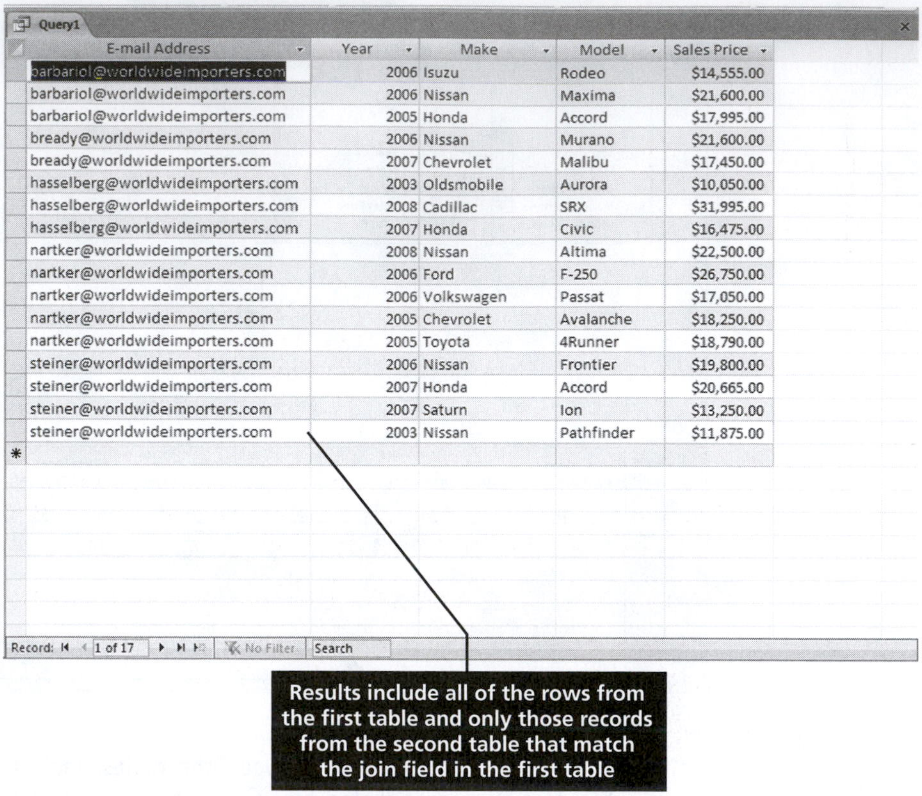

Results include all of the rows from the first table and only those records from the second table that match the join field in the first table

10. Save the query as **Join Query** and close.

11. **LEAVE** the database open.

PAUSE. LEAVE Access open to use in the next exercise.

CERTIFICATION READY?
How do you create joins?
4.2.3

Relational databases consist of tables that have logical relationships to each other. You use relationships to connect tables on fields that they have in common. A relationship between identical fields in different tables is represented by a *join* in Design view.

TAKE NOTE *

If the relationship is one-to-many, Access displays a "1" above the join line to show which table is on the "one" side and an infinity symbol (∞) to show which table is on the "many" side.

When you add tables to a query, Access creates joins that are based on relationships that have been defined between the tables. You can manually create joins in queries, even if they do not represent relationships that have already been defined.

The four basic types of joins are inner joins, outer joins, cross joins, and unequal joins. Inner joins are the most common type of join. An *inner join* includes rows in the query only when the joined field matches records in both tables.

Most of the time, you don't need to do anything to use an inner join. Access automatically creates inner joins if you add two tables to a query and those tables each have a field with the same or compatible data type and one of the join fields is a primary key.

An *outer join* includes all of the rows from one table in the query results and only those rows from the other table that match the join field in the first table. You create outer joins by modifying inner joins. Double-click the line joining the tables to display the Join Properties dialog box.

Option 1 represents an inner join. Option 2 is a *left outer join*, where the query includes all of the rows from the first table and only those records from the second table that match the join field in the first table. Option 3 is a *right outer join*, where the query includes all of the rows from the second table and only those rows from the first table that match the join field in the second table.

TAKE NOTE*

To tell which table is the left table or the right table in a given join, double-click the join to view the Join Properties dialog box.

Because some of the rows on one side of an outer join will not have corresponding rows from the other table, some of the fields returned in the query results from that other table will be empty when the rows do not correspond.

In a *cross join*, each row from one table is combined with each row from another table. Any time you run a query that has tables that are not explicitly joined, a cross join is produced. Cross joins are usually unintentional, but there are cases where they can be useful. A cross join can be used if you want to examine every possible combination of rows between two tables or queries.

If you want to combine the rows of two sources of data based on field values that are not equal, you use an *unequal join*. Typically, unequal joins are based on either the greater than (>), less than (<), greater than or equal to (>=), or less than or equal to (<=) comparison operators. Unequal joins are not supported in Design view. If you wish to use them, you must do so in SQL view.

TROUBLESHOOTING

If you create a join by mistake, for example, a join between two fields that have dissimilar data types, you can delete it. In the query design grid, click the join you want to remove and press Delete.

Creating a Calculated Query Field

You can create a new field that displays the results of a calculation you define with an expression or that manipulates field values.

➔ CREATE A CALCULATED QUERY FIELD

USE the database that is open from the previous exercise.

1. On the Create tab, in the Other group, click **Query Design**.
2. In the Show Table dialog box, double-click **Inventory** to add the table to the design grid.
3. Click **Close**.
4. In the Inventory field list, double-click **Year**, **Make**, **Model**, **AskingPrice**, and **TradeInValue**.
5. Click the Field cell in the first blank column and press $\boxed{\text{Shift}}$+$\boxed{\text{F2}}$ to open the Zoom dialog box.
6. In the Zoom dialog box, key the following expression:
   Markup: [AskingPrice] – [TradeInValue]
   Your screen should look similar to Figure 12-44.

Figure 12-44

Calculated field expression

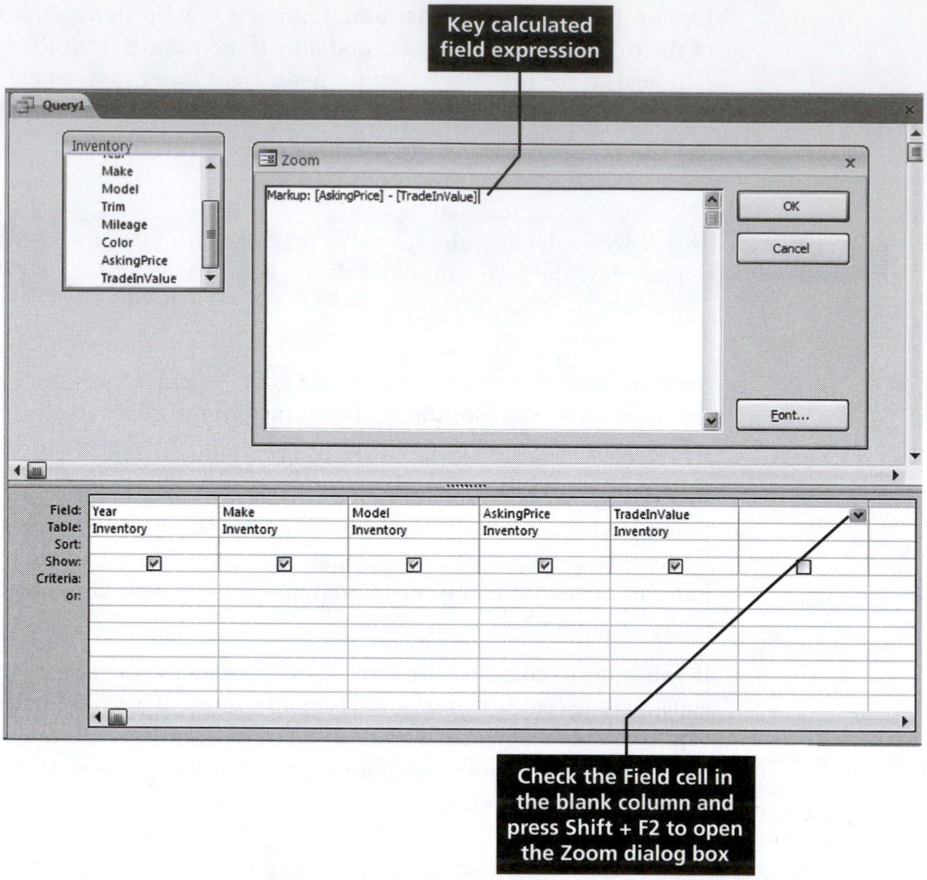

7. Click **OK**.

8. On the Design tab, in the Results group, click **Run**. The query with the new calculated **Markup** field is displayed, as shown in Figure 12-45.

Figure 12-45

Calculated field query results

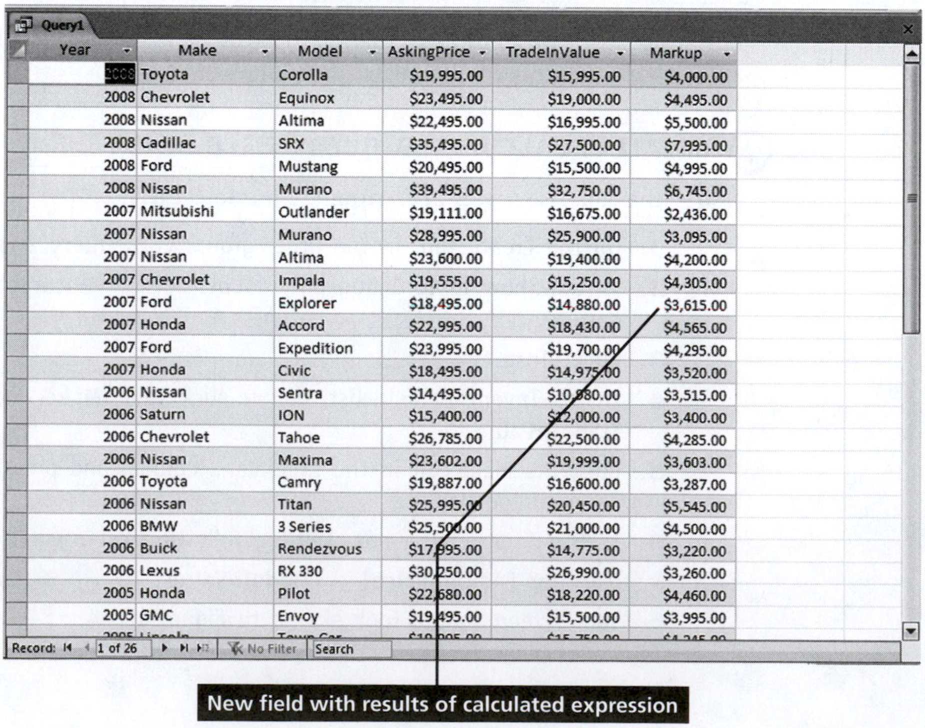

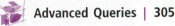

9. Save the query as **Calculated Query** and close.

10. **LEAVE** the database open.

   PAUSE. LEAVE Access open to use in the next exercise.

A *calculated field* is a column in a query that results from an expression. For example, you can calculate a value; combine text values, such as first and last names; or format a portion of a date. You can use expressions that perform arithmetic operations in calculated fields—to add, subtract, multiply, and divide the values in two or more fields. You can also perform arithmetic operations on dates or use expressions that manipulate text. Table 12-3 shows examples of expressions that can be used in calculated fields.

Table 12-3

EXPRESSION	DESCRIPTION
PrimeShip: [Ship] * 1.1	Creates a field called PrimeShip, and then displays shipping charges plus 10 percent in the field.
OrderAmount: [Quantity] * [Price]	Creates a field called OrderAmount, and then displays the product of the values in the Quantity and Price fields.
LeadTime: [RequiredDate] − [ShippedDate]	Creates a field called LeadTime, and then displays the difference between the values in the RequiredDate and ShippedDate fields.
TotalInventory: [UnitsInStock] + [UnitsOnOrder]	Creates a field called TotalInventory, and then displays the sum of the values in the UnitsInStock and UnitsOnOrder fields.
FullName: [FirstName] & " " & [LastName]	Creates a field called FullName that displays the values in the FirstName and LastName fields, separated by a space.
Address2: [City] & " " & [Region] & " " & [PostalCode]	Creates a field called Address2 that displays the values in the City, Region, and PostalCode fields, separated by spaces.

A well-designed database does not store simple calculated values in tables. For example, a table might store an employee's hire date, but not how long she has worked for the company. If you know both today's date and the employee's date of hire, you can always calculate her employment length, so there is no need to store that in the table. Instead, you create a query that calculates and displays the pertinent value. The calculations are made every time you run the query, so if the underlying data changes, so do your calculated results.

To create a calculated field, first open or create a query and switch to Design view. In the Field row of the first blank column in the design grid, key the expression. To name the field, key a name followed by a colon before the expression. If you do not supply a name, Access will use a generic name for the field, for example, EXPR1. The string following the colon is the expression that supplies the values for each record. To see the SQL code, you can switch to SQL View.

Adding an Alias to a Query Field

You can create aliases for query fields to make it easier to work with column names, calculations, and summary values.

⊕ ADD AN ALIAS TO A QUERY FIELD

USE the database that is open from the previous exercise.

1. On the Create tab, in the Other group, click **Query Design**.
2. In the Show Table dialog box, double-click **Inventory** to add the table to the design grid.
3. Click **Close**.
4. In the Inventory field list, double-click * to add all fields to the design grid.
5. Click the * in the Inventory field list and then on the Design tab, in the Show/Hide group, click **Property Sheet**. Your screen should look similar to Figure 12-46.

Figure 12-46

Field list properties

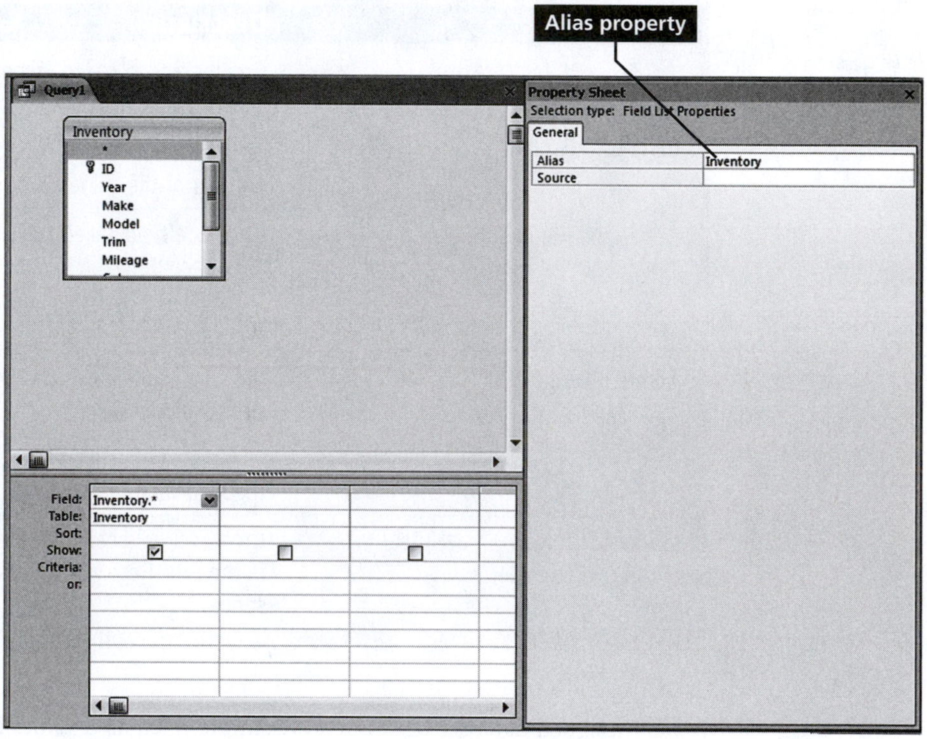

Alias property

6. Select the Inventory alias, key **CarsinStock**, and then click outside the cell. Notice the alias has changed, as shown in Figure 12-47.

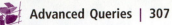

Figure 12-47

Alias changed

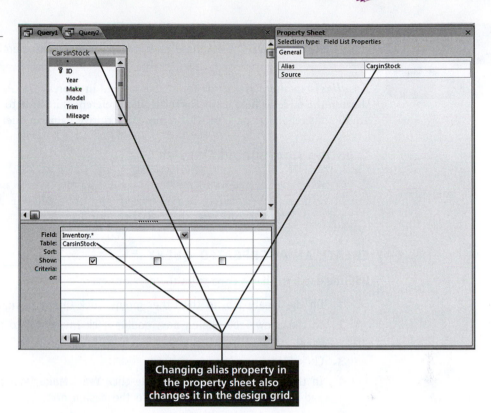

Changing alias property in the property sheet also changes it in the design grid.

7. Right-click the **Query1 tab** and click **SQL View** to view the code. Notice in Figure 12-48 that the alias is represented with the word "AS."

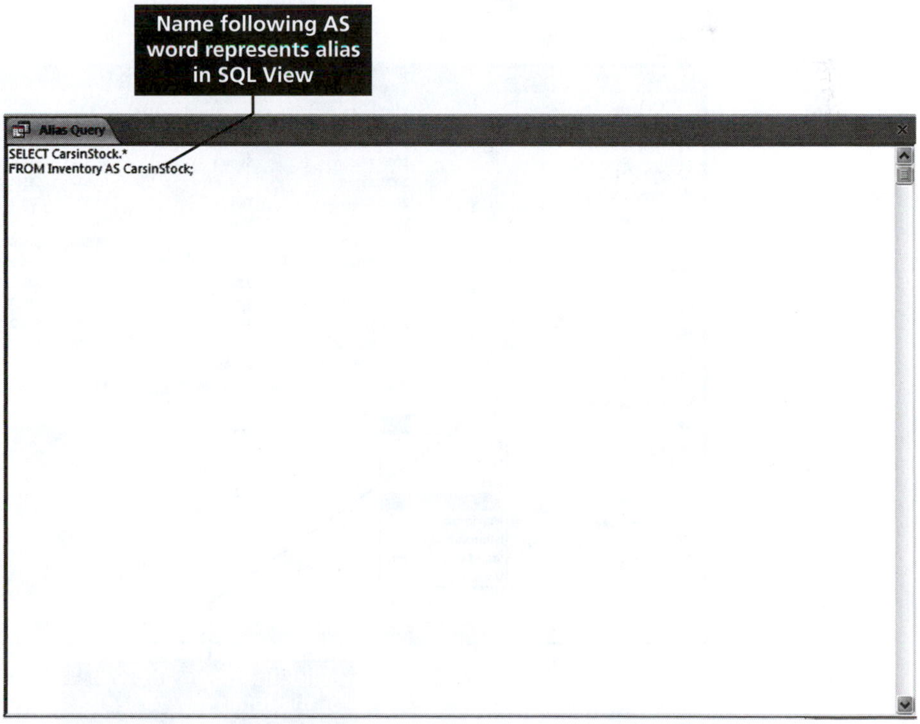

Figure 12-48

SQL View

Name following AS word represents alias in SQL View

Alias Query

SELECT CarsinStock.*
FROM Inventory AS CarsinStock;

CERTIFICATION READY?
How do you add an alias to a query field?
4.2.5

8. Save the query as **Alias Query** and close.

PAUSE. LEAVE the database open to use in the next exercise.

An *alias* is an alternative name for a table or field in expressions. Aliases are often used to shorten the table or field name for subsequent references in code to prevent possible ambiguous references or to provide a more descriptive name in query output.

Creating Aggregated Queries

You can use aggregated functions to count the data returned by a query, calculate average values, and find the smallest, largest, earliest, and latest values using a feature called the Total Row, which doesn't alter the design of your query.

→ CREATE AN AGGREGATED QUERY NEW FEATURE

USE the database that is open from the previous exercise.

1. On the Create tab, in the Other group, click **Query Design**.

2. In the Show Table dialog box, double-click **Inventory** to add the table to the design grid.

3. Click **Close**.

4. In the Inventory field list, double-click **Year**, **Make**, **Model**, **Mileage**, **AskingPrice**, and **TradeInValue** to add them to the design grid.

5. On the Design tab, in the Results group, click **Run**.

6. On the Home tab, in the Records group, click the **Totals** button. Scroll down to see the Totals row at the bottom of the result set.

7. In the Totals cell of the **Year** field, click the **down arrow** to display the menu and click **Count**, as shown in Figure 12-49.

Figure 12-49

Totals row menu options

	Year	Make	Model	Mileage	AskingPrice	TradeInValue
	2007	Ford	Expedition	37,550	$23,995.00	$19,700.00
	2007	Honda	Civic	24,925	$18,495.00	$14,975.00
	2006	Nissan	Sentra	42,344	$14,495.00	$10,980.00
	2006	Saturn	ION	45,682	$15,400.00	$12,000.00
	2006	Chevrolet	Tahoe	26,427	$26,785.00	$22,500.00
	2006	Nissan	Maxima	63,328	$23,602.00	$19,999.00
	2006	Toyota	Camry	33,986	$19,887.00	$16,600.00
	2006	Nissan	Titan	33,345	$25,995.00	$20,450.00
	2006	BMW	3 Series	50,145	$25,500.00	$21,000.00
	2006	Buick	Rendezvous	28,135	$17,995.00	$14,775.00
	2006	Lexus	RX 330	34,600	$30,250.00	$26,990.00
	2005	Honda	Pilot	57,606	$22,680.00	$18,220.00
	2005	GMC	Envoy	31,135	$19,495.00	$15,500.00
	2005	Lincoln	Town Car	30,087	$19,995.00	$15,750.00

Total menu options: None, Sum, Average, Count, Maximum, Minimum, Standard Deviation, Variance

All Tables field list:
- Inventory
  - Inventory : Table
  - Append Query
  - Alias Query
  - Calculated Query
  - Subquery
  - Inventory Query
- Sales Team
  - Sales Team : Table
  - Sales Team Query
  - Join Query
- Used Cars Sold
  - Used Cars Sold : Table
  - Used Cars Sold_Crosstab
  - Delete Query
  - Filter Query
  - Join Query
  - Used Cars Sold Query
- Sales Team Backup
  - Sales Team Backup : Table

Record: Totals   No Filter   Search

Click the down arrow in the Totals row to see aggregate function options.

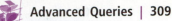

8. In the Totals row of the **Mileage** field, click the **down arrow** and click **Average**.

9. In the Totals row of the **AskingPrice** field, click the **down arrow** and click **Maximum**.

10. In the Totals row of the **TradeInValue** field, click the **down arrow** and click **Sum**. Your Totals row should appear similar to Figure 12-50.

Figure 12-50

Aggregate function results

Year	Make	Model	Mileage	AskingPrice	TradeInValue
2007	Ford	Expedition	37,550	$23,995.00	$19,700.00
2007	Honda	Civic	24,925	$18,495.00	$14,975.00
2006	Nissan	Sentra	42,344	$14,495.00	$10,980.00
2006	Saturn	ION	45,682	$15,400.00	$12,000.00
2006	Chevrolet	Tahoe	26,427	$26,785.00	$22,500.00
2006	Nissan	Maxima	63,328	$23,602.00	$19,999.00
2006	Toyota	Camry	33,986	$19,887.00	$16,600.00
2006	Nissan	Titan	33,345	$25,995.00	$20,450.00
2006	BMW	3 Series	50,145	$25,500.00	$21,000.00
2006	Buick	Rendezvous	28,135	$17,995.00	$14,775.00
2006	Lexus	RX 330	34,600	$30,250.00	$26,990.00
2005	Honda	Pilot	57,606	$22,680.00	$18,220.00
2005	GMC	Envoy	31,135	$19,495.00	$15,500.00
2005	Lincoln	Town Car	30,087	$19,995.00	$15,750.00
26			30,160	$39,495.00	$487,714.00

Record: Totals — No Filter — Search

Count — **Average** — **Maximum** — **Sum**

11. **SAVE** the query as **Aggregated Query** and close.

12. **CLOSE** the database.

> **PAUSE. LEAVE** Access running to use in the next exercise.

An *aggregate function* performs a calculation on a set of values and then returns a single value. You can add, count, or calculate other aggregate values, and display them in a special row, called the Total row, that appears below the asterisk (*) row in Datasheet view. You can use a different aggregate function for each column and you can also choose not to summarize a column.

Open your query in Datasheet view. On the Home tab, in the Records group, click Totals to add a Total row. The Total row allows you to use an aggregate function in one or more columns of a query result set without having to change the design of your query. Click in the Total row under a column and choose the function you want. To clear the total for a column, click in the Total row under that column, then select None from the dropdown list.

The following aggregate functions are available:

- **Count**—counts the number of items in a field (column of values)
- **Sum**—sums a column of numbers
- **Average**—averages a column of numbers
- **Maximum**—finds the highest value in a field
- **Minimum**—finds the lowest value in a field
- **Standard Deviation**—measures how widely values are dispersed from an average value (a mean)
- **Variance**—measures the statistical variance of all values in the column

Many of the aggregate functions work only on data fields set to specific data types. For example, if you are in a column that only displays text values, some functions—such as Sum or Average—are not relevant, and are therefore not available.

SUMMARY SKILL MATRIX

IN THIS LESSON YOU LEARNED	MATRIX SKILL	SKILL NUMBER
To create crosstab queries	Create crosstab queries	4.1.4
To create a subquery	Create subqueries	4.1.5
To save a filter as a query	Save filters as queries	4.1.6
To create action queries	Create action queries	4.1.3
To create a join	Create joins	4.2.3
To create a calculated field query	Create calculated fields in queries	4.2.4
To add an alias to a query field	Add aliases to query fields	4.2.5
To create aggregated queries	Create sum, average, min/max, and count queries	4.2.6

■ Knowledge Assessment

Fill in the Blank

Complete the following sentences by writing the correct word or words in the blanks provided.

1. A(n) _____ is a SELECT statement that is inside another select or action query.

2. A(n) _____ removes rows matching the criteria that you specify from one or more tables.

3. To minimize the risk of running an action query, you can first preview the data that will be acted upon by viewing the action query in _____ view before running it.

4. A(n) _____ includes all of the rows from one table in the query results and only those rows from the other table that match the join field in the first table.

5. A(n) _____ is a column in a query that results from an expression.

6. A(n) _____ is an alternative name for a table or field in expressions.

7. A(n) _____ performs a calculation on a set of values and then returns a single value.

8. A(n) _____ query always includes three types of data: the data used as row headings, the data used as column headings, and the values that you want to sum or otherwise compute.

9. To quickly add all the fields in a table to the design grid in Design view, double-click the _____ at the top of the list of table fields.

10. To be able to apply a filter when and where you want, save the filter as a(n) _____.

Multiple Choice

Select the best response for the following statements or questions.

1. What type of query displays its results in a grid similar to an Excel worksheet?
   a. crosstab
   b. append
   c. aggregated
   d. subquery

2. How many types of action queries are there?
   a. two
   b. three
   c. four
   d. five

3. Which action query does not make changes to the data in the tables that it is based on?
   a. append
   b. make table
   c. update
   d. delete

4. Which type of query can be thought of as a powerful version of the Search and Replace dialog box?
   a. filter
   b. calculated field
   c. update
   d. crosstab

5. Which of the following is *not* a type of join?
   a. inner join
   b. exterior join
   c. cross join
   d. unequal join

6. Which of the following is *not* an aggregated function?
   a. Lowest
   b. Sum
   c. Average
   d. Count

7. Which of the following SELECT statement selects all the fields from the Inventory table?
   a. SELECT all fields FROM Inventory
   b. SELECT [ALL] from [INVENTORY]
   c. SELECT from INVENTORY {all fields}
   d. SELECT * FROM Inventory

8. For more space in which to enter the SELECT statement in a field or criteria cell, what do you press to display the Zoom box?

   a. Shift+F2

   b. Ctrl+2

   c. Shift+Enter

   d. Ctrl+Spacebar

9. To undo the changes made by an action query,

   a. click the Undo button.

   b. restore the data from a backup copy.

   c. switch to Datasheet view.

   d. run the query again.

10. Which type of query adds the records in the query's result set to the end of an existing table?

    a. append

    b. make table

    c. update

    d. delete

■ Competency Assessment

Project 12-1: Create a Calculated Query Field

In your job as a travel agent at Margie's Travel, you are frequently asked the length of various trips. So that you don't have to calculate it mentally, create a calculated field that will give you this information.

GET READY. Launch Access if it is not already running.

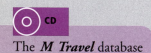

The **M Travel** database file is available on the companion CD-ROM.

1. **OPEN** the **M Travel** database from the data files for this lesson.
2. **SAVE** the database as **M TravelXXX** (where XXX is your initials).
3. On the Create tab, in the Other group, click **Query Design**.
4. In the Show Table dialog box, double-click **Events** to add the table to the design grid.
5. Click **Close**.
6. In the Inventory field list, double-click **Event**, **StartTime**, and **EndTime** to add them to the design grid.
7. Click the Field cell in the first blank column and press [Shift]+[F2] to open the Zoom dialog box.
8. In the Zoom dialog box, key the following expression:

   TripLength: [EndTime] – [StartTime]
9. Click **OK**.
10. On the Design tab, in the Results group, click **Run**. The query is displayed, with a new **TripLength** field calculating the number of days of the trip.
11. Save the query as **Calculated Query** and close.
12. **CLOSE** the database.

    LEAVE Access running for the next project.

Project 12-2: Save a Filter as a Query

As purchasing manager for the Coho Vineyard monthly wine, you frequently run the same filters on the database. Now that you have learned to save a filter as a query, you can save yourself some time.

1. OPEN *Wine Coho* from the data files for this lesson.
2. SAVE the database as *Wine CohoXXX* (where XXX is your initials).
3. On the Create tab, in the Other group, click the **Query Wizard** button.
4. In the New Query dialog box, click **Simple Query Wizard** and click **OK**.
5. In the Tables/Queries drop-down list, click **Table: Red Wine**.
6. Click the **>>** button to move all the fields from the Available Fields to the Selected Fields box and then click **Next >**.
7. Click **Next >** again and then click **Finish** to display a simple select query.
8. On the Home tab, in the Sort & Filter dialog box, click the **Advanced** button and then click **Filter by Form**.
9. In the Filter by Form, click the **down arrow** in the Country field and click **Italy**.
10. On the Home tab, in the Sort & Filter dialog box, click the **Toggle Filter** button to apply the filter. The results are displayed.
11. On the Home tab, in the Sort & Filter dialog box, click the **Advanced** button and then click **Advanced Filter/Sort** to display the new query design grid.
12. On the Home tab, in the Sort & Filter dialog box, click the **Advanced** button and then click **Save As Query**. The Save As Query dialog box appears.
13. Key **Filter Query** in the Query Name box and click **OK**.
14. Click the **Close 'Red Wines Queryfilter1'** button.
15. On the Home tab, in the Sort & Filter dialog box, click the **Toggle Filter** button to remove the filter.
16. Click the **Close 'Red Wines Query'** button and save the changes when prompted.
17. LEAVE the database open.

    LEAVE Access open for the next project.

■ Proficiency Assessment

Project 12-3: Create a Subquery

You are interested in extracting specific information about the wine prices from the database. Create a subquery to determine which white wines have a purchase price that is above average.

USE the database that is open from the previous project.

1. On the Create tab, in the Other group, click **Query Design**.
2. Use the Show Table dialog box to add the **White Wines** table to the upper section of the query design grid and then close it.
3. Add the **Bottled, Label, Type,** and **PurchasePrice** fields to the design grid.
4. Place the insertion point in the Criteria row of **PurchasePrice** field and display the Zoom dialog box.
5. Key the following expression in the Zoom dialog box:

   > (SELECT AVG([PurchasePrice]) FROM [White Wines])
6. Click **OK**.
7. On the Design tab, in the Results group, click **Run** to display the query results.

8. Save the query as **Subquery** and close.

9. **CLOSE** the database.

   LEAVE Access open for the next project.

Project 12-4: Create a Make Table Query

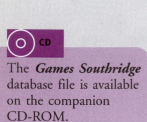

The *Games Southridge* database file is available on the companion CD-ROM.

As the manager at Southridge Video, you want to archive the current table with information about used games. Use the make table action query to create a backup table.

1. **OPEN** *Games Southridge* from the data files for this lesson.

2. **SAVE** the database as *Games SouthridgeXXX* (where XXX is your initials).

3. Create a simple select query named **Games Query** using all the fields in the **Games: Table**.

4. Display the query in Design View if it is not already.

5. On the Design tab, in the Query Type group, click **Make Table** to display the Make Table dialog box. (**Hint:** Be sure the content of the database has been enabled or the make table query will not run.)

6. In the Table Name box, key **Games Backup**. If it is not already selected, click **Current Database**, and then click **OK**.

7. On the Design tab, in the Results group, click **Run**. An alert message appears.

8. Click **Yes**. A new table appears in the Navigation Pane.

9. Close the **Games Query** and save the changes when prompted.

10. **CLOSE** the database.

    LEAVE Access open for the next project.

Mastery Assessment

Project 12-5: Create a Crosstab Query

The *Contoso Data* database file is available on the companion CD-ROM.

As a regional manager for Contoso Pharmaceuticals, you are in charge of overseeing the sales reps in your division. To determine the total samples given by each rep in the first two weeks of the quarter, you decide to create a crosstab query.

1. Open *Contoso Data* from the data files for this lesson.

2. Save the database as *Contoso DataXXX* (where XXX is initials).

3. Use the **Samples Given: Table** and the skills you have learned in this lesson to create the crosstab query named **Samples Given_Crosstab** shown in Figure 12-51.

Figure 12-51

Crosstab query

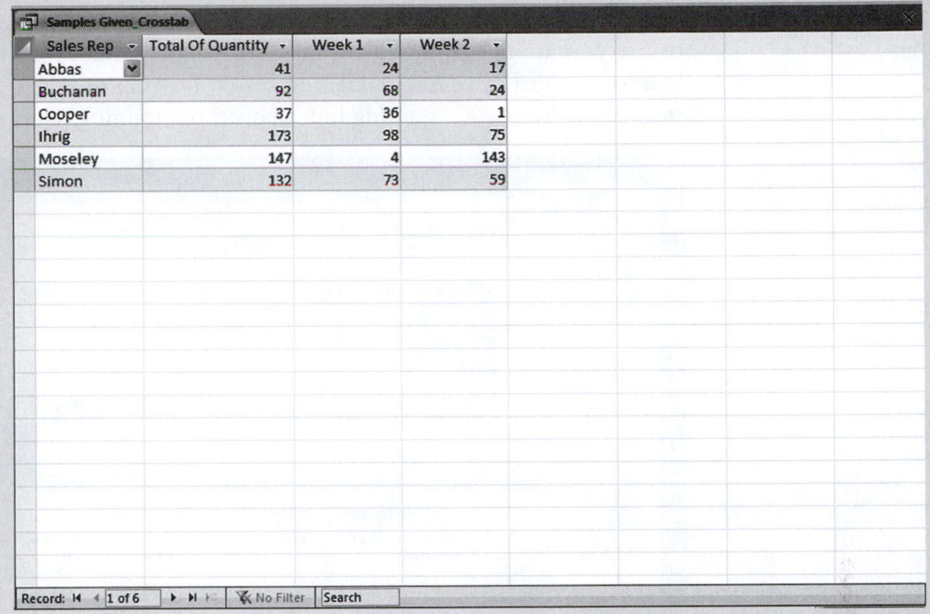

Sales Rep	Total Of Quantity	Week 1	Week 2
Abbas	41	24	17
Buchanan	92	68	24
Cooper	37	36	1
Ihrig	173	98	75
Moseley	147	4	143
Simon	132	73	59

Record: ◄ ◄ 1 of 6 ► ►► │ No Filter │ Search

4. **LEAVE** the database open for the next project.

LEAVE Access open for the next project.

Project 12-6: Create an Update Query

The name of one of the hospitals in your region has recently been changed. You need to create an update query to change the name in the database.

USE the database that is open from the previous project.

1. Create a select query named **Update Query** that includes all the fields in the **Doctors: Table**.

2. Switch to **Design View**.

3. Use criteria to select only the records that have "Community Medical Center" in the Hospital field.

4. Use the skills you have learned in this lesson to create an update query that will change the name of *Community Medical Center* to *Community Regional Hospital*. (**Hint:** Be sure the content of the database has been enabled or the update query will not run.)

5. Open the **Doctors: Table** to verify that the hospital name has been changed. Then, close the table and the query.

6. **CLOSE** the database.

CLOSE Access.

INTERNET READY

At this point in the book, you have learned a lot about using Access. If you need more practice or want to refresh your memory about some basic skills, Microsoft offers a training course containing self-paced lessons and practice sessions online for hands-on experience. Use Microsoft Office Access Help to search for "Up to speed" and then click on the *Up to speed with Access 2007* training link to open the training page, shown in Figure 12-52.

Figure 12-52

Up to speed with Access 2007

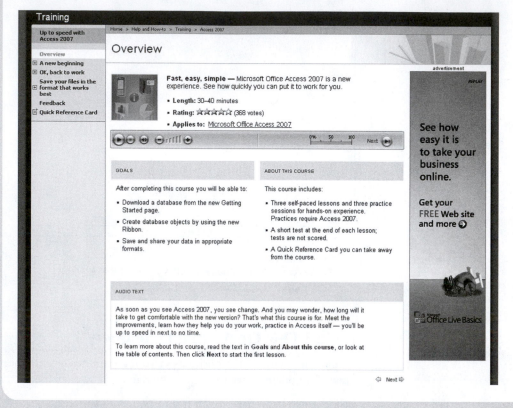

✳ Workplace Ready

Creating Mailing Labels in Access

Keeping track of sales data and contacts is vital to the success of any business. Access provides the tools you need not only to keep these records available and secure, but also to generate sales and provide customer service. Whether you need to mail a single sales brochure or do a mass mailing of two hundred, you can use Access to create the labels using the records you maintain in your Access databases.

Imagine you are a partner in a start-up software firm named Proseware, Inc., that has developed specialized software for colleges and universities. You have created an Access database with tables that include information for customers as well as sales leads for professors to whom you are marketing the product.

Using the Label Wizard in Access, you can create mailing labels and sort them by zip code for bulk mailing. You can create a parameter query that uses one or more criteria to select only certain records for labels. You can specify a label size that matches a brand of label sheets you can purchase at the office supply store, or you can choose to create a custom-size sheet of labels. With Access, you can produce professional, high-quality mailings to your targeted audience quickly and efficiently.

Display and Share Data

LESSON SKILL MATRIX

SKILLS	MATRIX SKILL	SKILL NUMBER
Creating a Chart Using the Chart Wizard	Create charts	5.3.1
Formatting a Chart	Format charts	5.3.2
Changing Chart Types	Change chart types	5.3.3
Build a PivotChart	Create and modify charts	5.3
Saving a Database Object as Another File Type	Save database objects as other file types	5.5
Printing a Database Object	Print database objects	5.6

Blue Yonder Airlines is a small but rapidly growing regional airline. In your position as Investor Relations Specialist, you assist in building investor relations programs, creating and distributing analyst reports, maintaining and updating databases, and preparing materials for conference presentations. In this lesson, you will create, save, and print charts that will be reproduced and included in a report detailing the growth of Blue Yonder Airlines.

KEY TERMS
chart
chart body
Chart Wizard
legend
PDF
PivotChart
XPS

■ Working with Charts

Charts are often used in the business world to give a visual representation of numeric data. Because a picture is worth a thousand words, charts play an important role in reports and presentations. In Access 2007, you can create charts in two ways. You can insert a chart into a new or existing form or report using the Chart Wizard control or you can create a PivotChart, which is a type of form.

Creating a Chart Using the Chart Wizard

The Chart Wizard lets you insert a chart into a new or existing report or form using a table or query as your data source. This allows you to insert a pictorial view of the data along with the numbers. The Chart Wizard asks you questions about the chart you want and then creates the chart based on your answers.

⊙ CREATE A CHART

GET READY. Before you begin these steps, be sure to turn on and/or log on to your computer and start Access.

CD

The *BlueYonderAirlines* database is available on the companion CD-ROM.

1. OPEN *BlueYonderAirlines* from the data files for this lesson.
2. Save the database as *BlueYonderAirlinesXXX* (where XXX is your initials).
3. Open the **Income & Expenses** report.
4. Switch to Design view.
5. On the Design tab, in the Controls group, click the **Insert Chart** button. The pointer changes to a plus sign with a chart icon.
6. Click in the upper left corner of the Page Footer section and drag to the lower-right corner to create a rectangular placeholder where the chart will be inserted, as shown in Figure 13-1.

Figure 13-1

Report in Design view

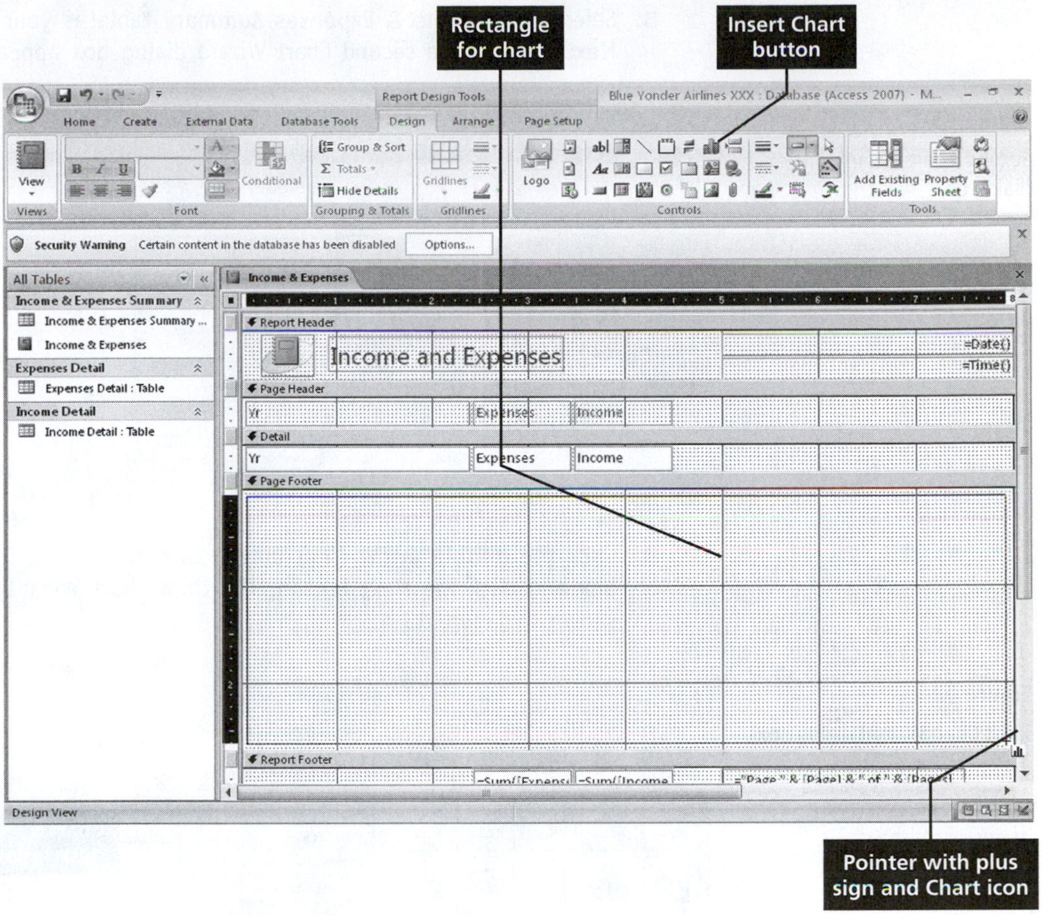

Rectangle for chart

Insert Chart button

Pointer with plus sign and Chart icon

7. Release the mouse button. The first Chart Wizard dialog box appears, as shown in Figure 13-2.

Figure 13-2

First Chart Wizard dialog box

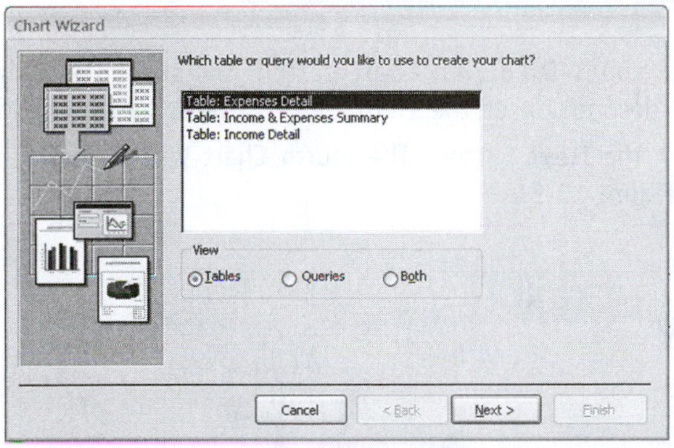

8. Select the **Income & Expenses Summary** table as your data source and click the **Next** button. The second Chart Wizard dialog box appears, as shown in Figure 13-3.

Figure 13-3

Second Chart Wizard dialog box

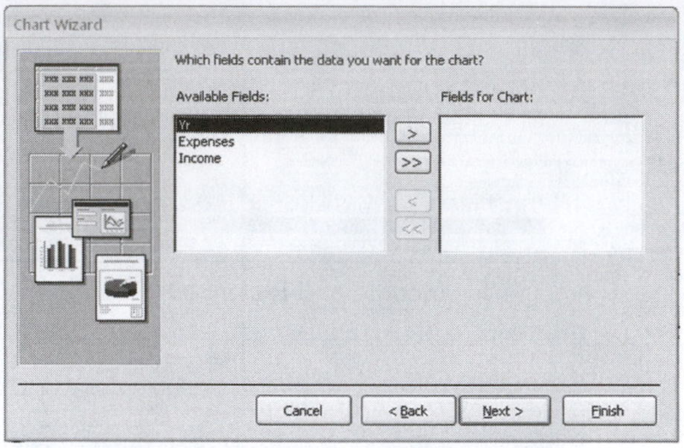

9. Click the **double arrow (>>)** button to move all the fields to the Fields for Chart box and click the **Next** button. The third Chart Wizard dialog box appears, as shown in Figure 13-4.

Figure 13-4

Third Chart Wizard dialog box

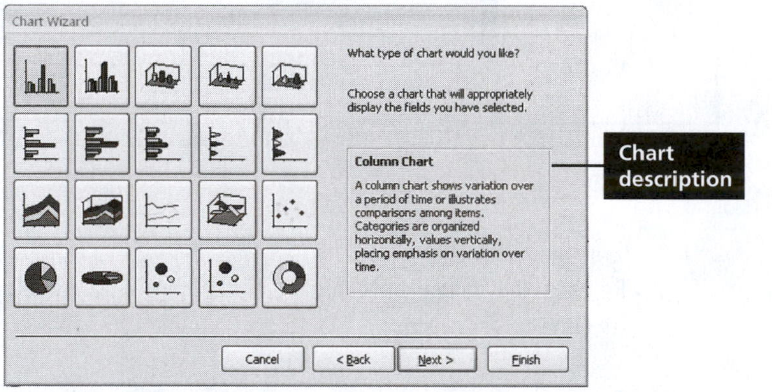

10. Click the **3-D Column Chart** button, the second icon in the first row. Notice that the description of the chart type is displayed on the right.

11. Click the **Next** button. The fourth Chart Wizard dialog box appears, as shown in Figure 13-5.

Figure 13-5

Fourth Chart Wizard dialog box

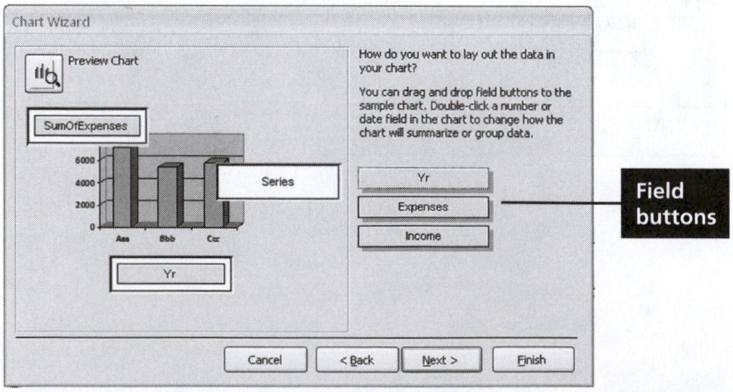

12. Click and drag the **Income** field button to the upper left of the chart and drop on the **SumofExpenses** data list. Both the **SumofExpenses** and **SumofIncome** fields should be listed.

13. Click the **Preview Chart** button. The Sample Preview dialog box appears, displaying a sample of your chart, as shown in Figure 13-6.

Figure 13-6

Sample Preview dialog box

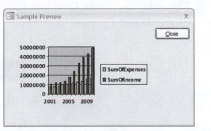

14. Click the **Close** button. The Sample Preview dialog box closes.

15. Click the **Next** button. The fifth Chart Wizard dialog box appears, as shown in Figure 13-7.

Figure 13-7

Fifth Chart Wizard dialog box

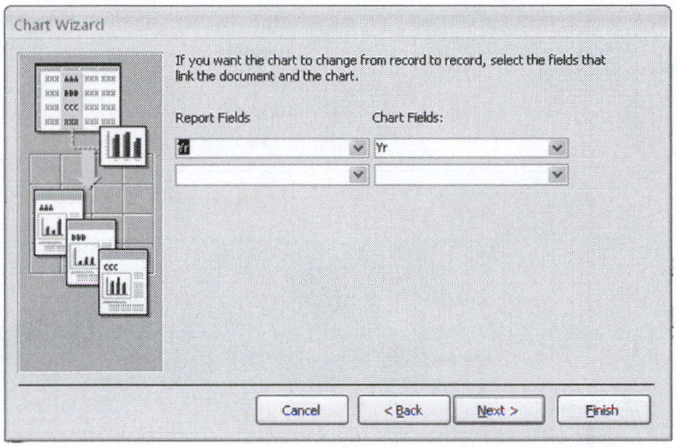

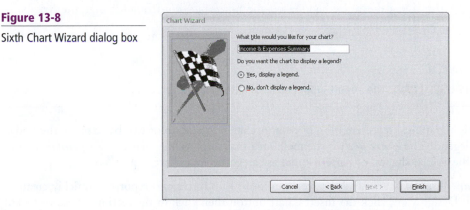

16. Click the down arrow in the **Report Fields** menu and select **<No Field>**.

17. Click the down arrow in the **Chart Fields** menu and select **<No Field>**.

18. Click the **Next** button. The Sixth Chart Wizard dialog box appears, as shown in Figure 13-8.

Figure 13-8

Sixth Chart Wizard dialog box

19. Key **2001-2010 Income and Expenses** in the Title box.

20. The **Yes, display a legend** button should be selected. If not, select it and click the **Finish** button. Access inserts your chart. Notice that in Design view the data from your chart is not displayed.

21. Click the chart to select it.

22. On the Design tab, in the Tools group, click the **Property Sheet** button.

Property Sheet

23. Click the **Data** tab of the Property Sheet. Click the down arrow at the end of the **Enabled** line and select **Yes**.

24. CLOSE the Property Sheet.

25. Switch to Report view.

26. On the Home tab, in the Records group, click the **Refresh All** button.

27. Scroll to the bottom of the report to view your chart, which should look similar to Figure 13-9.

Figure 13-9

Report with 3-D bar chart

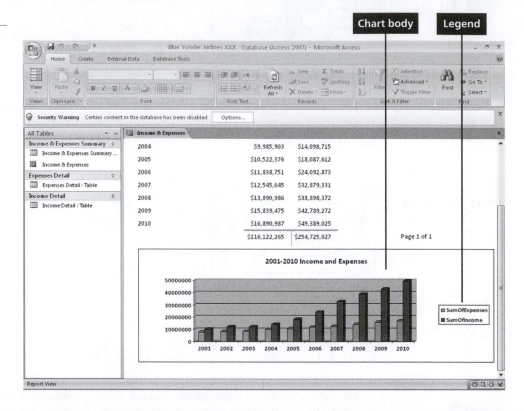

TROUBLESHOOTING If your chart is not displaying correctly, you probably need to increase the width and/or height of the placeholder. You do this the same way you resize any control. Switch to Design view and click the resize handles in the center of the vertical borders and drag to increase the size. Drag the resize handles on the horizontal borders to change the height. Then, return to Report view to see the results.

28. SAVE the report.

PAUSE. LEAVE the report open to use in the next exercise.

A *chart* is a graphical representation of data. A chart is made up of two basic parts, the body and the legend. The *chart body* is the main area that displays the chart. The *legend* displays a list of the colors, shapes, or patterns used as categories in a chart.

The *Chart Wizard* is a control that you can insert into forms and reports to quickly create charts. In Design view, click the Insert Chart button then click in the section where you want to insert the chart and drag to draw a rectangular placeholder large enough for your chart. If you need to resize it later, you can do so by clicking and dragging the selection handles to increase or decrease the height or width.

The Chart Wizard asks you to choose the table or query that you want to use as the data source for the chart, the fields you want to use in the chart, and the type of chart you want to create. You can also choose the layout you want for your chart and see a preview of it before creating it. If you want to display a chart for each record in the data source, you can specify the field that links the document and the chart. Choose a title and specify whether or not you want to display a legend. When you click Finish, the chart is inserted into the report or form.

In the previous exercise, you inserted the chart into the Page Footer section of the report because it is a one-page report and it is helpful to show the data at the bottom of the page after the columnar data. You could also place the chart in the Detail section of the report and set the chart to change with each record, so you would have a report displaying the record data and a chart for each record.

You can create 20 different charts using the Chart Wizard, including column, bar, area, line, XY scatter, pie, bubble, and doughnut charts.

To delete a chart, right-click it in Design view and select Delete from the shortcut menu.

CERTIFICATION READY?
How do you create a chart?
5.3.1

Formatting a Chart

You can use Microsoft Graph to change the formatting of charts created with the Chart Wizard. You can change chart options such as how the title and labels are displayed and where you want the legend located. You can also change formatting options, such as the color or the chart's background and the color and size of the data blocks in the chart.

⊖ CHANGE CHART OPTIONS

USE the report open from the previous exercise.

1. Switch to Design view.
2. Double-click the chart. The Microsoft Graph software launches, displaying the chart in a view similar to Design view, as shown in Figure 13-10.

Figure 13-10

Chart displayed in Microsoft Graph

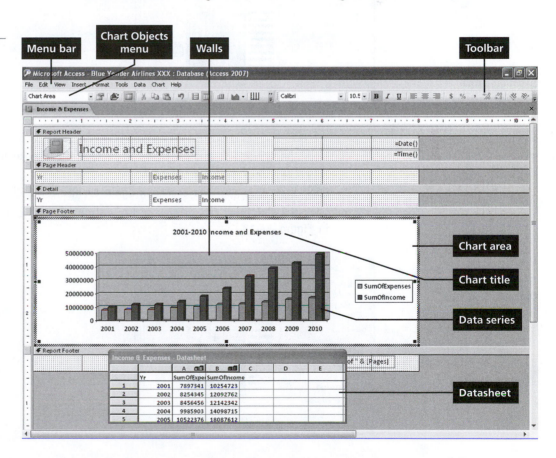

3. Click the **Chart** menu and select **Chart Options**. The Chart Options dialog box appears, as shown in Figure 13-11.

Figure 13-11

Titles tab of the Chart Options dialog box

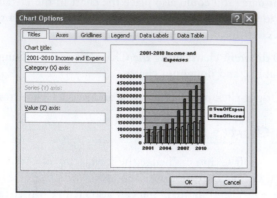

4. Select **2001-2010** in the Chart title box and press the Delete key. Notice that the preview on the right adjusts to show the change.

5. Click the **Axes** tab to display the options on the Axes tab, as shown in Figure 13-12.

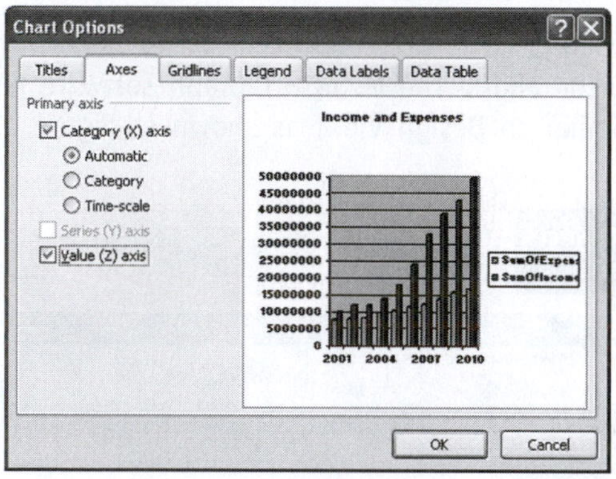

Figure 13-12

Axes tab of the Chart Options dialog box

6. Click the **Value (Z)** axis checkbox to remove the checkmark. Notice that the values on the Z axis are removed.

7. Click the **Value (Z)** axis checkbox again to insert the checkmark.

8. Click the **Gridlines** tab to display the options on the Gridlines tab, as shown in Figure 13-13.

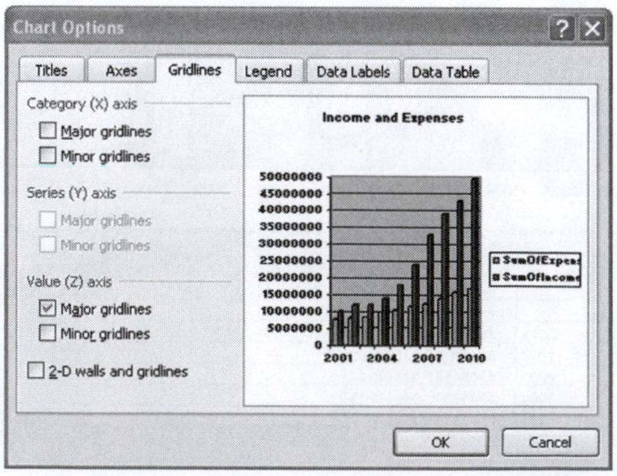

Figure 13-13

Gridlines tab of the Chart Options dialog box

9. Click the **Major gridlines** checkbox in the Category X axis section. Notice that gridlines are added to the preview.

10. Click the **Legend** tab to display the options on the Legend tab, as shown in Figure 13-14.

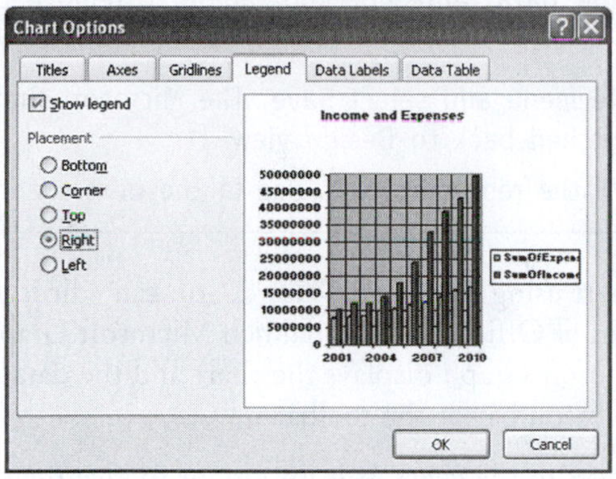

Figure 13-14

Figure 13-14

Legend tab of the Chart Options dialog box

11. Click the **Show legend** checkbox to remove the checkmark. Notice that the legend is removed from the chart.

12. Click the **Show legend** checkbox again to insert a checkmark. The legend is displayed in the preview.

13. Click the **Bottom** button to move the legend to the bottom of the chart.

14. Click the **Data Labels** tab to display the options on the Data Labels tab, as shown in Figure 13-15.

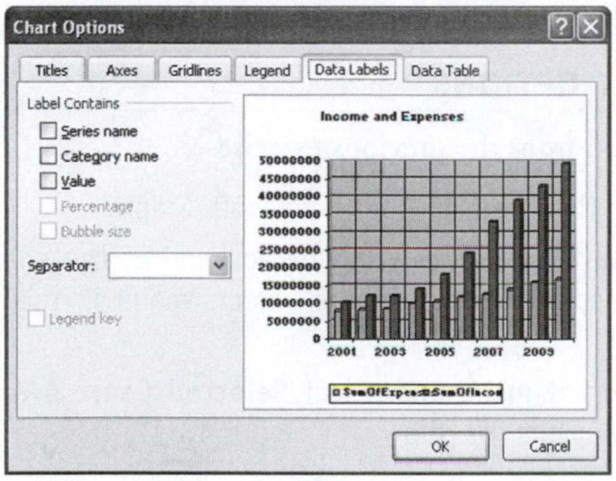

Figure 13-15

Data Labels tab of the Chart Options dialog box

15. Click the **Value** checkbox to insert a checkmark. Notice that values are added to the columns in the chart.

16. Click the **Value** checkbox again to remove the checkmark.

17. Click the **Data Table** tab to display the options on the Data Table tab, as shown in Figure 13-16.

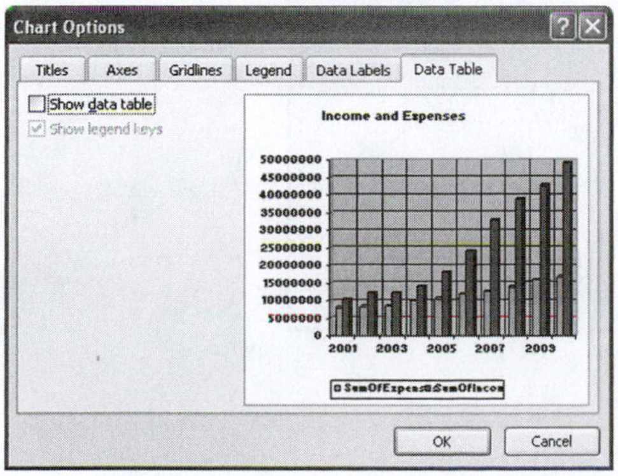

Figure 13-16

Data Table tab of the Chart Options dialog box

18. Click the **Show data table** checkbox to insert a checkmark. Notice that the datasheet is added to the bottom of the chart.

19. Click the **Show data table** checkbox again to remove the checkmark.

20. Click **OK.**

21. Click the **File** menu and select **Save.** The Microsoft Graph software closes and the report is switched back to Design view.

> **PAUSE. LEAVE** the report open to use in the next exercise.

After you create a chart using the Chart Wizard, you can edit it using Microsoft Graph, which is a component of Office 2007. To launch Microsoft Graph, double-click a chart in Design view. Microsoft Graph displays the chart and the datasheet. You can choose commands from the menu bar or the toolbar.

After you make changes to the chart, it is important to save the changes using the Save command on the File menu. After you save a chart, Microsoft Graph closes and switches you back to Design view.

CERTIFICATION READY?
How do you format a chart?
5.3.2

The Chart Options dialog box has six tabs with options for changing the look and layout of a chart. You can access the Chart Options dialog box from the Chart menu or by right-clicking the white Chart Area and selecting Chart Options from the shortcut menu.

TROUBLESHOOTING Microsoft Graph has its own Help system. To access it, double-click a chart to launch Microsoft Graph and choose Microsoft Graph Help from the Help menu or press **F1.**

⊙ CHANGE FORMAT OPTIONS

USE the database open from the previous exercise.

1. Double-click the chart to open Microsoft Graph.

2. Click the **Chart Area**, the white background of the chart, to select it. Chart Area should be displayed in the Chart Objects menu in the upper-left corner of the toolbar.

3. Click the **Format** menu and select **Selected Chart Area.** The Format Chart Area dialog box appears, as shown in Figure 13-17.

Figure 13-17

Format Chart Area dialog box

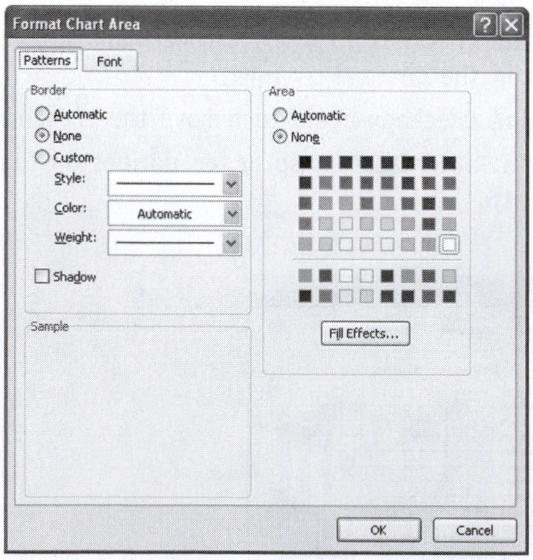

4. Click the **Fill Effects** button. The Fill Effects dialog box appears, as shown in Figure 13-18.

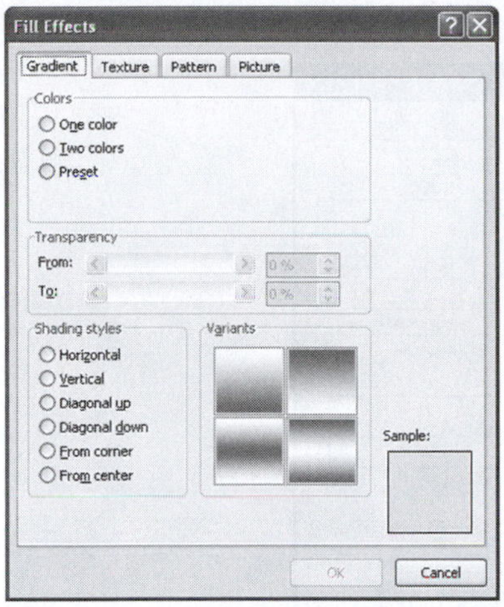

Figure 13-18

Fill Effects dialog box

5. Click the **Horizontal** button in the Shading styles section and click **OK**.

6. Click **OK** in the Format Chart Area dialog box.

7. Right-click any of the **purple** Data Series columns in the chart to display the shortcut menu. Notice that Series "SumOfIncome" is displayed in the Chart Objects menu.

8. Select **Format Data Series** from the shortcut menu. The Format Data Series dialog box appears.

9. Select the **Green** color, as shown in Figure 13-19.

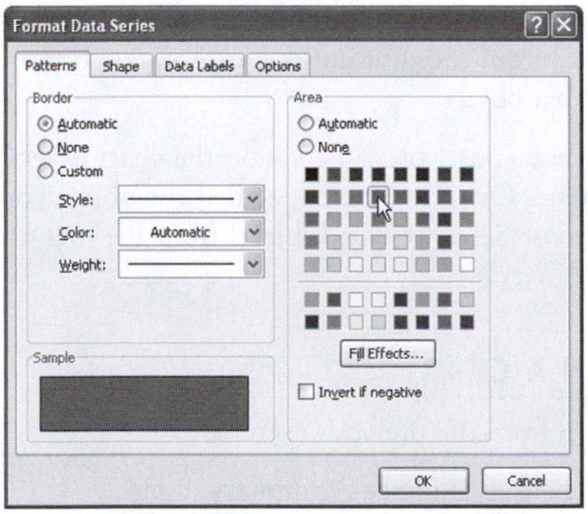

Figure 13-19

Format Data Series dialog box

10. Click **OK** in the Format Data Series dialog box.

11. Right-click the gray grid background of the chart, called the Walls, and select **Format Walls** from the shortcut menu.

12. Click the **Fill Effects** button.

13. Click the **From center** button in the Shading Styles section and click **OK**.

14. Click **OK** in the Format Walls dialog box.

15. Right-click the **Legend** and select **Format Legend** from the menu. The Color dialog box appears. Select the **Font** tab if it is not already displayed. The Color dialog box now appears, as shown in Figure 13-20.

16. Select **10** in the Size menu and click **OK**.

17. Click the **File** menu and select **Save**.

18. **SAVE** the report.

PAUSE. **LEAVE** the report open to use in the next exercise.

Microsoft Graph makes it easy to format a chart. Each part of the chart is an independent object, so you can simply right-click the chart object that you want to change and choose Format [Chart Object] from the shortcut menu. A dialog box appears with the formatting choices available for that object.

If you prefer to use the menus, you can click on the chart object to select it or choose it from the Chart Objects menu. Once you have specified the object you want to change, click the Format menu and choose Select [Chart Object] from the menu to launch the dialog box of available options.

➔ REFRESH DATA IN A CHART

USE the database open from the previous exercise.

1. **OPEN** the **Income & Expenses Summary** table.

2. In the first row, in the Income column, select the data and key **9004523** and press the (Enter) key.

3. **SAVE** and **CLOSE** the table.

4. Click the **Income & Expenses Report** tab. Notice that the numbers in the report data and the numbers in the chart have not changed.

5. On the Home tab, in the Records group, click the **Refresh All** button. The data in the report and in the chart are updated.

6. **SAVE** the report.

PAUSE. **LEAVE** the report open to use in the next exercise.

The Refresh All button can be a useful tool when working with charts. When you make a change to the data source of a chart, be sure to save the new data in the table or query. When you switch back to the form or report containing your chart, click Refresh All to update the data in the chart.

Changing Chart Types

Access provides many different chart types and variations of those chart types for you to choose from in the Chart Type dialog box. Access makes it easy to experiment with different configurations before you decide on the chart that best displays the data you want to emphasize.

→ CHANGE CHART TYPES

USE the database open from the previous exercise.

1. Switch to Design view.
2. Double-click the chart. Microsoft Graph opens.
3. Click the **By Row** button. The chart is changed to show all the expenses together and all the income together.
4. Click the **By Column** button to change it back to the original chart.
5. Click the **Chart Type** button and select **3-D Area Chart** from the menu, as shown in Figure 13-21. The chart changes to an area chart.

Figure 13-21

Chart Type button and menu

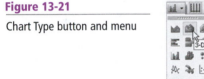

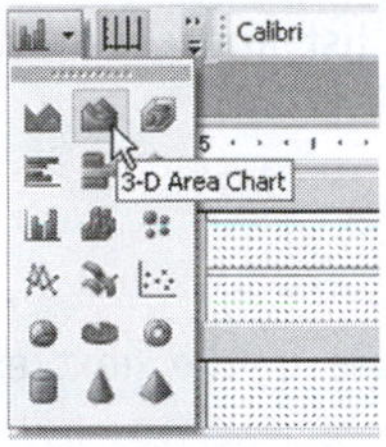

6. Click the **Chart** menu and select **Chart Type**. The Chart Type dialog box appears, as shown in Figure 13-22.

Figure 13-22

Chart Type dialog box

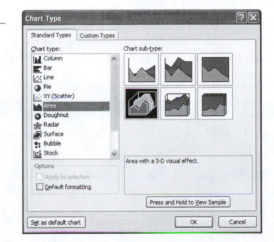

7. On the Standard Types tab, click **Pie** in the Chart type list. In the Chart subtype section, click the **Pie with a 3-D visual effect**, the second icon on the first row.

8. Click and hold the **Press and Hold to View Sample** button to see a preview of the chart, as shown in Figure 13-23.

Figure 13-23

Sample pie chart

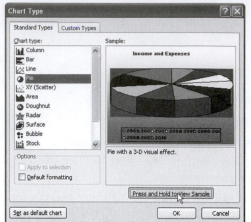

9. Click the **Custom Types** tab.
10. Click **Colored Lines** in the Chart type list and click **OK**.
11. Click the **File** menu and select **Save**.
12. Switch to Report view to see the chart.
13. **SAVE** and **CLOSE** the report.

    PAUSE. LEAVE the database open to use in the next exercise.

CERTIFICATION READY?
How do you change chart types?
5.3.3

Access 2007 has many different types of charts you can choose from. The key is to choose one that displays your data in a meaningful way. Often, you have a specific chart in mind that you want to use, but sometimes it requires experimentation, choosing and changing chart types until you get the results you want.

You can use the Chart Type menu to select a chart, or you can choose the Chart Type command from the Chart menu. The Chart Type dialog box has Standard Types and Custom Types of charts to choose from. Table 13-1 shows the standard chart types.

Table 13-1

Standard Chart Types

Button	Chart	Description and Use
	Column	Shows data changes over a period of time or illustrates comparisons among items. Categories are organized horizontally, values vertically, to emphasize variation over time.
	Bar	Illustrates comparisons among individual items. Categories are organized vertically, values horizontally, to focus on comparing values and to place less emphasis on time.
	Line	Displays trends over time or categories.
	Area	Emphasizes the magnitude of change over time. By displaying the sum of the plotted values, an area chart also shows the relationship of parts to a whole.
	XY Scatter	Either shows the relationships among the numeric values in several data series or plots two groups of numbers as one series of xy coordinates. It shows uneven intervals, or clusters, of data and is commonly used for scientific data.
	Pie	Shows the proportional size of items that make up a data series to the sum of the items. It always shows only one data series and is useful when you want to emphasize a significant element.
	Doughnut	Shows the relationship of parts to a whole, but it can contain more than one data series. Each ring of the doughnut chart represents a data series.

Building a PivotChart

PivotCharts are a type of form that you can create using data from a table or PivotTable. The difference between a regular chart and a PivotChart is that a PivotChart can be interactive. You can create, format, and change chart types for PivotCharts much like you did with the charts you created with the Chart Wizard.

⊕ **CREATE A PIVOTCHART**

USE the database open from the previous exercise.

1. Open the **Income Detail** table.

2. On the Create tab, in the Forms group, click the **PivotChart** button. A blank PivotChart appears and the PivotChart Tools appear in the Ribbon.

3. On the Design tab, in the Show/Hide group, click the **Field List** button to display the Chart Field List if it isn't displayed already. Your screen should look similar to Figure 13-24.

Figure 13-24

Blank PivotChart

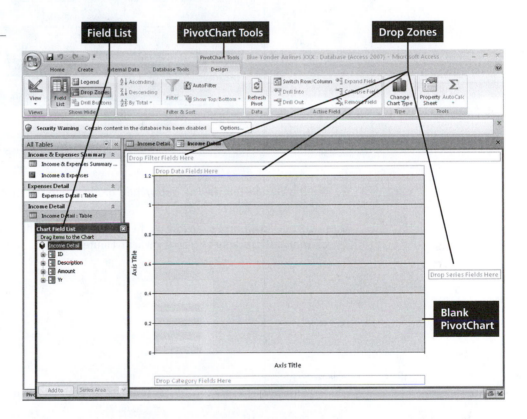

4. In the Chart Field List, click the **Amount** field and drag it to the **Drag Data Fields Here** drop zone box and release the mouse button.

5. Click the **Description** field and drag and drop it in the **Drop Series Fields Here** drop zone.

6. Click the **Yr** field and drag and drop it in the **Drop Category Fields Here** drop zone. Your screen should look similar to Figure 13-25.

Figure 13-25

PivotChart

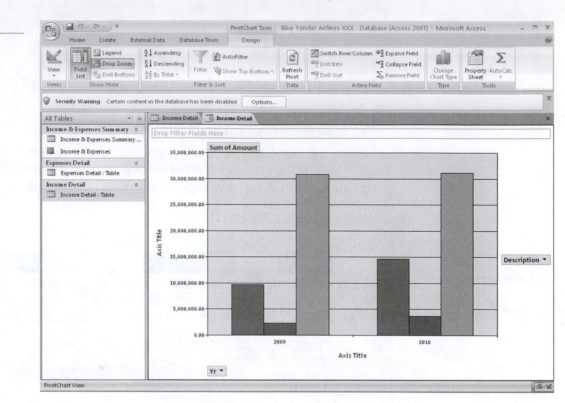

7. On the Design tab, in the Show/Hide group, click the **Legend** button. A legend is added to the chart.

8. Click the **down arrow** on the **Yr** field button at the bottom of the chart. A menu of year options appears, as shown in Figure 13-26.

Figure 13-26

Yr menu

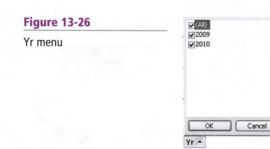

9. Click the **2009** checkbox to remove the checkmark, and click **OK**. Only the 2010 data is displayed in the chart.

10. Click the **down arrow** on the **Yr** field button. Click the **2009** checkbox again to insert the checkmark and click **OK**. The 2009 data is displayed along with the 2010 data.

11. Click the **Save** button on the Quick Access Toolbar. The Save dialog box appears.

12. Key **Income Chart** and click **OK**.

   PAUSE. LEAVE the chart open to use in the next exercise.

CERTIFICATION READY?
How do you create a chart?
5.3.1

A **_PivotChart_** is an interactive chart that shows data totals or summaries. When you view a PivotChart, you can change the chart to view different combinations of data, just as you chose to display only one year of data in the previous exercise.

To create a PivotChart, you need to select or open the data source before clicking the PivotChart button. Drag the fields you want to include from the Chart Field List and drop them into the appropriate drop zones. Like most charts, you can arrange the category, series, or data fields in different ways, depending on what you want to emphasize.

Like other database objects, you'll need to save and name the PivotChart after you make changes to it.

 FORMAT A PIVOTCHART

USE the chart open from the previous exercise.

1. Click the **Axis Title** at the bottom of the chart to select it.
2. On the Design tab, in the Tools group, click the **Property Sheet** button. The Properties dialog box appears, as shown in Figure 13-27.

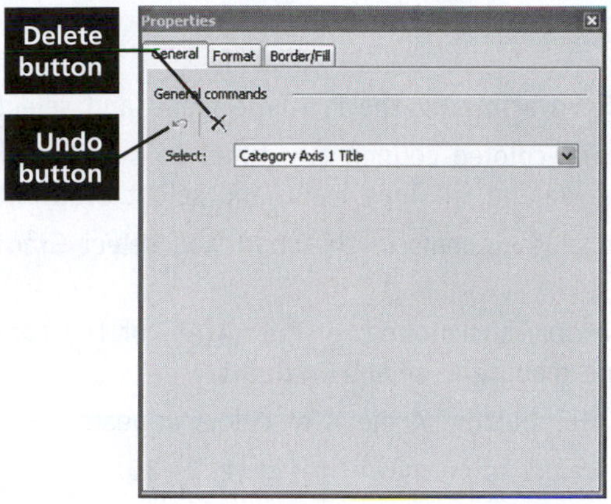

Figure 13-27

General tab of the Properties dialog box

| Delete button |
| Undo button |

Properties
General | Format | Border/Fill
General commands
Select: Category Axis 1 Title

3. Click the **Delete** button in the General Commands section. The Axis Title is removed from the screen. Leave the dialog box open on the screen.
4. Click the **Axis Title** on the left side of the chart to select it. The data in the Properties dialog box displays options for the selected title.
5. Click the **Format** tab on the Properties dialog box, as shown in Figure 13-28.

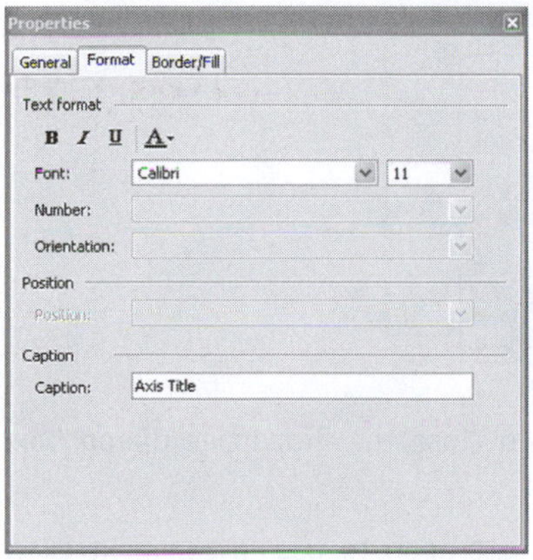

Figure 13-28

Format tab on the Properties dialog box

Properties
General | Format | Border/Fill
Text format
B *I* U A·
Font: Calibri   11
Number:
Orientation:
Position
Position:
Caption
Caption: Axis Title

6. Click the **Bold** button.
7. Click the **down arrow** on the Font size menu and select **14.**
8. Select **Axis Title** in the Caption box. Key **Amount** and press the [Enter] key. The changes you made are updated on the chart. Leave the Properties dialog box open on the screen. If you need to move it, click the top blue border and drag it to a new location.
9. Click the green **Passengers** column in the 2009 data to select it.

10. Click the same column again. Both green columns should now be selected.

11. Click the **Border/Fill** tab in the Properties dialog box, as shown in Figure 13-29.

Figure 13-29

Border/Fill tab on the
Properties dialog box

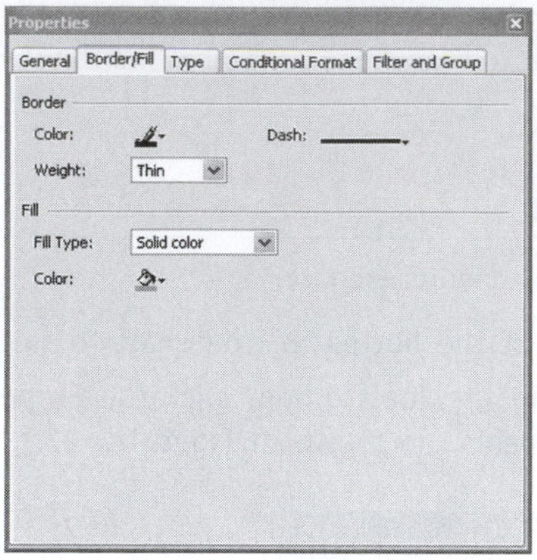

12. Click the **down arrow** on the Fill Type menu and select **Gradient**.

13. Click the coral-colored column two times to select both coral columns. Click the **down arrow** on the Fill Type menu and select **Gradient.**

14. Select both blue columns in the chart and select **Gradient** from the **Fill Type** menu.

15. Click in the gray background, or **Plot Area**, of the chart. Click the **down arrow** on the Fill Type menu and select **Gradient**.

16. Click the **Color** button. A menu of colors appears.

17. Select the **Khaki** color shown in Figure 13-30.

Figure 13-30

Color menu on the Border/Fill
tab of the Properties
dialog box

18. Click the **Close** box to close the Properties dialog box.

19. **SAVE** the chart.

    PAUSE. LEAVE the chart open to use in the next exercise.

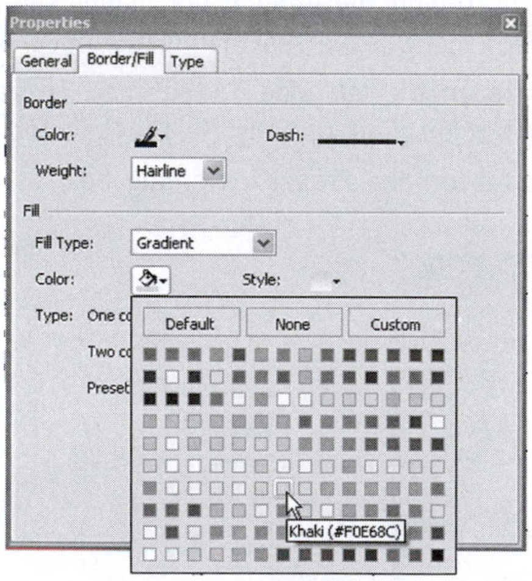

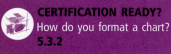

CERTIFICATION READY?
How do you format a chart?
5.3.2

You can easily change the format of data series, titles, and other chart objects using the Properties dialog box. Just select the object you want to change and click the Property Sheet button to display the Properties dialog box. You can leave the dialog box open while you make all your selections and formatting changes and then close it when you are finished. Remember to save your work.

CHANGE THE CHART TYPE

USE the chart open from the previous exercise.

Change
Chart Type

1. Click the white area on the chart, called the **Chartspace**.
2. On the Design tab, in the Type group, click the **Change Chart Type** button. The Properties dialog box appears with the Type tab displayed, as shown in Figure 13-31. Notice that the Clustered Column type is selected, because that is the current chart type.

Figure 13-31

Type tab of the Properties dialog box

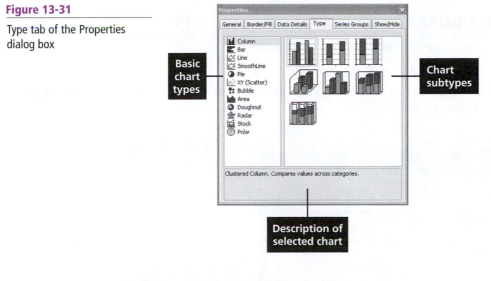

3. Click the **3D Stacked Column** type.
4. Close the Properties dialog box.
5. **SAVE** and **CLOSE** the chart.
6. **SAVE** and **CLOSE** the table.

   PAUSE. LEAVE the database open to use in the next exercise.

The same basic chart types are available for you to use as PivotCharts, as well as other charts, such as Radar and Stock charts. Additional variations are available for PivotCharts, too, as well as Custom Chart types, as you saw in the previous exercise.

The Type tab of the Properties dialog box lists each basic type of chart on the left and displays icons of subtype charts on the right. When you click an icon on the right, a description of the chart appears at the bottom of the dialog box. Your chart also changes to that chart type, so you can view your data in various configurations before you make your choice. Some types of charts may not fit the way your data is organized, so you can either rearrange the fields in your chart or try a different chart type.

CERTIFICATION READY?
How do you change chart types?
5.3.3

ANOTHER WAY   You can also access the Type tab of the Properties dialog box by right-clicking in the Chartspace and selecting Change Chart Type from the shortcut menu.

■ Saving a Database Object as Another File Type

THE BOTTOM LINE

Microsoft Access 2007 allows you to save database objects, such as tables, reports, and queries as other types of objects. For example, you can save a table as a report. You can also save database objects as PDF or XPS files.

Saving a database object as another file type allows you to share data with other users or repurpose the data in other ways.

➔ SAVE A DATABASE OBJECT AS ANOTHER FILE TYPE

USE the database open from the previous exercise.

1. Open the **Income & Expenses Summary** table.
2. Click the **Office Button**, point to **Save As**, and select **Save Object As**, as shown in Figure 13-32.

Figure 13-32

Save As command on the Office menu

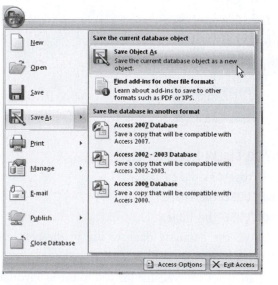

3. The Save As dialog box appears, as shown in Figure 13-33.

Figure 13-33

Save As dialog box

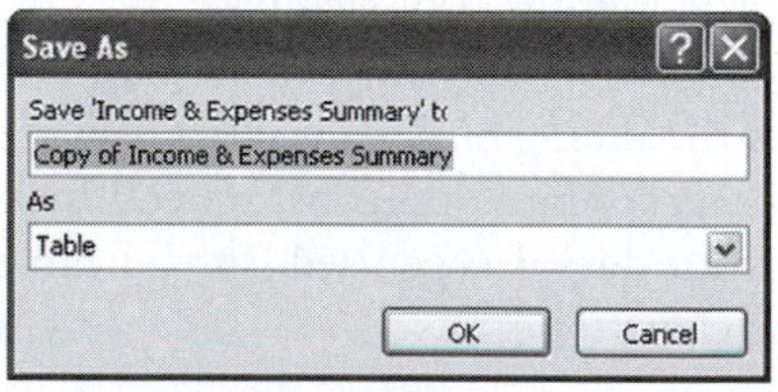

CERTIFICATION READY?
How do you save a database object as another file type?
5.5

4. Key **Summary Report** in the Save box.
5. Click the **down arrow** on the **As** menu and select **Report**.
6. Click **OK**. The table object is saved as a report object.

   PAUSE. LEAVE the report open to use in the next exercise.

In the previous exercise, you saved a table object as a report object using the Save As command on the Office button. Access also gives you the option of saving a database object in Portable Document Format (PDF) or XML Paper Specification (XPS) file formats. You might already be familiar with PDF files from documents you view on the Internet or share via emails. The **PDF** file format maintains the exact layout of the original file and can easily be shared.

A new alternative to PDF, the *XPS* file format preserves document formatting, can be easily shared, printed, and archived, and is more secure.

Before you can save a file in the XPS or PDF file format, you need to download the add-in software from Microsoft that will allow this type of save. To access the add-in, click the Office button, point to Save As, and select Find Add-ins for Other File Formats. Access Help will appear on your screen with information about the file formats and links to the add-in.

■ Printing a Database Object

THE BOTTOM LINE

You are probably familiar already with printing various kinds of documents from your computer. Printing a database object uses the same print options and settings you use with other types of documents.

You can choose various printing options before sending your document to the printer, such as the number of copies, size of the paper, or the range of pages to print.

➔ PRINT A DATABASE OBJECT

USE the report open from the previous exercise.

1. Click the **Office Button** select **Print** on the menu. The Print dialog box appears, as shown in Figure 13-34.

Figure 13-34

Print dialog box

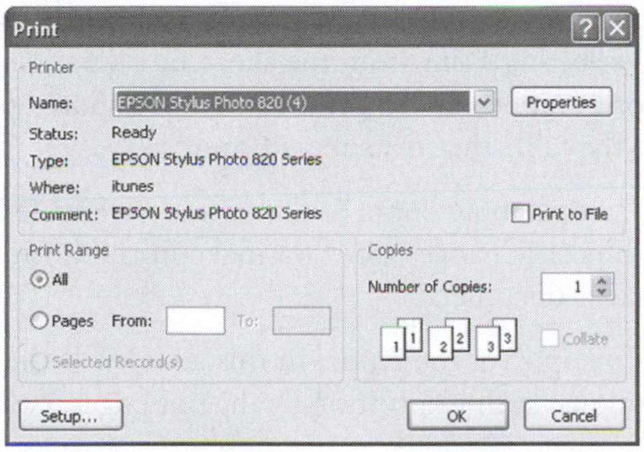

2. Click the **Properties** button. The Properties dialog box appears, as shown in Figure 13-35. Depending on your type of printer, the Properties box could be different. You can change the quality, paper, printing, and orientation options available for your printer. Click the **Cancel** button.

Figure 13-35

Properties dialog box

3. Click the **Setup** button. The Page Setup dialog box appears, as shown in Figure 13-36. Click the **Cancel** button.

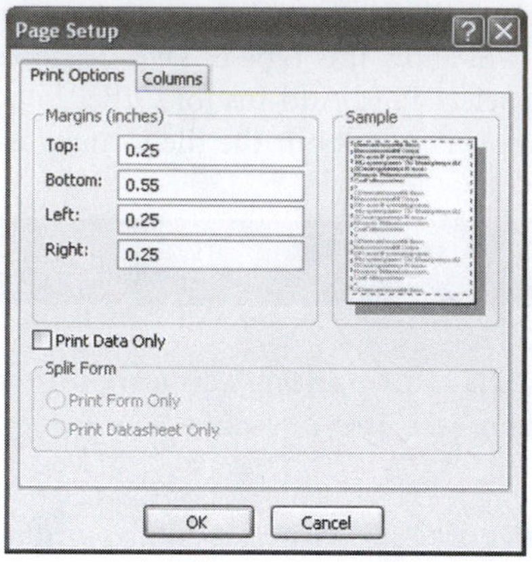

Figure 13-36

Page Setup dialog box

4. In the Copies section of the Print dialog box, click the **up arrow** in the Number of Copies menu to change the number of copies to **2.**

5. Click **OK.** Two copies of the report will start printing.

6. **CLOSE** the report and table.

CLOSE the database.

You can print tables, queries, forms, reports, or macros just by right-clicking the object in the Navigation pane and selecting Print from the shortcut menu. You can also select Print from the Office menu to print an object. To print charts, you must open either the form that contains the chart or the table that is its record source.

In this exercise, you learned about some of the options available in the Print dialog box when you print a database object. Changes that you make in the Print dialog box will only be applied to that particular document.

You chose to print two copies of the report in this activity. If the report was longer, you could have chosen other options, such as printing a range of pages, collating the pages, or printing multiple pages per sheet.

TROUBLESHOOTING

You may need to set up a new printer before you can choose it. To add a printer:
In Microsoft Windows Vista,
1. Click the Start button and then click Control Panel.
2. In the Control Panel, double-click Printers.
3. In the Printers dialog box, click Add Printer.
4. Follow the instructions in the Add Printer Wizard.
In Microsoft Windows XP,
1. Click the Start button and then click Printers and Faxes.
2. Under Printer Tasks, click Add a Printer.
3. Follow the instructions in the Add Printer Wizard.

TAKE NOTE *

To set a printer as the default, right-click the printer icon and click **Set as Default Printer** on the shortcut menu. A checkmark will appear next to the default printer.

ANOTHER WAY

You can also press **Ctrl+P** to display the Print dialog box.

ANOTHER WAY To print a document quickly, you can skip the Print dialog box and use the default settings by clicking the **Print** button on the Quick Access toolbar.

CERTIFICATION READY?
How do you print a database object?
5.6

SUMMARY SKILL MATRIX

IN THIS LESSON YOU LEARNED	MATRIX SKILL	SKILL NUMBER
To create a chart	Create charts	5.3.1
To format a chart	Format charts	5.3.2
To change chart types	Change chart types	5.3.3
To build a PivotChart	Create and modify charts	5.3
To save a database object as another file type	Save database objects as other file types	5.5
To print a database object	Print database objects	5.6

■ Knowledge Assessment

Matching

Match the term in Column 1 to its description in Column 2.

Column 1	Column 2
1. chart	**a.** a control that you can insert into forms and reports to quickly create charts
2. chart body	**b.** an interactive chart that shows data totals or summaries
3. Chart Wizard	**c.** a file format that maintains the exact layout of the original file and can easily be shared
4. legend	**d.** a file format that preserves document formatting, can be easily shared, printed, and archived, and is more secure
5. PDF	**e.** a component of Access 2007 used to make changes to a chart created by the Chart Wizard
6. PivotChart	**f.** a graphical representation of data
7. XPS	**g.** a type of chart that shows the proportional size of items that make up a data series to the sum of the items
8. Refresh All button	**h.** the main area that displays the chart
9. Microsoft Graph	**i.** displays a list of the colors, shapes, or patterns used as categories in a chart
10. pie	**j.** updates the data in a chart

True / False

Circle T if the statement is true or F if the statement is false.

T | F   **1.** You can choose from 20 different chart types in the Chart Wizard.

T | F   **2.** The Chart Wizard is a control.

T | F   **3.** A legend can be displayed only on the right side of a chart.

T | F   **4.** Microsoft Graph displays the chart and the datasheet of the underlying data source.

T | F   **5.** The Refresh All button displays an object's Property Sheet.

T | F   **6.** PivotCharts are a type of report.

T | F   **7.** You can save a table as a report.

T | F   **8.** You can print tables, queries, forms, reports, or macros by right-clicking the object in the Navigation pane and selecting Print from the shortcut menu.

T | F   **9.** An Axis is a type of chart.

T | F   **10.** After you save a chart in Microsoft Graph, Microsoft Graph closes.

■ Competency Assessment

Project 13-1: City Power & Light Salary Pie Chart

The City Power & Light human resources department is reviewing the salary budgets for the office. Your supervisor asks you to create a pie chart within a report to show the distribution of funds for each employee.

GET READY. Launch Access if it is not already running.

CD

The *City Power & Light* database is available on the companion CD-ROM.

1. Open the *City Power & Light* database.
2. Save the database as *City Power & Light XXX* (where XXX is your initials).
3. Open the **Salary** report in Design view.
4. Click the **Insert Chart** button and draw a large rectangle in the space provided in the Page Footer section. The Chart Wizard dialog box appears.
5. Click the **Next** button.
6. Move the **Employee ID** and **Salary** fields to the Fields for Chart list and click **Next**.
7. Click the **Pie Chart** button and click **Next**.
8. Drag and drop the **Salary field** button to the Data box.
9. Drag and drop the **Employee ID field** button to the Series box.
10. Click the **Preview Chart** button.
11. Click **Close**.
12. Click **Finish**.
13. Switch to Report view.
14. **SAVE** the Report.
15. Click the **Office Button** and select **Print** from the menu.
16. Click **OK**.
17. **CLOSE** the report.

    LEAVE the database open for the next project.

Project 13-2: Change the City Power & Light Chart Type

You decide to create a variation of the pie chart that will more clearly show the salary amounts in relationship to each other.

USE the database open from the previous exercise.

1. **OPEN** the **Salary** report in Report view.
2. Click the **Office Button**, point to **Save As**, and select **Save Object As.**
3. Key **Salary Line Chart** in the name box and click **OK.**
4. Switch to Design view.
5. Double-click the chart to launch Microsoft Graph.
6. Click the **Chart** menu and select **Chart Type** from the menu.
7. Click **Line** in the Standard types list.
8. In the Chart subtype list, click the **Line with markers displayed at each data value** button.
9. Click **OK.**
10. Click the **Chart** menu and select **Chart Options** from the menu.
11. Click the **Legend** tab and click the **Bottom** checkbox.
12. Click **OK.**
13. **SAVE** the chart.

   CLOSE the database.

■ Proficiency Assessment

Project 13-3: Create and Format the Expenses PivotChart

You created a chart representing the Income Detail table for Blue Yonder Airlines earlier, now you need to create a chart for the Expenses.

1. **OPEN** *Blue Yonder Airlines XXX* that you saved in an earlier exercise.
2. Create a blank PivotChart using the **Expenses Detail** table as the data source.
3. Drag the **Yr** field to the Series drop zone, drag the **Amount** field to the Data drop zone, and drag the **Description** field to the Category drop zone.
4. Click the **Legend** button to add a legend to the chart.
5. Click the **Yr** field button and click the **2009** checkbox to remove the checkmark so that only the 2010 data is displayed.
6. Click the **Change Chart Type** button and change it to a pie chart.
7. Close the **Properties** dialog box.
8. Save the chart as **Expenses Chart.**
9. **CLOSE** the chart.

   CLOSE the database.

Project 13-4: Create a PivotChart for Lucerne Publishing

The *LucernePublishing* database is available on the companion CD-ROM.

As a sales manager for Lucerne Publishing, you are constantly analyzing and sharing sales data in meetings with the sales force as well as other departments in the corporation. Create a chart for your presentation at the next sales meeting.

1. **OPEN** *LucernePublishing* from the data files for this lesson.
2. Save the database as *LucernePublishingXXX* (where XXX is your initials).

3. Create a new PivotChart using the **Sales** table.

4. Use the **Gross Sales**, **Cost of Goods**, and **Net Sales** fields as the Data fields. Drag and drop them side by side in the Data Fields drop zone.

5. Use the **Area** field as the Category field.

6. Add a legend to the chart.

7. **SAVE** the chart as **Sales Chart.**

   LEAVE the chart open for the next project.

■ Mastery Assessment

Project 13-5: **Format the Lucerne Publishing PivotChart**

The chart you created worked fine for your presentation; however, you have just been asked to present the information at a meeting with your boss, so you decide to add formatting to make it look more professional.

USE the chart open from the previous exercise.

1. Save the chart object as **Formatted Sales Chart.**

2. Change the Chart to a new Chart Type of your choice.

3. Format the plot area and blocks of data with your choice of colors, patterns, etc.

4. Change the Category Axis Title to **Area** and the Value Axis Title to **Amount**, using the color, size, style, and font of your choice.

5. **SAVE**, **PRINT**, and **CLOSE** the chart.

   CLOSE the database.

Project 13-6: **Fix the Wingtip Toys Yearly Sales Chart**

The *WingtipToys* database is available on the companion CD-ROM.

You asked an assistant to create a chart for the Yearly Sales Report, but it isn't exactly what you wanted. Fix the chart.

1. **OPEN** *WingtipToys* from the data files for this lesson.

2. Save the database as *WingtipToysXXX* (where XXX is your initials).

3. Open the **Yearly Sales Report**.

4. Launch Microsoft Graph and remove the data table at the bottom of the chart.

5. Move the legend to the bottom of the report.

6. Change the background color and pattern of the chart area to a solid light gray.

7. **SAVE** and **CLOSE** the report.

   CLOSE Access.

INTERNET READY

With your instructor's permission, download the Microsoft add-in for saving files in the PDF or XPS format. With Access open, click the Office button, point to Save As, and select Find add-ins for other file formats. Access Help will appear. Follow the instructions for downloading and installing the add-in. Then, open a chart from this lesson and save it as a PDF or XPS file.

Import and
Export Data

LESSON SKILL MATRIX

SKILLS	MATRIX SKILL	SKILL NUMBER
Importing Data	Import data	3.5
Importing Data from a Specific Source	Import data from a specific source	3.5.1
Linking to an External Data Source	Link to an external data source	3.5.2
Saving and Running Import Specifications	Save and run import specifications	3.5.3
Exporting Data	Export data	5.4
Exporting from a Table	Export from tables	5.4.1
Exporting from a Query	Export from queries	5.4.2
Saving and Running Export Specifications	Save and run export specifications	5.4.3

You are the human resources coordinator at Humongous Insurance, a private company dedicated to offering products that provide quality protection with value pricing for rural and low-income families, as well as senior citizens on fixed incomes. Your department has just begun to use Access, but you still receive data in different formats that must be merged with your Access databases. At times, you also want to distribute information that your manager prefers to view in a different format. In this lesson, you will learn how to import data, link to an external data source, and save and run import specifications. You will also learn how to export data from a table and from a query, as well as how to save and run export specifications.

KEY TERMS
delimited file
delimiter
fixed-width file
linked table
specification

■ SOFTWARE ORIENTATION

External Data Tab

The External Data tab contains commands that will be used to import and export data in various formats.

Figure 14-1

External Data tab

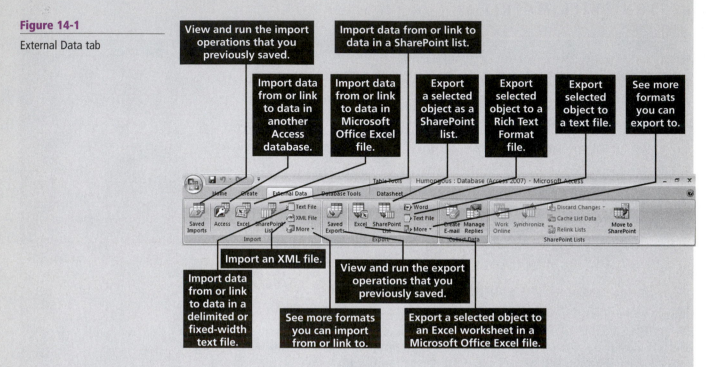

Use this figure as a reference throughout this lesson as well as the rest of this book.

■ Importing Data

THE BOTTOM LINE

To store data from an external source in Access, you can import the data into a new or existing database. After you run an import operation, you can save the import settings for reuse. You can also link to data from an external source without actually maintaining a copy of the data in the database.

Importing Data from a Specific Source

You can import data from a variety of sources into an Access database. When you import data, Access creates a copy of the data in a new or existing table without altering the source file.

⊙ **IMPORT DATA FROM EXCEL**

GET READY. Before you begin these steps, be sure to launch Microsoft Access.

1. **OPEN** the *Humongous* database from the data files for this lesson.
2. **SAVE** the database as *Humongous XXX* (where XXX is your initials).

3. On the External Data tab, in the Import group, click **Excel**. The Get External Data - Excel Spreadsheet dialog box appears, as shown in Figure 14-2.

Figure 14-2

Get External Data - Excel Spreadsheet dialog box

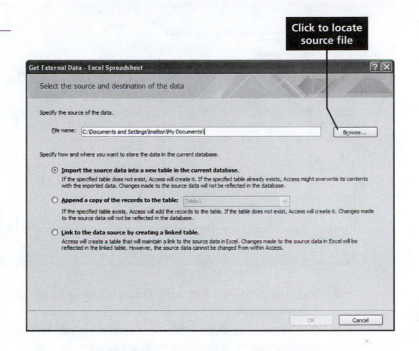

4. Click **Browse** to open the File Open dialog box.

 CD

The *New_Employees* spreadsheet file is available on the companion CD-ROM.

5. Use the Look in box to locate the **New_Employees** spreadsheet file and then click **Open**.

6. Click **Import the source data into a new table in the current database** and click **OK**. The Import Spreadsheet Wizard appears, as shown in Figure 14-3.

Figure 14-3

Import Spreadsheet Wizard, first screen

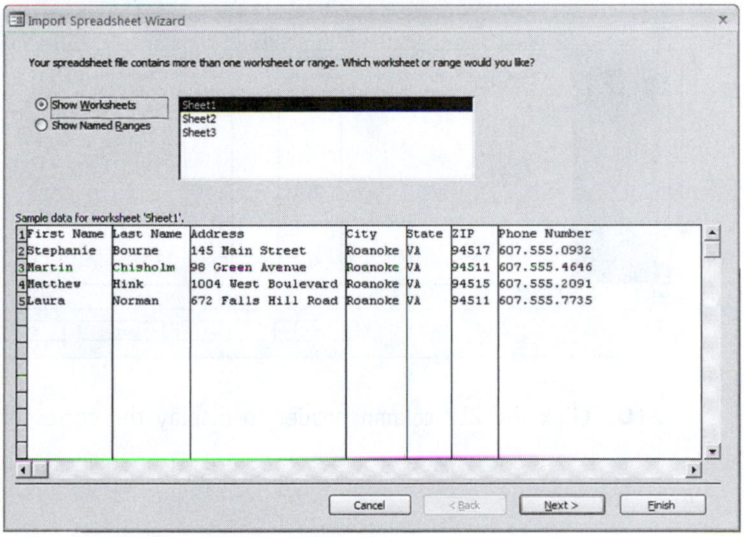

7. Click **Next >** to display the next screen, as shown in Figure 14-4.

Figure 14-4

Import Spreadsheet
Wizard, second screen

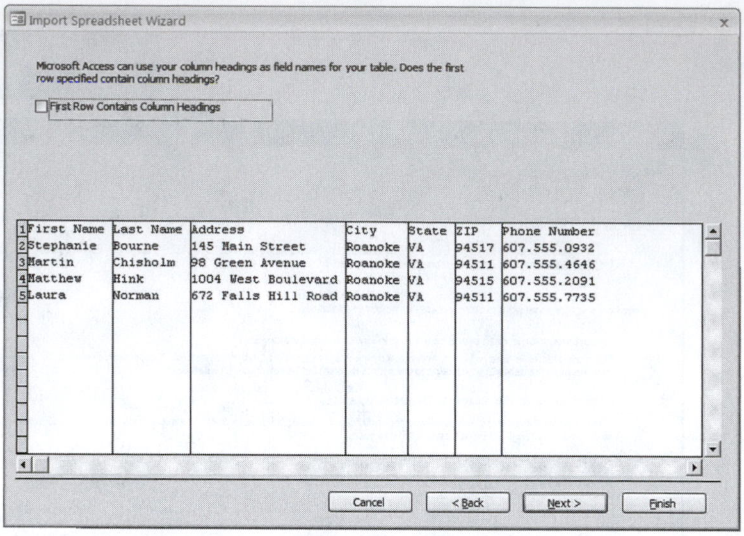

8. Click the **First Row Contains Column Headings** checkbox. Access uses these column headings to name the fields in the table.

9. Click **Next >** to display the next screen, shown in Figure 14-5, where the wizard prompts you to review the field properties.

Figure 14-5

Import Spreadsheet
Wizard, third screen

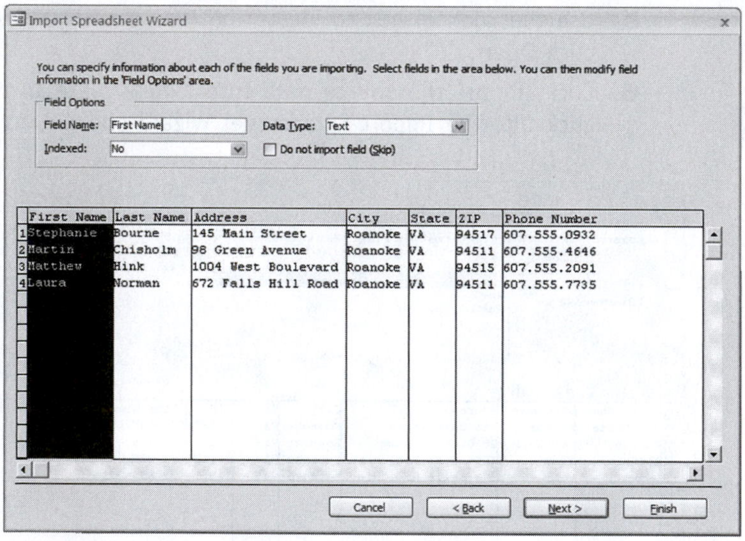

10. Click the **ZIP** column header to display the corresponding field properties.

11. Click the **Data Type down arrow** and click **Text**, as shown in Figure 14-6.

Figure 14-6

Change field properties

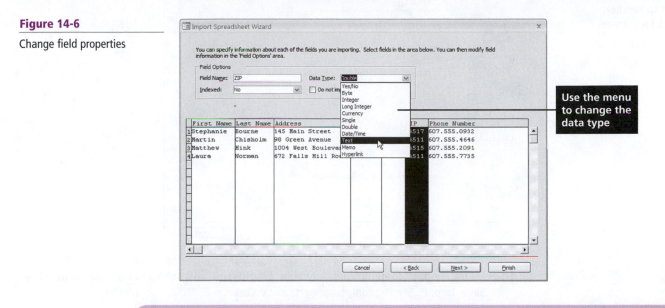

Use the menu to change the data type

TAKE NOTE

Access reviews the first eight rows in each column to suggest the data type for the corresponding field. If the column contains different types of values, the wizard suggests a data type that is compatible with all of the values in the column—usually the text data type. Although you can choose a different data type, values that are not compatible with the chosen data type will be ignored or converted incorrectly during the import process.

12. Click **Next >** to display the next screen, as shown in Figure 14-7.

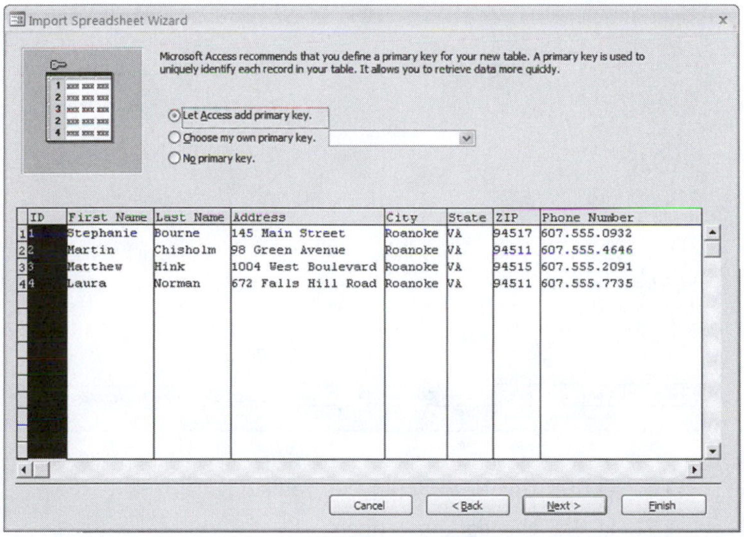

Figure 14-7

Define a primary key

13. Click **Next >** to let Access add the primary key. The final screen appears, as shown in Figure 14-8.

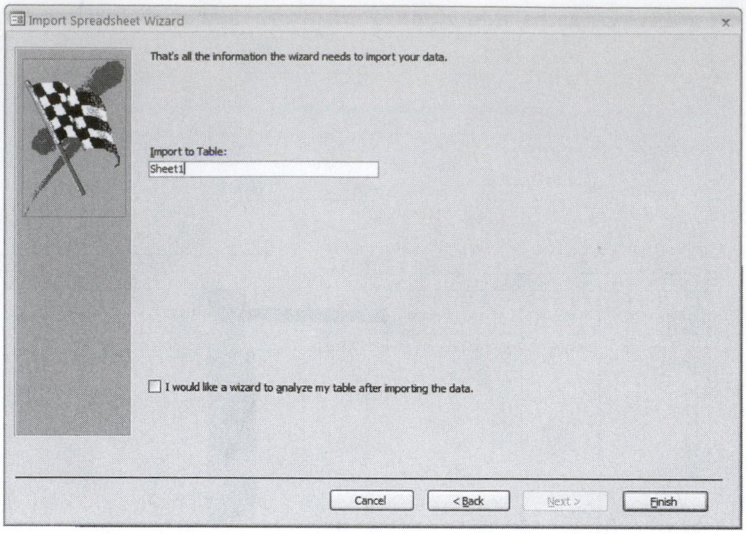

Figure 14-8

Import Spreadsheet
Wizard, final screen

14. In the Import to Table box, key **New Employees** and then click **Finish**. When the Save Import Steps prompt appears, click **Close**.

15. In the Navigation pane, double-click the **New Employees: Table** to open the new table with imported data, as shown in Figure 14-9.

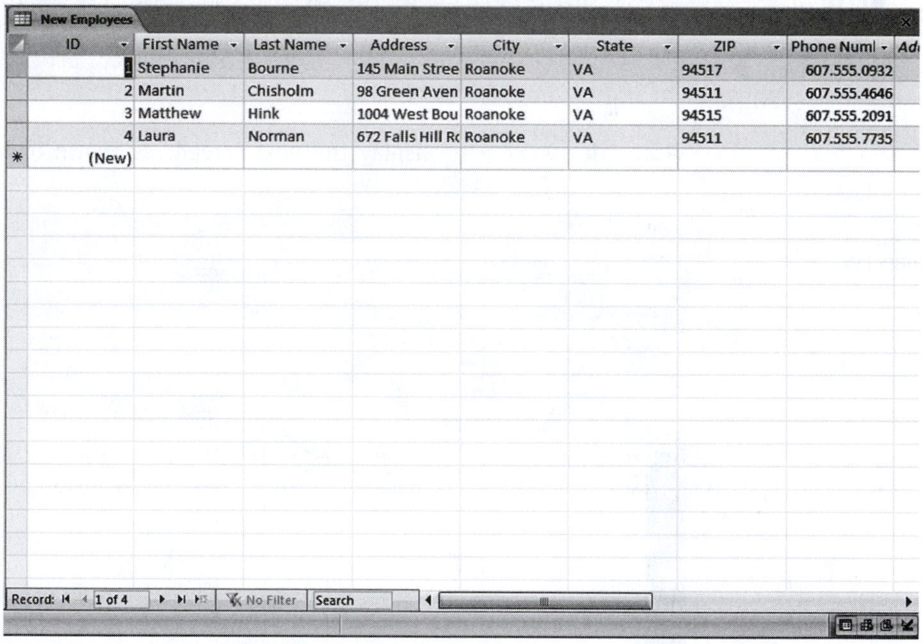

Figure 14-9

New table with imported data

ID	First Name	Last Name	Address	City	State	ZIP	Phone Numl	Ad
1	Stephanie	Bourne	145 Main Stree	Roanoke	VA	94517	607.555.0932	
2	Martin	Chisholm	98 Green Aven	Roanoke	VA	94511	607.555.4646	
3	Matthew	Hink	1004 West Bou	Roanoke	VA	94515	607.555.2091	
4	Laura	Norman	672 Falls Hill Rc	Roanoke	VA	94511	607.555.7735	
*	(New)							

Record: 1 of 4 — No Filter — Search

CERTIFICATION READY?
How do you import data from a specific source?
3.5.1

16. **CLOSE** the New Employees table.

17. **LEAVE** the database open.

PAUSE. LEAVE Access open to use in the next exercise.

In this activity, you learned how to import data from an Excel worksheet. You can also import data from other specific sources, such as a SharePoint list, a Word file, another Access database, or a text file. The same general process is used for importing data, regardless of the source. On the External Data tab, in the Import group, click the More button to see additional formats that you can import from or link to, as shown in Figure 14-10.

Figure 14-10

Import More menu

You can import only one worksheet at a time during an import operation. To import data from multiple worksheets, repeat the import operation for each worksheet.

To import data from Excel, first prepare the worksheet for an import operation. Locate the source file and select the worksheet that contains the data you want to import into Access.

Table 14-1

Source data elements

Review the source data and make any necessary modifications, as described in Table 14-1.

ELEMENT	DESCRIPTION
Number of columns	You cannot import more than 255 source columns, because Access does not support more than 255 fields in a table.
Skipping columns and rows	It is a good practice to include only the rows and columns that you want to import into the source worksheet or named range. Note that you cannot filter or skip rows during the import operation. If you choose to add the data to an existing table, then you cannot skip columns during the operation either.
Tabular format	Ensure that the cells are in tabular format. If the worksheet or named range includes merged cells, the contents of the cell are placed in the field that corresponds to the leftmost column, and the other fields are left blank.
Blank columns, rows, and cells	Delete all unnecessary blank columns and blank rows in the worksheet or range. If the worksheet or range contains blank cells, try to add the missing data. If you are planning to append the records to an existing table, ensure that the corresponding field in the table accepts null (missing or unknown) values. A field will accept null values if its Required field property is set to No and its ValidationRule property setting does not prevent null values.
Error values	If one or more cells in the worksheet or range contain error values, such as #NUM and #DIV, correct them before you start the import operation. If a source worksheet or range contains error values, Access places a null value in the corresponding fields in the table.
Data type	To avoid errors during importing, ensure that each source column contains the same type of data in every row. It is a good practice to format each source column in Excel and assign a specific data format to each column before you start the import operation, especially if a column includes values of different data types.
First row	If the first row in the worksheet or named range contains the names of the columns, you can specify that Access treat the data in the first row as field names during the import operation. If your source worksheet or range does not include the names, it is a good idea to add them to the source before you start the import operation. Note: If you plan to append the data to an existing table, ensure that the name of each column exactly matches the name of the corresponding field. If the name of a column is different from the name of the corresponding field in the table, the import operation will fail. To see the names of the fields, open the table in Design view in Access.

TROUBLE**SHOOTING** The worksheet should be closed before beginning the import operation. Keeping the source file open can result in data conversion errors.

Before you start the import operation, decide whether you want to store the data in a new or existing table. If you choose to store the data in a new table, Access creates a table and adds the imported data to this table. If a table with the specified name already exists, Access overwrites the contents of the table with the imported data. If you choose to add the data to an existing table, the rows in the Excel file are appended to the specified table.

Open the Access database where the imported data will be stored or create a blank database. On the External Data tab, in the Import group, click the Excel button to begin the import operation. After you specify where you want to store the data, the Import Spreadsheet Wizard leads you through the rest of the process.

TROUBLE**SHOOTING** After an import operation, you should review the contents and structure of the table to ensure that everything looks correct before you start using the table. If you see the message *An error occurred trying to import file*, the import operation failed. If the data imports and you find just a few missing values, you can add them directly to the table. However, if you find that entire columns or a large number of values are either missing or were not imported properly, use Access Help to troubleshoot the results and correct the problem in the source file. After you have corrected all known problems, repeat the import operation.

Linking to an External Data Source

By linking an Access database to data in another program, you can use the querying and reporting tools that Access provides without having to maintain a copy of the external data in your database.

➔ LINK TO AN EXTERNAL DATA SOURCE

USE the database that is open from the previous exercise.

1. On the External Data tab, in the Import group, click **Excel** to open the Get External Data - Excel Spreadsheet dialog box.
2. Click **Browse** to open the File Open dialog box.
3. Use the Look in box to locate the **Benefit_Providers** spreadsheet file and then click **Open**.
4. Click **Link to the data source by creating a linked table** and click **OK**. The Link Spreadsheet Wizard appears, as shown in Figure 14-11.

CD

The *Benefit_Providers* spreadsheet file is available on the companion CD-ROM.

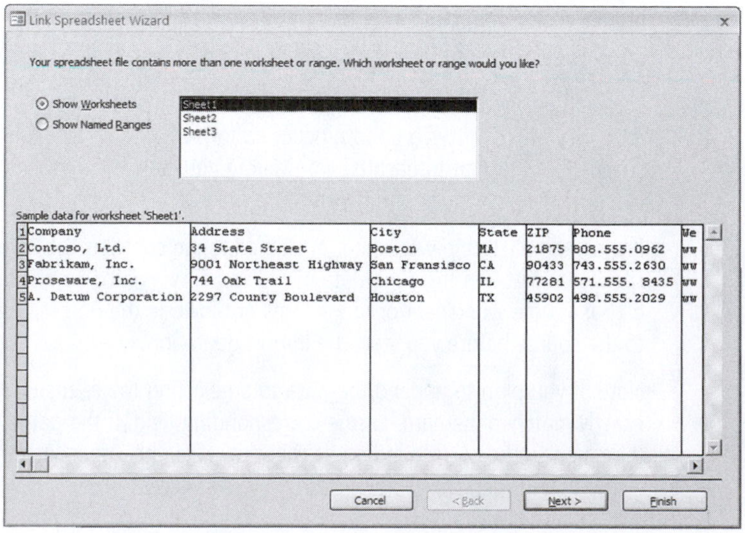

Figure 14-11

Link Spreadsheet Wizard, first screen

5. Click **Next >** to display the next screen.

6. Click the **First Row Contains Column Headings** checkbox, shown in Figure 14-12, to use the first row data as field headings in the table.

Figure 14-12

Link Spreadsheet Wizard, second screen

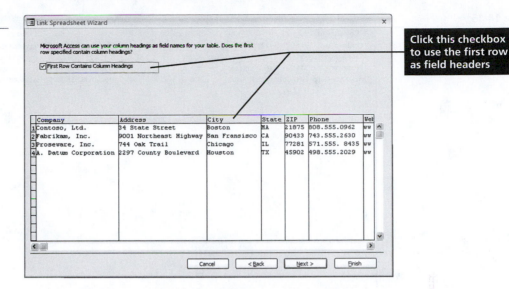

7. Click **Next >** to display the next screen.

8. In the Linked Table Name box, key **Benefit_Providers**, as shown in Figure 14-13.

Figure 14-13

Link Spreadsheet Wizard, final screen

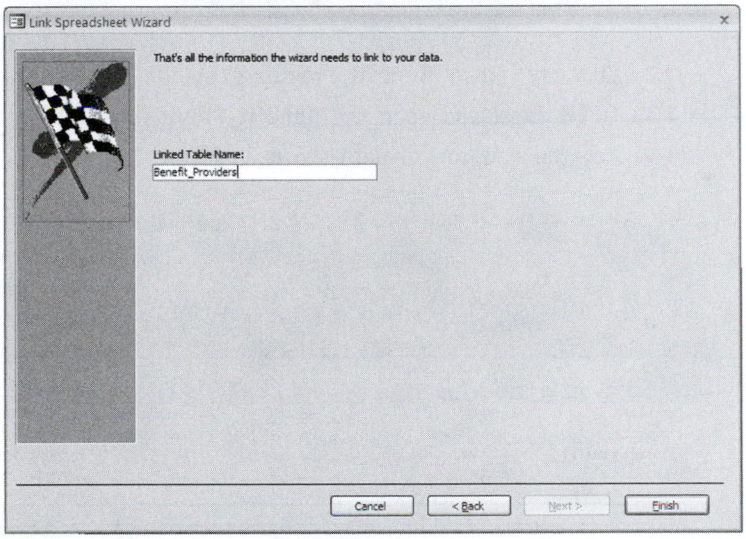

9. Click **Finish**. A Link Spreadsheet Wizard message appears, similar to the one shown in Figure 14-14.

Figure 14-14

Link Spreadsheet Wizard message

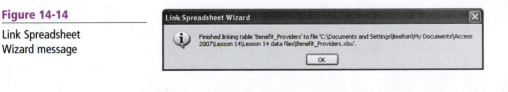

10. Click **OK**.

If the table with the name you specified already exists, you are asked if you want to overwrite the existing file. Click *Yes* if you want to overwrite the file; click *No* to specify a different filename.

11. In the Navigation pane, double-click **Benefit_Providers** to open the new linked table, shown in Figure 14-15. Notice that there is not an *Add New Field* column because the structure of a linked table cannot be changed.

Figure 14-15

New linked table

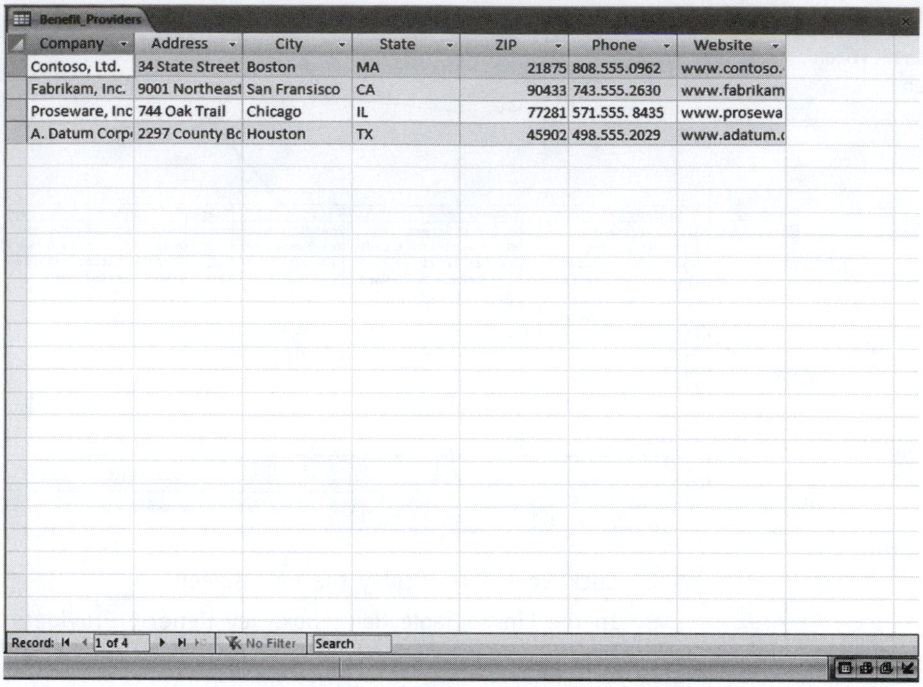

12. Click the **Close 'Benefit_Providers'** button to close the table.

13. **OPEN** Excel and open the **Benefit_Providers** spreadsheet.

14. Key the new row of data shown in Figure 14-16.

Figure 14-16

New Excel data

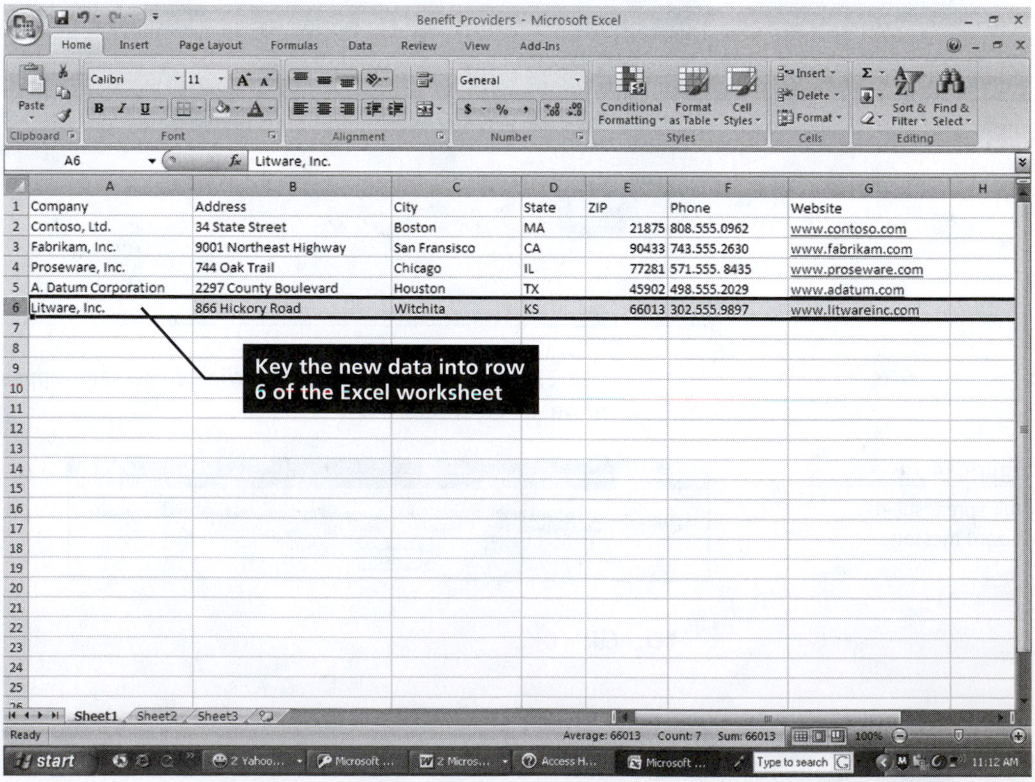

15. **SAVE** and **CLOSE** the spreadsheet.

16. **CLOSE** Excel.

17. In the Navigation pane of Access, double-click **Benefit_Providers** to open the linked table. Notice that the new row of data has been added, as shown in Figure 14-17.

Figure 14-17

New Excel data added to linked table

Company	Address	City	State	ZIP	Phone	Website
Contoso, Ltd.	34 State Street	Boston	MA	21875	808.555.0962	www.contoso.
Fabrikam, Inc.	9001 Northeast	San Fransisco	CA	90433	743.555.2630	www.fabrikam
Proseware, Inc	744 Oak Trail	Chicago	IL	77281	571.555. 8435	www.prosewa
A. Datum Corp	2297 County Bc	Houston	TX	45902	498.555.2029	www.adatum.c
Litware, Inc.	866 Hickory Ro	Witchita	KS	66013	302.555.9897	www.litwarein

New data appears in a linked Access table

Record: ◄ ◄ 1 of 5 ► ►► ☒ No Filter   Search

18. **CLOSE** the **Benefit_Providers** table.

19. **LEAVE** the database open.

PAUSE. LEAVE Access open to use in the next exercise.

In this activity, you linked an Access database to an Excel worksheet. You can also link to other external data sources, such as linking tables in another Access database (although you cannot link to queries, forms, or reports), HTML documents, or text files.

When you link to an Excel worksheet, Access creates a new table that is linked to the source cells, called a ***linked table***. The table shows the data in the source worksheet, but it doesn't actually store the data in the database. Any changes you make to the source cells in Excel appear in the linked table. However, you cannot edit the contents or structure of the corresponding table in Access. If you want to add, edit, or delete data, you must make the changes in the source file.

TAKE NOTE *

If you don't want to link to the entire worksheet, define a range that includes only the cells you want to link to. To create a named range, select the cells, right-click, and click Name a Range. In the New Name dialog box, key a name for the range and then click OK.

On the External Data tab, in the Import group, click the Excel button. When you choose to link to the source data by creating a linked table, the Link Spreadsheet Wizard leads you through the rest of the process. If the operation succeeds, Access displays the Finished linking table message. Open the linked table and review the fields and data to ensure that you see the correct data in all the fields. If you see error values or incorrect data, use Access Help to troubleshoot the source data and then try linking again.

Saving and Running Import Specifications

When you run an import wizard, you can save the settings you used as a specification so that you can repeat the operation at any time without having to provide any additional input.

 SAVE IMPORT SPECIFICATIONS

USE the database that is open from the previous exercise.

The *Applicants* text file is available on the companion CD-ROM.

1. On the External Data tab, in the Import group, click **Text File** to open the Get External Data - Text File dialog box.

2. Click **Browse** to open the File Open dialog box.

3. Use the Look in box to locate the **Applicants** text file and then click **Open**.

4. Click **Import the source data into a new table in the current database** and click **OK**. The Import Text Wizard appears, as shown in Figure 14-18.

Figure 14-18

Import Text Wizard, first screen

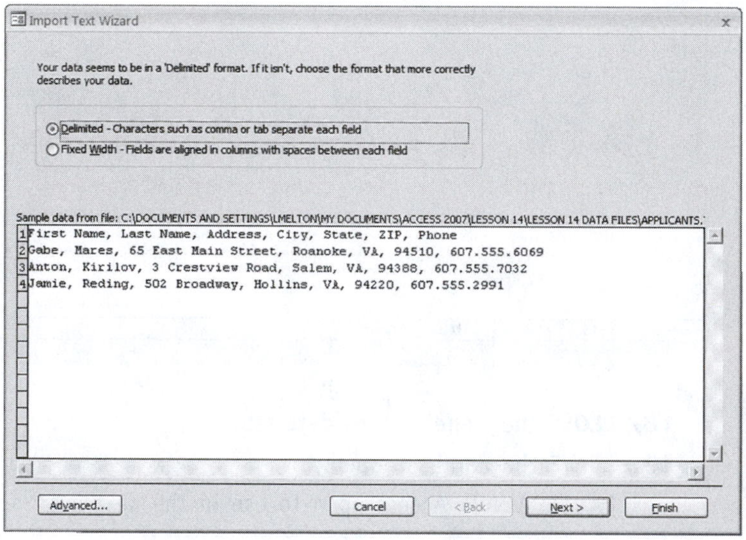

> **Import Text Wizard**
>
> Your data seems to be in a 'Delimited' format. If it isn't, choose the format that more correctly describes your data.
>
> ⊙ Delimited - Characters such as comma or tab separate each field
> ○ Fixed Width - Fields are aligned in columns with spaces between each field
>
> Sample data from file: C:\DOCUMENTS AND SETTINGS\LMELTON\MY DOCUMENTS\ACCESS 2007\LESSON 14\LESSON 14 DATA FILES\APPLICANTS.
> 1 First Name, Last Name, Address, City, State, ZIP, Phone
> 2 Gabe, Mares, 65 East Main Street, Roanoke, VA, 94510, 607.555.6069
> 3 Anton, Kirilov, 3 Crestview Road, Salem, VA, 94388, 607.555.7032
> 4 Jamie, Reding, 502 Broadway, Hollins, VA, 94220, 607.555.2991
>
> [Advanced...]   [Cancel] [< Back] [Next >] [Finish]

5. Click **Next >** to display the next screen, shown in Figure 14-19.

Figure 14-19

Import Text Wizard, second screen

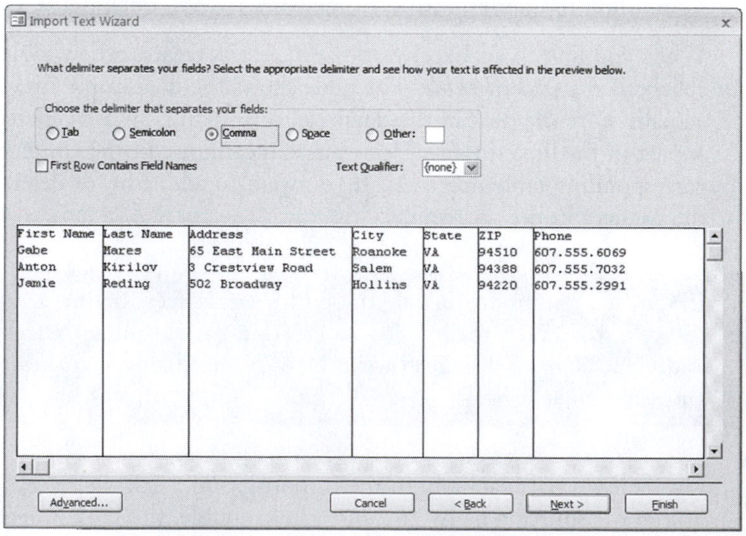

> **Import Text Wizard**
>
> What delimiter separates your fields? Select the appropriate delimiter and see how your text is affected in the preview below.
>
> Choose the delimiter that separates your fields:
> ○ Tab   ○ Semicolon   ⊙ Comma   ○ Space   ○ Other: [ ]
>
> ☐ First Row Contains Field Names   Text Qualifier: {none} ▾
>
> | First Name | Last Name | Address | City | State | ZIP | Phone |
> | Gabe | Mares | 65 East Main Street | Roanoke | VA | 94510 | 607.555.6069 |
> | Anton | Kirilov | 3 Crestview Road | Salem | VA | 94388 | 607.555.7032 |
> | Jamie | Reding | 502 Broadway | Hollins | VA | 94220 | 607.555.2991 |
>
> [Advanced...]   [Cancel] [< Back] [Next >] [Finish]

6. **Comma** should be selected as the delimiter. Click the **First Row Contains Field Names** checkbox to use the first row data as field headings in the table.

7. Click **Next >** to display the next screen, shown in Figure 14-20, where you can specify field information.

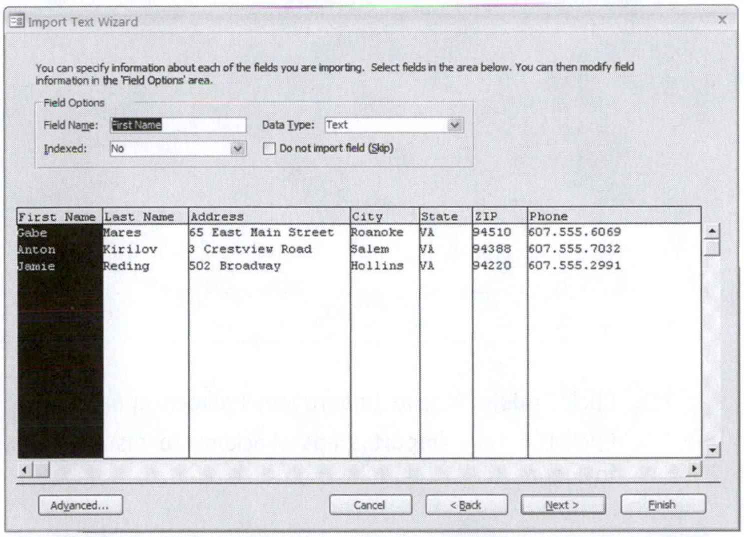

Figure 14-20

Import Text Wizard, third screen

8. Click **Next >** to display the next screen, shown in Figure 14-21, where you can define a primary key.

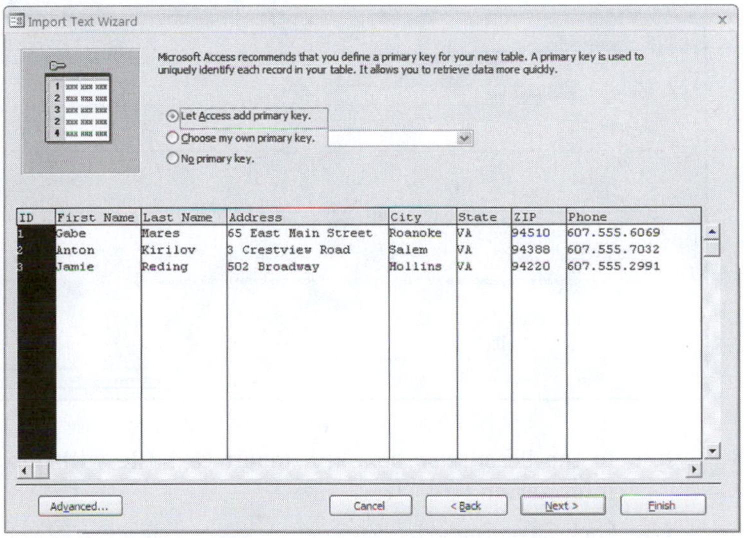

Figure 14-21

Import Text Wizard, fourth screen

9. Click **Next >** to display the final screen, shown in Figure 14-22.

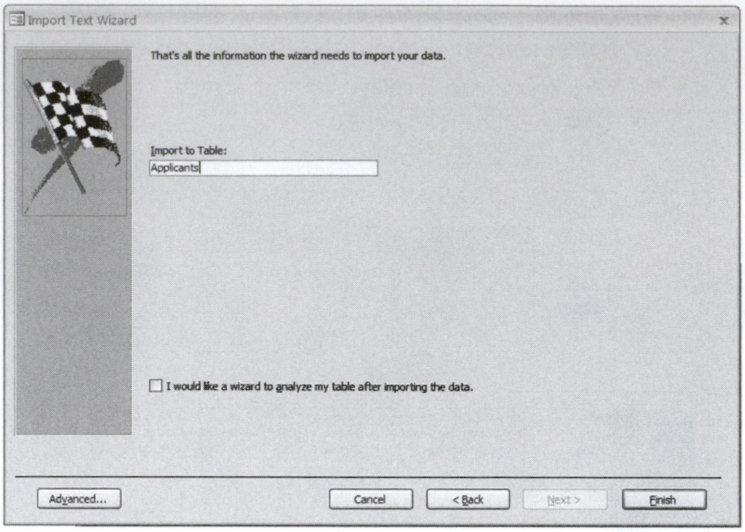

Figure 14-22

Import Text Wizard, final screen

10. Click **Finish**. A Save Import Steps screen appears.
11. Click the **Save import steps** checkbox to display the specification details, shown in Figure 14-23.

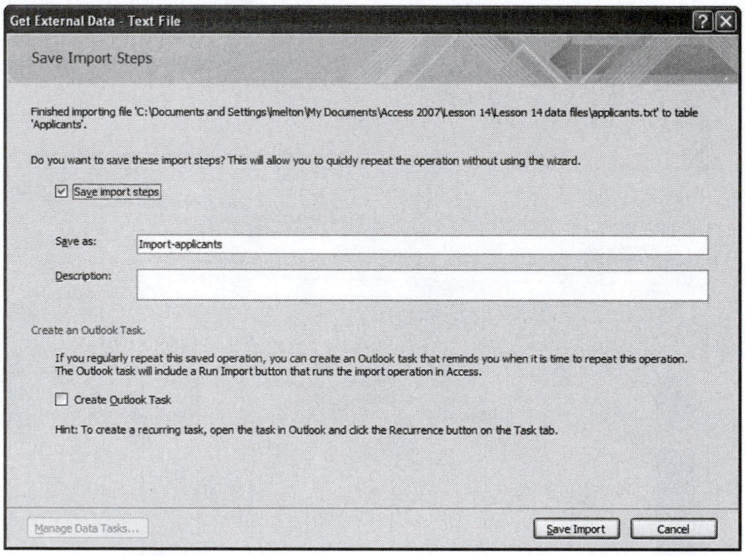

Figure 14-23

Save Import Steps screen

12. In the Description box, key **Import text file with job applicant contact information**.
13. Click **Save Import**.

14. In the Navigation pane, double-click the **Applicants: Table** to open the new table with imported data, as shown in Figure 14-24.

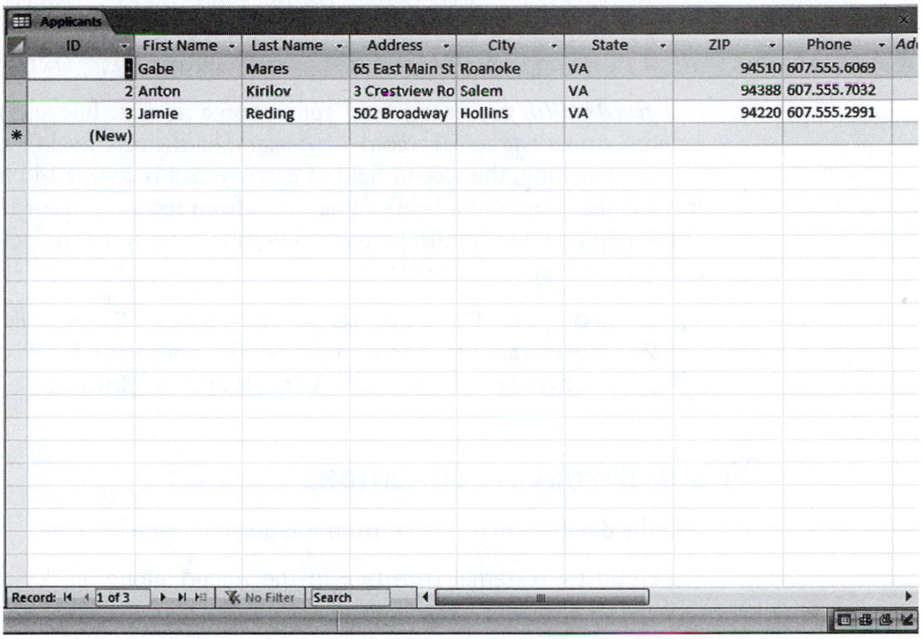

Figure 14-24

New table with imported data

ID	First Name	Last Name	Address	City	State	ZIP	Phone	Ad
1	Gabe	Mares	65 East Main St	Roanoke	VA	94510	607.555.6069	
2	Anton	Kirilov	3 Crestview Ro	Salem	VA	94388	607.555.7032	
3	Jamie	Reding	502 Broadway	Hollins	VA	94220	607.555.2991	
*	(New)							

Record: 1 of 3   No Filter   Search

15. CLOSE the Applicants table.

16. LEAVE the database open.

PAUSE. LEAVE Access open to use in the next exercise.

CERTIFICATION READY?
How do you save and run import specifications?
3.5.3

Saving the details of an import operation as a specification allows you to repeat the operation at any time. A *specification* contains all the information Access needs to repeat an import or export operation without user input. You can save an import or export operation involving any of the file formats supported in Access, but you cannot save the details of a linking operation or an operation where you export only a portion of a datasheet.

A specification is flexible. For example, you can change the name of the source file or the destination file before you run the specification again. This way, you can use a single specification with several different source or destination files.

To create an import specification, start the import operation and run the Import Wizard. After you click Finish, if Access successfully completes the operation, the Save Import Steps page appears in the wizard. Click Save import steps to save the details of the operation as a specification. Key a name and a description and then click Save Import to store the specification in the current database.

TAKE NOTE * If you regularly repeat this saved operation, you can create an Outlook task that reminds you when it is time to perform this operation by clicking the Create Outlook Task checkbox.

In this activity, you imported data from a text file. To use a text file as a source file for importing, the contents of the file must be organized in such a way that the Import Wizard can divide the contents into a set of records (rows) and each record into a collection of fields (columns). Two types of text files that are organized for importing are delimited files and fixed-width files.

In a *delimited file*, each record appears on a separate line and the fields are separated by a single character, called the delimiter. The *delimiter* can be any character that does not appear in the field values, such as a tab, semicolon, comma, space, and so on. The following is an example of comma-delimited text:

```
1, Fourth Coffee, Dana, Burnell, Sales Manager
2, Woodgrove Bank, Michael, Emmanuel, Vice President
3, Wingtip Toys, Billie, Murray, Owner
```

In a *fixed-width file*, each record appears on a separate line and the width of each field remains consistent across records. For example, the first field of every record is always 9 characters long, the second field of every record is always 14 characters long, and so on. If the actual length of a field's value varies from record to record, the values that fall short of the required width must be padded with trailing space characters. The following is an example of fixed-width text:

```
1   Fourth Coffee Dana   Burnell  Sales  Manager
2   Woodgrove Bank Michael Emmanuel Vice  President
3   Wingtip Toys  Billie  Murray   Owner
```

⊙ RUN IMPORT SPECIFICATIONS

USE the database that is open from the previous exercise.

1. On the External Data tab, in the Import group, click **Saved Imports** to open the Manage Data Tasks dialog box, shown in Figure 14-25.

Figure 14-25

Manage Data Tasks dialog box

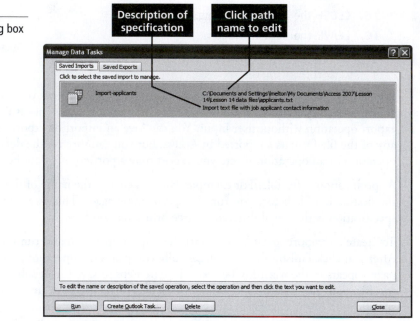

2. Click the file path and edit it by changing the source file name to **marchapplicants.txt**, as shown in Figure 14-26.

Figure 14-26

Manage Data Tasks dialog box

Edit file name

Manage Data Tasks

Saved Imports | Saved Exports

Click to select the saved import to manage.

Import-applicants

C:\Documents and Settings\melton\My Documents\Access 2007\Lesson 14
\Lesson 14 data files\marchapplicants.txt

Import text file with job applicant contact information

To edit the name or description of the saved operation, select the operation and then click the text you want to edit.

Run | Create Outlook Task... | Delete | Close

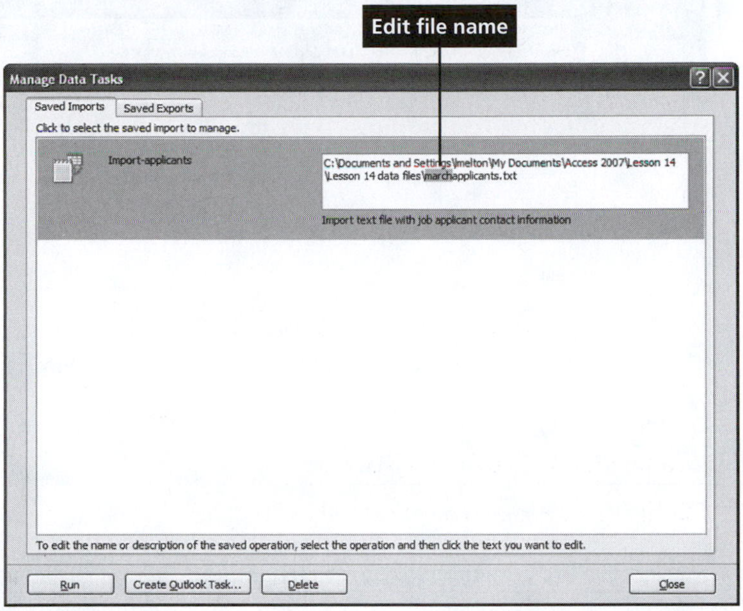

3. Click **Run**. A message appears asking if you want to overwrite the existing table, as shown in Figure 14-27.

Figure 14-27

Overwrite message

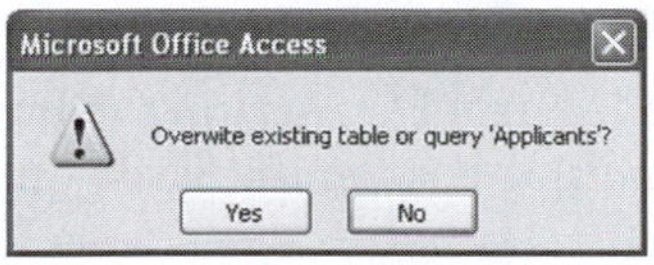

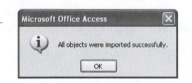

Microsoft Office Access

Overwrite existing table or query 'Applicants'?

Yes | No

4. Click **Yes**. A message appears confirming that all objects were successfully imported, as shown in Figure 14-28.

Figure 14-28

Successful import message

Microsoft Office Access

All objects were imported successfully.

OK

5. Click **OK**.

6. Click **Close** to close the Manage Data Tasks dialog box.

7. In the Navigation pane, double-click the **Applicants: Table** to open the table. The existing data has been replaced with new imported data, as shown in Figure 14-29.

Figure 14-29

Table with new imported data

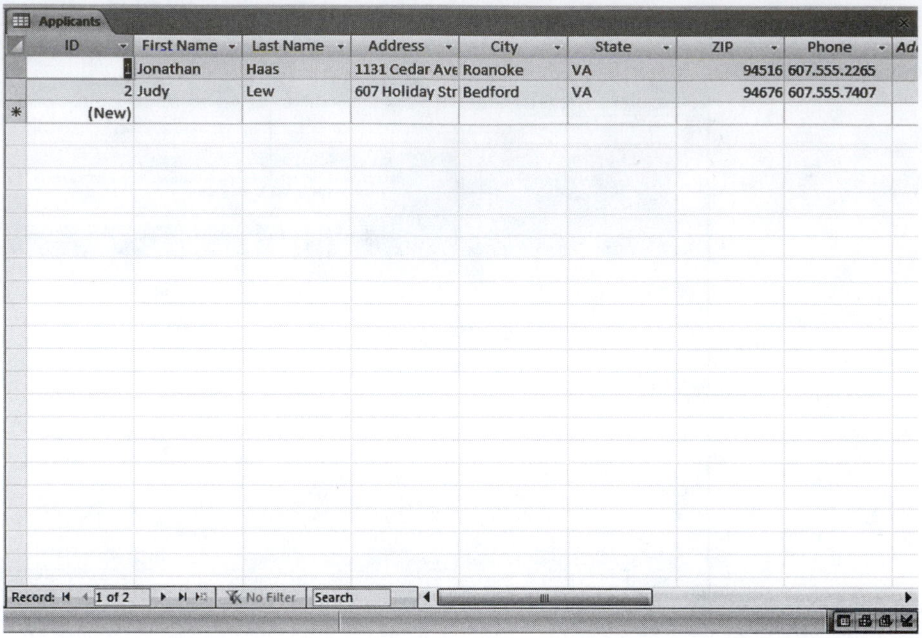

ID	First Name	Last Name	Address	City	State	ZIP	Phone	Ad
1	Jonathan	Haas	1131 Cedar Ave	Roanoke	VA	94516	607.555.2265	
2	Judy	Lew	607 Holiday Str	Bedford	VA	94676	607.555.7407	
*	(New)							

Record: I◄ ◄ 1 of 2 ► ►I ►⋇   ⨯ No Filter   Search   ◄   III   ►

CERTIFICATION READY?
How do you save and run import specifications?
3.5.3

8. CLOSE the Applicants table.

9. LEAVE the database open.

PAUSE. LEAVE Access open to use in the next exercise.

To run a saved specification, on the External Data tab, in the Imports group, click Saved Imports. In the Manage Data Tasks dialog box, on the Saved Imports tab, click the specification that you want to run.

If you want to change the source file, click the path of the file to edit it. The new file you specify must satisfy all the requirements essential for successfully completing the operation.

Before you click Run, make sure that the source and destination files exist, that the source data is ready for importing, and that the operation will not accidentally overwrite any data in your destination file. Do everything that you would do to ensure the success of a wizard-driven operation before running any saved specification and then click Run.

If you no longer need to perform a specific operation, you can delete the specification by selecting it and clicking Delete.

■ Exporting Data

↓ THE BOTTOM LINE
To use Access data in another program, you can use the various commands in the Export group to export the selected object in the format you want.

Exporting from a Table

When you export data from a table to Excel, Access creates a copy of the data and then stores the copy in an Excel worksheet.

➔ **EXPORTING FROM A TABLE**

USE the database that is open from the previous exercise.

1. In the Navigation pane, select the **Part-Time Employees: Table**.
2. On the External Data tab, in the Export group, click **Excel**. The Export - Excel Spreadsheet dialog box appears, as shown in Figure 14-30.

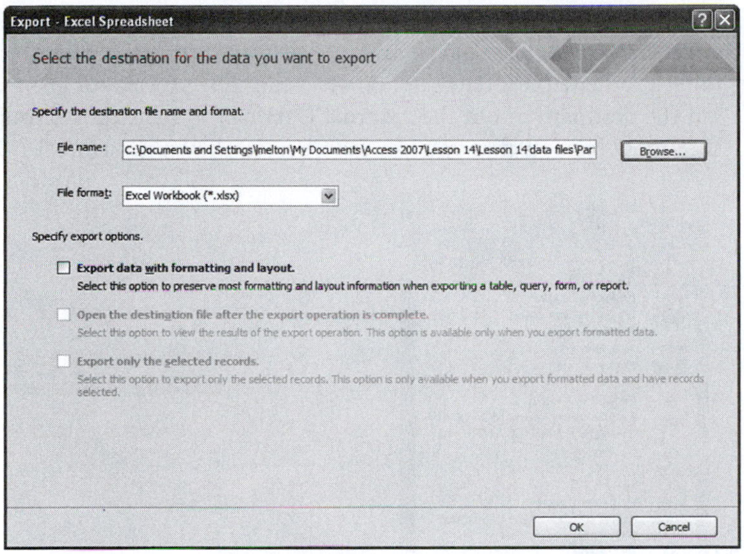

Figure 14-30

Export - Excel Spreadsheet dialog box

3. If you want to specify a different destination, click **Browse** to open the File Save dialog box, use the Save in box to choose a folder, and then click **Save**.
4. Click the **Export data with formatting and layout** checkbox and then click the **Open the destination file after the export operation is complete** checkbox.
5. Click **OK**. Excel opens and the new worksheet with exported data displayed, as shown in Figure 14-31.

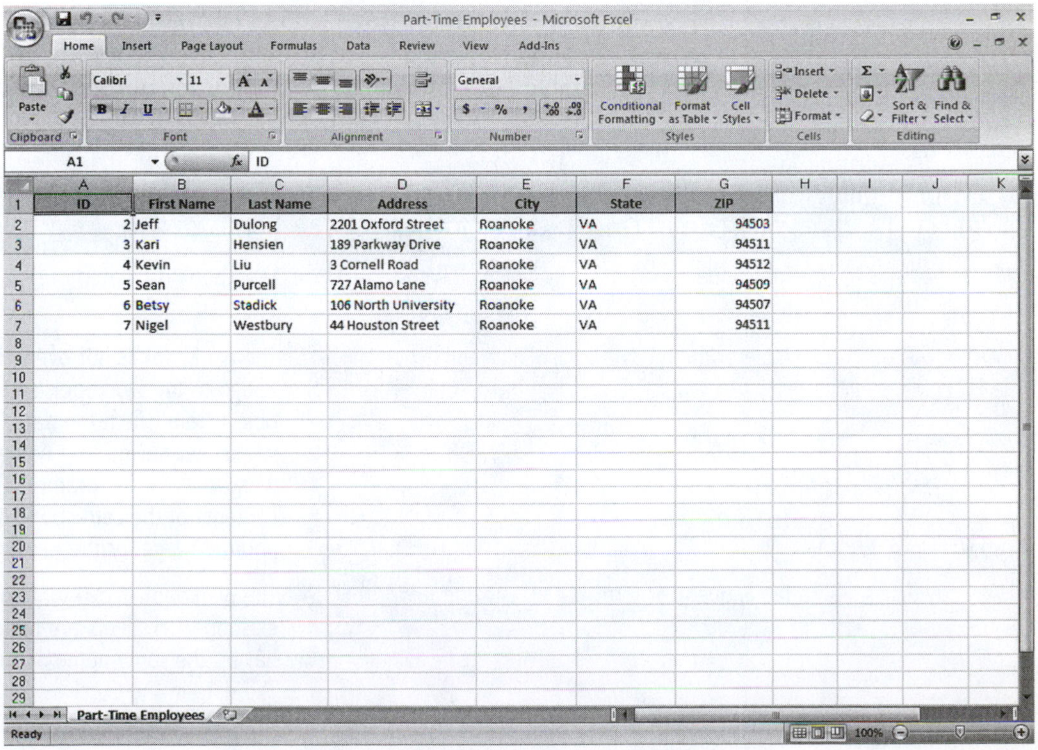

Figure 14-31

Excel worksheet with exported data

6. **CLOSE** the worksheet and **CLOSE** Excel.
7. Switch to Access.
8. On the Save Export Steps screen, click **Close**.
9. **LEAVE** the database open.

PAUSE. LEAVE Access open to use in the next exercise.

CERTIFICATION READY?
How do you export data from tables?
5.4.1

In this activity, you learned how to export data from an Access table to an Excel worksheet. You can also export data to other destinations, such as a SharePoint list, a Rich Text Format file, another Access database, or a text file. The process for exporting data is similar, regardless of the destination. On the External Data tab, in the Export group, click the More button to see more formats that you can export to, as shown in Figure 14-32.

Figure 14-32
Export More menu

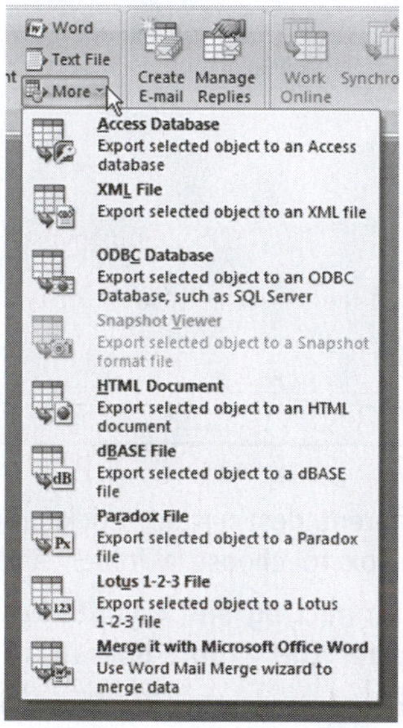

Open the Access database and select the table in the Navigation pane that contains the data you want to export. On the External Data tab, in the Export group, click the Excel button to begin the export operation. Access prompts you to specify the name of the destination workbook. Table 14-2 summarizes the options for creating or overwriting a workbook.

Table 14-2
Destination workbook options

Destination Workbook	Source Object	Data To Be Exported	Result
Does not exist	Table, query, or form	With or without formatting	Workbook is created during the export operation.
Already exists	Table or query	Without formatting	The workbook is not overwritten. A new worksheet is added to the workbook and is given the name of the object from which the data is being exported. If a worksheet having that name already exists in the workbook, Access prompts you to either replace the contents of the corresponding worksheet or specify another name for the new sheet.
Already exists	Table, query, or form	With formatting	The workbook is overwritten by the exported data. All existing worksheets are removed, and a new worksheet having the same name as the exported object is created. The data in the Excel worksheet inherits the format settings of the source object.

If the source object is a table or a query, decide whether you want to export the data with or without its formatting. If you choose without formatting, all fields and records in the underlying object are exported and the Format property settings are ignored during the operation. If you choose with formatting, only the fields and records displayed in the current view are exported and the Format property settings are respected.

You can export a table, query, or form to Excel. You can only export one database object in a single export operation. However, you can merge the data in multiple worksheets in Excel after completing the individual export operations. The data is always added in a new worksheet. You cannot append the data to an existing worksheet.

Exporting from a Query

> You can export data from an Access query to a variety of formats, just as you can export data from an Access table.

⊕ EXPORT FROM A QUERY

USE the database that is open from the previous exercise.

1. In the Navigation pane, select the **Part-Time Employees Query**.

2. On the External Data tab, in the Export group, click **Word**. The Export - RTF File dialog box appears, as shown in Figure 14-33.

Figure 14-33

Export - RTF File dialog box

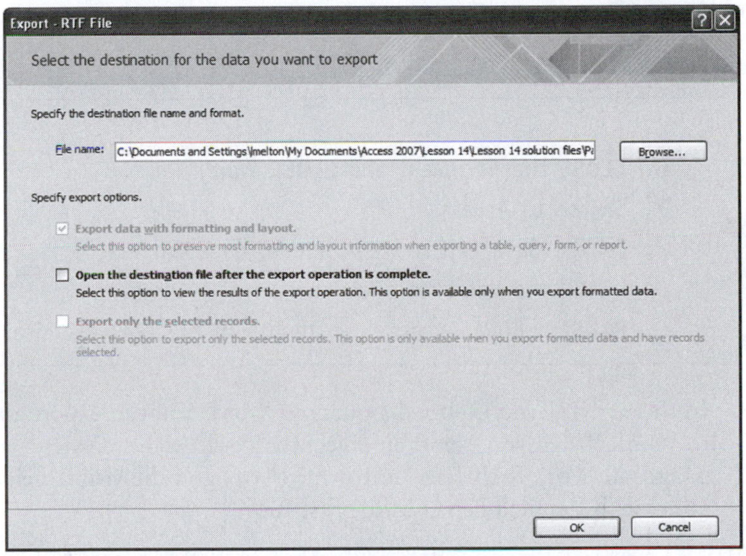

3. If you want to specify a different destination, click **Browse** to open the File Save dialog box, use the Save in box to choose a folder, and then click **Save**.

4. Click the **Open the destination file after the export operation is complete** checkbox.

5. Click **OK**. Word opens and the new document with exported data is displayed, as shown in Figure 14-34.

Figure 14-34

Word document with exported data

First Name	Last Name	Address	City	State	ZIP
Jeff	Dulong	2201 Oxford Street	Roanoke	VA	94503
Kari	Hensien	189 Parkway Drive	Roanoke	VA	94511
Kevin	Liu	3 Cornell Road	Roanoke	VA	94512
Sean	Purcell	727 Alamo Lane	Roanoke	VA	94509
Betsy	Stadick	106 North University	Roanoke	VA	94507
Nigel	Westbury	44 Houston Street	Roanoke	VA	94511

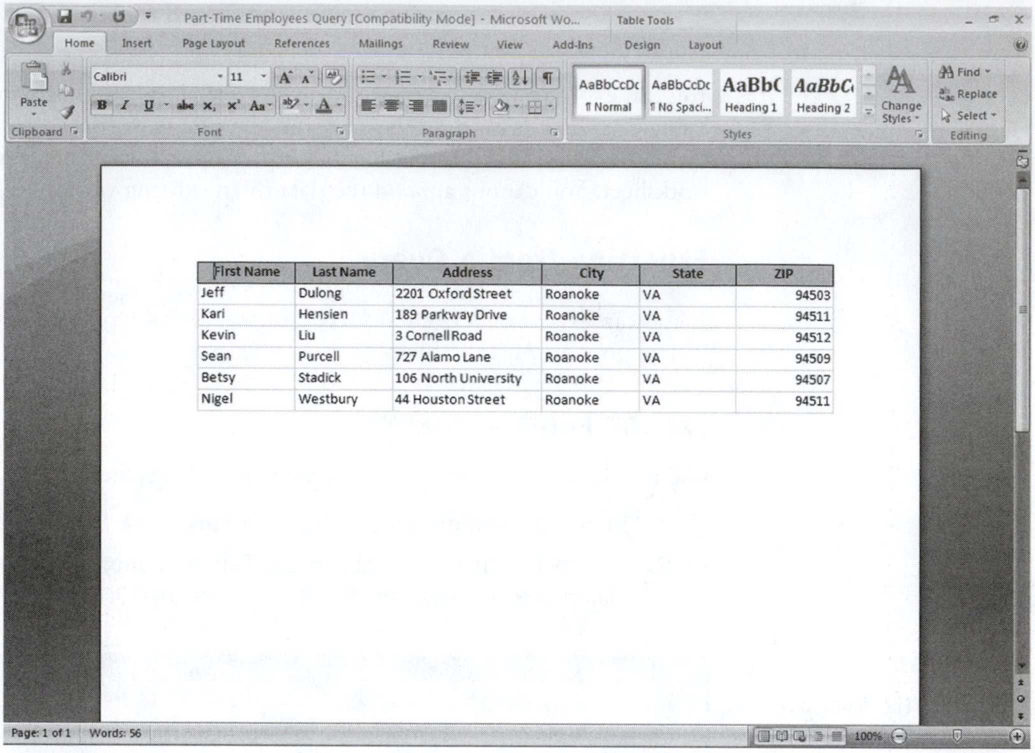

6. **CLOSE** the document and **CLOSE** Word.

7. Switch to Access.

8. On the Save Export Steps screen, click **Close**.

9. **LEAVE** the database open.

PAUSE. LEAVE Access open to use in the next exercise.

CERTIFICATION READY?

How do you export data from queries?

5.4.2

In this activity, you exported a query to Word. You can export a table, query, form, or report to Word. When you export an object to Word, Access creates a copy of the object's data in a Microsoft Word Rich Text Format file (*.rtf) and the visible fields and records appear as a table, with the field names in the first row.

TAKE NOTE*

Pictures or attachments that are part of the source data are not exported to Word. Expressions are not exported either, but the results are.

When you export from Access to a Word document, the Export Wizard always exports formatted data and the data is always exported into a new Word file. You cannot append data to an existing Word document.

In the Navigation pane, select the query that contains the data you want to export. On the External Data tab, in the Export group, click Word. In the Export Wizard, specify the name of the destination file. If you want to view the Word document after the export operation is complete, select the Open the destination file after the export operation is complete checkbox.

Saving and Running Export Specifications

When you perform an export operation, you can save the details for future use so you can repeat the operation at a later time without having to walk through the steps in the wizard each time. You can even schedule the export operation to run automatically at specified intervals by creating an Outlook task.

SAVE EXPORT SPECIFICATIONS

USE the database that is open from the previous exercise.

1. In the Navigation pane, select the **New Employees: Table**.
2. On the External Data tab, in the Export group, click **Text File**. The Export - Text File dialog box appears, as shown in Figure 14-35.

Figure 14-35

Export - Text File dialog box

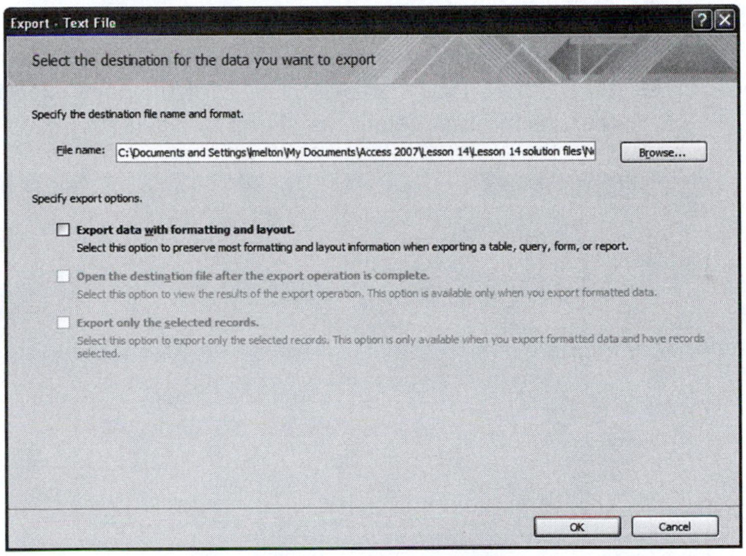

3. If you want to specify a different destination, click **Browse** to open the File Save dialog box, use the Save in box to choose a folder, and then click **Save**.
4. Click the **Export data with formatting and layout** checkbox and then click the **Open the destination file after the export operation is complete** checkbox.
5. Click **OK**. The Encode 'New Employees' As dialog box is displayed, as shown in Figure 14-36.

Figure 14-36

Encode 'New Employees' As dialog box

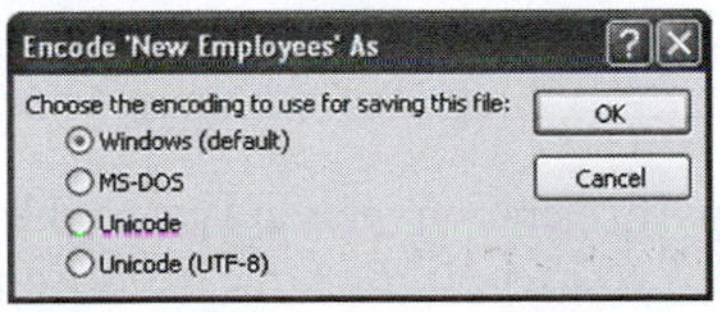

6. **Windows (default)** should be selected. Click **OK**. Notepad opens and the new file with exported data is displayed, as shown in Figure 14-37.

Figure 14-37

Notepad with exported data

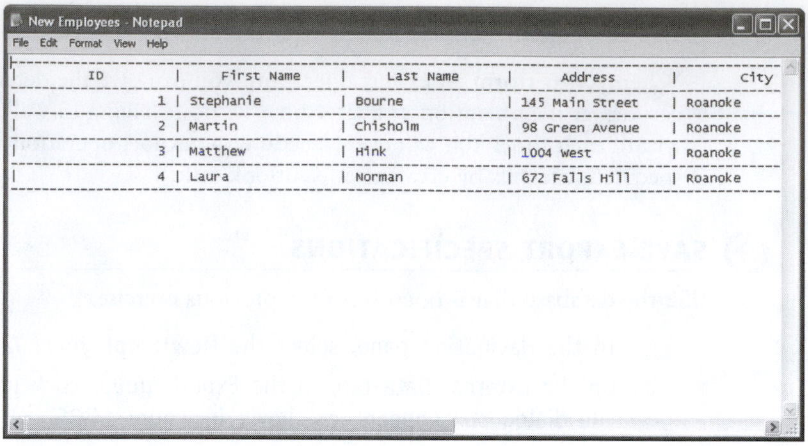

7. **CLOSE** Notepad.

8. Switch to Access.

9. On the Save Export Steps screen, click the **Save export steps** checkbox to display the specification details, as shown in Figure 14-38.

Figure 14-38

Save Export Steps screen

10. In the Description box, key **Export new employee information to a text file**.

11. Click **Save Export**.

12. **LEAVE** the database open.

PAUSE. **LEAVE** Access open to use in the next exercise.

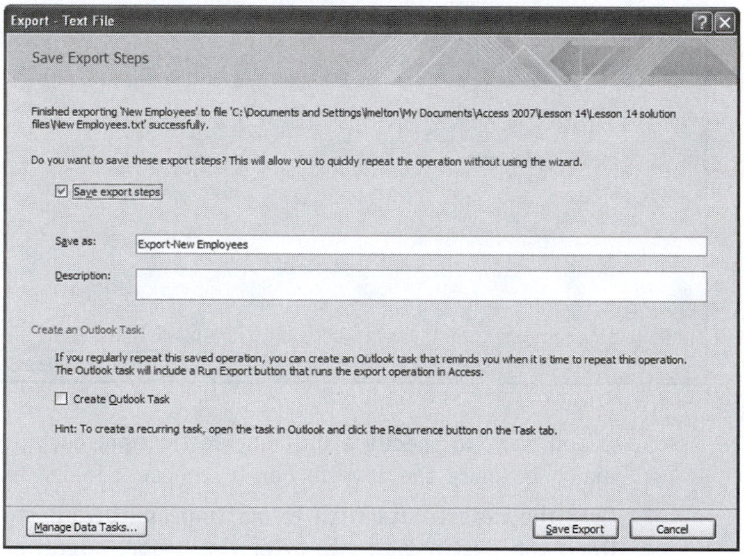

CERTIFICATION READY?
How do you save and run export specifications?
5.4.3

After you have performed an export operation, you are given the opportunity to save it for future use. Saving the details helps you repeat the same export operation in the future without having to step through the wizard each time.

In the Save as box, type a name for the export specification. Optionally, type a description in the Description box. If you want to perform the operation at fixed intervals, such as weekly or monthly, select the Create Outlook Task checkbox. Doing this creates an Outlook task that lets you run the specification by clicking a button.

➔ RUN EXPORT SPECIFICATIONS

USE the database that is open from the previous exercise.

1. In the Navigation pane, double-click the **New Employees: Table** to open it.

2. Add another record with the following information:

First Name: **Rachel**

Last Name: **Valdez**

Address: **39 Vista Drive**

City: **Roanoke**

State: **VA**

ZIP: **94510**

Phone Number: **607.555.1218**

3. Click the **Close 'New Employees'** button to close the table.

4. On the External Data tab, in the Export group, click **Saved Exports** to open the Manage Data Tasks dialog box, shown in Figure 14-39.

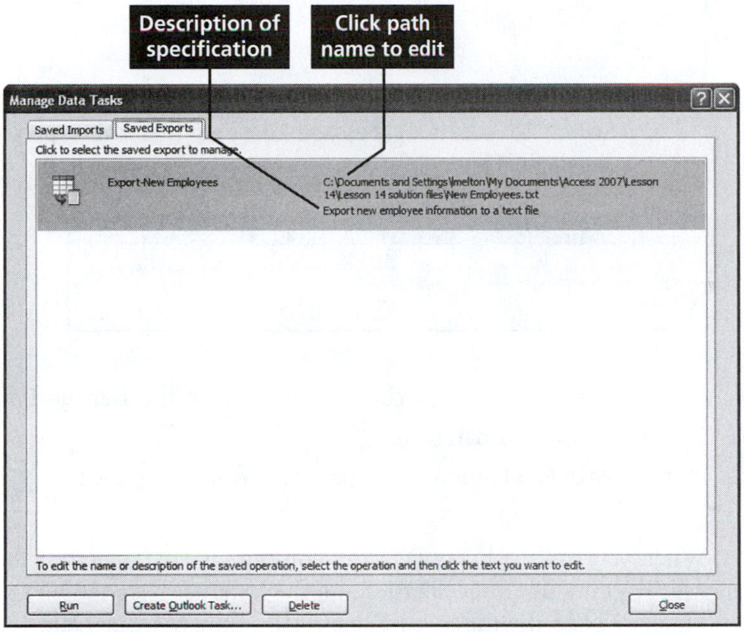

Figure 14-39

Manage Data Tasks dialog box

Description of specification

Click path name to edit

Manage Data Tasks

| Saved Imports | Saved Exports |

Click to select the saved export to manage.

Export-New Employees   C:\Documents and Settings\melton\My Documents\Access 2007\Lesson 14\Lesson 14 solution files\New Employees.txt
Export new employee information to a text file

To edit the name or description of the saved operation, select the operation and then click the text you want to edit.

Run   Create Outlook Task...   Delete   Close

5. Click the file path and edit it by changing the destination file name to **New Employees 2.txt**, as shown in Figure 14-40.

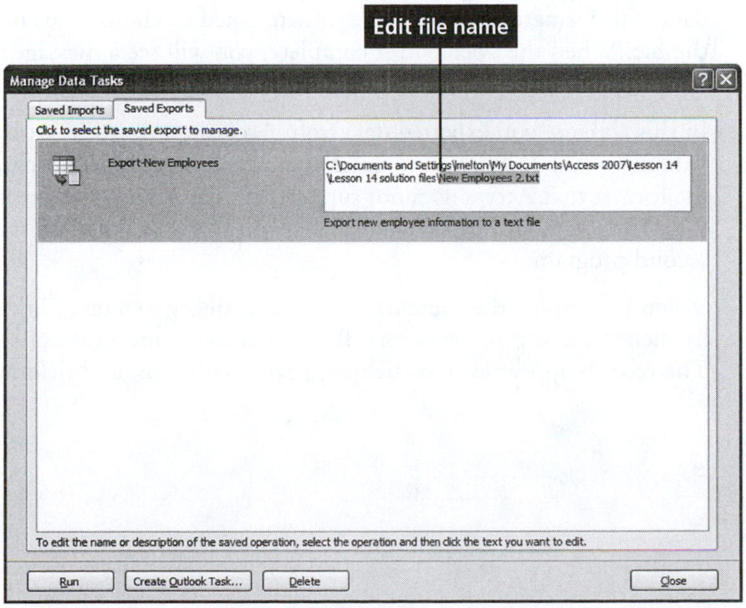

Figure 14-40

Edit destination file

Edit file name

Manage Data Tasks

| Saved Imports | Saved Exports |

Click to select the saved export to manage.

Export-New Employees   C:\Documents and Settings\melton\My Documents\Access 2007\Lesson 14\Lesson 14 solution files\New Employees 2.txt

Export new employee information to a text file

To edit the name or description of the saved operation, select the operation and then click the text you want to edit.

Run   Create Outlook Task...   Delete   Close

6. Click **Run**. Notepad opens and the new file with exported data is displayed, as shown in Figure 14-41.

Figure 14-41

Notepad with exported data

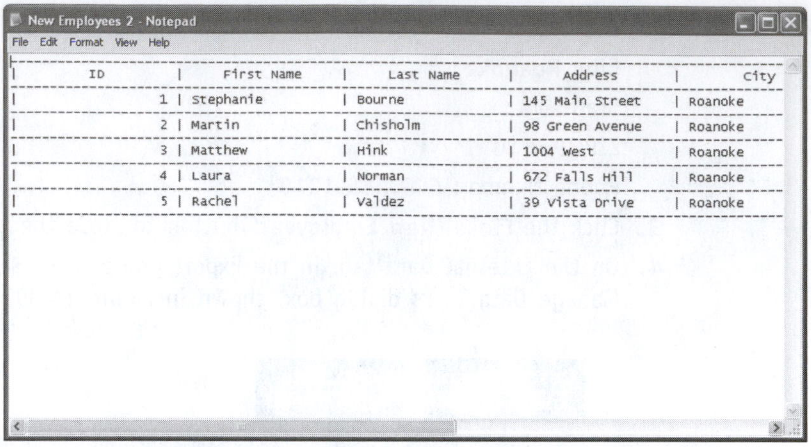

7. Switch to Access. A message confirms that the export operation was successful, as shown in Figure 14-42.

Figure 14-42

Successful export operation message

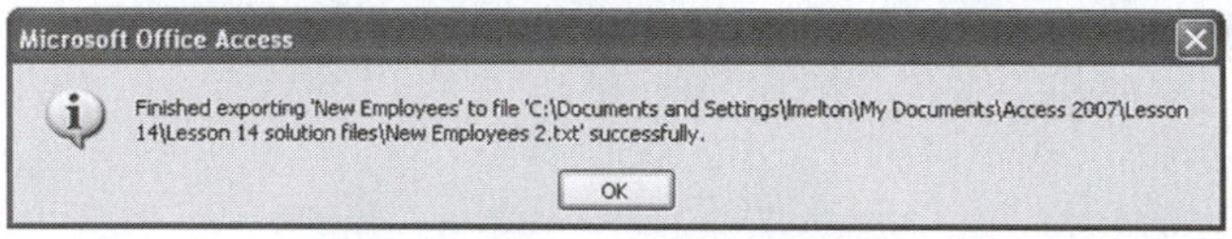

CERTIFICATION READY?
How do you save and run export specifications?
5.4.3

8. Click **OK** and then click **Close** to close the Manage Data Tasks dialog box.
9. **CLOSE** the database.

PAUSE. LEAVE Access open to use in the projects.

When you run the Export Wizard, you can save the operation as a specification for future use. To run a saved specification, on the External Data tab, in the Imports group, click Saved Exports. Then use the Saved Exports tab of the Manage Data Tasks dialog box to view and manage export specifications that you have created for the current database.

You can change the name of the specification, its description, and the path and file name of the destination file by clicking and making changes in the text box and then pressing Enter. Repeat an operation by clicking the specification and then clicking Run. If you are exporting data with formatting and layout, you are asked to choose the encoding to be used for saving the file. When the operation is complete, you will see a message that communicates the status of the operation.

In this activity, you exported data from Access to a text file. Although you can export Access data in various formats, sometimes you might need to export data to a program that uses a file format that Access does not support. In that case, if the destination program can use text (*.txt) files, you can export your data in that format and open the resulting file with the second program.

When you export the contents of a table or query to a text file with formatting and layout, hyphens (-) and pipe characters (|) are used to organize the content in a grid in the text file. The records appear as rows, fields appear as columns, and field names appear in the first row.

When exporting without formatting or layout, the Export Wizard gives you the option of creating a delimited file or a fixed-width file, as shown in Figure 14-43.

Figure 14-43

Export Wizard text file options

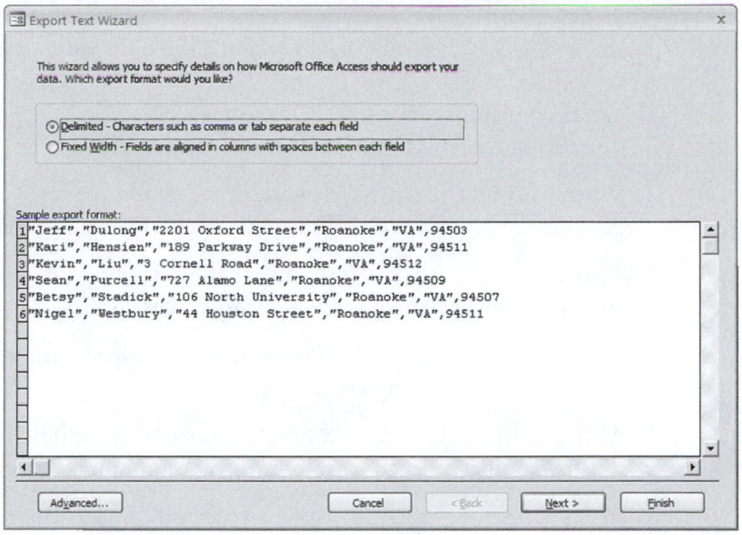

```
Export Text Wizard                                                          x

This wizard allows you to specify details on how Microsoft Office Access should export your
data. Which export format would you like?

  ⊙ Delimited - Characters such as comma or tab separate each field
  ○ Fixed Width - Fields are aligned in columns with spaces between each field

Sample export format:
1 "Jeff","Dulong","2201 Oxford Street","Roanoke","VA",94503
2 "Kari","Hensien","189 Parkway Drive","Roanoke","VA",94511
3 "Kevin","Liu","3 Cornell Road","Roanoke","VA",94512
4 "Sean","Purcell","727 Alamo Lane","Roanoke","VA",94509
5 "Betsy","Stadick","106 North University","Roanoke","VA",94507
6 "Nigel","Westbury","44 Houston Street","Roanoke","VA",94511


    Advanced...            Cancel    < Back    Next >    Finish
```

The choice you make usually depends on the system that works with the exported files. If users need to look at the data, a fixed-width file can be much easier to read than a delimited file.

SUMMARY SKILL MATRIX

IN THIS LESSON YOU LEARNED	MATRIX SKILL	SKILL NUMBER
To import data	Import data	3.5
To import data from a specific source	Import data from a specific source	3.5.1
To link to an external data source	Link to an external data source	3.5.2
To save and run import specifications	Save and run import specifications	3.5.3
To export data	Export data	5.4
To export from a table	Export from tables	5.4.1
To export from a query	Export from queries	5.4.2
To save and run export specifications	Save and run export specifications	5.4.3

■ Knowledge Assessment

Fill in the Blank

Complete the following sentences by writing the correct word or words in the blanks provided.

1. When you import data, Access creates a(n) _____ of the data in a new or existing table without altering the source file.

2. When you link to an Excel worksheet, Access creates a new table, called a(n) _____, that is linked to the source cells.

3. A(n) _____ contains all the information Access needs to repeat an import or export operation without user input.

4. In a(n) _____ file, each record appears on a separate line and the fields are separated by a single character.

5. A(n) _____ is any character that separates fields and does not appear in the field values, such as a tab, semicolon, comma, or space.

6. In a(n) _____ file, each record appears on a separate line and the width of each field remains consistent across records.

7. You can schedule an import or export operation to run automatically at specified intervals by creating a(n) _____ task.

8. When you export the content of a table or query to a text file with _____ and _____, hyphens (-) and pipe characters (|) are used to organize the content in a grid.

9. When exporting to Excel, the data is always added in a new _____.

10. To repeat an import or export operation, click the specification and then click _____.

Multiple Choice

Select the best response for the following statements or questions.

1. Which tab contains options for importing or exporting data?
   a. Manage Data
   b. Database Tools
   c. External Data
   d. Create

2. Before beginning an import operation, the source file should be
   a. open.
   b. closed.
   c. copied.
   d. backed up.

3. If you want to add, edit, or delete data in a linked table, you must make the changes in the
   a. first row of data.
   b. Access object.
   c. field headers.
   d. source file.

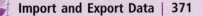

4. You can save an import or export operation involving any of the file formats supported in Access, but you cannot save the details of a

    a. linking operation.

    b. text file import operation.

    c. query export operation.

    d. fixed-width file.

5. The following is an example of what kind of text?

    1, Fourth Coffee, Dana, Burnell, Sales Manager

    a. HTML

    b. linked

    c. fixed-width

    d. comma-delimited

6. How many database objects can you export in a single export operation?

    a. one

    b. two

    c. three

    d. unlimited

7. When you export an object to Word, Access creates what type of file?

    a. MS-DOS Text

    b. Rich Text Format

    c. HTML

    d. linked

8. If you choose to store imported data in a new table, Access

    a. links the new table to an existing table.

    b. overwrites the data in the existing table.

    c. creates a table and adds the imported data to this table.

    d. gives you an error message.

9. What is an advantage of linking an Access database to data in another program?

    a. maintaining a copy of the external data in Access

    b. being able to use Access querying and reporting tools

    c. being able to edit the linked table in Access

    d. easily being able to change the structure of the Access table

10. Which dialog box allows you to manage saved import and export specifications?

    a. External Data

    b. Saved Specifications

    c. Import/Export Tasks

    d. Manage Data Tasks

■ Competency Assessment

Project 14-1: Import Data from Excel

You are the purchasing manager for Coho Wine Club and an associate has provided some information about champagne and sparkling wines that are being considered for the monthly wine club. The data is in an Excel worksheet and will need to be imported into the database.

GET READY. Launch Access if it is not already running.

🔘 **CD**

The *Coho Wine Club* database file is available on the companion CD-ROM.

1. **OPEN** the *Coho Wine Club* database from the data files for this lesson.
2. **SAVE** the database as *Coho Wine Club XXX* (where XXX is your initials).
3. On the External Data tab, in the Import group, click **Excel** to display the Get External Data - Excel Spreadsheet dialog box.
4. Click **Browse** to open the File Open dialog box.
5. Use the Look in box to locate the **Champagne_Sparkling** spreadsheet file and then click **Open**.
6. Click **Import the source data into a new table in the current database** and click **OK**. The Import Spreadsheet Wizard appears.
7. Click **Next >** to display the next screen.
8. Click the **First Row Contains Column Headings** checkbox.
9. Click **Next >** to display the next screen where the wizard prompts you to review the field properties.
10. Click the **Bottled** to display the corresponding field properties.
11. Click the **Data Type down arrow** and click **Text**.
12. Click **Next >** to display the next screen.
13. Click **Next >** to let Access add the primary key. The final screen appears.

🔘 **CD**

The *Champagne_Sparkling* spreadsheet file is available on the companion CD-ROM.

14. In the Import to Table box, key **Champagne_Sparkling** and then click **Finish**. When the Save Import Steps prompt appears, click **Close**.
15. In the Navigation pane, double-click the **Champagne_Sparkling: Table** to open the new table with imported data.
16. **CLOSE** the Champagne_Sparkling table.
17. **LEAVE** the database open for the next project.

    LEAVE Access open for the next project.

Project 14-2: Export Data to Word

Your supervisor at Coho Vineyard wants a list of the distributor information in a Word file. Use the Distributor table in the Access database to export the data to a Rich Text Format file.

USE the database that is open from the previous project.

1. In the Navigation pane, select the **Distributors: Table**.
2. On the External Data tab, in the Export group, click **Word** to display the Export - RTF File dialog box.
3. If you want to specify a different destination, click **Browse** to open the File Save dialog box, use the Save in box to choose a folder, and then click **Save**.
4. Click the **Open the destination file after the export operation is complete** checkbox.
5. Click **OK**. Word opens and the new file with exported data is displayed.
6. **CLOSE** the file and **CLOSE** Word.
7. Switch to Access.
8. On the Save Export Steps screen, click **Close**.
9. **CLOSE** the database.

    LEAVE Access open for the next project.

■ Proficiency Assessment

Project 14-3: Save Export Specifications

As a travel agent at Margie's Travel, a client asks you to email information about the dates for available travel packages. Because you don't know what program the client will use to open it, you export the data to a text file. Because you do this frequently, you decide to save the export operation as a specification that can be used later.

CD

The *Trip Events* database file is available on the companion CD-ROM.

1. **OPEN** the *Trip Events* database from the data files for this lesson.
2. **SAVE** the database as *Trip Events XXX* (where XXX is your initials).
3. In the Navigation pane, select the **2008 Events: Table**.
4. On the External Data tab, in the External group, click **Text File** to display the Export - Text File dialog box.
5. Specify the location where you want to store the file.
6. Click the **Export data with formatting and layout** checkbox and then click the **Open the destination file after the export operation is complete** checkbox.
7. Click **OK**. The Encode '2008 Events' As dialog box is displayed.
8. **Windows (default)** should be selected. Click **OK**. Notepad opens and the new file with exported data is displayed.
9. **CLOSE** Notepad.
10. Switch to Access.
11. On the Save Export Steps screen, click the **Save export steps** checkbox.
12. In the Description box, key **Export event information to a text file**.
13. Click **Save Export**.
14. **LEAVE** the database open.

    LEAVE Access open for the next project.

Project 14-4: Run Export Specifications

One of the trip packages is no longer available. Delete the information from the table and run the export specification to create a new text file with the updated information.

USE the database that is open from the previous project.

1. Open the **2008 Events: Table**.
2. Delete the **World Series** record from the table.
3. Close the **2008 Events** table.
4. On the External Data tab, in the Export group, click **Saved Exports**.
5. Click the file path and change the destination file name to **2008 Events updated.txt**.
6. Click **Run**. Notepad opens and the new file with exported data is displayed.
7. Switch to Access. A message confirms that the export operation was successful.
8. Click **OK** and then click **Close** to close the Manage Data Tasks dialog box.
9. **CLOSE** the database.

    LEAVE Access open for the next project.

■ Mastery Assessment

Project 14-5: Export Data to a New Database

You are the manager at Southridge Video. You have created a new database to store information about new video games. You want to export the Games table to the new database. You have exported an Access table to other destinations, but not to another Access database. Use Access Help if you need more information.

1. Create a new file called *New Games XXX* (where XXX is your initials).
2. **CLOSE** the *New Games* database.
3. Open *Sale Games* from the data files for this lesson.
4. Save the database as *Sale Games XXX* (where XXX is your initials).
5. Use the export skills you have learned in this lesson to export the data and definition of the Games table to the *New Games XXX* database.
6. Do not save the export steps.
7. **OPEN** the *New Games XXX* database to be sure the Games table was successfully exported.
8. **CLOSE** both the databases.

   LEAVE Access open for the next project.

Project 14-6: Appending Data to a Table

You are the human resource manager for Contoso, Inc. You have received information about new employees that needs to be imported into the employee database. You already have a table with information about sales reps, so you want to append the information instead of creating a new table. Because you have never appended data before, use Access Help if you need additional information.

1. **OPEN** the *Contoso Employees* database from the data files for this lesson.
2. **SAVE** the database as *Contoso Employees XXX* (where XXX is your initials).
3. Choose to import from Excel using the **New_Contoso** spreadsheet file.
4. Choose the options necessary to append the spreadsheet data to the Sales Rep table.
5. Do not save the import steps.
6. Open the **Sales Reps: Table**. The data from the Excel spreadsheet should be appended to the table, as shown in Figure 14-44.

Figure 14-44

Appended data

ID	Last Name	First Name	E-mail Address	Mobile Phor	Add New Field
1	Abbas	Syed	sabbas@contoso.com	405-555-2302	
2	Buchanan	Nancy	nbuchanan@conto4so.co	806-555-3167	
3	Cooper	Scott	scooper@contoso.com	405-555-8731	
4	Ihrig	Ryan	rihrig@contoso.com	405-555-9119	
5	Moseley	Julia	jmoseley@contoso.com	405-555-0405	
6	Simon	Britta	bsimon@contoso.com	806-555-6136	
7	Petculescu	Cristian	cpetculescu@contoso.co	405-555-6670	
8	Cao	Jun	jcao@contoso.com	806-555-0119	
9	Berry	Jo	jberry@contoso.com	405-555-3454	
*	(New)				

Record: 1 of 9   No Filter   Search

7. **CLOSE** the Sales Reps table.
8. **CLOSE** the database.

   CLOSE Access.

INTERNET READY

To open the Access Options dialog box, click the Office Button and then click Access Options. The Resources tab of the Access Options dialog box, shown in Figure 14-45, is where you can contact Microsoft, find online resources, and maintain health and reliability of your Office applications.

Figure 14-45

Resources tab in Access Options dialog box

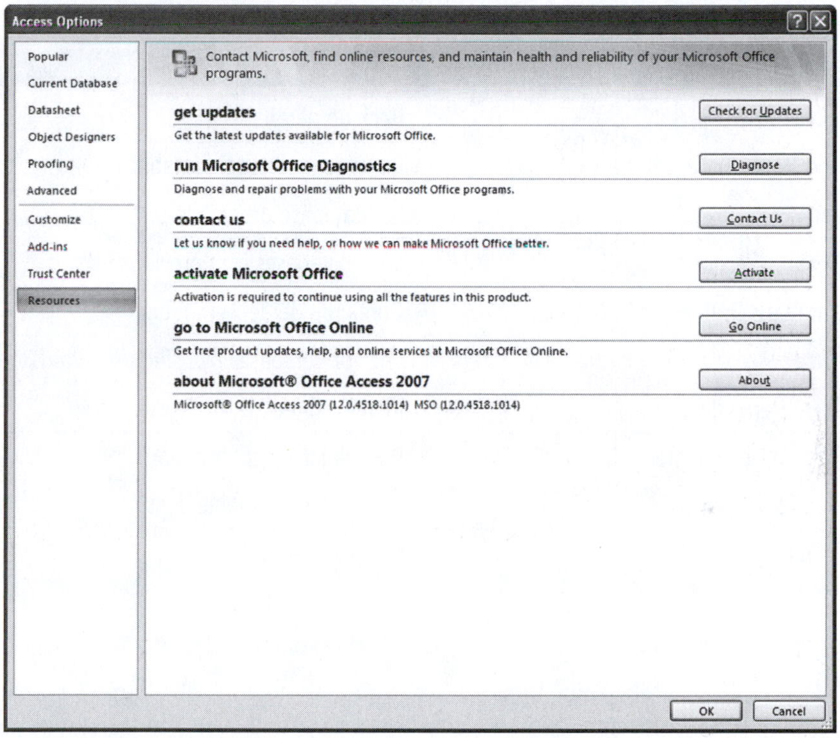

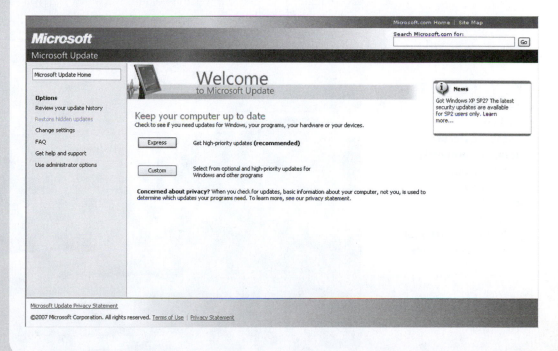

To keep your computer up-to-date, click the Check for Updates button to go to the Microsoft update site, shown in Figure 14-46. Here you can check to see if you need updates for your programs, hardware, or devices.

Figure 14-46

Microsoft update site

15 Database Tools

LESSON SKILL MATRIX

Skills	Matrix Skill	Skill Number
Backing Up a Database	Back up databases	6.1.2
Compacting and Repairing a Database	Compact and repair databases	6.1.3
Setting Database Properties	Set database properties	6.2.3
Saving as a Previous Version	Save databases as a previous version	6.1.4
Configuring Database Options	Configure database options	6.2.2
Encrypting a Database	Encrypt databases by using passwords	6.2.1
Identifying Object Dependencies	Identify object dependencies	6.2.4
Using the Database Documenter	Print database information	6.2.5
Using the Linked Table Manager	Reset or refresh table links	6.2.6
Splitting a Database	Split databases	1.4

Fabrikam, Inc. is a furniture manufacturer that supplies new lines, or collections, of furniture to showrooms each season. As an intern in the office, you help maintain the records related to the furniture collections and the showrooms that sell them for your company. Your supervisor is concerned about the maintenance, security, and the overall integrity of the database files, so your assignment is to safeguard these files. In this lesson, you will learn to back up a database, compact and repair a database, set database properties, and save databases in previous versions of the software. You will also learn to use database tools to configure database options, encrypt a database, identify object dependencies, document a database, refresh linked tables, and split a database.

KEY TERMS
back-end file
backup
Database Documenter
database properties
Database Splitter
decrypting
encrypting
front-end file
Linked Table Manager
object dependencies

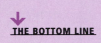

■ Maintaining a Database

<table>
<tr><td>↓
THE BOTTOM LINE</td><td>You can maintain some important aspects of a database by using the Manage menu on the Office Button. Though they might not seem as important as the actual data in your database, these commands allow you to provide protection of all the data in the file, and that is important. You can create a backup copy of your database, compact and repair the database, and set database properties. The Save As command on the Office Button lets you save a database in a previous file format.</td></tr>
</table>

Backing Up a Database

After all the work you have put into a database, you start to depend on being able to access and update the data and the information in it on a regular basis. To protect your work, it is a good idea to back up a database. Essentially, you are making another copy of the database that you can store on your computer, on a network drive, or in another safe location to prevent the loss of your data.

⊕ BACKUP A DATABASE

GET READY. Before you begin these steps, be sure to turn on and/or log on to your computer and start Access.

1. **OPEN** *Fabikam* from the data files for this lesson.
2. Save the database as *FabrikamXXX* (where XXX is your initials).
3. Click the **Office Button** and point to **Manage**. The Manage this database menu appears, as shown in Figure 15-1.

CD

The *Fabrikam* database is available on the companion CD-ROM.

Figure 15-1

Manage This Database menu

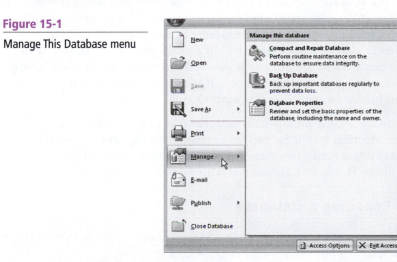

4. Click **Back Up Database**. The Save As dialog box appears, as shown in Figure 15-2. Notice that Access automatically adds the current date to the end of the filename.

Figure 15-2

Save As dialog box

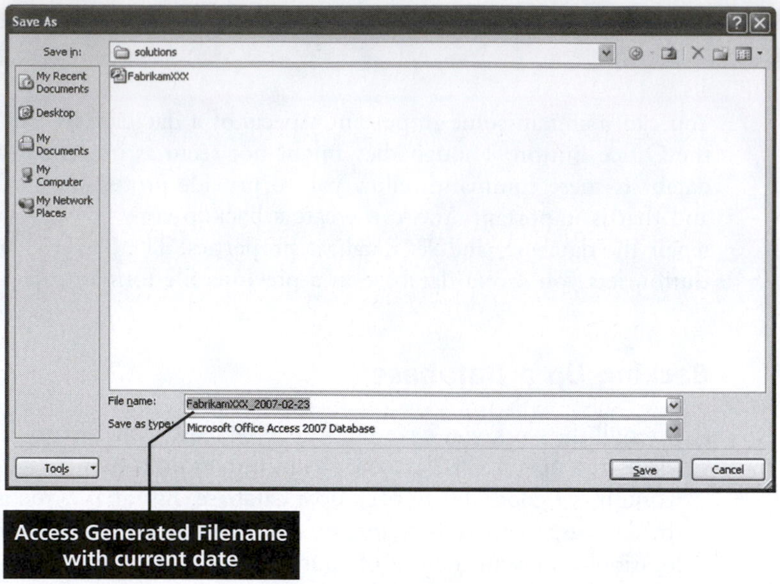

Access Generated Filename with current date

5. Click the **Save** button to accept the generated filename.

   PAUSE. LEAVE the database open to use in the next exercise.

A *backup* is a copy of a file. It is a good idea to create backup files of all your databases and continue to back them up on a regular basis.

You can store a backup copy in the same place as your original file, such as on your computer. However, if something happened to your computer, both files would be affected. A better solution is to save a backup copy to a network drive or removable media that is stored in a different physical location. For example, some companies that maintain sensitive client data have elaborate backup processes in place to store backup copies on computers or other media off premises in another part of the city or in another part of the country. If an entire office building is destroyed by fire or a city is involved in a natural disaster, the backup files containing client data are safe in another location. It is a good idea to consider the appropriate precautions needed for even a small company's data.

When backing up a database, Access automatically adds the date to the filename. You can keep this filename as an identifier for the backup file or change the filename to something else. Just keep in mind that you need a new name or location so that you aren't just overwriting your original file. In the Save In box, choose the location where you want to save the file.

CERTIFICATION READY?
How do you back up a database?
6.1.2

Compacting and Repairing a Database

The Compact and Repair command optimizes files and fixes minor problems in the file structure that may result from normal, everyday use of a database file.

COMPACT AND REPAIR A DATABASE

USE the database open from the previous exercise.

1. Click the **Office Button**, point to Manage, and select **Compact and Repair Database.** Access compacts and repairs the database.

   PAUSE. LEAVE the database open to use in the next exercise.

As records or objects in a database are deleted, the empty space within the file might not be replaced right away, leaving the file fragmented or with large empty spaces within the file structure. In databases with many records and objects, these issues can affect the database's performance over time. In the same way, minor errors can occur in any file, especially when it

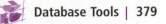

is shared by many different users on a network drive. Using the Compact and Repair command on a regular basis will help to optimize the file and repair minor problems before they become major ones.

Before you use this command on a shared file, make sure no one else has the file open.

ANOTHER WAY

You can set Access to compact a database every time you close it. On the Office Button menu, click the Access Options button and select Current Database. Click the Compact On Close checkbox and click OK.

TROUBLESHOOTING

If Access detects a problem with a file, or if you suspect a problem, the Office Diagnostics program may help repair the file. On the Office Button menu, click the Access Options button and select Resources. Click the Diagnose button and click OK. It is a good idea to search Access Help for more information about the Office Diagnostics program and any special precautions you should take before running the program.

Setting Database Properties

Using database properties makes it easier to organize and identify databases later. Some properties can be specified by you and some are automatically updated by Access. You can search to find files that contain certain properties, such as keywords, file size, or creation date. Standard properties are those such as author, title, and subject that are associated with a document by default.

⊙ SET DATABASE PROPERTIES

USE the database open from the previous exercise.

1. Click the **Office Button**, point to Manage, and select **Database Properties.** The FabrikamXXX.accdb Properties dialog box appears, as shown in Figure 15-3.

Figure 15-3

Summary Tab of the FabrikamXXX.accdb Properties dialog box

FabrikamXXX.accdb Properties	? X
General Summary Statistics Contents Custom	
Title:	I
Subject:	
Author:	Dawna Walls
Manager:	
Company:	
Category:	
Keywords:	
Comments:	
Hyperlink base:	
Template:	
	OK Cancel

2. Key **Fall Collection** in the Title box.
3. Key **preview** in the Subject box.
4. Select the text in the Author box and key **Your Name.**
5. Key **Britta Simon** in the Manager box.
6. Key **Fabrikam, Inc.** in the Company box
7. Click the **General** tab. Notice that this tab displays the file type, location, and size as well as the dates the file was created, modified, and accessed.

8. Click the **Contents** tab to view a list of the types of objects within the database file.

9. Click **OK.**

   PAUSE. LEAVE the report open to use in the next exercise.

You have just set some of the basic properties for a document that will help you identify and organize it later. ***Database properties*** are details about a file that describe or identify it. Table 15-1 describes each Standard property in the Summary tab of the Properties dialog box. These properties can all be changed by the user; however, some properties in the General, Statistics, and Contents tabs—such as the file size and date the document was created or updated—are Automatically Updated Properties that are updated by Access and cannot be changed. In the Custom tab, you can define Custom properties by assigning a text, time, numeric values, or yes or no values to custom properties.

All Microsoft Office documents have document properties. The descriptions of each Standard database property are listed in Table 15-1.

Table 15-1

Standard Database Properties

PROPERTY NAME	DESCRIPTION
Title	Title of the database
Subject	Topic of the contents of the database
Author	The name of the individual who has authored the database
Manager	The name of the manager who is responsible for the database
Company	The name of the company
Category	The category in which the database can be classified
Keywords	A word or set of words that describes the database
Comments	The summary or abstract of the contents of the database
Hyperlink base	The path to the destination of the file; the path may point to a location on your hard drive, a network drive, or the Internet

Saving as a Previous Version

Access 2007 allows you to save a database in a previous Access file format so that those using earlier versions of the software can use the database. However, some new features of Access 2007 cannot be converted to a previous file format. Access will alert you when this is the case, and you can always remove that new feature in order to save the database as a previous version.

⊙ SAVE AS A PREVIOUS VERSION

USE the database open from the previous exercise.

1. Click the **Office Button** and point to **Save As.** The Save As menu appears, as shown in Figure 15-4.

Figure 15-4

Save As menu

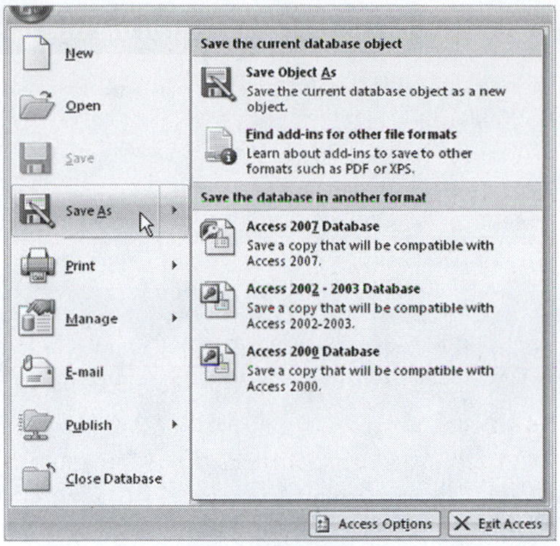

2. Select **Access 2002-2003 Database**. The Save As dialog box appears, as shown in Figure 15-5. Notice that Microsoft Access Database (2002-2003) is displayed in the Save as type box.

Figure 15-5

Save As menu

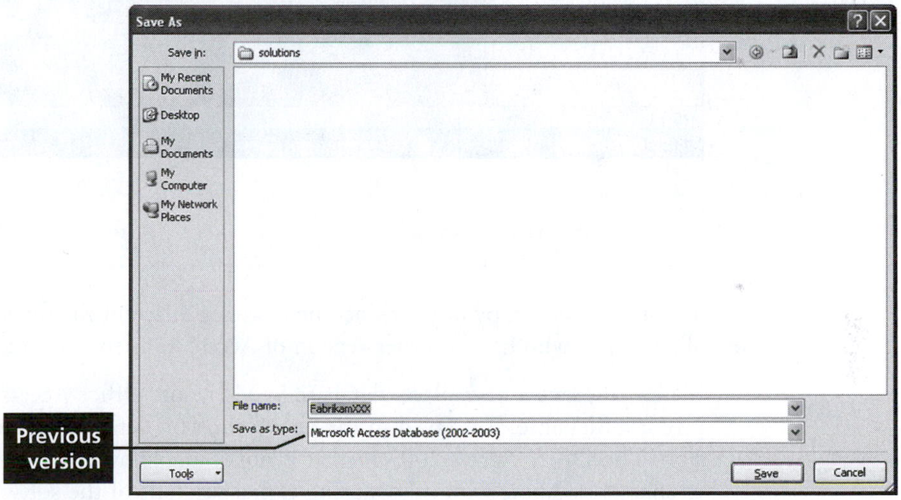

3. Key **Fabrikam2002-2003** in the filename box.

4. Click the **Save** button. Notice the filename and format change is displayed in the title bar, as shown in Figure 15-6.

Figure 15-6

Database saved in Access
2002-2003 format

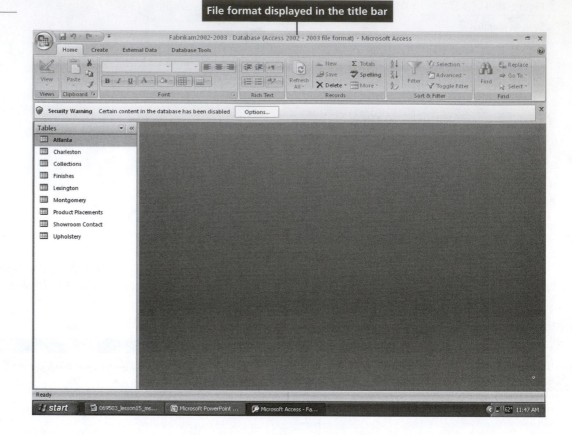

5. CLOSE the database.

You just saved a copy of your document with a different file format. The one you chose will allow a user who has an earlier version of Access to open your document without any difficulty.

When you save a new, blank database in Microsoft Office Access 2007, you are prompted to give it a filename. It is saved in the new format by default, which gives it the .accdb extension. The Office Access 2007 format is not readable by earlier versions of Access. If you need to share a database with others using earlier versions of the software, the Save As command allows you to save the database in the Access 2000 format or the Access 2002-2003 format, both of which have the extension .mdb. When you use the Save As command to save a database in an earlier format, it preserves the original database file in its format and creates a copy in the format you choose.

Before you can save a database in a previous file format, you should open the database, but make sure all objects are closed.

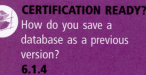

CERTIFICATION READY?
How do you save a
database as a previous
version?
6.1.4

TAKE NOTE If an Access 2007 database file contains complex data, offline data, or attachments created in Access 2007, you will not be able to save it in an earlier format.

■ Configuring Database Options

↓

THE BOTTOM LINE

The Access Options dialog box provides many ways to customize Access. From changing popular options to specific or advanced options for databases, you can specify many options for customizing your copy of Access for the way you use it on a daily basis.

Through the Access Options dialog box, you can enable error checking, show/hide the Navigation pane, and select a startup display form.

The *FabrikamInc* database is available on the companion CD-ROM.

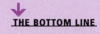

→ CONFIGURE DATABASE OPTIONS

OPEN *FabikamInc* from the data files for this lesson.

1. Save the database as *FabrikamIncXXX* (where XXX is your initials).
2. Click the **Office Button** and click the **Access Options** button. The Access Options dialog box appears. 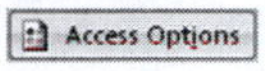
3. Click the **Current Database** button on the left to display the Current Database section of the Access Options dialog box, as shown in Figure 15-7.

Figure 15-7

Access Options dialog box

[Display Form menu]

[Display Navigation Pane checkbox]

Access Options dialog box showing Current Database options including Application Options, Application Title, Application Icon, Display Form, Display Status Bar, Document Window Options, Navigation, and Ribbon and Toolbar Options sections.

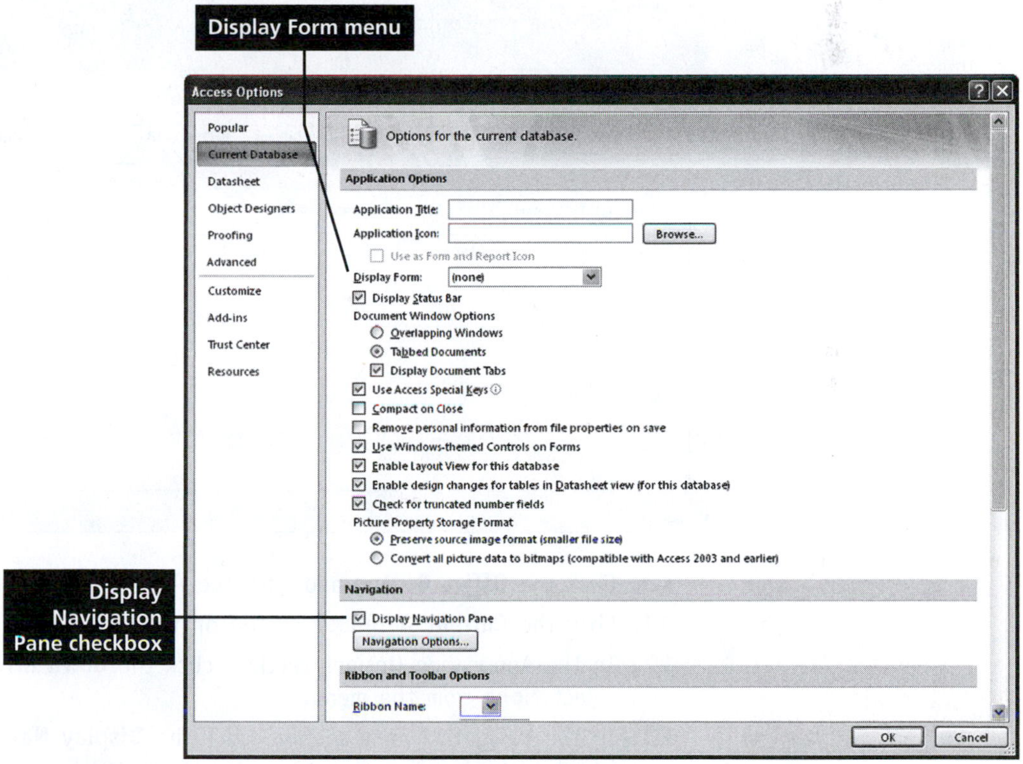

4. In the Application Options section, click the **down arrow** beside Display Form and select **Showroom Contact Form** from the menu.
5. In the Navigation section, notice that the Display Navigation Pane is turned on by default.

6. Click the **Display Navigation Pane** checkbox to remove the checkmark and click **OK**. A Microsoft Office Access dialog box appears, as shown in Figure 15-8, saying you need to close and reopen the database for the changes to take effect.

Figure 15-8

Microsoft Office Access dialog box

Microsoft Office Access

You must close and reopen the current database for the specified option to take effect.

OK

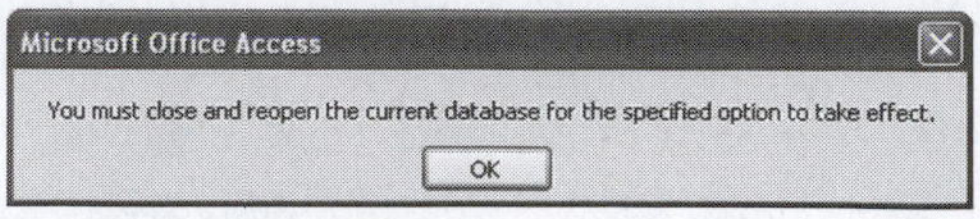

7. Click **OK**.
8. **CLOSE** the database.
9. Open the *FabrikamIncXXX* database. Notice that the Navigation pane is not visible and the Showroom Contact Form is displayed, as shown in Figure 15-9.

Figure 15-9

Showroom Contact form

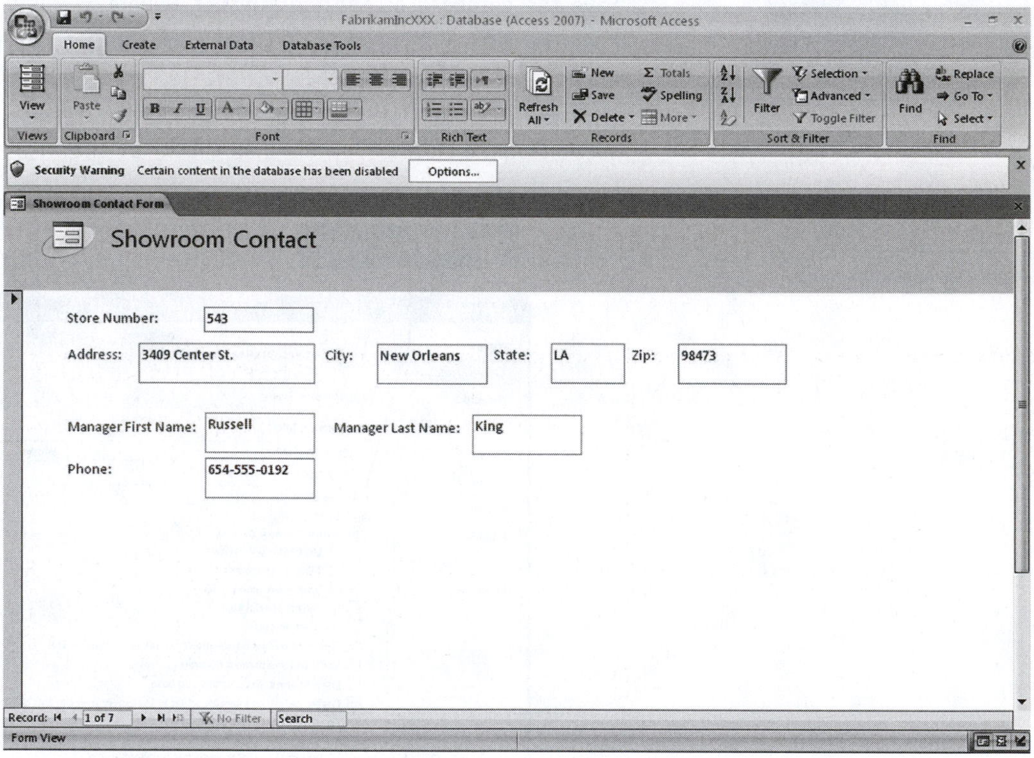

10. Click the **Office Button** and click the **Access Options** button.
11. Click the **Current Database** button on the left.
12. In the Application Options section, click the **down arrow** beside Display Form and select **None** from the menu.
13. In the Navigation pane section, click the **Display Navigation Pane** checkbox to insert a checkmark.
14. Click the **Navigation Options** button. The Navigation Options dialog box appears. Notice the grouping and display options available and click **Cancel**.
15. Click the **Object Designers** button on the left.
16. Scroll to the bottom of the window to see the Error checking section. The Enable Error Checking options are turned on by default.
17. Click **OK**. The Microsoft Access dialog box appears again.
18. Click **OK**.
19. **CLOSE** the database.
20. **OPEN** the *FabrikamIncXXX* database. Notice the Navigation pane is displayed and the form is not.

PAUSE. LEAVE the report open to use in the next exercise.

The Access Options dialog box lets you customize certain aspects of Access and your data-bases. The Access Options dialog box has 10 sections of customizable options, including Popular, Current Database, Datasheet, Object Designers, Proofing, and Advanced. In the previous exercise, you used the Current Database options to set a display form and hide the Navigation pane.

If you want a form to be displayed automatically when you open a database, the Display Form menu lets you choose from available forms in the database. You can choose none if you do not wish to display a form.

The Display Navigation Pane option is turned on by default, but if you don't want the Navigation pane to be displayed when you open your database, click the Display Navigation Pane checkbox to remove the checkmark. You must close and reopen the current database for these settings to take effect.

Enable error checking, located in the Object Designers options, is another feature you can change. Error checking is on by default, but you can clear the checkbox to disable all types of error checking in forms and reports. For example, Access places error indicators in controls that encounter one or more types of errors. The indicators appear as triangles in the upper-left or upper-right corner of the control, depending on text direction. The default indicator color is green, but you can change that to another color if you choose.

CERTIFICATION READY?
How do you configure database options?
6.2.2

■ SOFTWARE ORIENTATION

Database Tools Tab

The Database Tools tab on the Ribbon contains advanced commands for maintaining documents.

Figure 15-10

Database Tools tab

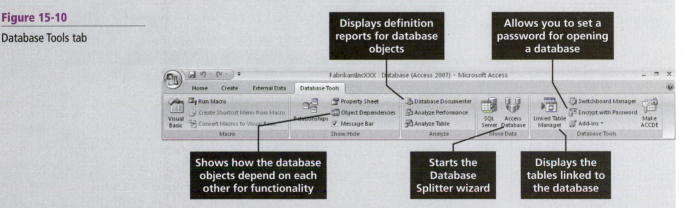

Use this figure as a reference throughout this lesson as well as the rest of this book.

■ Using Database Tools

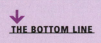
THE BOTTOM LINE

The Database Tools tab has advanced commands for maintaining databases. These tools allow you to encrypt and decrypt a database, identify object dependencies, create object reports with the Database Documenter, refresh links with the Linked Table Manager, and split a database.

Encrypting a Database

When you need to protect a database from unauthorized users, you can encrypt it with a password and only provide that password to authorized users. Encrypting a database can provide security for sensitive data. You can use the decrypt database command to change the password on a regular basis or to remove it.

⊕ ENCRYPT AND DECRYPT A DATABASE

USE the database open from the previous exercise.

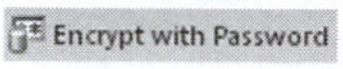

⬚ Encrypt with Password

1. On the Database Tools tab, in the Database Tools group, click the **Encrypt with Password** button. The Microsoft Office Access message box appears saying you must open the database in Exclusive mode, as shown in Figure 15-11.

Figure 15-11

Microsoft Office Access Message box

> **Microsoft Office Access**
>
> ⓘ **You must have the database open for exclusive use to set or remove the database password.**
>
> To open the database exclusively, close the database, and then reopen it by clicking the Microsoft Office Button and using the Open command. In the Open dialog box, click the arrow next to the Open button, and then select Open Exclusive.
>
> [OK]

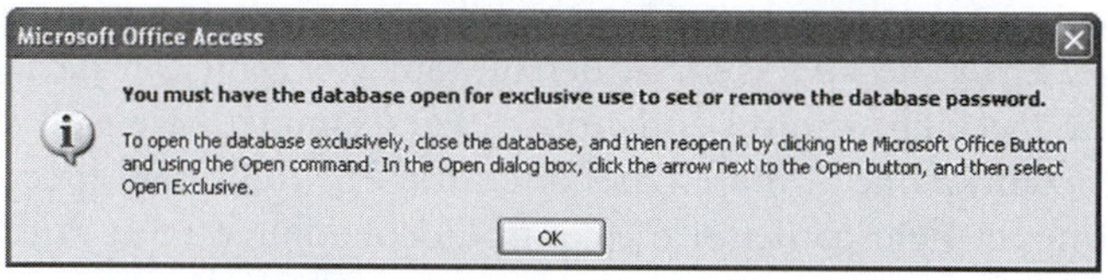

2. Click **OK**.
3. **CLOSE** the database.
4. Click the **More** link in the Open Recent Database list. The Open dialog box appears.
5. Navigate to the data files for this lesson and select **FabrikamIncXXX.**
6. Click the **down arrow** on the **Open** button and select **Open Exclusive** from the menu, as shown in Figure 15-12. FabrikamXXX opens in exclusive mode.

Figure 15-12

Open menu

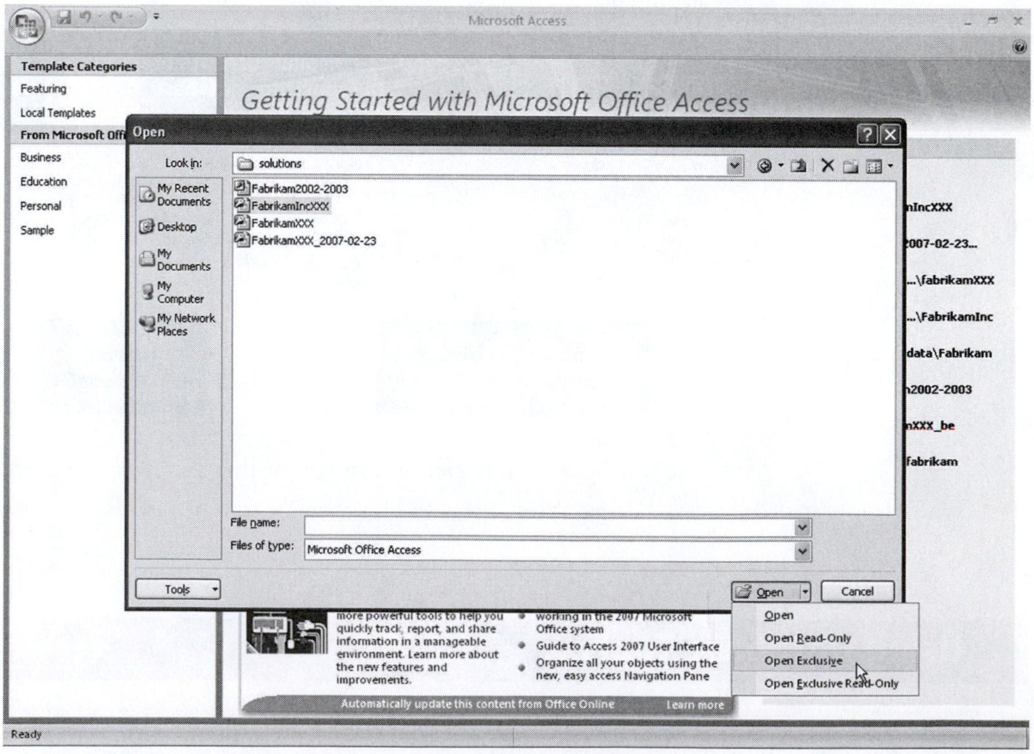

7. On the Database Tools tab, in the Database Tools group, click the **Encrypt with Password** button. The Set Database Password dialog box appears, as shown in Figure 15-13.

Figure 15-13

Set Database Password dialog box

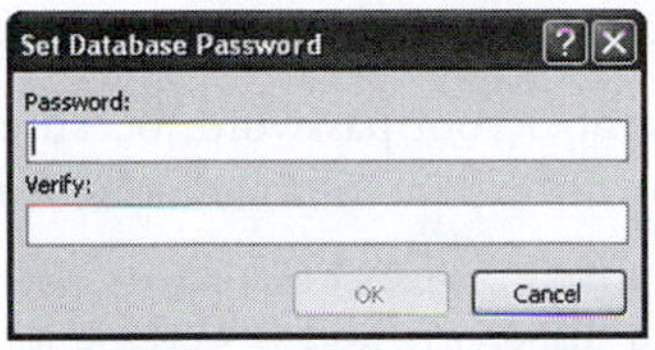

8. Key **$Fabrikam09fc** in the Password box.

TROUBLESHOOTING Be careful to key the passwords exactly as printed throughout this exercise to avoid error messages.

9. Key **$Fabrikam09fc** in the Verify box.
10. Click **OK.** The database is now encrypted with a password.
11. **CLOSE** the database.
12. **OPEN** the database in Exclusive mode again. The Password Required dialog box appears, as shown in Figure 15-14.

Figure 15-14

Password Required dialog box

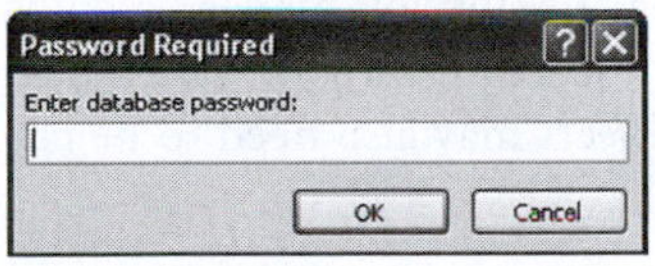

TAKE NOTE* You only need to open the database in Exclusive mode if you are going to set or unset a password. The database will be protected with the password in any mode.

13. Key **$Fabrikam09fc** and click **OK.** The database opens.
14. On the Database Tools tab, in the Database Tools group, click the **Decrypt Database** button. (If you hadn't opened the database in Exclusive mode, you would get a message prompting you to do so.) The Unset Database Password dialog box appears, as shown in Figure 15-15.

Figure 15-15

Unset Database Password dialog box

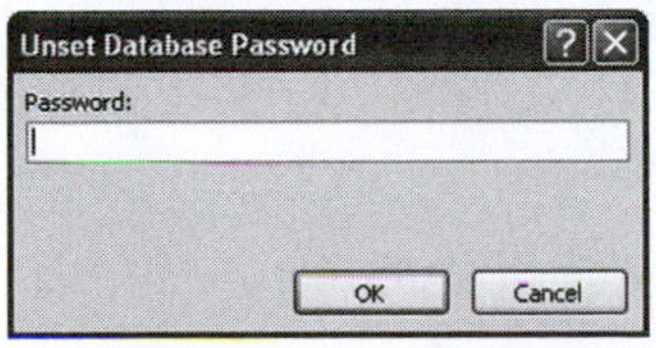

15. Key **$Fabrikam09fc** and click **OK.**
16. **CLOSE** the database.
17. **OPEN** the database in regular mode. Notice that a password is no longer required to open the file.

   PAUSE. LEAVE the database open to use in the next exercise.

Encrypting a database means to scramble the data in a way that can only be reconverted by an authorized user who has the password. When you use a database password to encrypt a database, you make all data unreadable by other tools and you force users to enter a password to use the database.

To encrypt a database, you first need to open it in Exclusive mode.

It is very important for you to remember your password, because if you forget it Microsoft cannot retrieve it for you. Write down the password and store it in a safe location.

TAKE NOTE * Use strong passwords that combine uppercase and lowercase letters, numbers, and symbols. Weak passwords do not mix these elements. Strong password: W5!dk8. Weak password: CAR381. Passwords should be 8 or more characters in length. A pass phrase that uses 14 or more characters is better.

When you open an encrypted database, the Password Required dialog box appears where you key the password. Passwords are case sensitive, meaning you can use uppercase and lowercase letters as well as numbers and symbols, but you must enter them exactly as they were entered when the password was set in order for there to be a match.

CERTIFICATION READY?
How do you encrypt a database?
6.2.1

Decrypting a database is removing the password from a file that has been encrypted. If you want to remove a password, open the database in Exclusive mode, then click the Decrypt Database button from the Database Tools group and key the password in the Unset Database Password dialog box exactly as it was entered to encrypt the database.

Identifying Object Dependencies

The Object Dependencies task pane helps you manage a database by displaying how all its components interact. This can be helpful if you want to delete a table or form. You will be able to see which other objects may also need to be changed so that they will still function without the deleted table.

⮕ IDENTIFY OBJECT DEPENDENCIES

USE the database open from the previous exercise.

1. Click the **Produce Placements Table** in the Navigation pane to select it.

Object Dependencies

2. On the Database Tools tab, in the Show/Hide group, click the **Object Dependencies** button. The **Object Dependencies pane** displays dependency information for the selected table, as shown in Figure 15-16. Notice that the *Objects that depend on me* button is selected.

Figure 15-16

Object Dependencies task pane

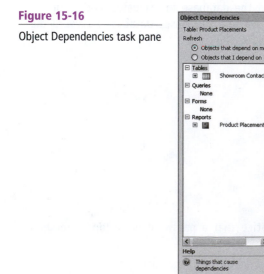

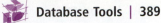

3. Click the **Objects that I depend on** button. Notice the changes in the Reports section.

4. Click the **Objects that depend on me** button. Click the **plus sign (+)** beside the Showroom Contact table to see the tables and forms that depend on the Showroom Contact table.

5. Click the **Showroom Contact** link to display it in Design view where you could make any necessary changes regarding dependencies.

6. **CLOSE** the Object Dependencies pane.

PAUSE. LEAVE the database open to use in the next exercise.

Object dependencies describe how objects in a database rely on other components to function properly. The Object Dependencies task pane displays how database objects, such as tables or forms, use other objects. This process helps keep databases running smoothly by preventing errors that could result when changes or deletions are made to objects in a database. The Object Dependencies task pane works only for tables, forms, queries, and reports in an Access database.

Using the Database Documenter

The Database Documenter provides detailed information about a database and presents it as a report that can be printed. Use the Database Documenter when you need to have a printed record of this information, such as for record-keeping purposes or as insurance in case you have to re-create the database or object.

➔ USE THE DATABASE DOCUMENTER

USE the database open from the previous exercise.

🖺 Database Documenter

1. On the Database Tools tab, in the Analyze group, click the **Database Documenter** button. The Documenter dialog box appears, as shown in Figure 15-17.

Figure 15-17

Documenter dialog box

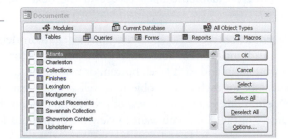

2. Click the **All Object Types** tab.

3. Click the **Tables** tab.

4. Click the **Showroom Contact** checkbox.

5. Click the **Options** button. The Print Table Definition dialog box appears, as shown in Figure 15-18.

Figure 15-18

Print Table Definition dialog box

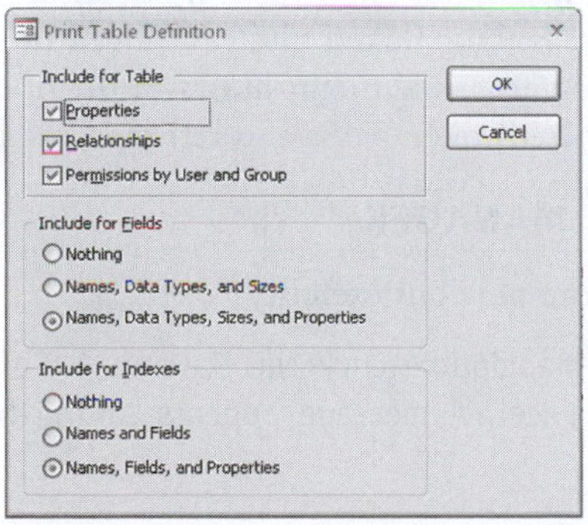

6. Click **OK.**

7. Click **OK.** The Object Definition report appears in Print Preview.

8. Click the **Zoom magnifying glass pointer** to view the report, as shown in Figure 15-19. At this point, you could print the report or make any changes to the layout and then print it.

Figure 15-19

Object Definition report

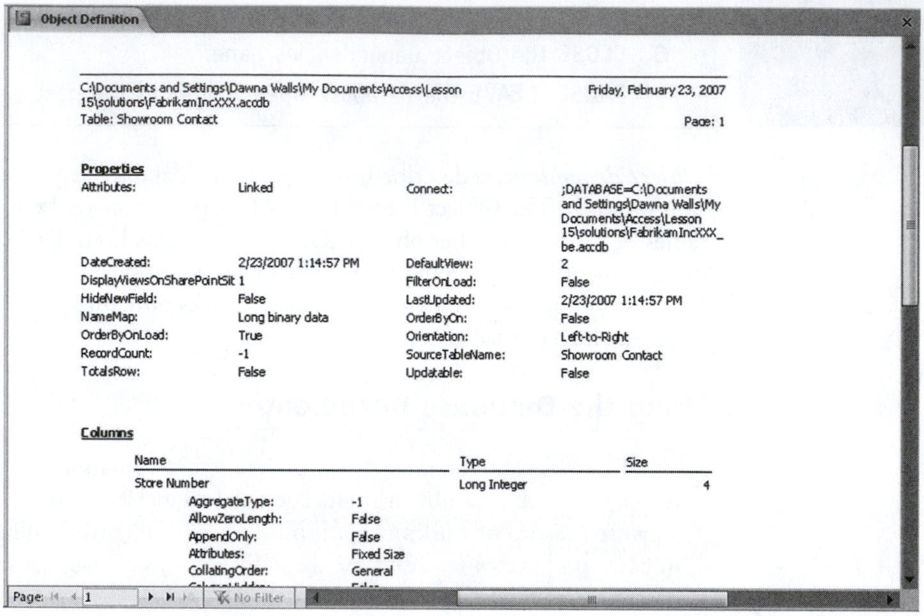

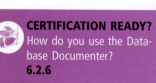

9. Click the **Last Page** button on the record navigation bar to move to page 4. Notice the relationship diagram included in the report.

10. Click the **Close Print Preview** button.

PAUSE. LEAVE the database open to use in the next exercise.

The ***Database Documenter*** creates a report that shows details, or definitions, about a selected object and opens it in Print Preview. You can view the properties for a form as well as properties for each section of the form and each label, button, or control on the form. The Documenter dialog box contains tabs for each type of object, as well as a tab that displays all objects. Select the object whose definitions you want to view or print. The Options button lets you further specify which features of the object you want to view the definitions for.

CERTIFICATION READY?
How do you use the Database Documenter?
6.2.6

> TAKE NOTE* Some object definitions can be several pages long, so it is a good idea to check the length of the report before printing.

Using the Linked Table Manager

> As you learned in Lesson 14, you can import and link data from other applications into your Access 2007 databases. If these linked files get moved to a new folder or other location, the Access database you are using might have trouble finding them. The Linked Table Manager identifies these broken paths and refreshes the links.

⊕ USE THE LINKED TABLE MANAGER

USE the database open from the previous exercise.

1. In the Navigation pane, double-click the **Savannah Collection** table, which has been imported from Excel. A message appears saying that Access cannot find the file. Click **OK.**

2. On the Database Tools tab, on the Database Tools group, click the **Linked Table Manager** button. The Linked Table Manager dialog box appears, as shown in Figure 15-20.

Figure 15-20

Linked Table Manager dialog box

Linked Table Manager

Select the linked tables to be updated:

☐ ▸ Savannah Collection (C:\Documents and Settings\Dawna Walls\My Documents\Access\Lesso

OK
Cancel
Select All
Deselect All

☐ Always prompt for new location

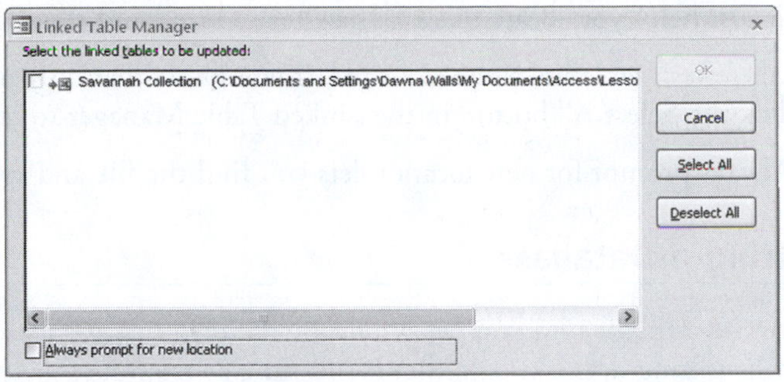

3. Click the **Savannah Collection** checkbox.

4. Click the **Always prompt for new location** checkbox and click **OK**. The Select New Location of Savannah Collection dialog box appears.

5. Navigate to the data files for this lesson on the companion CD-ROM. Open the New Collections folder, and click the **savannah** Excel file, as shown in Figure 15-21.

Figure 15-21

Select new location of Savannah Collection

Select New Location of Savannah Collection

Look in: ☐ New Collections

My Recent Documents
Desktop
My Documents
My Computer
My Network Places

savannah

File name:
Files of type: Microsoft Excel

Tools   Open   Cancel

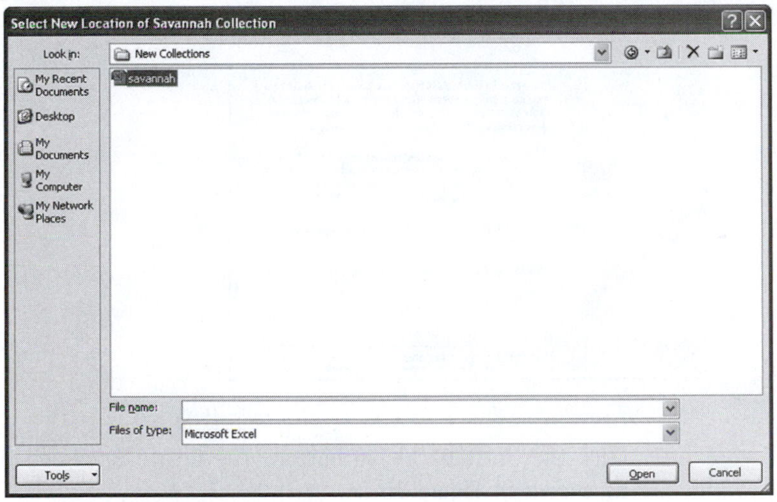

6. Click **Open**. The Linked Table Manager dialog box appears, as shown in Figure 15-22.

Figure 15-22

Linked Table Manager dialog box

Linked Table Manager

ⓘ All selected linked tables were successfully refreshed.

OK

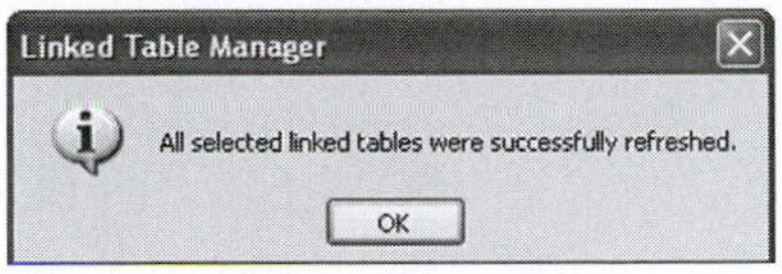

7. Click **OK**.

8. Click the **Close** button.

9. In the Navigation pane, double-click the **Savannah Collection** table. Notice it opens this time.

10. **CLOSE** the **Savannah Collection** table.

PAUSE. LEAVE Access open to use in the next exercise.

The *Linked Table Manager* lists the paths to all currently linked tables and refreshes any links for tables that have moved. If several selected tables have moved to the new location that you specify, the Linked Table Manager searches that location for all selected tables and updates all links in one step. The Linked Table Manager does not move database or table files, it just helps you locate them if they have moved and refreshes that path.

CERTIFICATION READY?
How do you use the Linked Table Manager?
6.2.6

You can refresh table links one at a time, if you know that only one has been moved, or you can click the Select All button in the Linked Table Manager to refresh all the links at once.

The Always prompt for new location lets you find the file and specify its new location.

Splitting a Database

It can be difficult for many people to use the data in a database at the same time. Synchronizing data can be difficult and time consuming. To avoid slowing down the network because of constant changes being made to a database, the Database Splitter wizard can split the database in two.

⊕ SPLIT A DATABASE

USE the database open from the previous exercise.

1. On the Database Tools tab, in the Move Data group, click the **Access Database** button. The Database Splitter Wizard appears, as shown in Figure 15-23.

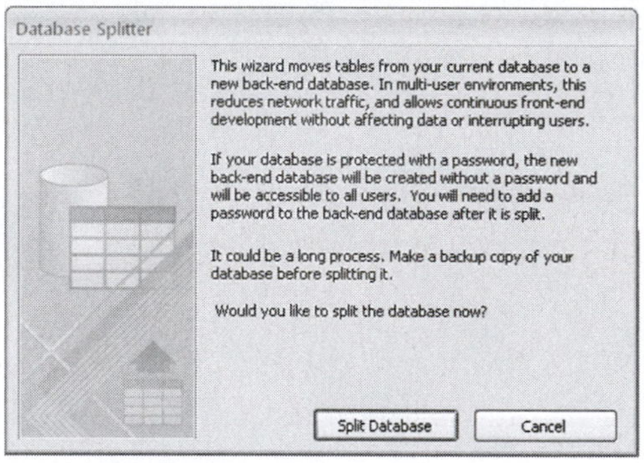

Figure 15-23

Database Splitter Wizard

Database Splitter

This wizard moves tables from your current database to a new back-end database. In multi-user environments, this reduces network traffic, and allows continuous front-end development without affecting data or interrupting users.

If your database is protected with a password, the new back-end database will be created without a password and will be accessible to all users. You will need to add a password to the back-end database after it is split.

It could be a long process. Make a backup copy of your database before splitting it.

Would you like to split the database now?

[Split Database] [Cancel]

2. Click the **Split Database** button. The Create Back-end Database dialog box appears, as shown in Figure 15-24.

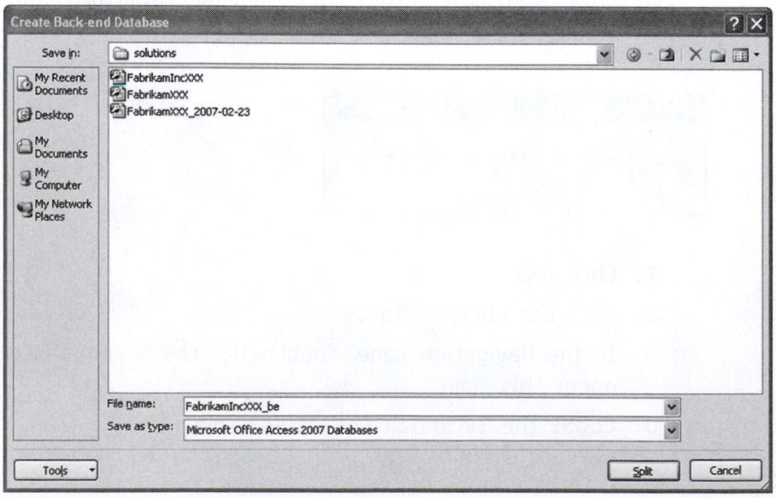

Figure 15-24

Create Back-end Database dialog box

Create Back-end Database

Save in: solutions

My Recent Documents
Desktop
My Documents
My Computer
My Network Places

FabrikamIncXXX
FabrikamXXX
FabrikamXXX_2007-02-23

File name: FabrikamIncXXX_be

Save as type: Microsoft Office Access 2007 Databases

Tools   [Split] [Cancel]

3. Navigate to the location where you want to save the back-end file and click **Split**. After a few moments, the Database Splitter dialog box appears, as shown in Figure 15-25.

Figure 15-25

Database Splitter dialog box

4. Click **OK**.
5. **CLOSE** the database.
6. **OPEN** *FabrikamXXX_be*. Notice that it contains only the tables for the database.
7. **CLOSE** the database.

   CLOSE Access.

CERTIFICATION READY?
How do you split a database?
1.4

The ***Database Splitter*** is a wizard that splits a database for you. You can split a database into two files: one that contains the tables, called the ***back-end file***, and one that contains the queries, forms, reports, and other objects created from the tables, called the ***front-end file***. Users who need to access the data can customize their own forms, reports, pages, and other objects while maintaining a single source of data on the network. It is a good idea to back up the database before splitting it.

SUMMARY SKILL MATRIX

IN THIS LESSON YOU LEARNED	MATRIX SKILL	SKILL NUMBER
To back up a database	Back up databases	6.1.2
To compact and repair a database	Compact and repair databases	6.1.3
To set database properties	Set database properties	6.2.3
To save as a previous version	Save databases as a previous version	6.1.4
To configure database options	Configure database options	6.2.2
To encrypt a database	Encrypt databases by using passwords	6.2.1
To identify object dependencies	Identify object dependencies	6.2.4
To use the Database Documenter	Print database information	6.2.5
To use the Linked Table Manager	Reset or refresh table links	6.2.6
To split a database	Split databases	1.4

Knowledge Assessment

Matching

Match the term in Column 1 to its description in Column 2.

Column 1	Column 2
1. backup	a. in a split database, the file that contains the queries, forms, reports, and other objects created from the tables
2. back-end file	b. details about a file that describe or identify it
3. front-end file	c. lists the paths to all currently linked tables and refreshes the links to any tables that have moved
4. database properties	d. to scramble data in a way that can only be reconverted by an authorized user who has the correct password
5. Database Splitter	e. removing the password from an encrypted file
6. Linked Table Manager	f. describe how objects in a database are dependent on or rely on other components to function properly
7. encrypting	g. creates a report that shows details, or definitions, about a selected object and opens it in Print Preview
8. object dependencies	h. a copy of a database file
9. Database Documenter	i. the file that contains the tables in a split database
10. decrypting	j. a wizard that splits a database for you

True / False

Circle T if the statement is true or F if the statement is false.

T | F 1. Backing up files on a regular basis is really not necessary.

T | F 2. When you back up a database, Access automatically adds the date to the filename.

T | F 3. Compacting and repairing a database leaves the file fragmented.

T | F 4. Some database properties are updated by Access and cannot be changed.

T | F 5. The .accdb extension is for the Access 2002-2003 file format.

T | F 6. Access Options allow you to customize Access.

T | F 7. If you forget a password for a database, Microsoft can retrieve it for you.

T | F 8. You can print a report from the Database Documenter.

T | F 9. The Linked Table Manager moves databases and tables then refreshes the path.

T | F 10. It is a good idea to back up a database before splitting it.

■ Competency Assessment

Project 15-1: Set Database Properties and Compact and Repair the Blue Yonder Database

As an investor relations specialist for Blue Yonder Airlines, you need to maintain and safeguard the databases that you use. Set the database properties and compact and repair the Income and Expenses database.

GET READY. Launch Access if it is not already running.

The *BlueYonder* database is available on the companion CD-ROM.

1. Open the *BlueYonder* database from the data files for this lesson.
2. Save the database as *BlueYonderXXX* (where XXX is your initials).
3. Click the **Office Button**, point to Manage, and select **Database Properties.**
4. Key **Income and Expenses** in the Subject box.
5. Key **Your Name** in the Author box.
6. Key **Andrew Lan** in the Manager box.
7. Key **BlueYonder Airlines** in the Company box.
8. Click **OK.**
9. Click the **Office Button**, point to Manage, and select **Compact and Repair Database.**
   CLOSE the database.

Project 15-2: Back Up and Split the WingTip Database

As part of your maintenance of database files at WingTip Toys, you decide to create a backup of a database and split it so that others in the company can create their own forms and reports using the data in the tables.

GET READY. Launch Access if it is not already running.

The *Wingtip* database is available on the companion CD-ROM.

1. **OPEN** the *Wingtip* database from the data files for this lesson.
2. Save the database as *WingtipXXX* (where XXX is your initials).
3. Click the **Office Button**, point to Manage, and select **Back Up Database.**
4. Use the generated file name with the date and click **Save.**
5. On the Database Tools tab, in the Move Data group, click the **Access Database** button.
6. Click the **Split database** button.
7. Accept the *WingtipXXX_be* file name and click **Split.**
8. Click **OK.**
   CLOSE the database.

■ Proficiency Assessment

Project 15-3: Encrypt the Blue Yonder Database

Create a password to protect the data in the Income and Expenses database.

USE the *BlueYonderXXX* database that you saved in a previous exercise.

1. **OPEN** the *BlueYonderXXX* database in Exclusive mode.
2. On the Database Tools tab, in the Database Tools group, click the **Encrypt with Password** button.
3. Key **#1BlueYonder$87** in the Password box.
4. Key **#1BlueYonder$87** in the Verify box.

5. Click **OK.**

6. **CLOSE** the database.

7. Open the database in regular mode.

8. Key **#1BlueYonder$87** in the Password box.

9. Open the **Database Documenter.**

10. Select the **Income & Expenses Summary** table and click **OK** to view the report.

11. Print the report.

12. **CLOSE Print Preview.**

CLOSE the database.

The *Lucerne* database is available on the companion CD-ROM.

Project 15-4: Save the Lucerne Database in a Previous File Format

OPEN the *Lucerne* database from the data files for this lesson.

1. Save the database in the Access 2002-2003 Database file format with the file format **Lucerne2002-2003.**

CLOSE the database.

■ Mastery Assessment

Project 15-5: Decrypt and Back Up the Blue Yonder Database

Password protection for the Blue Yonder Income and Expenses database is no longer necessary. Remove the encryption.

USE the *BlueYonderXXX* database that you saved in a previous exercise.

1. Remove the encryption with a password from the Blue Yonder database.

2. Create a backup file for the database using the generated file name. Save it in the same location as the original version.

CLOSE the database.

Project 15-6: Refresh Links and View Object Dependencies in the Humongous Database

An assistant at Humongous Insurance has moved some files around on the computer you share. Use the Linked Tables Manager to refresh a link to an Excel file that has been imported.

The *Humongous Insurance* database is available on the companion CD-ROM.

OPEN *HumongousInsurance* from the data files for this lesson.

1. Save the database as *HumongousInsuranceXXX* (where XXX is your initials).

2. Refresh the link for the **Benefit Providers** Excel file, located on the companion CD-ROM, using the Linked Table Manager.

3. View the Object Dependencies Information for the Part-time Employees Table.

4. **SAVE** the database.

CLOSE the database.

INTERNET READY

On the Office Button menu, click the Access Options button to launch the Access Options dialog box. Click the Trust Center button on the left. In the Security & more section, click the Microsoft Trustworthy Computing link and read the online article. Browse other links that interest you at the Trust Center.

Circling Back

As Woodgrove Real Estate grows, you continue to learn more about Access and use the database for more advanced tasks.

Project 1: Create a Grouped Report

You want to see the houses that have been sold each month. Use the Report Wizard to create a report that groups the data according to the closing date. Then create an aggregate field that will sum the total amount of sales for each month.

GET READY. Launch Access if it is not already running.

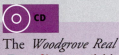

The *Woodgrove Real Estate* file is available on the companion CD-ROM.

1. **OPEN** the *Woodgrove Real Estate* database from the data files for this lesson.
2. **SAVE** the database as *Woodgrove Real Estate XXX* (where XXX is your initials).
3. Open the **Houses Sold** table.
4. On the Create tab, in the Reports group, click the **Report Wizard** button to display the first screen in the Report Wizard.
5. Select the **Listing Agent** field and click the **single right arrow** to move the field to the Selected Fields list.
6. Using the same method, move the **Address**, **Selling Price**, and **Closing Date** fields from the Available Fields list to the Selected Fields list.
7. Click the **Next >** button to display the second screen in the Report Wizard.
8. Select the **Closing Date** field and click the **single right arrow** to move it to the grouping levels box.
9. Click the **Next >** button to display the third screen in the Report Wizard.
10. Click the **down arrow** on the Sort menu and select **Closing Date**.
11. Click the **Next >** button to display the fourth screen in the Report Wizard.
12. In the Layout section, the **Stepped** option button should be selected and in the Orientation section **Portrait** should be selected.
13. Click the **Next >** button to display the fifth screen in the Report Wizard.
14. Select the **Trek** style.
15. Click the **Next >** button to display the sixth screen in the Report Wizard.
16. Click the **Finish** button to accept the settings and create the report.
17. Close Print Preview.
18. Switch to Layout view.
19. Right-click the **Selling Price** header to display the shortcut menu.
20. Click **Total Selling Price** and then click **Sum**. The totals for each month are displayed. Your report should look similar to Figure 1.

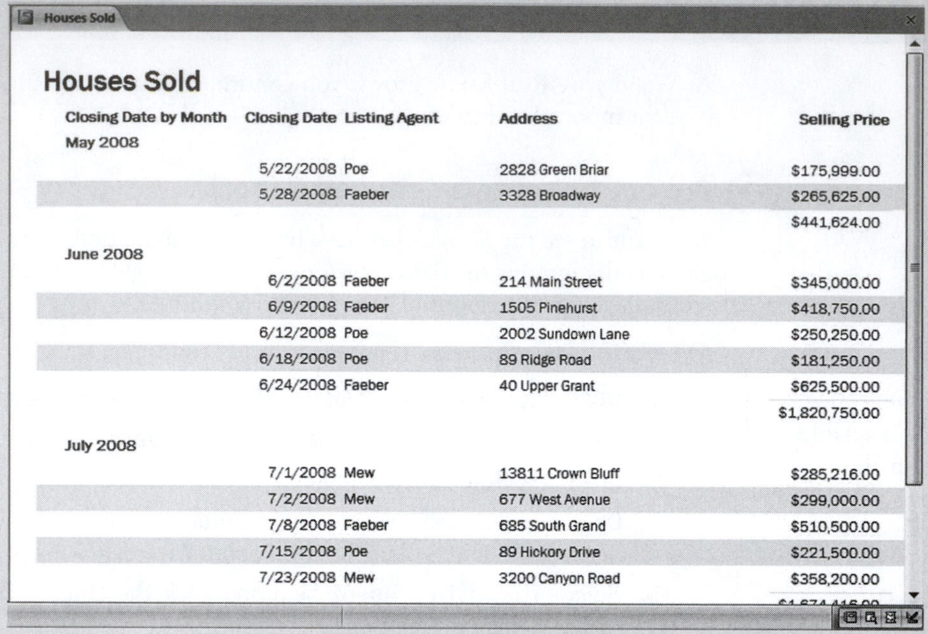
Houses Sold

Closing Date by Month	Closing Date	Listing Agent	Address	Selling Price
May 2008				
	5/22/2008	Poe	2828 Green Briar	$175,999.00
	5/28/2008	Faeber	3328 Broadway	$265,625.00
				$441,624.00
June 2008				
	6/2/2008	Faeber	214 Main Street	$345,000.00
	6/9/2008	Faeber	1505 Pinehurst	$418,750.00
	6/12/2008	Poe	2002 Sundown Lane	$250,250.00
	6/18/2008	Poe	89 Ridge Road	$181,250.00
	6/24/2008	Faeber	40 Upper Grant	$625,500.00
				$1,820,750.00
July 2008				
	7/1/2008	Mew	13811 Crown Bluff	$285,216.00
	7/2/2008	Mew	677 West Avenue	$299,000.00
	7/8/2008	Faeber	685 South Grand	$510,500.00
	7/15/2008	Poe	89 Hickory Drive	$221,500.00
	7/23/2008	Mew	3200 Canyon Road	$358,200.00

Figure 1

Sales report grouped by month

21. CLOSE the report and **CLOSE** the table.

PAUSE. LEAVE the database open to use in the next project.

Project 2: Create a Calculated Query Field

You are interested in knowing the difference between each house's asking price and selling price. Create a query with a calculated field that will give you this information. Then add a totals row so you can find the average asking price, selling price, and difference.

USE the database that is open from the previous project.

1. On the Create tab, in the Other group, click **Query Design**.
2. In the Show Table dialog box, double-click **Houses Sold** to add the table to the design grid.
3. Click **Close**.
4. In the Inventory field list, double-click **Address**, **Bedrooms**, **Bathrooms**, **Asking Price**, and **Selling Price**.
5. Click the Field cell in the first blank column and press **Shift** + **F2** to open the Zoom dialog box.
6. In the Zoom dialog box, key the following expression:

   Difference: [Asking Price] - [Selling Price]
7. Click **OK**.
8. On the Design tab, in the Results group, click **Run** to create a query with the new calculated **Difference** field.
9. On the Home tab, in the Records group, click the **Totals** button. Scroll down to see the Totals row at the bottom of the result set.
10. In the Totals cell of the **Asking Price** field, click the **down arrow** to display the menu and click **Average**.
11. In the Totals row of the **Selling Price** field, click the **down arrow** and click **Average**.

12. In the Totals row of the **Difference** field, click the **down arrow** and click **Average**. Your query should look similar to Figure 2.

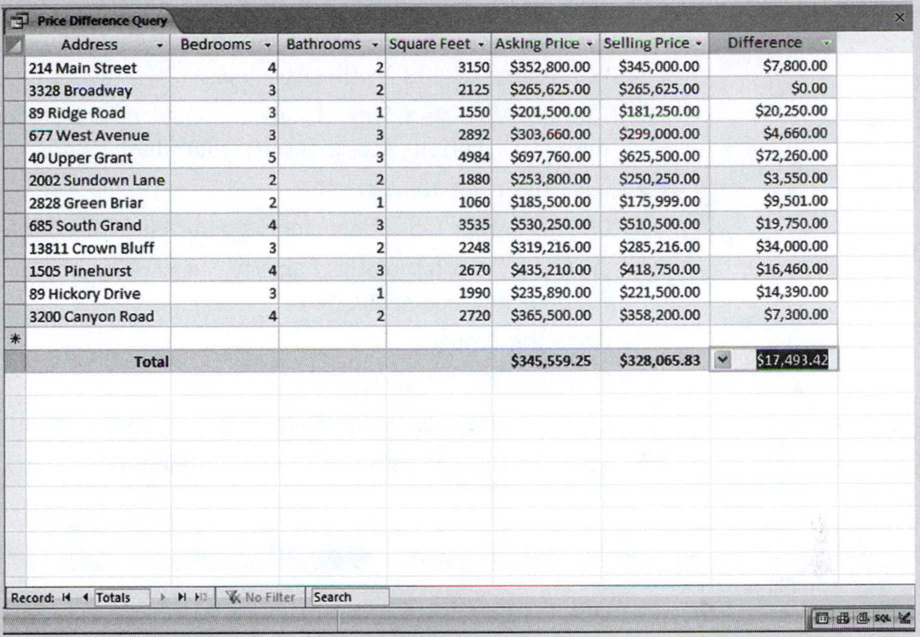

Figure 2

Query results

Address	Bedrooms	Bathrooms	Square Feet	Asking Price	Selling Price	Difference
214 Main Street	4	2	3150	$352,800.00	$345,000.00	$7,800.00
3328 Broadway	3	2	2125	$265,625.00	$265,625.00	$0.00
89 Ridge Road	3	1	1550	$201,500.00	$181,250.00	$20,250.00
677 West Avenue	3	3	2892	$303,660.00	$299,000.00	$4,660.00
40 Upper Grant	5	3	4984	$697,760.00	$625,500.00	$72,260.00
2002 Sundown Lane	2	2	1880	$253,800.00	$250,250.00	$3,550.00
2828 Green Briar	2	1	1060	$185,500.00	$175,999.00	$9,501.00
685 South Grand	4	3	3535	$530,250.00	$510,500.00	$19,750.00
13811 Crown Bluff	3	2	2248	$319,216.00	$285,216.00	$34,000.00
1505 Pinehurst	4	3	2670	$435,210.00	$418,750.00	$16,460.00
89 Hickory Drive	3	1	1990	$235,890.00	$221,500.00	$14,390.00
3200 Canyon Road	4	2	2720	$365,500.00	$358,200.00	$7,300.00
Total				$345,559.25	$328,065.83	$17,493.42

13. Save the query as **Price Difference Query** and close the query.

PAUSE. Leave the database open for the next project.

Project 3: Create a Chart

In the report you created, you want to have a pictorial view of the data along with the numbers. Use the Chart Wizard to insert a 3-D column chart into your existing report.

USE the database that is open from the previous project.

1. Open the **Houses Sold** report.
2. Switch to Design view.
3. On the Design tab, in the Controls group, click the **Insert Chart** button. The pointer changes to a plus sign with a chart icon.
4. Click in the upper-left corner of the Page Footer section and drag to the lower-right corner to create a rectangular placeholder where the chart will be inserted.
5. Release the mouse button. The first Chart Wizard dialog box appears.
6. Select the **Houses Sold** table as your data source and click the **Next >** button. The second Chart Wizard dialog box appears.
7. Double-click the **Asking Price**, **Selling Price**, and **Closing Date** fields to move them to the Fields for Chart box and click the **Next >** button. The third Chart Wizard dialog box appears.
8. Click the **3-D Column Chart** button, the second icon in the first row.
9. Click the **Next >** button. The fourth Chart Wizard dialog box appears.
10. Click and drag the **Selling Price** field button to the upper-left of the chart and drop on the **SumofAskingPrice** data list. Both the **SumofSellingPrice** and **SumofAskingPrice** fields should be listed.
11. Click the **Preview Chart** button. The Sample Preview dialog box appears, displaying a sample of your chart.
12. Click the **Close** button. The Sample Preview dialog box closes.

13. Click the **Next >** button. The fifth Chart Wizard dialog box appears.

14. Click the **down arrow** in the **Report Fields** menu and select **<No Field>**.

15. Click the **down arrow** in the **Chart Fields** menu and select **<No Field>**.

16. Click the **Next >**. The Sixth Chart Wizard dialog box appears.

17. Key **Summer 2008** in the Title box.

18. The **Yes, display a legend** button should be selected. If not, select it and click the **Finish** button. Access inserts your chart.

19. Click the chart to select it.

20. On the Design tab, in the Tools group, click the **Property Sheet** button.

21. Click the **Data** tab of the Property Sheet. Click the **down arrow** at the end of the **Enabled** line and select **Yes**.

22. Close the Property Sheet.

23. Switch to Report view.

24. On the Home tab, in the Records group, click the **Refresh All** button.

25. Scroll to the bottom of the report to view your chart, which should look similar to Figure 3.

Figure 3

Report with 3-D Column Chart

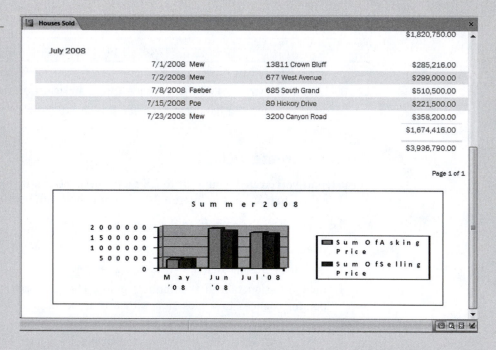

26. **SAVE** and **CLOSE** the report.

   PAUSE. LEAVE the database open for the next project.

Project 4: Export Data and Save Specification

You need to provide listing information to the agents in your office in another format, so you export the data to Excel. Because you will perform this export operation on a regular basis, you save the specification for future use.

USE the database that is open from the previous project.

1. In the Navigation pane, select the **Listings: Table**.

2. On the External Data tab, in the Export group, click **Excel**. The Export - Excel Spreadsheet dialog box appears.

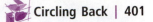

3. If you want to specify a different destination, click **Browse** to open the File Save dialog box, use the Save in box to choose a folder, and then click **Save**.

4. Click the **Export data with formatting and layout** checkbox and then click the **Open the destination file after the export operation is complete** checkbox.

5. Click **OK**. Excel opens and the new worksheet with exported data is displayed.

6. **CLOSE** the worksheet and **CLOSE** Excel.

7. Switch to Access.

8. On the Save Export Steps screen, click the **Save export steps** checkbox to display the specification details.

9. In the Description box, key **Export listing information to Excel**.

10. Click **Save Export**.

   PAUSE. LEAVE the database open for the next project.

Project 5: Maintain, Back Up, and Split a Database

You regularly perform routine maintenance on the database to ensure data integrity. You decide to split the database into two files to reduce network traffic, but after all the work you have put into the database you first want to protect your work by backing it up to prevent data loss.

USE the database that is open from the previous project.

1. Click the **Office Button**, point to Manage, and click **Compact and Repair Database.** Access compacts and repairs the database.

2. Click the **Office Button**, point to Manage, and click **Back Up Database** to display the Save As dialog box. Access automatically adds the current date to the end of the filename.

3. Click the **Save** button to accept the generated filename.

4. On the Database Tools tab, in the Move Data group, click the **Access Database** button to display the Database Splitter Wizard.

5. Click the **Split Database** button to display the Create Back-end Database dialog box.

6. Navigate to the location where you want to save the back-end file and click **Split**. After a few moments, the Database Splitter dialog box appears.

7. Click **OK**.

8. **CLOSE** the database.

9. **OPEN** *Woodgrove Real Estate XXX_be*. Notice that it contains only the tables for the database.

10. **CLOSE** the database.

   STOP. CLOSE Access.

MATRIX SKILL	SKILL NUMBER	LESSON NUMBER
Define data needs and types	1.1	1
Define table fields	1.1.1	1
Define appropriate table field data types for fields in each table	1.1.2	1
Define tables in databases	1.1.3	1
Define and print table relationships	1.2	3
Create relationships	1.2.1	3
Modify relationships	1.2.2	3
Print table relationships	1.2.3	3
Add, set, change, or remove primary keys	1.3	3
Define and modify primary keys	1.3.1	3
Define and modify multi-field primary keys	1.3.2	3
Split databases	1.4	15
Create databases	2.1	2
Creating databases using templates	2.1.1	2
Create blank databases	2.1.2	2
Create tables	2.2	2
Create custom tables in Design view	2.2.1	9
Create tables by copying the structure of other tables	2.2.2	2
Create tables from templates	2.2.3	2
Modify tables	2.3	4
Modify table properties	2.3.1	4
Evaluate table design by using the Table Analyzer	2.3.2	9
Rename tables	2.3.3	4
Delete tables	2.3.4	4
Summarize table data by adding a Total row	2.3.5	9
Create fields and modify field properties	2.4	4
Create commonly used fields	2.4.1	4
Modify field properties	2.4.2	4
Create and modify multi-valued fields	2.4.3	4
Create and modify attachment fields	2.4.4	4
Create forms	2.5	5,10
Create forms using Design View	2.5.1	5
Create datasheet forms	2.5.2	5
Create multiple item forms	2.5.3	10
Create split forms	2.5.4	10
Create subforms	2.5.5	10
Create PivotTable forms	2.5.6	10

continued

MATRIX SKILL	SKILL NUMBER	LESSON NUMBER
Create forms using Layout view	2.5.7	5
Create simple forms	2.5.8	5
Create reports as a simple report	2.6.1	6
Create reports by using the Report Wizard	2.6.2	6
Create reports by using Design view	2.6.3	6
Define group headers	2.6.4	11
Create aggregate fields	2.6.5	11
Set the print layout	2.6.6	11
Create labels by using the Label Wizard	2.6.7	11
Add controls	2.7.1	7
Bind controls to fields	2.7.2	7
Define the tab order of controls	2.7.3	7
Format controls	2.7.4	7
Arrange controls	2.7.5	7
Apply and change conditional formatting on controls	2.7.6	7
Apply AutoFormats to forms and reports	2.7.7	5, 6
Enter, edit, and delete records	3.1	3
Navigate among records	3.2	3
Find and replace data	3.3	3
Attach documents to and detach from records	3.4	3
Import data	3.5	14
Import data from a specific source	3.5.1	14
Link to an external data source	3.5.2	14
Save and run import specifications	3.5.3	14
Create queries	4.1	8
Create queries based on a single table	4.1.1	8
Create queries based on more than one table	4.1.2	8
Create action queries	4.1.3	12
Create crosstab queries	4.1.4	12
Create subqueries	4.1.5	12
Save filters as queries	4.1.6	12
Modify queries	4.2	8
Add tables to and remove tables from queries	4.2.1	8
Add criteria to queries	4.2.2	8
Create joins	4.2.3	12
Create calculated fields in queries	4.2.4	12
Add aliases to query fields	4.2.5	12
Create sum, average, min/max, and count queries	4.2.6	12
Sort data within tables	5.1.1	3
Sort data within queries	5.1.2	8
Sort data within reports	5.1.3	6
Sort data within forms	5.1.4	5
Filter data within tables	5.2.1	3

continued

Matrix Skill	Skill Number	Lesson Number
Filter data within queries	5.2.2	8
Filter data within reports	5.2.3	6
Filter data within forms	5.2.4	5
Remove a filter	5.2.5	3
Create and modify charts	5.3	13
Create charts	5.3.1	13
Format charts	5.3.2	13
Change chart types	5.3.3	13
Export data	5.4	14
Export from tables	5.4.1	14
Export from queries	5.4.2	14
Save and run export specifications	5.4.3	14
Save database objects as other file types	5.5	13
Print database objects	5.6	13
Open databases	6.1.1	1
Back up databases	6.1.2	15
Compact and repair databases	6.1.3	15
Save databases as a previous version	6.1.4	15
Encrypt databases by using passwords	6.2.1	15
Configure database options	6.2.2	15
Set database properties	6.2.3	15
Identify object dependencies	6.2.4	15
Print database information	6.2.5	15
Reset or refresh table links	6.2.6	15

TO USE MICROSOFT OFFICE PROFESSIONAL 2007, YOU WILL NEED:

COMPONENT	REQUIREMENT
Computer and processor	500 megahertz (MHz) processor or higher[1]
Memory	256 megabyte (MB) RAM or higher[1,2]
Hard disk	2 gigabyte (GB); a portion of this disk space will be freed after installation if the original download package is removed from the hard drive.
Drive	CD-ROM or DVD drive
Display	1024x768 or higher resolution monitor
Operating system	Microsoft Windows XP with Service Pack (SP) 2, Windows Server 2003 with SP1, or later operating system[3]
Other	Certain inking features require running Microsoft Windows XP Tablet PC Edition or later. Speech recognition functionality requires a close-talk microphone and audio output device. Information Rights Management features require access to a Windows 2003 Server with SP1 or later running Windows Rights Management Services. Connectivity to Microsoft Exchange Server 2000 or later is required for certain advanced functionality in Outlook 2007. Instant Search requires Microsoft Windows Desktop Search 3.0. Dynamic Calendars require server connectivity. Connectivity to Microsoft Windows Server 2003 with SP1 or later running Microsoft Windows SharePoint Services is required for certain advanced collaboration functionality. Microsoft Office SharePoint Server 2007 is required for certain advanced functionality. PowerPoint Slide Library requires Office SharePoint Server 2007. To share data among multiple computers, the host computer must be running Windows Server 2003 with SP1, Windows XP Professional with SP2, or later. Internet Explorer 6.0 or later, 32 bit browser only. Internet functionality requires Internet access (fees may apply).
Additional	Actual requirements and product functionality may vary based on your system configuration and operating system.

[1] 1 gigahertz (GHz) processor or higher and 512 MB RAM or higher recommended for **Business Contact Manager**. Business Contact Manager not available in all languages.

[2] 512 MB RAM or higher recommended for **Outlook Instant Search**. Grammar and contextual spelling in **Word** is not turned on unless the machine has 1 GB memory.

[3] Office Clean-up wizard not available on 64 bit OS.

A

action query changes the data in its data source or creates a new table

aggregate field a field that uses an aggregate function to calculate data

aggregate function performs a calculation on a set of values and then returns a single value

alias an alternative name for a table or field in expressions

append query an action query that adds the records in a query's result set to the end of an existing table

ascending sorts data from beginning to end

AutoFormat command that applies a predefined format to a form or report

B

back-end file in a split database, the database that contains the tables

backup a copy of a database file

badges small square labels that contain Key Tips

Blank Form tool that creates a new blank form in Layout view

bound control uses a field in a table or query as the data source

C

calculated control a control that displays the result of a calculation or expression

calculated field column in a query that results from an expression

chart a graphical representation of data

chart body the main area that displays the chart

Chart Wizard a control that you can insert into forms and reports to quickly create charts

common filters popular filters available as context menu commands, depending on the type and values of the field

composite key two or more primary keys used in a table

conditional formatting changes the appearance of a control or the value in a control when certain conditions are met

Connection Status menu a menu that lets you choose between searching help topics online and help topics offline

control an object that displays data, performs actions, and lets you improve the look and usability of a form or report

control layouts use to align your controls horizontally and vertically to give your report or form a uniform appearance

control tab order the order in which the selection moves from field to field when the Tab key is pressed

Control Wizards help you create controls such as command buttons, list boxes, combo boxes, and option groups

cross join each row from one table is combined with each row from another table

crosstab query a query that calculates a sum, average, count, or other type of total on records and then groups the results by two types of information: one down the left side of the datasheet and the other across the top

D

data type kind of information a field contains—whether text, number, date/time, or some other type

database tool for collecting and organizing information

Database Documenter creates a report that shows details, or definitions, about a selected object and opens it in Print Preview

database management system (DBMS) a system for managing data that allows the user to store, retrieve, and analyze information

database properties details about a file that describe or identify it

Database Splitter a wizard that splits a database into two files

datasheet visual representation of the data contained in a table or of the results returned by a query

decrypting removing the password from a file that has been encrypted

delete query an action query that removes rows matching the criteria that you specify from one or more tables

delimited file text file where each record appears on a separate line and the fields are separated by a single character

delimiter a character that separates fields in a delimited file and does not appear in the field values, such as a tab, semicolon, comma, or space

descending sorts data from the end to the beginning

desktop the first screen you see after you start the computer

dialog box launcher a small arrow in the lower-right corner of a group that you click to launch a dialog box

E

encrypting to scramble data in a way that can only be reconverted by an authorized user who has the password

Expression Builder a feature that provides the names of the fields and controls in a database, lists the operators available, and has built-in functions to help you create an expression

F

field column in a database table

field list a window that lists all the fields in the underlying record source or database object

filter a set of rules for determining which records will be displayed

filter by form tool that creates a blank form similar to the original; useful for filtering on several fields in a form or to find a specific record

fixed-width file text file where each record appears on a separate line and the width of each field remains consistent across records

foreign key a primary key from one table that is used in another table

form database object that simplifies the process of entering, editing, and displaying data

Form Design tool that creates a new blank form in Design view

Form tool creates a simple form that includes all the fields from the underlying data source

Form Wizard form-building tool that allows you to choose the form fields, style, and layout

front-end file database that contains the queries, forms, reports, and other objects created from the tables

G

group a collection of records separated visually with any introductory or summary information displayed with it

group footer the section of a report where data in the group is summarized

group header the section of a report where the name of a grouped field is displayed and printed

grouping field a field by which data is grouped

grouping intervals the way that records are grouped together

grouping levels the nested arrangement of the groups in a report

groups related commands within the tabs on the Ribbon

H

hierarchical form a form/subform combination, also called a *master/detail form* or a *parent/child form*

I

inner join most common type of join; includes rows in the query only when the joined field matches records in both tables

innermost field secondary sort field in a multifield sort

input mask a set of placeholder characters that force you to enter data in a specific format

J

join relationship between identical fields in different tables

K

KeyTips small letters and numbers that appear on the Ribbon when you press ALT; used for executing commands with the keyboard

L

Label Wizard a wizard that asks questions about the labels you want to create and the data you want to display on them; it creates the labels based on the answers

left outer join includes all of the rows from the first table in the query and only those records from the second table that match the join field in the first table

legend displays a list of the colors, shapes, or patterns used as categories in a chart

linked table a new table created when a database is linked to an Excel worksheet

Linked Table Manager lists the paths to all currently linked tables

M

main form primary form in a form/subform combination

make table query an action query that creates a new table and then creates records in it by copying records from an existing table

multivalued field a field that allows you to select more than one value from a list

Multiple Items tool to create a customizable form that displays multiple records

N

normal forms standards and guidelines of database design that can be used to determine if a database is structured correctly

normalization process of applying rules to a database design to ensure that information is divided into the appropriate tables

O

object dependencies describes how objects in a database are dependent on or rely on other components to function properly

objects elements in a database, such as tables, queries, forms, and reports

Office Button a menu of basic commands for opening, saving, and printing files, as well as more advanced options

outer join includes all of the rows from one table and only those rows from the other table that match the join field in the first table

outermost field primary sort field in a multifield sort

parameter query query in which the user interactively specifies one or more criteria values

P

PDF a file format that maintains the exact layout of the original file and that can easily be shared

PivotChart an interactive chart that shows data totals or summaries

PivotTable a type of form that allows you to reorganize columns and rows to analyze data

primary key column in a database that uniquely identifies each row

Print Preview displays a report as it will look when printed

Q

query database object that enables stored data to be searched and retrieved

query criterion a rule that identifies the records that you want to include in the query result

Quick Access Toolbar a toolbar at the top left of the screen that contains the commands that you use most often, such as Save, Undo, Redo, and Print

R

record row in a database table

record source tables or queries from which a query gets its data

redundant data duplicate information in a database

referential integrity prevents orphaned records

relational database group of database tables that are connected or linked by a defined relationship that ties the information together

report database object that presents information in a format that is easy to read and print

Ribbon located across the top of the screen, it contains tabs and groups of commands

right outer join includes all of the rows from the second table in the query and only those records from the first table that match the join field in the second table

S

select query most basic type of Access query that creates subsets of data, displayed in Datasheet view, that can be used to answer specific questions or to supply data to other database objects

SELECT statement a SQL command that instructs the Microsoft Access database engine to return information from the database as a set of records

sort to arrange data alphabetically, numerically, or chronologically

specification details of an import or export operation that contain all the information Access needs to repeat it without user input

split form feature that gives you two views of your data at the same time—in both Form view and Datasheet view

stacked layout a layout in which the controls are arranged vertically with a label on the left and the control on the right

subform a form that is inserted into another form

subquery SQL SELECT statement that is inside another select or action query

T

tab area of activity on the Ribbon

table most basic database object; stores data in categories

Table Analyzer a wizard that performs the normalization process by examining a table design and suggesting a way to divide the table for maximum efficiency

tabular layout a layout in which the controls are arranged in rows and columns like a spreadsheet, with labels across the top

template ready-to-use database that contains all of the tables, queries, forms, and reports needed for performing a specific task

Totals row a row inserted at the bottom of a table that provides a menu of functions for each column in the row

U

unbound control displays information such as lines, shapes, or pictures; not bound to a field

unequal join join that is not based on the equivalence of the joined fields

update query an action query that changes a set of records according to specified criteria

V

validation rule expression that limits the values that can be entered in the field

validation text specifies the text in the error message that appears when users violate a validation rule

W

wildcard characters used to find words or phrases that contain specific letters or combinations of letters

X

XPS a file format that preserves document formatting; can be easily shared, printed, and archived and is more secure

Z

zero-length string contains no characters and is used to indicate that no value exists for a field

Index

Photo Credits

Lesson 1
PhotoDisc/Getty Images

Lesson 2
Digital Vision

Lesson 3
"PhotoDisc, Inc."

Lesson 4
"PhotoDisc, Inc./Getty Images"

Lesson 5
ImageState

Lesson 6
Corbis Digital Stock

Lesson 7
PhotoDisc/Getty Images

Lesson 8
Corbis Digital Stock

Lesson 9
(c) Royalty-Free/CORBIS

Lesson 10
"PhotoDisc, Inc."

Lesson 11
Purestock

Lesson 12
Purestock

Lesson 13
Digital Vision

Lesson 14
Corbis Digital Stock

Lesson 15
"PhotoDisc, Inc."

Microsoft Office Ultimate 2007

To use Microsoft Office Ultimate 2007, you will need:

COMPONENT	REQUIREMENT
Computer and processor	500 megahertz (MHz) processor or higher[1]
Memory	256 megabyte (MB) RAM or higher[1, 2, 3]
Hard disk	3 gigabyte (GB); a portion of this disk space will be freed after installation if the original download package is removed from the hard drive.
Drive	CD-ROM or DVD drive
Display	1024x768 or higher resolution monitor
Operating system	Microsoft Windows(R) XP with Service Pack (SP) 2, Windows Server(R) 2003 with SP1, or later operating system[4]
Other	Certain inking features require running Microsoft Windows XP Tablet PC Edition or later. Speech recognition functionality requires a close-talk microphone and audio output device. Information Rights Management features require access to a Windows 2003 Server with SP1 or later running Windows Rights Management Services.

Connectivity to Microsoft Exchange Server 2000 or later is required for certain advanced functionality in Outlook 2007. Instant Search requires Microsoft Windows Desktop Search 3.0. Dynamic Calendars require server connectivity.

Connectivity to Microsoft Windows Server 2003 with SP1 or later running Microsoft Windows SharePoint Services or Office SharePoint Server 2007 is required for certain advanced collaboration functionality. PowerPoint Slide Library requires Office SharePoint Server 2007. Connectivity to Office SharePoint Server 2007 required for browser-enabled InfoPath forms and additional collaboration functionality. Groove Messenger integration requires Windows Messenger 5.1 or later or Communicator 1.0 or later. Includes a 5 year subscription to the Groove relay service.

Some features require Microsoft Windows Desktop Search 3.0, Microsoft Windows Media Player 9.0, Microsoft DirectX 9.0b, Microsoft Active Sync 4.1, microphone[1], audio output device, video recording device (such as a webcam), TWAIN-compatible digital camera or scanner, Windows Mobile 2003 powered Smartphone or Windows Mobile 5 powered Smartphone or Pocket PC, or a router that supports Universal Plug and Play (UPnP). Sharing notebooks requires users to be on the same network.

Internet Explorer 6.0 or later, 32 bit browser only. Internet functionality requires Internet access (fees may apply). |
| Additional | Actual requirements and product functionality may vary based on your system configuration and operating system. |

[1] 2 gigahertz (GHz) processor or higher and 1 GB RAM or higher recommended for **OneNote Audio Search**. Close-talking microphone required. Audio Search not available in all languages.
[2] 1 gigahertz (GHz) processor or higher and 512 MB RAM or higher recommended for **Business Contact Manager**. Business Contact Manager not available in all languages.
[3] 512 MB RAM or higher recommended for **Outlook Instant Search**. Grammar and contextual spelling in *Word* is not turned on unless the machine has 1 GB memory.
[4] Send to **OneNote 2007** print driver not available on a 64 bit operating system. Groove Folder **Synchronization** not available on 64 bit operating system. Office Clean-up wizard not available on 64 bit OS.